THE RULES ARE NO GAME

P9-DCX-412

FRONTISPIECE overleaf: The celebrated Chinese strategist, Sun Tzu, author of *The Art of War* (4th century BCE), the first book of its kind. Sun Tzu says: 'Generally in war the best policy is to take a state intact: to ruin it is inferior to this. To capture the enemy's army is better than to destroy it . . . For to win one hundred victories in one hundred battles is not the acme of skill. To subdue the enemy without fighting is the acme of skill'. The flag bears the legend 'Command'. The illustration is taken from a set of 50 cigarette cards, 'China's Famous Warriors', packed with W. D. and H. O. Wills' (Overseas) Pirate Cigarettes in 1911. The original is lithographed in color with a gold lamé overlay (65 × 25 mm).

孫武子

THE RULES ARE "NO GAME

THE STRATEGY OF COMMUNICATION

BY
ANTHONY WILDEN

WITH

*Women in Production: The Chorus Line
1932–1980*

BY RHONDA HAMMER AND ANTHONY WILDEN

INTRODUCED BY

The Naming of Parts and the 20th Century War

BY ANTHONY WILDEN

ROUTLEDGE & KEGAN PAUL
London and New York

First published in 1987
by Routledge & Kegan Paul Ltd

11 New Fetter Lane, London EC4P 4EE
Published in the USA by
Routledge & Kegan Paul Inc.
29 West 35th Street, New York, NY 10001

Set in Linotron Sabon 10 on 12pt
by Input Typesetting Ltd, London
and printed in Great Britain
by The Thetford Press Ltd, Thetford, Norfolk

© Anthony Wilden 1987

No part of this book may be reproduced in
any form without permission from the publisher,
except for the quotation of brief passages
in criticism

Library of Congress Cataloging in Publication Data

Wilden, Anthony.
The rules are no game

Bibliography: p.
Includes indexes.
1. Communication. 2. Linguistics. 3. Sociology.
I. Hammer, Rhonda. II. Title.
P91.W457   1986   001.51   85–30169

British Library CIP data also available

ISBN 0–7100–9868–5

Visual Studies Workshop
Research Center
Rochester, N.Y.
January 1989
Gift of the publisher

For Mark and Paul

Doucement allé loin   Softly takes you far
Patience bat la force   Patience masters force
Motto of General Toussaint L'Ouverture (1743–1803)

BOOK COVER: 'This is not a pipe' (1928–9) by René Magritte (1898–1967),
entitled *The Treachery of Images*. The image is a report, a command, and
a question about itself, and thus self-referring, creating the oscillation of a
double bind between 'pipe' and 'not a pipe' (a paradoxical injunction like 'Do
not read this'). The content level of the message – the supposed text – is
placed in a 'strange' or self-reflexive loop with the relationship level of the
message – the supposed context. See pp. 210, 244, 256–7.

Contents

Acknowledgments   (ix)

To the reader   (xi)

PART 1

The naming of parts and the 20th century war   (1)

PART 2

The strategy of communication   (65)

CHAPTER 1

Levels of reality   (67)

1.1 Symbolic, imaginary, and real   (67)
1.2 The human context   (70)
1.3 Energy and information   (71)
1.4 Orders of complexity   (73)
1.5 Freedom and constraint   (77)
1.6 Opposites   (79)
1.7 The rational and the real   (82)
1.8 Form and matter   (88)
1.9 Chhi and Li   (89)

CHAPTER 2

Kith and kin   (91)

2.1 Origins   (91)
2.2 Memory   (96)
2.3 Rules and rules   (102)
2.4 Marriage and descent   (105)
2.5 Mapping   (107)
2.6 Orientation   (112)
2.7 Power   (117)

CHAPTER 3

Language and communication   (122)

3.1 Symbolization in nature   (122)
3.2 Subjectivity and objectivity   (124)
3.3 Science and theology   (126)
3.4 A discourse has a subject   (132)
3.5 The lasting word   (133)
3.6 Language and communication   (136)
3.7 Signs   (140)
3.8 Semiotics   (142)
3.9 Joseph Priestley on universal grammar   (143)

CHAPTER 4

System and structure   (146)

4.1 Map and territory   (146)
4.2 Code and message   (151)
4.3 Mediation   (160)

CHAPTER 5

The principle of requisite diversity **(167)**

5.1 Logical types (167)
5.2 Complexity and constraint (172)
5.3 Levels of structure (176)
5.4 Variety, information, and noise (182)
5.5 Redundancy, entropy, and evolution (184)
5.6 The principle of requisite diversity (189)
5.7 Reductions of diversity (193)

CHAPTER 6

Metaphor and metonymy (196)

6.1 Metaphor and metonymy (196)
6.2 The verbal image (207)
6.3 The art of blazon (208)
6.4 Condensation and displacement (214)
6.5 Emblems (219)

CHAPTER 7

On telling left from right (222)

7.1 Coding (223)
7.2 Neurons and hormones (226)
7.3 Emulation (229)
7.4 Left brain, right brain (231)

CHAPTER 8

Montage analytic and dialectic: The right-brain revolution (243)

8.1 Negation (245)
8.2 Framing and punctuation (254)
8.3 Cliché clinches (259)
8.4 Film stereotypes of American women (261)
8.5 Montage (269)
8.6 Both-and and either/or (276)
8.7 Montage analytic and dialectic (277)

ENVOI

Women in Production: The Chorus Line 1932–1980 (283)
a videotape montage by Rhonda Hammer and Anthony Wilden

POSTSCRIPT

Context theory/Théorie des contextes: The new science (301)

BIBLIOGRAPHY

Part A The 20th century war (323)
Part B Illustrated media (343)
Part C The strategy of communication (366)
Part D Reference works (390)

Name index (399)

Index of battles, campaigns, and wars (405)

Subject index (407)

Illustrations

Figures

Frontispiece: Sun Tzu   ii

Frontispiece to Part I: I Want Out   xvi

Figure I.1 Inflation in history   34

Figure I.2 The Kondratieff wave   35

Frontispiece to Part II: Tiffany & Co.   64

Figure 1.1 (a) and (b) The Phantasmagoria   68

Figure 1.2 The structure of complexity   74

Figure 2.1 Personal adornment   97

Figure 2.2 Village plans: (a) Cheyenne; (b) Pygmy; (c) Bororo   99

Figure 2.3 Kinship. The Kariera system   106

Figure 2.4 Kinship. The Ambrym-Pentecost system   108

Figure 2.5 Kinship. The Tarau system   108

Figure 2.6 Kinship. The Arunta system   108

Figure 2.7 A Micronesian stick chart   109

Figure 2.8 Wave patterns   111

Figure 3.1 Quality and quantity   126

Figure 3.2 Language, discourse, and speech   133

Figure 3.3 A Dogon village   136

Figure 4.1 Stonehenge   147

Figure 4.2 The four elements   155

Figure 4.3 Elements and correspondences   157

Figure 4.4 *Melencolia* I (1514)   158

Figure 4.5 Code and message   161

Figure 4.6 Form and matter   162

Figure 4.7 Microcosm and macrocosm   164

Figure 5.1 Emergent qualities and logical types   168

Figure 5.2 Combination without complexity   174

Figure 5.3 Levels of semiotic freedom   182

Figure 5.4 Feature recognition of printed letters   187

Figure 5.5 The centrifugal governor   191

Figure 6.1 Metaphor and metonymy, or selection and combination   202

Figure 6.2 Artforms: (a) bear; (b) pipe   210

Figure 6.3 The heraldic points   210
Figure 6.4 Chimerical charges   214
Figure 6.5 A condensation joke   215
Figure 6.6 A medieval picture puzzle   216
Figure 6.7 Crest of Sir John Hawkins   220
Figure 8.1 The treachery of images   243
Figure 8.2 'Lips are the doorway to the heart'   262
Figure 8.3 *Angel*, 1937   266
Frontispiece to Envoi: The commander of the guard   280
Figure E.1 *Chorus Line* program   284
Figure E.2 *Dames*, 1934   289
Figure E.3 *Footlight Parade*, 1933   290
Figure E.4 Leni Riefenstahl   292
Figure E.5 Police units, 1934   292
Figure E.6 The mass ornament   294
Figure E.7 *Ku Klux Kuties*, 1980   296

Tables

4.1 Elements and correspondences   156
4.2 Qualities and elements   159
5.1 Distinctive features   179
7.1 Functional distinctions between the cerebral hemispheres (Bakan, 1971)   235
7.2 Hearing and vision (Kimura, 1973)   236
7.3 Psychological distinctions (Bogen, 1977)   237
7.4 General distinctions (Campbell, 1982)   240
8.1 Analytic and dialectic   278

For information on *Women in Production: The Chorus Line 1932–1980*, please write to:
'The Chorus Line'
c/o Dept. of Communication
Simon Fraser University
Burnaby, BC V5A 156
Canada

Acknowledgments

If I had to put into a list the names of at least some of the people who have helped me work this out over many years – and I do have to – I would thank Sushil Anand, Nancy Armstrong, Godwin Assogba, Yves Barel, Gregory Bateson, Michel Benamou, Len Berggren, Janet Blanchet, Robert C. Brown, Paul Bouissac, Diana Burfield, Amoy Chan, Victoria Chen, Michael Cherniavsky, Jimmy Cliff, Linda Clarke, Rick Coe, Bill Cooper, Jeff Couser, Larry Crawford, Creedence Clearwater, Dorothy Cruikshank, Gill Davies, Ioan Davies, Nathan Edelman, Tom Edens, Robert Elliott, Anne Fleming, René Girard, Jack Goellner, Lucien Goldmann, Lionel Gossman, Kate Guiton, Patrick Guiton, Takeo Hagikawa, Elizabeth Hall, Rhonda Hammer, Michael Harding, Clarke Harmeson, Newton Harrison, John Harvard-Watts, Harry Hickman, Peter Holland, Ray Holland, Peter Hopkins, Hidetaka Ishida, Glyn Jones, Dennis Judd, Maxine Judd, Georges Khal, Kirby, Hermann Kocnig, Alistair Lachlan, Ned Larsen, Nigel Lawson, Keith Lowe, Edith E. Lucas, Dean MacCannell, Juliet MacCannell, Jane-Anne Manson, Brian Markham, Glen Markham, Michael Marland, Lucie Menkveld, William Miller, Edgar Morin, Ray Morris, Nikko-houye Panahi Hassan, Joseph Needham, Nyree, Taku Oikawa, Steve Osborne, Pamela Parford, Jean Petitot, Massimo Piatelli-Palmarini, Gary Pitcher, J.-B. Pontalis, Kathleen Porter, the President's Research Grant Committee at Simon Fraser University, G. van Praagh, Terry Quigley, Roy A. Rappaport, Joan Rayfield, Anthony Read, Otis Redding, Klaus Rieckhoff, Klaus Riegel, Philip T. Rogers, David Roberts, Judy Rosenthal, Norbert Ruebsaat, Bob Scholte, Thomas Sebeok, Bob Seeds, Harley Shands, Nina Simone, Marie-Hélène Simonis, Yvan Simonis, Peter Smith, Jim Sturgeon, Mark Thomas, Ron Tippe, Mathilde Vilas, Thanh H. Vuong, An Wang, Julia Warner, Mrs Watson, Chester Wickwire, Patricia Wilden, Tim Wilson, Kathleen Woodward, Mr Yardley, Sylvia Yip, and many students at the University of California at San Diego and Simon Fraser University. The errors are of course my own.

To the Reader

Basic training

I count among many blessings the fact of having somehow fallen in step from time to time with several of the finest teachers in the world – and this in spite of class and other conflicts with some of them you could have cut with a knife.

The best teacher I ever had was David Roberts, or 'DSR', Head of the History Department at Christ's Hospital, one of the religious and royal charity schools set up in England by the Tudors in the sixteenth century.

Recently integrated, Christ's Hospital boarded 800 boys in sixteen 'houses' near Horsham, West Sussex, not far from Brighton. The main aim of the institution in the 1950s, as I recall it, was to teach you everything – from drilling and Divinity to fortitude and Foundry and the 1895 model Lee-Enfield rifle – you might possibly need to know to keep the Empire going.

Entering Christ's Hospital on a scholarship at ten years old in 1946 was like being parachuted into hell. Mental and physical torture by the older boys in strict rank order was a matter of ordinary survival at that time. The result was that as you grew older and bigger you yourself insensibly became part of the evil.

Praise the Lord, but three or four ethical radicals of my generation revolutionized the place by breaking up the worst of the bully system. Within a year or so they had argued everybody in the house into cutting it out.

You had to learn individual defensive guerrilla warfare just to survive in a place like that – being short I had my own system of judo – but whatever they did to your body, it was above all your mind, your identity, your personal dignity, your capacity to be a real person, that you had to protect. Psychologically and morally you had to have secure, secret, impregnable, and invisible guerrilla bases. We did, of course, and they never found us out.

One ought never to underestimate the importance of morale in life, nor the significance of simple acts – like breaking all the rules at school – in maintaining it.

Our local radicals took to offensive guerrilla war in the fight against the bully system. And that required words, not weapons. They had to argue their case for co-operation, i.e. prove their policy better than any other, with boys and masters who generally couldn't have cared less, provided it was not their ox being gored.

Words too win wars.

As Sun Tzu would say, our radicals attacked not the enemy – the individual bully – but the enemy's strategy – the system of bullying individuals. Here practically everyone becomes *somebody's* victim, except at the top, and you insensibly retaliate against the system by creating your own victims as you grow older.

As long as the pain is personalized and individualized, and as long as there is no political and strategic analysis of the system as a whole, then the reproduction of violence in the system is self-organizing, self-perpetuating, requiring no directions, no planning, no particular leaders, and nobody's conscious consent.

The fact is that male supremacy – for that is what it is – is the longest running system of organized bullying ever to arise on earth.

The school – and it really was a *school*, you had to hand it that – had as its Headmaster in 1946–53 a nineteenth-century fanatic – a man with 'wild staring eyes', to use Peter Holland's recent formulation, the eyes that blazed the way for the British Empire around the conquest of the world. Blue-eyed devils, the Chinese say. The Head, who had eyes that popped out on stalks, was a man who rejoiced in 'blow-ups', in a voice audible for miles, i.e. verbal assassinations usually ending with the victim in tears, the ultimate humiliation.

The worst aspect of the school, no doubt, was our systematic training in class prejudice, intellectual elitism, snobbery, racism, monarchism, authoritarianism, general savagery, and vicious misogyny – all communicated via the 'brotherhood of men', the biggest and most complex secret society in the world.

I was so insulted at the injustice I suffered at that school, not to mention the self-righteousness of most of the English public school teachers as a class, that I took my personal revenge on the place by continuing to prepare for history at Oxford and then refusing to go. After deciding not to be a jet pilot, I dropped out in midterm in the summer of 1953 to go to work for Mobil Oil in London but within a matter of months was timber cruising in the wilds of central British Columbia.

That was the best decision I ever made, and I guess I really did get to the Head. He blew me up the day I left his bloody school.

Let these sober facts cast no shadows on the man I honor here, born a Welshman in 1900 and tragically dead of a wasting disease at fifty-six. David Roberts specialized in people in trouble, and when I went into the advanced French and History program – Christ, they called us 'Modern Grecians'! – he very soon began specializing in me.

After I had already made one successful escape by train, DSR also saved my bacon at a later time when I became so instantaneously fed up that I grabbed a woman's bicycle from the rack by the Kitchens and pedalled off for home, at Three Cups Corner about 40 miles due east of the school, between Heathfield and Battle, on the road to Hastings. Hours later, in the dark, with two flat tires, no map, no money, completely lost, and very hungry, I gave myself up to the police, saying it was *home* I had run away from the idea being that they should put me in a car and take me back right away. Needless to say, I ended up back at school in disgrace, and when threatened with expulsion, replied that that was just fine with me. They could have their school, I said. DSR saved me from the troubles I courted with that act of defiance.

In the system of teaching history alongside modern languages that DSR devised at Christ's Hospital, other than some hours in French Literature – Corneille, Molière, Racine, and Victor Hugo – and Major Rider's French Prose Composition, along with some of Caesar's Gallic Wars (they had already taught us the Retreat of the Ten Thousand under Xenophon in Greek), we had the divine right of not having to go to classes at all.

You were given a question, some books to consult in the library, and ten days to come back with an essay arguing your point of view, after which you spent a more or less comfortable hour or so talking with your supervisor about getting reality right. All this beginning in my case at fourteen.

Nobody at Christ's Hospital ever taught us to write English. They just read a resounding chunk of the Revised Version every day (twice on Sundays) – the Lesson – and had us memorize plenty of poetry, mainly Shakespeare, Chaucer, and Romantic.

We weren't taught Chemistry the ordinary way, either, but by Dr Van Praagh's personal historical method, in which the first dialectical loop in learning – seeing the pattern which connects – the Aha! experience – came the day we suddenly realized that this gas we had discovered by following Joseph Priestley's experiments was actually oxygen.

As DSR's fondly remembered colleague Michael Cherniavsky points out in his 1980 essay on David Roberts, the magical touch of this marvelous man was that

> he treated each boy from first to last as an individual, whose
> individual needs, academic and personal, were studied with
> infinite patience. This was as apparent to his colleagues as it was
> to his pupils; marks and orders interested him little, but to get an

ever fuller picture of a boy's individual qualities mattered to him enormously, and was worth any amount of discussion and exchange of impressions.

That was not all:

In a beginner, he was better pleased by lively if erratic work than by careful reproduction of what the textbook said; he wanted essays about real people, by real people. Then, once a boy had shown he was prepared to 'use his own wits', his work would be judged by more exacting standards; vitality remained essential, but the approach to a real historical and critical sense had begun.

The secret was that you had to dig the story out and make the argument yourself.

And what of the inevitable Why study History (Art or Science)? I quoted a progressivist male supremacist passage from R. G. Collingwood (1889–1943) at the time:

Knowing yourself means knowing what you can do; and since nobody knows what he can do until he tries, the only clue to what men can do is what men have done.

As Schiller (1759–1805) had put it: 'Thinking is comparing with the past.'

History, symbolic, imaginary, and real, is the social memory without which communication would be impossible. It is also the locus of the later realization of present goals, and the wellspring of unexpected future events.

What we learned in the 1950s in modern English and European history (800–1500 Common Era) was not terribly near the whole truth, of course, nor free of fable or lie – one can easily rip apart the facile ideological content of my 1950s history essays, for instance, or heap scorn upon the whole nineteenth-century romantic image of the land of the Mother of Parliaments therein – but DSR's method was a critical and open-ended conflict approach to real conflict in real history, with due attention to economics, classes, and personalities: real struggles for real rights and powers between real people for real ends. (We dealt mainly with popes, bishops, barons, parliaments, and kings, it is true.) But not a word of tactical history: every question eventually demanded an understanding of the strategic 'patterns that connect' that change the future of the world.

He returned their written work not just marked and corrected, but enlivened with his characteristic marginal exclamations, exhortations, expostulations; even the most middling piece of work moved him to positive reactions!

Next to an ignorant remark by me about the English constitutional historian, Bishop William Stubbs (1825–1901), I find in DSR's hand: 'Bishop Stubbs was a great man! You'll never be as great!'

Let me conclude this tribute with some of DSR's 'General' questions from examinations in the early 1950s:

GENERAL PAPER: FOUR questions ONLY to be attempted

1 The Colour Bar.
2 Television and society.
3 How far would you accept Toynbee's definition of Communism as a 'Western criticism of the West's failure to live up to her own Christian principles in the economic and social life of this professedly Christian society'?
4 What would Marx have thought of modern Russia?
5 'Games are all right for those who haven't the brains to spend their time more profitably'. Do you agree?
6 How far do you think it true to say that the main hope for Britain lies in the revival of the Liberal Party?
7 Consider critically the presupposition lying behind the statement: 'Boys will be boys'.
8 Was it right to hang Bentley?
9 Are there any occasions when it is right to tell a lie?
10 What would you regard as some (at any rate) of the Seven Blunders of the World?

FRONTISPIECE: 'I Want Out': One of the posters created in 1971 by The Committee to Help Unsell the War, a group formed by 35 American advertising agencies. Reprinted from Gary Yanker's *Prop Art* (1972).

PART ONE

The Naming of Parts and the 20th Century War

If there's a hole in a' your coats,
  I rede you tent it:
A chield's amang you taking notes,
  And, faith, he'll prent it.

ROBERT BURNS: *On Captain Grose's Peregrinations Thro' Scotland* (1793)

My earliest memories are a child's memories of war — we drew swastikas on unwashed cars and collected shrapnel — memories that include the rules you follow to avoid getting hit by bombs. The radio and the films and the newspapers told us that we had to respond in kind, that we had to kill as many Germans as possible — at the time I thought Germans came from Germs — or else they'd be on top of us, perhaps forever.

At night you could see the fires burning in the working-class and slum districts in southern and eastern London, close to the river, the factories, and the docks. We knew from our parents that it was the working class, at home and abroad, who were bearing the brunt of the fighting and dying. We were much safer in the suburbs north and west.

When the nightly sirens made that noise you never forget, my mother carried us pick-a-back to the shelter, then brought down 'the boys'. 'The boys' were our stuffed animals, ten of them, each of whom had a distinct and engaging personality. You always felt better after a talk with the boys. When you were asleep, and they weren't working for your imagination, they came alive and played with each other all they wanted, with no grown-ups to interfere.

One night Child's Way elementary school was flattened by a land mine. I had left Rupert Bear at school the day before. This was my first death in the family, a casualty of war. My brother Alan lent me his Winnie-the-Pooh until I got over it.

One cloudy day later in the war a doodle-bug chased me on the way to school, where I fell down the steps of the shelter. At least the flying bombs gave you a warning: the engine cut out the moment they dived. The V-2 rockets were much worse because you couldn't hear them coming, and the AA guns were silent.

The firing of the guns was wonderful to hear. It meant our boys were fighting back. One sparkling summer's day our class went to see an anti-aircraft gun on Hampstead Heath. It was manned by women. They laughed and smiled and called you 'ducks' and 'dear' and let you try on their tin hats and gave you tea so hot it burnt your tongue.

Rule of war

In the summer of 1914, my grandfather on my mother's side, George Harold Ballard, was 29. Son of a London policeman, he had left school at the age of 11. Now he was married, with three children, aged 8, 6, and 4, driving for MacNamara's Motor Transport in Camden Town – until one day he and his mate had one too many drinks with an Army recruiting sergeant and gaily signed up for the Army Reserves. The attraction was two weeks at summer camp, with pay.

Three weeks later the Austro-Hungarian Empire declared war on Serbia. Grandpa had got himself a front row seat in World War One, where the machine gun reigned supreme. Army Reserve units were thrown into battle by a panicky British government. The untrained troops suffered heavy casualties. Along with many others, George Ballard arrived in France not even knowing how to fire a rifle. Fortunately for us, he did know how to handle a truck.

The family did not see him again until he appeared out of the blue one day in May 1919. In the meantime Ada Ballard went to work to support the children – they thought he'd gone forever. George Ballard took the pledge – he never touched another drop.

On August 23, 1914, the German infantry and artillery overwhelmed the French and British forces in Belgium, driving them backwards almost to the gates of Paris. This was the terrible two-week Retreat from Mons. Here Private Ballard drove food and ammunition through the chaos to wherever the fighting happened to be. Among the wounded he carried back were men who swore they had seen the fabled 'Angels of Mons' – come down to earth to carry the dying men to heaven.

What had merely been awful now became appalling. By the end of November 1914, barely three months after the first shots were fired, the Allies had suffered nearly a million casualties – a figure never to be matched in so short a period throughout the rest of the war.

By 1915, now an NCO in the Army Service Corps and eventually to become Company Sergeant-Major, Corporal Ballard was running motor transport in a battalion supporting the Dardanelles Campaign of 1915–16 (Gallipoli). He spent the rest of the war on the Balkan Front, in Salonika in Macedonia, where the Allies had landed in an abortive attempt to support Serbia against the Austro-German and Bulgarian offensives of 1915.

For over two thousand years, Salonika has been a strategic center of communication. In the fourth century BCE, the city was part of the empire of Alexander the Great, son of Philip of Macedon. After the collapse of the Roman Empire in the fifth century CE the city fell to the Byzantine Empire, centered in Constantinople (modern Istanbul). Many barbarities were committed against its inhabitants by Bulgarians, Normans, and others. In 1430 the Turks took the city with a terrible massacre. From the fifteenth century until the Balkan Wars of Independence in 1912–13, when it became part of Greece, Salonika remained part of the Turkish or Ottoman Empire, the Muslim power that had controlled much of southeastern Europe, the Middle East, Asia Minor, and North Africa for some four hundred years. Salonika had been a haven for twenty thousand of the Jews expelled from Spain in 1492, until the Nazis captured it in 1941 and exterminated their descendants, a community of sixty thousand souls.

The Dardanelles, called the 'Hellespont' by the ancient Greeks, are the narrow straits lying between Europe and Asia Minor, which with the Bosphorus and the Sea of Marmora, control the access of Russian and other shipping to the Mediterranean from the Black Sea. After the fall of Constantinople in 1453, the straits were controlled by the Ottoman Empire, which collapsed in stages in the last half of the nineteenth century. The sultanate was eventually overthrown by the Young Turks – the 'new men' with old prejudices who ordered the massacre of the Armenians of Asia Minor in 1915. Amid terrible atrocities a million died.

Today, a body of water with a strategic importance comparable to the military and commercial importance of the Dardanelles in 1915 is the Strait of Malacca between Malaysia and Indonesia, through which pass the supertankers on their way from the Persian Gulf to Japan.

Germany had persuaded Turkey to come into the war against France, Britain, and Russia in October 1914. The fortifications in the Dardanelles were defended by Turkish troops commanded by German advisors. The war in France had already settled into deadly stalemate, and when Churchill and Kitchener pressed the idea of an attack on the straits, it was mainly in the hope of raising British morale and helping the Russians against the Turks – by a quick and easy victory over an enemy assumed to be cowardly, lazy, and inferior.

On the Allied side, the Dardanelles Campaign of 1915–16 was fought by young men from Britain and the Empire. For the Empire troops, this was their first experience of war. British and Colonial casualties in the first two weeks were 20,000, of whom 6,000 were killed, out of the original force of 70,000. Three British battleships were sunk, depriving the army of the physical and psychological support of the big guns of the fleet.

At the end of 1915, after eight months of mistakes at every level of the British command, most of the British and Empire troops, and the small French contingent, were still on the beaches where they had landed: Ari Burnu, Anzac Cove, Cape Helles, Sedd-el-Bahr, Suvla Bay, Gallipoli. Diseases such as dysentery and typhoid increased the casualties. Assault after assault had failed because of reckless commanders, bad planning, lack of coordination, the awful terrain, the excellent defenses, and the skill and bravery of the Turks.

The massive failure of the Dardanelles Campaign brought down the British government, and Churchill was forced to resign as First Lord of the Admiralty. Admittedly this was the first modern amphibious operation, but on land also the tactical failures of the officers were fatal. No worse display of incompetence in military and civilian leadership had occurred since the war in the Crimea, some 450 miles northeast of Gallipoli, when the Turks were allied with the British and the French against the Russians, in 1854–56.

The Dardanelles Campaign was not quite as sudden a disaster as the bungling – strategic and tactical – that led to the appalling loss of Canadian troops at Dieppe on August 19, 1942 – 3367 killed, wounded, and captured out of 4963 Canadians embarked – but the pattern was the same: the use of 'colonial troops' to assault practically impregnable positions.

(Lord Louis Mountbatten was the man in charge of Combined Operations in 1942. General Montgomery approved the original plans for the Dieppe assault. The Canadian generals involved were Crerar and Roberts.)

Canadians who know their history recall a similar pattern in the war in South Africa: Lord Kitchener's abuse of his troops, including the Royal Canadian Regiment, in the frontal attacks on the Boers entrenched in the bed of the Modder River, during the Battle of Paardeberg, February 18–27, 1900, the last year of the nineteenth century.

Paardeberg is not a popular battle with English-speaking military historians. But the further one looks into this apparently minor event, the more it tells us about the nature of war in the twentieth century.

The British and Colonial casualties on the first day at Paardeberg were the subject of an official British cover-up. As they had done about Lord Raglan's responsibility for the destruction of the Light Brigade in charging the Russian guns at Balaklava in 1854, the British army and government sought to protect Lord Kitchener by claiming that it was not clear whether he or Lord Roberts had been in direct command of the action on the first day of the battle. At Balaklava they also blamed the disaster on the man who carried the ambiguous order to charge the guns, Captain Nolan, who was killed in the first minutes of the action.

The American army and government used both techniques in 1969, when their policy against Vietnamese civilians was exposed by the truth about the My Lai massacre of 1968. They protected General Westmoreland and, indeed, the whole chain of command from President Johnson on down, by court-martialling and convicting only the man who put into effect the unwritten orders to kill prisoners and civilians, Lieutenant Calley.

In February 1900, through blazing days and sleepless nights, a Boer force of 4000 men and 50 women (and some children), commanded by General Piet Cronje, had been fighting a brilliant rearguard action – one of the most difficult manoeuvres of war – as they retreated in their ox-wagons before a force of between 15,000 and 20,000 sunburnt 'rednecks' (as the Boers called the English), drawn from an army of 40,000 British and Colonial troops.

Cronje decided to make a stand at Paardeberg entrenched in the bed of the Modder River, with a laager of wagons drawn up on the riverbank. On Sunday, February 18, 1900, Kitchener's force surrounded the Boer laager and entrenchments. His force included the Royal Canadian Regiment, the Gordons, the Shropshires, and the Cornwalls (forming the 19th Brigade), as well as the 1st Welsh, the 1st Essex, the Buffs, the Norfolks, the Oxfords, the Yorkshires, the East Lancashires, the South Wales Borderers, the Argyll and Sutherlands, the Highland Light Infantry, the Seaforths, and the Black Watch.

Had Cronje and his force abandoned their lumbering wagons, they would almost certainly have got away. By not doing so, Cronje made the strategic error that lost the Boers the battle before it began.

Even when Christiaan De Wet's mounted commando of about 400 men came up and captured the tactical key to the battlefield – a hill from which they could not be dislodged, called 'Kitchener's Kopje' by the troops because Kitchener had failed to see its military importance – and thus gave the trapped force a chance to escape on horseback, Cronje and his remaining men refused to go. They did not see that the answer to superior numbers is superior mobility. Mobility was the key to the successes of the Boer guerrillas, who kept fighting for two long years after the British captured Pretoria in 1900 and announced that they had won the war.

To experienced officers and other ranks at Paardeberg, it was evident that Cronje's error in battle strategy had made a Boer surrender inevitable, a matter of time requiring no special exertions on the part of the British and Colonial troops. The Boers could be starved into submission, if need be, or intimidated or shelled into surrender by artillery – which is largely how the battle ended anyway, the Boer position reduced to indescribable conditions by the heavy guns of the Naval Brigade, nine days later.

Cronje's error was a failure of nerve: He had stopped and refused to budge, not because it was the best alternative, but because his morale had failed him. But Cronje's error was nothing compared to

Kitchener's. In facing Cronje, said Arthur Conan Doyle in 1900 in *The Great Boer War* (he was knighted for his services in South Africa), 'there was only one thing which apparently should not have been done, and that was to attack him'.

By most accounts, 'attack' may have been the only intelligible word in Kitchener's tactical vocabulary. Instead of taking advantage of his opponent's mistake, and saving lives and suffering, and money too, Kitchener chose the worst of all alternatives, a frontal assault on a fortified position.

As the most visible of the new modern organization men, an expert in army structure and supply (and later in police work against the Boer population), Kitchener was a technocrat of mechanical bent, not a skilled field commander and not a strategist. He had won the Battle of Omdurman against the Dervishes in the Sudan in 1898 by brute force and ignorance, with massive fire-power brought up past the Nile cataracts and across the desert by a special railroad 385 miles long built by a Canadian engineer, Lieutenant Edouard Percy Cranwell Girouard, afterwards knighted, who became Kitchener's Director of Railways in South Africa. The Boers were the first whites Kitchener had faced in battle.

Kitchener was the image of the New Model General, one of the modern apostles of total war, a doctrine derived first from Napoleon and the theories of Carl von Clausewitz (1780–1831), and secondly from the huge casualties and great destructiveness of the American Civil War, where General William T. Sherman's 'locust strategy' – sixty thousand Union troops burning and plundering their way through Georgia on a sixty-mile front in the 'march to the sea' in 1864–65 (Sherman was the man who said 'War is hell') – provided military observers with a real example of a modern army's capacity to terrorize women and children, humiliate their men, destroy their homes and farms, smash the means of communication, and thus to cripple the industrial, commercial, and agricultural capacity of an enemy state.

Kitchener's actions in South Africa show that he did not understand the technological and tactical revolution produced by magazine rifles and smokeless powder in the hands of invisible sharpshooters concealed in miles of trenches – the revolution through which the strategic advantage in warfare had passed to the defense.

Yet it was Kitchener, as Secretary of State for War, who dominated British strategy in World War One. He went down with HMS *Hampshire* when it struck a German mine in June 1916, which was probably just as well, but his simple-minded doctrine of conquest at any cost by any means and to hell with the casualties and the civilians is still the dominant doctrine of offensive warfare today.

The Boer entrenchments at Paardeberg were protected on every side by two to four thousand yards of barren plain, devoid of cover. Most of the attacking force had marched all night without food, and many were already out of water. At seven o'clock on what became known as 'Black Sunday', Kitchener ordered the 1st Welsh and the 1st Essex to the attack. Glancing at his watch, he announced, 'We shall be in the laager by half past ten'. The charge failed. So did the next, and the next, and the next. At two o'clock, after seven hours of uncoordinated action and contradictory orders (most of which he was careful not to put in writing), amid casualties that observers attributed to the lust for blood (a male pathology), Kitchener suddenly ordered Colonel O. C. Hannay's Mounted Infantry to rush the laager 'at all costs'.

Hannay, a Highlander, treated the order as the act of a madman. To refuse the order would be mutiny or cowardice. He gathered a small detachment of men, less than fifty, and said quietly, 'We are going to charge the laager'. He then registered his protest against his superior officer by putting spurs to his horse, riding far ahead of his men, and charging the Boers alone. He was shot with the majority of his followers.

Towards four o'clock, without telling the commanding officer of the brigade, Kitchener ordered the Canadians under Colonel Otter and three companies of the Cornwalls of the 19th Brigade to take the Boer positions at bayonet point. Major-General Smith-Dorrien watched in horror as half of his brigade advanced to the 500-yard fire zone and charged into a hail of bullets. Colonel Aldworth of the Cornwalls was killed instantly, the charge failed after 200 yards, the recall was sounded, and as many men as could broke and retreated. But like many other men that day, the Canadians had carried their charge too close to the Boer firing line to be able to retreat. Wounded and not, they lay on open ground, swept by rifle fire, without cover, under a scorching sun, without water, until darkness covered the withdrawal of the survivors. Thus ended the first day of the first experience of battle for the volunteers of the Royal Regiment of Canada. Nine days later they insisted on leading the final infantry charge against the laager (February 27).

On the first day at Paardeberg some 1210 men were killed or wounded, with 60 missing, the worst day's casualties for the entire war (1899–1902), worse even than the disaster visited on the Lancashire Fusiliers and other North Country regiments – 1700 killed and wounded – by incompetent officers at Spion Kop the previous month (January 22–24), where Winston Churchill and the war correspondents were horrified to see the dead piled three deep in the shallow trenches on the rocky top.

There could be no excuse for ordering the charge of the 19th Brigade at Paardeberg, said a Canadian chronicler, T. G. Marquis, an ardent

Imperialist. Writing in 1900, in *Canada's Sons on Kopje and Veldt* (p. 250), he compared it with the charge of the Light Brigade at Balaklava in 1854 ('Cavalry do not charge artillery from the front', Lord Cardigan had protested to Lord Lucan), where Lieutenant A. R. Dunn of Toronto won the Victoria Cross.

Marquis concluded:

> The soldier dearly loves the spectacular in war, and nothing is so magnificently inspiring or picturesque as a bayonet charge; but whatever it may have been in the days of the 'thin red line', it has a place in modern war only on the rarest occasions. Of all the blunders of this war that at Paardeberg is perhaps the most unpardonable. Magersfontein has its excuses, but Paardeberg has none. However, the mistakes of England's leaders have been the glory of the English soldier; and this charge gave Canada a permanent place in British history. 'The Men of Paardeberg' will stand out in bold characters on the future pages of the story of the Empire. But there was a terrible butcher's bill for the renown they gained. Seventy-five per cent of all who fell on that black Sabbath met the fatal blow in this mad charge.

It was later proved that the British knew absolutely nothing of the character of the Boers' position at Paardeberg. In the frontal assault on Dieppe forty years later, the British intelligence was that the port was weakly defended, the highly complicated plan of the raid was so rigid that even a few minutes meant success or failure, the almost 200-page operation order was so detailed that it allowed for no mistakes and no accidents, the troops had been inadequately trained and briefed, the fleet ran into a German convoy in the middle of the night, the preliminary saturation bombing of the German defenses had been called off in June (in spite of warnings of disaster and without objection from either General Crerar or General Roberts, the Military Force Commander), the tactical air support from Spitfires and Hurricanes had no visible effect on the German positions, the only naval support was the 4-inch guns of destroyers, many of the Canadians' Sten guns jammed on the first magazine, tactical communications between the different units and forces became hopelessly tangled, orders and reports were repeatedly garbled, leading to further loss of life, the RAF lost more aircraft over Dieppe (in the biggest air action since the Battle of Britain) than on any other day in the entire war (106 machines, the Luftwaffe lost 48), the Churchills manned by the Calgary Tanks were prevented by tank traps from getting beyond the Dieppe promenade (most of the engineers assigned to blow up the obstacles were either wounded or dead), the South Saskatchewans, who did achieve surprise (as did the British Commandos), were landed on the wrong side of their objective, and the Fusiliers Mont Royal, tactical reserves committed to a lost cause by General Roberts because of a confused report, were landed on the wrong beach, right under the guns of the West headland. Most of the defenders were on full alert as the first wave of wooden landing craft approached, and many of these touched down late, riddled with bullets, as daylight was breaking.

When it was decided to try to withdraw the remaining men at 11 o'clock, the wholesale confusion led a number of landing craft to return empty to England instead.

The Germans were amazed at the folly of the attack. One survivor of the main landing recalls that the water ran red with blood as far as you could see. Men were wounded twice, three times, six times and more – one trooper survived twenty-three wounds. Most of the men in the main landing were pinned down behind wrecked tanks and landing craft, or at the foot of the Dieppe sea wall, by pill boxes with criss-cross fields of fire, enfiladed at the same time by artillery, mortars, and heavy machine guns from the headlands overlooking Dieppe on either flank. For nine hours the Canadians died at the rate of a man a minute.

The task of the Royal Regiment of Canada was to seize the guns of the East headland so as to protect the left flank of the frontal assault across Dieppe beach. Their landing craft were at first taken the wrong way by the Royal Navy. The fifteen-minute delay cost them the critical necessity of surprise. The sixty-odd Germans on the heights had only to sit still and shoot straight. Of the 554 men of the regiment, only 65 got back to England, and 33 of them were wounded. In just over three hours at Puys, they had suffered 94 per cent casualties. The official Canadian casualty rate (made more favorable by the inclusion of men who never landed) was 68 per cent (3367 Canadians killed, wounded, and captured, of whom 906 died in the action itself, 2000 or more were wounded, and 2195 were captured). The British planners had predicted 10 per cent. Casualties much over that are usually described as 'heavy'.

On the German side General Conrad Haase found the assault 'incomprehensible'. He added: 'The fact that the Canadians did not gain any ground on the main beaches was not due to any lack of courage but because of the concentrated defensive fire. . . . The British rather seriously underestimated the quantity of weapons required for such an attack. The strength of the naval and air forces was *entirely insufficient* to suppress the defenders during the landings.'

Quoted by Ronald Atkin in *Dieppe 1942*, Captain Richard Schnösenberg, who had watched the whole affair from the vantage point of the East headland, came right to the point:

The main thing people don't realize is that the outcome was decided after half an hour. It was a stupid thing to do, to land in daylight on an open beach (p. 179).

Churchill later demanded to know who had been responsible for making and approving the plans (a matter never fully decided, although Roberts was made the scapegoat). He added that

> it seemed to a layman hardly in accord with the principles of war to attack a strongly fortified town front without first securing the cliffs on either side, and to use tanks in a frontal assault instead of landing them a few miles up the coast and entering the town from the back (p. 261).

One of the men of the Royal Hamilton Light Infantry told Atkin:

> People felt they had been abandoned. Later on they realised they were sacrificed. We felt it in retrospect and we feel it today.

As in 1900, so in 1942: the Battle of Dieppe was the Canadians' first experience of war – a battle for which many of them were issued with weapons at the last minute, so choked with preservative grease that men were still cleaning them on the way across. But whereas the bravery and skill of the Canadian troops in South Africa was everywhere recognized, as also in World War One, the Battle of Dieppe turned into a colonial nightmare. The victims of the tragedy were blamed for the failure of the assault – the official whisper being 'incompetence or cowardice'.

Only the colonized know how deep such wounds can go. The standard Canadian account of the disaster is called *The Shame and the Glory*.

Secrets rule

On April 29, 1984, John Ezard reported in the *Guardian Weekly* that

> a former German E-Boat commander has apologised after hearing, for the first time, evidence that his torpedoes killed 700 US servicemen off the Devon coast [in April 1944] in one of the worst and most secret Allied disasters of the second world war.

He continues:

> In the middle of the rehearsal for the D-Day landings Oberleutnant Hans Schirren's E-boat appeared on convoy patrol and sank two landing craft. A British warship was unable to defend them because

its guns were pointing the wrong way. The warship made no effort to pick up survivors.

Moreover,

> earlier in the exercise, which was carried out with live ammunition, some 36 GIs died when mines exploded during a lecture on mine safety.

His source, the Television Southwest documentary *The Sands of Silence*, written by Leslie Thomas, says that this 'astounding catalogue of incompetence and misunderstanding' caused a higher death list than the real Normandy landing on Utah Beach on June 6, 1944. It quotes official papers stating that medical officers dealing with the carnage were ordered: 'Ask no questions, take no histories. Anyone who talks about these casualties will be the subject of a court martial.'

The official records 'contain savage criticism by General Eisenhower's naval aide, Harry Butcher, of the quality of officers involved', says Ezard.

> In an interview transcript the warship commander said that if he had fired at the E-boat he would have hit the landing craft. He made no effort to pick up survivors because of new general instructions that this should be delayed until an attack was over.

> > Eternal Father, strong to save:
> > Aid those in peril on the wave.

Murphy's Rule

In a letter published in the May 6, 1984 *Guardian*, Master Mariner J. R. B. Towner reports on another source of casualties beside the torpedoes of the E-boat:

> I took part in the famous 'balls up' of the battle of Slapton Sands [April 29, 1944] whilst serving as sub-lieutenant in HMS Hawkins, which was controlling ship for the exercise. As far as I recall the cause for the heavy casualties amongst the American lads who went ashore, was that the US army commander, who conducted the exercise from the bridge of my ship, decided at the last moment to advance 'H' hour by one hour. Now most of the bombarding units who were shelling the foreshore got the orders and lifted the range to half a mile inland. Each broadside from each ship contained one live [high explosive] projectile to indicate the fall of shot.

Unfortunately,

> one of the inshore support destroyers did not receive the order and
> continued shelling the beach as the assault troops were landing
> there.
>
> Needless to say that the captain and others on our bridge were
> considerably shaken when they realised the enormity of the
> tragedy that was going on ashore. However, one top brass US army
> wallah is reported to have said that he didn't give a damn, and
> that as long as he got through the first day with ten per cent of his
> men he'd be satisfied.

Casualty rules

Like Paardeberg and other actions against the Dutch-descended Boers
in South Africa in 1899–1902, the campaign against the Turks in the
Dardanelles in 1915–16 was fought by British and Empire troops, and
once again this was the Colonials' first experience of war. Accurate
reports of the casualties from battle and disease are not available – as
in the Crimea in 1854–55 the medical and supply services repeatedly
collapsed – but in *Gallipoli* (1956) Alan Moorehead gives a figure of
252,000 killed or wounded out of 489,000 troops embarked, a casualty
rate of just over 50 per cent.

(*The Times History of the War* notes that the official total of casualties in action in the first six weeks in the Dardanelles – 38,636 killed,
wounded, and missing – was larger than the losses in action, not
counting disease – 38,156 killed and wounded – in the entire three
years of the South African War.)

At Gallipoli the Anzac force fought desperately to hold a beachhead
about the size of Regents Park. Commanded by General Ian Hamilton,
the expedition included the 4th Australian Infantry Brigade; the Otago
Mounted Rifles, the New Zealand Field Troop, and the Maori Contingent; the 29th Indian Infantry Brigade with the Indian Mountain Artillery; the Manchester Brigade and the Lancashire Fusiliers; the South
Wales Borderers; the Anson, Drake, Howe, Collingwood, and Hood
battalions of the Naval Division and the Royal Marine Brigade; the
14th Sikhs and the 6th Ghurkas; the 29th Irish Brigade, including the
Munsters, the Dublins, and the Royal Inniskillings Fusiliers; the 5th
Royal Scots and the King's Own Scottish Borderers; and finally, a
contingent from the Crown Colony of Newfoundland (which joined
Canada in 1949).

Most of the British force thus came from Ireland, Scotland, Wales,
and Lancashire – the oldest domestic colonies of London and the
South of England. The smaller French force at Sedd-el-Bahr included

Senegalese, Zouaves, and the 1er Régiment de Marche d'Afrique (the Foreign Legion).

All these men, on all sides, were victims of the Rule of War. What they faced seems incredible today. Nobody put it better than H. G. Wells, in *The Shape of Things to Come*, in 1933. In the Great War, he said,

> millions of human beings went open-eyed to servitude, bullying, hardship, suffering and slaughter, without a murmur, with a sort of fatalistic pride. In obedience to the dictates of the blindest prejudices and the most fatuous loyalties they did their utmost to kill men against whom they had no conceivable grievance, and they were in their turn butchered gallantly, fighting to the last.

According to Purnell's *20th Century*, whose figures seem conservative, in World War One some 17 million people of many nations, mostly peasants and other working people, died of shot, shell, and starvation. This figure includes the massacre of 4 million Armenians, Syrians, Jews, and Greeks.

In World War Two nearly 44 million human beings, again mostly working people, were killed from all causes. This figure includes 20 million Russians and 6 million Jews (3 million from Poland alone).

In both wars, Russia, Germany, France, and most of Europe were all invaded. The United States and Britain were not. Thus Anglo-American casualties from all sources were relatively low.

In 1914–18, the military death toll for the British was 760,000. For the Americans, who were in economic and imperial terms the real winners, it was 114,000. Canada, with one-tenth the US population, lost 60,000 men.

In the same four years, the French lost 1.4 million men; the Russians, 1.7 million; the Germans, 2 million.

In 1939–45, the military and civilian toll for Britain was 388,000. For the United States, again the winners, it was 406,000.

In the same six years, besides the staggering Russian loss (more than the entire total of the 1914–18 war), the Japanese death toll was 1.2 million. Yugoslavia lost 1.7 million. Invaded by Japan in 1932, China's losses against the Japanese are unknown, but must have been at least 15 million men, women, and children. Germany and Poland each lost over 4 million people.

Note that these figures refer to deaths only. They do not include the bodily and mentally wounded.

(For a conservative estimate of physically wounded, except in colonial and other wars where no quarter is given and civilians are treated as personal and military targets, multiply deaths by two.)

For both wars the British total is about 1 million dead (in World War Two, Commonwealth casualties were lumped in with British casualties). The American total is about 520,000 dead. Thus, of the world total of 61 million deaths in two world wars, 97 per cent of the people who died were neither British nor American.

We would do well to remember that leaders of nations that have not suffered on their own soil the killing and mutilating of soldier and civilian alike, and the mental and physical atrocities of twentieth century total war, are neither the wisest, the most experienced, nor the most competent people to be entrusted with guarding the peace — viz. the startling strategic envelopment of the Reagan Administration by Iran in 1986 in the $100 million guns-for-hostages swaps.

Family rules

My lasting impression of my grandfather, who was one of the best known men around — he used to let us ride round London hanging over the tailgate of his moving vans — is that whenever he had money he gave some away, bought presents all round, and gambled the rest on a horse or some new business scheme, but he never went completely broke. Until their very last plunge into business, the Ballards had risen from Camden Town to the suburban perfection of Finchley, where we used to go to get our groceries during the war.

On the mantelpiece in the impeccable interior stood two fluted vases of beaten brass, with 'Macedoine 1919' embossed in a Turkish-looking script, formed out of two 4-inch navy shell cases by a Greek craftsman working with hammer, hand anvil, and punch.

In World War Two their son George Edward Ballard served as a master mechanic with the rank of sergeant in the Royal Fusiliers. He married Sergeant Jowett of the Women's Auxiliary Air Force in 1945. After that war, father and son tried their hands at business again, this time as offtrack bookmakers, or 'turf' accountants'. The front for the betting shop was a used furniture store. Here we boys were allowed to play with the rubber stamps, the carbon paper, the typewriter, and sundry other marvels of the world of commerce. This venture collapsed because Grandpa was the proverbial soft touch. He let his 'good customers' lay bets on tick, and they didn't pay up.

During the 1939–45 war, my father, Frank Clover Wilden, was a radar and bombsight technician in the Royal Air Force, an NCO like the Ballards. Born on Alderney in the Channel Islands off the coast of France, he is the son of a French teacher, née Jessie Le Breton Raffray, and an English émigré from Suffolk, Dennis Wilden, son of a postmaster, who died during the German occupation of the Islands in the war.

Jersey rules

Jessie Le Breton Raffray was the daughter of a millwright. She was a strong and forthright woman much respected and feared by my brother and me, and a stickler for 'the right way' of doing whatever it was you were doing. She lived in St Helier in Jersey, where we used to go before and after the war, myself hopelessly seasick until I learned the rules of avoiding it, which consist mainly of staying on deck, not looking at the water, and breathing in every time the bow goes down.

The Le Bretons are an old Jersey family. In the tenth century they were obliged to become feudal vassals of the Dukes of Normandy. (In French, the Islands are the *Iles normandes*.) A Le Breton is depicted in the Bayeux Tapestry, fighting for the Normans in the invasion of Britain in 1066.

The most famous member of the Le Breton family was Mrs Lillie Langtry (1853–1929). Mrs Langtry, 'the Jersey Lily', was the most successful woman of her day, a master of management and finance, the stunning consort of the Prince of Wales (later Edward VII), and the first 'society woman' to appear professionally on the stage. One of her loyal admirers was 'Judge' Roy Bean, who saw her perform in Chicago during her American tour in 1882–3. 'Judge' Bean, a Canadian saloon-keeper, knockabout, and murderer who had somehow been appointed justice of the peace, had declared himself 'the law west of the Pecos River' in 1882. He is said to have named the hamlet of Langtry, Texas, after her. He called his saloon-courtroom 'The Jersey Lilly'. After Roy Bean died, the citizens of Langtry made Lillie a present of the judge's revolver, which, they said, 'aided him in finding some of his famous decisions'.

Jessie Raffray's mother, Jane Le Breton, was the daughter of a sea captain. He took her under sail all over the world. The Raffrays were marine engineers. Jessie's brothers, Herbert and Jack, constructed the first automobile in the Islands, an 1899 English Benz. They both became Chief Engineers in the Merchant Navy. Herbert was lost in the war at sea in 1916; Jack died when his ship was torpedoed in 1940.

In 1929, when he was 22, my father emigrated to London. Before he left the Islands, he had learned all that the Islanders teach their menfolk: how to fish, how to grow food, how to run a boat, how to look after machinery, how to handle deadly weapons, and how to guard yourself against unwelcome surprises.

In every situation and in every trade there was a code of rules to abide by. In every code, the Rule of Rules told you how to protect yourself against the unexpected. (Murphy's Law: If anything can go wrong, it will.) Bad luck aside, these rules guaranteed that you wouldn't lodge a hook in someone's ear, or lose your fingers to a machine, or get caught on a lee shore, or blow your foot off.

These rules were no game. They were all legitimate, and still are. Some codes of rules, like some authorities, are legitimate, some are not. The test of legitimacy is the actual effect of a rule in a real context. Legitimate codes of rules enable people to express their creativity and to protect themselves and each other. Illegitimate rules serve the tyrants who create them. They drive people to destruction.

Magic rules

My mother, Lilian Elizabeth Ballard, born within sound of Bow Bells, had to leave school at 14 and go to work. She was the mediator between everyone and everyone else, including the adults and the children, a tower of strength, may I say, and always the popular favorite, someone people told you they were honored to know. For her myriads of friends and relations, Lily stands for tea and sympathy and just what you need to hear. An eternal optimist like her mother, Ada, if Lily has a single rule of life it is 'Never mind, dear, it's probably for the best and it'll all turn out right in the end.'

The Ballards were a diverse and happy family – Lily's older sister, Peggy, almost won the ballroom dancing contest at the Albert Hall in 1933. My mother's sunny and resourceful character has a lot to do with my great aunt Lizzie, Grandma Ballard's sister. Great Aunt Lizzie was a wizard – our personal medium of communication with the spirit world. All the spirits she knew were good, kind, and helpful, and, as she used to say, 'great buck-me-ups'. Her go-between was called Topsy, who I suspect came straight from Harriet Beecher Stowe's *Uncle Tom's Cabin: Or, Life Among the Lowly*. When Aunt Lizzie read fortunes, she warned you about dangers in your future – Be Prepared – but being a magical person, she never told a bad one.

In her daily work, which was against the law, Aunt Lizzie was in fact a therapist for the lonely and distressed. Her art and science was the practice of communication, and this she saw from the sunny side of life. For her the nature of life was an open book in which those who run may read. In 'reading the signs' she gave me my first lessons in the fact that reading is not confined to language, that codes and messages, including written messages, are not confined to words.

When Aunt Lizzie read your fortune, she took you on a voyage of discovery, with the 'fall of the cards' as the chart for the day. By working her creative imagination and life experience into the rules of the code of map-reading she followed, Aunt Lizzie could always uncover in the images of the cards the 'pattern that connects' – with you.

Home rule

Like all the women on the Ballard side, my mother Lily complemented the sterner traditions of the Wilden women. Frank Wilden's older sister, Dorothy, is my godmother. Tough-minded like her mother, Dorothy was for many years a school headmistress in Essex, always devoted to the welfare of the young. This stern tradition was in fact quite unconventional. Dorothy Wilden is the kind of woman who can say 'I am who I am' because she had used her education to free herself from any kind of dependence on men.

The Wilden women stood for freedom and self-respect to be gained by schooling in the strategy of education. The equally strong Ballard women stood for freedom and self-respect to be gained by learning how to break oppressive rules and get away with it – using tactical or strategic withdrawals when necessary. Where the Wilden women taught the strategy of position, the Ballard women taught the strategy of manoeuvre.

Seven years at Christ's Hospital (1946–53) gave me every opportunity to put those strategies to the test.

The Wilden family, more frugal and more rigorous, stood for the challenge of life outside the home, and they took great care to prepare us for it. The Ballards, who prepared us in other ways, were always in the hole. They rarely paid cash for anything if you could get it 'on the never-never'. 'Life is for the living' was their banner and device: They stood for getting as much fun out of life as you could while it lasted.

Propaganda rules

My father was a watchmaker. If he had the means to make a thing, he could make it. During the war, when he came home on leave from the instrument shops at Farnborough, he brought finely painted scale models – a Ventura, a Stirling, a Sunderland flying boat, two motor torpedo boats – astounding in their detail and carved from the block.

For my mother he made bracelets, rings, and brooches out of brass buttons, cap badges, and burnished perspex from aircraft windscreens. For the house he made a chromium-plated table lighter out of an unidentified explosive device, and he usually came home on leave with some entrancing new machine, say an electric motor out of a Lancaster, or the box of switches and colored pilot lights we installed in an orange box and hooked up to make our 'instrument panel', or the hand-wound crystal set on which you could pick up the BBC news read at dictation speed for the forces overseas.

After Frank Wilden was demobilized in 1945, his sister Dorothy helped him start a repair business. My image of this two-year venture is the upstairs back bedroom at 8 Clifton Gardens, Golders Green, a room full of the outsides and insides of every kind of watch and clock, as well as his collection of antique hands and dials. There was a watchmaker's lathe, on which he machined the parts that couldn't be bought, a blow-pipe, spirit-lamp, and lump of charcoal for silver-soldering, sets of tiny graduated screwdrivers, drill bits of every shape and size, a whetstone, assorted types of files, burnishing tools, reamers, saws, tweezers, clamps, vises, side-cutters, pliers, punches, drifts, awls, gauges, and calipers along with all the other delicate instruments of his craft, everything in miniature. To drill the holes to rebush worn-out brass or jeweled pivots he used a bow drill no different from that used by Egyptian artisans 5000 years ago.

There were also magnifying glasses and jewellers' loupes that were just right for looking at other miniature things, such as the fine engraving and lithography on the stamps and cigarette cards he taught us to collect.

The stamp catalogues divided the world into two parts: Foreign Countries, and the British Empire and its Colonies. Invented in the United States during a tobacco war, cigarette cards are part of the archeology of the social media in the United States and Britain, tens of millions being issued between 1880 and 1939. The first cards were pictures of actresses.

Cigarette cards became the smoker's encyclopedia. They provided information, written and pictured with marvelous technical skill, on thousands of subjects. These included daring escapes, myths and legends, kings and queens, stars and constellations, believe it or not, pirates and highwaymen, Highland clans, Irish patriots, Chinese warriors, characters from Dickens, cries of London, VC heroes, military motors, the story of Napoleon, peeps into many lands, wings over the Empire, eastern proverbs, treasure trove, antique pottery, garden hints, breeds of dogs, garden flowers, birds and their eggs, butterflies and moths, life on the seashore, animals of the countryside, the story of navigation, wonderful railway travel, Empire air routes, overseas dominions, polar exploration, famous bridges, British locomotives, railway working, the world's dreadnoughts, international airliners, flags and funnels of leading steamship lines, life in the Royal Navy, the RAF at work, semaphore signalling, wireless telegraphy, this mechanized age, shots from famous films, builders of the Empire, soldiers of the king, women on war work, transportation then and now, celebrated ships, posters by famous artists, wonders of the world, famous inventions, fire-fighting appliances, engineering wonders, how-it-works, how-it-is-made, where-it-is-from, helpful hints around the home, safety first, arms and armor, the Boer War, the Boxer Rebellion, our colonial troops, riders of the world, national flags and arms, Derby winners, tennis tips, association footballers, sporting personalities, and science and technology – the 'dirty thirties' were also called 'The Age of Speed'

– and of course the other media, such as the stars of radio, stage and screen, and British warriors through the ages. Apart from war subjects, the largest categories of all were famous beauties and women of all nations. One of the very last issues, widely distributed in 1938, was Air Raid Precautions.

Goebbels used this medium also. A set of cards I came across recently consists of 50 real photographs of the Party Days of the NSDAP – the National Socialist German Workers Party – in Nuremberg in 1933. One card shows the Graf Zeppelin, symbol of German engineering, far in advance of the rest of the world. Another shows the film director, Leni Riefenstahl, shooting up into the blond arrogance of a Hitler Youth leader in the making of *Triumph of the Will* (1934).

Begged by boys from relatives, from smokers leaving tobacco shops, and from likely-looking men in the street – 'Any cigarette pictures, guv'nor?' – British and Empire cigarette cards taught manliness, monarchism, militarism, and imperialism. But they were also the best textbooks of general knowledge available to us. They had use value: they helped us pass exams. The quest for the unusual card or the card needed to complete a set was a daily adventure. Duplicates and unwanted cards had exchange value, like shrapnel. You could also win cards by gambling or testing skills with other boys in the underground economy in cards at school.

In World War One cigarette cards communicated optimism and solidarity between the Front Lines and the Home Front. In World War Two the government had full control of the immense resources of radio and film. By 1941 cigarette cards had been abolished to save paper.

Grandpa with his rhyming slang and endless friends operated in underworlds we never knew. If he wasn't grinning, he was winking, and if he wasn't winking, he was laughing, and he told the best stories I ever heard – better than any we read in the British Boys' Weeklies – the *Wizard*, the *Champion*, the *Hotspur*, the *Rover*, the *Adventure* – whose social values George Orwell analyzed in a biting essay on ideology in 1939. From these weekly serials and short stories (the *Rover* was founded in 1921, the *Hotspur*, in 1933) we received up-to-date instruction in imperialism, especially male imperialism. A favorite character was Lionheart Logan of the Royal Canadian Mounted Police.

Outside the movies, the medium of our outlook on America during the war was the Yank Mags: *Captain Marvel* (really a boy, Shazam!), the Marvel Family, the *Green Hornet*, *Superman*, *Superboy*, and – to keep up the morale of women on war work – *Wonder Woman*, *Superwoman*, and *Supergirl*. These we were given by endlessly cheerful and generous Canadian and American servicemen. There was an agreed-on signal for entering into close communication with these big tall men from overseas: 'Got any gum, chum?'.

The first black man I ever saw and talked to was a sergeant in the American Army Air Corps. He bought us ginger beer. I asked him for his autograph. He wrote: 'May all your troubles be little ones.'

Wizard and *Adventure*: Orwell published his analysis of the English-language boys' media in 1939. I read it in the 1950s. It rang true. Anglo-American movies and television have made it truer yet. Much like *Punch* at the turn of the century, and much like the religious weekly, *The Boy's Own Paper* (later a Boy Scout organ), the older papers, such as the *Gem* and the *Magnet* (1908–40), displayed traditional English attitudes: prejudice, scorn, and ignorance aimed at non-white, non-English, and non-upper-class people (social racism or its equivalent). Women and girls appear strictly in supporting roles. The working class is comic, criminal, deferential, or invisible. But in the 'modern' papers of the 1930s – seven of them the property of the Amalgamated Press combine, and thus linked to the *Daily Telegraph* and the *Financial Times* – there also emerge new themes: bully-worship and the cult of violence.

The readers (mostly males) are led to identify with 'a G-man, with a Foreign Legionary, with some variant of Tarzan, with an air ace, a master spy, an explorer, a pugilist – at any rate with some single all-powerful character who dominates everyone about him and whose usual method of solving any problem is a sock on the jaw.' In the Yank Mags of the same period (*Action Stories*, *Fight Stories*), says Orwell, 'you get real blood-lust, really gory descriptions of the all-in, jump-on-his-testicles style fighting, written in a jargon that has been perfected by people who brood endlessly on violence.'

When hatred of Hitler eventually became popular in the United States in the late 1930s, the Yank Mags quickly adapted 'anti-fascism' to pornographic purposes. By pornography (as distinct from eroticism), Orwell means violence against women – real or simulated, physical or mental, verbal or non-verbal, painted or pictured – or in other words, pain, degradation, and humiliation masquerading as sex, much like the all-star, all-media pornography of the 1980s.

He gives as an example a Yank Mag story of about 1938, called 'When Hell Came to America'. In it the agents of a 'blood-maddened European dictator' are trying to conquer the United States with invisible airplanes and death rays:

There is the frankest appeal to sadism, scenes in which the Nazis tie bombs to women's backs and fling them off heights to watch them blown to pieces in mid-air, others in which they tie naked girls together by their hair and prod them with knives to make them dance, etc., etc. The editor comments solemnly on all this, and uses it as a plea for tightening up restrictions against immigrants.

Irregular rules

When my grandfather told you stories, he had such perfect timing, you never missed a beat. One of his favorite subjects was a far-off desert people called the 'Fuzzy-Wuzzies', or Dervishes, whose great bravery was much talked about in the British Army in his day. Browsing through a used bookshop thirty-five years later, I came across the Dervishes again – in a old news clipping from the *Daily Telegraph*, the more gung-ho of the traditional Tory papers. Dated 1944, the item was reprinted in the Canadian Army newspaper, *The Maple Leaf*, and circulated during the Army's bitter struggle against fire and flood and crack German troops – the best in the world – on the way from Normandy to the liberation of the Netherlands in 1944–5. The headline ran:

Canucks Fight Like Dervishes, Writes Englishman.

Through this one connection – 'colonial troops fight like savages' – a new pattern, a pattern of patterns, suddenly made sense. (This is called 'learning-after-the-event', one of Freud's more useful contributions to understanding education.)

According to H. D. Ziman, the *Telegraph* correspondent:

It is no wonder the German troops believe Nazi propaganda about Canadian soldiers being savages with scalping knives. Many of the captured enemy are quite surprised to find that these Canadians who have fought like wild dervishes are really quiet, civilized, calm and well-disciplined when one meets them after the battle.

The truth is that the British invented the story about 'Canadian savages with scalping knives' in 1899, as part of their propaganda against the Boers, before the deployment of the First Canadian Contingent of 1000 largely upper-class volunteers in South Africa in January 1900.

I also met Grandpa's heroes in Kipling's 'Barrack-room Ballads', written in 1892, where Kipling accorded them an imperial salute:

So 'ere's *to* you Fuzzy-Wuzzy, at your 'ome in the Sowdan;
You're a pore benighted 'eathen but a first-class fightin' man;
An' ere's *to* you, Fuzzy-Wuzzy, with your 'ayrick 'ead of 'air –
You big black boundin' beggar – for you bruk a British square.

The 'Fuzzy-Wuzzies' were the Moslem followers of Mohammed

Ahmed, the Mahdi (d. 1885), in the Sudanese War of Independence. The Mahdists had driven the British and Egyptians out of the Sudan in 1881–5. The square they 'bruk' is a tactical formation to be used when surrounded, outflanked, or attacked from several directions. Scarcely used since Wellington's squares stopped the repeated onslaughts of the French at Waterloo in 1815, the square was revived in the colonial wars in Africa, as in the Zulu War of 1879. Its concentrated and disciplined fire power could stop a cavalry charge dead in its tracks.

In the teeth of breech-loading rifles and machine guns, the Dervishes (literally 'preachers') broke British squares at Tamai in 1884 and Abu Klea in 1885. As Douglas G. Browne recounts in *Private Thomas Atkins* (1941):

> It was a high tribute to the Mahdi's almost naked warriors, had they known it, that the famous two-deep line, which had been good enough for the French, the Russians, the Sikhs, the Afghans, and all the rest of the world, was not thought good enough for them (p. 251).

In 1884, as the British force of about 3000 men marched towards Tamai in two squares (a difficult mode of movement), the leading square at first advanced in good order, the ranks keeping their dressing and the Navy bluejackets pushing and hauling their Gatling and Gardner machine guns at the angles.

> Then, as thousands of yelling Dervishes appeared in the low scrub, waving swords and spears, the banners of their chiefs borne aloft, the front face of the square, and then the flanks opened a rapid fire. The men became excited, and got out of hand, blazing away so hotly, in spite of bugle calls and orders, that in a few minutes the whole square was wrapped in smoke. No one could see what was happening at a few yards distance (p. 257).

The companies of the York and Lancasters and the Black Watch which formed the front of the square continued to push on eagerly.

> But their ranks grew disordered, while their other companies, on the flanks, had failed to keep up. The rough ground and clinging scrub further disturbed the formation, and what had been a solid rectangle of red coats and white helmets assumed an irregular shape, with dangerous bulges and gaps. In vain officers yelled themselves hoarse; in vain the buglers blew the 'cease fire' again and again (p. 258).

No one heard them, and the blinding smoke was denser than ever.

And then out of the reek, from the scrub on either flank and from the deep gulley in front, leaped a horde of black figures, yelling like demons. In an instant the disordered square was broken, cracked like an egg. The York and Lancasters were flung staggering back upon the Marines, and through the gap the Mahdi's swordsmen poured in a flood, slashing and stabbing. Others got in at the angles, creeping under the very bayonets and the hot, smoking muzzles of the machine guns.

Then followed a blind, furious struggle, hand to hand, amid a hideous din of yells and rifle shots, and in a baffling fog of smoke.

Redcoats and naked black Hadendowas jabbed and wrestled breast to breast, and many of our men owed their lives to the crush, for, given sword- or spear-room, the muscular, lightly clad Arab was more than a match for the British private with his uniform and equipment and his heavy rifle. Pushing a bayonet-lunge aside with his circular hide shield, the former could get in several thrusts or slashes before his opponent recovered. Thus writhing and struggling, with this ravening swarm in its midst, the whole square was pressed back in increasing confusion, the men . . . jammed together in an unwieldy mob against the mounted officers and the frightened animals of the ammunition train.

Private Edwards of the Black Watch held off a dozen swordsmen to save a Gatling gun and won the V.C. Many of the Scots had their kilts torn right off, 'presenting a most unmilitary appearance'.

It was their rear companies, with those of the York and Lancasters, that saved the situation: they had time to face about, and kept formation; and the broken companies were able to rally on them as the brigade, in its confused retreat, got clear of the smoke and the huddle of fallen men, and saw, coming up on its right, as if on parade, the Royal Irish, the [King's Rifles], and the Gordons of the second square.

The second square, with better discipline and fire control, stopped charge after charge, and sent the cavalry sweeping round the Dervish flank, threatening their line of retreat. The Dervishes then withdrew; no one dared pursue them (p. 259).

Named by the British after the Afros and Dreadlocks sported by the Hadendowa tribe, the 'Fuzzies', both Arab and Nubian, were also the people – civilians, warriors, and wounded – who were slaughtered by lance, bayonet, rifle, and machine gun on the orders of General Herbert Kitchener during and after their final defeat at the Battle of Omdurman in 1898. Contemporary sources speak of 25,000 to 30,000 Mahdists killed, wounded, and captured. Of these only 3,000 or 4,000 were taken prisoner. Nearly 11,000 bodies were counted on the battlefield. Kitchener's British and Egyptian force lost 48 killed and 382 wounded.

Winston Churchill was there. He joined the 21st Lancers in one of the last cavalry charges in British military history. This was a tactical error, for which Kitchener was much criticized. The Lancers charged unbroken infantry of unknown quantity over unknown ground. The Mahdist infantry put the Lancers out of action.

Humanists said at the time that the slaughter at Omdurman was premeditated. One official story is that the killing was done in revenge for the annihilation of Hicks Pasha's army by Mahdist guerrillas in 1883. Another is that it was done in revenge for the death at Khartoum in 1885 of General 'Chinese' Gordon, a popular British mercenary and mystic who with the French had helped put down the Taiping Rebellion (1851–64) during the British Opium Wars (it is said that he personally directed the burning of the Emperor's summer palace in 1860, after its looting by French and British officers and men), when the British and Egyptian relieving force, transported up the Nile cataracts by Canadian voyageurs under the command of Lord Wolseley, who had learned to use river transport in suppressing the Red River Rebellion of Louis Riel and the Métis against English Canada in 1870, failed to reach Khartoum in time to save the Egyptian garrison.

The real reason is more simple. The Mahdist population were victims of the Rules of War When Fighting Irregular Troops. They were victims of the official policy of 'pacification' followed in every imperial war, including Algeria, Indochina, Zimbabwe, and Afghanistan.

Although he said little in public about the Battle of Omdurman, Winston Churchill did not keep it from his mother. He wrote to her from India on January 6, 1899:

> I shall merely say that the victory of Omdurman was disgraced by the inhuman slaughter of the wounded and that Kitchener was responsible for this.

Colonial warfare has become vastly more violent since the nineteenth century. In the Algerian War of Independence (1954–62), for one example, the French were responsible for the deaths of at least a million men, women, and children, out of a population of 9 million, and for the mental and physical maiming of untold numbers of the eventual survivors. The methods of interrogation used by the French in Indochina and Algeria, including half-drowning (the Americans used water torture in the Philippines, 1898–1906) and electrode shock (Franco's men used electric torture in the Spanish Civil War, 1936–39), are universally used by fascist armies, police forces, and governments today.

A fascist I define as anyone who enjoys inflicting violence or suffering, physical or mental, on other living beings.

In 1975, in an unforgettable book *Against Our Will*, Susan Brownmiller spelled out in horrifying detail the secret history of the grand strategy used by imperial generals in wars of conquest, colonial warfare, slave rebellions, peasant revolts, and people's wars.

The objective is to destroy the will to resist; the target is the entire population; the strategy is terror; the means is torture; the usual end is death; most of the victims are women and children; the worst instrument is rape.

To do this, you simply let your men loose on anyone they choose. You use men and boys you have brutalized through race and class oppression and the army, police, and prison systems as your instruments of imperial terror against young and old.

As the men say, 'All's fair in love and war.'

Rape is not a crime of passion, but a crime of power, a deliberate, conscious act of torture and degradation. Rape is the cross-burning and the lynching that keeps every woman in her place – and dependent on some men (father, brother, boyfriend, husband, son, police) to protect her from other men.

As the women say: 'Pornography is the theory, rape is the practice.'

In colonial war and banditry, individual men and often gangs of men rape and mutilate women and children, girls and boys, and, less often, other men. For imperial troops and bandits this is an act of 'manhood' – meaning here the power of God over anyone and everyone without a weapon or the strength to fight back.

In basic training with the US Army, the first definition in the Naming of Parts has long been this one:

> This is my rifle (18-year-old holds up M-16)
> This is my gun (puts hand to crotch)
> One is for killing
> The other for fun.

'All's fair in love and war' is the manifesto of the mercenary, the bandit, the free fire zone, the death squad. Imperial troops and bandits fight for the power to do with other people exactly what they please. People's armies obey strict codes of ethics – and above all Chu Teh's Tenth Rule: 'Never take liberties with women'.

General Chu Teh (b. 1886) laid down his fifteen Rules of Discipline in 1928, as his peasant guerrillas battled the Nationalist forces of Chiang Kai-shek and the warlords in the rural uprising whose failure led to the formation of the celebrated 4th Red Army and the 22-year-long guerrilla partnership between Chu Teh, the soldier, and Mao Tse-Tung, the commissar.

Chu Teh's Tenth Rule was implicitly observed by the Viet Cong guerrillas and the North Vietnamese regulars throughout the Vietnam war, as the Saigon correspondents knew very well, but did not care to report – perhaps because among American troops rape was known as 'SOP' or 'standard operating procedure'. The man who broke the Saigon press corps' silence was Peter Arnett, a New Zealander, who told Susan Brownmiller, who put it in her book.

Anglo-American rules

The Moslems of the Sudan were victims of the ruthlessness with which the English upper class built their Empire – now largely reduced to Southern England's oldest colonial dependencies, the Northern and Celtic parts of the British Isles.

Their American counterparts have behaved no differently. As Gary Cooper reminded us in 1939 in *The Real Glory*, the year of the Battle of Omdurman also marks the expansion of the United States into the Caribbean (Cuba and Puerto Rico) and the Pacific (Guam and the Philippines), where the Americans seized the remnants of the Spanish Empire in the Spanish-American War of 1898.

Vividly etched in my memory is the scene in which Gary Cooper, playing an Army doctor, humiliates a Moro, and therefore Moslem, guerrilla in front of a crowd of Catholic Filipinos, by threatening to bury him in a pigskin. The man is not afraid of death, but in terror of being defiled, he begs for mercy, and is denounced as a coward.

Four years before, while playing an Indian Army officer on the North West Frontier in the days of Victoria, Captain Cooper had been directed to use the same mental torture to show Lieutenant Franchot Tone how to get information out of an Afghani rebel in *The Lives of a Bengal Lancer* (1935) – a film the *Daily Telegraph* reviewed as 'the best army picture ever made'.

Every culture distinguishes between honorable and dishonorable death, and between ordinary death or execution and a death that is like no other. The British in India knew this when they used religion as a weapon in putting down the 'Indian Mutiny' of 1857–9. In front of disarmed sepoy regiments, they blew Hindu and Moslem rebels from the mouths of guns. Moslem and Hindu were mingled together in the growing pile of dismembered bodies, the worst kind of death Indians of either religion could imagine.

The Philippine-American War, officially known as the 'Philippine Insurrection', lasted from 1899 to 1906, with active resistance continuing until 1912. In that war the guerrillas fighting for independence were Christians and Moslems, just as they were when the Huks and others, aided by US training, communications, and arms, fought the Japanese occupiers in World War Two, and just as they are today. But *The Real Glory* (a few weeks in the South in 1906) makes the entire war of the independence fighters against the Americans, their colonial troops, and their collaborators appear to be a religious war (as in Ulster), a civil war between different Philippine islanders, with bad, dark, fanatical, and evil-looking Moslems on one side, and good, light, polite, and angelic-looking Catholics on the other.

David Niven – graduate of Sandhurst and veteran of four years with the Highland Light Infantry (he resigned his commission in 1932) – is there to see fair play, while Broderick Crawford tends an orchid collection and slaps Moro prisoners around. There follows in the film all the obligatory images of white hospitals, devoted priests, happy villagers, kind soldiers, and handsome children – a black and white version of the official picture of the Americans in Vietnam before the Tet Offensive in 1968.

No empire ever expanded so rapidly and with so little effort as did the American empire in 1898. With the annexation of the Hawaian Islands completing the chain of island bases across the ocean, the United States set out to seize strategic control of the Pacific via the Philippines – next door to China, Southeast Asia, and Japan – while also opening new markets to American trade.

The official American story, beginning with President McKinley, is that the United States got into the Philippines by accident – just as the English say they 'muddled into' the British Empire – and that once they were there they had to stay to teach the people freedom. But General Arthur MacArthur, father of General Douglas MacArthur and military governor of the Philippines between 1898 and 1900, explained it differently to a Senate committee in 1901. The Philippine group of islands, he said, 'is the finest in the world'.

> Its strategic position is unexcelled by that of any other position on the globe . . . It affords a means of protecting American interests which, with the very least output of physical power, has the effect of a commanding position in itself to retard hostile action.

Viewed as a military, naval, and commercial base facing China and Southeast Asia, the Philippines lie in the center, the most favored position, he said, of thousands of miles of Asian coastline, with Japan on one flank and British India on the other.

The presence of the United States in the islands, MacArthur said, 'is one of the results, in logical sequence, of great national prosperity'. Moreover, he added, in an ingenious explanation of imperialism,

to doubt the wisdom of the United States remaining in the islands
is to doubt the stability of republican institutions, and amounts
to a declaration that a nation thus governed is incapable of
successfully resisting strains that arise naturally from its own
freedom, and from its own productive energy.

The senator from Indiana, Albert J. Beveridge, spoke more directly
in 1900. He described the Philippine Islands as 'a self-supporting,
dividend-paying fleet, permanently anchored at a spot selected by the
strategy of Providence, commanding the Pacific'. The power that rules
the Pacific, he said, is the power that rules the world. God had been
preparing the English-speaking and Teutonic peoples for a thousand
years to be the 'master organizers' of the world, to 'establish system
where chaos reigns', to govern 'savage and senile peoples', and to
become the 'trustees of the world's progress, guardians of its righteous
peace'. The Philippine Islanders have no right to independence, he
declared, because they are not a 'self-governing race':

> What alchemy will change the Oriental quality of their blood and
> set the self-governing currents of the American pouring through
> their Malay veins?

The United States, he argued, has a 'divine mission': to lead 'the
regeneration of the world' and to become 'the arbiter of the destinies
of mankind'. In this divine mission, he concluded, lie 'all the profit, all
the glory, all the happiness possible to man'.

The Chicago *Times-Herald*, an Administration paper, simply said:

> We find that we want the Philippines . . . We also want Porto
> Rico . . . We want Hawaii now . . . We may want the Carolines,
> the Ladrones, the Pelew, and the Marianna groups. If we do we
> will take them . . . Much as we deplore the necessity of territorial
> acquisition, the people now believe that the United States owes it
> to civilization to accept the responsibilities imposed on it by the
> fortunes of war.

The question of which foreign power would control the Philippines
was last settled when the United States recovered the islands from
Imperial Japan in 1945. The colony has supposedly been independent
since 1946.

Kipling seems to have recognized at the turn of the century that the
mantle of world empire was passing from Britain to the United States.
His 'White Man's Burden', published in 1899 with the subtitle, 'The
United States and the Philippine Islands', was addressed to the new
colonizers. The first, third, and last verses run like this:

Take up the White Man's burden –
　Send forth the best ye breed –
Go bind your sons to exile
　To serve your captives' need;
To wait in heavy harness
　On fluttered folk and wild –
Your new-caught, sullen peoples,
　Half devil and half child.

Take up the White Man's Burden –
　The savage wars of peace –
Fill full the mouth of Famine
　And bid the sickness cease;
And when your goal is nearest
　The end for others sought,
Watch Sloth and heathen Folly
　Bring all your hope to nought.

Take up the White Man's burden –
　Have done with childish days –
The lightly proffered laurel,
　The easy, ungrudged praise.
Comes now, to search your manhood
　Through all the thankless years,
Cold-edged with dear-bought wisdom,
　The judgment of your peers!

The 15th edition of the *Encyclopedia Britannica* tells us that at least 200,000 women, children, and men were killed between 1898 and 1906 by the American counter-insurgency program in the Philippines. Repression has continued practically ever since. I have seen somewhere a photograph of an American soldier standing on a heap of Filipino bodies. So terrible were the massacres that one of the American generals seems to have been made a scapegoat for the official strategy. He was actually convicted by court martial of using 'indiscriminate ferocity', and forced to retire.

During the Philippine War, the United States announced its 'Open-Door Policy' on China, designed to forestall any further partition of that country by other powers. In 1900, as you may not have guessed from *55 Days at Peking* (1963), with Charlton Heston and David Niven, a six-nation army invaded China to put down a peasant rebellion against foreigners and foreign influence. The rebels were the Chinese nationalists of the Society of Righteous and Harmonious Fists (the 'Boxers' of the Rebellion of 1899–1901). Manipulated by the Empress, the rebels retaliated against a century of foreign outrages by killing hundreds of foreigners, especially missionaries, as well as the Chinese nationals associated with them.

The Allied Expeditionary Force relieved the legations in Peking, sacked the Chinese fortifications, and again reduced China to subservience. For several months, North China was given over to rape and plunder by the foreigners, civilian and military, high and low.

The Boxer Rebellion became a repetition of the Opium Wars (1839–42, 1856–60), when the British, with the help of the French later on, had used force to impose on China the British opium trade from India – a combination of high profits and effective psychological warfare. The British seized Hong Kong in 1842 and the Kowloon Peninsula in 1860. They also secured crippling indemnities, and expanded the British and European penetration of the huge Chinese market.

According to G. A. Henty's account, *With the Allies to Pekin*, the punitive expedition that marched against the Boxers to Peking was composed of 8000 Japanese, 4500 Russians, 3000 British, 2500 Americans (including three regiments of regulars from the Philippines), and 800 Frenchmen. (The German contingent operated separately.) With them were 1200 Chinese troops under British officers. Each nation exacted a financial indemnity. The Chinese were still paying the interest on these reparations after China became a republic in the Revolution of 1911 led by Sun Yat-Sen (1866–1925).

During the Boxer Rebellion, knowing that Japan had its eyes on Manchuria, the Czar completed the Russian occupation of that Chinese province, from which his forces were partially dislodged by the devastating victory of Japan on land and sea in the Russo-Japanese War of 1905, after which Japan annexed Korea. This was the first modern war in which a non-white nation defeated a nation ruled by whites.

At the same time, half a world away, the British were still bogged down in the Second South African War (1899–1902) against the Boer republics of the Orange Free State and the Transvaal. It was in the last two years of this war, the guerrilla war, that the British commander-in-chief, now Lord Kitchener of Khartoum, copied the system the Spanish had used against Cuban guerrillas, the *reconcentrado* or concentration camp, to break the popular support for the Boer commandos. Between 18,000 and 28,000 Boer civilians, mostly women and children, and uncounted Africans, died in these camps from hunger and disease.

The official story is that the 'Boer War' was a 'white man's war', a war between whites. In actual fact, blacks were dragooned into forced labor by both sides in South Africa. They were forced to fetch and carry, to drive army ox-wagons, to act as couriers, guides, and spies, and to dig the trenches from which the Boers on the regular front, with smokeless powder and magazine rifles, could hold a position against greatly superior forces. When captured by either side, blacks who had been forced to work for the other side were commonly shot out of hand for 'collaborating with the enemy'.

Seventy-eight years after the Siege of Mafeking (1899–1900), it was revealed in Pakenham's *Boer War* that the garrison commander, Colonel Robert Baden-Powell (1857–1941), fresh from the campaigns against the Ashanti and Matabele in 1896 – and founder of the Boy Scouts in 1908 – had systematically starved his 'Kaffir' troops and laborers to feed the whites. A number of starving Africans caught stealing food were shot. He had 115 others flogged. As the siege wore on, the black members of the garrison were faced with death by starvation in the town or running the gauntlet of the Boers surrounding it.

No one has any idea how many thousands of Africans were executed, died in battle, or died of starvation in this war. The rape of African women by Boers and British is rarely even hinted at in the official histories.

In August 1901, in keeping with the unwritten but no less official British policy, the men of the Bush Veldt Carabineers, a special anti-commando unit from Australia, were ordered by their officers to shoot twelve captured Boer guerrillas. In February 1902, the British court-martialled six of the Carabineers' officers, five Australians and one Englishman. Not being generals, two of the Australian scapegoats, Lieutenant Handcock and Lieutenant Breaker Morant, were convicted of multiple murder and shot.

Some 7360 Canadians volunteered to serve in South Africa, mostly with the regulars. There is every reason to believe that the same unwritten and all-too-regular rules of colonial warfare were followed by other special service units besides the Bush Veldt Carabineers, including the Canadian and South African irregular units, and the British regulars as well.

Production rules

I can still see the diagram explaining the atomic bomb printed in the *Daily Express* in August 1945. I was nearly 10. I was quite surprised that the newspapers kept on coming out, because now the war was over, how could there be any news? There was of course, but there was never a diagram explaining war. And if we hated the Germans and the Japanese so much that we had a war with them, and dropped that bomb on Japan, how was it possible for us to become friends after it was over? I didn't mean we shouldn't be friends. I meant that if we could be now, after all that killing, we could have been before, so why had we had a war at all?

In Canada ten years later, I began reading about war, beginning with

FIGURE I.1: War, inflation, and prosperity: a general view. Periods of higher prices represent times of expansion; periods of lower prices represent times of recession or depression. A depression differs from a recession in being widespread or world-wide, as in the period 1980–83, rather than being localized or regional. Additional dates: the US-Mexican War (1846–48), the American Civil War (1861–65), and the Franco-Prussian War (1870).

World War Two. In the United States ten years after that, I was again in a country in the middle of a war: the Second Indochina War (1957–75), and now it was on television. (The French Empire had been defeated in the war of 1946–54 by General Vo Nguyen Giap and the Viet Minh at the siege of Dien Bien Phu.) The average age of Americans serving in World War Two was about 26; in Vietnam it was about 19.

Until 1965 all the books I read accepted war as necessary, normal, and inevitable. Necessary for whom? Arms races leading into major wars have coincided with major economic booms (Figure I.1). War production has brought economies out of serious depressions and massive unemployment. As the *Bank Credit Analyst* for October 1974 pointed out, citing the work of N. D. Kondratieff in the 1920s, over the two hundred years since the present economic system became dominant over most of the world, one can distinguish a long-term pattern of major booms and busts, about 54 years from peak to peak. Long-term depressions and expansions have each led to wars (Figure I.2). This pattern suggests that war is an essential component of the long-term business cycle under capitalism, state and private.

The idea of a supposedly rational economic system being dependent on destruction goes against common sense. Such a system must surely

THE KONDRATIEFF WAVE

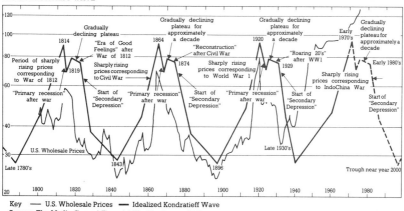

Key — U.S. Wholesale Prices — Idealized Kondratieff Wave
Source: *The Media General Financial Weekly*, August 1972.

FIGURE I.2: The Kondratieff Wave, as manifested in the economic history of the United States. In the diagram an idealized K-wave is superimposed over actual US wholesale prices since the 1780s. The pattern of the K-wave is as follows: (1) a 20- to 30-year period of rising prosperity and prices ending in a major war (e.g. the period 1843–64); (2) then a period of about ten years consisting of a brief 'primary recession' after the war, a short recovery, and then a slowly declining 'plateau' (e.g. 1864–74); and finally (3) a long decline in prosperity and prices (the 'secondary depression') ending in another war (e.g. the Spanish-American War of 1898). Kondratieff, who first published his findings in the 1920s (he died soon after, purged by Stalin), argued that the 'peak' wars, bigger and more violent than the 'trough' wars, are the result of a boom with no further place to go. The trough wars, in contrast, smaller and cheaper, help the system to recover from its long decline. (The three longest and worst depressions in the US all came 8 to 10 years after the peak, in 1825–29, 1874–79, and 1929–33, each followed by a further period of deflation.) In US economic history the peak wars are the Revolutionary and Napoleonic Wars (1789–1815), the Civil War (1861–65), World War One (1914–18), and the escalated Vietnam War (1965–74). The trough wars are the Mexican War (1846–8), the Spanish-American and Philippine Wars (1898–1906), and World War Two (1941–45) – the latter coming a little earlier than the pattern strictly suggests.

be inhuman – unless, of course, you have been taught that human beings are born evil, born sinners. Major and minor scientists and certain religions have done much to make Original Sin popular, but there's no good evidence that the problem of imperial war is an individual, genetic, or 'sociobiological' matter. In contrast, the evidence against the modern economic system – both capitalist and state-capitalist – is simply damning.

After the Great Depression of 1873–96, when British capitalism first began losing its industrial and technological monopoly to German,

Japanese, and American competition, the boom and the arms race of the late 1890s led step by step into World War One via the colonial wars at the turn of the century. The boom began to collapse soon after the military truce in 1918. The early 1920s were years of deep depression with high unemployment. The recovery after 1925 – 'the roaring twenties' – led via the crash of 1929 to the long, deep, and worldwide Great Depression that lasted in the United States until 1941, the year America entered the war.

Social unrest was widespread. When the arms race was renewed during the early 1930s, H. G. Wells and many others saw that another world war was on its way. Like the 1920s *Punch* cartoonist who told us to expect another war when the post-war babies reached military age – in 1940 – Wells almost got the dates right. The problem is to know whether he was right about a question of much greater generality: Does the grand strategy of capitalism – state or private, East or West – depend on war?

From his study of history, Wells became convinced that the modern economic system is unstable, prey to inflation and unemployment. He argued that it seeks to overcome its oscillations by expanding production. But in the process it eventually produces more goods than can be profitably sold. The result is depression. To expand production the system must expand consumption. One of the system's ways of expanding consumption is to pour tax money into arms production, and eventually to use labor and capital to destroy labor and capital by means of war, which also serves as a weapon in the arsenal of social control.

By 1933, when Hitler came to power in Germany, new wars were already under way. In 1931 the Japanese had invaded and occupied Manchuria. By 1933 they had begun the invasion of China, with the objective of enslaving the Chinese nation to Japanese industry. In 1936 Fascist Italy set out to conquer and colonize the people of Abyssinia (Ethiopia).

In Spain in 1936 General Franco and other Fascist army officers rebelled against the elected government of the Spanish Republic, using German help to airlift Moroccan forces from the colonial troops in Spanish Africa to invade Spain itself. In the three years' civil war that followed, the United States, Britain, and France tacitly allowed Hitler and Mussolini to use Spain as a testing ground for weapons and tactics developed with World War Two in mind, and forced the Republicans into dependence upon Stalin, who soon betrayed them. Some 1200 Canadian volunteers fought for the Republic in the Abraham Lincoln, George Washington, and Mackenzie-Papineau battalions of the International Brigades before the Republic was defeated in April 1939.

Also in 1939, besides Hitler's invasion of Poland on September 1, German troops occupied the rest of Czechoslovakia, Italy invaded

Albania, Japan cut China off from French Indochina, and Russia invaded Finland.

In 1933, in *The Shape of Things To Come*, analyzing the arms race of the 1890s that led directly into the First World War, Wells had written:

> Without this cancer growth of armies and navies, the paradox of over-production latent in competitive private enterprise would probably have revealed itself in an overwhelming mass of unemployment before even the end of the nineteenth century. A social revolution might have occurred then. Militarism, however, alleviated these revolutionary stresses, by providing vast profit-yielding channels of waste. And it also strengthened the forces of social repression.

As Cecil Rhodes (1853–1902) had said at the time: 'You have to be an Imperialist to avoid civil war.'

(Between 1881 and 1905 – including the 'Gay Nineties' – there were some 37,000 strikes in the United States, violently opposed by local police, the state-based National Guards, and company goon squads.)

Almost exactly a hundred years before, Carl von Clausewitz, Prussian student of Napoleon (first modern dictator) and modern apostle of total war, had said that war is 'a real political instrument, a continuation of political commerce, a carrying out of the same [ends] by other means'. Wells has taken this candid analysis much further. He is saying in effect that war is a real commercial instrument, a continuation of ordinary business, a carrying out of commercial ends by military means.

We can add some recent evidence to Wells' argument about economic instability, armaments, unemployment, and war. According to the CBS television program, *60 Minutes* (May 4, 1980), the original escalation of the price of oil in 1973 had to do with armaments, and specifically with the overproduction associated with Vietnam.

In 1971 the British withdrew from the Persian Gulf. In 1972 the United States was 'winding down' the Vietnam War. In that same year, Richard Nixon and Henry Kissinger stopped off on the way back from the Moscow summit conference to see the Shah of Iran. They invited him to look after American political and business interests in the Gulf. They offered him all the 'high-tech' American military equipment and counter-insurgency training programs he wanted, much of which was the most sophisticated in the world, and some of which was still too secret for general export.

The Shah began to buy arms like a man possessed. But the only way that Iran could afford to pay for this vastly expensive equipment was by raising the price of oil. Saudi Arabia, financially conservative and a strong supporter of the United States, was opposed to such a move, fearing its destabilizing effects. So were a number of highly qualified American specialists, including William E. Simon, later Secretary of the Treasury. But President Nixon and Secretary of State Kissinger over-rode all opposition. The result was that in October 1973, aided and abetted by the energy companies, the Shah personally led the Organiz-ation of Petroleum Exporting Countries (OPEC) into quadrupling the price of oil.

Oil inflation multiplied already existing world inflation, which began as a result of Vietnam. The dislocation of trade and markets, US government borrowing to fight the war, and the war economy had produced an inflation rate of about 5 percent in the late 1960s, which was considered very serious at the time. By the early 1970s the export of American inflation into Europe, much of it via the French banks in Saigon, had destabilized and then wrecked the world monetary system of stable exchange rates set up at Bretton Woods in 1944.

(Between 1957 and 1967 in Canada, rents rose by an average 4 per cent a year; the Consumer Price Index rose an average of 2.3 per cent a year. At the same time personal net income was rising on the average by a little over 5 per cent a year.)

The multiplier or compounding effect of inflation means that at a rate of 7 percent per year, prices will double about every ten years. (The rule of thumb to calculate this kind of growth – exponential growth – is the same as for compound interest. The doubling time is approximately equal to 70 divided by the growth rate. For example, at its estimated annual rate of increase of 1.9 per cent, the world population will double in 37 years.)

In the 1970s price increases, high profits, the price of oil, and continued government borrowing produced double-digit inflation (about 13 per cent in North America in 1980), which in turn produced interest rates of 20 per cent and more as the banks simply added the rate of inflation to the rate of interest. The three-year depression that followed drove unemployment in the industrialized countries to its highest levels since the Great Depression, and inflation down to the 5 per cent level we began with in the late 1960s.

Apart from the defeat in Vietnam, the increases in the price of oil in 1973 and after were the most important events in the series of events that brought to a halt the longest general economic boom in American history (1941–74), which began with World War Two and continued after the war with the replacement of destroyed capital and the rebuilding of production in Europe through the Marshall Plan of 1948–51, by which the Allied countries were assisted in paying their debts to the United States. Between 1945 and 1965 American industry gained greater economic and technological power over Western Europe, notably Britain, increased its power in Australia, and took strategic economic control of Canada, its markets, and the use of its resources.

The postwar boom continued with most people's taxes being diverted into greater defense spending, and the rise of the modern arms industry. With American military aid and advisers being sent to 'trouble spots' all over the world – in the last years of the First Indochina War (1946–54) the French forces were largely financed and supplied with weaponry and air support by the United States, and in 1954 President Eisenhower actually considered 'loaning' France a couple of atomic bombs – the boom continued with minor ups and downs through the Chinese people's victory in the civil war against the US-supported forces of Ch'iang Kai-shek (1945–49) and through the Korean War (1950–53) – where twenty-four nations killed or wounded nearly 2 million working men, and killed, wounded, or made homeless several million civilians. United States deaths were about 55,000.

W. Averell Harriman called Korea 'a sour little war'; Republicans referred to Truman's and Acheson's action as 'the foreign policy blunder of the century'. Commented General Omar Bradley, Chairman of the Joint Chiefs of Staff, of the 'unvictorious conclusion' of the war: 'Frankly, a great military disaster. The wrong war, in the wrong place, at the wrong time, with the wrong enemy' (China). Or as the college boys put it: 'There's two things we gotta avoid: Korea and gonorrhea'.

Two months after the start of fighting in Korea (June 25, 1950), the United States gave the first military assistance to the French in their new colonial war of conquest in Indochina (1946–54).

Moreover, as Joseph Goulden reports in *Korea: The Untold Story* (1983, p. xv):

> The Korean War marked the start of the construction of a military juggernaut the support of which consumed half the annual federal budget, even in 'peacetime' years, and found American men and women at posts in the farthest reaches of the world.

Of the phoney 'missile gap' between the US and Russia that helped get John Kennedy elected over Richard Nixon in 1960 (by the barest of margins), and the Bay of Pigs disaster, followed by the Cuban Missile Crisis of October 1962, the current edition of the *Encyclopaedia Britannica* (1974) comments, under 'International Relations':

> With its global ring of Strategic Air Command (SAC) bases, the United States had always possessed an overwhelming strategic advantage in its ability to deliver nuclear warheads to targets in the Soviet Union.

Nonetheless, in 1961,

when Kennedy took office, he began a vigorous upgrading of the strategic missile program, a prodigious expansion of the conventional forces, the development of a new 'counterinsurgency' arm [the Special Forces or Green Berets] to deal with civil revolts, and, on the political front, an Alliance for Progress [and Peace Corps] economic-aid program to offer a long-term free world alternative to Communist revolution in Latin America and the underdeveloped world.

John Kennedy was also responsible for the deepening American military commitment to Laos, Thailand, South Vietnam, and Cambodia.

Of the escalation of the arms race by the United States in the 1980s, The *Guardian Weekly* of January 15, 1984, has this to say, in an article by Harold Jackson:

The United States, which already has 26,000 nuclear bombs and warheads in its arsenal, has embarked on the biggest production programme since the early days of the nuclear era, according to a privately sponsored academic report released in Washington on [January 9, 1984].

The US is producing eight new nuclear weapons per day, and these are a new generation of the technology of destruction.

The report is the *Nuclear Weapons Databook* (1984). The Chairman of the Federation of American Sciences, Dr Frank von Hippel, comments in a foreword that this is 'the most authoritative and complete reference work available on US forces and capabilities'.

It is the first volume of an eight-volume encyclopedia of world nuclear weapons. The White House says that the study is 'not in America's national interest'.

In Vietnam the United States was assisted by troops from Thailand and South Korea, by about 8,000 men and women committed by the governments of Australia and New Zealand, by a contingent from the Philippines, under General Fidel Ramos, and by about 15,000 Canadian volunteers, while the Green Berets used the Montagnards (despised by the Vietnamese) as mercenaries.

The first US advisers were formally requested by South Vietnam in 1955. In 1960 adviser strength was increased from 327 to 685. The first American to die in Vietnam was an OSS officer accidentally killed by the Viet Minh in 1945; the first of the new advisers was killed in 1961. In 1962 President Kennedy increased the military commitment to 4000 men. By 1963 there were 15,000 American troops in the country, and Secretary of Defense Robert McNamara predicted an end to the war by 1965. At the end of 1965, after President Johnson's dramatic escalation of the conflict, the troop total was 181,000. It rose to 385,000 in 1966 and to 536,100 in 1968. Figures vary widely, but not counting the thousands of American civilians in the country, some 3 million American troops served in Vietnam between 1964 and 1975. According to the *National Geographic* for August 1985 'nine million men and women . . . were involved in the 18-year course of the war . . . nearly three million in the combat zone.'

Other casualty figures also vary from source to source, and few armies concern themselves with recording civilian deaths, especially in colonial wars.

In eight years of war (1946–54) the French metropolitan and colonial troops lost about 75,000 killed; their opponents, the Viet Minh, are said to have lost 150,000 or more.

In the eighteen years of the American commitment between 1957 and 1975 an estimated 400,000 South Vietnamese troops died. I have seen no figures for the Viet Cong. According to *Soldier of Fortune* (December 1984), more than 57,000 Americans were killed (actually 57,939) and 300,000 wounded. An accepted estimate for the North Vietnamese forces is over 1 million dead (*Mother Jones*, April/May 1986).

In *The Ten Thousand Day War: Vietnam 1945–1975* (1981), Michael Maclear reports a North Vietnamese estimate that 15,000,000 Vietnamese died in the Indochina wars.

Carl and Shelley Mylands estimated in the 1968 edition of *The Violent Peace* that between 1945 and 1968 there were some fifty military conflicts big enough to be called wars. Sixteen of them were fought between sovereign nations, the others were anti-colonial liberation movements or anti-governmental uprisings, and twenty of these involved foreign troops. More recent estimates give a figure of 150 serious military conflicts, including civil wars, since the end of World War Two. In 1983 the Hudson Institute estimated that 32 million people had died in 130 wars since 1945.

The oil price rise of October 1973 was a multinational coup d'état. Supply and demand had nothing to do with it. When the price went up, the market was glutted with oil – the result of overproduction. The oil glut is still with us, and finally the price has fallen. But most prices are still rising while real wages are falling behind the rate of inflation; most profits are either very large or very uncertain; spending on arms and military communications is increasing to new and unprecedented levels; the banks have kept the price of money up, in spite of reduced inflation; supposedly stable First World governments are creating larger and larger deficits, keeping interest rates higher than a healthy world economy would require; many Third World countries are effectively bankrupt; vast sums of money are still seeking investment (by the logic of the system, they ought to be placed in new production, but most are being wasted in speculation and mergers); smaller competitors are being wiped out; economic and political power is becoming even more concentrated in fewer and fewer hands, mostly male; more and more philosophical, scientific, and strategic talent is being swallowed up by stock trading and the defense-destruction industry, to the detriment of the arts, sciences, and world society; and increasing world-wide unemployment is forecast for the mid-1980s and long after. These are ingredients for war.

There is of course no guarantee that past trends will continue their full course. The system could collapse first, or blow itself to pieces.

The immediate strategic deficiency in the world economic system is the vast loads of debt carried by most countries, debts resulting from irresponsible lending by banks awash in petrodollars in the seventies and early eighties, and continuing government deficits, of which the most dangerous to world stability is that of the United States, much of it directly attributable to massive expenditures for arms, including the scientific fraud called Star Wars ('celestial snooker' says Richard Ennals).

Besides its massive tax cut for the rich, the Reagan administration's four-and-a-half year, $1 trillion arms escalation has resulted in annual deficits which have soared from $79 billion in 1981 to an estimated $213 billion in 1985 – 'doubling the national debt and equaling all the debt piled up by previous administrations' (*U.S. News + World Report*, July 29, 1985).

According to the economist and philosopher John Kenneth Galbraith, the military, in both the US and the Soviet Union, has escaped the control of its governments and is now 'a force on its own'.

Traditionally, military expenditure – weapons development, weapons purchases – were in response to international tension. We have now moved into different mode where the tension is created to promote the military expenditure (*Vancouver Sun*, April 25, 1986).

This is a system set to escalate exponentially to infinity or oblivion.

We know from modern ecology that competition in nature leads to diversity of species, sharing of territory, and long-range survival. We know from modern history that competition under capitalism leads to monopoly in business, struggles for territory, and uncertain survival. The concentration of capital destroys the diversity needed for flexible responses to future uncertainties.

Except for the new and dangerous fact that we now have inflation and unemployment at the same time – both undoubtedly much higher than is officially admitted by any country – the present world situation fits in well with the beginning of *The Shape of Things to Come* (1933).

Popular rules

The rules of thumb passed on in my family combined the artisan ethic
with the popular sayings of the 1930s and the 1940s. These maxims
can be understood in many ways, including the way a man like Kipling
might understand them. But in their positive sense they are practical
guides to that combination of respect for self, respect for others, and
respect for quality that makes for sensible relations with other people.

They also help to maintain morale – with high morale success may
still be difficult, but without it there will be no victory at all – for they
are above all anti-defeatist. As hopeless as matters may appear, an
extra effort can bring about the success that lies just around the corner:

– Stick to your guns.
– Don't give up the ship.
– Turn adversity to advantage.
– It's a bad workman blames his tools.
– A job worth doing is worth doing well.
– If at first you don't succeed, try, try, try, again.
– It's an ill wind blows nobody any good.
– Where there's a will, there's a way.
– Actions speak louder than words.
– You can't win 'em all.
– Don't panic.

When we moved to Sussex from Golders Green in northwest London
in 1949, I learned another one:

– Sussex wunt be druv.

By 1952, the year before I dropped out of school and left on the SS
Arosa Kulm for Wolfe's Cove, Québec, and thence via Canadian Pacific
for Vancouver, British Columbia, we were living at Three Cups Corner,
East Sussex, named after the roadside inn my father and mother leased
from the Star Brewing Company of Eastbourne. People were shorter
in the old days. Anyone over six feet had to duck the roofbeams to get
from the front door to the bar. Over the inglenook fireplace in the
public bar someone had carved initials and a date, 1696.

The hamlet of Three Cups was largely inhabited by gypsies, stigma-
tized in those days as 'diddy-guys', who had settled down and taken
up the art of buying and selling junk, and in whose richly decorated
homes my brother, born in 1937, and myself, born in 1935, first saw
television.

The traditions of the Sussex coast are shipwrecking, smuggling, and
privateering. At the farm near Heathfield owned by Mr English French,

where Alan and I hunted rabbit and pigeon with a 32-inch 12-bore with external hammers and a stock bound up with copper wire, the house had been built out of great oak beams from ancient shipwrecks. In years gone by, when the sea came up much closer inland, the Three Cups Inn had been a haunt of those the Sussex people called 'the gentlemen'. Protected from the revenuers by many a parish priest – they paid their friends in kind – the gentlemen were the land-smugglers who took the cargoes landed on the beach, lace, brandy, tobacco, and all the rest, along the Sussex byways up to London.

Imperial rule

If you turn northwest at Three Cups Corner and head for Punnett's Town, you pass the stone memorial to Jack Cade at Cade Street near Heathfield. Jack Cade was the Irishman who led the Kentish Rebellion against the government of Henry VI – a major rebellion of middle-class property-holders that contributed to the outbreak of the Wars of the Roses (1455–85), the civil war between feudal factions that paved the way for the autocracy of the Tudor monarchs, notably Henry VIII and Elizabeth I. Jack Cade died of his wounds somewhere near this spot on July 12, 1450, as his captors were taking him to London. Shakespeare tells the story in *Henry VI, Part 2*.

If you turn south-east at Three Cups and head for the sea, you arrive at Battle, the site of the battle of Hastings, north of Pevensey Level, where William the Conqueror landed in 1066.

The Saxons who lost to William at Hastings were descended from the Germanic tribes who had invaded and conquered half of Celtic Britain in the seventh century of the Common Era (CE). The ancient and loosely connected Celtish imperium, centered on the present frontier between France and Germany, had lasted some six hundred years. Until the expansion of the Roman Empire in the first and second centuries CE, the Celts had dominated most of Europe and part of Asia Minor. Celtish peoples include the Celto-Iberians of Spain, the Celts of Italy, the Gauls of France, the Bretons of Brittany, the ancient Britons, the Manx of the Isle of Man, the Irish, the Scots, the Cornish, and the Welsh.

The greatest of the Celtic queens of the ancient Britons was Boudicca (Boadicea), Queen of the Iceni in what is now the county of Norfolk. Left defenseless by the death of her husband against outrages by the Roman conquerors in garrison in Britain, she raised a rebellion in 61 CE. As the Roman historian Tacitus tells the tale, bringing as her allies the Trinovantes of Essex, Boudicca and her forces sacked Londinium, massacred 70,000 Romans and Britons – the Celtic tribes collaborating in the Roman policy of divide and rule – and cut the Roman 9th

Legion to pieces. The reason for her fury? The Romans had raped her daughters.

William of Normandy was a Viking, a Northman, descended from the pirates of Scandinavia. In the ninth century CE, one group of Vikings had established the Danish Empire over Anglo-Saxon England and half of Celtic Ireland. Just two centuries old, the Danish Empire in Britain collapsed in 1042, opening the way for William's invasion and claim to the crown. The group of Norsemen William was descended from had colonized Normandy and the Channel Islands under Rollo in the tenth century, adopting a new military religion, Christianity, and learning to speak French. The Duke of Normandy paid homage to just one man, beside the Pope, the King of France.

Normandy was the most centralized state in Europe. After his victory at Hastings, the new King William I of England imposed on the Anglo-Saxon class structure, nobles and serfs alike, an absolutist, centralist, and ruthlessly efficient version of the new feudalism in which every inch of tenured land was held in homage by a vassal of his lord, and every lord was a vassal of the king.

William I was an incarnation of the 'divine right of kings', a principle of inherent royal supremacy not laid to rest until long after the execution of Charles I (1649) during the English Revolution (1642–88). The legacy of supremacy passed into the hands of Parliament in the nineteenth century, thence into the hands of the Cabinet, and finally, in the twentieth century, into the hands of the Prime Minister in power.

(In the United States, the most advanced of the capitalist democracies, the constitutional division of powers obliges the President, the executive, to share power with the Congress, the legislature, and the Courts, the judiciary.)

Once England had been pacified, William invaded the remaining Celtic parts of the British Isles, Scotland, Wales, Cornwall, and Ireland, and annexed them to his portion of the Norman Empire. From here began the 900-year-long struggle of the modern Celts against the imperialism of Westminster and the magnates of the South of England.

In the early 1800s, the Napoleonic Empire menaced the English imperium, and the most likely spot for an invasion was exactly where William had landed. A Sussex rhyme we learned in the 1950s went something like this:

> If Bona-parte
> Shud zummon th'eart
> T'land'n Pevensey Level
> I'ave three sons
> 'oo with thurr guns
> 'll blow 'um to the Devull.

Anti-defeatism again.

True, the English do tend to overdo it. In the English imperial tradition, now the Anglo-American tradition, important defeats are treated like victories, or simply not remembered as defeats at all. Most Americans think they really could have won the Vietnam War (Baritz, 1985). But the truly classic example is the Norman victory at Hastings. The way the English call themselves 'Anglo-Saxons', you have to believe that the Norman Conquest – the Norman Colonization – never really happened.

Colonial rule

In his *Dictionary of Catch Phrases* (1977), Eric Partridge lists three versions of the saying 'you can't win 'em all':

• *you can't win 'em all.* American catch phrase from about 1940, adopted in Britain about 1955, yet not widely used there before about 1960.
• *you can't win.* Canadian, from about 1950.
• *you can't win 'em all – but one now and again would break the monotony.* British, about 1975.

'You can't win 'em all' is classic Yankee common sense, part of a positive national and personal identity. It comforts, it keeps you going. Success is merely delayed, a matter for new initiatives, and not to be begrudged to others.

'You can't win' is classic Canadian defeatism, part of a negative national and personal identity. It intimidates, it stops you dead. Success is out of the question, not to be thought of, something to hate in others.

Defeatism is part of every colonial ideology. Although she doesn't use the word, and although she is talking only about women, colonization is the source of what Colette Dowling has aptly called *The Cinderella Complex* (1981). The Cinderella Complex stands for woman's hidden fear of independence, her training in dependency at home, in school, and on the job, by mothers, fathers, and employers, her lack of self-esteem or fear of such a lack, the loss of self when separated from the significant man, her hostility to, and fear of, other women (women being brought up to hate women), her lack of political consciousness, her lack of the real sense of sisterhood (compare the brotherhood of men), her conscious and unconscious desire for a Prince Charming to solve her troubles, relieve her of responsibility, but still provide her with significance, and above all wash away her fear of fear itself – the very fear that makes subjection and defeatism the price of survival as an auxiliary species in a world she has been trained to misunderstand.

The Cinderella Complex – not a disease or a thing, but a set of pathological incapacities in the real world of relationships – is one effect of the original imperial strategy of divide and rule. The big lie behind the psychological warfare of defeatism is that no human relations better than the present have existed or can exist. War is as inevitable as rape, they tell us, so we'd better make the most of it.

When we ask for proof, we are told that the present is the result of the will of God, original sin, wicked Eve, Pandora's box, innate evil, natural selection, the survival of the fittest, might is right, the Soviet Union, cherchez la femme, or the 'determinism' of our genes.

Defeatism is a denial of personal dignity which cripples the creative faculties. But to attack it and go beyond it does not mean wrapping ourselves in chauvinism, defined by the men at the top in the Present Rule:

The Present Rule: My country (religion, race, class, sex) – right or wrong.

Nor does it mean deluding oneself or others with imaginary hopes and denials of reality. It does mean recognizing that every unjust system seeks to deny even the idea of hope, dignity, and self-determination to the peoples it oppresses.

It also means recognizing that the strategy of domination teaches the colonized to prefer their oppressors to themselves, to dislike or even hate their own kith and kin, that it teaches the privileged to blame the victims for their plight, and that it teaches the victims to blame each other and fight among themselves (divide and rule). When the victims come to believe that they suffer because they 'really' are (inherently or genetically) inferior or because they deserve whatever they get ('s/he was asking for it'), then the circle of destruction is complete. One is collaborating in one's own oppression.

In *The Art Of War*, written over two thousand years ago, Sun Tzu says:

Weapons are ominous tools to be used only when there is no alternative.

Sun Tzu says:

Know the enemy and know yourself; in a hundred battles you will never be in peril.

Sun Tzu says:

To win one hundred victories in one hundred battles is not the acme of skill. To win over the enemy without fighting is the acme of skill.

Sun Tzu says:

Thus, what is of supreme importance in war is to attack the enemy's strategy.

You cannot beat strategy with tactics.

If you are tactically illiterate you know how to change it. If you are strategically illiterate you don't know you don't know, and cannot find out unless aided by some person or event that is not.

In China the leaders have all read Sun Tzu. Sun Tzu is required reading in Russian military and political circles.

Strategy is not confined to generals. We all use strategies and tactics – conscious and unconscious, individual and collective – every second of our lives. ('Tactics', the act of putting a strategy into practice, is not to be confused with 'stratagems', the use of duplicity.) In the simplest, conscious, personal sense, a strategy is what we want to do, tactics are how we do it.

Strategy without tactics is imaginary, tactics without strategy is impossible.

Or as Jomini defined them in the world's best footnote in his *Précis de l'art de guerre* in 1837, tactics is learned from the bottom up (dominated by mainly left-brain procedures), whereas strategy is learned from the top down (a mainly right-brain capacity) (see below).

Winning is not confined to win-lose, zero-sum, either/or conflicts in which whatever one party gains the other loses. As Tessa Albert Warshaw shows in *Winning by Negotiation* (1980) one can adopt both-and, win-win strategies. Win-Win negotiators

have fought the conventional professional and social battles, seen the flow of blood, tossed through sleepless nights, and decided that no prize can be worth the cost of relentless tension and minimal joy. Survival, they have learned, depends on other people.

But mere survival is not their objective:

They want a balanced life, the kind achieved only in community with other people, who believe as they do that caring and nurturing are reciprocal.

Make no mistake, however. Win-Win negotiators want their share:

If they are committed to mutuality, it's not primarily because they're charitable but because they're eminently pragmatic. They've learned the hard way that, in the long run, winning and survival depend not just on themselves but on others (pp. 61–2).

How strategies and tactics are employed is a matter of ethics. The basis of a truly democratic and human ethic and pride in who we are is not the imperial belief that we are superior to some other group of people. It is the belief that we are just as good and just as human as everyone else. In the democratic ethic, the Rule of Rules is simple and direct:

The Democratic Rule: Everyone a strategist.

This contrasts with the Colonial Rule:

The Colonial Rule: Teach tactics, and above all kamikaze tactics; make strategy and the very idea of strategy a secret never to be revealed.

Everyone educated as a strategist and serving their own best interests will follow the humanistic aspects of Sun Tzu. Strategists brought up on Sun Tzu meeting in conflict will not go to war. They will adopt win-win strategies and negotiate, demonstrating their mastery of the art of strategy by winning without fighting at all.

Mercenary rules

Today, with the United States trying to shore up a weakened economic and technological empire by means of a newly belligerent and profitable escalation of arms races – divide and rule – all over the world (between the nations of Latin America, between Israel and the Arab states in the Middle East, between India and Pakistan, besides the nuclear race with Russia), along with encouragement for industry and agriculture to step up the war on nature, we know as a fact what every humanistic thinker in this century has been afraid of: That the capitalist and state-capitalist empires are still fighting the First World War, the war for the domination of the planet.

Without going into the saga of the unprovoked torpedoes that set off the killing in the 1982 Falklands War (had the Argentines properly set the fuses on their plain iron bombs, it might have had another outcome), Anglo-American war fever in the 1980s might have come right out of *Beau Geste*, *The Real Glory*, *The Four Feathers*, or *Gunga Din* (all 1939). What is the Reagan Revolution but a series of punitive expeditions against people at home and abroad who cannot fight back?

Mother Jones analyzed the first domestic goals of the Reagan Administration: to dismantle 50 years of civil rights, environmental, anti-trust, and New Deal legislation, little enough as it is, protecting Americans and the American environment from American-based corporations – and the American government.

The mutinies and other social unrest surrounding the German defeat in World War One were the origin of Hitler's 'stab-in-the-back' explanation of the German defeat. The Imperial German Army had not been defeated in the field in 1918, it had really been defeated at home – by Jews, foreigners, traitors, outside agitators, 'half-breeds', criminals, socialists, unions, 'inferior races', communists, 'mental defectives', anarchists, gypsies, homosexuals, atheists, leftists, marxists, liberals, and other infidels. And if Germany still had economic and social problems when Hitler came to power in 1933, then it was because these same people – the scapegoats of the State – were still undermining the German version of totalitarian capitalism.

Today, as we can see from many sources, including the television documentary *Vietnam 1945–75: The 10,000 Day War* and the magazines *Soldier of Fortune* and *Gung-Ho*, a similar stab-in-the-back story, with the same motif of excuse for failure and revenge for defeat, has been adopted by American dupes to explain away the catastrophic tactical victory and unstoppable strategic defeat in Southeast Asia (Kolko, 1985).

Gung-Ho, subtitled 'The Magazine of the International Military Man', began its career as the mercenary's *Time-Life*. The magazine is a well-illustrated monthly much respected (and promoted and assisted) at all levels of the American military and intelligence command, as well as being welcomed, like its highly competitive and successful rival *Soldier of Fortune* (which in April 1983 sent a team of privately armed specialists to train and evaluate army units in El Salvador) by the security services and armed forces of Central American and other countries said to be fighting communist aggression.

Gung-Ho takes the same position against the Russians and other certified enemies as the US Cavalry took against the Indians in the nineteenth century. When practised by the United States, the principles of strategy are honest, above-board, and legitimate acts of self-defense. When practised by the Russians, however, the very same principles are godless, vicious, and diabolical forms of treachery.

Gung-Ho is a tag first used by the US Marine Corps in World War Two, meaning 'work together' in Chinese.

The mercenary magazines are symptoms of the escalation in the scope and intensity of violence, and in the toleration of violence, since 1965, when President Lyndon Johnson, elected on the promise not to send American boys to die in the jungles of Southeast Asia, made the decision that eventually destroyed him, and sent 150,000 of 'his boys' to South Vietnam.

Soldier of Fortune and *Gung-Ho* reflect and glorify the brutalization of ignorant and frightened young men in Vietnam and the other colonial wars since 1945. They combine authoritarianism and hero worship, hatred and cynicism, evangelical certainty about the identity and intentions of the 'enemies of freedom' ('the communist as gook'), the ever-insecure desire for recognition as a man among 'real men', and the exaltation of bullying and coercion as the arbiter of truth and killing as the ultimate experience in the life of Man.

In his editorial in the August 1983 issue, Jim Shults begins by quoting the well-known patriot General John Singlaub (USA, retd) on the subject of the Tet Offensive of 1968, a turning point in the Vietnam War:

> 'We were killing tens of thousands of communists. We'd been hoping for this open battle, and we were *destroying* them. Yet after a week the TV media in the U.S. started telling us and the world we were losing – and the people of America believed it.'

On the military side this is correct. In spite of the dramatic (but unsuccessful) Viet Cong attack on the US Embassy in Saigon, an event that drew vastly more attention from the US and other media than was warranted by its strictly military significance, the surprise assault by the Viet Cong on more than 100 towns and villages in South Vietnam on January 31, 1968 was a crushing tactical failure that practically destroyed them as a fighting force. The expected general rising of the population did not take place, and from this point on the bulk of the fighting in the South was done by North Vietnamese regulars.

On the surface Shults' statement about the media is also correct. On March 12, 1968, for example, the New York *Times* carried the following headline, quoted by Don Oberdorfer in *Tet!* (1971):

U.S. Is Losing War in Vietnam, NBC declares.

But as Oberdorfer records, already in 1967 a number of influential US newspapers, including the conservative and Republican Los Angeles *Times*, had begun to doubt the wisdom of the war, months before Tet, and when the doubters were joined by *Time*, *Life*, and *Fortune* in the fall of 1967, the suspicion that the US was in deep trouble was already widespread. In August 1967 the Gallup Poll reported that for the first time more Americans thought the war was a mistake (46 per cent) than did not (44 per cent).

What was significant about Tet was not the fact that it was defeated, but the fact that it happened at all. For years the media had faithfully reported the official view (Time Incorporated being one of the war's most enthusiastic supporters) – increased 'body counts', more villages 'pacified', more Viet Cong defections, and so on. We were told that the United States was not only winning the military war, but also the political war for the 'hearts and minds' of the South Vietnamese. As US officials put it year after year: 'American troops can soon be withdrawn. There's light at the end of the tunnel.'

We were encouraged to think of the Viet Cong as some thousands of scattered guerrillas, but I can recall no image whatsoever of the size of their forces before the Tet attack. (One reason for this was that the true figures were not being reported.) But in the first two weeks of Tet they and the North Vietnamese Army regulars (NVA) involved (principally in the northern provinces) suffered 32,000 killed and 5,800 captured.

(The South Vietnamese eventually lost 2,788 killed; the Americans, 1,536; and the Viet Cong and NVA, about 45,000 – their overall losses in the 25 days of Tet were higher than those of the US forces in the entire Korean War.)

What was significant about these huge casualties was not simply that so many actual and supposed Viet Cong were being slaughtered, soldiers and civilians alike, but that so many Viet Cong had existed in the first place. (A total of 84,000 men and women took part in the Tet attack.) The strategic fact, then, was that President Johnson, General Westmoreland, Secretary Rusk, Ambassador Bunker, and any number of other soldiers and officials were either lying about the war to us and to each other or deluded about it or both.

The *coup de grâce* for American and South Vietnamese policies and credibility in 1968 was delivered by the Saigon police chief, who blew the brains out of a handcuffed Viet Cong prisoner in front of Eddie Adams, the AP photographer, producing an unforgettable image seen by millions of people around the world.

And the US really was losing the war. The Tet Offensive complied with the principles of guerrilla strategy in revolutionary war – where the guerrillas seek, not military success, but political victory – an objective that includes winning the hearts and minds of the foreigners whose children are fighting the war. Militarily Tet was an invitation to a massacre, a terrible mistake. But its effect on the way Americans and others thought about the war, the Army, the President, and the United States was a huge political, psychological, and strategic success. This it could not have been, of course, had the war been actually winnable by available US methods, nuclear and not.

Jim Shults continues:

> Vietnam is pretty much behind us now, but the despicable 'loser attitude' continues to be drilled into us every day. *Every single day* we hear from our 'media' how our great country is sliding into ruin: how we're going broke, becoming 'immoral, imperialist

oppressors', and generally up to our asses in alligators with no way out – and no hope.

So Shults is talking about defeatism, saying in effect that the United States, surely the least defeatist country in the world, is sliding from 'you can't win 'em all' to 'you can't win (at all)'.
To this he responds:

Well, *goddammit*, I'm sick of it. Who the hell are we anyway? We're *Americans*, that's who! We're the people who taught the world about freedom and generosity and wealth and the ability to achieve anything you believe you can.

A plain statement of a familiar theme, that of the solipsistic moral superiority of the imaginary 'city on the hill' (Baritz, 1985).

We're the people who live in the country more people the world over want to live in than any other.

No argument with that.

We're the people who are tougher, meaner, and more feared than any other in the world. As a former Warsaw Pact soldier put it: 'You Americans seem to *enjoy* fighting. You go to war wearing jewelry and bandanas, with a machine gun in your hand, a cigar between your teeth, and a big grin on your face!'

The Americans are not the most violent people in the world, but they are the most powerful violent people in the world.
'The media', he continues,

keep harping on the 'guilt' we should feel toward the Poor of both our country and the rest of the world. How we should 'atone' for this guilt by shouldering an increasingly heavy tax burden to support those who refuse to work – and how we should take the crap the Third World countries hurl at us in the United Nations.

A classic instance of the old right argument for which colonialism and recession and depression mean nothing, and for which unemployment is the fault of the unemployed, just as poverty is the fault of the poor and starvation the fault of the starving.
Shults goes on to condemn the 'bastards who are betraying our country' (the 'media' and the 'professional career diplomats'), and then explains why these 'slimy' people are so dangerous to America:

No matter how strong and tough and able we may still be, if Americans (or anybody else) hear how awful and worthless they are enough times, they will probably start believing it: it will become a self-fulfilling prophecy. And then we'll *really* be up the creek.

Quite right. He has restated the basic psychological principle, the ideology of defeatism, in the strategy of colonialism.

So it's time to start fighting back. It's time to start kicking ass on the wimps and naysayers who are infecting our national psyche with their pessimism and guilt. We need to stop apologizing to the world and take charge again.

We might be listening to a modern translation of Senator Albert J. Beveridge expounding on the 'divine mission' of the United States as the 'master organizer' of the world, the 'trustee of the world's progress' and the 'guardian of its righteous peace' when the US seized the Philippines in 1898.

Shults continues:

It's time to get started: We have a true American in the White House and millions more of us just waiting for the word.

And concludes:

And the word is 'Let's go!' After all we're Americans. Who's going to stop us? Sure as hell, not any communists! The next time you are exposed to lies or propaganda, counter it: don't *let* people BS you any more.

You can't object to that last sentence, can you?

Finally here, a word from Europe: In 1980 a German banker told us in the May 19 issue of *Fortune* that with the installation of the new Reagan régime America had recovered her manhood. As it was in the last verse of Kipling's 'White Man's Burden' in 1899, where the test of 'manhood' is the conquest of empire, that one word 'manhood' is the smoking pistol, the proof positive of the intimate connection between imperialism in the state and male supremacy in the individual.

In February 1984, in an editorial celebrating the American victory over Grenada ('a crucial turning point'), *Soldier of Fortune* put it more directly:

'It's great to be an American again', remarked a friend when he heard about the Grenada operation.

'It's great to have a president with balls', said an unknown trooper from the 75th Rangers on Grenada.

Morale rules

To organize against imperial war, we might begin by looking at some of the qualities that the multinational generals use negatively, with such deadly success, and start thinking about how to use them positively. So long as we understand their context, we can read between the lines of the war manuals to see what positive qualities are needed for organized resistance against the makers of imperial war, military and economic.

My copy of the British *Field Service Regulations* for 1912 – the complete do-it-yourself battle manual, made pocket size, just in case the officers needed to look anything up – begins like this:

> Success in war depends more on moral than physical qualities. Skill cannot compensate for want of courage, energy, and determination; but even high moral qualities may not avail without careful preparation and skilful direction. The development of the necessary moral qualities is therefore the first of the objects to be attained; the next are organization and discipline, which enable those qualities to be controlled and used when required.

Every word of this can be read in the positive terms of popular struggle against tyrannies. In popular struggles, it is always the tyrants, not the tyrannized, who start the war. It is always the tyrants who commit the first atrocity.

Popular struggle is collective self-defense. When the tyrants and their collaborators will not make peace, counter-warfare becomes unavoidable. When unavoidable, popular war against foreign or domestic tyranny is justified war.

Part of the next rule I've picked is similar to the one just quoted. Part of it is not:

> Superior numbers on the battlefield are an undoubted advantage, but skill, better organization, and training, and above all <u>a firmer determination in all ranks to conquer at any cost, are the chief factors of success. Half-hearted measures never attain success in war, and lack of determination is the most fruitful source of defeat</u>.

We have to agree that skill, organization, training, and determination are necessary to success in any enterprise, including the anti-war movement. Except when they are deliberate policy, half-hearted measures in any enterprise, military or not, bespeak incompetence and defeatism.

And bravery and numbers alone are never enough. If they were, then women would have put an end to war long ago. The Mahdists were brave beyond belief and superb with sword or spear, but they fought as a mass of individuals, without the strategic direction and tactical discipline that would have made up for their inferior weaponry, and enabled them to defeat a Western imperial army and its mercenaries.

The key words in the second passage are 'conquer at any cost'. The word 'conquer' tells us that by 'war' this passage means offensive, imperial war. 'At any cost' is further madness. No war, no battle, can be won 'at any cost'. Kamikaze strategies lead to collective suicide. But this maxim tells us why 17 were killed in 1914–18, 44 million people in 1939–45, and, as estimated by the Hudson Institute, 32 million people in 130 wars between 1945 and 1983.

In their purges, both Stalin and Mao killed millions.

Today, 'conquer at any cost' threatens everyone on earth. No previous system of competing imperialisms, and no single empire, was ever before powerful enough to threaten all life on earth, whether by industrial and agricultural pollution, or by war, or by both. But 'conquer at any cost' is once again the official strategy of the Anglo-American Empire – whether in the military, in politics, in business, in the global economy, in foreign and colonial affairs, or in all that affects the ecology of the earth.

For many millions of people there is no longer any choice about fighting back. Their lives and dignity as human beings are at stake: Afghanistan, Angola, Brixton, El Salvador, Namibia, Nicaragua, the Philippines, Poland, the western Sahara, Toxteth, Ulster, West Berlin, even Zurich – that was 1981.

As the Welsh say: 'We Welsh, we give a little, we take a little, but we never give up.'

We, the peoples, did not start the Twentieth Century War, but we, the peoples, will be its casualties if it is not brought to a stop. The plain fact is that the world empires are not in the end at war with one other. The men in charge of the state and private corporations that run those empires and their client states are really at war with everyone else on earth.

Machine rules

During the war, many of our toys were treasured examples of the clockmaker's art. Some of the best were tinplate cars from Germany, Schucos I believe, purchased at third or fourth hand. Mine had a clutch, a gearshift, four forward speeds and reverse, removable tires, and rack-and-pinion steering. I remember wondering whether the patriotic thing to do would be to sacrifice it to the war effort, in the spirit of the times, but it was just too beautifully made for that.

The best clockworks of all were grandfather clocks. After 1945 they would arrive at the upstairs workshop in a state of sad neglect, occasioned by the war, and we were given the task of soaking, brushing, and buffing the larger pieces of dingy brass. This was a step up from cleaning our collection of cap badges. That was play. This was work. But before you can really qualify as a clockmaker's helper, you have to master the first rule of every kind of art or science: the Naming of Parts.

My father was not a believer in the bits-and-pieces or accumulator theory of education, by which the teacher supposedly fills the student up with knowledge bit by bit. Knowing as he did the strategy of machines, he didn't expect us to learn the names of all the detailed parts. Instead we learned mechanical structure: how to take a quick look at a clockwork and decide whether it was driven by springs or weights, whether it was regulated by pendulum or balance wheel, whether it was silent, alarm, or chiming, whether the main drive was by gearing or by chain and fusee, whether the escapement was designed to compensate for changes in temperature, and whether it was designed to be infinitely repairable or thrown away. We then learned the names of the principal parts of these basic assemblies, which distinguish one kind of clock from another.

The elegant images of clockworks remain engraved in my memory to this day. Like the steam locomotive and even the car engine – and two hundred years of marvelous mechanical toys – this is a visible technology. You can understand it, follow its logic, and appreciate its beauty by seeing it at work or taking it apart, for where form follows function the parts actually look like what they do. You can see why every mechanical whole is distinct – by the ways its parts are organized – from the mere sum or aggregate of its parts.

In helping my father and watching him at work, we saw a box of obstinate-looking bits and pieces turn back into the insides of a grandfather clock. When he was finished, he put it through its paces. We had before us another shining example, and I do mean shining, of precision engineering and mechanical perfection. We would watch its motions and levels of motion – for a clock is a mechanical hierarchy – as it correctly performed every operation and level of operation its creator had designed it to perform.

Engineering rules

One Christmas soon after the war, when Alan was 8 and I was 10, the men of the family gave us a Meccano set, which got bigger and more complex year by year. We read the instructions, chose a model, and built our very first machine that very same day: an aeroplane that circled around a miniature Eiffel Tower on the end of a horizontal arm and dropped a bomb when you switched the motor off.

The instructions were ambiguous, however. It took me three hours to get that bomb to drop.

Scientia potestas est: 'Knowledge is power'. So said Sir Francis Bacon (1561–1626), pioneer of modern science. But not all knowledge is equally powerful. Knowledge of principles, knowledge of codes, knowledge of structure, knowledge of strategy – this is not mere knowledge, but literacy. Literacy is power. Literacy gives one power over the details, the messages, the parts, the tactics of whatever topic, activity, field, or discipline is concerned. And in our society machine literacy is part of the male strategy that separates 'boys' from 'girls', 'men' from 'boys', and 'men and boys' from 'women'.

From Meccano we learned to name and use the five simple machines known to the ancient Greeks: the lever, the wheel and axle (the windlass), the wedge (the inclined plane), the pulley, and the screw. Selections and combinations of the principles expressed in these five simple machines form the moving parts of the more complex mechanical devices. We also learned to use the balance, the crank, the eccentric, the cam, the pawl-and-ratchet, the chain and sprocket. We learned how to convert rotary motion into other forms, how to use the relationship between speed and power, and how to take advantage of the principles of gearing.

For motive power we had the choice of rubber bands, clockwork, electric motor, steam engine, or a Pelton wheel water turbine (the latter making more mess than motion).

In putting energy to work mechanical machines make use of just three basic devices (we had one of each): the tension or potential energy stored in wound-up weights or springs and released through gearing as in clockworks; the pressure of a fluid against a piston in a cylinder (derived from the water pump), as in steam, diesel, or gasoline reciprocating engines; and the pressure of a fluid against a rotating vane, as in the waterwheel, the windmill, the ship's screw, the aircraft propellor, the steam turbine, the jet turbine, and the fanjet.

As with clocks, so with Meccano: the first rule in machine literacy is the naming of parts. Surrounded by the bits and pieces of our first set (there are about 150 categories of parts in the Meccano system), we were doing just what the builder of a famous steamboat, Robert Fulton (1765–1815), told his apprentices to do:

> The mechanic should sit down among levers, screws, wedges,
> wheels, etc., like a poet among the letters of the alphabet,
> considering them as an exhibition of his thoughts, in which a new
> arrangement transmits a new Idea.

From Meccano we learned to follow the recipes for the construction of the models pictured in detail in the instruction book. We learned the rules of the Meccano code so that we could use its system of interchangeable parts to create our own mechanical messages. We didn't realize it then, but the Meccano people were teaching us creative engineering.

Time Life's *Machines* says (1964, p. 15):

> As a musician writing a score composes music, so an inventor designing a machine composes *motion*.

Model building is a mainly visual, spatial, three-dimensional, and non-verbal mode of expression – all the more so when your prototype is imaginary, existing only as information in an image and not as matter-energy in reality as well. It is an activity dominated by the right hemisphere of the brain and best learned by what artisans call 'emulation' and learning by doing: copying a piece of work made by a master in the craft, just as we copied the models in the Meccano instruction book.

Some years later we were given an electric train, which emphasizes a different mode of thought. We became quite skilled in freightyard switching problems, using the network of railroad switches and track circuits to sort our strings of cars into different orders (or 'consists'). Switching problems on one-dimensional tracks are governed by 'either/ or' logic: on a railway a contradiction is a collision. Here we were exercising the left brain, the mainly analytic and verbal hemisphere, more than the right, in an activity logically identical to that of a digital computer – with this difference, that freight cars carry matter as well as information.

Model building and railroad switching were central aspects of our education in the exercise of power. Ideally, machines are designed to be used by human beings in the expression of their creativity – and mechanical toys are of course ideal machines.

Naturally, we didn't approach our playthings in the spirit of this retrospective analysis. But as Athelstan Spilhaus remarks in *Those Wonderful Old Mechanical Toys* (1983), 'All toys are inherently educational. The best teach subliminally – while one is having fun.' 'Toys stimulate the imagination', he continues, 'and are enormously satisfying because they take the place of the real thing that is unobtainable.' 'They can bring a whole circus onto a little table, and exotic characters can bring the world into your hand. They can do things we cannot do in real life, thus keeping us in touch with fantasy.'

Analytic rules

The amazing thing about well-made machines is that they never present a problem without a solution. Basically,

— if you understand the principles involved;
— if you learn to see, hear, and get the feel of the thing through the medium of the necessary tools and instruments, from fingertips and feeler gauges to calipers and torque wrenches, from socket sets to stethoscopes, from pressure gauges to voltmeters and electronic analyzers on up;
— if you follow the correct hierarchy of logical and practical steps, dis-assembling from the (general) whole to the (particular) parts, and re-assembling in the same linear and lineal sequence, but in reverse;

and if you know when to ask for help; the process always leads to success: It works!

One of our toys would break. Here my father taught us the basic rules you follow to diagnose the symptoms of a mechanical complaint. Without a strategy of diagnosis, you cannot know where to begin, or what to look and feel and listen for.

To diagnose what ails a machine, you do pretty much the same, in a small way, as an experimental physicist does, except that a machine is designed, and nature, although organized, is not.

You run through a hierarchy of variety, moving step by step from one class of variety to another, going from the general to the particular. You test one variable, or one system of variables, at a time, just as you do in checking the gas tank, the ignition system, the fuel flow, and so on, when the car won't start.

Assembly by sub-assembly, constraint by mechanical constraint, you use the standard either/or tests of analytic logic to rule out uncertainties until you reach the solution you are converging on, where what had previously been noise turns into information.

Just as analytic logic is the simplest of all logics, the machines and physical systems to which it is applied with such success in science and technology are among the simplest of all systems. Machines and ordinary physical systems are closed systems; closed or self-contained systems can exist independently of their environments. In contrast, living systems, at the organic level, and social systems, at the person level, are open systems. They depend for their structure and survival on the exchange of matter, energy, and information with their environments.

Given adequate information about it, a closed system can be understood without reference to its environment, its context. But no amount of information is adequate to understand or analyze an open system — an organism, a person, a family, a corporation, a natural ecosystem, a society, a system of ideas — unless its context is also part of the explanation.

Context rules

The Wildens and the Ballards taught us strategies and tactics rooted in everyday life and tempered by a healthy respect for the powers of nature and machinery and the realities of war.

They could not of course have said so in so many words, but they taught us machine logic for machines and human logic for people. And in keeping with the artisan tradition, their teaching was ultimately based on the imitation or emulation of examples, and thus on visual, spatial, non-verbal, and other mainly right-brain forms of communication, rather than simply on left-brain language and left brain logic. We may not always recognize it, for most learning takes place unconsciously, but we learn more this way than in any other way.

There is a great deal more to the diverse logics of communication – and therefore to the strategies and tactics of life – than the dominant logic in our society, the left-brain logic of analytic and digital communication, usually permits us to be aware of.

Analytic logic is one-dimensional, as if truth and falsity were the opposite ends of a magnet, or the terminal points on a spectrum from black through grey to white. While it can be used to proper effect within particular levels of communication and reality, analytic logic is poorly equipped to explain the relationships between these levels, which it commonly passes over in silence.

You use analytic logic to connect the patterns of the stars, measure out the land, aim a siege engine, chart the seas, construct a railway network, discover the malaria parasite, dig a canal, organize communications, find your way to the moon, design an army, build a prison, or structure a corporation.

Used alone, analytic logic, static logic, ignores the context of natural and social relationships and fails to recognize the realities of change. It treats every relationship or situation it singles out as a unique, closed, and separate event, as if it is not related to its past and present contexts, and not part of any pattern of events.

You cannot use analytic logic by itself to understand a feeling, to teach a child, to love a person, to appreciate beauty, to understand history, to enjoy a film, to analyze nature, to explore imagination, to explain society, to recognize individuality, to communicate with others, to create novelty, or to learn the principles of freedom.

We have to be careful at this point not to throw common sense out the window. The 'either/or' of analytic logic is essential to every process of decision; the digital computer could not exist without it. But in the either/or thinking of analytic logic, the 'either' usually excludes the 'or'. Don't let that ingrained pattern of 'all-or-none' thinking lead you to assume that we should try to do without analytic logic or replace it with another one. What I am saying is that we should use analytic logic where it works, and contextual and many-level logics, including both-and logic – dialectical logic – where it doesn't, just as I have done throughout this essay.

You may rightly ask how a non-contextual, one-dimensional, static, and closed-system logic, based on the principles of the watertight compartment, has continued to dominate our ways of thinking, to the point of ruling contextual and relational views out of court. The answer is that those who presently define what is logical and what is not, have the power to make it so. They have so far had at their command the physical force, the organization, and the means of communication and representation to make this domination real.

Above all, they have controlled the general styles and contents of the most influential of the social media – including the family, the schools, the history books, the comic books, the movies and television, and organized entertainment in general.

They cannot go on forever.

Orwell's rule

In human affairs, using or stating a rule implies a code of rules. In the human context, rules are never divorced from values. Three of the most important ethical values I learned as a boy can be summarized as follows:

- The end cannot justify the means.
- Those with more power are responsible to those with less.
- Violence, of whatever kind, is never justified except in self-defense against a real aggressor with real power, for whom you should always be prepared.

Other reliable rules of life can be set out in the proverbial twenty-five words or less: Honesty is the best policy; quality, the best argument; diversity, the best method; experience, the best reference; example, the best teacher; reality, the best proof.

These rules of thumb are subject to the Rule of Rules, which I call Orwell's Rule, after a man who tried to make it his rule of life:

Orwell's Rule: Break any rule – not including this one – rather than do wrong.

In *Nineteen Eighty-Four*, published in 1949, Orwell gave us what I think is best called the Media Rule. It reminds us that one of the greatest of television's threats to personal and public sanity has to do with history.

In print and image, a book is medium, message, and memory. And hundreds of the movies of the past fifty years can still be seen through repertory theatres, film clubs, night school courses, and of course and especially through television and videocassette, by which the medium does great service. But television as television, television as the most subtle and powerful source of information, education, and ideology in history, is here today, gone tomorrow. Television is a medium that leaves behind no written record, no visible artefacts, no historical trace, no publicly available memory.

The Media Rule: Those who control the present control the past. Those who control the past control the future.

Nowhere more tragically defeatist than in his last work, *Nineteen-Eighty-Four* in 1949, George Orwell died of tuberculosis in 1950, at the age of 46. Had he lived he would be the same age as my parents.

Now to the main text. Like my father, of course, I have to begin this too with the Naming of Parts.

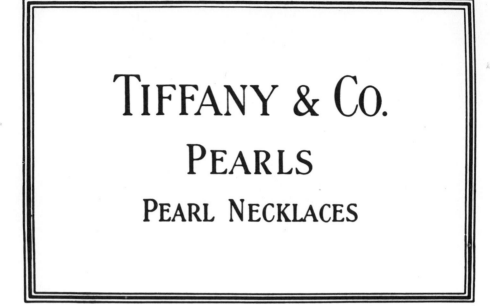

TIFFANY & CO.

PEARLS

PEARL NECKLACES

PART TWO

The Strategy of Communication

CHAPTER 1

Levels of reality

The world of reality has its bounds, the world of the imagination is boundless; as we cannot enlarge the one, let us restrict the other; for all the sufferings which really make us miserable arise from the difference between the real and the imaginary.

JEAN-JACQUES ROUSSEAU: *Emile, or Education* (1762)

1.1 Symbolic, imaginary, and real

Let me begin with three working definitions, definitions of the symbolic, imaginary, and real relationships we find in living and social systems, but without asking you to take them up in detail at the moment:

Reality, real: What trips you up when you don't pay attention to it – includes matter, energy, and the communication of many kinds of information, whether biological like the genetic code, or social like the exchange of goods; thus includes nature, society and technology; other people and other minds; food and shelter; race, class, and sex; a wealth of wasted human creativity; and the need to change most of it for something better.

Imaginary: What originally exists only for the mind or the mind's eye and may not be capable of real existence – includes the communication of many kinds of information in society and some in nature, such as mimicry; is dominated by visual imagery but not necessarily expressed in that form of communication; includes in its general aspects camouflage, fiction, and fantasy; in its negative aspects error, illusion, obsession, and terror without a name; and in its positive aspects imagination, innovation, and invention.

Symbolic: Any kind of information standing for information of another kind or level, whether that information is real, imaginary, or already symbolic – includes simple symbolization in nature, as when male dance flies present the female with a gift of silk before mating; complex symbolization in society, as when money stands for price standing for real, imaginary, or symbolic value, or when communication and behavior are regulated by conventional rules, as in manners, kinship, and the experimental method; is essential to communication and exchange between human subjects in society, whether through

FIGURE 1.1: The magic lantern horror show called *La Fantasmagorie* (the Phantasmagoria), invented by the Belgian illusionist Etienne Robertson (later a balloonist). Housed in a deserted chapel surrounded by tombs, this show amazed and terrified audiences in Paris in the 1790s for six successful years. Robertson used rear projection on translucent gauze and enlarged or decreased the image at will. Not yet literate in this form of communication, and unable to see the projector, spectators could not tell the distance between themselves and the images, and would reach out to touch them. The use of smoke as a screen made the images appear to move and change expression. Developments of the same device were immensely popular in Europe and the United States throughout the nineteenth century (and were still popular with

language, moving pictures, humor, useful goods, or other means; and is represented above all by our ability not just to talk about the world and ourselves, but also to think about what and why we do as we do, and about where and how our creativity might be best directed.

Consider the symbolic, imaginary, and real relations of the magic lantern shows depicted in Figure 1.1. (Along with language, the visual faculty is our most important medium of learning and understanding; and the visual imagination is as complex and creative as any other kind of thought.) The engravings themselves are acceptably real images of real performances. The monster and the winged death's head projected onto the smoke in the first picture are visual images of imaginary beings with symbolic meanings. The attitudes of the audience tell us that some are confusing the imaginary images with real ones.

The ghost projected onto the angled sheet of glass in the second picture, probably symbolizing divine or human retribution, is a real image of a real actor, but optically displaced so as to create an imaginary image on a real stage. Assuming the play is a fictional representation of life, then the actor with the pistol is presenting us with a real image of himself disguised for the part, but playing an imaginary character in an imaginary story in a real play, with meanings symbolic of the author's view of life.

I'll return to the symbolic, the imaginary, and the real in later chapters.

Accept now that all behavior, beside whatever else it is (including action), is communication, with message value, whether intended or conscious or not. From this it follows that it is impossible for an organism or a person *not* to communicate. We communicate both by what we do and by what we do not do.

Silence is not only a message, but often a weapon too, as the film editor Ralph Rosenblum (*Annie Hall, A Thousand Clowns, The Producers*) remarks in his 1979 autobiography, *When the Shooting Stops . . . the Cutting Begins*, an initiation into a hidden art with vast powers over the audience. The subject is Woody Allen the well-known misogynist (*The Purple Rose of Cairo*, 1985):

---

children in the 1940s). After 1840 the powerful beams of limelight replaced the flickering images of oil lamps, which permitted even grander effects, as in the second picture, which is from a book on the magic lantern published in 1880. The Jesuit scholar Athanasius Kircher discussed the principles of the magic lantern in 1646, the Dutch scientist Christian Huyghens described it in detail in 1659, and Samuel Pepys the diarist bought one from the optician and telescope maker Richard Reeves in 1666 (Barnouw, 1981). Reprinted from: Erik Barnouw: *The Magician and the Cinema* (1981).

With colleagues, silence is his primary tool for both protection and control, and it works an unsettling devastation whether on a room full of smooth executives at United Artists or a group of garruluous production people on the set. I knew from my own experience that this was the strategy of a proud but insecure man. As a boy I found that if I got angry, I stammered, I blocked, I made a fool of myself. But shut up, and the effect is potent. Maintain that silence, keep from saying the words that put others at their ease, that grease the social flywheels [sic], and more sociable people falter and even go to pieces. In Woody, I'd found a man who had taken my own nonverbal protection to its extreme . . . (p. 263).

We find it difficult to sympathize with the emotions of a potato; so we do with those of an oyster. Neither of these things makes a noise on being boiled or opened.

SAMUEL BUTLER: *Erewhon* (1872)

1.2 The human context

The human context includes all the symbolic, imaginary, and real relations of daily life. Our context of information thus includes dreams, hopes, visions, and fantasies; art, science, and artefacts; speech, music, print, and image; verbal and non-verbal information; analytics and dialectics; theory and practice; conscious and unconscious communication; emotion, feeling, and reason; production and reproduction; time past, time passing, time present, time future.

Nature, society, and individual human beings are linked together *both* by the transformation of matter-energy *and* by the communication of information.

Communication signifies literally 'to share, to make common'. As the term is used here, it means the sending and receiving of information. It does not necessarily imply conscious awareness, understanding, or recognition. A failure of understanding is not a failure of communication – in animal mimicry, camouflage, and military deception a misunderstanding is a successful communication, and in human affairs failures of understanding may be the result of paradoxical or pathological and often unconscious communication.

Context is essential. Newborn children are human, of course, but they are at first simply human organisms (products of nature and natural evolution), and not yet social individuals (products of society and history). The biological media constrain and condition life; the social media constrain and condition persons.

Besides the familiar media of print, image, disc, tape, film, and television, the social media include the family, the neighborhood, and the schools; myth, religion, ritual, and received ideas; the architecture of the local environment; music, painting, dance, and the other arts; the existing relations of class, race, and sex; work and play, of course; and finally the information of what we isolate as 'entertainment', which is probably the most influential teacher of them all.

Within these and other constraints – indeed by using these constraints – we seek to express our creativity as individuals.

Nature is the environmental system that supports society as a whole, as well as our existence as a biological species, as humankind. I do not say 'man'. 'Man' confuses the male organism and the male person; confuses society, a product of history, with the species, a product of natural evolution; and by implying that 'man' is the same in all times and all places ignores the diversity of the social record and the role of novelty in history.

If we had a keen vision of all that is ordinary in human life, it would be like hearing the grass grow or the squirrel's heart beat, and we should die of that roar which is the other side of silence.
GEORGE ELIOT: *Middlemarch* (1872)

1.3 Energy and information

Energy is the capacity of a system to do physical work – essentially its capacity to set matter in motion. Information is the capacity of a system to do logical or structural work – its capacity to organize matter, energy, and/or information in ways not found in ordinary physical or chemical systems.

Matter-energy and information are thus functionally distinct. The medium is not the message, it is the means of communication.

Unlike matter-energy, which we transform, exchange, and use, but cannot create or destroy (energy is conserved, says the first axiom of thermodynamics), information is continually created and destroyed – and negated, distorted, falsified, and misread – in ordinary human and biological activities.

For all practical purposes the amount of energy in the cosmos is constant; in its interactions it simply changes form. In contrast, the amount and the diversity of information in the cosmos has been increasing since the beginning of time (the origin of organization) – more so since the beginning of life (biological organization) and the evolution of increasingly complex organisms, and yet more so since the emergence of human social systems at the beginning of history.

Information is characteristic of living and open systems – organisms, populations, persons, classes, societies, systems involving or simulating life or mind, and the value systems that arise from them. Open systems depend for their existence on exchanges of matter, energy, and information with their environments. In open systems information is used to trigger, guide, structure, and organize the matter-energy exchanges and transformations within the open system and between the system and its environment. Information also organizes information. In open systems information of one kind, or at one level, is used to read, punctuate, translate, edit, reproduce, store, and remember information of other kinds, or at other levels. In such systems information governs growth, metabolism, production, consumption, and reproduction.

Information in the simplest sense is a pattern of variety (such as the number of this chapter) carried by a matter-energy marker or medium (in this case ink and paper). Information is in no intrinsic way distinct from any other kind of variety. For a given goalseeking system, however, information is *coded* variety (relative order); *uncoded* variety (relative disorder) is noise.

(Two or more kinds of variety produce one or more kinds of diversity: Chapter 5.)

Variety has no intrinsic sense, meaning, or signification. For a pattern of variety or diversity to be acted on as information, it must form part of a coding system in a context. It must be part of a sender-receiver relationship organized by a goal or goals.

A single sender-receiver may produce and exchange information alone (as when the hermit admires the sunset). But a sender-receiver is by definition a participant in a system of communication populated by other sender-receivers. It is therefore the whole system of communication, not the individual goalseeker, that is both the necessary and the sufficient condition for the communication of information. The system of communication, with its levels and types of coding, mediates the relationships of all its communicants.

Matter-energy is real and does not depend for its existence on being perceived by living creatures or human minds or senses. Information may be symbolic, imaginary, or real and does depend for its existence on being perceived by living creatures or human minds or senses.

Consider in this light the paradox of the falling tree in the forest: If a tree should fall in the forest unheard by any living creature, would it make a noise? As matter-energy the falling tree would create real vibrations in earth and air and alter its real environment, whether perceived or not. But in the absence of any living creature to translate those vibrations into information the tree would fall without a sound.

Matter-energy and information are distinct from each other both in kind and level of reality. There is no causal relation between the marks on this page and the information they communicate. Nor is there any rule of linearity or proportion between the domain of matter-energy and that of information. The Washington Monument uses vast amounts of matter to convey very little information, principally Freudian phallic; the Lincoln automaton at Disneyland uses very little matter-energy to convey a great deal of information, principally American democratic.

The distinction between matter-energy and information, and many other distinctions between levels, are crucial to the strategy of life, as also to its understanding. Distinctions between levels, and especially between levels of complexity, are equally important if we wish to understand the communication and exchange between society and nature.

'Level' in 'level of complexity' refers to distinct levels in a hierarchy, and not to continuous changes in degree, as in 'sound level'.

The art of seeing nature is a thing as much to be acquired as the art of reading the Egyptian hieroglyphics.

JOHN CONSTABLE (1776–1837)

1.4   Orders of complexity

We can employ the term 'order of complexity', meaning 'more than one level of complexity' to label the four major orders of complexity in the cosmos:

- *the inanimate order of complexity* (closed systems of inorganic relations independent of their environments)
- *the organic and ecological order of complexity* (open systems of organic relations within and between organisms, and between organisms and the environment(s) they depend on)
- *the social order of complexity* (open systems of social, economic, political, interpersonal, and other relations between human beings)
- *the cultural order of complexity* (open systems of human relations making similar societies, with similar economic systems, e.g. the Trobrianders and the Dobu, or the US and Germany, distinct from one another).

The hierarchy of orders of complexity in Figure 1.2 forms a dependent hierarchy. It is called 'dependent' because each lower order of complexity, being an open system, depends on (and is therefore constrained by) the orders above it (its environments) for the matter-energy and information required for its existence, survival, and eventual reproduction.

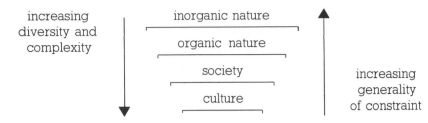

FIGURE 1.2: The four major orders of complexity, a dependent hierarchy. It is called 'dependent' because the open systems of the lower orders in the diagram depend for their existence on the environment of the higher ones. (Open systems depend on their environments for production, reproduction, and survival.) Complexity increases downwards; the generality of the constraints increases upwards. Note that since the human individual includes all four of these orders of complexity, and the individual organism a complex of two of them, the individual cannot be fitted into this kind of hierarchy. (The diagram is modified from one originally published by me in *Recherches sémiotiques/Semiotic Inquiry*, vol. 1, no. 1, 1981.)

The fact that these four orders of complexity are distinct from each other does not make them separate from each other. The boundaries between them are open-system boundaries, not barriers or adamantine spheres.

Nor are these orders 'opposed' to each other – although this framing of their relationships has a long and often tedious history, as C. K. Ogden showed in *Opposition* in 1932. Above all, they are not related to each other by 'either/or' relations of exclusion. Every person, for instance, is a complex of 'both-and' relationships between all four orders of complexity.

To know whether we have this dependent hierarchy the right way up, we apply the Extinction Rule:

> *The Extinction Rule*: To test for the orientation of a dependent hierarchy, mentally abolish each level (or order) in turn, and note which other level(s), or order(s), will necessarily become extinct if it becomes extinct.

Since we know that society is dependent on nature for its survival, then we know that the extinction of the life-sustaining activities of nature (by the entropic disorder of pollution, for example), necessarily entails the extinction of society. In contrast, if human society becomes extinct, nature simply takes over where we left off. Nature therefore belongs at the top of this dependent hierarchy, and its position there is the result of necessity, not of theory.

Or as Goethe (1749–1832) put it: 'Nature is always right.'

The first three orders of complexity of Figure 1.2 are distinguished from each other by clearly defined boundaries.

The outer boundary of the inorganic order, the least complex order and the environment of all the others, is that of the expanding universe itself. It is not known whether this boundary is open or closed.

The boundary between life and non-life (at the micro level) is defined by the presence of the genetic code, the DNA-RNA communication system within the cell that stores, copies, and transmits the instructions for organic production and reproduction. At the macro level, with some exceptions, life is defined by its dependence on photosynthesis in green plants and marine algae.

The boundary between nature and human society, or between the natural ecosystem and the social ecosystem, is defined by the emergence of kinship, language, and labor, which together give rise to systems of value and belief (Chapter 2).

Photosynthesis signifies literally 'creation by light'. This living process of energy transformation is the only way in which the energy of solar radiation can enter the biological cycle. Photosynthesis uses the energy of sunlight to produce organic compounds from water and carbon dioxide, principally energy-rich carbohydrates such as sugars, starch, and cellulose. In the process, plants, algae, and certain bacteria liberate oxygen. (In evolution, they are the original source of the oxygen in the atmosphere, beginning some two billion years ago.) Photosynthesis thus creates the macro-conditions for most other kinds of life. It is also the original source of our non-renewable fossil fuels (stored sunlight). The energy used by your nervous system to read this sentence has the same source: it was once sunlight trapped on earth by a plant.

The boundary between an open system and its environment is a locus of communication and exchange. As Daniel Mazia said of the cell membrane in 'The Cell Cycle' in 1974:

> The cell membrane is not a wall or a skin or a sieve. It is an active and responsive part of the cell; it decides what is inside and what is outside and what the outside does to the inside. Cell membranes have 'faces' that enable cells to recognize and influence one another. The membranes are also communications systems. Things outside a cell do not necessarily act on the cell interior by passing through the membrane; they may simply change the membrane in some way that causes the membrane, in turn, to make changes in the cell interior.

The invisible and intangible boundary between nature and society is also a boundary between open systems. Across that boundary, in an immense and staggering diversity of forms of organization, and at a vast number of levels, matter-energy and information are continuously communicated and exchanged.

For human beings, a simpler but still similar boundary of communication and exchange distinguishes the social self from the biological individual.

The human biological individual is a visible and tangible organism with a complex brain and nervous system and many other modes and systems of communication, bounded by the skin (including the alimentary canal: our 'insides' are in fact 'outside'), and defined by a real and ecological network of relationships with nature and society at many levels. The biological individual is a product of natural selection – the survival of the fittest ecosystem (Gregory Bateson) – in natural evolution.

The social self is an invisible and intangible open system with a complex mind and emotional system and many other modes and systems of communication, but without any boundary in any way similar to the biological boundary of the skin. And rather than existing 'in our head' or 'inside the body', the social self exists only in relationships, relationships between selves and others in society in history.

According to the 'central dogma' of molecular biology, evolution is Darwinian. The genetic information passes from the genes to the organism and never in the other direction. A change in the genetic information thus precedes any change in organic structure.

Evolution in society, culture, and history, however, is Lamarckian, based on the inheritance of acquired characteristics: the discoveries, innovations, and inventions of one generation are passed on to the next. Thus while the evolution of the brain and the organism is Darwinian, that of the mind and the self is Lamarckian.

Both 'nature' and 'nurture' are involved in the development of the self, and it is goalseeking and constraint, rather than physical causality and determinism, that define the results of their interaction (next section). The genes define a vast array of biological potential; environment and experience define an even more complex and extensive array of social potential; the interaction between them is the source of human creativity.

The boundary between society and culture, the two most complex systems on earth, is more difficult to define: at last count there were 164 definitions of culture. The definition that provokes the least disagreement is that culture is what makes societies with the same kind of economic system, the Trobrianders and the Dobu, for instance, or Italy and France, distinct from each other. This implies that culture is symbolic and imaginary, as well as real.

To avoid all misunderstanding, I use the word 'society' in this text to refer to human society, including culture, rather than to groups of animals and insects with social organization or the rudiments of culture.

The world around us is extremely rich in constraints. We are so familiar with them that we take most of them for granted, and are often not even aware that they exist. To see what the world would be like without its usual constraints we would have to turn to fairy tales or to a 'crazy' film, and even these remove only a fraction of all the constraints.

W. ROSS ASHBY: *An Introduction to Cybernetics* (1956)

1.5 Freedom and constraint

For goalseeking, adaptive open systems – systems involving or simulating life or mind – constraints are the basis of complexity and the conditions of creativity. Only by using the constraints of the code of English can I write this sentence, for example. And only by manipulating the constraints of the machine I'm working on can I type it.

Figure 1.2 is not only a hierarchy of orders of complexity; it is also a hierarchy of constraints. Each open-ended bracket in the diagram denotes the boundary of a set of constraints related to the order of complexity involved. A constraint both limits and defines the relative 'semiotic freedom' of the goalseeking subsystems in the systems it constrains; it is at the same time a principle of organization.

'Semiotic' comes from the Greek *sema*, 'sign'; it is used here to mean 'characterized by communication'. By relative 'semiotic freedom' I mean the relative freedom to use information to organize matter-energy or the relative freedom to use one kind or level of information to organize another kind or level.

In complex systems, relative semiotic freedom describes a bounded 'sphere of possibilities', or a many-dimensioned 'function space', through which goalseekers may trace an infinite diversity of pathways in space and time, without going beyond the system's constraints.

A constraint is not a cause, like a physical force, nor a positive control, like steering, that makes something happen. Constraints are limits, like grammar, conscious or not, that define the conditions of what is not allowed or not supposed to happen.

The negative character of constraints has positive results. Consider driving home from work. Consciously and unconsciously, one is constrained by the road network, by cautionary and directional signs (mandatory signs can be considered controls), by the highway code, by driving etiquette, by other drivers, and by the characteristics of cars. But without this network of constraints, driving in traffic would be impossible.

As we near our goal, the constraints defining our relative freedom to choose other routes converge, fewer and fewer outcomes are possible, and our arrival on the doorstep eventually becomes the only solution to our quest. Thinking only of the beginning and the end of the journey, we might regard our departure as the cause of our arrival, when in fact our arrival was the cause of our departure.

There is thus a fundamental distinction between a matter-energy process caused by a physical force and a matter-energy process triggered or organized by information. Kicking a rock is a matter-energy transaction with nature; kicking an attacking dog is a communication between organisms as well.

Semiotic freedom in general is the relative freedom of a goalseeking adaptive subsystem to obtain and use matter-energy, at one level, and to obtain, create, and use information, at other levels, within the limits on behavior and communication defined by one or more constraints. It is called 'semiotic' because in living and social systems the use of matter-energy is governed by information.

Ordinary physical or Newtonian causality (also called 'efficient causality') is a matter-energy relationship determined by the past: the cause is 'behind' the effect, as when cue-ball strikes eight-ball, and the effect always follows the cause. Causality here is positive and mechanical: it is the result of the presence of a cause, the result of something actually happening. In contrast, cybernetic causality, or goalseeking within constraints, is an informational relationship defined by the future: the goal exists before the effects that result from seeking to achieve it. Causality here is negative: it is the result of the absence of the goal, the result of something not yet happening. Cybernetic causality does not however contradict or nullify ordinary physical causality; it complements it at another level of reality.

Goalseeking within constraints is characteristic of all systems involving or simulating life or mind, and occurs on millions of levels in living nature and society. Goalseeking behavior (or at simpler levels, goal directed behavior) means behavior organized towards an end, as in protein synthesis in the cell, the growth of an embryo, breaking out of the egg, building a nest, spinning a web, hunting for food, seeking a mate, or caching nuts to last the winter.

Goalseeking behavior in this sense has no connection with religious or philosophical 'teleology' (from Greek *telos*, 'goal' or 'end'), the idea that the cosmos (or natural evolution, or history) is the working out of a pre-established harmony, or predestined plan, or a Grand Design established by God, Providence, or Mother Nature. (The technical term used for 'goalseeking' is 'teleonomy'.)

Human behavior is thus neither determined nor the product of free will; it is the product of goalseeking within constraints. What distinguishes us from animals and microbes in this respect is the vast extent and great complexity of human goalseeking, which does not simply include the capacity to change goals but also the capacity to invent entirely new ones.

From this we can conclude that freedom is not, as Hegel said, 'the recognition of necessity', but rather the recognition of constraint.

'What is the use of a book', thought Alice, 'without pictures or conversations?'

LEWIS CARROLL: *Alice in Wonderland* (1865)

1.6 Opposites

The dependent hierarchy between nature and society is commonly spoken of as an 'opposition', at a single level. The failure to distinguish an opposition at a single level from a relation between levels is deeply rooted. We find it in ancient Athens, a slave-supported state – like Plato's ideal Republic – and eventually an empire, which collapsed after defeat by Sparta in the Peloponnesian War (431–404 Before the Common Era [BCE]).

Plato's great pupil, Aristotle (384–322 BCE), was the son of a physician to the King of Macedonia. He became tutor to Alexander the Great, who conquered an empire stretching from Greece to India before his death from malaria in Babylon in 323 BCE.

The key comment on Aristotle I have chosen is from George Boas, who was, with A. O. Lovejoy and Alexandre Koyré, a pioneer in the history of ideas. Boas is analyzing one of the basic assumptions of Aristotle, his metaphysical – and ultimately, ideological – belief in the 'fundamental character' of the binary opposition, in belief reasserted in contemporary structural linguistics and structural anthropology.

Etymologically an opposite is something which is placed in a position facing something else, which means along the same straight line and facing in the reverse direction. If up and down, or left and right, are opposites, their opposition must be defined geometrically. . . . The geometrical structure of [Aristotle's] world permits him to interpret opposition in spatial terms (Boas, 1959, p. 26).

C. K. Ogden remarked in 1932 in *Opposition* that Aristotle 'was obsessed with the problem of opposition' (p. 21). Boas's analysis shows that the basic orientation of Aristotle's world view is a left-right symmetry between pairs of so-called opposites. In his *Physics* (literally 'the study of nature'), the four Greek elements are said to be opposed in pairs: Fire/Earth and Air/Water, as are full/empty, dense/rare, and high/low. In his *Metaphysics*, the major oppositions (so-called) are form/matter, unity/variety, natural/unnatural, active/passive, before/after, whole/part, being/not-being, and so on.

('Metaphysics', the title given by scholars in the first century CE to Aristotle's works on the foundations of philosophy, literally means 'after physics', i.e. the work next to Aristotle's work on physics on the shelf in the library. Later on 'metaphysics' came to mean 'beyond physics', i.e. 'beyond nature'. It is used to refer to speculative thought in philosophy and hidden assumptions in science.)

For Aristotle then, up and down are simply a left-right horizontal symmetry stood on edge, like the vertical axis of a graph. In this two-sided (bilateral) symmetry, the 'oppositions' face each other as if across a circle: they are 'diametrically opposed'. Up and down are seen as two poles, 'up' on the one hand, and 'down' on the other, just like the magnetic poles, where 'north' is of the same level of reality as 'south'. Here Aristotle's approach makes no distinction between levels of existence, logic, or reality.

A major reason for the circularity of this point of view has to do with Greek views of perfection. For Aristotle, the 'most perfect' kind of motion is circular motion – largely because for him as for Plato it represents the ideal of eternal motion in a changeless world. In this view, which still survives in modern thought, rotation is defined as the primary kind of movement.

In human reality, however, up and down are not symmetrical, except in mechanics and the like. With the help of Boas, we see that in Aristotle there is no significant distinction between a hierarchy and a series – except when he is explaining the 'natural baseness' of slaves, or the 'natural inferiority' of women.

In social relations, Aristotle's viewpoint encourages us to see real conflicts between dominant and subordinate – between master and slave, or man and woman, for instance – as pairs of apparently equal imaginary opposites at a single level, rather than as real relations between levels in (illegitimate) hierarchies of power.

Two millennia after Plato and Aristotle, in his seventeenth-century *Pensées* (1670, no. 50), the French mathematician, mystic, and philosopher Gabriel Pascal comments on the origin of our faith in bilateral symmetries, while remarking on the asymmetry of up and down and back to front:

[Our notion of] symmetry is derived from the human face. The result is that we demand symmetry horizontally and in breadth only, not vertically nor in depth.

Aristotle also insists that change, which is for him a form of motion (of quality, quantity, or place), is always into opposites or intermediates between them. Boas concludes, as many others have done, that Aristotle's basic assumptions, including those he derived from Plato, make up 'the nucleus of whatever is permanent in the philosophic traditions of the Occident' (1959, p. 8).

Imaginary oppositions

From Cardinal Nicholas of Cusa to Lenin, from the Taoist *ch'i wu* to Engels, from William Blake to Mao, and from the eighteenth-century German 'nature philosophers' to the French anthropologist Claude Lévi-Strauss, the doctrine that binary oppositions are basic to human relationships – they are often called the 'unity (or identity) of opposites' – has consistently confused our understanding of the relationships between organisms and environments in nature, between people and groups in society, and between reality and the domain of images and ideas (whether in verbal, visual, logical, or sensual thought).

Consider as examples the following pairs of terms:

culture	nature
mind	body
reason	emotion
conscious	unconscious
white	non-white
capital	labor

We have only to apply the Extinction Rule to realize that not one of these pairs is a real opposition. They are the symmetrization – the reduction to a single level – of a dependent hierarchy. Only in the imaginary can these categories be seen as symmetrical opposites rather than as relations between levels. The second term in each pair (e.g. emotion) is in fact the environment that the first term (e.g. reason) depends on for subsistence and survival. (Similarly labor is the source and sustenance of capital.) But by turning each hierarchy upside down like the inverted image of a camera obscura, the first term (e.g. culture) either appears to dominate the second (e.g. nature), or does in fact dominate it (e.g. white and non-white). Each term on the left-hand side is an open system apparently free to exploit whatever it defines as its environment; and any open system that exploits its environment in the short range inevitably exploits itself in the long range.

No one can answer what nature is unless he knows what history is.

R. G. COLLINGWOOD: *The Idea of Nature* (1945)

1.7 The rational and the real

The passage to be remarked on here is taken from the *Philosophy of History* by G. W. F. Hegel (1770–1831), the German idealist philosopher who ended his days as an apologist for the Prussian State, an absolute monarchy tempered by aristocracy.

The term 'idealism' was introduced into philosophy in the eighteenth century. It refers to perspectives based on the assumption that ideas and spiritual values are the controlling factors in society, history, or the world as a whole. In idealism change begins as an idea, often attributed to a single person; in realism change begins as action, the action of many people, and is only later expressed as an idea. Extreme idealists deny that anything exists independently of its perception. *Esse est percipi* – 'to be is to be perceived', said Bishop Berkeley (1685–1753).

Philosophical idealism has dominated western ideology and education since the days of Plato. It is usually contrasted with (or opposed to) materialism, which is the foundation of modern physical and biological science and the experimental method.

(The two terms do not mean the same in philosophy as they do in ordinary conversation, where idealism usually means striving for the best, and materialism, the almighty dollar or godless communism.)

Today these two terms do little but create confusion. Now that we understand that information can be every bit as real as matter-energy, the imaginary and usually either/or opposition between ideas and reality, or that between idealism and materialism, disappears from serious science.

Hegel was born in the century in which the French invented the word 'ideology', and from which there emerged the modern doctrine of (infinite) 'progress'. The medieval cosmology in Europe had taught that space was finite, that the cosmos was closed, and that perfection lay only in God and the after-life. A common medieval argument runs: Only God can be infinite, therefore the cosmos is finite.

With the 'Age of Discovery' of the fifteenth and sixteenth centuries, leading to the European colonization of other worlds, and with the European social revolutions of the seventeenth and eighteenth centuries, notably in England, America, and France, the previously dominant view of a limited and unchangeable universe was rejected. Both in 'the heavenly city of the eighteenth century philosophers' (Carl Becker, 1932), and in the world of commerce, there emerged the doctrine that 'the progress of civilization', based on new technologies, would eventually lead to perfection here on earth.

Hegel's great influence on the modern world view and on political attitudes, left and right, stems from the fact that, until the 1870s, he was the greatest and the most systematic of the philosophers of change. For Hegel being is a process of becoming, and change is created by conflict. Conflict at one level of development in history is transcended by its resolution and restatement at another level of development, at which point conflict begins anew (Chapter 8).

The Hegelian dialectic is a dialectic of concepts. In *The Phenomenology of Mind* of 1807 (meaning simply 'the study of the phenomenon or manifestation of mind or spirit'), which is also an abstract history of literature, the dialectic is expressed as an ascending process of ever more complex arguments between pairs of abstract individuals representing the progress of the spirit. These abstractions stand for stages in the evolution of human consciousness, meaning 'consciousness-of-self' (as distinct from animals, which display only a 'sentiment-of-self'). Each pair in conflict stands for a 'critical moment' in a grand dialectic of ideas from the time of the Greeks to the present day. The resolution of the conflict at any one level prepares the way for it to be restated in a more complex form at another level.

'Dialectic' in Greek is simply 'conversation' or 'argument'. As Bertrand Russell explains in *The Wisdom of the West* (1959), the Hegelian dialectic is based on the development of Greek philosophy. Greek thought throughout its stages was influenced by a number of dualisms, says Russell, the most basic being the distinction between truth and falsehood. Closely connected with that were the dualisms of good and evil, harmony and strife, appearance and reality, mind and matter, and freedom and necessity. There were also cosmological questions as to whether the world is One (as Parmenides believed) or Many (as Heraclitus said), or simple or complex. Finally there were the dualisms of chaos and order, and the boundless and the limit.

One Greek philosopher or school of philosophy

might come down on one side of a dualism, another subsequently would raise criticisms and adopt the opposite view. In the end a third would come along and effect some kind of compromise, superseding both the original views. It is by observing this see-saw battle between rival doctrines amongst the pre-socratic philosophers that Hegel first developed his notion of the dialectic (pp. 14–15).

What Russell in his English way calls a 'compromise' between opposed views is better understood as a battle followed by a transcendence, or 'going beyond' them. The truth on one side and the truth on the other are 'overcome' and yet still retained in the truth of a new position at a new level. (For this double process, Hegel uses the verb *aufheben*, which conveniently means both 'to abolish' and 'to conserve'.)

The idea of the 'dialectical leap' or 'discontinuity' is commonly expressed as a process by which a 'thesis' (taking a stand) is opposed by an 'antithesis' (taking a stand against), which by their conflict are transformed into a new level of becoming, a 'synthesis' (standing together). The synthesis carried them forward while going beyond them (Chapter 8).

Hegel held that mind or spirit (*Geist*) is the only true reality. 'The real is rational', he said, 'and the rational is real.' He believed that the 'essence' of history is not the real people who make and live it, but rather a disembodied *Geist* that uses people as the agents of its own operations. The aim of the Mind or Spirit in history is its transformation into the changeless world of the Absolute, where all desires are one. The most important manifestation of this 'world spirit' or 'world mind' is Reason, for it is by 'the cunning of reason' (*der List der Vernunft*) that the Spirit operates unconsciously in every person.

Politically, Hegel's Absolute is the State: 'the divine idea as it exists on earth'. Prussia, he said, was the highest yet 'self-realization' of the ideal of the Absolute Spirit.

What Hegel teaches in spite of all this is a sense of change quite unlike tradition; an understanding of life as a quest, just as *Don Quixote* in 1605 or *Madame Bovary* in 1857 are quests for meaning and sanity; an understanding of mediation, meaning that the relationship between two or more associated terms at one level is mediated by a third term at another level (Chapter 4); and an initiation into the psychology of imaginary relations between individuals, where each plays the part of an opposing mirror image of the other.

The following passage is taken from Hegel's *Philosophy of History*, as compiled from his students' notes (1832, pp. 9–11). It outlines his view of the relationship between culture, society, and nature.

> The only Thought which Philosophy brings with it to the contemplation of History, is the simple conception of *Reason*; that Reason is the Sovereign of the World; that the history of the world, therefore, presents us with a rational process ... [In Philosophy it is] proved by speculative cognition, that Reason ... is *Substance*, as well as *Infinite Power*; its own *Infinite Material* underlying all the natural and spiritual life which it originates, as also the *Infinite Form* – that which sets this Material in motion. On the one hand, Reason is the *substance* of the Universe; viz., that by which and in which all reality has its being and subsistence. On the other hand, it is the *Infinite Energy* of the Universe; since Reason is not so powerless as to be incapable of producing anything but a mere ideal, a mere intention – having its place outside reality, nobody knows where; something separate and abstract, in the heads of certain human beings. It is *the infinite complex* of things, their entire Essence and Truth. ... It supplies its own nourishment, and is the object of its own operations. ...

Hegel goes on to reveal the mixture of Newtonian and Cartesian mechanism and Greek and Chinese organicism in his philosophy of nature (Chapter 3). The planets themselves demonstrate the 'laws of reason' as if they were alive:

> The movement of the solar system takes place according to unchangeable laws. These laws are Reason, implicit in the phenomena in question. But neither the sun nor the planets which revolve around it according to these laws, can be said to have any consciousness of them.

As Morton White points out, in Hegel's view

> the universe is not unlike an animate being that has a soul, desires, aims, intentions, and goals. The universe is spiritual; it has direction; and the explanation of ordinary facts, human actions, historical changes, and institutions may be grasped once we recognize how they are embedded in this cosmic organism, how they are directed by the cunning of the Absolute, how they play their part in the Universe's progressive realization of the World Spirit (1957, p. 13; quoted in Hammer, 1981, p. 129).

Hegel's reductionism is drastic. In the passage quoted, whether viewed mechanically or organically, he makes reason its own context, its own environment. No such self-referring living system can exist; it is cut off from any source of real energy and real information. Whether they are believed to be conceptual or real or both at once, the operations of Hegel's 'reason', and indeed the basic assumptions of his entire philosophy, are imaginary, as imaginary as perpetual motion.

We may now write the Environment Rule:

> *The Environment Rule*: The environment of an open system or systems is of a higher logical type, or level of reality, than the systems that depend on it for their existence. Open system and environment form a dependent hierarchy. To test orientation of levels, apply the Extinction Rule.

From the Environment Rule follows the Inevitable Rule:

> *The Inevitable Rule*: The system that destroys its environment destroys itself.

The Hegelian view is not restricted to philosophers. The following extract is from *Arthur Mee's Wonderful Day*, by the Editor of *The Children's Newspaper*, published in the 1930s:

Mind Marching On

From the creeping life of the ocean bed to the beautiful life of a
child we have seen Mind making its way. By laws that never fail,
by ways that no man knows, impelled by a power beyond our
understanding, Mind climbs ever upward.

. . . Mind has never turned back; it has never been beaten; and
today it is the master of all the universe we know.

. . . 'In the beginning was the Word', says the Gospel of St John;
but the original Greek for Word means reason and speech, or
mind and the expression of mind, so that it served to suggest Mind
expressing God in the world.

Mind has come into its own. It dominates the living world. It
moves and moulds and changes matter to its will. How it has
conquered, the marvellous mechanism it has built up for itself
throughout the Animal Kingdom, is a long tale to tell . . .

Note in this passage the central assumption of 'rationalism' – as in
Hegel and many modern and recent writers, especially in France – the
idea that the only faculty of communication really worthy of mind, or
reason, or thought, is language. In this view, promoted by many
modern linguists, thought is simply 'inner speech'.

(The Greek Logos or 'Word' is not confined to language or conversation. It also means thought, referent (what is spoken of), computation, measure, proportion, analogy, plea, reputation, ground, principle, and (human or divine) reason, and may well be translated 'information', meaning literally 'given form'.)

In the mainly left-brain perspective of linguistic rationalism, the non-
verbal thinking, feeling, seeing, sensing, and other kinds of mainly
right-brain communication – the basis and the immediate environment
of verbal thought and linguistic communication – are simply ruled out
of court (Chapter 8).

Indeed, the Austro-British philosopher of language Ludwig Wittgenstein (1889–1951), true to the dominant mental bent, went so far as
to say at the end of his *Tractatus Logico-Philosophicus* (1921):
'Whereof we cannot speak, thereof we must be silent.'

It is so then, that in the work of the creation we see a double
emanation of virtue from God, the one referring more properly
to power, the other to wisdom, the one expressed in making the
subsistence [the substance] of the matter, and the other in
disposing the beauty of the form.

SIR FRANCIS BACON: *The Advancement of Learning* (1605)

1.8 Form and matter

The passage from Hegel in the preceding section illustrates the collapsing of the form/matter distinction by what Gregory Bateson (1904–80) has called the 'bioenergetic epistemology'. Largely derived from the 'mechanical philosophy of nature' developed in the seventeenth and eighteenth centuries (Cartesianism and Newtonianism), the bioenergetic viewpoint does not distinguish between matter-energy and information, nor between objects and the communicational relations they represent.

The following passage will provide a significant contrast with Hegel's perspective. It is taken from Giambattista della Porta's *Magia naturalis* (1558–89), as translated into English in 1658, a decade after the execution of Charles I in the midst of the English Revolution (1642–88), and only thirty years before the publication of Newton's *Principia* (1687).

The Italian 'natural philosopher', Giambattista della Porta (1535?–1615), was the first scientist to recognize the heating effects of light rays. A classic example of the upper-class 'renaissance man', Porta also wrote some of the best Italian comedies of his day. He produced an agricultural encyclopedia; a work on optics; a design for a steam engine anticipating the first commercially successful engine (Thomas Savery's, patented in 1698); a work on chemistry; a discussion of magnetism; an attack on astrology; and a work on the theory of secret codes and ciphers (1563).

The passage chosen from *Natural Magick* provides a renaissance transformation of the traditional Greek world view that was to be replaced by the scientific revolution of the 'mechanical philosophy of nature' associated with Galileo (1564–1642), Descartes (1596–1650), and Newton (1642–1727). In the dominant discourse of Greek antiquity, all of nature is said to be infused with mind (*nous*) or spirit (*pneuma*: breath). Nature and society are a complex of organicist relations in which mind is the medium of the Forms or Ideas or Patterns that inform the cosmos.

In the renaissance view, form and matter are clearly distinct from each other, but they are not opposed to each other as they would be in a one-dimensional way of seeing. Their relationship is hierarchical. Shorn of its religious and alchemical trappings, the 'both-and' or 'co-operative' viewpoint expressed by Porta is not fundamentally different from the modern understanding that in living and social systems, information organizes matter-energy:

> Every natural substance (I mean a compound body) is composed
> of matter and form, as of her principles . . . But the Form hath

such singular vertue, that whatsoever effects we see, all of them first proceed from thence; and it hath a divine beginning; and being the chiefest and most excellent part, absolute of herself, she uses the rest as her instruments, for the more speedy and convenient dispatch of her actions: and he which is not addicted nor accustomed to such contemplations, supposeth that the temperature and the matter works all things, whereas indeed they are but as it were instruments whereby the form worketh . . . Therefore whereas there are three efficient and working causes in every compound, we must not suppose any of them to be idle, but all at work, some more and some lesse; but above all other, the form is most active and busie, strengthening the rest; which surely would be to no purpose if the form should fail them, in as much as they are not capable of heavenly influences. And though the form of its self be not able to produce such effects, but the rest must do their parts, yet are they neither confounded together, nor yet become divers things; but they are so knit among themselves, that one stands in need of anothers help. . . . Wherefore that force which is called the property of a thing, proceeds not from the temperature, but from the very form it self.

Note that, as Reason has been for many western writers, Form is feminine first, and neuter second.

He plants trees to benefit another generation.
CAECILIUS STATIUS (220–168 BCE)

1.9 Chhi and Li

In his *Science and Civilisation in China*, Joseph Needham provides a comparison between the kind of organicism represented by della Porta and the dominant patterns of thought and explanation in China.

(The more important passages will be found in volume two (1956, pp. 472–93, 253ff., 273ff., 279–303.)

Needham discusses the use of the basic Chinese concepts, Chhi (氣) and Li (理), by the Sung Neo-Confucians, and particularly by the naturalist philosopher Chu Hsi (1130–1200), contemporary with the twelfth-century renaissance in the European middle ages. Needham notes the similarity between Chhi and the Greek *pneuma* (breath), but rejects this as a possible translation. Li, he points out has been translated 'form' by many writers, 'reason' (in the Hegelian sense) by others, and also by the completely innappropriate 'law' and 'soul' ('the great tradition of Chinese philosophy had no place for souls'). Needham continues:

> . . . The word *li* in its most ancient meaning signified the 'pattern' in things, the markings in jade or the fibrous texture of a muscle, and only later required its standard dictionary meaning of 'principle' (p. 473).
> . . . The distinctive importance of Li is precisely that it was not intrinsically soul-like or animate. . . . Chhi did not depend on Li in any way. Form was the 'essence' and 'primary substance' of things, but Li was not itself substantial or any form of Chhi or *chih* ['solid, hard, or tangible matter']. . . . I believe that Li was not in any strict sense metaphysical, as were Platonic ideas and Aristotelian forms, but rather the invisible organising fields or forces existing at all levels within the natural world (p. 475).

He quotes Chu Hsi: 'Throughout the universe there is no Chhi without Li, nor is there any Li without Chhi.'

The association with patterns in jade — order in disorder — recalls the advice to artists of Leonardo da Vinci (1452–1519) in the *Notebooks*:

> . . . Look into the stains of walls, or ashes of a fire, or clouds, or mud or like places, in which, if you consider them well, you may find really marvellous ideas. The mind of the painter is stimulated to new discoveries . . . because by indistinct things the mind is stimulated to new inventions (quoted in March and Steadman, 1971, pp. 31–1).

Needham, who is also a renowned biologist well-acquainted with cybernetics and levels of organization, goes on to consider other explanations of these two terms and their relationships. After a masterly sweep through world philosophies of nature and natural science, Needham concludes that the classic 'body/soul' and 'matter/form' arguments about their signification must be given up, and that Chhi and Li should be translated as 'matter-energy' and 'organization'. Since information is the instrument of living, social, and theoretical organization, we might also translate Li as 'pattern', 'order', or 'information'.

CHAPTER 2

Kith and kin

The image of a scene, a sequence, of a whole creation, exists not as something fixed and ready-made. It has to arise, to unfold before the senses of the spectator.

SERGEI EISENSTEIN: *The Film Sense* (1942)

2.1 Origins

The question of the origin and organization of nature and society – 'why things are the way they are' – is the origin of ideology. The desire to know why, and the mere fact that we ask such questions, are what most obviously distinguish us from animals and computers. Ideologies are systems of rules, structures, images, ideas, values, feelings, and beliefs – conscious and unconscious, left and right brain – that are essential to the organization of all human societies.

An ideology is a prescription for a way of life. Every society displays a general or 'dominant' ideology: a code of general values most of its people share, consciously and unconsciously, and within which various group and individual ideologies arise.

A general ideology acts as the ground of truth itself, and so profoundly so that most people remain unaware of its existence.

A general ideology is not necessarily entirely imaginary, erroneous, oppressive, or violent; but wherever violence exists an ideology exists to justify it. In oppressive societies, ideologies make physical and other forms of violence seem ordinary or inevitable, a part of the 'natural order of things'. Violence is blamed on its victims; the victims are taught to take responsibility for it on themselves.

Ideologies are by nature symbolic: what they symbolize may be both imaginary and real, reality being the ultimate test of their validity. They are transmitted between people by every available means: ritual, schooling, clothing, religion, jokes, games, myths, gestures, ornaments, entertainment.

A dominant ideology arises out of the real relationships between people in society, and those between society and nature. The task of a general ideology is to explain the past, the present, and the expected future of the system one is in, whether fully, reliably, usefully, or not. Imaginary ideologies invariably include enough elements of truth to be plausible to most people most of the time, however implausibly these elements may be interpreted and arranged.

Any ideology may be subverted and transformed by social change, at which times it will be refuted by the emerging ideology of the changes taking place.

(This view of ideology is not part of a 'conspiracy theory' of society. To conspire means literally to 'breathe together': i.e. to do what one normally does with other people who share one's general values, whether deliberately or not.)

An ideology begins with a 'myth of origins' – as the story of Aeneas of Troy was for Imperial Rome, as Genesis is for Jews and Christians, as the Liberty Tree and the Grand Old Flag are for Americans, as the Angles and the Saxons and the unwritten constitution – but not the Ancient Britons, who went in for human sacrifice – are for the English.

For the Bororo Indians of the Mato Grosso of south central Brazil the myth of origins is an explanation of the origin of kinship itself:

> After a flood, the earth became so full of people that the sun
> decided to reduce their number. All perished by drowning in a
> river at his command, except Akaruio Bokodori. Those who were
> lost in the rapids had wavy hair; those who were lost in the pools
> had straight hair. Akaruio Bokodori then brought them all back to
> life, but accepted only those clans whose gifts to him he liked. All
> the others he killed with arrows.

This is a summary of a myth analyzed by Claude Lèvi-Strauss in *Le Cru et le cuit* (*The Raw and the Cooked*), published in 1964 (pp. 58–63).

Translated into modern terms, as Lévi-Strauss makes clear, the Bororo myth is an explanation of the logical foundations of kinship that is as much to the point as any to be found in western anthropology.

The myth tells us that is became necessary for people to become less numerous so that neighboring physical types, and later whole groups of individuals, could be clearly distinguished from one another. Without distinction there can be no identity, and in kinship identity is all-important. Identity in the myth is defined by the gifts one bears; giftgiving is the rationale of kinship and many other activities in band and village societies.

By his decisions about the value of the different gifts the ancestors offer, Akaruio Bokodori is defining kinship categories. He is creating a system of discrete distinctions between groups – just as 'foreigner', 'mother', 'cousin', 'mother's brother', and so on are discrete distinctions between members of groups – out of a series of apparently continuous differences between people. By inserting intervals into a continuum, he turns differences into distinctions.

The independently evolved myth of origins of the Arunta of the central Australian desert tells the same story, but in a different way. The ancestors of the Arunta are eternally existing supernatural beings who appeared 'in the beginning': in the mystic paradise in space, time, and memory called 'the Dreaming' or 'the Eternal Dream Time'. The Dreaming is both past, present, and future, and attainable through ritual and self-discipline.

As Mircea Eliade explains in *Australian Religions* (1973, pp. 44–50), quoting W. E. H. Stanner, the Dreaming at the origins stands for

> a kind of charter of things that still happen, and a kind of *logos* or principle of order transcending everything significant for aboriginal man.

The Dreaming is the precedent for all behavior, the time when the patterns of living and the rules of Arunta society were laid down, and the origin of reality itself. Says Eliade:

> Everything that fully *exists* – a mountain, a water place, an institution, a custom – is acknowledged as real, valid, and meaningful because it came into being *in the beginning*.

In the beginning the earth was a desolate plain. The only living beings were masses of half-developed infants, lying helplessly at places later to become salt lakes or waterholes. Quoting T. G. H. Strethlow, Eliade explains that besides transforming the earth and populating it with animals and plants, the ancestors of the Arunta

> sliced massed humanity into individual infants, then slit the webs between their fingers and toes, and cut open their ears, eyes, and mouths.

The basic principle here – making discrete distinctions in a continuum of difference (like counting time) – is the same as the Bororo conception of the origins of kinship, except that in this case, by opening eyes, ears, and mouths, and freeing fingers and toes, the ancestors of the Arunta are made responsible for the origin of human communication as well.

Like the alphabet, the whole numbers, the genetic code, or the pieces in chess, a kinship system is a digital system. A digital system is made up of discrete units separated by distinct gaps, that between 'a' and 'b', for instance, or that between dot and dash in Morse. The gaps are a necessary part of the syntax or ordering principles of the system

(Chapter 4). In digital systems goalseekers select and combine discrete categories according to codes of rules in ways that create and recreate complexity, in this case the complexity of a kinship system that includes levels of relationship.

That a kinship system is a communication system the Bororo myth makes clear: Akaruio Bokadori is using the gifts borne by the ancestors as information about life and death.

We cannot know the actual origins of society, but we can know a great deal about what distinguishes society from nature. Four apparently inseparable conditions, each of which involves a system of communication, make society possible: kinship, language, the division of labor, and an ideology that explains and justifies it all, whether correctly or not.

'Labor' should be understood to include mental, manual, and emotional labor, besides the labor of economic production and the preparation of food, as well as the labor of bearing and rearing children.

In non-state (and non-capitalist) societies – the so-called 'primitive' societies – the rules of kinship are codes of instructions about permitted, prescribed, and prohibited relations of communication and exchange between persons and groups. In patriarchal societies, the practically universal form known to us, this means a system of marriage and descent founded on the exchange of women between men.

(In Lévi-Strauss's strictly formalist analysis of kinship, wrongly based on a language model, kinship becomes 'a matrimonial dialogue in which women are exchanged like spoken words'.)

The expression 'band and village societies' will serve to distinguish non-state societies from state societies. In band and village societies kinship is more important than any other ideological value, social bond, political position, or economic relation, except for the relationship between the sexes, which is of course the basis of kinship and society itself.

The Hawaiian system of Polynesia once stood on the boundary between state and non-state societies, having a hereditary aristocracy and kingship (signs of a state society) constrained by collective kinship relations (the sign of a non-state society). These constraints included successful popular revolts supported by aristocratic families and death sentences against kings who rose above their station (Sahlins, 1972, pp. 139–48).

In state societies like our own, which are not necessarily civilized societies, social, political, and economic constraints – and many thousand years of despotism – play a far more important role in life than kinship relations – except for the 'in-marrying' kinship systems of the ruling classes, past and present, who rarely speak of kinship with those they rule, except in time of war.

Kinship relations in the 'other' societies are both interpersonal and collective; they involve degrees of complexity, distance, and intimacy not generally found in modern society. Besides the organization of marriage and descent, kinship relations influence and constrain etiquette, ceremony, joking, sexual liberties, ritual, games, and play, as well as one's manner of speaking and one's role in production and reproduction.

Kinship sets the rules for kith and kin and distinguishes 'us' from 'others'. Kinship is so important in band and village societies that strangers on meeting may not be able to begin a conversation until they know their kin relationship and, from that, the correct terms to address each other with. Thus the first words of an Australian aborigine to a stranger are: 'Who is your father's father?'.

(Four thousand years ago, in the city states of Sumer near the Tigris-Euphrates delta – which invented (among other things) the wheel, sailing ships, the priesthood, writing, grammar schools, and what the nineteenth century called 'civilization' (i.e. the state) – it used to be said: 'Friendship lasts a day; kinship lasts forever'.)

Above all, kinship rules and customs (they are not laws) play a dominant role in governing – not determining – who does what, and when and where, in economic production, biological reproduction, and the reproduction of the society itself.

Kinship supposes language, which is unique to human beings. Kinship is communication rather than language, but the two systems of communication are similar in that each depends on rules and structures that are largely unconscious.

Language provides:

- the capacity to name distinct categories of relationship, and to forbid certain of them, with great subtlety when necessary, by means of 'not' (syntactic negation: Chapter 8);
- the capacity to select and combine linguistic information at many levels according to a complex syntax (rules of order), and thus to creat messages with meaning (Chapter 5);
- the capacity to codify rules and levels of rules about social relationships, including rules about the permissible uses of language, discourse, and other means of communication (Chapter 6).

Language also provides the means of defining and justifying, by verbal means, the unspoken values – social, economic, ecological, and ethical – implicit in the kinship system itself.

Thinking is comparing with the past.

FRIEDRICH VON SCHILLER (1759–1805)

2.2 Memory

Along with myth and ritual, the constraints of kinship are the most important part of the 'unwritten' social memory of the 'primitive' society. Without memory life, communication, kinship, identity, and society itself are all impossible.

Memory organizes space and time. A memory system depends on recording or writing, on lasting memory traces, whether imprinted in the brain, or (in our society) on paper, tape, stone, metal, film, concrete, and other media of record.

In societies without writing as we know it, the social memory is recorded in many ways: in the memories of individuals; in the structure and design of tools and ornaments handed down the generations; in the body image and its adornment (Figure 2.1); in the kinship identity of the person; in the assignment of roles in myth and ritual; in the division of labor; in the wisdom of the past; in the topological organiz-ation of the dwelling place; and in the perceived organization of the natural environment in myth and reality.

The *marae* of the Tahitians of Polynesia provides an example of a consciously recorded system of memory traces in a society without writing as we know it. Tahitian society is a highly stratified system of continuous degrees of rank, generally classified into nobles and commoners. Polygyny – one man, several or many wives – is permitted and practiced. Tahitian social status, which is simultaneously economic, political, and religious, is believed to be based on the spiritual power called *mana* possessed by all individuals in degrees according to rank, and is fixed by birth and inheritance.

In such a society the ability to tell one's genealogy is a statement of identity over time that is of great importance for many other relation-ships: people of high status can often trace their ancestors as far back as fifty generations. (The system of ranks and titles used by the Tahitian aristocracy is not very different from that of the European nobility.) The *marae* or assembly places assist in this remembrance of things past (Service, 1963, pp. 258–62):

> Here is laid a ring of stone seats, each inherited by the various chiefs, who sit on them at the religious ceremonies, arranged in the order of social importance and sanctity. In the early days of the expansion of Tahitian society, kinship groups which emigrated to another place took with them the stone of their own leader from the ancestral marae to establish a new one where they settled. The position of the stone in the original marae was retained, however, so that the precise social position of a new lineage settlement relative to the original families was never lost. Thus, by visible

MANYEMA ADULT.

(BY-ZANZI) A CONGO DANDY.

A BATOKA.

A NATIVE OF RUA, A VISITOR AT UJIJI.

A NATIVE OF UHHA.

FIGURE 2.1: Personal adornment: Images of Africans as seen by English-speaking readers in the late nineteenth century. Taken from *Africa and its Exploration, As Told by its Explorers* (London, 1892), principally Richard Burton and David Livingstone, and from H. M. Stanley's *Through the Dark Continent* (1878).

objective means, the whole genealogical system is graphically symbolized, no matter how widely separated in space the component lineages become.

Among the North American Indians, as Lt Col. Lewis F. Acker explained in an article on their communication systems in the *Signal Corps Bulletin* for January–March 1939:

> Belts of wampum were frequently passed from tribe to tribe as a signal of record and as a token on occasions of the greatest importance. They were used generally in connection with the sale of property, the making of treaties, the confederation of tribes, and as declarations of war and peace.

Information was recorded on the belts by patterns of shell beads of various colors set on contrasting backgrounds of skin, so as to

> convey and record permanently the story of events of the past and plans for the future. Great care was exercised in the construction of wampum belts and they were held in great reverence as archives.

The width and length of a belt depended on the importance of its purpose or record. The chiefs and elders of the people were accustomed to assemble at intervals 'to rehearse the matters' conveyed by the belts in the keeping of the tribe – so that the codes in use, besides the pleasure and the drama of the memories themselves, might not be forgotten.

Memory, like information, is not a thing, but a relationship to an environment, without which it is reduced to noise.

Our daily environment is for us also a message system, a memory, and a map. As a topological map of a system based on hierarchies of wealth and power, the messages of our daily environment provide us with explicit and implicit instructions about contexts, situations, statuses, and directions, and about available and preferred pathways through the system it stands for. Few of the messages of this network – this ideostructure – are translated into words, and many of them cannot be communicated in language at all.

('Topology' means literally the 'science of places' (*topoi*). In botany in the seventeenth century it meant 'plant ecology'. In modern mathematics and philosophy, topology is the study of relationships such as surfaces, shapes, and boundaries, continuity and discontinuity, and neighborhood.)

In Figure 2.2 the plan of the Cheyenne camp circle and that of the Bororo village illustrate the topological memory of kinship by the individual's orientation in the dwelling place. The third plan, from the

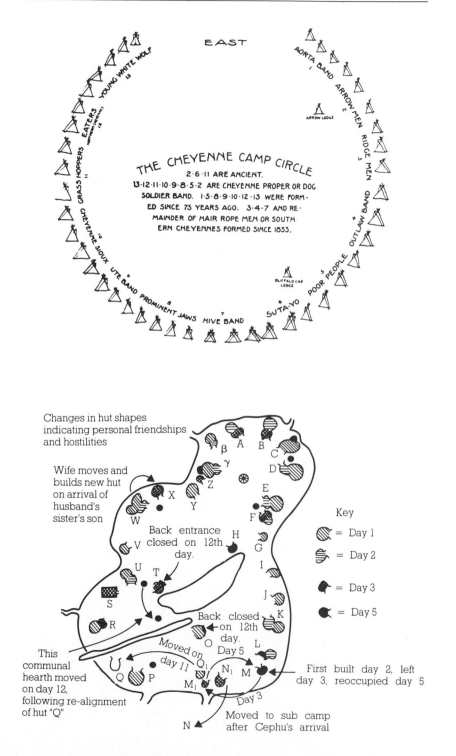

EAST

THE CHEYENNE CAMP CIRCLE

2·6·11 ARE ANCIENT.
13·12·11·10·9·8·5·2 ARE CHEYENNE PROPER OR DOG
SOLDIER BAND. 1·5·8·9·10·12·13 WERE FORM-
ED SINCE 75 YEARS AGO. 3·4·7 AND RE-
MAINDER OF HAIR ROPE MEN OR SOUTH-
ERN CHEYENNES FORMED SINCE 1855.

YOUNG WHITE WOLF 13

EATERS (HEVIKSNIPAHIS) 12

GRASS HOPPERS 11

CHEYENNE SIOUX 10

UTE BAND 9

PROMINENT JAWS 8

HIVE BAND 7

SUTA·YO 6

POOR PEOPLE 5

OUTLAW BAND 4

RIDGE MEN 3

ARROW MEN 2

AORTA BAND 1

ARROW LODGE

BUFFALO CAP LODGE

Changes in hut shapes
indicating personal friendships
and hostilities

Wife moves and
builds new hut
on arrival of
husband's
sister's son

Back entrance
closed on 12th
day.

Back closed
on 12th
day.
Day 5

This
communal
hearth moved
on day 12,
following re-alignment
of hut "Q"

Moved on day 11

Day 3

Moved to sub camp
after Cephu's arrival

First built day 2, left
day 3, reoccupied day 5

Key

⬟ = Day 1

⬟ = Day 2

⬟ = Day 3

⬟ = Day 5

β A B
  γ   C
Z   D
  E
X Y
W   F
  V
   H
      G
U T   I
 S
      J
R   K
      O   L
   Q₁ N₁ M
Q P   M₁   N

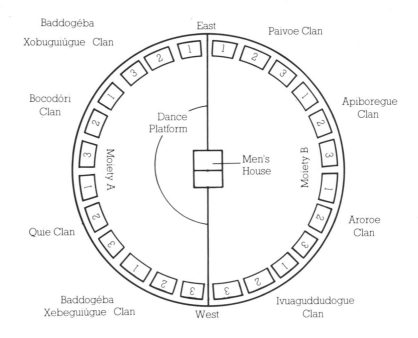

Baddogéba
Xobuguiúgue Clan

East

Paivoe Clan

Bocodóri
Clan

Dance
Platform

Apiboregue
Clan

Moiety A

Men's
House

Moiety B

Quie Clan

Aroroe
Clan

Baddogéba
Xebeguiúgue Clan

West

Ivuaguddudogue
Clan

FIGURE 2.2: Village plans, topological indicators of the social memory of kinship and community: (a) Cheyenne camp circle, Western Plains, United States; (b) Bororo village, south central Brazil; and (c) Mbuti Pygmy huts, Lelo River, Ituri Forest, north-eastern Congo. (a) The Cheyenne were originally woodland hunter-gatherers, later farmers and hunters, and, after the introduction of the horse (*c.* 1830), nomadic hunters. Except for the subordination of women, there is no social stratification; families are large extended families with polygyny (a man takes more than one wife). Like other Plains Indians, the Cheyenne used the circular plan when their various bands assembled as one tribe for ritual and ceremony. It might consist of a thousand *tipis*, three and four deep, a mile in diameter. The diagram records some of the history of the bands. (b) The Bororo are hunter-gathers of the Mato Grosso of Brazil, with settled villages. Details are given in the text. (c) The Mbuti Pygmies are forest-dwelling hunter-gatherers who have lived in the north-eastern Congo for thousands of years, as Egyptian, Greek, and Roman records testify. There is no social stratification between men; families are nuclear, with limited polygyny. The plan of their huts illustrates the use of the dwelling place as a communication system day by day. *Reprinted from*: Douglas Fraser: *Village Planning in the Primitive World* (1968).

Mbuti Pygmies of the Congo, illustrates a system in which the shape, organization, and orientation of the huts make up a simple coding system permitting individual families to exchange unspoken messages about day-to-day relationships.

The Bororo village plan is an explicit map of their kinship structure. The Bororo, who numbered about 4000 in the early 1970s, were originally nomadic hunter-gatherers (the men hunt, the women gather) who later decided to take up agriculture as well and founded permanent villages. The same plan is reproduced even in overnight encampments.

Like most of the Indian societies in the Amazon basin and the Mato Grosso, and except for the subordination of women, the Bororo display little social stratification. They form mostly monogamous extended families, but older men and chiefs may take more than one wife (polygyny). They reckon descent of children, obligations, and rights through the female line, as do about a third of all known band and village societies. (This is matrilineal descent; it does not signify matriarchy.) One result of matrilineal kinship among the Bororo is that the women, while still subordinate to the men, have control over the houses of the village.

The Bororo kinship system is probably the most diverse and complex among the Indians of South America. Claude Lévi-Strauss, the founder of modern French structuralism in the 1950s, studied them in the 1930s. Analyzing the village plan in his *Structural Anthropology* (1958, pp. 124, 137–60), Lévi-Strauss argues that the Bororo kinship system is based on a combination of a two-way or dualist concentric structure with several diametric structures, as well as a triadic or three-way structure.

The concentric structure of the village plan and kinship system is what Lévi-Strauss calls an 'opposition' – it is really a contradiction between levels in a hierarchy – primarily between men and women, and between 'sacred' and 'profane', symbolized by the relationship between center (the dancing place and men's house) and circumference (the forest).

(As is sadly the case in many societies, the subordinate status of Bororo women includes their exclusion from the secrets of Bororo religion.)

One of the several diametric structures is the division of the eight clans along the east-west axis into two intermarrying halves or 'moieties', labelled A and B, making two groups of four clans.

Another diametric structure (not shown and apparently no longer functioning) is the division of the eight clans along the north-south axis into two other groups of four, the 'upper' (upstream) and the 'lower' (downstream).

Concealed within the dual structures, each one of the eight clans is itself divided into three hierarchical classes (1, 2, 3), which Lévi-Strauss calls 'upper', 'middle', and 'lower'. (This hierarchy is a tradition in a system largely egalitarian between males, rather than a class structure like that of our society.) Since upper class marries only upper class, and the same for the other two classes, Bororo society has concealed within it, he says, three 'subsocieties' that in spite of appearances, do not exchange marriage partners and have no kinship ties with one another.

Note that the Bororo village diagram is indeed a diagram of a structure, not a diagram of a system. A system minimally consists of structure, rules, content, and a relationship to one or more environments. To understand the Bororo system in any detail, we would have to know the kinship rules governing the exchanges between the categories defined by the kinship structure, the actual relations between people 'on the ground' (which would include exceptions), and the system's social, economic, and ecological context. Rules may be strategic or tactical.

To explain clearly the idea of method . . . we must be allowed to cast a hasty glance at the logical hierarchy by means of which, as if by regularly constituted authorities, the world of action is governed.

CARL VON CLAUSEWITZ: *On War* (1832)

2.3 Rules and rules

Like language, kinship is a revolution rather than an invention, and one that no doubt occurred in many different times and places in the past. In every human society there is a rule about kinship that has no parallel in nature, a rule so universally accepted that it is not even mentioned in the Ten Commandments: the prohibition of incest.

Incest is at one and the same time regarded with general horror around the world, and much more commonly practiced in our own society, notably by fathers and other male relatives on children, than we suspect. Traditional penalties for incest in traditional societies include banishment and death.

Because it is a spoken rule hemmed about by social sanctions, and not just a habit or a tendency, and certainly not an 'instinct' or a genetic program (which would require no rules or penalties), the prohibition of incest is quite distinct from the 'incest avoidance' (usually resulting from dominance hierarchies such as that between mother and son) found among primates, and even there father-daughter and brother-sister mating is quite common (Harris, 1971, p. 288).

The incest rule does not always concern incest as we now conceive it; in some societies kin that we would consider distantly related come under its ban; and in other systems what we call incest is permitted or required. To maintain and consolidate the power of the Egyptian royal family, for example, the Pharaoh commonly married his sister. Brother-sister marriage was also the preferred form among the ruling families of other despotisms, notably the royal families of the Hawaiians, the Inca of Peru, and the Azande of Africa.

Even these are exceptions to just one category of incest, while prohibitions against sexual relations with other nuclear relatives were observed. The association with royalty and power is no accident: one explanation for these practices is that the power of kings, like gods, depends on their being venerated exceptions to everyone else's rules.

No doubt the incest prohibition exists for more than a single reason, just as it has more than a single result. But it is not necessary to know all the reasons for a rule to understand its most significant levels and kinds of implications and results.

The prohibition of incest is a special kind of rule, a 'rule of rules', a rule about all other kinship rules, and the basis of their existence. The prohibition of incest operates at a higher level of communication and behavior than that of the hierarchy of rules it contextualizes, orients, and constrains.

Rules are information about information, stored information that is remembered and expressed every time a rule is used. They are informational constraints that goalseeking adaptive systems observe in the creation of structure: organization, complexity, meaning.

Every system of rules depends on rules about rules, including the very idea of rule itself. The following might be called the Rules Rules:

- No rule without exceptions.
- Rules are made to be broken.
- The exception tests the rule.
- A rule to which there are no actual or imaginable exceptions ceases by that fact to be a rule (after Benjamin Lee Whorf).

By recognizing that rules may be broken, we recognize that rule-governed systems are open to innovation.

Society and culture are more complex than any other order of complexity we know of. Social and cultural systems are governed by levels upon levels upon levels of rules — including rules for breaking rules — and involve many special conditions, exemptions, and exceptions.

In everyday arithmetic the special rules for zero, such as the prohibition against dividing by zero, are exceptions to the rules that govern all the other integers. Whole numbers are either odd or even, but zero is neither one nor the other. Whole numbers are either positive or negative, but zero is not – it is the boundary between positive and negative.

And whereas the other digits (literally 'fingers') are simply whole numbers, zero – an idea inconceivable to the ancient Greeks – is a whole number, a digit or digital symbol, and a rule about arranging numbers – a 'metanumber'. The revolutionary idea of a number for nothing – the marker of the empty place – was not invented until quite recently, in Hindu India about two thousand years ago.

Surviving records suggest that zero was first written down about 800 CE. Whether as a number, an empty place, or a rule, zero was unknown in Europe until the Arab civilizations of Africa, the Middle East, and Spain adopted the idea from the Indians in the tenth century CE, from which it eventually appeared in Italian banks (counting houses) in the thirteenth century.

Along with language and labor, themselves intimately bound up with marriage and descent, the prohibition of incest marks the boundary between nature and society.

Rules about rules like the incest rule can be called 'metarules', just as 'communication about communication' can be called 'metacommunication', or the philosophy of mathematics can be called 'metamathematics'. (This use of the prefix 'meta-' is derived by analogy with 'metaphysics' in the sense of 'beyond physics': Greek *physis*, 'nature'.)

Psychological reasons excepted, the prohibition of incest is not so important for what it tells kinfolk not to do, as for what it is they do do. Its 'yes' is more important than its 'no'. A prohibition against certain kinds of marriage and/or sexual relations requires a group to 'marry out' of their immediate social grouping, and thus to enter into social exchanges with another group using similar, or at least compatible, kinship rules. When a man gives his sister to the man who will become his brother-in-law (like our own society, the other societies are patriarchal), he is giving a gift from one family or group to another. That gift will be returned in the form of another brother's sister in the same or another generation.

The prohibition of incest is not genetically necessary in nature, as mammalian groups and domestic animal breeding show, which can be understood to mean that it is not genetically necessary in society either. (As Lévi-Strauss put it in irrefutable form in a lecture in 1960, 'The enigma of the prohibition of incest is that it is an answer for which there is no question'.)

The necessity for the incest rule is human and social, for in the 'primitive' societies it touches on every other aspect of social life – quite unlike its minor role in our society, where kinship is dominated by the economic and political relations of class, caste, race, and sex.

The social prohibition does of course have beneficial genetic effects, but these are a consequence of kinship exchange, not the cause of it. The prohibition increases the diversity of the society's 'gene pool', and thus helps to maintain the biological flexibility of the group's response to nature, to other societies, and to its own changes over time.

The genetic diversity of an individual or a population is guided, translated, and transformed by the social diversity that also results from kinship exchange. Social diversity works to preserve the system's personal, psychological, and economic flexibility, and thus helps to maintain the single most important condition for long-range survival in relation to the environment, which is of course all the more significant if the environment is changing or being changed (by society): what Gregory Bateson called our 'uncommitted potential for future change'.

Unlike our own society many of the other societies never chose to go beyond relationships of co-evolution and co-adaptation with the natural environment, choosing instead what might be called 'social symbiosis' ('symbiosis' from the Greek meaning 'together with life'). Thus their kinship systems were one very important set of rules governing – but not determining – the economic and ecological relations of those types of society that if undisturbed by catastrophe, can last forever.

It may be objected here that the other societies did not develop the flexibility to know how to survive modern capitalism, but then as yet we don't know how to survive it either.

Co-evolution did not of course exclude war, ritual murder, slavery, or cannibalism – we are not talking about the 'noble savage' of sixteenth- to eighteenth-century romanticism. As Marvin Harris argues most convincingly in *Cannibals and Kings* (1977), individual human beings and entire societies can be brought up to love war, killing, brutality, or human flesh as easily as they can be brought up to hate and detest them, such is the vast power of society and culture over the actual expression in real life of our genetic potential as organisms.

The worst thing is not giving presents.

KUNG BUSHMAN of the Kalahari Desert

2.4 Marriage and descent

A kinship system minimally consists of structure, strategic and tactical rules, content, and a relationship to one or more environments, notably nature, other groups, other societies, history, the future.

X	A	B	C	D	(man's section)
marriage: m	C	D	A	B	(woman's section)
descent: c	D	C	B	A	(children's section)

FIGURE 2.3: Kinship: the Kariera system of western Australia (four sections). In the four kinship systems illustrated in Figures 2.3 to 2.6, the broken lines marked m indicate the exchanges and connections resulting from the rules governing marriage; the solid lines marked c indicate the results of those governing the descent of children. The table below each figure gives the marriage rules in another form: X stands for the father's section; m for that of the women he marries; and c for that of their children. The diagrams used here are modified from André Warusfel's *Les Mathématiques modernes* (1969, pp. 166–9). Warusfel derives them from André Weil's application of group theory to kinship in the Appendix to Part One of Lévi-Strauss's *Elementary Structures of Kinship* (1949, 1967, pp. 157–168, 221–9). These diagrams are sychronic models (relations considered independently of the passage of time).

Figure 2.3 displays at a glance in simplified form the kinship structure governing relationships among the Kariera of Australia, studied in detail in 1910. In 1865 about 650 Kariera lived near the coast on the western edge of the central Australian desert, about 1300 km north of what is now the city of Perth.

The Kariera are hunter-fisher-gatherers who for some hundreds of years used stone-age technology and a precise and subtle adaptation to the local environment to maintain themselves, their pleasure in life, and thus their relationship to nature. Except for the subordination of women, which is far from total, they are, like other hunter-gatherers, among the most egalitarian of all known societies.

The Kariera reckon descent of personal property, names, obligations, and rights in the male line (patrilineal descent). As men do in many of the other aboriginal societies of Australia – before the catastrophic effects of the arrival of Europeans in 1788 there were some 500 distinct kinship groups and a total of about 300,000 people – most Kariera men take more than one wife. Polygyny in these societies is usually restricted to two or three wives, but the maximum recorded amongst the Murgnin of Arnhem Land in the north is as high as 20 or 25, with many men having 10 or 12 wives; and the maximum recorded among the Tiwi close by the Murngin is 29.

In Figure 2.3, the Kariera system, as in those following, the broken lines marked m indicate the exchanges and connections resulting from the rules governing marriage; the solid lines marked c indicate the results of those governing the descent of children.

Kariera society is divided into two intermarrying halves or moieties:

AB and DC, which are themselves divided in two by means of distinctions between generations, giving four exogamous sections (sections that 'marry out').

Following the arrows in the diagram in Figure 2.3, one sees that a Kariera man of section A in one moiety must marry a woman from section C in the other one; and that their children will become members of section D.

In the next generation, a male child from section D will marry a woman from section B. Their children will become members of section A. A male child from section A will marry a woman from section C, and so on *ad infinitum*.

The table next to the diagram in Figure 2.3, as in the figures following, gives the Kariera rules of marriage and descent in another form: X stands for the father's section: m for that of the women he marries; and c for that of their children.

'Marrying out' is called 'exogamy'. As Marvin Harris points out in *Culture, Man, and Nature* (1971, pp. 301–2), among band-organized people like the Australians, the general function of exogamy is to widen the network of kinship relations to permit efficient utilization of the habitat's carrying capacity. Band organization is capable of expansion and contraction in conformity with changes in local ecological conditions; it also draws on the reproductive potential of the people of a whole region, rather than simply on that of a local band.

Bands do not 'own' their territory: they are in fact rather open communities whose prime characteristic is not their territoriality, but their ability to expand, break into small groups, mix, and reassemble as conditions require (p. 300). People 'marry out' of the nuclear family, the extended family, and the local band because these three types of exogamy maintain maximum flexibility and adaptivity in relation to the natural environment.

Mapping is a fundamental act in any process of abstraction or pattern recognition . . . Mapping is not necessarily a means of visual representation. It is a way of structuring information.
LIONEL MARCH and PHILIP STEADMAN: *The Geometry of Environment* (1971)

2.5 Mapping

The topological diagrams of kinship in Figures 2.3 to 2.6 are maps of the basic kinship structure of each society. A map is a translation from code to code – a translation of selected features of a 'territory' into

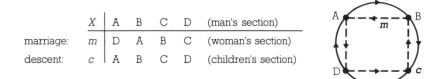

X	A	B	C	D	E	F	(man's section)
marriage: m	D	E	F	A	B	C	(woman's section)
descent: c	F	D	E	B	C	A	(children's section)

FIGURE 2.4: Kinship: the Ambrym-Pentecost system in the New Hebrides of the South Pacific, almost halfway between Fiji and Australia and south-east of Guadalcanal, another notably complex system (six sections). The Ambrym are gardeners (rather than farmers), and dependent on root crops such as yams, rather than grains. Ambrym men exchange sisters or other female relatives on marrying; the society consists of nuclear families with limited polygyny. Social status is a function of wealth, judged by possession of personal property and generosity in giving it away, without hereditary class distinctions, other than the relation between men and women.

X	A	B	C	D	(man's section)
marriage: m	D	A	B	C	(woman's section)
descent: c	A	B	C	D	(children's section)

FIGURE 2.5: Kinship: the Tarau system of India-Burma (four sections). In spite of its apparent similarity, this system is unlike the others illustrated. Intermarriage is not reciprocal between moieties but takes place in only one direction, the sister given by A to D being eventually replaced by a sister given by B to A.

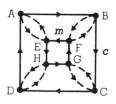

X	A B C D E F G H	(man's section)
marriage: m	E F G H A B C D	(woman's section)
descent: c	H E F G B C D A	(children's section)

FIGURE 2.6: Kinship: the system of the northern Arunta in the central Australian desert, near Alice Springs (eight subsections). The Arunta are hunter-gatherers similar to the Kariera who live about 1600 km to the west. The eight subsections are formed out of a four-section system by introducing an extra distinction between generations. (The northern Arunta system is believed to be a development of the Kariera system.) In the four-section system groups exchange women in adjacent generations; here they exchange women in alternating generations. In the four-section system sisters are given in one generation and their daughters are taken back. In the eight-subsection system sisters are given in one generation and their granddaughters are taken back.

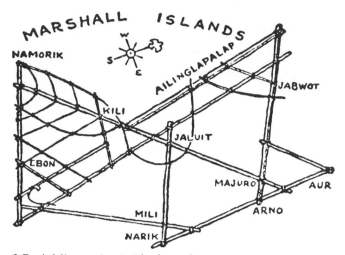

FIGURE 2.7: A Micronesian 'stick chart' for open ocean navigation. The intersections mark the positions of the islands; the sticks map the wave and current patterns to be followed in tracing a given course.

another medium or another code of representation, or the translation of one kind or level of mapping into another kind (Chapter 4).

Mapping at one or several levels – which is taken to include reconnaissance – is one of the most important activities of systems dependent on information. These include (in order of increasing diversity and complexity) cybernetic machines (including robots with feedback), computers, organisms, persons, corporations, armies, and societies.

Mapping varies from the simplest of mechanical simplicities in the mapping of temperature by a household thermostat, to the relative simplicity of the mapping of patterns of numbers in a computer, to the more complex mapping of the immediate environment (what Jakob von Uexküll called the organism's *Umwelt* or milieu) by a microbe or a cell, to the high complexity of the many maps of many territories at many levels characteristic of human beings.

Mapping is necessary for the replication of the four-unit code of DNA in cell division, for its transcription into the slightly different code of RNA, and for the translation of that message into the 20-unit code of the amino acids to form the linear molecular chain that precedes the formation of a fully structured protein. The two-dimensional linear molecule becomes the final product of the original genetic instructions by mapping itself onto itself: it folds in on itself in three dimensions according to the topology of its chemical bonds and 'active centers', vastly increasing its capacity to store information in the process. Wherever one may find it, the most complicated molecule in the cosmos is probably a protein, and in simple creatures like bacteria protein molecules may function as primitive nervous systems.

Figure 2.7 is a blue-water chart from Micronesia, the scattered groups of islands lying north of New Guinea and east of the Philippines. Called a 'stick chart' it is made of interwoven strips of a local wood studded with cowrie shells. The shells mark the positions of the various islands; the sticks map the wave patterns to follow in tracing a given course from place to place.

As the World War Two navigator Guy Murchie explains in *Song of the Sky: An Exploration of the Ocean of Air* (1954, pp. 22–7), we owe our original understanding of South Sea Island navigation to research by Captain Winkler of the nineteenth-century German navy, amongst others, and in more detail more recently, to the New Zealander Harold Gatty, who navigated Wiley Post in their record-breaking flight around the world in the Lockheed craft the *Winnie Mae* in 1931.

Murchie says:

> To the islander the wave was like a tool, for it was studied and measured to a degree not to be exceeded anywhere until the latter days of oceanography. In fact, as we use radio and radar today so did the South Sea navigator a thousand years ago use the ocean wave. He did not merely steer by the angle of the wave, but he observed the whole pattern it made around an island . . .

Moreover:

> He recognized the differences between the ripple, the wave, and the swell – how the tiny ripples change with each puff of breeze as it laces the greeny slope of the wave, how the wave keeps on rolling despite a momentary lull or sideways gust until the wind as a whole shifts to another quarter, and how the great swell may persist in one direction all day or night against wind and even waves which have swung round the compass to oppose it, sometimes outrunning the wind altogether to give warning of the unseen typhoon like a dog before his master.

This 'wonderful stability of the swell', Murchie continues,

> gave the navigator a system of sea marks around an island almost as reliable as the complex radio pattern around a modern airport, including two narrow fixed beams of eddies equipped with direction finders, and a special pointed swell aiming precisely at the safe lagoon channel.

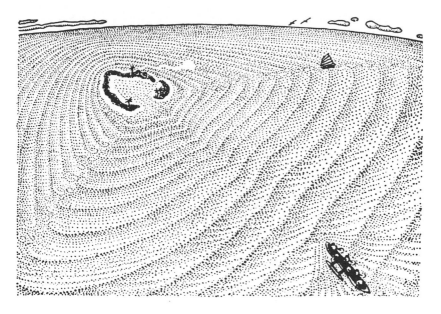

FIGURE 2.8: Wave patterns: A simplified illustration of the topography of the waves used in inter-island navigation by the South Sea Islanders, as depicted in Guy Murchie's *Song of the Sky* (1954).

This telltale swell pattern (Figure 2.8) went far beyond the sight of land,

> for the nature of the swell was to bend itself invariably around each piece of shore, shaping its contour to the smallest reef, sending a counterswell in to the land against the wind from the leeward side, its shape transmitting itself backward revealingly, betrayingly, suggestively in all directions – ever fainter but ever farther – detectable under ideal conditions perhaps twenty miles at sea.

The South Sea people who advanced this particular study to its greatest perfection, Murchie notes, were the Marshall Islanders. He goes on to spell out the rest of the extraordinary details of their wave-reading art. (They also named and knew the varying positions of 150 stars, and they used land birds, set free from the boat like the dove released by Noah from the Ark, as flying signposts pointing the way to the nearest land.) Murchie adds that only from an aircraft can we today appreciate even a part of the patterns of information the islanders saw inscribed in motion on the great south sea.

Micronesia includes the US Trust territories of Guam, the Gilberts, the Carolines, the Marianas, and the Marshalls: some 2,100 islands with about 100,000 inhabitants. The island-to-island counteroffensive against Japan in 1943 began in the Gilberts; the Marianas became the air base for the B-29 Superfortresses that bombed Hiroshima and Nagasaki on August 6 and 9, 1945. After the war Bikini and Eniwetok Atolls in the Marshalls were the site of nuclear tests (1946–58). The first H-bomb was exploded over Eniwetok in 1952.

> In absorbing his food, the 'primitive' partakes in the sacredness of the world. Living as a human being is in itself a religious act.
> MIRCEA ELIADE: *Australian Religions: An Introduction* (1973)

2.6 Orientation

The original Australian societies are some thousands of years old. The Arunta and others share with the Bushmen of the Kalahari Desert in Africa the distinction of living in one of the world's harshest environments, with a simple stone age technology, a rich store of ceremony, myth, and ritual and plenty of leisure time.

The Australian societies also exclude women from religious mysteries and tribal knowledge, most practice some infanticide, and some, including the Arunta, match male initiation through circumcision with female initiation through clitorectomy (female castration). Boys go through initiation as a band of brothers; girls go through alone.

Most of their 260 or so languages are more complex in their grammar than Latin or English; their kinship systems are the great classics of anthropology, raising disputes between anthropologists that continue today.

On 'primitive' societies in general:

Item: There are no societies or peoples with primitive languages, primitive thought processes, or primitive economies.

Item: Although still subject to natural selection mediated by cultural and technological evolution, the human brain has not evolved for many thousands of years. No human society and no human race is any less capable of brainwork than any other.

Item: The idea of civilization, coupled with the idea of empire and progress, is quite a recent invention: in the eighteenth century Dr Johnson considered the word too barbarous for inclusion in his dictionary, choosing 'civility' instead.

Item: There has never been any 'normal' or 'natural' or 'necessary' course of 'progressive' social evolution, supposedly leading from hunting to herding to farming, or from Savagery to Barbarism to Civilization.

Item: Life in 'primitive' societies is far from being 'nasty, brutish, and short'. Marshall Sahlins has argued persuasively in *Stone Age Economics* (1972) that even stone age societies never involved the desperate, unending struggle to survive depicted in modern ideology, but were in fact relatively affluent societies in which most people were better off most of the time and had greater control over their own lives than most people in most countries today.

Item: No 'primitive' society depends on a mere 'subsistence economy'. Band and village societies produce their subsistence with relative ease, direct their surplus production to support social and cultural activities, including entertainment, and can if they wish produce a greater surplus than they actually choose to do. (They generally underuse the productive capacity of their technology, population, and natural environment, in some cases by over 50 per cent.)

Item: Imaginary views of other societies are part of imaginary views of our own.

We may now return to the question of ideology, drawing once more on Mircea Eliade's *Australian Religions* (1973, pp. 44–83). In the beginning, says one Arunta myth, communication with heaven was possible and even easy – by climbing a tree, a vine, a ladder. But when death came into the world, says another myth, communication with heaven was cut off.

According to the traditions of another Arunta group, one of the supernatural beings called Numbakulla (meaning 'always existing' or 'out of nothing') arose and went to the north, making mountains, rivers, animals, and plants on the way. At this time, before people existed, he also created the 'spirit children' (believed by the Australians to be the origin of pregnancy), certain of the mythical ancestors, the *churinga* (visible manifestations of a person's spirit in the form of flat, oval pieces of wood or bone, carved with symbolic designs, some of which are whirled about on a string to make the whirring noise of the 'bull-roarers'), and taught the first ancestors the ceremonies of the totems (names of animals, birds, insects, even clouds and rain, that are used to identify the kinship groups said to be descended from the totem).

Numbakulla then planted a pole in a sacred ground, anointed it with blood and began to climb it, telling the first ancestor to follow him. But the man slid down. Numbakulla 'went on alone, drew the pole up after him, and was never seen again'.

(Compare Lucien Goldmann's *Le Dieu caché* (1955), translated into English in 1964, on the *deus absconditus* (Isaiah 45: 15) or 'hidden God' of the seventeenth century Jansenists in France, of whom the most prominent was Pascal.)

Eliade comments (p. 52) that the sacred pole can be considered to be an *axis mundi* (world axis, cosmic axis) uniting heaven and earth:

> Elsewhere, and particularly in the Oriental cultures . . . the *axis
> mundi* (conceived as a pillar, a tree, a mountain, etc.) actually
> constitutes a 'center of the world'. This implies, among other things,
> that it is a consecrated place from which all orientation takes
> place.

'Orientation' is of course originally a religious word meaning 'turning
to the East', i.e. turning towards the Holy Land, the center of
Christendom, from the direction of Western Europe. Others turn to
Mecca.

This 'center', says Eliade, 'imparts structure to the surrounding
amorphous space'. Both the myths associated with the sacred pole and
the ceremonial use of a representation of it in initiation rites suggest
its double function of a means of communication with heaven and a
means of orientation on earth.

The *axis mundi* is in other words the mediator of other significant
relationships (Chapter 4).

It is through the *rite de passage* of initiation into adulthood that
the (male) initiate is first introduced to the tribal traditions, sacred
knowledge, and 'the origins'. This knowledge is total knowledge of the
group's environments, mythical, ritual, and geographic: the initiate
begins to learn the mythical mapping, in time and space, of the territory
of the band (which is not 'owned', but held in collective trust for future
generations).

In learning about the Dream Time the initiate also learns what must
be done in order to maintain the living, productive world on which
the group depends. He is introduced to the topology of the innumerable
sites in the territory where the supernatural beings once performed a
ritual or some other significant act. Thus, says Eliade, the sacred history
of the world makes everywhere meaningful; it is always possible to be
'oriented' in a world in which every prominent physical feature is
associated with a mythical event (pp. 54–6).

For the Australians the natural environment is thus transformed into
system of secret signs in the individual and social memory, a network
of memory traces eternally inscribed on nature in the Dream Time.
The symbolic geography is also the means to memorize the topology
of every significant feature – many invisible to Europeans – of the real
environment, which is a desert not rich in obvious distinctions, so that
no one gets lost and everyone knows where to find food and especially
water.

Of another Australian group, the Murinbata, W. E. H. Stanner
writes: 'The Murinbata considered the countryside filled with plain
evidence that the [mythical] dramas had occurred. The places of climax
were known and named, and each one contained proof – a shape, or
form, or pattern of a great event' (p. 56).

T. G. H. Strethlow says of the native Australian:

> The whole countryside is his living, age-old family tree. The story
> of his own totemic ancestor is to the native the account of his
> own doings at the beginning of time. . . . He himself has played a
> part in that first glorious adventure, a part smaller or greater
> according to the original rank of the ancestor of whom he is the
> present reincarnated form (quoted in Eliade, 1973, pp. 57–8).

The landscape is the written part of the social memory.

The disclosure of the sacred history of the tribe takes many years; it is a lifelong task and goal, the way to wisdom. In the process the male individual learns through ritual how to relive the Dreaming. Eventually he will be totally immersed in the tribe's mythical history and topography, in the mapping of the cosmos, that explains 'why things are the way they are'. He will 'know the origin and understand the meaning of everything from rocks, plants, and animals to customs, symbols, and rules' (p. 64).

This implies, says Eliade, not simply that the world has a past that explains the present, but also that the people of the tribe have taken on the responsibility of maintaining the world in being.

This they do in life by accepting the stewardship of nature in terms not very different from the interpretation of Genesis by the philosopher Philo Judaeus, also called Philo of Alexandria (*c.* 30 BCE – 30 CE), in his *On the Creation*:

> So the Creator made man last of all things, as a sort of driver and
> pilot [*kybernetes*], to drive and steer [*kybernai*] the things on
> earth, and charged him with the care of animals and plants, like a
> governor or steward subordinate to the chief and great King.

In religion the Australians remember and renew their responsibility to nature by continuously re-enacting the great events of the beginning of time, 'and by endlessly infusing the land with the powers of "Dreaming" ':

> When man ceases to communicate with the Dream Time and to re-
> enact his mythical history, the world will disintegrate and life will
> wither, to disappear eventually from the surface of the earth (p.
> 66).

And throughout it all the totemic ancestor is the mediator at the boundary between nature and society. As Lévi-Strauss put it in 1962 in *La Pensée sauvage* (p. 128), it is the system of named totemic distinctions between social groups, not the particular content of totemism, that is significant: 'the totemic representations amount to a code which makes it possible to pass from one system to another regardless of whether it is formulated in natural terms or cultural terms' (quoted in Eliade, 1973, p. 199).

But all or most of this is denied to women, and the men blame the women for being denied. Said one Arunta man to T. G. H. Strethlow (quoted in Eliade, 1973, p. 122n):

> Our women are of no use at our ceremonial gatherings. They are altogether ignorant of the sacred *tjurungas* [*churingas*]. They have fallen from the estate of our great feminine ancestors. Why, we do not know.

Outside the question of male supremacy, to which I shall return, the key relationship between the ideology of the Australians and their reality is reciprocity, reciprocity between brothers, between families, between generations, between society and nature. This relationship is not in the least mythical, whatever one might call its rationale, because it is the product of co-evolution and co-adaptation − co-operation − with the natural environment.

Thus we do not ask whether this ideology is true, but how well it works in reality over time − because if it works, there is no reason to change it. Nothing is more scientific than survival.

The Arunta ideology may well be imaginary, but its imaginary content is symbolic of real relations.

Elman R. Service, in *Profiles in Ethnology* (1971, p. 4), has this to say about the Arunta:

> Everything about this culture, from the technical means of acquiring food from a niggardly nature to the codes of social living − the kinship system, rules of etiquette, beliefs and sentiments, religious ceremonies − seems to have been a functional apparatus which was nearly the ultimate in efficiency for survival under the conditions imposed by the nature of the Australian habitat and the limitations of the native tool kit.

We understand here also the now obvious reason why the Northern Arunta developed an eight-subsection system, whether they did so intentionally or consciously or not. Beside all else, a kinship system organizes co-operation between individuals and groups; it orients and identifies the individual in space and time; it is the adaptable reference point or mediator one counts on to weather every crisis.

By doubling from four sections to eight, the Arunta doubled the kinship information and thus the connections borne by every participant in the system, and in that way strengthened and reaffirmed the network of the ties that bind kinfolk together. In the midst of one of the most difficult environments in the world, this adaptation too was made – consciously or not – in the interests of long-range survival.

These links are both material and ideological: Ties that bind are the most important of the many relationships that define and mediate one's identity-for-others and one's original orientation in life. The ideology adapts to change also, as Eliade explains (1973, p. 67):

> There exists no culture without history. . . . But the 'history' is not acknowledged as such by the primitives; although they are aware of the modifications that have taken place in a more or less remote past, they telescope these modifications into a primordial and ahistorical time and interpret them as the acts of mythical Beings.

(This can be true of our own society, also.)

> In sum, by the simple fact that the innovation has been accepted and absorbed into the traditional pattern, it is considered to have taken place in the Dream Time . . .

The disorder or 'noise' of the innovation is converted into order and information just as a successful mutation in nature becomes inscribed in a novel message in the genetic code, just as a social, political, or economic revolution re-orders the significance of past events and projects a new future. This is the principle of 'order from disorder', or 'information' from 'noise' (as distinct from 'order from order' and 'order from oscillation').

Under civilization poverty is born of superabundance itself.

CHARLES FOURIER (1772–1837)

2.7 Power

The original Australians map their environment in space and time by means of a mythology constrained in its organization and values, if not in its content, by an intimacy with the real. We do the same for the geography of our environment: our personal and collective maps are topological translations of what is significant for us in the territory they represent. That our geography is also scientific is the result of the fact that our society seeks to manipulate the real.

The same cannot so easily be said for the way we map our history and social structure. Many people, many historians included, believe that the course of history and the structure of society are defined by the ideas people have about them. But it is surely obvious that society and history as we know them are in fact defined by power.

Power is not simply an idea. In our society power is the barrel of a gun, it is command, control, communication, and intelligence, it is information, organization, money, and production, it is the capacity to coerce and ultimately the capacity to kill.

The basic distinction between state and non-state societies lies in their organization and use of power. Consider briefly the background of the 'original states' – the 'pristine states', as Marvin Harris calls them in *Cannibals and Kings* (1977) – the first states to emerge in history.

The word 'state' (literally 'standing') first became usual in Europe in the sixteenth century, partly as a result of its use by Machiavelli (1469–1527) in his handbook of statecraft, *The Prince*, referring to the warring and commercially competitive city-states of Renaissance Italy.

The Greeks called their city-states 'polities', from the word for 'city' ('politics' means literally 'relating to citizens'); the Romans called their state and later empire the *res publica*, the 'common or public matter'; the seventeenth-century English revolutionists called their republic the 'commonwealth'; others preferred the 'body politic'.

The classic example of the modern nation-state is the centralized dictatorship established in England by Henry VIII (reigned 1509–47), who took ruthless advantage of the fact that the feudal magnates had exhausted themselves and the country in the civil strife of the Wars of the Roses (1455–85). Henry amalgamated Church and State by breaking with Rome over his divorce; he paid for his extravagances, including his wars, largely by stealing the vast wealth of the English monasteries; he crushed rebellion with a terrible ferocity; and he maintained his power over the nobility by legalized assassination on Tower Hill.

The Tudor state – with a population of a mere two-and-a-half million – was raised to new heights of commercial and military power under his brilliant daughter Elizabeth I, who reigned from 1558 to 1603. The Stuart dictatorship that followed was broken by Parliament with the execution of Charles I in 1649 and the forced abdication of James II in 1688, when the decision to change dynasties and draw up a new contract between King and Parliament brought William and Mary to the throne from Holland.

An 'original' or 'pristine' state is a state not influenced in its origin and early development by the existence of other states. A state so influenced is a 'secondary state', a category which includes the 'primitive states' of the African kingdoms and empires.

The army of the Zulu Empire, for one example, a conquest state created between 1816 and 1828 and destroyed by British rifles, organization, and Gatling guns in 1879, was modeled on that of the Portuguese colony of Mozambique. It was a trained and disciplined conscript army capable of co-ordinated flanking movements – a strategic innovation that made the Zulus invincible against other Africans and serious trouble for the Boers and British seeking control of Zululand.

There is general agreement that original states appeared in Mesopotamia about 3300 BCE, in Peru about the time of Christ, and in Mesoamerica (Central America including Mexico) about 100 CE.

Most scholars also agree that original states arose in Egypt about 3100 BCE, in the Indus Valley of India just before 2000 BCE, and in the Yellow River basin of northern China shortly after 2000 BCE. States may also have arisen in Crete and the Aegean about 2000 BCE and perhaps in the Lake Region of East Africa about 200 CE (Harris, 1977, p. 103).

Harris argues that the original states were products of the intensification of production in agriculture that resulted from population increase. For reasons unknown the population of the Middle East increased fortyfold between 8000 and 4000 BCE. The population of Egypt probably doubled between 4000 and 3000 BCE. In the highland zones of early state formation in Mexico, the population probably tripled, and similar estimates are made for Peru, China, and the Indus Valley (pp. 117–18).

By way of comparison and contrast with the characteristics of state societies that I'll list in a moment, we find among non-state societies the following range of social and economic relations, as defined by George P. Murdock in his indispensable *Ethnographic Atlas* (1967, pp. 57–9):

(1) An absence of significant class distinctions between freemen in systems where variations in individual repute and status are achieved by skill, valor, piety, or wisdom;

(2) Wealth distinctions based on status earned through the generous distribution of personal property, but not based on the existence of distinct classes or a hereditary class structure ('big man' systems);

(3) Dual stratification into a hereditary class of nobles and a lower class of commoners or 'freemen', where noble status is at least as decisive in the division of power as is control over scarce resources;

(4) More complex stratification into several classes;

(5) A caste system with several levels and one or more despised occupations (e.g. smiths, leatherworkers, latrine orderlies), or a dual and ethnic caste system in which a dominant caste treats the other caste as an alien, inferior, and conquered people, as if they were another species, or a more complex caste system based on occupation and including a despised 'untouchable' lower caste, as in India;

(6) More rarely, various forms of slavery, usually non-hereditary and including adoption into the family, existing alongside other distinctions.

To this typology of social structure we must add (7) the subjugation of women, the original working class, providing mental, manual, biological, and emotional labor under the rule of men.

In some non-state societies, the office of 'local headman' or band or village chief is entirely absent; in others it is a non-hereditary position achieved through informal consensus or through some form of election; in others it is achieved through influence, such as wealth or status, or through seniority or age; and in others it is hereditary.

Male supremacy relies on male leadership. In non-state societies where the status of women was much higher than elsewhere, as it was among the Iroquois, women could nominate men for leadership, and act indirectly, through men, as influential advisers in councils, but they could not become council members themselves.

In the anthropological sense the term 'state' is equivalent to 'civilization'. The major and typical features of the early civilized states are the following: a monopoly of rights over land, labor, commerce, and other resources exercised by a head of state and usually a ruling class; a highly stratified class structure; the existence of more or less magnificent cities dependent on the labor of peasants, artisans, and other workers, very often including slaves; a well-developed trade with other regions through merchants; a state religion and priesthood; a professional army (including mercenaries if necessary); the protection of the head of state by a 'palace guard' loyal to him, rarely her, and to him alone; a royal court of ministers, advisers, and hangers-on; an organized government staffed by professional bureaucrats (often priests at first); codes and courts of law; a police force to compel obedience (which may be part of the army); secret police and spies; a system of forced tribute or taxation and often forced labor as well; often slavery in one form or another (but not as ruthless and barbaric as modern slavery); a system of writing, or if not that, at least a record-keeping system (such as the knotted strings or 'quipu' of the Inca of Peru); a mathematical notation; a geometry adequate for measuring land and constructing monuments, tombs, and temples; a calendar based on (often very precise) observations of the heavens; a road system and official messengers for communication; usually an official language; an advanced technology, often including irrigation, which is further advanced by innovations (the institutionalization of what A. N. Whitehead called the invention of invention); expansive ambitions, territorial aims, client states, and the imperial strategy of divide and rule; and finally in some such empires the equivalent of 'bread and circuses' – like the 'soma' in Aldous Huxley's *Brave New World* (1932) or the Victory Gin and the hate sessions in George Orwell's *Nineteen Eighty-Four* (1949) – to keep the lower classes from rising up against their masters.

The original states were empires committed to conquest, to the intensification of work and production, to the exaction of tribute and taxes, and to territorial expansion.

In contrast, band and village societies fight wars but not wars of conquest; they systematically underuse their productive capacity; they engage in reciprocity not in exaction; and they do not seek political expansion. As a rule their entire mode of existence is dominated by the need *not* to expand, so that they can preserve the existing favorable relationships between people and resources, between society and nature, and thus maintain their accustomed standard of living (Harris, 1977, p. 55; Sahlins, 1972).

Generosity is almost always one of the supreme virtues in band and village societies, and all the more so when the subject of the highest generosity is the chief. In fact, it was without much doubt a wrinkle in the development of originally egalitarian generosity that gave rise to chiefs – and thus to the origins of social and economic inequality between men and groups of men.

In Melanesia, in non-chief societies, we find the age-old institution of the 'Big Man', and it is the amount of labor required to make the holder a truly generous 'big man' that opens the egalitarian system to exploitation. Polygyny is extremely common. Thus in some societies it will take the labor of several wives working for one man to produce enough useful and exchangeable goods to give away for 'big man' status. In the more complex of such systems, it takes the labor of whole families, even extended families, to meet the big man's obligations to the communal system. Where there is an entire class of big men – an embryonic ruling class – they can elect a chief, who will co-ordinate the entire production of a village, or several villages, or more. For the people doing the actual work, that might already be too much.

A multitude of kin-dominated class relations may ensue. In the best case, the chief or chiefly class express their generosity as mediators in a system of *redistribution*. They receive obligatory gifts of food and other products from the family-centered production units of the village economy and then return the gift by sharing the general wealth throughout the community, equalizing differences, and making sure that no one lives in hunger, poverty, or humiliation. Of course the system is open to overt exploitation if the chiefly dues become a tax. But not until a ruling class gains control of the means of production, as well as distribution, and economics begins to dominate kinship, can we expect to find the beginnings of a class-based, imperial, conquest state.

CHAPTER 3

Language and communication

One hundred tellings are not so good as one seeing.

Traditional Chinese Proverb

3.1 Symbolization in nature

Communication between organisms in nature is particularly important in the competitive sexual selection that decides which combination of genes is passed on to the next generation.

Many species of carnivorous 'dance flies' of the Empididae family engage in biologically programmed mating rituals. In some species this is no more than a simple approach by the male, followed by copulation. In others, the male first captures an insect that is the species' usual prey and presents it to the female before mating (Wilson, 1972).

In other dance fly species, the male fastens threads or globules of silk to the offering, which as Wilson says, is clearly a step in what Thomas Huxley in 1914 called the 'ritualization' of a biological process. Offering a dead insect provides both matter-energy and information. Adding decoration to the offering not only increases the information it bears, but also introduces a new form of information by means of a rudimentary process of symbolization.

In another species of dance fly the male encloses the dead prey in a sheet of silk. In another yet, the size of the dead insect is smaller but the covering is as large as before, so that the offering is a partly empty balloon of silk. The male of another species simply offers the female an empty silk balloon. Here what is in other species a food offering has evolved into a symbol of food. It is no longer matter-energy for the female, but entirely information, and there is no direct connection between the information and what it symbolizes or stands for.

The male black-tipped hangingfly, a species of 'daddy long legs', also offers food to the female before mating (Thornhill, 1980). Females choose to mate with males bearing prey they consider suitable, feeding on it while mating, and thus select against males offering prey that is distasteful or too small.

Males capture prey and judge its size, discarding about a third as inadequate. They obtain prey by catching it themselves, or by stealing it from mating couples or from other males. The more males (or the fewer prey) there are the more competition there is between them in stealing prey – competition so conventionalized, however, that it looks like play.

A male with prey emits a chemical message (a pheromone) to attract a female. Males are not sensitive to the odor signal, but they can tell by sight when another male is sending it. About half the time a male stealing from males will simply try to grab the prey from the other one who is expecting a female.

At other times, the male attempting to steal prey will mimic a distinctive female pattern of behavior. About two-thirds of the signalling males are fooled by the false information sent by the mimic, and try to mate with it, sometimes for several minutes. When this happens, the mimic is usually successful in wresting the prey away from the other male, and sets off to attract and mate with a real female – provided another mimic does not show up instead.

Mimicry, the capacity to pretend, often associated with camouflage, is found in many animal and insect species. It is in some cases entirely genetic, as when a butterfly of one species looks like another, and in others voluntary, as when an opossum 'plays possum'. The distinctive human capacity here is not pretending, however, it is rather the capacity of pretending to pretend:

> 'Two Jews met in a railway carriage at a station in Galicia. "Where are you going?" asked one. "To Cracow", was the answer. "What a liar you are!" broke out the other. "If you say you're going to Cracow, you want me to believe you're going to Lemberg. But I know that in fact you're going to Cracow. So why are you lying to me?" '

The example is taken from Chapter 3 of Freud's *Jokes and their Relation to the Unconscious* (1905). Freud remarks that truth must depend on both speaker and listener, and that this kind of 'absurd' or 'sceptical' joke attacks the very notion of truth itself. The joke is paradoxical, he says: The man going to Cracow 'is lying when he tells the truth and is telling the truth by means of a lie'.

Most people reason dramatically, not quantitatively.

OLIVER WENDELL HOLMES, JR. (1841–1935)

3.2 Subjectivity and objectivity

Language is one type of communication and one type of semiotic – or 'sign-using' – activity. Although the analysis of language provides us with insights into the vast domain of communication, it is generally agreed that language cannot usefully serve as a general model of communication or semiotics.

To 'communicate' means:

> To make common to many; to share, impart, divide, exchange; to unite, join together, consult; to partake of, to participate in; to talk, converse, transmit; to use or enjoy in common; to have intercourse with; and, in Christianity, to partake of the body and blood of Christ in holy communion.

Communication is goalseeking activity. This is to say that every message has a referent (what it is about) and an address (where or to whom it is sent) – the addressee of general messages being 'to whom it may concern'. There are no intransitive systems of communication, and no intransitive messages.

(Let it be emphasized that the communication of information does not necessarily imply the use of (human) language, nor consciously perceived sending or receiving, nor consciously intended communication, nor consciously noted understanding.)

As already noted, every act, every pause, every movement in living and social systems is also a message; silence is communication; short of death it is impossible for an organism or a person *not* to communicate. As Ray Birdwhistell, author of *Kinesics and Context* (1972), a study of the infinite complexities of body communication, put it in the 1960s: 'In a communications system, nothing never happens.'

The foregoing remains true for human beings whether the referents or addressees of a particular discourse – or of any other type of communication – are symbolic, imaginary, or real. By 'talking to ourselves' we create an imaginary self to correspond with; when we dream we exchange symbolic messages (usually desires) with real or imaginary 'others' or the Other (an authority figure, for example); and even when we are apparently alone, we are in fact in communication with many other people – parents, bosses, lovers, ideals, judges – some of whom are elsewhere, some of whom never existed, and some of whom are dead. The mediation of communication by particular others, by the Other or by Others, and by otherness in general is essential to our humanity (Chapter 4).

No single historical influence on our beliefs about language, communication, and knowledge has been more striking than that of Jewish, Christian, and Greek theology (literally, 'the science of gods'). Theology was after all the 'queen of the sciences' in the West, the dominant discourse in science and society, for fifteen centuries and more, and it is still taken seriously by many people. We should not therefore be surprised to discover that certain patterns of thought, originally derived from the religious perspective, still survive in modern science – the commonest being the belief in 'objectivity', originally the province of God and God alone.

Objectivity in communication is as imaginary as perpetual motion in mechanics. Because communication involves goals, it necessarily involves values. But the critique of objectivity does not imply that all knowledge and communication are subjective (relative to the individual). Taking refuge from 'objectivity' in 'subjective relativism' (or 'cultural relativism') is simply a switch between imaginary opposites. Subjectivity is real and unique, but it is not strictly subjective, and it has no opposite. Many of our apparently unique personal opinions are in fact derived from social conditioning by dominant codes of values transmitted by others, beginning in the cradle and including the media of family, school, and popular entertainment, rather than from personal and informed decisions that we actually made for ourselves.

True subjectivity, like true self-interest, is a 'self-and-other' relationship. The so-called 'autonomous subject' is another figment of the imaginary. Much of what we believe to be 'subjective' or 'objective' is really collective, mediated by communication with our environments and other people, conscious or not.

The imaginary opposition between subjectivity and objectivity may be usefully compared with the similar confusion between quality and quantity. In logic as in life quality precedes and constrains quantity. Any decision about quantities is based on prior decisions about the (general) framing and the (detailed) punctuation of the subject matter by decisions about qualities, whether these are consciously made or not (Figure 3.1).

Quality and quantity are not opposites: the second depends on the first. Faced with measuring an object, we have to decide what quality to measure – matter, energy, or information, weight, size, or exchange value, and so on – before making any decisions about quantities. Objectivity is itself a quality, if an imaginary one, as is the assumption that objectivity speaks – or ought to speak – in numbers.

In ordinary arguments objectivity and subjectivity quickly reveal their sources. Objectivity says in effect, '*This* is the only reliable context for judgments', i.e. the objects, the events, the facts. Subjectivity replies, '*This* is the only reliable context', i.e. the subject, the opinions about the objects, the events, the facts. (Each fails to recognize what the Gestalt psychologists demonstrated in the early years of this century:

FIGURE 3.1: Quality and quantity, a dependent hierarchy. Quality and quantity are not of the same level of communication or reality. (In the terminology originally used by Bertrand Russell to distinguish between a class and its members, they are not of the same logical type: Chapter 5) The relationship between quality and quantity is not symmetrical: the one cannot legitimately take the place of the other. (Quantity is a kind of quality, but quality is not a kind of quantity.) Quality and quantity do not exist in an 'either/or' relationship of opposition, but in a 'both-and' relationship between levels. Only in the imaginary do the two appear to be opposites.

that we perceive relationships in reality, rather than objects, events, or facts.) Within the constraints of this imaginary opposition there is no appeal from the dogmatism of the two positions. As often as not each is a kind of 'security operation' (Harry Stack Sullivan's definition of schizophrenia) – meaning by that a supposedly unassailable perspective on the real.

> Generally speaking, we can observe that the scientists in any particular institutional setting move as a flock, reserving their controversies and particular originalities for matters that do not call in question the fundamental system of biases they share.
> GUNNAR MYRDAL: *Objectivity in Social Research* (1967)

3.3 Science and theology

Theology traditionally implied that there was some perfect (and there-fore 'objective') language available to the initiated, the Word of God or some equally metaphysical equivalent. For Pythagoras (sixth century BCE), as also for Galileo (1564–1642), the secret language spoke in numbers and geometry. Combined in mathematical forms and musical harmony, the Pythagorean numbers were the constituents of the 'deep structure' of reality, the components of the 'really real', which was itself conceived to be a living, breathing, and divine creature displaying order, beauty, and structural perfection (three meanings of the Greek term *kosmos*).

For the equally ancient Jewish tradition, the perfect language was the voice of God inscribed on nature and in human hearts. The Jewish perspective is an example of the semiotic (or communicational) perspec-

tives independently evolved in many different societies. Unlike the
largely mechanistic viewpoint that has been dominant in our own
society only since the eighteenth century, the semiotic perspective of
the Bible, like that of the non-state societies and ancient and early
modern China, is based on an organicist conception of the cosmos:

> The heavens declare the glory of God; and the firmament sheweth
> his handywork. Day unto day uttereth speech, and night unto
> night sheweth knowledge. There is no speech nor language; their
> voice cannot be heard. Their line is gone out through all the earth,
> and their words to the end of the world.
>
> Psalm 19. 24

> I will put my law in their inward parts, and in their hearts will I
> write it.
>
> Jeremiah 31. 33

> He searcheth out the deep, and the heart,
> And he hath understanding of their cunning devices:
> For the Most High knoweth all knowledge,
> And he looketh into the signs of the world,
> Declaring the things that are past, and the things that shall be,
> And revealing the traces of hidden things.
>
> Ecclesiasticus 42. 18–19

For the Christian Hellenists of the first century CE and later, the
cosmos, and therefore the truth, was the Logos, the articulation of the
Word of God:

> In the beginning was the Word, and the Word was with God, and
> the Word was God. The same was in the beginning with God.
> All things were made by him; and without him was not anything
> made that hath been made. In him was life; and the life was the
> light of men.
>
> Gospel According to St John 1. 1–4

> Ye are our epistle, written in our hearts, known and read of all
> men; being made manifest that ye are an epistle of Christ,
> ministered by use, written not with ink, but with the Spirit of the
> living God; not in tables of stone, but in tables that are hearts of
> flesh.
>
> Second Epistle of Paul the Apostle to the Corinthians 3. 2–3

For the Neoplatonists, from the *Enneads* of Plotinus (205–270 CE)
to Wordsworth's *Intimations of Immortality* (1807) and after, the

universe was an emanation from the Deity by the medium of mind (*nous*), while in the world the individual soul sought an eternal return to the celestial home that gave it birth.

For many of the medieval and renaissance scientists and philosophers called 'natural magicians', the cosmos was a text informed by the written script of the Author of Nature, or an ordered whole governed by the 'natural laws' of the Supreme Lawgiver. For others the cosmos was an idea in the mind of God, a reflection or mirror-image of the deity, or a poem written by the first *poeta* (literally 'maker').

In his encyclopedia *The French academie*, published in English in 1601 (quoted in Heninger, 1977, p. 11), Pierre de la Primaudaye says that by God's great book of nature, he means

> the admirable frame of this Univers, or whole world. Wherein the infinite varieties and sorts of creatures, like so many visible words, doe proclaime and publish unto man the eternitie, infinitie omnipotency, wisedome, justice, bountie, and other essentiall attributes of his dread and soveraigne creatour.

The physician Sir Thomas Browne (1605–82) provides an example of the transformation of the linguistic metaphor of the divinely written text we have to learn to read (whether by science or revelation) into the communicational or semiotic metaphors of the doctrine of signatures. In his *Religio Medici* (1643), Browne speaks of Physiognomy, the art of judging character by reading facial expressions and interpreting body communication. Experienced beggars know it well:

> . . . Master Mendicants . . . instantly discover a mercifull aspect, and will single out a face wherein they spy the signatures and markes of mercy: for there are mystically in our faces certaine characters which carry in them the motto of our Souls, wherein he that cannot read A.B.C. may read our natures. I hold moreover that there is a . . . Physiognomy, not onely of men, but of Plants and Vegetables; and in every one of them, some outward figures which hang as signes and bushes of their inward formes. [A hanging bush used to signify a tavern.] The finger of God hath left an inscription upon all his workes, not graphicall or composed of Letters, but of their severall formes, constitutions, parts, and operations, which aptly joyned together doe make one word that doth expresse their natures. By these Letters God cals the Starres by their names, and by this Alphabet *Adam* assigned to every creature a name peculiar to its Nature.

The *lingua Adamica* turned out to be the information of DNA.

The semiotic (and usually teleological) viewpoint of the traditional organicist perspective is well stated by John Norris (1657–1711), Rector in the Church of England and sometime Fellow of All Souls College, Oxford.

In *The Unconscious before Freud* (1960, pp. 86–98) Lancelot Law Whyte discusses Norris and the English Platonist (or Idealist) school, whose adherents were among the first to remark on the existence of unconscious communication. The Platonist School included Sir Thomas Browne, Henry More, Ralph Cudworth, and A. A. Cooper, third Earl of Shaftesbury.

Whyte cites Norris's anticipation of Leibniz (1646–1716) on the concept (and the reality) of the unconscious and the non-conscious orders of communication:

- 'We may have ideas of which we are not conscious.'
- 'There are infinitely more ideas impressed on our minds than we can possibly attend to or perceive.'
- 'There may be an impression of ideas without any actual perception of them.'

In the second edition of his *Collection of Miscellanies* (1692, pp. 320–22), Norris defines the nature of God in the following way:

As for the Nature of God, it involves, as in *Notion* and Conception, so likewise in *Truth* and reality . . . absolute and infinite Perfection; and consequently, includes a *Beneficient* and *Communicative* disposition, this being a *Perfection*.

Nor does the Superlative eminency of the Divine nature only argue him to be *Communicative*, but to be the most *Communicative* and Selfdiffusive of all Beings.

. . . *Light*, which of all Bodies is nearest ally'd to Spirit, is also most diffusive and self-communicative. God therefore, who is at the very top [of the great chain of being] . . . and who lastly is such *pure Light* as in which *there is no darkness at all*, must needs be infinitely self-imparting and Communicative; and consequently, wants nothing to qualifie him to be the true End and Center of Man.

In this context, 'end' (Greek *telos*) signifies a teleological or 'final' cause (as distinct from 'goalseeking' or 'teleonomy'). According to the contemporary definition given by John Harris in 1704, in his *Universal English Dictionary of Arts and Sciences*, final or teleological causes are

such great, wise and good Ends as God Almighty, the Author of Nature, had in Creating and Proportioning, in Adapting and

Disposing, in Preserving and Continuing all the several Parts of the Universe.

In his classic work, *The Great Chain of Being* (1936, pp. 87–8), A. O. Lovejoy quotes part of the passage from Norris as an early modern illustration of the ancient idea that there is a gradual or graduated 'scale of being' joining the lowest Matter, without Form (the element Earth), to pure Form without Matter (God, the highest Form). Every element and creature finds its place in the hierarchy in proportion to its degree of 'perfection', and the hierarchy is immobile and eternal.

The scale of being, an accurate metaphor of the structure of the societies that reproduced it for over two thousand years, can be seen in two ways: as a continuum of differences, expressing the idea that nature is 'full', with no gaps between its parts (what Lovejoy calls 'the principle of plenitude'), or as a scale of discontinuous distinctions, like Jacob's Ladder. In either case the hierarchy emanates from God (communication descending) and ultimately returns to God (communication ascending).

It is worth noting that Brute Matter, situated at the bottom of the great chain of being, stands for the inorganic order of complexity in nature; and that God, the pure Form at the top, stands for an idea produced by culture. The hierarchy of the great chain of being is in fact a classic example of metaphysical idealism (Chapter 1): it is a dependent hierarchy turned upside down.

These deeply rooted systems of theological and spiritual metaphors had three main implications for language and communication, one mainly negative and two mainly positive.

The negative implication was that a 'perfect' and 'objective' 'language', all-present and all-powerful, did indeed exist – and that it was not the language spoken by ordinary human beings. Unlike the perfect system designed by the Divinity, ordinary language was believed to be a distortion of reality, a misrepresentation of the really real. In the minds of influential latter-day saints, including logical positivists and empiricists, language came to be regarded as an obstacle in the path of science.

The plain truth, however, is that every language is as adequate and appropriate to its socioecological context as it needs to be. No language is ultimately 'better' in this than any other. Language has ecological validity. For human beings, then, language is neither a copy of reality, nor a misrepresentation of reality; it is part of human reality.

The second and positive implication, evident in organicist and animist ideologies all over the world, is that what we may not understand through language and linguistics, we can expect to understand through communication and the study of systems of signs (semiotics).

The third is that communication, including the signs written out on nature, is not confined to human beings.

The organicist view remained in conflict with the mechanical view throughout the nineteenth century, but its association with religion and the 'argument from design' (said to prove the existence of God and the fixity of species) doomed it to defeat in science until its transformation by the rise of modern systems theory in the 1930s, originally developed and named by Ludwig von Bertalanffy, himself a biologist.

In Parker Gillmore's *Days and Nights by the Desert*, published by Kegan Paul, Trench & Co in 1888, we hear the oldest version of organicism, where the inanimate becomes animate (literally, 'full of soul'):

> At length the great voice spoke. So short and concise was its utterance that all stood aghast. Its emphasis, its power, and its sublimity were such that every one, regardless of colour and creed, were overpowered with dismay. I have frequently stood by the side of the heaviest siege guns and mortars while they were fired, but they were a bagatelle to the voice of the raging elements. The detonation lasted little more than an instant; but, short as was that time, what terrible force and power of destruction it heralded! For a moment after, all was a death-like stillness, then the echoes took up the thunder roar, and every tree, rock, and hill reverberated with its ironical applause, ha! ha! ha!

Gillmore, a.k.a. 'Ubique' ('Everywhere'), was a retired military man who mounted expeditions, consisting of himself and up to 200 Africans from different tribes, into the southern African interior. The desert in the book is the Kalahari, one of the least hospitable of environments. Gillmore's expeditions were organized like an army on the move, complete with a requisite diversity of kinds of warriors for defense against predators and hostile Africans. He travelled with foot scouts, mounted scouts, trackers, baggage train, herds of animals for food, ox-drawn Cape carts, a diversity of weaponry (from spears to the most accurate of available rifles and the heaviest shotguns made), and camp followers. The expedition marched with advance guard, flank guards, and rear guard, and fortified its camps every night.

Any mental activity is easy if it need not take reality into account.
MARCEL PROUST (1871–1922)

3.4 A discourse has a subject

Language is not the problem in our understanding of reality, the problem is discourse (*Rede*). What may or may not be adequate to a given social, historical, and ecological reality is the dominant discourse of a given society, a discourse created out of the infinite potential of the language(s) in use. Time is a factor also. What separates our talk from that of the middle ages is not so much how we talk – linguistic changes in grammar, spelling, basic vocabulary, and so on, real as these may be – but radical changes in what we talk about and how we do it.

The 'Sapir-Whorf hypothesis' tells us that languages impose structure and content on our relationship to reality, and therefore on our understanding of reality. This is not only true, it is precisely what makes languages part of human reality. But the real issue has repeatedly been confused by the reduction of language and discourse the one to the other. This appears to be the reason why the hypothesis has been difficult to demonstrate in concrete terms.

It is the task of language to bring its structure to the representation of reality, for where there is no structure, there is no sense. Structure structures content. And any language can be restructured, in both form and content, so as to deal with changing ecological, economic, and historical realities.

Language is in any case only one of many ways of communicating with and about reality. In our present context, then, the role of language as language is not particularly significant. In contrast, the diverse discourses created in different times and places are always significant. For, unlike a language, a discourse has a subject and a subject-matter. A discourse is some people talking to some other people about some relationship or other.

In any society, we can expect to find dominant and subordinate discourses, the most universal of these relations being the dominance of the male discourse over the female discourse.

The dominant values of a society are ultimately derived from its most important social and economic relations, as well as from their history. The dominant forms of communication in a given society (verbal and non-verbal) define and constrain its ways of seeing and believing, and knowing and judging. They form the ground of what the dominant members of the society accept as true and false, legal and illegal, legitimate and illegitimate. For whereas language or communication in general are neither of them statements at all, dominant discourses and dominant communications are always statements – ultimately about survival value, both long-range and short-range.

The relationship between language in general (French *langage*), a

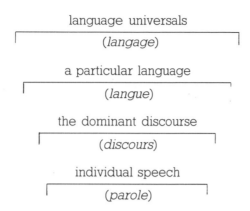

language universals
(langage)

a particular language
(langue)

the dominant discourse
(discours)

individual speech
(parole)

FIGURE 3.2: Language in general, language in particular, the dominant verbal discourse, and individual speech: a dependent hierarchy. This schema represents the general case: the dominant language and dominant discourse can be remade – are remade – by individuals and groups in history. The schema does not include the non-verbal communication that accompanies every verbal communication and fills every silence between words.

particular tongue (*langue*), a dominant verbal discourse (*discours*), and individual speech (*parole*) can be represented by a dependent hierarchy (Figure 3.2).

> The organism is a message . . . We are not stuff that abides, but patterns that perpetuate themselves.
> NORBERT WIENER: *The Human Use of Human Beings: Cybernetics and Society* (1950)

3.5 The lasting word

One of the aspects of social life that most sharply distinguishes western and westernized societies from most non-state societies is the way of seeing and knowing expressed in their respective attitudes to communication, itself a statement about relations between persons and between society and nature. Whereas we have come to value language over all other forms of communication, many band and village societies value communication over language. Let me cite two examples.

In one of the societies of New Caledonia studied by the missionary Maurice Leenhardt at the turn of the century (published in French in 1947 as *Do Kamo*), the word *no*, translated by Christianized islanders as *parole* (word, speech, faculty of speech), stands for 'word', 'thought', 'act', 'gift', and the 'object' or 'content' of an exchange or communication. An artefact may be called a word because it is a manifestation or expression of a person. Children who closely resemble one of their parents, or who act or think like one of them are said to 'enwrap' the word of the parent. Memories and myths are 'the lasting word' – or as one might now translate it, with more accuracy but less elegance, 'the lasting message'.

In Lifu in the Loyalty islands, the term *ewekë* embraces a similar domain, as well as defining the male supremacist values of Lifu society (male supremacy varies in degree and danger to life and limb, but is sadly characteristic of all contemporary societies):

> The 'word' has its source in one's 'insides', since the heart is called 'the basket of words'. All that pertains to man is *ewekë*: his eloquence, the object he fashions, what he creates, what he owns personally, his work, his statements, his goods, his garden, his wife, his psychic well-being, his sex . . . [The phrase) *ekon ewekë* is a euphemism for the male sex and the male genitals (p. 221).

(The power of the 'word', besides being equated with the father, is often equated with the phallus (symbol of the penis): in Sanskrit, the scholarly language of the Hindus, which is of the same general family as Greek and English, the noun *lakshana* means 'mark', 'token', 'sign', 'symptom', 'definition', 'name', 'sign or organ of virility'.)

For both New Caledonian societies, says Leenhardt, the 'word' (speech, communication, message) is a manifestation of the human and the social. It is the essence of gifts, pledges, and ritual obligations, the essence of social activity, the rhythm of life, and continuity down the generations.

In the words of a New Caledonian ritual saying used to punctuate the non-verbal communication of ceremonial feasting and gift-giving, cited by Marcel Mauss in his classic essay, *The Gift* (1925):

> Our feasts are the movements of the needle which serves to bind together the parts of [our] reed roofs, making of them one single roof, one single word. The same things return, the same thread runs on through.

The image serves to remind us that the word 'context' comes from the Latin verb *contexere*: to 'braid', 'weave', 'connect', or 'unite'; and the word 'text', from *textus*: 'web', 'tissue', 'texture', or 'structure'.

In the *Guardian* for February 6, 1983 the indigenous people of New Caledonia are reported to be engaged in a war of independence against the French and the European 'caldoches' (locally born whites, like the 'pied noirs' ('black feet') of Algeria).

Victor Turner, citing the work of the French anthropologist G.

Calame-Griaule and his own investigations among the Dogon, who live in the neighborhood of Mali and Upper Volta, has pointed out in his *Dramas, Fields, and Metaphors* (1974, pp. 156–65) that the Dogon term *sɔ:*, translated by *parole*, covers language in general, particular tongues, speech, including the faculty and act of speech, as well as word and message. He likens it to the doctrine of signatures and correspondences held by the mystic Jakob Boehme (1575–1624), besides the tradition of the Gnostic Gospels. Calame-Griaule says of the Dogon, who distinguish between twenty-two major parts of the body and personality and forty-eight types of speech:

> Man seeks his reflection in all the mirrors of an anthropomorphic universe where each blade of grass. each little fly is the carrier of a word (*parole*). The Dogon call it *adhunc sɔ:*, word of the world (*parole du monde*), the symbol.

Much like the orienting function of the Australian Dream Time, the Dogon 'word' acts as a reference point mediating between natural kingdoms, animal, vegetable, and mineral, which are themselves regarded as parts of a gigantic human organism (Turner, 1974, p. 160). As in the European tradition of alchemy, cosmology, and magic, the microcosm of the person has correspondences with the universe, the macrocosm. Correspondence with nature means co-operation with nature. The Dogon 'word' runs throughout the Dogon universe as a cosmic, creative, and fertilizing principle (recalling the doctrine of the Logos), but human language is just one of its many manifestations (cf. Figure 3.3).

In Marcel Griaule's 1948 interpretation of the Dogon 'word' (quoted by Turner on p. 157), it represents the 'spirit of order, organization and universal reorganization which contains everything, even disorder'. It is thus the logical and cosmological equivalent of 'variety' and 'diversity' in cybernetic and systems theory, where coded variety means information, organization, or (relative) order, and uncoded variety means noise, unperceived organization, or (relative) disorder (Chapter 5).

> Truly admirable is [the] varied structure [of the Paraguayan languages], of which no rational person can suppose these stupid savages to have been the architects and inventors. Led by this consideration, I have often affirmed that the variety and artful construction of languages should be reckoned amongst the other arguments to prove the existence of an eternal and omniscient God.
> MARTIN DOBRIZHOFFER: *Account of the Abipones* (1822). Quoted by Marvin Harris in *The Rise of Anthropological Theory* (1968)

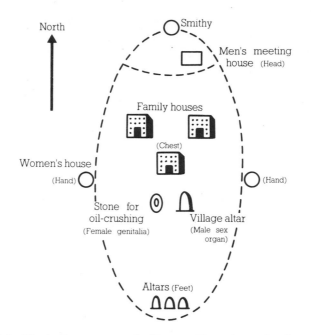

North

Smithy

Men's meeting
house (Head)

Family houses

(Chest)

Women's house
(Hand)

(Hand)

Stone for
oil-crushing
(Female genitalia)

Village altar
(Male sex
organ)

Altars (Feet)

FIGURE 3.3: The basic structure of a Dogon village, icon of male supremacy. The actual village may contain many hundreds of houses. *Reprinted from*: Douglas Fraser; *Village Planning in the Primitive World* (1968).

3.6 Language and communication

There is no communication system between animals, insects, or computers that remotely approaches the complexity, flexibility, and capacities of language. And while there are simple and complex forms of communication in nature, there are no 'primitive' or 'advanced' forms of language in society, as Freud, for one, believed.

For Freud (1856–1939) the 'content' of a dream is a translation (*Übertragung*) of the verbal 'dream thoughts' of the dreamer into a nonverbal means of representation or expression. It is a translation of a communication (*Mitteilung*) encoded in language into a communication encoded in visual imagery. The task of the dreamer seeking to understand the messages of the dream is therefore to recover the original and unconscious thoughts by endeavoring to translate the dream images back into words.

In the *New Introductory Lectures* of 1933, Freud drew an analogy between the grammar (or syntax) of visual imagery – of which more later – and that of a supposedly 'primitive' language:

[In dreams] all the linguistic instruments by which we express the subtler relations of thought – the conjunctions and prepositions, the changes in declension and conjugation [noun and verb endings] – are dropped, because there is no means of representing them. Just as in a primitive language without any grammar, only the raw material of thought is expressed, and abstract terms are taken back to the concrete ones that are at their basis.

In contrast a decade earlier the American linguist Edward Sapir (1884–1939) had written in *Language* in 1921:

There is no more striking general fact about language than its universality. . . . We know of no people that is not possessed of a fully developed language. The . . . South African Bushman speaks in the forms of a rich symbolic system that is in essence perfectly comparable to the speech of the cultivated Frenchman.

Modern languages are among the simplest of all languages; those of many band and village societies are among the most complex.

Nor do the thought processes of so-called 'primitives' provide examples of 'savage' or 'pre-logical' thought, as the French anthropologist Lucien Lévy-Bruhl maintained, and as was long accepted in social science, philosophy, and psychology, besides the movies and popular imagination. The thought processes of so-called 'primitives' were likened to pathological communication in schizophrenia and to the incompletely developed thought processes of children.

We are more intimately involved in language and communication, including verbal and non-verbal thinking, than in any other activity besides love and work – both of which are modes of communication and usually require language anyway. We know more about language and communication than we do about any other activity, but most of this knowledge is unconscious.

Communication is the general category within which language appears as a special case, inextricably bound up with mind (distinct from brain) and society (distinct from nature). Among systems of communication between organisms, language is the most complex, largely because of its powerful syntax (its capacity to select and combine sound and sense, words and images, meanings and ideas).

All language is communication but very little communication is language. With the five senses and body communication in general, our non-linguistic modes of communication in society include music, the visual arts, and the visual aspects of film and television; kinship, status, money, sex, and power; accent, height, shape, and beauty; much mathematics, dreams, and fantasy; images, ideals, emotions, and desires; the production and exchange of commodities; and class, caste, race, and sex.

We share with other species non-linguistic modes of communication that include song, tone, key, rhythm, timing, intonation, loudness, silence, color, odor, taste, touch, shape, gesture, facial expression, body posture, movement, displays, dance, drumming, clicks, whistles, sighs, cries, screams, mimicry, and play.

In western society, notably since the scientific revolution of the seventeenth century, language has been commonly identified with 'thought' or 'reason', and assumed to be more important or more significant than other modes of communication, such as the environment of non-verbal communication that makes thought and language possible. In his useful textbook, *Culture, Man, and Nature* (1971, p. 107), Marvin Harris, for one example, defines meaning in language (semantics) in the broadest of terms:

> Human languages are unique among communication systems in possessing *semantic universality* (Greenberg 1968). A communication system that has semantic universality can convey information about all aspects, domains, properties, places, or events in the past, present, or future, whether actual or possible, real or imaginary.

(Semantics refers to the various forms of meaning.)

It is certainly true that the infinite possibilities of meaning in language are quite staggering, but we have only to think of going to the movies to realize that we cannot claim universality of meaning for language. There are other and non-verbal communication systems in society, such as touch, that manifest a richness of sense and meaning that language can neither reach nor reproduce. Visual communication is perhaps the richest of all. But we writers and teachers tend to overvalue words, which are of course our stock-in-trade. Thus we often fail to recognize the importance and influence of other modes of communication, especially those associated with popular culture.

Moving pictures rival language as the most powerful system of communication between people ever created. Nine-tenths of a movie cannot be translated into words, and if you want to experience its meaning, you cannot have it explained or read to you, you have to go and see it yourself. A movie is neither a conversation, nor a script, nor a poem, nor a book, and although the verbal syntax of language (the rules governing the structure of verbal messages) is more complex than the visual syntax of film, the semantics of language are far less rich in levels and types of meaning than the semantics of film.

Moreover, whereas verbal syntax is the same for all speakers of a given dialect, the visual syntax of film is far less constrained. It is open to level upon level of innovation, as Abel Gance showed in *Napoleon* in 1927, undoubtedly the greatest tribute to visual communication ever made.

Language and communication do however share a number of basic features, of which the most important are:

- symbolization (representation by means of information);
- syntax (the organization or patterning of information; in iconic and digital systems, such as film and language, syntax governs the selection and combination of information to make messages according to rules);
- semantics (the translation of information into one or more levels or kinds of meaning).

Human language is distinguished from animal communication by the following basic features:

- double articulation: the use of combinations of meaningless sounds (phonemes) to create combinations of words with meaning;
- a complex syntax involving levels of rules, from the level of sound to that of signification;
- the capacity to refer to past, present, and future;
- the use of 'not', whose signification depends on its placing in the sentence (syntactic negation, as distinct from 'no' or refusal, which can be communicated without using words);
- the capacity to talk about symbolic and imaginary relationships, as well as real ones;
- the capacity to talk about itself (metalanguage);
- the capacity for wit and jokes, which play on levels of language.

The visual communication of film excludes negation but includes the following, taken up again in Chapter 8:

- a syntax distinct from that of language but including levels of communication;
- the capacity to refer to past, present, and future;
- a much richer capacity than language to represent feelings, motives, and meanings and to communicate about symbolic, imaginary, or real relations;
- a more limited capacity than language to communicate about itself, but, like music and painting, a capacity to communicate about examples of itself;
- the capacity to switch between levels of communication.

Human language is distinguished in many ways from the communication of apes taught to use American Sign Language, colored chips, or keyboards to communicate with humans. Recent critiques have shown that much of their 'talk' is in fact imitative behavior cued by the unconscious communications of the experimenters or others present. (This is called the 'Clever Hans effect', named after a famous 'thinking horse' trained to respond to the body communication of its owner.) The critiques, some based on close analysis of unedited videotapes, suggest that the apes are more literate in communication and relationship than their trainers.

What seems always to be lacking in the 'talking apes' is the capacity to select and combine discrete signs independently of accident, unconscious cuing, or imitation. They do not display the capacity to use even the simple syntax of three-word sentences, much less the capacity to use levels of language (Gardner, 1980).

The problem here is not whether apes can be trained to 'talk', for that would make no difference to the validity of the distinctions between human language and animal communication. It is rather the naïveté about the complexity of language and communication between humans displayed by many scientists experimenting with communication between primates (see p. 321).

In battle all appears to be turmoil and confusion. But the flags and banners have prescribed arrangements; the sounds of the cymbals, fixed rules.

LI CH'ÜAN: Comment on Sun Tzu: *The Art of War* (c. 400–320 BCE)

3.7 Signs

A sign is a marker of information. It is a marker that may trigger action or other response, including the transformation of matter-energy, the reorganization of other information, and the production, exchange, or reproduction of other signs.

The simplest kind of sign is a signal. Depending on circumstances, any sign or signifier (a linguistic sign) may act as a signal.

Most signs are highly complex, however. Consider the example of the visual icons called flags:

... Flags represent or identify the existence, presence, origin, authority, possession, loyalty, glory, beliefs, aspirations, or status of a person, an organization, or a political entity. They are

employed to honor and dishonor, warn and encourage, threaten
and promise, exalt and condemn, commemorate and deny; they
remind and incite and defy the child in school, the soldier, the
voter, the enemy, the ally, and the stranger. Other flags of this
kind authenticate claims, dramatize political demands, establish a
common framework within which interest groups are willing to
confront one another and work out mutually agreeable solutions –
or postulate and maintain irreconcilable differences that prevent
such agreements from occurring (Smith, 1975).

In classic battles up to the end of the nineteenth century, 'the colors',
regimental, royal, or national, were much more than a simple sign of
identity, they were the center of tactical communication on the
battlefield. General Sir Charles Napier (1782–1853) describes the
organizing function of the battle standard (Wise, 1977, p. 26):

Great is the value of the standard; it is the telegraph in the centre
of battle, to speak of changes in the day to the wings. Its
importance has therefore been immense in all ages, and in all kinds
of wars. 'Defend the Colours!' 'Form upon the Colours!' is the
first cry and first thought of a soldier when any mischance of battle
has produced disorder: then do cries, shouts, firing, blows and all
combat thicken around the standard; it contains the symbol of the
honour of the band, and the brave press round its banner.

Honor and bravery are of course relative to the values of the victors.
Sir Charles Napier first saw active service in Ireland during the United
Irish Rebellion against English rule (1798–9), led by the Protestant
Theobald Wolfe Tone, amongst others. Shortly before the rebellion,
the Earl of Moira detailed in the Irish house of peers the 'abominable
acts of cruelty and torture, flogging, picketing, [and] half-hanging' used
to extort confessions from Protestant and Catholic suspects, wherever
the king's garrisons and the Orange volunteer militia, Protestant and
anglophile, prevailed. He urged conciliation. The Lord-Chancellor of
Ireland, Fitzgibbon, Earl of Clare (1749–1802), replied that the English
policy was already conciliatory. Furthermore:

He did not justify the proceedings of the Orange-men, but he
asserted that they were not enemies to their country. He did not
approve the tortures, burnings, assassinations, and murderings, of
which the noble lord had spoken: but he was compelled to
observe, that when treason and rebellion make it necessary to call
out the military, it is not always possible to restrain their
resentments (Belsham, 1805, vol. 5, pp. 462–3).

The Irish patriot Henry Grattan (1746–1820) had an answer: 'The Irish Protestant can never be free until the Irish Catholic ceases to be a slave.'

The organizing center of any utterance, of any experience, is not within but outside – in the social milieu surrounding the individual being

V. N. VOLOSHINOV: *Marxism and the Philosophy of Language*
(1929)

3.8 Semiotics

Semiotics, from the Greek noun, *sema*, is the art and science of sign-systems. It was originally a medical term, signifying 'the art of diagnosing symptoms' (the signs of disease). It was first used in its modern sense by John Locke, the British 'empiricist' philosopher, in about 1690.

The vocabulary of semiotics is extensive and ancient. Words for 'sign' in the sense of 'indicator' include the Greek *sema* and *semeion*, the Gothic *taikns* (English 'token'), the Latin *signum* (French *signe*), and the German *Zeichen*. These words are generally derived from verbs for 'to point out, observe, see, know, teach'.

The term *sema* in classical Greek may be translated in a variety of ways, depending on its context:

a sign, mark, token (e.g. the star or blaze on a horse's forehead);
a sign from heaven, omen, portent; a sign to do or begin
something, a watchword, a battle-sign, signal; the sign by which a
grave is known, a mound, cairn, barrow, tomb; a token by which
any one's identity was certified, including both pictorial and written
tokens, and scars or marks on the body; the mark on a lot in
drawing lots; the device or bearing on a shield; the seal impressed
on a letter (cf. signet); a constellation.

Similarly with *semeion*, which, besides many of the above, may be translated as:

a sign or signal to do a thing, made by flags; a battle standard,
flag, ensign; a boundary, limit; a ship's figurehead; a proof in
reasoning.

The German *Zeichen* is more extensive: 'sign, symbol, mark, token;

indication, proof, testimony, evidence; symptom (physiology); brand, stamp, badge; signal, call-sign; omen, portent.'

The English noun 'sign' has had and may have the following meanings:

> a gesture; a show or pretence; a signal; an indicator; a distinctive mark, device; a bookmark; a 'conventional symbol' (as in science and mathematics); a mark of attestation or ownership written or stamped on a document, a seal; a figure, image, statue, effigy, imprint; a device borne on a banner or shield, a cognizance (token of recognition) or badge; (in the plural) insignia; a characteristic device marking a house, inn, or store; an emblem, standard, ensign; a token or indication (visible or otherwise) of some fact, quality, etc.; the trail or trace of wild animals; a portent of the future; a divine message (e.g. the 'signs and tokens' of the God of the Old Testament, such as the rainbow); a miracle, marvel, or wonder; a distinction in the circle of the Zodiac.

And as the Anglican catechism has it, 'A sacrament is an outward and visible sign of an inward and invisible grace.'

What a grammar is to language, a constitution is to liberty.

THOMAS PAINE (1737–1809)

3.9 Joseph Priestley on universal grammar

Joseph Priestley (1733–1804) was with Lavoisier one of the discoverers of oxygen (1774–89). As the *Encyclopedia Britannica* (1974) points out, Priestley's textbooks, teaching, and classroom demonstrations in science were major innovations in education. Besides teaching astronomy and anatomy, he pioneered the teaching of modern history and practical science. His *Rudiments of English Grammar* (1761) radicalized language teaching, and remained in use for some 50 years.

Unlike Galileo, who was persecuted by the Inquisition for his scientific beliefs, Priestley was persecuted for his religious and political beliefs, and not by the Church, but by his own country.

A genuinely devout man, Priestley was ordained a minister in one of the dissenting (nonconformist) churches, the Unitarians (1762), where he was a radical in theology as well. In preparation for his ministry, he tells us, he studied 'Hebrew, Chaldee, Syriac, and a little Arabic', as well as Greek, Latin, and modern languages. As an educator, he sought to prepare students for practical life with the best education possible, giving judicious attention to both theory and practice. Against the classical university curriculum, Priestley emphasized history, science, technology, and the arts.

Since he was not a member of the Church of England, most scientific and educational posts were closed to him. Nevertheless, he became a member of the celebrated Birmingham Lunar Society and the Royal Society of London (elected 1766). Priestley counted among his colleagues the naturalist Erasmus Darwin (grandfather of Charles Darwin and Francis Galton), the pottery manufacturer Josiah Wedgwood, and the Scottish engineer James Watt.

Priestley had been encouraged in his scientific pursuits by Benjamin Franklin (1706–90), who lent him essential books (notably on electricity). Priestley was well known as an outspoken defender of civil and religious liberties, and greatly sympathized with the ideals of the French Revolution. In 1791, Priestley denounced the Tory principles of Edmund Burke's attack on the French, *Reflections on the Revolution in France* (1790).

(Burke's tract inspired Thomas Paine to refute him in *The Rights of Man* (1791), in which Paine went on to propose the elimination of poverty, illiteracy, unemployment, and war. Threatened by arrest, he fled England for France. He was convicted of treason in his absence, declared an outlaw, and the book ordered to be permanently suppressed. One of the most influential books ever written, it sold thousands upon thousands of copies in Europe, Britain, and the United States. Of Burke Paine said: 'It is power, and not principles, that Mr Burke venerates; and under this abominable depravity, he is disqualified to judge between them.')

On July 14, 1791, the second anniversary of the Fall of the Bastille, an organized Tory mob attacked Priestley's home in Birmingham. They destroyed his house, library, and laboratory. He immediately left England, never to return, and settled in the United States, where he was a friend of Thomas Jefferson (1743–1826) and John Adams (1735–1826).

In 1762, Priestley published his course of lectures on *The Theory of Language and Universal Grammar*, from which the following extracts are taken (pp. 10–13, 16, 21–3):

> The kind author of nature hath given to every animal that is capable of any kind of society, a power of communicating his sensations and apprehensions, at least, to every other animal he is connected with: and this power is more or less extensive in proportion as the animal is fitted for a more perfect or imperfect state of society. An animal that hath little connection with, or dependance upon any others, either of his own or a different species, as he hath little to communicate, hath a power of communication proportionately small: but when the connections of any animal are more numerous,

and the dispositions and actions of others are of more consequence
to him, it is requisite that, for his own advantage, he be furnished
with a greater power of affecting them, by communicating his
own ideas, apprehensions, and inclinations to them.

The *instrument* and *medium* of this communication are different,
according to the different situations of animals: in some it being
most convenient to apply to one sense, and in others to another.
E. G. *Fishes*, which, it is supposed, have no organs of hearing,
probably give all the information they can give to one another by
motion, perceived by the sight or feeling: but the *air* . . . affords
to all animals that live in it a most convenient medium of
communication by *sounds*. . . .

. . . From the voices and gestures of brute animals, others . . .
may understand the whole of what they mean to convey: and
even men, who have given sufficient attention to them, may be able
to decypher their meaning to a considerable degree. [Animals have
strong expressions for] joy, sorrow, surprize, with the various
subdivisions of those passions, hope, fear, love, anger, jealousy,
and the like. . . .

Brute animals . . . have very little power of modulating their
voices; which is called *Articulation*. Of this men are capable. . . .

It is observable that dogs and other animals, not having the
power of articulation, make use of various *gestures*, and motions
to express their meaning. With men too gestures and postures of
the body, and particularly motions of the hands, and of the
features of the countenance, are strongly associated with particular
states of mind; and being in a less degree voluntary, are often a
surer indication of a man's real internal feelings than words, which
are more at his command. . . .

Amazing as is the power and advantage of *speech* for the
communication of ideas, it is, in several respects, infinitely inferior
to the art of *Writing* . . . By the one the power of communication
is confined both in point of time and place, and in the other it is
absolutely unconfined with respect to both . . . [Writing] connects,
as it were, the living, the dead, and the unborn: for, by writing
the present age can not only receive information from the greatest
and wisest of mankind before them, but are themselves able to
convey wisdom and instruction to the latest posterity.

. . . [But] letters can only express the simple sounds of words,
without the particular tone and inflection of the voice in which
they are spoken; on which, notwithstanding, very often, the most
important part of the meaning depends: for, in conversation, we
attend as much to the manner in which a thing is said, as to the
words themselves. By the tone of voice we can vary, and modify
our ideas in a manner that no power of letters can ever equal.

CHAPTER 4

System and structure

The map is not the territory.
The name is not the thing.
The word is not the relationship.
The signal is not the sign.
The sign is not the signified.
The figure is not the speech.
The symbol is not the symbolized.
The imaginary is not the real.
The figurative is not the literal.
But many metaphors are meant.

TWENTIETH CENTURY APHORISM

4.1 Map and territory

Ninety years ago the astronomer Samuel P. Langley, third secretary of the Smithsonian Institution and founder of its Astrophysical Observatory, was the first major scientist to recognize that the stone circles of Stonehenge on England's Salisbury Plain were of possible astronomic significance, as Gerald S. Hawkins pointed out in 1966 in his *Stonehenge Decoded*.

Stonehenge was built in several stages between about 1800 and 1400 BCE (estimates differ), during the late New Stone Age and the early Bronze Age in Europe, at a time when Salisbury Plain was a part of a network of trade and communication from the Baltic to the eastern Mediterranean. The stone circle is surrounded by burial grounds – the long barrows of the Windmill Hill People, the round barrows of the Beaker People – as well as other monuments: a 'Woodhenge' was found close by in 1925 through the new science of aerial photography.

Built a thousand years or so after the pyramids, Stonehenge is contemporary with the Harappa civilization in the Indus valley of modern Pakistan, with the lawmaker Hammurabi of Babylon, with Israel's bondage in Egypt, and with the Minoan and Mycenaean civilizations of Crete and Greece. (The latter appear to have influenced the mode of dressing the stones.) Stonehenge went through three major building periods and three variants of the last, called Stonehenge III, when the structure was extensively remodelled (Figure 4.1).

Hawkins showed that Stonehenge is a massive celestial observatory. Sunrise on Midsummer's Day occurs at precisely the point indicated by a line of sight along the central axis of the structure. A whole series

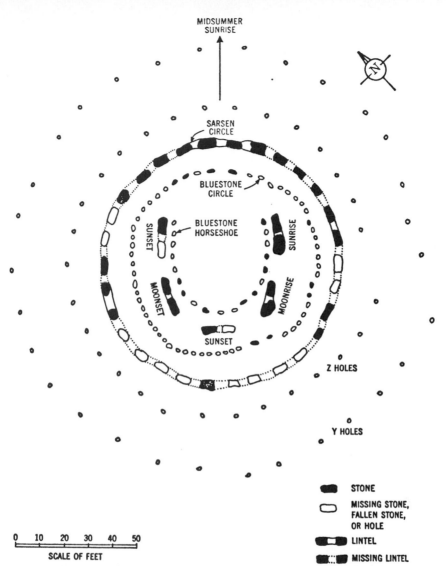

MIDSUMMER
SUNRISE

SARSEN
CIRCLE

BLUESTONE
CIRCLE

BLUESTONE
HORSESHOE

SUNSET

SUNRISE

MOONRISE

MOONSET

SUNSET

Z HOLES

Y HOLES

STONE

MISSING STONE,
FALLEN STONE,
OR HOLE

LINTEL

MISSING LINTEL

0 10 20 30 40 50
SCALE OF FEET

FIGURE 4.1: A plan of Stonehenge III (c. 1600–1400 BCE) according to the
state of archeological knowledge at the time of *Stonehenge Decoded* (1966).
The plan is an example of the map-territory (or code-to-code) relationship.
Every relation selected from the structure of the territory (Stonehenge) is
represented by a corresponding relation in the structure of the map (the plan
or representation). The translation of information from territory to map is a
translation from code to code, and in this instance the translation is also one-
to-one. This plan translates from the real to the symbolic, as an ordinary map
does, as the symbolic codes of mathematics do when they are used to represent
real relations. In other kinds of code-to-code relations we translate not from
reality, but from one symbolism (or code of representation) to another, as
when we translate from language to language, or from the code of the
alphabet to the code of Morse, or from plaintext to cipher in secret codes.
Stonehenge itself maps a territory: it translates a celestial topology into an
earthly one. As explained below code-to-code translations are utterly unlike
the generative grammars of code/message relations. *Reprinted from*: Gerald
S. Hawkins: *Stonehenge Decoded* (1966).

of other alignments indicate the extreme positions of sun and moon in the sky around the year. Stonehenge was thus an annual clock, providing orientation in time, as well as an instrument of orientation in space.

Stargazing must have been an important medium of entertainment in those times: some 600 simpler structures like Stonehenge and contemporary with it have been found in Britain and Brittany. On the north-central plains of North America, not inhabited until much later than Europe, the so-called 'Indian medicine wheels' are other examples of the skyward orienting devices invented by aboriginal peoples – and not by imaginary visitors from outer space – for social, economic, and ideological uses.

During its three hundred years of on-and-off construction – about as long as it took to finish a Gothic cathedral – many people of many thoughts and cultures came to Stonehenge. Different rulers, priests, artisans, and common workers (possibly serfs or slaves) built and built again on the same spot, which was perfectly situated for its purposes. In time

> the great monument grew from a simple circle open toward the midsummer sunrise to a rectangle-within-a-circle to a massive and complex cathedral of stones standing in arched circles and horseshoes. Yet the oldest orientation of all, the axis alignment to the summer solstice, was never lost; rather it was maintained, duplicated, emphasized (Hawkins, 1966, p. 114).

As the structure grew in complexity, its original symmetry, economy, and simplicity were retained: every single stone, for example, is used in one alignment or another.

Hawkins was able to do the number-crunching computations necessary to uncover the secret of Stonehenge with the help of the Harvard-Smithsonian IBM 704, which, he notes in an aside, was 'as obsolete as the hand-crank telephone' even in 1964. Using the results of actual tests, he estimates that about a million and a half person-days went into the physical work of the several stages of building the great stone machine, including transporting stones weighing from 5 to 30 tons by raft and roller from as far as 240 miles away, but not counting the brainwork of the planning, geometry, and engineering.

As for the capacity of people in Europe to construct such an observatory 4000 years before our time, Hawkins reminds us of Alexander Marschak's discovery that the beginnings of writing are many times older than originally thought: Marschak found a whole series of markings on bone recording the phases of the moon and other astronomical events, written down some 20,000 years ago. The evidence suggests that number systems and written symbols for numbers preceded the invention of writing itself, which came about independently in different societies in different times and places (cf. Schmandt-Besserat 1978).

In a more speculative interpretation of Stonehenge that can never be proved, but one would enjoy believing, Hawkins also argued that the outer circle of 56 regularly placed sockets for markers made of wood or stone show Stonehenge to be a giant digital computer as well, capable of calculating periods of eclipse and the major events of the moon (pp. 140–8).

Hawkins suggests one reason and two conjectures for the pattern of the sun-moon alignments of Stonehenge, which was also a temple: the structure made a calendar, useful for planting crops; it helped to create and maintain the power of the priests who operated it, who could use as evidence of their divine and magical power the spectacular risings and settings of the sun and moon as seen by line of sight between certain stones; and – possibly – it served its adepts as a 'intellectual' (read 'computer') game (p. 117).

Stonehenge, says Hawkins, was a marvel (p. 118):

As intricately aligned as an interlocking series of astronomical
observing instruments (which indeed it was), and yet
architecturally perfectly simple, in function subtle and elaborate, in
appearance stark, impressive, awesome, Stonehenge was a thing
of surpassing ingenuity of design, variety of usefulness and grandeur
– in concept and construction an eighth wonder of the world.

Finally, for every significant relation in space and time selected by its engineers, there is a corresponding alignment in Stonehenge. And one alignment above all, the place of sunrise on Midsummer's Day, serves a crucial double purpose: it testifies to the continuing good order of the universe year by year and at the same time casts in stone for those who used it the orientation of the whole – the *axis mundi*, the center of the world.

Although the material of Stonehenge has an 'inward' physical structure (molecules, atoms, and so on), this is effectively irrelevant to the way the structure itself is used. There is no hidden level of structure 'lying behind' the visible structure of Stonehenge that we need to understand in order to use it to observe the heavens, there is no code of rules governing the generation of messages – as there is in the case of kinship structure.

In Stonehenge system and structure are one, like an engine; form follows function, like a wheel; and deep structure and surface structure exist at the same level, like a clock. As a mechanical device Stonehenge involves only code-to-code translations (the mapping of territories, the use of one code to represent another); it does not involve the use of a code to create messages. Stonehenge simply translates from the code of a celestial territory to that of an earthly map.

Until recently in transformational linguistics Noam Chomsky (b. 1928) used the expressions 'deep structure' and 'surface structure' to refer to the structure of sentences or messages. The two sentences following are almost identical on the surface, but their deep structures – the abstract or conceptual plan of the sentence and the speaker's intended meaning – are quite different:

John is easy to please
John is eager to please

In the next two sentences, however, surface structures are distinct but deep structures are the same:

The boy chased the angry dog
The angry dog was chased by the boy

The conversion of the deep structure of the message into its surface structure is governed by the transformational rules in the generative grammar.

In the work of Marx, Freud, and the French structural anthropologist Claude Lévi-Strauss, however, the concept of deep structure refers not to the deep structure of a message but to the deep structure of a system – economic, psychic, social, ideological, mythological, and so on.

In this sense, the one I shall use here, the deep structure corresponds to the codes of constraints that permit goaldirected adaptive subsystems to create a vast diversity of messages, or great complexities of organization, by the repeated application to the available variety of a finite number of rules. Deep structure in this sense encompasses the entire grammar of the economic, psychic, social, ideological, or other system under consideration. It refers to the rule-bound codes of information, beginning with DNA, that make production, reproduction, consumption, and exchange possible in biological and social systems.

The primary colours are only five in number but their combinations are so infinite that one cannot visualize them all.

In battle there are only the ordinary (*cheng*) and the extraordinary (*ch'i*, unique, rare, wonderful) forces, but their combinations are limitless; none can comprehend them all.

SUN TZU: *The Art of War* (c. 420–360 BCE)

4.2 Code and message

Language, and with it, communication, is perhaps the greatest mystery of modern science. Beside language, black holes, quarks, and quasars pale to insignificance, and yet most of us, including many scientists, are more naive about language and communication than we are about almost any other activity. Barring accident or misfortune, we all learn to speak our native tongue with great fluency, but no one, not the linguists and least of all ourselves, knows how we do it.

In speaking English we must be using a grammar not like that we learned in school, even if we studied a foreign language, a deep structure grammar intimately known but unconsciously expressed, and we must know certain fundamental principles of that grammar – including the relationship between sound and sense and other people – before we come to say anything at all. Unlike apes, we are born with a genetic propensity to learn language from others of our species, and that potential must be based on inborn neurological and other structures, later elaborated by learning, the success and extent of which depends on adequate nutrition, diversity of stimulation, and – dare one say – happiness while the brain is rapidly growing in complexity during the 'once-only opportunity' for proper brain development in the first two years of life (Chase, 1980, pp. 551–5).

It is usually said that the code of rules in the deep structure grammar of a language or communication system governs the permissible organization of a 'repertoire' made up of a limited number of discrete or digital units or elements: elements of sound, at one level of language, for example, elements of syntax or ordering, at another, and elements of meaning, at yet another level. By analogy with the alphabet (or DNA), the repertoire is assumed to consist of discrete or digital units existing separately from the rules that govern their selection (from the code) and their combination (in the message) – selection and combination being basic to all systems of communication. But it is likely that in language and other complex systems certain of the rules exist to create the apparently discrete elements that other rules provide with grammatical structure (4.5).

Consider the first and most important principle of cartoon animation (there are twelve in all), called 'squash and stretch'. This principle was discovered and developed in the Disney studios in the early 1930s, following the stilted and mechanical animation of early Mickey Mouse shorts like *Steamboat Willie* (1928) – a piece that also set the style for the unremitting violence and cruelty depicted in the cartoon film in the name of childhood fun.

At this point my explanation of code/message relations in non-verbal communication was itself expressed non-verbally by means of three illustrations I had hoped to use from the extensive resources of *Disney Animation: The Illusion of Life* (1981) by Frank Thomas and Ollie Johnston. Two of these pictures illustrated the radical difference between cartoons made before and after the discovery of the principle of squash and stretch. If you have seen *Steamboat Willie* and/or any of Max Fleischer's rather mechanical cartoons and can compare either or both with the Disney cartoons of the early thirties and after, you will have no difficulty in imagining the change – pictured on page 33 and page 50 of *Disney Animation* – even if you cannot tell why.

The secret lies in the third and most important of the illustrations (p. 49 of *Disney Animation*): the half-filled floursack, the code/message system used to test, develop and teach the communication of meaning and emotion (called 'attitudes' by Disney) by simple changes in form. To avoid bloated-looking squash and stringy-looking stretch, the shape or volume of the cartoon figure is compared to a half-filled floursack. If dropped, the sack will squash into its fullest shape; if lifted by its two top corners it will stretch into its longest shape. In these two shapes, or in any intermediate shape, the floursack acts as a 'guide to maintaining volume in any animatable shape', as well as proving that 'attitudes can be achieved with the simplest of shapes' (p. 50).

In the artist's depiction of the floursack in the book, the first five sketches respectively illustrate full squash, squash and bend, full stretch, stretch and lift (the sack leaves the ground), and stretch, squash, and twist. The two top ears of the sack assume various positions in the process. The results communicate a vast potential of meanings, which might be labeled, respectively, bloated contentment (full squash), oppression (squash and bend), *qui vive?* (full stretch), dance the light fantastic (stretch and lift), and what was that? (stretch, squash, and twist around).

The artist then proceeds to illustrate, with ten different combinations in ten different drawings, the following 'attitudes': dejection (stretch, squash, and bend inwards), joy (stretch and bend outwards), a tantrum (flattened stretch lying on the ground with ears up like little fists), curiosity (one corner stretched into a point), cockiness (full chested stretch and bend), laughter (squash and bend flat on the back, with lines indicating vibration), belligerence (stretch and bend, ears thrust forward), more laughter (the sack dances doubled up), crying (horizontal stretch and twist), and finally, happiness (stretch, expand, curve, and lift – the sack gambols before your eyes).

In Disney's terminology, the goal of animation is to communicate 'attitudes' to the audience, to communicate meaning and emotion simply, directly, lucidly, and completely, without the use of words, through the body attitudes of the cartoon characters. Disney believed that animation can explain whatever the human mind can conceive.

But 'we cannot do fantastic things based on the real', he said, 'unless we first know the real'.

Newcomers to the Disney studio were amazed at the amount of time the animators spent analyzing body movement and communication in nature in order to create the 'caricature of reality' on which successful animation depends. The animated floursack was invented to demonstrate, teach, and test the role of squash and stretch in producing the illusion of life in the animated film.

One may not be quite sure at first whether the code/message system of the animated floursack is based on discrete elements, like an alphabet, or on the creation of form by the continuous transformation of shape, as in topology, resulting in a series of iconic combinations of continuity (shape) and discontinuity (outline). But there is no such ambiguity between continuity and discontinuity in the imaginary grammar of the four elements, earth, air, fire, and water, that for over two thousand years were believed to be the deep structure of reality.

The doctrine of the four (unchanging) elements probably originated with the Greek poet, Pythagorean philosopher, and democrat, Empedocles of Agrigentum in Sicily (fifth century BCE). In his and later versions, it was an elegant way of explaining the unity and diversity of reality, as well as change. (Heraclitus had said that change alone existed; Parmenides, who greatly influenced Empedocles, had dismissed it as an illusion.) Empedocles is also the first Greek to posit the existence of an invisible, incorporeal spirit pervading all of nature, a principle, we would say, of information: 'a holy mind (*phrēn*) alone, darting through the whole cosmos with rapid thoughts'.

Change is the result of combinations and separations of the four indestructible elements, like a painter mixing colors, said Empedocles; it is governed by two cosmic principles, Love (attraction, or Aphrodite), the original source of organic unity and creative combination, and Strife (repulsion, or Quarrel), the principle of diversity and differentiation. The life cycle of the cosmos thus oscillates in cycles between unity and diversity (Kahn, 1968).

(In the Chinese tradition the cosmic principles are yin and yang, and the elements are five: earth, fire, water, wood, and metal. Aristotle reserved a fifth and unchanging element, the 'quintessence' or 'ether', whose 'nature' is to move in circles, for the heavenly bodies, which he held to be perfect and imperishable.)

Matter-energy systems include what might be called a deep structure and a surface structure. But they cannot legitimately be viewed as code/message systems. Matter-energy systems exist whether life or society exists or not; code/message systems exist only when goalseeking or goaldirected subsystems exist to use them.

In considering the theory of the four material elements in ancient and medieval physics, we are only apparently dealing with a matter-energy system. The reason we can correctly regard this system as code/ system, or as a grammar with deep structure, surface structure, and a set of rules, is that in the organicism of the traditional view, matter, energy, planets, elements, and so on are treated as if they are alive and exist with purposes: each of the elements, for instance, 'naturally' seeks to reach its proper goal, fire seeking to rise just as water seeks to flow, air to float, and earth to fall. These goals are those of the eternal purpose of the Grand Designer; the elements, the raw materials of the Master Artisan; the cosmos, the speech of the Divine Author, by whose word all things consist.

> Bless the Lord, O my soul.
> O Lord my God, thou art very great;
> Thou art clothed with honour and majesty.
> Who coverest thyself with light as with a garment;
> Who stretchest out the heavens like a curtain:
> Who layeth the beams of his chambers in the waters;
> Who maketh the clouds his chariot;
> Who walketh upon the wings of the wind:
> Who maketh winds his messengers;
> His ministers a flaming fire. . .
>
> Psalm 104: 1–4

Figure 4.2, taken from the work of the sixteenth-century humanist Charles de Boulles, depicts an Aristotelian version of the structure formed by the four elements and the four qualities. Fire is depicted as the opposite of water, and air as the opposite of earth. Similarly, hot is the opposite of cold, and moist is the opposite of dry.

Figure 4.3 is taken from the work of Archbishop Isidore of Seville (?560–636), whose *Etymologiae* or 'Origins', a human and divine encyclopedia in 20 parts covering matters from medicine and the liberal arts to agriculture, furniture, and warfare, was for six centuries one of the reference books most often consulted by students. In Isidore's diagram the supposed oppositions or antipathies between the elements take their usual form. Integrated with the four elements in the (Pythagorean) tetrad are the four seasons of the year and the four humours of the body – an early version of the doctrine of correspondences between humanity and nature, similar to the Dogon ideology remarked on in Chapter 3.

Since the human organism is made up of the same elements as the world organism, the microcosm or 'little world' and the macrocosm or 'big world' correspond: both have souls. Through correspondence or correlation, human life in space and time is governed by the orientation of the universe and the motions of the stars. Conversely, the human form and its proportions are 'a pattern for all structure, including the

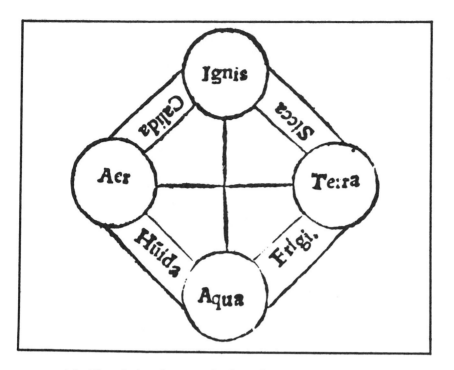

FIGURE 4.2: The relations between the four elements, earth, air, fire, and
water (*terra, aer, ignis, aqua*), themselves composed of the four qualities,
hot, cold, moist, and dry (*calidus, frigidus, humidus, siccus*), and believed
for 2000 years to be the deep structure of reality. The diagram depicts the
Aristotelian oppositions between the qualities hot and cold, and moist and
dry, and between the elements fire and water, and air and earth. It is taken
from *On Generation*, a work of about 1540 by Charles de Boulles, an early
French humanist. The rules of selection and combination applicable to this
code/message system are explained in the text. Here the elements form a
Pythagorean 'fourness' or 'tetrad'. (The number 4 was a 'mystery of mysteries'
for the Pythagoreans of the fifth century BCE and after; they believed it to
be the cause, root, and foundation of nature and of everything said or
done.) The ancient theory of the elements was not entirely given up until the
eighteenth century, when it was displaced by the new chemistry of scientists
like Robert Boyle (1627–91). *Reprinted from*: S. K. Heninger, Jr.: *The
Cosmographical Glass* (1977).

structure of the universe' (Byard, 1977). The disposition of the body
and the complexion of the personality are also regulated by the combinations of the four humours or body fluids, and by the cycle of the
seasons (others will later add the four ages of the person and the four
winds). These correspondences are given in Table 4.1.

elements	humours	seasons	ages	cardinal points
fire	choler (yellow bile)	summer	childhood	East Wind
air	blood (sanguine)	spring	adolescence	South Wind
earth	melancholia (black bile)	fall	middle age	North Wind
water	phlegm	winter	old age	West Wind

Table 4.1: Some of the traditional correspondences or correlations between humanity and nature in space and time. The correspondences between matter and time, as for instance between air and spring, are logically deficient, and the doctrine of oppositions (Table 4.2) begins to fail. While one can see an opposition in space between East and West, which are directions and thus of the same kind or quality, one cannot legitimately create an opposition between periods in time, such as childhood and old age, which are distinct in kind. And even if there is some 'natural' flavor to the idea of an opposition between fire and water, the relationship between them is in fact a mere distinction.

Along with astrology, the theory of the humours provided a theory of psychology and psychosomatic medicine: A choleric person or state of mind is impatient, passionate, and quick to anger; sanguine is courageous, hopeful, and amorous; phlegmatic is even-tempered, hard to move, and perhaps cold and dull; melancholy speaks of creativity and madness.

Commenting on Albrecht Dürer's *Melancolia* of 1514, with its magic square and black sun (Figure 4.4), and using sixteenth-century theories of the personality, Walter L. Strauss suggests that the engraving depicts 'melancolia imaginativa', a condition 'particularly affecting artists, architects, and artisans'. (A second kind of melancholy was said to affect doctors, scientists, and statesmen; a third kind, theologians and divines.)

The central figure is 'a strong, bright-eyed woman, sitting in contemplation, her wings locked in by the hourglass, her face darkened by melancolia' (literally, in Greek, 'black bile'). Earthbound for the moment, seated amid the artefacts of science and technology (including a millstone), framed by the hourglass, balance scales, and bell of the new time of the commercial revolution, surrounded by the tools of the crafts, a book in her lap, holding in one hand the dividers that in the Age of Discovery charted the way around the world, she seems to personify the combined power of theory and practice in the creative imagination – and for a Hegelian perhaps the Spirit of Capitalism.

Drawing on S. K. Heninger's analysis of medieval and Renaissance cosmology as pictured in printed books, in his *Cosmographical Glass* (1977, pp. 99–113), the rules of selection and combination that make

FIGURE 4.3: Elements and correspondences: An expanded tetrad of the elements from *On the Nature of Things* by Isidore of Seville (?560–636 CE), with the usual arrangement of the supposed opposites or antipathies. The center label reads: Cosmos, Year, Man, for Isidore includes in this model the doctrine of correspondences in space and time between humanity and nature, between microcosm and macrocosm. The four elements correspond to the four humours (*colera, sanguis, humor* or *phlegma,* and *melancholia*) and to the four seasons (Table 4.1). Reading clockwise from the top, the outer labels read: Fire, hot, hot, Air, moist, moist, Water, cold, cold, Earth, dry, dry. In his *Cosmographical Glass* (1977, p. 109), Heninger says of this diagram: 'No representation of infinite variety could be simpler'.

the structure of the qualities and the elements into a system, a grammar of the cosmos, can be quickly summarized.

The qualities and the elements are organized around two circles of affinities and two pairs of oppositions (Table 4.2).

Hot, dry, cold, and moist, in that order, form the circle of affinities between the qualities. Fire, earth, water, and air form the circle of affinities between the elements.

Fire is hot and dry; earth is dry and cold; water is cold and moist; and air is moist and hot.

A typical 'proof' of the existence of these relationships might be seen in placing a green log on the fire: as it heats up, water will ooze from its ends; smoke will rise as it burns, smoke being a kind of air;

FIGURE 4.4: Albrecht Dürer's *Melencolia I* of 1514, said to depict the 'imaginative melancholy' of the artist and the artisan (Strauss, 1972). The May issue of *Science 83* reports that art scholars have puzzled over the identity of the oddly shaped solid in the picture for over a century, some believing it to be a mystical symbol. Philip Ritterbush, a cultural historian, has identified it as an acute rhombohedron – a six-sided solid with a rhombus for each face – with two corners of the rhombohedron cut off.

Table 4.2: Qualities and elements: affinities and oppositions (sympathies and antipathies). Affinities read clockwise in a circle; oppositions face each other along the solid lines.

flames will appear, being fire; and ashes will be left behind, which are earth.

Rules for qualities

- Elements consist of qualities combined in various proportions.
- One quality cannot form an element.
- Hot and cold are opposites, as are dry and moist.
- Unmediated opposites are mutually exclusive.
- No more than two qualities can be combined into one element, for otherwise incompatible opposites will come together and annihilate each other (much like matter and anti-matter).
- Hot and cold are active; dry and moist are passive; active cannot be directly combined with passive.
- Adjacent qualities interact to create the elements: Hot and dry produce fire; cold and moist produce water; hot and moist produce air; cold and dry produce earth.

Rules for elements

- All earthly things consist of the four elements combined in various proportions.
- Fire and water are opposites, as are earth and air.
- Ummediated opposites are mutually exclusive.
- Adjacent elements share one quality: fire and earth share dry; earth and water share cold; water and air share moist; air and fire share hot.
- In fire hot is dominant over dry; in air moist is dominant over hot; in water cold is dominant over moist; in earth dry is dominant over cold.
- By varying the degree of one quality in relation to another, elements may be transmuted into each other and eventually even into their opposites.
- Whatever their transmutations, the amount of each element in the

universe remains constant (as energy does according to the first axiom of thermodynamics).

• Opposites are driven apart by Strife, which brings corruption and decay; they are brought together by Love, which brings synthesis and generation.

• The relative powers of Love and Strife, or attraction and repulsion, wax and wane with the seasons and the cycle of life and death, creating an oscillation like that between yin and yang.

• Opposites are connected, and opposition transcended, by mediation. As a third term or mean, fire mediates between air and earth; earth mediates between fire and water; water mediates between earth and air; and air mediates between water and fire.

'Thirdness is mediation, generality, order, interpretation, meaning, purpose. The Third is the medium or bond which connects the absolute first and last, and brings them into relationship. Every process involves Continuity, and Continuity represents Thirdness to perfection'.

EUGENE FREEMAN: *The Categories of Charles S. Peirce* (1931)

4.3 Mediation

Considering the symbolic importance of the number three in the Christian religion – Father, Son, and Holy Ghost; Father, Son, and Virgin Mother – it is not surprising that the doctrine of the four elements includes the rule of the transcendence of opposition by mediation. Just as fire in the medieval view is the third term mediating between air and earth, or water that between earth and air, Christ is the third term or mediator between humanity and God, the Virgin Mary is for millions of Catholics the mediator between the Church and the faithful, and the Holy Ghost, as the English say, is the Comforter.

'Mediate', which used to be a common technical term, means 'not immediate'. 'Mediation', in its logical and scientific sense of a medium, channel, agency, means, third term, or other indirect relationship by which two or more subjects, objects, patterns, systems, or other relationships are connected or communicate with one another, first went out of style with the nineteenth-century legacy of Hegel, the 'philosopher of mediation'. There is no article on the subject (nor is there one on communication), and no index entry either, in the otherwise excellent *Dictionary of the History of Ideas* (1968), where I came across Peirce's definition of 'Thirdness' placed at the head of this section, in the article on continuity.

Since the 1960s mediation has become a technical term more and

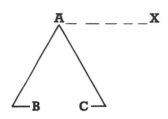

A: level of the code, deep structure (locus of mediation)
B, C.   goalseeking sender-receivers mediated by the code
B–C.   level of the messages, surface structure (message channels)
A–B, A–C.   coding channels
X.   relationship to an environment via the code

FIGURE 4.5: Code and message: the triangle of mediation. The level of the code, or deep structure, is not of the same logical type as the level of the messages, or surface structure. This diagram also defines the minimum requirements of a system of communication: a structure of constraints utilized by goalseekers subject to rules and open to its environment(s) via the mediation of its code.

more favored by neurologists in discussing the communication and control systems of the body, notably the systems of intercellular communication within and between the central nervous system and the hormone system.

Charles Sanders Peirce (1839–1914), the founder of American pragmatism and semiotic theory, saw that in living and social systems mediation or 'Thirdness' is essential to relationship itself. Thirdness mediates between first and second just as a code mediates between communicators. And just as a code is distinct in its level of logic, communication, and reality from the messages it makes possible, as we saw with the simple four-unit code of the element theory, so too is mediation distinct in its level of relationship from what it mediates.

In the element theory mediation has no orientation, no 'handedness': by changing levels an element can be the mediator in one relationship and the mediated in another. In communication and behavior, however, mediation does have an orientation: a code mediates its messengers and their messages, but messengers and messages cannot ordinarily change levels so as to mediate their code. Figure 4.5 is a useful way of representing these relationships. Using the terminology of the next chapter, we can say that the mediator and the mediated, the code and the message, are not of the same logical type.

With the concept of mediation, we can modify the metaphor of the *axis mundi*, as used by Mircea Eliade (b. 1907), the much-respected analyst of the structure of the religions of the world. As we saw in Chapter 2, Eliade uses the term to denote the center and centrality of the Eternal Dream Time in the orientation of the original Australians

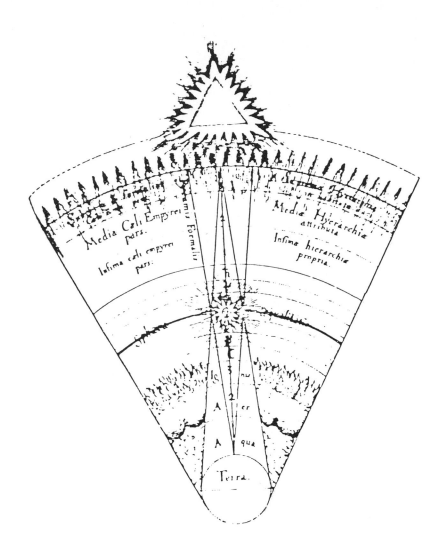

FIGURE 4.6: Form and matter. Taken from Robert Fludd's encyclopedia of matters 'metaphysical, physical, and technical' (1617–19), this classic diagram shows the traditional western view of the cosmic relations between form and matter (Chapter 1). Earth, at the bottom, represents brute Matter, without Form, while God, at the top, represents pure Form, untainted by Matter. As Heninger explains:

> The pyramid of pure form reaches down from the Holy Trinity [the equilateral triangle representing the Father, Son and Holy Ghost] until it diminishes to nothingness at the surface of the earth, while the pyramid of material substance [matter] reaches upward from our planet until it disappears at a point where the empyrean [the celestial sublime] begins.

to the environment of nature, the environment of the past, and the replication of the past in the environment to come, the future. Eliade, who believes the sacred to be truly sacred, is well known as the philosopher of the 'myth of the eternal return', a pattern of cyclical time appearing in many religions, but not found in the dominant judeo-christian mythology, which is linear and progressive, rather than repetitive.

Along with its use to label the dimensions of a graph, the metaphor of the 'axis' of a system is appropriate to the rotation of a wheel about its axle, the movement of the hands of a clock, or the rotation of the earth about its poles. But as a mechanical metaphor it is inappropriate to the vastly more complex relations of nature and society, myth and meaning, individual and value.

The metaphor of the *axis mundi* also implies a fixed and unchanging center or point of reference, a concept inapplicable to the ideology of societies which, like the Australian societies, have co-evolved with nature over time, adapting to new conditions as required for long-range survival. There will be more to say on the topic of faith in misplaced metaphors later on, but it is surely obvious that the ecology of the Australian Dream Time is best described, not as a center of rotation and repetition, but as a locus of mediation adaptable to changing realities over time (Chapter 5).

The religious ideology of the Dreamtime and its mystical geography may appear to us to be imaginary, but that is only because we can no longer see the way the Australian sees. Unlike the Australians and many of the 'other societies', most of which we have managed to

---

By emanation, God informs the Cosmos (Chapter 3). Heninger continues by pointing to

> the reciprocal relation between conceptuality [in-formation] and materiality [matter-energy] throughout the three levels of our universe – at any level in creation the greater the conceptuality, the less the materiality, and vice versa. (p. 144).

The sphere immediately beneath the Godhead is one part of the 'empyrean', or highest of the high: the 'abode of the highest angelical hierarchy' (numbered 3); next is that of the middling angels (numbered 2); and below it, numbered 1, is that of the lower angels. There follow the spheres of the seven 'planets' in this earth-centered sector of the circle of creation: Saturn, Jupiter, Mars, the Sun, Venus, Mercury, and the Moon. Beneath these are the spheres of the elements, fire, air, and water (numbered 3, 2, 1), with earth (implicitly zero) at the bottom. The orbit of the Sun is the 'sphere of equality', where conceptuality and sensuality (form and matter) are exactly balanced, the centre of an absolute symmetry.

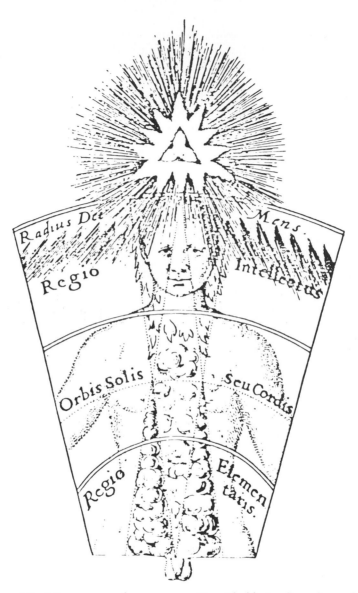

FIGURE 4.7: Microcosm and macrocosm. Here Fludd visualizes the analogy (*analogia*) between the human sphere and the cosmic sphere. In Heninger's words:

> Man is divided into three regions: 'the intellectual region', comparable to the angelic [or empyrean] world in the macrocosm; 'the middle region', through which runs 'the sphere of the sun or the heart', comparable to the celestial world in the macrocosm; and 'the elementary region, comparable to the sublunary world [the world beneath the moon] of [the] four elements in the macrocosm (p. 144).

destroy, we live, not in a co-evolved society, but in a de-evolved one: in a system in competition with its human and natural environments.

(In *Talking Drums to Written Word* (1950), Gordon Baldwin notes that three to four hundred years ago, before European exploration and expansion exterminated the Caribs, the Tasmanians, and hundreds of other societies, there were probably 5000 languages in use in the world. Today, with several billion more people, there are less than 3000. Some 2000 of these are spoken by band and village societies: about 1000 among the North, Central, and South American Indians; perhaps 500 among the blacks of Africa; another 500 in Australia, New Guinea, and the South Seas; and several hundred in Asia.)

As the product of a society tested by hundreds upon hundreds of years of long-range survival in nature, the dominant ideology of the Australians cannot be symbolic of an imaginary reality. It must be symbolic of the real structure of their real environment, and of the relationships between themselves, their society, and nature.

Thus the real counterpart of the locus of mediation in the Australian ideology lies not in individual minds, as Claude Lévi-Strauss (b. 1908) would have us believe; but rather at the ultimate locus of mediation in reality, the system-environment relationship itself. This relationship is universally defined as the product of the creative or carrying capacity of nature and the creative capacity of the society living in it.

NOTE

I chose Stonehenge as a model of what I do *not* mean by 'structure' in code/message relations, and used Hawkins and White's *Stonehenge Decoded* (1966) to do it for two important but perhaps not sufficient reasons: The book was the first I had ever seen that paid proper respect to the creative faculties of our remote ancestors – they were no less intelligent and imaginative than we – and also because it made a charming story.

As I feared and finally found out when I asked, the book is also the

---

The inversely related 'pyramid of form' and 'pyramid of matter' in Figure 4.7 are represented here by dotted lines, with the sphere of exact equilibrium between form and matter, or between form and sensation, running through the heart. At the top, a 'refulgent [or communicative] equilateral triangle' represents 'the mind, the light of godliness', completing Fludd's visual analogy.

focus of controversy. The English Heritage Foundation notes on page 28 of its 1978 guidebook, *Stonehenge and Neighbouring Monuments*:

Studies of other stone circles in Britain do suggest that their builders in Late Neolithic and Early Bronze Age times may have had a surprisingly exact knowledge of the way in which the directions of the risings and settings of the sun and moon vary with time. We cannot therefore reject out of hand the idea that the builders of Stonehenge used parts of it to mark and to record similar observations. We must admit, however, that Stonehenge is today so ruined that it is no longer possible to recover with certainty the sight-lines to the horizon that may have been built into it originally. The use of Stonehenge as an astronomical observatory in prehistoric times must remain a matter of speculation.

CHAPTER 5

The principle of requisite diversity

> We must not stop at the testing of a means for the immediate goal, but test also this goal as a means to a higher one, and thus ascend the series of facts in succession, until we come to one so absolutely necessary as to require no examination or proof.
>
> CARL VON CLAUSEWITZ *On War* (1832)

5.1 Logical types

Figure 5.1, showing the logical typing of complexity, is a simple development of the dependent hierarchy between society and nature originally put forward in Chapter One (Figure 1.2). In a dependent hierarchy the lower orders depend on the higher orders for structure and survival. The Extinction Rule tells us that nature's position at the top of the dependent hierarchy is the result of necessity, not of theory.

It will be seen from Figure 5.1 that the greater the qualitative complexity of any given level or order in a dependent hierarchy, the lower, or less abstract and inclusive, is its logical type. A logical type is a device originally invented by Bertrand Russell (1872–1970) primarily to distinguish between levels of logic and reality, as when we say that the logical typing of a class is distinct from that of its members (the class is distinct from its members by being the whole of which they are parts), or that the logical typing of a society is distinct from that of its citizens.

Looking at logical types in another way, consider the relative logical typing of the body parts attached to the trunk and chest. The logical typing of the head is obviously distinct from that of the legs. Or consider the Catholic doctrine of 'transubstantiation' which declares that in the communion the Wine *is* the Blood and the Bread *is* the Body of Christ – a confusion of the logical typing of the literal and the figurative in which, as Bateson puts it, 'the metaphor is meant'.

In Figure 5.1 society is shown as divided into (1) the means of production and reproduction (the natural environment, humans as organisms, materials, technology, productive capacity); (2) the social relations of production and reproduction (the relations between people in the course of work and marriage, including kinship and structures

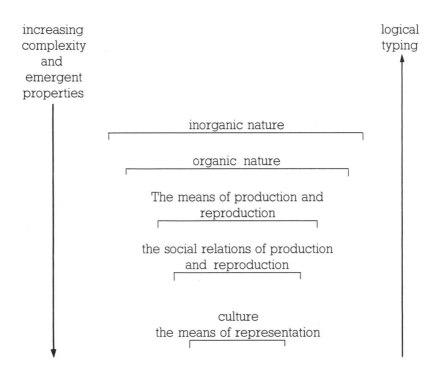

FIGURE 5.1: The emergent qualities and the logical typing of complexity in the dependent hierarchy between nature and culture, a development of Figure 1.2. In the diagram lower orders (as systems) depend on higher orders (as environments) for structure and survival. Complexity and diversity increase qualitatively from top to bottom, giving rise to emergent qualities: the RNA molecule at the origin of life, for instance, the rule against incest at the origin of society. The ultimate constraint is the principle of entropy. The lower the complexity of any level or order in a dependent hierarchy, the higher (more general, more abstract, more inclusive) is its logical type. The means of production and reproduction and the social relations of the same make up a particular mode of production and reproduction (slavery, feudalism, capitalism, and so on). Complex societies usually consist of dominant and subordinate modes of production and reproduction (see text). As noted in Figure 1.2, the human individual cannot be included in this hierarchy, not because the individual is not important, but because an individual is a complex of all the levels in it. The logical typing of each level in the diagram is distinct from that of the others, but they are all of the same family of logical types. The organism and the individual are part of another family of types.

of class, caste, race, and sex where they exist); and (3) culture (the means of representation). These three levels together make up the *mode of production and reproduction* of a given society (e.g. kinship and gender-dominated hunter-gathering, feudalism based on serfs tied to the soil, agrarian capitalism based on slavery and share-cropping, industrial capitalism based on wage labor). Complex societies generally consist of dominant and subordinate modes of production (e.g. relations of bondage, vassalage, and slavery co-existing with wage labor, as in modern society).

Lewis Carroll (1832–1898) set out another kind of hierarchy of logical types in *Alice Through the Looking Glass* in 1871: 'You are sad', said the White Knight to Alice, 'let me sing you a song to comfort you':

> 'The name of the song is called *"Haddock's Eyes"* '.
> 'Oh, that's the name of the song is it?' Alice said, trying to feel interested.
> 'No, you don't understand', the Knight said, looking a little vexed. 'That's what the name is *called*. The name really *is "The Aged Aged Man"* '.
> 'Then I ought to have said "That's what the *song* is called"?' Alice corrected herself.
> 'No, you oughtn't: that's quite another thing! The *song* is called *"Ways And Means"*: but that's only what it's *called*, you know!'
> 'Well, what *is* the song, then?' said Alice, who was by this time completely bewildered.
> 'I was coming to that,' the Knight said. 'The song really *is "A-sitting On A Gate"*: and the tune's my own invention'.

What the name of the song is called is not of the same logical type as what the name [of the song] really is, which is not of the same logical type as what the song is called, which is not of the same logical type as what the song really is.

This hierarchy of labels – labels labeling labels – is not a dependent hierarchy; it is a hierarchy of logical types between things, names of things, and names of names of things. In the grammar of English the name of a person or thing is a noun; the name of the name of a thing is a word.

As Martin Gardner points out in his delightful *Annotated Alice* (1960), the label 'Haddock's Eyes' – the name of the name of the song – is a statement in a 'metalanguage' about statements at other levels of language. A simple example of the use of metalanguage is a sentence referring to itself: 'This message is in English.' An infinite number of levels of language are logically possible: 'The message "This message is in English" is in English' – and so on.

The artless complexity of the conversation between Alice and the White Knight is quite striking. Each of the first three names is a statement, at its own level of language, about a statement at another level (another name). In addition to these three levels of language, the final name is a statement about the song (making four levels), which is of course itself a statement about its subject matter (making five levels):

'I'll tell thee everything I can:
  There's little to relate.
I saw an aged aged man,
  A-sitting on a gate.
'Who are you, aged man? I said.
  'And how is it you live?'
And his answer trickled through my head,
  Like water through a sieve . . .

And so on.

But Gardner tells us that the White Knight's song is a revised and expanded version of an earlier poem published by Carroll in 1856, which we could count as another level of communication. The poem of 1856 is moreover a parody of William Wordsworth's poem about the aged leech-gatherer, *Resolution and Independence*, which we could count as two more levels, one for Wordsworth's poem and one for the old man, not to mention resolution and independence . . .

The increases in order of complexity in Figure 5.1 are accompanied by 'emergent qualities'. Emergent qualities, which are found in every corner of complexity in the universe, are qualities not included in, and generally not predictable from knowledge of, the qualities of the systems in which they arise. The emergent qualities of the simple chemical combination H_2O, for example, are not found in the two gases taken separately or mixed together. Similarly, complete physical and chemical knowledge of the DNA molecule would not predict its function in reproduction.

As the product of the interaction between a genetic program and the internal and external environments of the organism, the developing embryo is the classic example of emergent qualities in biology. In life and society, meaning is a function of context. The qualities that emerge at each stage of organic development are the result of the reading and rereading of the same genetic message at higher levels of organization, that is to say, reading the same information in a new context. Depending on where it is in both space and time, the genetic information (identical in all the developing cells) takes on new meanings, and cell-differentiation – really cell-distinction – results.

The emergent qualities of classical physical and chemical systems are always in principle or in fact reversible: the parts can be recovered unchanged by reversing the motion, the reaction, or the combination. With the exception of reversible functional adaptations such as the increase in the number of red cells in the blood at high altitudes, the emergent qualities of living and social systems, are not reversible: the living parts cannot be recovered unchanged from the organization of the whole.

Apart from the thermodynamic irreversibilities inherent in biological and social organization – and in physics and chemistry the non-classical, non-equilibrium, and fluctuating systems ('dissipative structures') for which the Nobel Laureate Ilya Prigrogine and his associates in Brussels created the theory – the reason for the non-reversibility of emergent qualities in living and social systems is that such systems create system-dependent behavior between system-dependent parts – parts that cannot normally develop or exist outside the context they are in. The differentiated cell is a system-dependent component of tissue; the liver a system-dependent organ of the body; the organism a system-dependent part of the ecosystem; the person a system-dependent member of society. The moon or the earth, in contrast, are not system-dependent parts of the solar system, only their motion is dependent on the system they are in.

As we descend the dependent hierarchy from inorganic nature to society and culture, the relationship between matter-energy and information changes radically. The more complex a system is, the more distinctive is the relationship between the two. In the relatively simple inorganic order, matter-energy and information are not distinct from one another – except for the scientist who depends on the information to follow the tracks of the matter-energy (as in a cloud chamber, for example). This identity between matter-energy and information in classical and quantum physics is central to Heisenberg's principle of indeterminacy. Because the act of reading the signal (information) disturbs the carrier (matter-energy) it is impossible to know both the position and the velocity of an elementary wave-particle (such as an electron) at the same time.

In the organic order, where complexity is organized, remembered, and reproduced by information, the distinction between matter-energy and information is minimal in viruses and bacteria. But the more complex the organism, and the more extensive its relations with other organisms, the more abstract the information becomes, the more levels it involves, and the less it resembles the matter-energy that bears it.

In natural ecosystems, nevertheless, the communication of information usually depends on close connections in space and time between the reason for the communication, the sender, and the receiver, as is the case for the gibbon call signaling 'danger' and the response of gibbons within hearing, for the mating dance of sticklebacks, which uses body posture and color, for the 'wagging dance' of bees in the hive (each species with its own 'dialect'), which communicates to other bees the distance and direction of a source of nectar by reference to the polarized light of the sun, or for communication between ants, which includes touch, body posture, and odor (pheromones).

In the social and cultural order the relation between matter-energy and information becomes increasingly indirect and arbitrary, nowhere more so than in speech and language, where the matter-energy has no natural relation to what it symbolizes. And only in society does information become imaginary. It also becomes richer, more complex, more flexible, more ambiguous, and less dependent on close connection: continents or centuries may separate one sender-receiver from another.

When a constraint exists, advantage can usually be taken of it.

w. ross ashby: *An Introduction to Cybernetics* (1956)

5.2 Complexity and constraint

Complexity is a quality based on diversity. Diversity is the combination of two or more kinds of variety. A system displaying only one level or kind of variety – such as the 'organized simplicity' of the planets in mechanics or the 'unorganized variety' of the molecules in a gas in thermodynamics – is neither complex nor diverse. Considered simply as the means of counting, for example, the positive whole numbers display infinite variety. But all of this variety is of the same kind and exists at the same level: the whole number system does not display diversity.

Systems displaying one kind of diversity (two kinds of variety) are the least complex of complex systems. If we consider the variety of the positive integers, not on the basis of counting alone but also by the quality of being odd or even, then the whole number system displays two kinds of variety and one kind of diversity.

The more levels and kinds of variety a system displays – living systems operate on many thousands of levels (the average cell may contain 3000 different enzymes) – the greater is its diversity and thus its complexity.

Complexity and diversity are products of constraint. One kind of constraint produces one kind of variety. Complexity and diversity thus require the operation of more than one constraint. The more levels and kinds of constraint that govern (but do not determine) a system, the more levels and kinds of diversity it is sensitive to, and the more complex and diverse it is.

('Govern' is to be taken in the enlarged sense of communication, control, and constraint in living and social systems, as understood by systems cybernetics.)

The relation between complexity and constraint can be seen and heard in the following lines from Alexander Pope's *Essay on Criticism* (1711):

> True ease in writing comes from art, not chance,
> As those move easiest who have learned to dance.
> 'Tis not enough no harshness gives offence,
> The sound must seem an echo to the sense.
> Soft is the strain when zephyr gently blows,
> And the smooth stream in smoother numbers flows;
> But when loud surges lash the sounding shore,
> The hoarse, rough verse should like the torrent roar:
> When Ajax strives some rock's vast weight to throw,
> The line too labours, and the words move slow;
> Not so, when swift Camilla scours the plain,
> Flies o'er th' unbending corn and skims along the main.

Each line is subject to the constraints of sound, sense, and syntax in English, and to the constraints of the verse-form too, called the 'heroic couplet' (because it was used in so many 'heroic' dramas) – brought into English in the fourteenth century by Geoffrey Chaucer, who had it from the French poet and musician Guillaume de Machaut (1305?–77). The heroic couplet consists of two rhyming lines (called 'iambic pentameters'): two lines of five pairs of syllables apiece, with the beat on every other syllable (de dum, de dum, de dum, de dum, de dum) – you can hear Pope vary the numbers on that line – the same base beat as the blank verse used by Shakespeare.

In the 'closed couplet' favored first by Dryden in the eighteenth century, there were other constraints as well, notably the rule that each line express a single thought, and each couplet a complete idea, with balance, repetition, and antithesis within that frame. To the diversity of the verses created by taking advantage of these constraints, Pope adds yet another one: that every line will sound like what it says.

The combination of diversity that creates complexity is a qualitative process. In contrast a combination of variety may be simply quantitative. The eighteenth-century landscape game depicted in Figure 5.2 is such a combination. No matter how vast the number of possible combinations of the full set of 24 cards – 1 686 553 615 927 922 354 187 720 to be exact – these combinations do not increase diversity or create complexity.

We can define each card as equivalent to one 'bit' of information in the digital 'information theory' of Claude Shannon and Warren Weaver (1949). (One bit can stand for any kind or amount of information: we

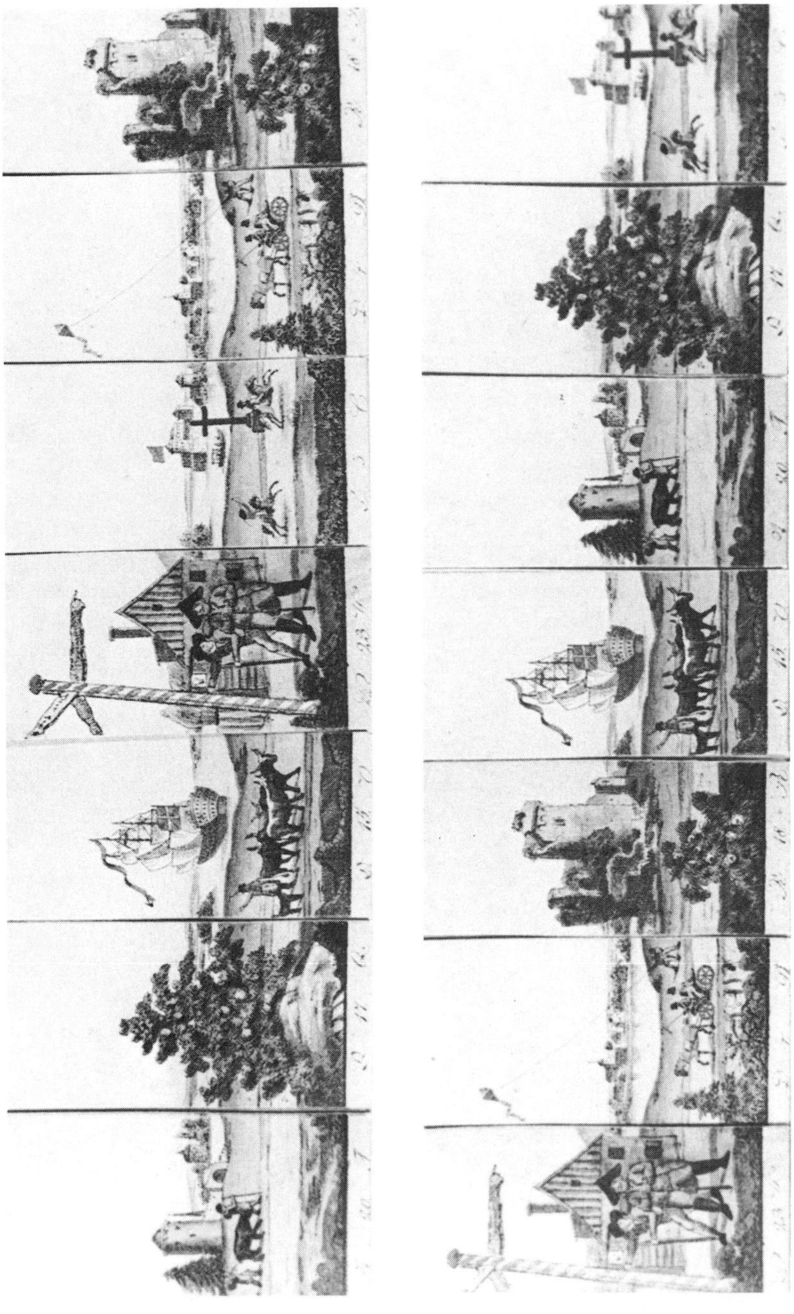

could define the Bible as one bit and the Koran as another.) Mathematical information theory is a part of the physics of communication, concerned with transmitting signals over the media, and not with the meaning or effect of the signals, nor with the sender-receivers exchanging them, nor with their purposes in communicating with each other. (For this reason the engineer and philosopher Heinz von Foerster has argued (1980) that this 'information' theory ought really to be called 'signal theory'.)

For Shannon and Weaver information is defined by its relative 'surprise value' (its statistical improbability). The greater one's freedom of choice in selecting a signal from the (digital) repertoire (from the 24 cards for example), the greater the quantity of physical 'information' the signal is said to represent. The greatest freedom of choice – and the highest surprise value – occurs when all signals are equally probable, as in the landscape game.

In the communication of meaning, however, constrained and therefore more probable choices (the genetic message, for instance) increase the quality and quantity of the information; and equiprobable choices decrease it (if all combinations of the four bases of DNA were equally likely, the resulting messages would be genetic gobbledygook). Mere mathematical combination, therefore, is not an index of complexity.

Constraints are neither causes, nor forces, nor obstacles, nor barriers. For the goalseeking subsystems they constrain – but do not determine – legitimate and natural constraints are part of the principles of creativity, the rules of organization, and the structures of complexity that make individuality and diversity possible. In systems of communication and exchange the constraints of the codes in use permit – and do not determine – the creation of mutually understandable messages by the living and social creatures who share the codes.

In his work on structure and transformation, *Zur Morphologie*, written in 1795 and published ten years later, in which he named and founded the transdisciplinary science of morphology (literally 'the study of form'), Goethe wrote about organisms in the following terms:

FIGURE 5.2 (opposite): Combination without complexity: an eighteenth-century game of landscapes. The second row of cards is a rearrangement of the first. The 24 cards in the whole set (not shown) may be arranged in any possible permutation and yet in each case a harmonious land- and seascape results. (There are 1 686 553 615 927 922 354 187 720 possible combinations.) This is accomplished by designing each card within the frame of the same limited number of 'planes of depth' – most show between four and six – such as one sees in 3-D stereoscope pictures or computer animation, and then aligning these planes throughout the set. But no amount of numerical combination can increase the complexity or diversity of the picture on these cards.

The more imperfect a being is, the more do [its] parts resemble the whole. The more perfect the being is, the more dissimilar are its parts. In the former case, the parts are more or less a repetition of the whole; in the latter case, they are totally unlike the whole. The more the parts resemble each other, the less subordination there is of one to the other; and subordination of parts is the mark of a high grade of organization.

One has only to substitute the modern term 'complexity' for the eighteenth-century term 'perfection' to see what Goethe is after. The simpler an organism is, he says, the more homogeneous are its parts and the fewer its levels of organization and constraint (its relative 'subordination of parts'). The more complex an organism is, the more heterogeneous are its parts and the greater the number of its levels of organization and constraint (its relative 'grade of organization').

Except for the underlying idea of inevitable progress in nature and in history based on increasing perfection – an eighteenth-century invention and a nineteenth-century article of faith – the structural relationships Goethe sees between degree of complexity, quality of diversity, and levels of organization are not essentially different from those put forward here.

(Note the change in the ideal of perfection; for Aristotle and Plato and the middle ages, it had been simplicity.)

Finally here, each of the orders of complexity and logical typing in Figure 5.1 includes levels and kinds of constraint. But the more general the order of complexity, the fewer levels and kinds of constraint it displays. There are fewer constraints in and over the world of physics and chemistry than there are in and over the world of biology and ecology. There are fewer constraints in and over living nature than there are in and over society. Culture displays the most levels and kinds of constraint – and therefore the greatest diversity and complexity – of all.

The more constraints one imposes, the more one frees one's self of the chains that shackle the spirit.

IGOR STRAVINSKY: *Poetics of Music* (1940). Quoted by H. H. Pattee in *Hierarchy Theory* (1973)

5.3 Levels of structure

Quite the most elegant discovery about language in this century is that all the basic sounds, or 'phonemes', of the known languages can be created out of a binary code of about twelve pairs of 'distinctive features', distinctive aspects of sound.

Distinctive features are either/or or more-or-less relationships between aspects of sound, such as nasal/not-nasal or tense/lax, all or most of which will be found in any given language. Some of the features, like the nasal/non-nasal distinction, are universal, others not. The twelve pairs established in 1956 and confirmed in 1966 are listed in Table 5.1.

The distinctive features are not the only important aspects of sound in language, for loudness, pitch, intonation, accent, and other continuous variations in sound, none of which have the apparently binary-digital characteristics ascribed to the distinctive features, also carry information. But the distinctive features are the basis of distinguishing one word from another – the major distinction between *dent* and *tent*, for instance, is that /d/ is voiced (the vocal chords vibrate) and /t/ is not – thus they are essential to the meaning of what we say.

The distinctive features form the acoustic deep structure or code of the phonemes; the phonemes, grouped in syllables, form the acoustic deep structure or code of words and parts of words. There are between 35 and 40 phonemes in English, for example, some 20,000 syllables, and about 300,000 words, 100,000 of which schooled individuals may know.

Linguistics, with mathematics, is one of the oldest of the sciences: There exists a grammar of Sumerian written some 4000 years ago. But the structural study of language systems came of age only in the twentieth century. The structural approach is called 'synchronic', meaning the study of a given language as a system 'at any moment of time'. Traditional historical linguistics is called 'diachronic', meaning the study of a language system 'through time'.

Among many pioneers, certain require mention: Charles Sanders Peirce (1839–1914), the physicist, mathematician, and semiotician already mentioned; Ferdinand de Saussure (1857–1915), the Swiss founder of European structural linguistics, whose development of synchronic linguistics decisively influenced the development of linguistics and semiotics, especially in France: Roman Jakobson (1896–1981) of the Prague School of linguistics, the Russian émigré who with Nikolai Troubetzkoy (1890–1938), also an émigré, founded the modern structural analysis of the phoneme, leading to the discovery of the distinctive features already mentioned; Noam Chomsky (b. 1928), who with *Syntactic Structures* in 1957 reframed the science of linguistics around the linguistic definition of surface structure and deep structure in transformational or generative grammar; and the anthropologist Claude Lévi-Strauss, who sought to apply to the (unconscious) deep structure of societies, kinship, myth, and even the mind the discoveries of Jakobson and Troubetzkoy in the sound structure of language, notably the so called 'binary opposition'.

Lévi-Strauss met Roman Jakobson at the New School for Social Research in New York during World War Two. As he explained in 'Structural Analysis in Linguistics and in Anthropology' in 1945 (published as Chapter 2 of his *Structural Anthropology* in 1958), the novelty of the structural linguistics of the Prague School was as follows:

- they passed from studying conscious linguistic matters to the unconscious infrastructure of language;
- they did not study linguistic terms as independent entities, rather they studied the relations between them;
- they treated the sound structure of language as a system with an internal logic;
- they searched for the general 'laws' of the system;
- they realized that the sound system was goalseeking or self-regulating, that it was a cybernetic system tending to maintain steady state and steady structure.

The notion of studying relationships, which is not of course restricted to linguistics, structural or otherwise, requires comment. In the early twentieth century the founder of phenomenology Edmund Husserl (1859–1938) raised the cry 'Zu den Sachen!' ('To the things themselves!' – the phrase also suggests 'get down to business', i.e. serious philosophy). The prevailing neo-Kantianism distinguished between the 'phenomenon' ('that which appears') and the 'noumenon' or 'the thing itself' and denied that the 'thing itself' could be known. Husserl simply denied this denial. Following his teacher Franz Brentano, who got the idea from the scholastics of the late middle ages, he defined consciousness as an 'intentionality' towards an object, as a transitive operation, as a goalseeking activity, as 'consciousness *of* . . .'. Jean-Paul Sartre, brought up in the tradition of the apparently autonomous subject (the *cogito*, or 'I think') of René Descartes (1596–1650), saw this as a great insight in 1939. Other thinkers applied the notion of intentionality to meaning: a message signifies something for someone. (Freud's concept of goalseeking, *Besetzung* or 'investment of interest', is similar in its sense and sources.) Phenomenology remained a world of subjects and objects, however, and failed to recognize the significance of the communication and exchange analyzed by the Anglo-American systemists and the French structuralists in the 1950s and 1960s, notably of course Lévi-Strauss. The structuralists soon raised the cry: 'Not the things themselves, but the relations between them!'.

This concern for relationships rather than entities or objects is recognizable in the 1930s in early information theory, general systems theory (Ludwig von Bertalanffy), and cybernetics, which influenced the Prague School. The systems-informational-cybernetic approach, the basis of the modern computer, greatly expanded during World War Two (early information processors were invented to crack the codes of the German Enigma machines). This perspective, the basis of the new view, became the dominant theory in Britain and the United States in the 1960s, linking with systems ecology in the 1970s. Given its emphasis on the system-environment relation, it was perhaps to be expected that in the 1970s the systemists would raise the cry: 'Not the relations between things, but the relations between relations!'

All of this was however foreshadowed in the work of the Prague school in the 1930s, for the phonological relations in language, are quite clearly relations between relations (Table 5.1).

vocalic/non-vocalic	checked/unchecked
consonantal/non-consonantal	voiced/voiceless
nasal/non-nasal	tense/lax
compact/diffuse	grave/acute (low-high frequency)
abrupt/continuant (non-abrupt)	flat/non-flat
strident/non-strident	sharp/non-sharp

TABLE 5.1: The twelve distinctive features, from which particular languages make their selection (Jakobson and Halle, 1956; revised 1966–67; reprinted 1971). Except for those involving the more-or-less of a continuum (e.g. grave/acute, tense/lax) each feature is defined by the presence or absence of one aspect of sound (the feature is thus either 'marked' or 'unmarked' in respect of that aspect). They are selected and combined simultaneously in bundles with other features to make phonemes (French consonants contain from two to five features, for example). Every phoneme is distinct from every other phoneme by at least one feature. The phonemes /b/, /d/, and /g/, for example, are marked by voicing (vocal chord vibration); the phonemes /p/, /t/, and /k/ are unmarked in that respect. Unlike letters or words or any other linguistic units, features and phonemes are entirely relational, with no individual existence, referring only to others of their kind. The ultimate significance of the distinctive features in communication is their semantic value: without them distinctions in meaning would not be possible. (The context-sensitivity of language at all levels means that every linguistic unit carries semantic information.) The distinctive features are commonly called 'binary oppositions' in the literature, which leads to logical and ideological problems.

In fact we can go even further back, to that extraordinary man, Saussure, (*Cours de linguistique générale*, 1915, p. 166):

> In language (*langue*) there are only differences. . . . A difference generally presupposes positive terms between which it is established, but in language there are only differences without positive terms . . .

Only when the sound and sense of a linguistic sign are united in speech does the sign have a positive value. Otherwise:

> Concepts . . . are purely differential. They are not defined positively by their content, but negatively by their relationships with the other terms of the system. Their most exact characteristic is to be what others are not.

The phonemic structure of language is the least complex and best understood of the three kinds of basic linguistic structure (the other two are syntactic and semantic). A phoneme (literally 'sound') is a simultaneous bundle of several distinctive features distinguished from every other phoneme by at least one feature. A distinctive feature is one of a pair of marked/unmarked kinds of sound. Phonemes are selected and combined in sequences, based on syllables, to make morphemes, which make words.

Castilian Spanish uses 24 phonemes; American Spanish, usually 22. Czech contains 33 phonemes. French people born before 1940 generally use 34 phonemes; those born later may use only 31. English uses between 33 and 40 phonemes (depending on the authority). Hawaiian uses 13, the fewest of all.

Like the distinctive features, and unlike all other language units (including the letters of the alphabet), a phoneme is purely relational, without independent or individual existence, defined or specified only by its distinction from every other phoneme in the language. As Jakobson and Halle put it (1971, pp. 22, 28), 'phonemes denote mere *otherness*'.

Morphemes (literally 'forms') are the minimum units with meaning; they include words without meaningful parts, such as *cat*, *and*, *dog*; word prefixes, such as *pre-* and *un-*; and word endings, such as *-ed*, *-s*, *-ly*, *-ing*, and so on.

The twelve pairs of distinctive features form an optimal acoustic code. Since each feature is defined as either marked or unmarked, each can be specified by one yes/no question (marked or unmarked?). The answer to this question makes up one 'bit' (or 'binary digit') in mathematical information theory (Shannon and Weaver, 1949). Every phoneme can thus be specified by a definite number of 'bits'. Fifteen of the French consonantal phonemes, for example, can be fully defined by only five binary decisions: either nasal or non-nasal; if non-nasal then either continuant or abrupt and either tense or lax; either compact or diffuse, and if diffuse then either grave or acute (p. 59).

The principle of marked/unmarked distinctions operates at many levels of language: just how far it extends into meaning, concepts, and life, and whether the distinctions 'marked/unmarked' or 'black/white' and so on are 'oppositions' are questions of logic, perspective, and value that divide many of us from the previous generation. In English the present tense is unmarked; the past is marked; similarly the active voice is unmarked; the passive marked. Singular is unmarked; plural marked; male is unmarked, female marked.

In language, rather than being either (relatively) 'free' or 'not free' to create meaning, we are both relatively free and not free, depending on the level we look at. Our semiotic freedom to select and combine distinctive features into phonemes is zero (Figure 5.3). In combining phonemes into words, it is not much greater, although we can invent new combinations of phonemes, such as 'Kleenex', but these are of course governed by the sound structure of English. We may say 'lips of the stung' in error for 'slips of the tongue', for example, but we will not say 'tlips of the sung', not because we cannot pronounce the sound 'tl', but because it is not permitted to begin a word in English (Fromkin, 1973).

At the level of words, we are constrained by the common code of meanings. In forming sentences from words, we are constrained by the syntax of word order, but this can be varied a good deal. In combining sentences into discourse, we are freed from the constraints of syntax; here our semiotic freedom is constrained mainly by our linguistic competence, as well as by the limits of language itself.

Since the 1960s linguists have agreed that all levels of language and all three kinds of structure influence each other, and that they cannot legitimately be studied separately from one another. Little is in fact known about the way a speaker's intention is translated into expression; it is recognized that every aspect and level of language carries some aspect of meaning (Jakobson, 1972).

It is the common wonder of all men, how among so many millions of faces, there should be none alike. Now [on the] contrary, I wonder as much how there should be any [the same]; he that shall consider how many thousand severall words have been carelessly and without study composed out of 24 Letters; withall how many hundred lines there are to be drawn in the fabrick of one man; shall easily finde that this variety is necessary.

SIR THOMAS BROWNE: *Religio Medici* (1643)

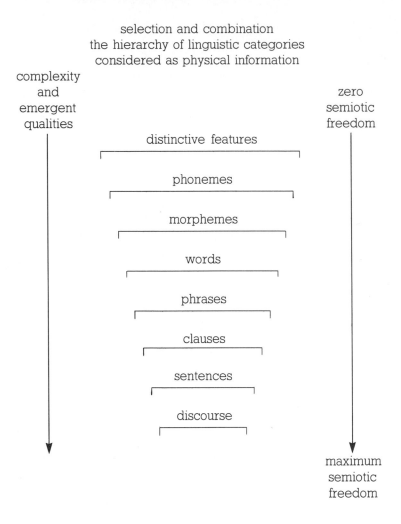

selection and combination
the hierarchy of linguistic categories
considered as physical information

complexity
and
emergent
qualities

zero
semiotic
freedom

distinctive features

phonemes

morphemes

words

phrases

clauses

sentences

discourse

maximum
semiotic
freedom

FIGURE 5.3: Levels of semiotic freedom in the eight-level hierarchy of the linguistic categories considered as the organization of physical information, a dependent hierarchy. Complexity and relative semiotic freedom increase from top to bottom. For the equivalent hierarchy of writing in alphabetic languages, substitute 'alphabet' for the first three levels; for ideographic languages like Chinese, substitute 'radicals' and 'characters' for the first four levels.

5.4 Variety, information, and noise

Variety, the basis of diversity, is a pattern borne by a matter-energy medium or marker; it is both matter-energy and information. Which of these two aspects is its dominant aspect in any particular case depends on the context.

In the case of a Yale key, the matter-energy and information of its pattern of notches are distinct but not separate. As matter, the notches act as wedges which physically rearrange the tumblers when the key is pushed into the lock. As information, the notches are messages in a code shared by the lock. If key and lock are parted, then the information of the notches is reduced to noise.

Information is in no intrinsic way distinguishable from any other form of variety (W. Ross Ashby). Information is not inherently distinct from noise. In and for a given observer and a given system-environment relation, variety recognized as information is *coded* variety, and variety not so recognized is noise, i.e. *uncoded* variety.

What is noise in one context may be information in another. The variety in the observed orbit of Mercury, for example, is noise for Newtonian mechanics. For Einsteinian relativity this variety is not only information, but information crucial to the experimental verification of the theory itself.

For organisms and human beings, much of the environment is noise, some of it uncoded variety and some of it variety that cannot be coded at all. And even in the relatively limited domain of coded variety, most of the information actually available is not attended to. Organic and human open systems must constantly select particular patterns of information at particular levels at particular times. If they were sensitive to all of the information all of the time, they would perish in confusion. Protecting ourselves against overloads of information may be one reason we need to sleep.

Information is a relationship, not a thing. For a given system, information represents order or organization, and noise, disorder or disorganization, or more strictly non-order or non-organization. The relationship between order and disorder is relative to its context — physical, biological, human, historical. Disorder does not necessarily mean randomness or chaos, only that it is not perceived or not perceivable as order.

Information may be degraded into noise; under the right conditions noise may be translated into information. Consider the genetic message in evolution. If the genetic message of DNA becomes mispunctuated or otherwise disordered, perhaps by radiation or by uncorrected errors in replication, translation, or transcription, in most cases the garbled instructions will not produce an organism capable of surviving. But in a minute number of cases, the disordered instructions will result in the novelty of a surviving mutation, and what was originally noise will be passed on to the next generation as information.

This is an example of the principle of 'order from disorder' in natural evolution, where the source of the noise is logically or otherwise external to the system it comes to alter. (The same is true of social evolution resulting from outside events or unexpected innovations, such as the invention of gunpowder.) In history, whenever the source of the noise is the system itself, order from disorder is the principle of revolution.

Once it is agreed that information and noise are not inherently distinct, then it follows that without context, there can be no information — i.e. no distinction between information and noise.

For any biological or social system, the existence of coded and uncoded variety or diversity presupposes the existence of goalseeking subsystems dependent on communication for survival. Communication is impossible without coding, and coding is impossible without context. We see, therefore, that information, communication, context, order, and goalseeking are all implicit in the original distinction between coded and uncoded variety. They are all implicit in the fact of coding itself.

Arrangement, configuration, organization, structure, ordering – these are now key words. What underlies this verbal fashion? Greater attention to complexity.

LANCELOT LAW WHYTE: 'Atomism, Structure and Form' (1965)

5.5 Redundancy, entropy, and evolution

Thermodynamics means literally 'the power of heat'; entropy means 'transformation'; 'energy' literally means 'action'.

Entropy is a measure of relative disorder. To people literate in playing cards a pack of cards arranged in numerical order by suits displays low entropy and high order. A shuffled pack displays high entropy and low order.

The first axiom of thermodynamics states that energy is conserved. The second axiom of thermodynamics states that in the physical universe the entropy of isolated systems tends irreversibly to increase towards a state of complete disorder or randomness (complete positive entropy). In the process the energy of the system remains constant in quantity, but changes irreversibly in quality.

In energy and engineering terms entropy means that the 'free' energy available to do work in a given system (e.g. fuel) is transformed by use into 'bound' energy (e.g. waste heat) from which no further work can be obtained in the system in question.

In the physical universe disorder is more probable than order – Eddington called entropy the arrow of time – hence the principle of entropy is a principle of probability.

In natural evolution, however, as well as in the evolutions and revolutions of societies, we find that order, organization, information, and complexity are more probable than disorder, disorganization, noise, or randomness. In evolution and history, biological and social complexity have increased over time. This process of increasing organization through the constant creation of novel information in life and society (Erwin Schrödinger called it 'negative entropy') does not violate the second axiom, however. Systems whose entropy remains constant, increases, or fluctuates are open systems dependent on their environments. They take order from the environment (matter-energy and information), re-order it to maintain or increase their own order, and return to the environment the resulting disorder. Entropy does not increase in the open system; it increases in the system's environment.

After thermodynamic entropy was recognized as a measure of the disorder in a closed system, the Scottish physicist James Clerk Maxwell (1831–1879) raised the 'thought experiment' as to whether the second axiom's rule of increasing entropy could be evaded by the introduction into the system of an 'intelligence' (the Maxwell Demon) to sort the system's disorder (noise) into order (information). This was the first stated connection between entropy and information. In 1922 Leo Szilard showed that the 'intelligence' would create at least as much entropy in obtaining the information necessary to sort the disorder as it would reduce by the creation of order through sorting. Like work, like order, information can be obtained and communicated only at the cost of disorder somewhere else in the system or in its environment.

In 1894 the Austrian physicist Ludwig Boltzmann (1844–1906) defined entropy, not as an 'objective' quantity and not as a result of energy at work, but as a relationship to an observer. Entropy, he said, is a matter of 'missing information' (information unavailable to the observer about the system's randomly ordered microstates). The higher the entropy, the greater the amount of unobtainable information.

At high entropy the system is so disordered that the observer can perceive in it no structured variety. At low entropy the system is highly structured and thus rich in potential information.

Information (coded variety) is qualitatively distinct from sensing (perception), meaning (connotation), and signification (denotation) – the three components of knowledge, each dependent on a distinct level of information.

Sensing is coded information; meaning is coded sensing; and signification is coded meaning. The three form a dependant hierarchy supported by information.

Shannon's information is physical, quantitative, statistical, and one-dimensional (it deals only with variety, not with diversity). The physical 'amount of information' is defined as a measure of one's freedom of choice, on the average, in selecting a particular sign or symbol from the (digital) 'repertoire' (e.g. the alphabet) of the information source. This is a statement of probability. The greater the freedom of choice permitted by the repertoire, the more improbable any particular choice will be. The more improbable the choice, the greater the physical quantity of information (Shannon called it 'surprise value') it carries, and the greater the uncertainty (in the recipient) that the message actually selected is any particular one. The communication of information reduces that uncertainty to certainty.

The meaning, utility, or value of the messages transmitted, and the desires or skills or relationships of the communicators, have no significance in Shannon's theory (which is why Heinz von Foerster prefers to call it 'signal theory'). Here, says Weaver, the word 'information' relates not so much to what you *do* say (as the qualitative concept of meaning would do), as to what you *could* (statistically) say: The 'amount of information' is a function of the freedom of choice available on the average in the whole repertoire – which is reduced wherever previous choices influence later ones (as in the case in language, for example).

The statistical measure of the physical amount of information is the 'bit' (the binary digit): the logarithm to the base 2 of the number of available choices. A two-unit repertoire (dots and dashes, for example) in which each unit is equally probable allows two choices, and $\log_2 2 = 1$ bit. Putting it another way, the quantity of information is the same as the number of yes/no questions required to uniquely identify a particular unit of the repertoire. With a two-unit repertoire, one question suffices: each unit carries one bit. If the repertoire is the alphabet (26 letters plus the space), and if all letters are considered to be equally probable, then each letter or space carries about 4.76 bits of information ($\log_2 27 = 4.755$): between four and five yes/no questions will uniquely identify any particular letter.

Some of Shannon's intuitions were shared by the mathematician Norbert Wiener (1894–1964), who published his *Cybernetics: Or Control and Communication in the Animal and the Machine* in 1948, a year before the appearance of Shannon and Weaver's *Mathematical Theory of Communication*. Just five years later, in 1953, the American biochemist James Watson (b. 1928) and the British biophysicist Francis Crick (b. 1916) discovered the double helix of DNA, then recognized that DNA is a system of information storage and communication. For this, the greatest discovery in biology in the twentieth century, they shared the 1962 Nobel Prize for medicine with the New Zealander Maurice Wilkins (b. 1916).

In the single and quantitative dimension of Shannon's theory, if every selection were equally probable, one would enjoy the maximum possible freedom of choice, the greatest possible quantity of infor-

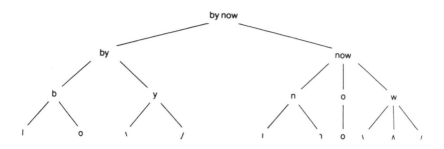

HIERARCHICAL ANALYSIS, in this case of the phrase 'by now', views reading as a progressive feature-recognition process in which a few basic 'modules of form' (curves, angles, vertical lines and so on) serve as the cues for the recognition of letters, which in turn serve as the cues for recognizing syllables and words, which in turn serve as cues for recognizing phrases.

FIGURE 5.4: Feature recognition of printed letters. The distinctive features of letters (called 'modules of form') shown at the bottom of the hierarchy serve as cues for the recognition of letters, which serve as cues for recognizing syllables and words, which serve as cues for recognizing phrases, and so on. (This process is almost certainly concurrent, rather than sequential.) Letters can be seen as made up of various rotations of five simple components, or modules of form, each represented in the word 'loves': a vertical line (l), a closed circular curve (o), an angular intersection (v), a horizontal line with a curve (e), and a cyclical curve (s). Almost all English lower-case letters can be constructed by varying the orientation of these five basic forms. In the printed word it seems clear that letters are recognized as integrated gestalts or wholes (rather than as associations of elements) – or in another terminology, as visual icons (combinations of analog and digital information, or continuous and discontinuous codings). Most handwriting, in contrast, is analog in form (continuously coded), much more complex than print, and only intelligible because of our vast capacity for recognizing essential patterns amidst an infinity of transformations and distortions. Presumably we extract visual icons from the continuous script. Reprinted from: Peter Dunn-Rankin: 'The Visual Characteristics of Words' (1978).

mation, the most surprise value (negative entropy), the greatest uncertainty in the recipient, the widest variety of ways of arranging the information, and the minimum of context or structure. Every choice would be as important (and as improbable) as every other, with the result that every single error in transmission would change the original message into another one.

The protection against errors required here is redundancy, which is one of the most important concepts in information theory, and the subject of Shannon's 'second theorem', which Campbell calls 'one of the major intellectual discoveries of the time' and 'Shannon's most elegant and profound discovery' (1982, pp. 78, 80). Shannon showed that it is always theoretically possible to protect a message from any amount of noise, provided only that the message be supplied with requisite redundancy.

Redundancy is potential information. Unlike noise, which remains outside the code in use and can be converted into information only by a restructuring of the code, redundancy is coded diversity available for use as required, notably in protecting the message against noise.

Redundancy is structure.

Redundancy means that more signals are sent than are strictly necessary to transmit the information in the message. Written English, for example, considered apart from meanings, is about 50 per cent redundant when one considers the statistical regularities or context of sequences of eight letters; the redundancy rises to about 75 per cent for sequences of 100 letters.

(The amount of physical information carried by each of the 26 letters of the alphabet considered as equally probable is $\log_2 26$, or 4.70 bits. The redundancy (or structure) of actual letter frequencies (where e, the most frequent, carries 2.98 bits and z, the least frequent, 10.71 bits) reduces this to 4.15 bits. The redundancy of two-letter sequences gives a figure of 3.57 bits per letter, and that of eight-letter sequences, 2.35 bits per letter, half of the first figure: Hassenstein, 1970.)

Since redundancy is potential information, it is not intrinsically distinct from any other form of coded diversity. What is redundant in one context may be information in another. In Shannon's theory, the transmission of a message between sender and receiver means an increase in the quantitative redundancy occupying the available channels (a reduction of surprise value). From the semiotic point of view, however, the transmission means an increase in qualitative information (an increase of structure in the sender-receiver relation).

Redundancy is relative to the system in which it occurs. In the context of communication the information carried by particular sign or symbol is less significant than the overall redundancy of the message, for it is redundancy that makes understanding possible. Redundancy permits the receiver to anticipate the meaning or signification of a message – to see the pattern that connects – and thus to link its diverse parts together in a comprehensible whole.

As Jeremy Campbell takes pains to point out (1982), in nature and society it is redundancy that makes complexity possible. Complexity is generated by rules, which are a form of stored information acting as constraints on other information and thus themselves forms of redundancy too. 'The power of a small number of fixed rules to produce an *unpredictable* amount of complexity is very striking' (p. 105).

A rule operates at a level of communication and reality distinct from the level of what it rules. It appears, moreover, that there is a hierarchy of levels (statements and metastatements) encoded in the DNA of complex organisms, some genes being concerned with protein synthesis, others with the regulation of other genes – and perhaps even with the regulation of the rules of the genetic grammar itself. It may be that it was changing levels of gene activity, and not simply changing genes, that led the way from the biological simplicity we find in microbes to the complexity of later forms of life (p. 133).

All that is not information, not redundancy, not form and not restraints – is noise, the only possible source of *new* patterns.
GREGORY BATESON: 'Cybernetic Explanation' (1967)

5.6 The principle of requisite diversity

In his elegant exposition of the theory of cybernetic systems 'closed to information and control' in 1956 in *An Introduction to Cybernetics* (pp. 186–7, 206–11), the British engineer and philosopher W. Ross Ashby based what he called the 'law of requisite variety' on the fact that only variety can diminish or destroy (i.e. control) variety. He left unstated the fact that only variety can increase or create – or re-create – variety.

Cybernetic or self-regulating devices using negative feedback (deviation reduction) to maintain a steady state (homeostasis) were invented by the Greeks, as in the needle-and-seat level regulators for water clocks devised by the engineer Ctesibius of Alexandria in the second century BCE.

In windmills of the 1760s and 1770s flyball or centrifugal governors – derived from the centrifugal pendulums (ball-and-chain flywheels) of Renaissance technology – were invented by English and Scottish millwrights to replace the child-controlled 'lift-tenters' used to regulate the distance between the millstones. (The upper stone tended to ride up the shaft in high winds so that the grain in the middle was not properly ground.)

Robert Hilton took out a patent for an automatic or self-regulating lift-tenter in 1785. This was followed by a new design by Thomas Mead in 1787, and a new patent by Stephen Hooper in 1789. The first steam-powered mill, the Albion Mill developed by Boulton and Watt and erected in London in 1786 by John Rennie (1761–1821), was equipped with a governor like Mead's. Boulton reported on this novelty (presumably installed by Rennie, who was 27 years old at the time, and later to become famous as a bridge-builder) in a letter of 1788 to Watt in Birmingham. Watt's 30-year-old assistant John Southern designed the first 'Centrifugal Speed Regulator' for the stationary steam engine from an engineering drawing in 1788, one of several cybernetic devices invented by that firm (De Bono, 1974; Mayr, 1969).

Windmills, which before the rise of the factory were the most complex systems of automatic machinery in use in England and the Continent, used a number of other cybernetic devices, including 'patent sails' that spilled wind under heavy gusts and the 'fantail gear', patented in 1745 by Edmund Lee, a Wigan blacksmith, who called it the 'Self-Regulating Wind Machine'. This device kept the sails pointing into the wind on the same principle as the cybernetic wind vane used by long-distance solo sailors (Mayr, 1969).

James Clerk Maxwell (1831–1879), ranked with Newton for his development of the field theory of electromagnetism (1864) from Faraday's intuitions, initiated the theory of governors in an article published in 1868, but it was not until after the Second World War that cybernetics became a new (and transdisciplinary) branch of science, defined by Norbert Wiener in 1949 as 'communication and control in the animal and the machine'. As Ashby put it in 1956: 'The truths of cybernetics are not conditioned on their being derived from some other branch of science.'

Governors are negative feedback or 'deviation-reducing' devices designed to keep other systems under control. Cybernetics and systems theory did not take up the study of positive feedback or 'deviation-amplifying' systems – which include the processes of growth, creativity, and invention, as well as compound interest, cancers, exponential population growth, the multiplication of inflation by inflation, pathological conflicts leading to madness, the escalation of arms races, and in general all adaptive systems that have 'run away' or gone out of control – until the early 1960s.

(See Magoroh Maruyama's 1963 article 'The Second Cybernetics: Deviation-Amplifying Mutual Causal Processes', reprinted in the useful (and now historic) anthology edited by the systems sociologist Walter Buckley in 1968: *Modern Systems Research for the Behavioral Scientist.*)

Ashby wrote as an engineer concerned to suppress noise in systems of communication and control. His 'principle of requisite variety' states that if the variety which a given system is likely to encounter in its environment is greater in quantity than the variety the system can process, then the system's stability will be threatened, because it will not have the flexibility sufficiently to reduce, absorb, suppress, or transform the uncoded variety (the noise) that threatens it.

In another form, the principle says that the capacity of a system, R, to regulate or control or steer another system, S, cannot exceed the capacity of R as a channel of communication.

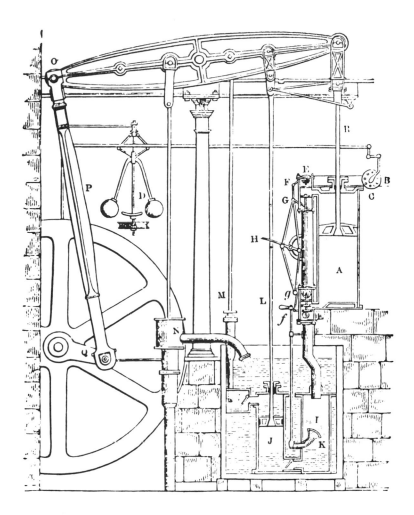

FIGURE 5.5: A double-acting stationary steam engine with a centrifugal governor (D), about 1800. When the engine falls below its operating speed, the rotating pendulums fall inwards, moving the slide up the governor shaft, closing the scissors linkage, and causing the horizontal link and crank to open the throttle valve C, increasing the supply of steam to the cylinder. Conversely, when the engine exceeds its desired speed, the balls fly outwards, closing the throttle valve and reducing the steam supply. The position of the balls at any moment represents the speed of the machine. As in all control devices, the feedback is 'negative': it opposes whatever the engine is doing. The linkage and crank form a closed feedback loop between the governor and the throttle. Feedback, says Weiner, 'is a method for controlling a system by reinserting into it the results of its past performance'.

In its ordinary, quantitative, sense, Ashby's principle is designed to be the cybernetic equivalent of Claude Shannon's Tenth Theorem in *The Mathematical Theory of Communication* (1949). This theorem states that the total amount of noise that can be removed by a correction channel from a main channel of communication transmitting discrete signals is limited to the number of quantitative bits of information that the correction channel can carry. In Ashby's words, 'the use of a regulator to achieve homeostasis [steady state] and the use of a correction channel to suppress noise are homologous' (1956, p. 211).

Control requires a representation of what is being controlled. In the case of the centrifugal governor, for example, the distance of the weights from their center of rotation represents the speed of the engine. Ashby's principle of 'requisite variety' can therefore be restated as a principle of representation, using the more general term 'requisite diversity':

The capacity of any system, R, to represent the diversity of another system, S, cannot exceed the flexibility of R as a coding system.
This is the principle of requisite diversity in representation.

Requisite diversity does not imply that the representing system has to represent all the diversity of the system being represented, but only that R must be capable of representing the basic codings of the types of variety found in system S. If S includes qualities, then R must contain corresponding representations. If S involves levels, then R must contain corresponding levels.

When this is not the case, the representing system – e.g. a scientific theory, a perspective, an ideology – will be reductionist. Reductionism crosses boundaries between levels and orders of complexity without recognizing their existence. This inevitably entails the neutralization of diversity, and therefore the loss of qualitatively significant information.

You have meddled with the primal forces of nature, Mr Beale, and I won't have it, is that clear? . . . The Arabs have taken billions of dollars out of this country, and now they must put it back. It is the ebb and flow, tidal gravity, it is ecological balance. There are no nations! There are no Arabs! There are no Third Worlds! There is no West!

There is only one holistic system of systems, one vast and immune, interwoven, interacting, multivariate, multinational domination of dollars! . . .

And you have meddled with the primal forces of nature. You get up on your little 21-inch screen and howl about America and democracy. There is no America! There is no democracy! There is only IBM, ITT, and AT&T, Dupont, Union Carbide, and Exxon. These are the nations of the world today!

Mr Jensen, Chief Executive Officer, to Howard Beale, Television Anchorman, in *Network* (1976). Script by Paddy Chayevsky.

5.7 Reductions of diversity

Reductionism – whether in science, society, or ideology – has real counterparts in socio-ecological relationships. Every natural ecosystem obviously displays the requisite diversity it needs for long-range survival in its general environment, whether that is the relatively simple ecosystem of the arctic tundra, the more complex and diverse ecosystems of the temperate forests or the coastal shelf, or the highly complex and diverse ecosystems of the coral reef and the tropical rainforest. Requisite diversity provides long-range stability in each ecological context. If undisturbed by natural or human catastrophe, these system-environment relations will last as long as there is life on earth.

The species inhabiting a natural ecosystem maintain a unity of diversity with each other within the general environment. When these complex relationships are disturbed by processes to which the ecosystem is not adapted, such as energy production in permafrost environments, industrial wastes dumped into seas and rivers and lakes, the use of petroleum-based or heavy-metal biocides in agriculture, and 'cut and run' logging in the rainforests, temperate and tropical, the ecosystem becomes unstable.

Instability breaks the unity of diversity between the various populations and communities of species inhabiting the ecosystem. Normal relationships of oscillation between populations may become converted into what cybernetics calls 'hunting': seeking to reach a dimension of stability that can no longer be attained.

Instability makes the ecosystem more likely to be forced into a more simplified state in which there are fewer ecological niches for fewer species. This reduction of ecological structure makes the ecosystem much less ecologically productive. It may not be able to recover from this loss of complexity in the foreseeable future (cf. N. Polunin, ed., *The Environmental Future*, 1972, pp. 33–52, 67–86).

Modern industrial strategies are anti-ecological. They reduce the maturity of ecosystems by destroying the qualitative diversity of their interrelations, as in the destruction of the original habitats of the Great Lakes by industrial wastes and sewage, as in the destruction of other lakes by acid rain resulting from smelting and power production by fossil fuels.

The modern world system has also destroyed the structural diversity of the many distinct social and economic systems that once existed. Historically, first mercantile and then industrial capitalism accomplished this by forcing every other economic system it encountered into a presently irreversible dependence on wage labor, exchange value, cash-cropping, and monoculture. Wage labor makes creative power into a commodity. Single cropping displaces the diversity of locally adapted plant strains with a less diverse array of hybrids. Hybrid monoculture requires huge petrochemical subsidies – insecticides, herbicides, and fertilizer – to protect the crop from its natural environment and force its growth. All of this has to be paid for in hard currency, usually by loans from the banks of the industrialized countries.

Competition in natural ecosystems leads by 'divergent evolution' (new species emerge to divide the available habitat in novel ways) to increasing diversity, complexity, and flexibility in nature. Competition under capitalism has led (by competitive exclusion) to increasing monopoly, simplicity, and rigidity in national and international economic systems.

Hybrid monoculture has lowered the energy conversion efficiencies of agriculture in many parts of the world, while forcing third-world countries into dependence on agricultural technology controlled by the industrialized countries and the multinational corporate states.

In these and other ways, social and economic systems that were once protected by their co-evolved relationships with their environment(s) have been deprived of their co-evolved protections. Third-world economies are 'underdeveloped', not because they are 'backward', but because they have been 'de-developed' by the more powerful industrial nations. They have been made increasingly dependent on a system of commodity relations in which exchange values dominate use values, and (long range) survival value is ignored. The modern economic system has replaced qualitative diversity with quantitative variety. It is homogenizing the diversity and rapidly increasing the entropy of the planet earth.

We may now state Bateson's Rule:

Bateson's Rule: In proportion as the structural diversity of a natural or social ecosystem is reduced, so also is its flexibility to survive future environmental uncertainties. Reductions of diversity deplete the ecosystem's resources of uncommitted potential for future change.

De-diversified systems have available to them fewer and fewer responses to perturbation, whether in quantity or quality. The range of possible outcomes of unexpected events thus becomes centered around drastic, structural change: evolution, revolution, or extinction.

Again drawing on Bateson, we can state the Survival Rule:

The Survival Rule: What survives in nature in the long range is not the fittest individual, organism, population, or species, but the fittest ecosystem: *both* system *and* environment.

Wiener named cybernetics after the Greek for helmsman, and cybernetics also means the art of government. We might venture to draw another conclusion from the principle of requisite diversity in representation and control: the Political Rule.

The Political Rule: In proportion as the diversity of a system of elected representatives is inadequate to represent the diversity of the people it governs, the more likely it is to be tyrannical.

CHAPTER 6

Metaphor and metonymy

A nerve stimulus first translated into an image! First metaphor!

NIETZSCHE: *Truth and Lie in an Extra-Moral Sense* (1873)

6.1 Metaphor and metonymy

A word portrait typical of the Russian novelist, Gleb Ivanovič Uspenskij (1840–1902), runs as follows:

> From underneath an ancient straw cap, with a black spot on its visor, peeked two braids resembling the tusks of a wild boar; a chin, grown fat and pendulous, had spread definitively over the greasy collar of the calico dickey and lay in a thick layer on the coarse collar of the canvas coat, firmly buttoned at the neck. From underneath this coat to the eyes of the observer protruded massive hands with a ring which which had eaten into the fat finger, a cane with a copper top, a significant bulge of the stomach, and the presence of very broad pants, almost of muslim quality, in the wide bottoms of which hid the toes of the boots.

A detailed head-to-toe description – about sixty words from the cap to the collar and about the same from the collar to the boots – but there is simply no one there. The most significant marker of an individual is the face. Babies are more fascinated by faces than by any other visual pattern; we remember faces better than almost any other image. A faceless person is worse off than a stateless person: without a face one has no identity at all.

Every detail in the portrait is contiguous to the hole in the middle of the pattern, the missing identity, either as a part of the body – a spreading chin, massive hands, a fat finger, a protruding stomach – or else as a piece of clothing in contact with head, neck, trunk, feet. The character is all context and no text.

The description itself moves from part to part, from contiguity to contiguity, but never from part to whole.

In the last years of his life Gleb Ivanovič Uspenskij suffered from a psychological illness involving a speech disorder. His first and second names, normally used together in polite conversation in Russian, split into names for two distinct selves. Gleb came to stand for all his virtues. Ivanovič – the name relating the son to the father – came to stand for all his vices.

Naturally one does not know precisely what he suffered from, but difficulties in maintaining the boundaries of one's self-identity in relation to others and a conflict between two imaginary selves would today be called schizophrenia.

Roman Jakobson cites the example of Gleb Ivanovič in his pioneering study of speech disorders, 'Two Aspects of Language and Two Types of Aphasic Disturbances' (1956, 1971, p. 94). The two aspects of language are *selection from the code* and *combination in the message*, the two basic operations in language and communication. The two types of aphasia are 'similarity disorder' and 'contiguity disorder'.

As the following summary explains, selection from the code corresponds to metaphor, where one word or image stands for another word or image; combination in the message corresponds to metonymy, where a word or image of a part is used to stand for a whole.

Gleb Ivanovič's speech disorder corresponds to 'similarity disorder', where selections from the code are impaired but combinations in the message are not (contiguity dominates similarity, metonymy dominates metaphor). In the other type of aphasia, called 'contiguity disorder', combinations in the message are impaired but selections from the code are not (similarity dominates contiguity, metaphor dominates metonymy).

Similarity disorder means the loss of mainly right-brain functions; contiguity disorder means losses mainly for the left brain (Chapter 7).

Selection and combination

We have seen that selection and combination impart structure and meaning to messages whether the repertoire of the code consists of discontinuous forms, like DNA, or of continuous forms, like squash and stretch in animation.

Jakobson's definition of selection and combination in language (and other forms of communication) can be summarized as follows (pp. 74–5):

- In the axis of the code *selection* corresponds to *substitution* and *similarity*, the axis of metaphor.

• In the axis of the message *combination* corresponds to *contexture* and *contiguity*, the axis of metonymy.

(As Norbert Wiener pointed out in *Cybernetics* in 1948 (pp. 127, 133), the principle of similarity and the principle of contiguity are derived most directly from the theory of the association of ideas of John Locke (1632–1704). Locke included a third principle, association by cause and effect, but this was reduced, notably by David Hume (1711–1776), to 'concomitance' or 'occurring together', i.e. to a special case of contiguity.)

(A similar theory was held by Plato, Aristotle, Condillac (from Locke), and Freud, the latter using it to explain relations between conscious and unconscious messages in 1895.)

Figure 6.1 illustrates these relationships, adding also the terms 'condensation' and 'displacement', the two fundamental operations Freud discovered in the construction of dreams, jokes, forgettings, slips of the tongue, and schizophrenic speech.

Beside being the axis of selection, the code is also the axis of *simultaneity* and *synchrony*. (All of its possibilities exist at the same time.) Beside being the axis of combination, the message is also the axis of *succession* and *diachrony*. (Its possibilities exist as a function of their place or order in time.)

Translated into the idiom of music the axis of the code stands for *harmony* (simultaneity); that of the message, for *melody* (succession).

Definitions

A metaphor is the illumination of one part of experience by another. It is a similarity or comparison without an 'as' or 'like', an analogy created by substituting word for word, image for image, or sign for sign. (It is also used to mean any figurative use of words, including metonymy.) A metaphor brings together in a single word or phrase (e.g. the Golden Gate) the image of two or more things or relationships (gold-sunset, gold-heaven, heaven's gate) and out of them creates a third.

Metonymy is the evocation of the whole by a connection. It consists in using for the name of a thing or relationship an attribute, a suggested sense, or something closely related, such as effect for cause, function for structure, the desired for the desire, the abode for the person, and so on, the imputed relationship being that of contiguity.

(Synecdoche, an ugly word, is a more accurate term for the relationship of whole and part. It means to replace the more comprehensive by the less comprehensive (or vice versa), the genus by the species (or vice versa), the whole by a part or the part by a whole, and so on.)

Two kinds of aphasia

Jakobson bases his analysis of aphasia on the extensive work on organic and psychological speech disorders by Kurt Goldstein (1878–1965) beginning in the 1920s, following the huge number of brain injuries and cases of 'shell shock' in World War One.

The two kinds of aphasia are:

- *Similarity disorder*: Here combination and contexture in the message are dominant; selection and substitution are deficient ('coding disorder'). Metonymy is dominant over metaphor.
- *Contiguity disorder*: Here selection and substitution from the code are dominant; combination and contexture are deficient ('message disorder'). Metaphor is dominant over metonymy.

(The terms 'coding disorder' and 'message disorder' are mine.)

Neither of the disorders entirely excludes the use of the other aspect of language. As in ordinary language the relationship between selection and combination in the two disorders is not 'either/or', nor is it 'all-or-none'. It is rather that the one aspect comes to dominate the other to a greater or lesser extent, depending on the seriousness of the illness or injury, and depending on changes in the speech disorder over time.

In severe cases of either disorder the patient loses control over the use of sound, sense, and syntax in precisely the reverse order from that in which children learn to speak.

> I'm an in divide you all.
> Julie in: R. D. LAING: *The Divided Self* (1960)

Similarity disorder

In similarity or coding disorder the context of the message is the decisive factor. Presented with scraps of words or sentences, the patient readily completes them; he or she easily carries on a conversation, but has difficulty starting a dialogue. The sentence 'it rains' cannot be pronounced unless the person sees it raining. The deeper an utterance is embedded in the verbal and non-verbal context, and the deeper a word is embedded in the context of the word order of the message itself, the higher the chances that the person will be able to use it successfully (p. 77).

The result is that in similarity or coding disorder words subordinated to other words in the sentence; words governed by grammatical agreement; and words like pronouns, adverbs, connectives, and so forth, with inherent reference to the context of the message, are the most likely to survive.

The main subordinating agent in the sentence, the subject, however, is most likely to be lost; the patient then finds great difficulty in starting a sentence, unless it happens to be a sequel to a previous sentence.

Patients with similarity or coding disorder tend to use context-bound words specific to their situation. Thus one patient of Goldstein's never uttered the general term *knife* alone, but, depending on its use and surroundings, called the knife *pencil-sharpener*, *bread-knife*, *knife-and-fork*, and so on, using a contextualized and particular equivalent of the general word designating the class of all knives (a switch in logical typing).

Similarly, the person may be able to use the word *bachelor* as it might occur in *bachelor apartments*, but be quite unable to define it or substitute for it the synonym *unmarried person*, which would involve making an equivalence between similar meanings in the code (p. 79). In similarity disorder *fork* may be used for *knife*, *table* for *lamp*, *smoke* for *pipe*, *eat* for *toaster* (p. 83).

Bilingual sufferers from similarity or coding disorder will lose the capacity to translate from code to code between languages: they will have lost the capacity for 'code-switching'.

In an even more significant difficulty with coding and substitution, the patient will not be able to name an object held up by the doctor, say a pencil, but will make a remark about its use or connections instead, such as 'for writing',. The same problem occurs with pictures. Coding or similarity disorder prevents the name from being selected from the code to label the thing or the visual representation of the thing. This is a problem with metalanguage (p. 80), as explained below.

Even simple repetition of words used by the doctor may be rejected by the patient. Told to repeat the word 'no', one patient replied 'No, I don't know how to do it'. He could use the word spontaneously in the context of his answer, but he could not produce the simplest form of similarity: '$a = a$': 'no' is 'no' (p. 81).

Other subjects will end up with an increasingly personal language pattern, not recognizing the messages of others. 'I can hear you dead plain', said one patient, 'but I cannot get what you say . . . I can hear your voice but not your words . . . It does not pronounce itself' (p. 82).

Goldstein said of patients with what Jakobson called similarity disorder that they 'grasped the words in their literal meaning but could not be brought to understand the metaphoric character of the same words'. (By 'metaphor' he means 'figure of speech'.) It is not implied that the subjects concerned are unable to use figurative language, but that they interpret it in their own way.

This loss of 'the capacity of naming' in similarity disorder, says Jakobson, is a loss of the capacity to use metalanguage (language about language). Using metalanguage is a normal and everyday event: When we say to someone 'Do you follow me?' or 'What do you mean?', we are using one level of language to check whether we are both using the same code of understandings at another level (pp. 81–2).

Interpreting one word by another is a use of metalanguage essential to children's language learning – and pre-school children spend a lot of their time talking about talking.

(Learning language depends on the pre-existing, but unconscious understanding of metalanguage. The simplistic idea that we learn language by naming objects pointed to fails to recognize the child's mastery of the grammar of levels of language that makes naming possible in the first place. We do not learn words first and grammar later. Our very first word is already a grammar.)

Naming objects pointed to is a reference to the code of English, and thus a statement in a metalanguage about the language of that code. Says Jakobson: Naming is the equivalent of saying: 'In the language code we use, the object you are holding is a pencil.'

Comment

The problem mentioned by Goldstein concerning the literal and the figurative is similar to a choice of language patterns often made by subjects in schizophrenia and psychosis: The subject confuses the representation (*Vorstellung*) of the word with the representation of the thing (*Sach*) (Freud); or confuses the Symbolic with the Real (Jacques Lacan); or the metaphor with what is meant (Bateson: by 'metaphor' he means 'figure of speech').

These are confusions between levels of language, between communication and reality, and between logical types.

Speaking in 1939, in a conference attended by Harry Stack Sullivan and published in 1944 as *Language and Thought in Schizophrenia*, edited by J. S. Kasanin (and not cited by Jakobson), Goldstein referred to a patient who called a bird 'le song', the summer 'le warm', the cellar 'le spider', and the physician 'le dance' (because 'during rounds the physicians dance round the professor') – surely a description of similarity disorder – and went on to describe this as metonymy, but without using the term:

A word when used by a schizophrenic appears as part of an object or a situation, not as representative of it, in the same way as it is used by some patients with irreversible organic diseases (pp. 26–7).

axis of the code
selection and substitution
similarity
langue (language)
simultaneity and synchrony
paradigmatic
metaphor
condensation
harmony

axis of the message
combination and contexture
contiguity
parole (speech)
succession and diachrony
syntagmatic
metonymy
displacement
melody

FIGURE 6.1: Metaphor and metonymy, or selection and combination: the two basic axes of language and communication ('axis' in the sense of the axis of a graph). Each sign communicated is interpreted by reference both to the code (the dictionary meanings of 'rules', for example) and to the message (the meaning of 'rules' in a given sentence). ('Context' for Jakobson refers to the context of the message.) The terms listed with each axis are not lists of synonyms, but one of a pair of terms between which the relationships are similar to those between code and message, similarity and contiguity, metaphor and metonymy, and so on. The two axes of this diagram are the same as those of the code/message triangle of mediation in Figure 4.5, but here the environment and the communicators mediated by the code are left out. 'Condensation' (*Verdichtung*) and 'displacement' (*Verschiebung*) are the two basic processes of dream and joke formation according to Freud. Jakobson cites Freud on this topic later in the monograph.

Goldstein calls this 'concrete thinking', not accepting the terms 'symbolic' or 'metaphoric', but points out that the 'average person' may well make the same kind of connections. It is characteristic of the 'impairment of the abstract attitude' that 'the subject is not able to give himself an account of what he is doing' (p. 29) (cf. Jakobson's remarks on metalanguage).

The same impairment of the 'abstract attitude', in both organic diseases and schizophrenia,

> disturbs the normal discrimination between the essential and the unessential in the given situation, between figure and ground (p. 32).

Goldstein adds that Norman Cameron had observed the striking inability of schizophrenic patients 'to maintain adequate boundaries'. Furthermore:

> Owing to this deficient figure-ground formation, objects or situations which can be grasped as concrete objects come abnormally into the foreground . . .

Many illusions and delusions of schizophrenics originate in this way, he says, as a result of the 'vagueness of the boundaries' between figure and ground. The further result is:

> the inversion, that is, the coming into the foreground of the ground instead of the figure, and the sudden and nearly permanent fluctuation between figure and ground (p. 33)

The 'schizophrenic' oscillation between levels of perception (figure and ground) noted in this passage – found again by accident fifteen years after I first read it – normally occurs only with paradoxical figures where the eye and brain cannot decide between figure and ground for normal physiological reasons.

Goldstein's use of the word 'inversion' (rather than 'reversal') to describe the oscillation between figure and ground – the Dutch artist M. C. Escher follows the same usage – indicates that he sees it as an oscillation between levels.

The most common oscillations found in nature are the sine waves (or combinations thereof) produced by what is called 'simple harmonic motion' – as with the oscillations of a pendulum, an ocean wave, a radio signal, alternating current, atoms, and the quartz crystals used in electronic watches. These are *matter-energy oscillations* produced by forces. In society the most common oscillations are cybernetic, and may also be paradoxical, or pathological. These are *semiotic oscillations* constrained by information. They include certain ritual cycles, the long- and short-term business cycles, paradoxical oscillations in logic, oscillations between figure and ground in paradoxical figures, and pathological oscillations resulting from double binds in schizophrenic relations (Bateson et al. 1956; Bateson 1972). These semiotic oscillations are analyzed in detail in *Man and Woman, War and Peace: The Strategist's Companion.*

> What is the characteristic of all *literary decadence*? It is that life no longer resides in the whole. The word gets the upper hand and jumps out of the sentence, the sentence stretches too far and obscures the meaning of the page, the page acquires life at the expense of the whole – the whole is no longer a whole; it is composite, summed up, artificial, an unnatural product.
>
> FRIEDRICH NIETZSCHE: *The Case of Wagner* (1888). Quoted by Sergei Eisenstein in *The Film Sense* (1942, 1947)

Contiguity disorder

From 1864 onwards, says Jakobson, it was repeatedly pointed out by the neurologist John Hughlings Jackson (1835–1911) that:

> It is not enough to say that speech consists of words. It consists of words referring to one another in a particular manner. . . . Loss of speech is the loss of the power to propositionize. . . .
> Speechlessness does not mean entire wordlessness (p. 85).

Impairment of the ability to use syntax to construct propositions, or, generally speaking, to combine simpler linguistic forms into more complex ones is typical of the second type of aphasia, contiguity or message disorder.

Contiguity disorder is context deficient. The item conserved in this type of disorder is typically the word selected from the code; the items lost from the message are precisely the contextual, contiguous, grammatical, prepositional, adverbial, joining, and other words that are retained in the similarity or coding disorder (p. 85).

In contiguity or message disorder the extent and diversity of sentences are reduced. Relations of grammatical co-ordination and subordination, agreement and government, are dissolved. The rules of syntax governing the construction of messages are lost. The result is a 'word heap', as Jackson called it, where word order becomes chaotic. The subject speaks in 'telegraphic style'. The more a word depends grammatically on its context in the message the less likely it is to be retained.

But while combination and contexture disintegrate, selection and substitution continue. 'To say what a thing is', said Jackson, 'is to say what it is like.' The patient with contiguity disorder deals with similarities: thus she or he chooses metaphoric selections from the code rather than the metonymic combinations of similarity disorder. *Spyglass* for *microscope*, or *fire* for *gaslight* are typical expressions (p. 86).

In contiguity disorder words lose their endings, inflections, plurals, markers of tense, and so on. Derivations of words from the same root, such as *employ* – *employer* – *employee*, related in their meaning by contiguity, are dropped. Even relations between two words may become irresolvable. Patients who were able to understand and utter such compounds as *Thanksgiving* or *Battersea*, understood as a single word, but unable to say or grasp *thanks* and *giving*, or *batter* and *sea*, as separate words, have often been cited (p. 87).

In contiguity or message disorder the aphasic becomes unable to resolve words into their constituent phonemes, with the result that she or he loses control over word construction. A French aphasic recognized, understood repeated, and spontaneously produced the words *café* 'coffee' and *pavé* 'roadway', but was unable to grasp, discern, or repeat nonsensical combinations of the same phonemes, such as *pafé* or *kéfa*, permitted by the sound structure of French.

Vocabulary weakens and disappears; the last residues of speech in contiguity or message disorder are one-phoneme, one-word, one-sentence utterances. The patient may finally lose all power to use or understand speech.

The person with contiguity disorder who loses control over combination and contexture in the message further tends to abolish the hierarchy of linguistic units in the sentence, and thus to reduce them all to a single level, abolishing syntax in the process (p. 89).

One notes that like the loss of control over metalanguage, the loss of the capacity to metacommunicate, and the confusion of levels between figure and ground in similarity disorder, the loss of grammatical levels in contiguity disorder is a confusion of logical types – or, as explained in the next chapter, an imaginary 'symmetrization' of levels in a real hierarchy.

The metaphoric way and the metonymic way

These relations between metaphor and metonymy are not confined to aphasia. Of Freud Jackobson says (p. 95): In an enquiry into the structure of dreams,

> the decisive question is whether the symbols and the temporal
> sequences used are based on contiguity (Freud's metonymic
> 'displacement' and synecdochic 'condensation') or on similarity
> (Freud's 'identification and symbolism').

Jacques Lacan read Jakobson in the 1950s. He replaced Jakobson's reading by one that identified the two major processes in dreams and jokes, condensation and displacement, with metaphor and metonymy respectively (cf. Lacan and Wilden, 1981).

All of us, says Jackobson, in ordinary speech and writing, tend to favor one orientation, the 'metaphoric way' or the 'metonymic way', over the other:

> Both processes are continually operative, but careful observation will reveal that under the influence of a cultural pattern, personality, and verbal style, preference is given to one of the two processes over the other (p. 91).

In using these two kinds of relationship (similarity and contiguity) in both of their aspects (positional [syntactic] and semantic) individuals exhibit their personal style and preferences.

Similarity in meaning connects the symbols of a metalanguage with the symbols of the language referred to. Similarity connects a metaphorical term with the term for which it is substituted. Consequently, when constructing a metalanguage to interpret tropes [figures of speech], the researcher possesses more homogeneous means to handle metaphor, whereas metonymy, based on a different principle, easily defies interpretation. Therefore nothing comparable to the rich literature on metaphor can be cited for the theory of metonymy. For the same reason, it is generally realized that romanticism is closely linked with metaphor, whereas the equally intimate ties of realism with metonymy usually remain unnoticed. Not only the tool of the observer but also the object of observation is responsible for the preponderance of metaphor over metonymy in scholarship. Since poetry is focused upon the sign, and pragmatical prose primarily upon the referent, tropes and figures were studied mainly as poetic devices. The principle of similarity underlies poetry; the metrical parallelism of lines, or the phonic equivalence of rhyming words prompts the question of semantic similarity and contrast; there exist, for instance, grammatical and anti-grammatical but never agrammatical rhymes. Prose, on the contrary, is forwarded essentially by contiguity. Thus for poetry, metaphor, and for prose, metonymy is the line of least resistance and, consequently, the study of poetical tropes is directed chiefly toward metaphor. The actual bipolarity has been artificially replaced in these studies by an amputated, unipolar scheme which, strikingly enough, coincides with one of the two aphasic patterns, namely with the contiguity disorder (pp. 95–6).

Preferences for the 'metaphoric way' or the 'metonymic way', or oscillations between them, are not confined to verbal art. Cubism in painting, with its many-sided figures, is clearly metonymic, Jakobson points out; the surrealists responded with a metaphoric attitude (cf. Figure 6.2). Moreover:

> Ever since the productions of D. W. Griffith, the art of the cinema, with its highly developed capacity for changing the angle,

perspective, and focus of 'shots', has broken with the tradition of the theater and ranged an unprecedented variety of synecdochic 'close-ups' and metonymic 'set-ups' in general.

In the early cinema, before Griffith made the close-up part of his cinematic syntax – he first used it to save money on actors – and before literacy in the silent film became the common link of every audience, no matter what their language, the close-up was declared unacceptable on the grounds that no one would believe it, since the rest of the actor was missing.

A 'set-up' is the arrangement of the scenery, props, performers, lights, and so on for a particular shot. A 'metonymic set-up' would include such shots as a house standing for a family, or a shot of a drunken black man standing for all black men, as in Griffith's masterful combination of cinema and intolerance, *Birth of a Nation* (1915).

Jakobson continues:

In such motion pictures as those of Charlie Chaplin and Eisenstein, these devices in turn were overlayed by a novel, metaphoric 'montage' with its 'lap dissolves' – the filmic similes.

He refers us to an article of 1944 by Sergei Eisenstein (1898–1948), in which Eisenstein explains at length how David Wark Griffith learned the technique of 'parallel montage' (intercutting between parallel action, as in chases) from reading Charles Dickens. The article, 'Dickens, Griffith, and the Film Today', appears in Eisenstein's *Film Form*, published in English in 1949.

Among all creatures, the *Head* is preferred above all other parts, both of Man and Beast; in Man, because it is the seat of the intellectual soul, and is the emblem of Sovereign jurisdiction, the Head being the Hieroglyphick of the beginning.

W. SLOANE SLOANE-EVANS: *The Art of Blazon* (1847)

6.2 The verbal image

The following passage from *Jerusalem* (1804) by the poet, artist, mystic, and democrat William Blake (1757–1827), who engraved it in his own handwriting, is an example of an almost perfect concord between the metaphoric and the metonymic ways, whether in sound, sight, or sense. The metaphors build the building by metonymy – part by part – before one's eyes.

What are those golden builders doing? . . .
  . . . is that Calvary and Golgotha?
Becoming a building of pit and compassion? Lo!
The stones are pity, and the bricks well wrought affections:
Enameld with love & kindness, & the tiles engraven gold
Labour of merciful hands: the beams and rafters are forgiveness:
The mortar & cement of the work, tears of honesty: the nails,
And the screws & iron braces, are well wrought blandishments,
And well contrived words, firm fixing, never forgotten,
Always comforting the remembrance: the floors, humility,
The ceilings, devotion: the hearths, thanksgiving.

In the next passage, metaphor and metonymy begin in conflict, with metonyms dominant, break apart at 'cruel works', but end in the unity of an ideal whole. Bacon, Newton, Locke, and the schools and universities of Europe stand as parts for the whole of the new ideology and system of values of early industrial capitalism, as well as for the power of science through technology. The looms, works, and wheels outside wheels stand as parts for the whole way of life being forced on the laboring poor:

For Bacon & Newton sheathd in dismal steel, their terrors hang
Like giant scourges over Albion, Reasonings like vast Serpents
Infold around my limbs, bruising my minute articulations

I turn my eyes to the Schools & Universities of Europe
And there behold the Loom of Locke whose Woof rages dire
Washd by the Water-wheels of Newton. black the cloth
In heavy wreathes folds over every Nation; cruel Works
Of many Wheels I view, wheel without wheel, with cogs tyrannic
Moving by compulsion each other: not as those in Eden: which
Wheel within Wheel in freedom revolve in harmony & peace.

The role of melody in music is precisely that of drawing in a painting.

JEAN-JACQUES ROUSSEAU: *Essay on the Origins of Languages* (1749–55)

6.3 The art of blazon

Heraldry or 'blazonning' ('to mark a shield with signs') is a system of visual metaphor and metonymy. Blazons were one of the earliest means of identifying warriors in the field. Heraldry, the 'armorie of honor', developed into a specialized way of displaying, asserting, and advertising the identity of the bearer of arms — by definition a member of the nobility.

By the seventeenth century this medium of personal and public communication had become a complex system of visual symbols and written mottoes, complete with a visual syntax and semantics, and a highly technical Anglo-French jargon to describe the results.

Armorial insignia were not simply products of the vanity, aggressivity, and high living of the feudal lords, for they had political, economic, and social functions as well. Coats of arms defined and permanently recorded kinship relations, dynastic and family histories and alliances, deeds of valor and posts of honor, claims to sovereignty over peoples and ownership of territory, and the minutest distinctions in status between members of the national aristocracies and royal families of Europe.

The pragmatic task of the herald — originally a messenger of peace and war between kings and of courtesy or defiance between knights, as well as a master of ceremonies at trials by battle, tournaments, and public ceremonies generally — was to display in unmistakable visual images the armsbearers' real and imaginary virtues, notably their good sense, intelligence, and discretion; their sense of justice, righteousness, and compassion; their firmness, strength and courage; and their sense of moderation (*prudentia, justitia, fortitudo, temperentia*).

The selection and combination of visual metaphors and metonymies in heraldry includes metals, furs, colors, textures, shadings, hatchings, chevrons, stripes, lozenges, checks, tiles, lattices, quarters, bends, bars, piles, crescents, crosses, circles, squares, triangles, curves, letters, numbers, trees, flowers, fields, mountains, lakes, legs, arms, heads, virtues, gems, the zodiac, earth, air, fire, and water, animals, persons, and supernatural beings, suns, moons, and constellations, arms, armor, tools, ships, and other machines, keys, cups, bells, and musical instruments, crowns, caps, and coronets, manors, fords, bridges, castles, towers, pillars, and many other things.

The shield — with the crests, helmets, wreaths, coronets, mantles, supporters, scrolls, and mottoes around it — is the frame constraining the articulation of the heraldic messages. Within these constraints the 'field' of the shield is divided into a hierarchy of nine or eleven 'points' (Figure 6.3), modeled on the human body, which punctuate — from medieval Latin, *punctuare*, to 'prick, point, appoint' — the partitioning of the field and the placing of its 'charges' (anything occupying the field) (Figure 6.4).

The images of heraldry are also constrained by the code of the 'tinctures': the two metals — or (gold) and argent (silver) — the five colors — azure (blue), gules (red), sable (black), vert (green), and purpure (purple) — and the several kinds of fur.

In combining selections on the field great attention is paid to figure-

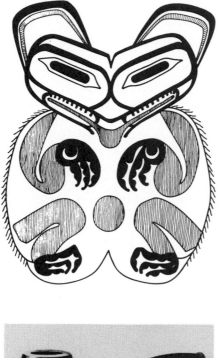

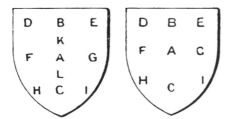

FIGURE 6.2: Artforms: (a) A bear as seen in the art of the Tsimshian Indians on the Pacific Coast of British Columbia. This is a 'split-style' and largely metonymic perspective (contiguity) common in non-western art and in the drawings of children of all cultures, even where adults openly disapprove (Deregowski, 1972). (b) 'This is not a pipe': A paradoxical metaphor playing on levels of communication and reality: *La Trahison des images* (*The Treachery of Images*), oil painting by the Belgian surrealist René Magritte (1898–1967), done in 1928 or 1929. The image is a report, a command, and question about itself, and thus self-referring, creating the oscillation of a double bind (a paradoxical injunction like 'Do not read this'). See pp. iv, 210, 244. (Double binds are analyzed in detail in *Man and Women, War and Peace*, 1987.)

FIGURE 6.3: The surface or 'field' of the heraldic escutcheon is punctuated by nine, and sometimes eleven, points. A, the 'fess point', represents the heart; D, B, E, the 'chief points', represent the head; F and G are the 'flank points'; K is the 'honor point'; and L is the 'nombril point' or navel.

ground relations. Shadings are often added to charges to provide depth, and outlines are used to separate charges from background. There are of course exceptions, but as a general rule metal is not to be placed on metal, nor color upon color. Since fur is regarded as a 'mixed tincture' (both metal and color) it may be used on both, though generally on certain colors only, attention being paid to its distinction from the ground. Within these constraints, other rules of descending generality govern the selection and combination of other visual images; a separate code of rules governs the jargon of the verbal description.

'Nothing is more certain', say Woodward and Burnett in their *Treatise on Heraldry* of 1892, 'than that by far the larger number of the arms assumed in early times were phonetic in character – *armes parlantes* – allusive to the name, title, or office of the bearer' (p. 671). These are called in English 'canting arms', cant being another term for jargon, and in his *New Science* (1725) the philosopher Giambattista Vico (1668–1744) – who influenced Rousseau in the latter's insistence that when humans first began to speak they spoke a poetic and thus metaphoric tongue – based his notion of the origins of language and letters on the origins of 'family arms', along with hieroglyphics, laws, names, medals, and money.

Woodward continues:

Some of the allusions may seem to us very far-fetched, but a pun was dear to the medieval mind (p. 672).

Everything in art or nature that could give birth to a double meaning was put to use (Figure 6.5):

I have engraved on Plate XXXVII., fig. 3, from EYSENBACH, a seal which, though not armorial, is an excellent instance of the taste of the time. It is that of *Gui de Munois*, monk of St. Germain l'Auxerrois. The cowled ape in the sky, scratching its back with its hand, was a hieroglyphic in which all might read: *Singe-air-main-dos-serre*, – Saint Germain d'Auxerre!

This is a picture puzzle such as one sees on the children's page in the newspaper, called a rebus, where images stand for sounds. Letters may also be used, as in this English one: 'If B mt put more: if the B.': 'If the grate be empty put more coal on if the grate be full stop'.

In the monk's seal the names of the parts of the picture (metaphors) are condensed to the level of sounds and combined by displacement (metonymy) from one to the other into a sentence in which the pictorial elements are irrelevant compared with their phonetic expression.

Like a good many jokes, all puns, and most dreams picture puzzles

1   2   3   4

5   6   7   8

9   10   11   12

13   14   15   16

17   18   19   20

like the rebus cannot be successfully translated into another language. In the example cited, translation gives: 'Ape-air-hand-back-scratch'.

Oh, God, not Blagoveshchensk!

HAROLD GATTY, Navigator, on sighting the mud at Edmonton Airport after the flight across Siberia: Wiley Post and Harold Gatty: *Around the World in Eight Days: The Flight of the Winnie Mae* (1931)

FIGURE 6.4: Some of the 'chimerical charges' of heraldry, all of great antiquity, taken from 'The Art of Blazon' in the *Grammar of British Heraldry, With an Introduction on the Rise and Progress of Symbols and Ensigns*, published in 1847 by The Reverend W. Sloane Sloane-Evans, K.C.T., B.A. of Trinity College, Cambridge, Curate of Cornworth, Devon, and Hon. Sec. of the Exeter Diocese Architectural Society, etc. In sequence: (1) a centaur; (2) a cockatrice (a dragon with the head of a cock); (3) a dragon; (4) a griffin (part eagle and part lion); (5) a male-griffin (with body spikes in place of wings); (6) a harpy (a monster with a woman's face and body and a bird's wings and claws); (7) a heraldick-antelope; (8) a heraldick-tiger; (9) a lion-poisson (lion-fish); (10) a merman (always bearing a trident); (11) a mermaid (always with comb and mirror); (12) Pegasus, the flying horse; (13) a phoenix (a half-body of an eagle issuing out of flames of fire); (14) a salamander; (15) a satyral (a lion with the horns and tail of an antelope and the face of an old man); (16) a sea-dog; (17) a sea-horse; (18) a sphinx (in Greece usually a winged lion with a woman's head, in Egypt a wingless body with a male head); (19) a unicorn (part lion, part horse, with horn); and (20) a wyvern or sea-dragon (a winged dragon with the feet of an eagle and the tail, barbed, of a serpent). The unicorn is said to symbolize strength of body, virtue of mind, and extreme courage. The dragon is the emblem of vigilancy, as is the griffin, which also displays eagerness in pursuit. The winged horse may represent 'exceeding activity and energy of mind, whereby we may mount to honor'. The mermaid is the symbol of eloquence. The harpy 'should be given to such as have committed manslaughter' so that 'they might be moved to bewail the foulness of their offence'. This mythological stereotype is described in the *Oxford English Dictionary* as 'a fabulous monster, rapacious and filthy, having a woman's face and body and a bird's wings and claws, and supposed to act as a minister of divine vengeance'.

6.4 Condensation and displacement

In Chapter 6 of *The Interpretation of Dreams* (1900), Freud says:

> The dream-content seems like a transfer or translation
> [*Übertragung*] of the dream-thoughts into another mode of
> expression, whose signs [*Zeichen*] and syntactic laws it is our
> business to discover.

The dream-content is expressed 'as it were in a hieroglyphic or picto-
graphic script [*Bilderschrift*]'.

> If we attempted to read these signs according to their pictorial
> value, instead of according to their sign-relationship, we should
> clearly be led into error . . . I have a picture-puzzle, a rebus, in
> front of me . . . [Its solution requires us] to try to replace each
> image [*Bild*] by a syllable or word that can be represented by that
> image in some way or other. The words that are put together in
> this way are no longer nonsensical . . .

In the picture puzzle, writing, images, and speech come together, and
the sound is the essential vehicle of the sense (see Figure 6.5).

> A dream is a picture-puzzle of this sort, and our predecessors in
> the field of dream-interpretation have made the mistake of treating
> the rebus as a pictorial composition: and as such it has seemed to
> them nonsensical and worthless.

For Freud the visual icons appearing in dreams are the result of the
translation of conscious and unconscious thoughts into images. Dreams
are imaginary representations of real wishes or desires. In his first
theory of dream symbolism, Freud insists that it is the spoken text
recounting the dream that must be interpreted, not the visual images
as images (and that it is the dreamer, not the analyst, who must do
the interpreting). The dream-text will reveal the desire of the dreamer
through its use of sound and sense.

One example Freud gives is the account by Artemidorus (second
century CE) of Alexander the Great's dream when he laid siege to King
Azemilcus and the citizens of Tyre, in what is now southern Lebanon,
in 322 BCE.

Alexander was uneasy and disturbed because his seven-month siege
with 250 ships and floating batteries attacking from seaward was going
badly. Tyre had walls 160 feet high and the most advanced defenses
of the day. The display of clever tricks, mechanical arts, new inventions,
and technical improvements by the Macedonian and Tyrian technicians

FAMILI ÄR
MILIONÄR
FAMILIONÄR

'R. treated me quite *familiär,*
that is, so far as a *Millionär* can.'

'R. treated me quite *famili* on *är.*

(*mili*)   (*är*)

FIGURE 6.5: Freud's graphic analysis of a 'condensation joke'.

and military engineers far exceeded anything either side had ever tried
before.

In the midst of this Alexander dreamed of a satyr dancing on his
shield. His soothsayer interpreted this, correctly, says Freud, as the
Greek words *sa tyros*, signifying 'Tyre will be thine'.

Alexander had his wish. He decided to change Tyre from an island
into a peninsula, building a causeway 2000 feet out from the mainland
to the city walls (it still exists). In the meantime the Tyrians had
overplayed their hand, showing contempt for Alexander by torturing
and executing prisoners in full view of the general and his men. When
he captured the city Alexander put 10,000 of its citizens to the sword,
and sold 30,000 into slavery. Just what happened to the Tyrian women
and children is not recorded.

The word 'satyr' is a condensation (similarity, substitution, metaphor); the visual image of the satyr is a displacement or diversion of
the wish (contiguity, context, metonymy).

In Lacan's interpretation of condensation and displacement already
referred to, condensation and metaphor are considered as equivalent to
the psychoanalytical symptom (the satyr is the symptom of Alexander's
anxiety); displacement and metonymy are considered as equivalent to
desire (the *sa tyros* is the message of Alexander's desire).

The connection with desire is implicit in the fact that for Freud
displacement also means the displacement (or diversion) of 'psychic
energy' or 'affect' – one would now say meaning – from the real center
of interest in the original dream thoughts to something as far removed
as possible, usually 'something small', in the dream text.

The following is a 'condensation joke' involving a play upon words,
analyzed by Freud at the beginning of *Jokes and the Unconscious*
(1905). One of Heinrich Heine's characters meets Baron Rothschild:
'The Baron', he says, 'treated me quite famillionairely [*familionär*]'.
Freud labels the joke a 'condensation accompanied by the formation
of a substitute' (similarity, metaphor); he depicts the condensation of
'familiar' and 'millionaire' into a 'composite word' as shown in Figure
6.6.

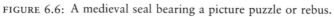

FIGURE 6.6: A medieval seal bearing a picture puzzle or rebus.

'Displacement jokes' are much less common. In this respect jokes differ from dreams, not only in being linguistic rather than imagistic, but also by the fact that although dreams favor condensation (similarity) above all, displacement (contiguity) is usually always associated with it.

The following is a displacement joke – and characteristically self-mocking:

Two Jews met in the neighborhood of the bathhouse. 'Have you taken a bath?' asked one of them. 'What?' asked the other in return, 'is there one missing?'

Freud explains the displacement is as follows:

The first Jew asks 'Have you taken a *bath*?' The second replies as though the question had been: 'Have you *taken* a bath?'

Unlike the condensation joke, which is a play on words, the displacement joke is a play on ideas. The train of thought is diverted or displaced so that the two sentences have different centers of meaning, the one emphasizing 'bath', the other, 'take'. The emphasis shifts by contiguity in the sentence, changing the effective context of the central term in each case, and making a part ('bath' or 'take') serve for the whole idea ('take a bath').

The interplay of displacement and meaning can be fully appreciated in Yiddish intonation. In *Hooray for Yiddish* Leo Rosten gives the following examples:

1

Q. Did you send your mother flowers on her birthday?
A. *Did* I send my mother flowers on her birthday? (Meaning 'Are you implying that I could forget an important occasion like that?')

2

Q. Did you send your mother flowers on her birthday?
A. Did *I* send my mother flowers on her birthday? (Meaning: 'What kind of monster do you think I am – not to send my mother flowers on her birthday?')

3

Q. Did you send your mother flowers on her birthday?
A. Did I *send* my mother flowers on her birthday? (Meaning: And suppose I didn't send them? Suppose I brought them in person? Is that a crime?)

4

Q. Did you send your mother flowers on her birthday?
A. Did I send *my* mother flowers on her birthday? (Meaning: 'Have

you forgotten that I sent *your* mother flowers on her birthday? If I sent flowers to your mother would I forget to send flowers to mine?')

5

Q. Did you send your mother flowers on her birthday?
A. Did I send my *mother* flowers on her birthday? (Meaning: 'You know that I always send flowers on their birthdays to my wife, my sister, my aunt, my cousins in New Jersey, so are you implying that I am the kind of *paskudnyak* who would send flowers to them and not to my own *mother*?')

6

Q. Did you send your mother flowers on her birthday?
A. Did I send my mother *flowers* on her birthday? (Meaning: flowers were just the *beginning* of what I gave my mother on her birthday!' Which suggests anything from a round-trip ticket to Israel to a condominium in West Palm Beach.)

7

Q. Did you send your mother flowers on her birthday?
A. Did you send your mother flowers on *her* birthday? Meaning 'If I always send my mother flowers on *my* birthday, what kind of *grubyan* would I be not to send her flowers on hers?')

8

Q. Did you send your mother flowers on her birthday?
A. Did I send my mother flowers on her *birthday*? (Meaning 'Flowers you don't have to send your mother on New Year's or the Fourth of July – but on her *birthday*?')

There are many other processes by which the dream work hides (and yet still expresses) the dream thoughts. (The best general summary is 'On Dreams', written in 1901; the most important later developments can be found in 'Repression', 'The Unconscious', and 'A Metapsychological Supplement to the Theory of Dreams', all dating from 1915; see also Lacan and Wilden, 1968; Wilden, 1980b.)

The other processes of the dream work include: indirect representation in general, the transformation of objects or persons (hiding identity, locality, importance, and often cause and effect), reversal or representation by the opposite, chronological reversal, contradiction or opposition represented by identification or substitution, the reproduction of logical connection by simultaneity or approximation in time and space, the representation of causal relations (often also reversed) by two or more separate dreams or two-part dreams, the construction of composite persons, composite ideas, and composite structures (the latter being the product of condensation and displacement when combined at the same time), the representation of opposites or contraries by composite structures, the use of the form of the dream to represent its subject matter (vagueness representing doubt, gaps in dreams representing real gaps), and the representation of contradiction or opposition by the inability to act or do something (the latter being the closest dreams can come to representing 'not').

As distinct from jokes, slips of the tongue, and schizophrenic speech, the dreamwork is not a language. Dreams thus have no way of expressing logical relations such as 'if . . . then', 'because', 'either/or', or any of the other linguistic conjunctions. In this logical and grammatical sense they suffer from contiguity disorder, favoring metaphor over metonymy.

The importance of Freud's work on jokes and dreams does not simply lie on the analyst's couch, nor only in the literary and artistic studies to which it is most commonly implied. Along with his analysis of repression, denial (unconscious contradiction), disavowal, rejection, and the maintenance of completely contradictory conscious attitudes on the same subject at the same time, his work on dreams and jokes is an analysis of the structures and processes involved in the verbal and non-verbal articulation of the dominant ideology of our society (and in that of others, no doubt), a subject I shall return to in a later work.

As the limestone of the continent consists of infinite masses of the shells of animalcules, so language is made up of images, or tropes, which now, in their secondary use, have long ceased to remind us of their poetic origin.

RALPH WALDO EMERSON: 'The Poet' in: *Essays* (1844). Quoted by Sergei Eisenstein in *Film Form* (1949)

6.5 Emblems

The heralds depict the codes and sub-codes of the rules of heraldry and the different parts of its 'repertoire' or 'lexicon' as a hierarchy of categories, classed according to their relative level of logical typing in the system, like a linguistic grammar. But heraldry, like dreams, is not a language, and both lack essentially the same logical and grammatical categories.

There are just four 'General Rules of Blazon' governing heraldic description. They are listed by Sloane-Evans in his *Grammar of British Heraldry* (1847, p. 25). One notes that they apply to any art or science whatever:

- The more compendious your description, by so much is it esteemed the more commendable.
- Shun a multiplicity of words.

FIGURE 6.7: The crest chosen by Sir John Hawkins (1532–95), chief architect of the Elizabethan fleet that faced the Spanish Armada in 1588 and the first English slave trader. Backed on his second expedition (1564–5) by a wealthy syndicate that included Queen Elizabeth, he was the originator of the fabulously profitable 'triangular trade' across the Atlantic. The English slavers bartered trade goods for human beings in West Africa, carried their cargo of slaves to the West Indies, traded for tobacco and sugar, carried sugar and other goods to England, where they paid off their backers and refitted, then took on another cargo of trade goods to be exchanged for a new cargo of slaves on their return to West Africa. Reprinted from *Patterns of Racism* (1982).

- Take care, lest in your endeavours to be compendious you omit something material or necessary to be expressed. 'So muste Blazonners blaze, as brieflye as may be, but with this care, that no different matter be omitted.'
- Let your selection of words be clear, and without repetition.

The heraldic signs form a dictionary of conventionalized visual symbols, visual icons. Here are some of the meanings attributed to the parts of the body in the heraldic code (Sloane-Evans, 1847, pp. 105–8):

By the Head is signified Honour; by the Heart, Magnaminity; by the Eye, Sincerity; by the Hand, Friendship and Fidelity; by the Right Hand, Faith; by the Left, Justice; by two Right Hands conjoined, Union and Alliance; by the Arm, Labour and Industry; by the Leg, Strength, Stability, Expedition, and (when bent), Obedience; by the Thigh, a Solemn Compact.

All are metaphors in one aspect and metonymies in another.

In Francis Markham's *Five Decades of Epistles of Warre* (London, 1622), the colors used in flags are given the following values (p. 75):

Yellow betokeneth *Honour* . . . White signifieth *Innocence*. *Blacke* signifieth *Wisedome* and *Sobrietie*. *Blew* signifieth *Faith*, *Constancie*. *Red* signifieth *Justice*, or noble and worthy Anger in defence of Religion or the oppressed, and *Greene* signifieth *Good Hope*.

The colors act as metaphors.

In the *Grammar of British Heraldry*, the virtues are symbolized as follows (pp. 108–9):

Hope, (for instance,) is represented by a Female Figure richly attired, resting the Hand upon the *Anchor*. *Truth* and *Fortitude* are represented by female figures: – the *former* vested in white, her head irradiated, on her breast *a Sun*, and in her right hand *a Mirror*; the *latter* clad in a corslet of mail, on her head a plumed casque, in her right hand *a branch of oak*, and her left arm resting on *a pillar*. And so, *Justice* and *Mercy* are beautifully expressed by female figures:– the *former* holding in the right hand *a naked sword erect*, and the left *a pair of scales*; while the *latter* bears the sword in a *reversed* position. Again, *Prudence* holds in her hand a *javelin* (sometimes a *mirror*), entwined with a serpent [Wisdom]. *Liberality* bears the *Cornucopia*: *Fame*, the *trumpet*: *Temperance*, the *bridle*.

. . . Nor has Old *Ireland* been forgotten in the Assignment of Emblematic representations. A female figure habited in a flowing azure vest, an antique crown upon her head, a spear in the left hand, standing in front of *a harp*, forms the symbol of the Green Isle.

Each of these emblems is a metaphor, an emphasis on selection and similarity that matches that of dreams.

Many of the heraldic symbols were taken up by the Hollywood motion picture companies in the 1930s: Warner Brothers, the shield; Metro-Goldwyn-Mayer, the lion; 20th-Century Fox, the fortress of light; Universal, the globe; Paramount, the mountain (the pyramid – stability – as depicted, with the eye – sincerity – on US banknotes); RKO, the lightning flash; and Columbia, truth and liberty.

CHAPTER 7

On telling left from right

There are not many differences in mental habit more significant than that between the habit of thinking in discrete, well-defined class concepts and that of thinking in terms of continuity, of infinitely delicate shadings-off of everything into something else, of the overlapping of essences, so that the whole notion of species comes to seem an artifice of thought not truly applicable to the fluency, the, so to say, universal overlappingness of the real world.

ARTHUR O. LOVEJOY: *The Great Chain of Being* (1936)

7.1 Coding

No two categories, and no two kinds of experience are more fundamental in human life and thought than continuity and discontinuity, the one full, complete, compact, dense, and infinitely divisible, the other partial, intermittent, atomic, discrete, and not divisible beyond the individual units that make it up. Similarly with information: analog coding, based on difference, is continuous; digital coding, based on distinction, is discrete; and iconic coding, based on both difference and distinction, is both continuous and discrete.

Analog differences, related by continuity, are 'more-or-less'; digital distinctions, separated by gaps, are 'either/or' (and often 'all-or-none'). Time and space as we perceive them are obvious examples of analog information; the alphabet and money are equally obvious examples of digital information. Perceptions consisting of analog differences organized and bounded by digital distinctions, as in visual images, distinct sensations, or specific events, are examples of iconic information.

The terms 'analog' and 'digital' were originally derived from the distinction between analog computers (computing by means of variations in continuous quantities, such as volume, potential, or length) and digital computers (computing by means of the selection and combination of discrete elements). 'Iconic', meaning 'form' or 'image', is derived from the visual and plastic arts, but may equally well be applied to dreams, music, meaning, ideas, any distinct bodily sensation, and so on.

Analog devices include the slide rule, the clock, the planimeter (designed to measure the area bounded by a continuous curve), the mechanical or electrical differential analyzer (designed to compute rates of change in continuous functions, as in ballistics), the traditional phonograph record, cybernetic control devices such as the centrifugal governor or the solo sailor's wind vane, and other devices based on analogic representations of one kind of information by other kinds, as with traditional television and radar. Seen in macroscopic perspective (as distinct from the molecular and pixel levels), audiotape, videotape, and photographic film are other examples of analog means of representation.

Since analog devices employ digital coding in computation and control (the divisions on the dial of a clock, the distances marked on a ruler, the opening or closing of the engine throttle by a governor), they are strictly speaking both analog and digital, or in other words, iconic devices.

Digital computers and digital devices include the abacus, the telegraph key, the punched-card-controlled Jacquard loom, the music box, the player piano, the pinball machine, and the recently developed digital radar, digital television, and digital phonograph records.

Other examples of digital coding include the oscillations of a door buzzer, traffic lights, the four-unit code of DNA, the 'on/off', 'yes/no', or '0/1' of the binary code in computers, exchange values in economics (as distinct from use values, which are analog and iconic), boundaries between states, boundaries between systems and environments, and distinctions between levels in hierarchies.

A digital computer or a digital means of representation can be used to simulate the continuities of analog and iconic information, provided that the amount of analog and iconic information is reduced to the point that it can be described in a finite number of words or their equivalents (McCulloch and Pitts' nerve-net theorem). The advantages of digitalization are a much better signal-to-noise ratio, a reduction in the power required to transmit the signals (as with the Voyager space probes), ease of interpolating boundaries (as with Landsat images), and ease of storing the information in digital memory (as with digital radar – storing images of analog radar requires cinematography or videotape).

The infinite sequence of the whole numbers is digital – each integer is separated from the next by a distinct and unfillable gap that is part of the syntax of the system. (The digital gap is not the same as the space between words, which is a gap with a gap on each side of it.) The infinite sequence of the real numbers is analog – there is an infinity of differences between every other difference in the system.

The phonemes of speech – bundles of distinctive relationships between types of sound such as grave/acute, compact/diffuse, voiced/unvoiced, and so on (Chapter 5) – are iconic or digital, as are morphemes (the minimal units with signification) and words considered as sentence units (meanings are more complex), as well as such basic concepts as present/absent, full/empty, closed/open, figure/ground, and so on.

In analog and iconic communication, as in dreams (Chapter 6), there is no tense, no negative, and no contradiction.

Digital coding is dominant in what Freud called the 'word-presentation' (*Wortvorstellung*) in his analysis of dreams and schizophrenic speech; analog and iconic coding are dominant in what he called the 'thing-presentation'. The secondary system, consisting of consciousness and the preconscious (ordinary memory), is both analog and digital; the primary system (the unconscious, the deep memory) is analog.

It is probable that the patterns of ordinary memory are iconic; the act of search and recall is probably digital.

Digital coding has at its command a precise and powerful syntax well suited for computation and the operations of analytic logic, but this is achieved only at the cost of an impoverished capacity to express meanings. Analog coding, in contrast, displays little syntax beyond succession, similarity, and simultaneity, but a rich and plentiful, if ambiguous, semantics. Because it lacks syntax and is unable to communicate the fundamental logical operation of identity, analog coding cannot represent zero, nor express three of the four truth functions of analytic logic (the fourth is 'and'):

either/or

if . . . then

not

for which a digital syntax based on identity and contradiction, and capable of distinguishing between levels of communication (or logical types), is required.

Analog coding maps continuums completely but is imprecise about boundaries; digital coding maps boundaries precisely but can only evoke or suggest continuity. Denotations and literal significations in language are predominantly digital, as are naming and definition: these are all well-bounded terms reminiscent of Descartes' ideal of 'clear and distinct ideas'. Connotations and meanings, however, including metaphors and other figures of speech, and of course rhetoric and poetic diction, are predominantly analog and iconic: these are loosely bounded terms reminiscent of Pascal's preference for the 'esprit de finesse' over the 'esprit de géométrie'.

Analog, iconic, and digital coding apply equally well to communication within organisms – the predominantly analog information of the chemicals secreted by the endocrine glands (hormones), for example, or the predominantly digital information communicated by the firing of the neurons in the brain and nervous system – as they do to communication between organisms. The 'wagging dance' of bees, for example, by which one bee communicates to others the distance and direction of a source of nectar (by reference to the polarized light of the sun), which is based on figure-8 patterns and frequencies, is analog-digital or iconic; the small repertoire of distinct calls in gibbon communication is predominantly digital.

In digital systems the discrete coding is supplied by the syntax; in interpreting analog systems, iconic or digital coding is supplied by the perceiver.

Analog coding leading to iconic gestalts selected by the perceiver is the basis of body communication between humans. Examples include intonation, emphasis, sighing, laughing, smiling, frowning, feeling, eyeing, rhythm, closeness, forwardness, backwardness, hesitation, non-conventionalized gestures, facial expression, pupil size, and most aspects of body posture, style, and motion. Conventional iconic coding in body communication includes handshaking, bowing, saluting, clapping, dancing, dressing, and so on.

Iconic communication in general includes sculpture, music, painting, photography, film, and video. Along with visual icons (the commonest kind) should be included images of touch, taste, smell, and hearing, and icons of orientation in space and time.

Three levels of knowledge can also be distinguished: sensing, where analog continuity dominates digital discontinuity; meaning, where analog and digital coding combine in iconic coding; and signification, where digital coding dominates analog coding.

Taking up again the definition of information as coded variety (or diversity), sensing can be defined as coded information, meaning as coded sensing; and signification as coded meaning.

In the analog and iconic domain it is impossible for a person or an organism *not* to communicate. Analog and iconic information generally form the context of digital communication, especially when language is involved. When language communicates content, analog and iconic information communicate relationship.

Analog and digital coding are found in all communication systems. Where the analog communicates context and relationship, the digital is its instrument: the two forms of coding do not oppose or contradict each other ('either/or'), but complement each other ('both-and').

In modern society, however, where emotion and feeling, which are typically analog or iconic states, are commonly disparaged and divorced from (digital) reason (in spite of their being its ultimate source, i.e. the reasons for reason), and where images and thoughts not expressed or expressible in words are commonly regarded as not worth thinking at all, digital information and digital coding – the form taken by signification in language, by commodities in production, by money in relations of price, and by value in relations of exchange – have come to dominate their context of analog and iconic communication, just as 'all-or-none' has come to dominate 'more-or-less', just as 'either/or' has come to dominate 'both-and', and just as competition has come to dominate co-operation.

More and more evidence is accumulating concerning the role of
the whole body, its muscular tones, tensions, and movements in
our perceiving and conceptualizing both ourselves and our world.
The body, in its parts and its functions, seems to be of central
importance in the formation of the semantic roots of verbal
language.

KRESTEN BJERG: 'The Hollow Men and the Public Speech Act'
(1975)

7.2 Neurons and hormones

Apart from the genetic memory in every cell and the vast diversity of
information that can be generated by genes coding for the immune
system (specifying literally billions of distinct antibodies to neutralize
invading 'non-self' molecules bearing antigens), there are two major
communication and regulatory systems in the body, the nervous system
communicating electrochemical messages mainly via the nerve fibers,
and the glandular or hormone system communicating chemically
mainly via the bloodstream.

It is estimated that the human brain contains 10^{12} nerve cells, or
neurons, connected in multiple layers in networks of amazing
complexity. Simplifying greatly, a neuron consists of a cell body, an
axon, and a set of dendrites. The axon is a fiber projecting from the
cell body that normally conducts frequency-modulated electrical signals
generated by the neuron away from the cell body to other nerve cells,
or to muscle cells, or to gland cells. The dendrites (literally 'tree-like')
are numerous short thread-like and branching processes extending from
the neuron that may receive signals from the axons or dendrites of
other neurons, as may the cell body itself.

The electrical message transmitted down the axon of one cell is
passed on to another cell across the synapse, a minute gap between the
end of the first cell's axon and the cell body (or the axon or a dendrite)
of the second cell. An axon and its branches may end in a few synaptic
junctions or in several thousand. The cell body of one neuron may
receive synaptic contacts from several hundred to as many as 20,000
other cells. The signal is transmitted across the synaptic gap by the
release from the first cell of a chemical called a neurotransmitter, which
binds to receptor sites on the synaptic membrane of the receiving cell
and, under appropriate conditions, evokes in it the electrical response
of another signal.

Nerve cell communication is thus point-to-point and fast. In the
endocrine system, in contrast, each gland cell releases its chemical
product – a hormone, such as adrenalin or insulin – into the bloodstream, where its circulation and eventual influence on its target cells

throughout the body may take several minutes or several hours. Hormone communication is often widely diffused and relatively slow. Nerve cell communication is electrochemical and apparently digital; hormone communication is chemical and apparently analogic.

Until recently, as Floyd Bloom explained in 'Neuropeptides' in the *Scientific American* for October 1981, the nerve cell was thought to be an all-or-none, digital device communicating in one direction and part of a system quite separate from the hormone system. Now these distinctions no longer hold. Certain substances thought to be only neurotransmitters (chemicals that communicate across the synaptic gap between cells) have turned out to be hormones as well, and substances once thought to be only hormones have turned out to be neurotransmitters also. These substances are amino acid chains called peptides.

As Gordon M. Shepherd had reported in the *Scientific American* in 1978, in 'Microcircuits in the Nervous System':

> The discovery of the dendro-dendritic synapses [in 1965], together with our functional model, contradicted the classical doctrine that the nerve cell could only receive signals with its dendrites and cell body and transmit them through its axon, since it suggested that neurons can communicate with each other through their dendrites without the intervention of an axon or [digital] nerve impulse. . . . Recently . . . several examples of neurons have been found that communicate only through graded [analog] potentials . . . It is becoming evident that the nervous system is built up of hierarchies of functional units of increasing scope and complexity (pp. 95, 100, 103).

James A. Nathanson and Paul Greengard put it more explicitly in 'Second Messengers in the Brain' in 1977:

> In this respect [the likelihood that a neuron will or will not fire] a neuron acts much like an analogue computer, integrating the many hundreds of inhibitory and excitatory chemical messages that impinge on its surface at any given moment before deciding whether or not to fire (cf. Wilden, 1972, p. 158).

Oldendorf and Zabielski (1982) point out that unlike the either/or nature of the electrical 'impulse' in the axon (which does however vary in frequency according to the strength of what triggers it), the chemical activity of the neuron at the synapse allows for a greater variety of possibilities. The neurotransmitter substances can diffuse across the synapse at different rates, or be neutralized by other chemicals, or even return to the neuron that first emitted them. And the second neuron may simply ignore the chemical messages of the first. There is no definite threshold of sensitivity at which the second neuron will always accept the message of the first, as was once assumed:

> There is almost no presetting in the real neuron, and it can change its sensitivity from moment to moment, dependent on what is happening in its environment (p. 83).

The system is more complex, more subtle, and more flexible than previously suspected. Each neuron, the two authors continue, is in a state of flux, influenced by thousands of signals from other neurons. The 'mood' or receptivity of each neuron is constantly changing.

(Some authors have suggested that every one of the billions of neurons in the brain is ultimately connected to every other one, an echo of Lashley's 'theory of mass action', according to which the more complex integrative activities of the cortex may be conditioned by the activities of all its other parts.)

Neurons may be capable of selecting between different *types* of messages. The complexity required presumably lies in the short chains of amino acids making up the neuropeptides. Peptides are fragments of protein whose amino acid sequence can be synthesized only by the ribosomes, following the instructions of a gene, and which are then transported to their point of action within the neuron.

> Peptides make good messengers because their complex structures seem to allow them to encode more complicated messages than simply 'become more sensitive' or 'become less sensitive' [as the simple neurotransmitters do] (p. 116).

(Oldendorf and Zabielski go on to say that a peptide consisting of 100 amino acids encodes (a quantity of) information equivalent to that of about three English sentences. When cells need to communicate information too complicated for simple excitatory or inhibitory substances to transmit, it is apparently peptides that do the job.)

Peptide messengers typically serve more than a single function. Some of the brain peptides called enkephalins and endomorphins have effects on cells similar to the effects of opiates ('endorphin' is a contraction of 'endogenous morphine'): they suppress the perception of pain. But they are also found in brain circuits involving the control of blood pressure and body temperature, the regulation of the secretion of hormones, and the governance of body movement (Bloom, 1981, p. 164).

It remains to remark on the extraordinary complexity and flexibility of the neural network. (If there are 10 billion neurons in the brain and each is connected to 1000 others, the number of synapses created is 10 trillion.) Not only does the complexity of the brain continue to increase until as late as puberty, as the nerve cells create new synaptic connections through the growth and branching of their axons and dendrites, but it is also capable of restructuring its connections throughout life, although with greater difficulty in adults than in children (if it were a computer we would say that it is capable of rewiring its own hardware).

The network is too complex to be the result of a simple genetic 'program', argues Jean Pierre Changeux in *L'Homme neuronale* (1983), and he puts forward the theory that the structure of the network of neural pathways is not simply *instructed* (as in the synthesis of a protein according to the instructions of DNA), but more importantly *selected* – selected through the interaction of the brain with the natural and social environments, learning, and life experience. In his theory of brain development, the network begins by greatly increasing in diversity, produces as a result a 'transitory redundancy' of synaptic connections, and through learning passes into a stage of 'selective stabilization' by the elimination of rarely used neural pathways.

Unlike other human cells, most kinds of neurons cease to reproduce through cell division before birth: we are born with all the neurons we will ever have. Neuron death is thus an essential part of the changing structure of the dynamic brain. Memory traces – functional events – notably the repeated use of particular pathways (what Freud in the *Project* of 1895 called 'facilitation' or 'grooving') – become translated into the ongoing organic structure by their frequency and utility.

It is difficult to distinguish between engineering innovators and toymakers – both leaven their practical ingenuity with a measure of fantasy.

ATHELSTAN SPILHAUS: 'Those Wonderful Old Mechanical Toys' (1983)

7.3 Emulation

As reported by Gerald Jonas in *Science Digest* for October 1983, Brook Hindle, Senior Historian at the National Museum of American History, is concerned that modern engineers are dominated by 'number crunching' approaches to research, design, and innovation, an activity dependent on the digital computer, and have failed to appreciate the importance of 'non-linear, spatial thinking'. Their nineteenth-century counterparts, in contrast, typically began with a rough sketch or a crude model, which evolved through a series of prototypes in a step-by-step, 'hands-on' process of development into the finished product.

'Engineering itself', he argues, 'is not in the scientific mode.' Science looks for 'the one best way to describe something', whereas in the real world of the engineer there can never be 'one determinate answer' to a particular design problem. The design of a new aircraft, for example, involves a series of compromises between weight, speed, safety, cost, and so on. With so many interrelated and not easily quantifiable variables, digital number crunching alone cannot do the job.

'The best way to proceed on a technological problem is to begin with the past technology and build on it.' Hindle thinks that engineers – without sacrificing scientific rigor – should pay closer attention to the traditional role of 'emulation' in the crafts. Emulation is a method of teaching technical skills that emerged from classical times. The essence of the method was that you learn by doing, by copying from the best models.

The first goal of the apprentice was to make exact copies of the master's work, learning to demonstrate a proficiency equal to that of the master. In the process apprentices would inevitably face many of the same technical and design problems as their predecessors, with the result that they would grasp the history of their trade, an essential component in their literacy as artisans.

At the same time, the focus on real models and actual experience would encourage in them the capacity to grasp spatial relations in three dimensions: the non-linear, non-verbal processes associated with the right cerebral hemisphere, and above all the ability to manipulate in the imagination an imaginary model of the desired product, whose characteristics cannot be reduced to the unambiguous verbal or numerical descriptions typical of the digital capacities of the left hemisphere. Few words exist to describe this concrete and contextual experience of getting the 'feel' of things, this 'fingertip knowledge' typical of the holistic capacities of the right hemisphere.

To become master artisans in their own right, apprentices were required to produce a 'masterpiece' – a work that was as good as the master's best and at the same time excelled it in some way. Inherent in learning by emulation, then, was a medium for the transfer of power between generations – for that is what teaching is – and an incentive to individuality and innovation.

Break the pattern which connects the items of learning and you necessarily destroy all quality.

GREGORY BATESON: *Mind and Nature* (1979)

7.4 Left brain, right brain

Few theories spring untutored from the human breast, and the several theories of the functional distinctions between the left brain and the right brain are no exception. In the first volume of R. Chambers' *Book of Days: A Miscellany of Popular Antiquities in Connection with the Calendar, Including Anecdote, Biography, & History, Curiosities of Literature, and Oddities of Human Life and Character*, published in London and Edinburgh in 1869, we find under date of February 17 and under the rubric of 'Mystic Memory', the following theory of the experience of *déjà vu*.

The occasion and the date come from the diary of Sir Walter Scott. On February 17, 1828, while in the company of three old friends, Scott had the feeling of 'being haunted by a sense of pre-existence', as if by a mirage in the desert, by a feeling what was being said and done at that moment had all been said and done before by the same people in the same way – the whole sensation being accompanied by 'a vile sense of want of reality'.

Pythagoras and many others regarded this kind of experience as conclusive evidence of the transmigration of souls, of existence in a previous life. Others believed it to be evidence of a 'genetic memory' of past stages in the evolution of human consciousness. For the poet Wordsworth (1770–1850) it confirmed the Christian and Neoplatonist myth, largely derived from Plato and Plotinus, of the 'eternal return'. At birth on earth the soul is said to leave its 'true ancestral home' in heaven, where it had previously existed at one with God, and is made to forget its heavenly origins. The soul then seeks to go beyond the toils and tribulations of earthly life by an unending quest to rejoin the divine unity from whence it came.

Chambers wrote (p. 269):

In a curious book, published in 1844 by Dr [L.W.] Wigan, under the title of *The Duality of Mind*, an attempt is made to account for the phenomenon [of mystic memory] in a different way. Dr Wigan was of opinion that the two hemispheres of the brain had each its distinct power and action, and that each often acts singly . . .

'The persuasion of the same being a repetition', says he, 'comes on when the attention has been roused by some accidental circumstance, and we become, as the phrase is, wide awake. I believe the explanation to be this: only one brain has been used in the immediately preceding part of the scene: the other brain has been asleep, or in an analogous state nearly approaching it. When the attention of both brains is roused to the topic, there is the same vague consciousness that the ideas have passed through the mind before. . . . The ideas *have* passed through the brain before: and as there was not sufficient consciousness to fix them in the memory without a renewal, we have no means of knowing the length of time that had elapsed between the *faint* impression received by the single brain, and the *distinct* impression received by the double brain. It may seem to have been many years.'

Wigan's notion derives some indirect support from recent Russian research showing that in the bottle-nosed dolphin the hemispheres sleep one at a time, displaying 'complementary dominance' by which one is dominant over the other at one time, and the other dominant at another time (Finn, 1983).

In his article on *déjà vu* first published in 1914, Freud summarized Wigan's anatomical hypothesis (put forward, he says, in 1860) by saying that it is 'based on an absence of simultaneity in the functioning of the two cerebral hemispheres'. In his own view, based on his structural distinction between the secondary system (consciousness and the preconscious) and the primary system (the domain of the unconscious), the feeling of having said something before (*déjà raconté*) is ascribed to an unconscious wish or intention never actually carried out; and the feeling of *déjà vu*, to a process of thought that we cannot consciously remember because it never was conscious. The feeling of *déjà vu*, he had concluded in *The Psychopathology of Everyday Life* (1901), 'corresponds to the recollection of an unconscious phantasy' on the very fringe of consciousness.

In 1936 Freud wrote that *déjà vu* is often accompanied (as it was in Sir Walter Scott's case) by a feeling of a loss of personal or external reality (depersonalization or derealization). Depersonalization can lead us on to 'the extraordinary condition of "*double conscience*" ['dual consciousness']', he adds, 'which is more correctly described as "split personality"'.

Complementary dominance of the cerebral hemispheres

It is generally accepted that the left hemisphere of the brain is specialized for language in over 95 per cent of all right-handed people and in about two-thirds of all left-handers.

Long ignored and misunderstood, the right brain plays a dominant role in vision and in our perception of context (including the natural and social environments). It is dominant in our ability to find our way and situate ourselves in context.

One might say that the left brain is mainly logical, whereas the right brain is mainly ecological.

Generally speaking, the left brain receives information from the right side of the body; the right brain receives information from the left side. The left brain controls body movements on the right side; the right brain controls body movements on the left.

By 'brain' in this context is meant the cerebral cortex, an intricately wrinkled sheet of gray matter about a tenth of an inch thick forming the outer covering of the brain. Beneath the cortex, which develops fully only after birth, is the so-called 'mammalian brain' controlling a host of biological functions from breathing to the 'wisdom of the body' (as Cannon put it in the 1930s). Within that is the so-called 'reptilian brain', said to control our most basic animal functions.

Spread out flat, the cortex is about the size of a regular newspaper page (three square feet). It contains some 10 billion nerve cells interacting with neurotransmitters and hormones. The nerve network is connected or potentially connected in every possible way – it is the most complex organic structure in the cosmos.

(The more complex the structure of a system is, the greater is the quantity of information it can store for future necessities (notably long-range survival), and the more diverse are its capacities to innovate and thus to use qualitatively distinct forms of information.)

Although the potential of the cortex is defined by the genes, and the relation between the two hemispheres is initially constrained by the effects of the sex hormones on the embryo, the recent discovery that the cortex is capable of restructuring its networks (changing its organization and orientations) in response to experience, change of context, change of goals, change of norms, and other forms of learning is one more example of the crucially important and powerful role that culture – social relations – plays in guiding, directing, orchestrating, and modulating the expression in society of the biological legacy of the genes.

Except under certain conditions – notably the neurological oscillation between the hemispheres that results when the brain is faced by left hemisphere coding (language) transmitted by a right hemisphere medium (the moving dot of light scanning the TV screen), as it is with the Video Display Terminals of computers and word processors – the relationship between the two hemispheres is not a conflict and not either/or. Nor is it an opposition, a dichotomy, a competition, or a contradiction. It is simply a distinction between two complementary forms of coding and two complementary sets of capacities: a distinction between relative specialization and relative dominance between parts constrained by the whole.

The two hemispheres are more flexible in their functions than any verbal 'splitting into lists' can possibly indicate; and the topic remains a controversial one. Damage to the language-oriented left hemisphere can result in the right hemisphere taking on linguistic functions; and damage to the visual and contextual right hemisphere can result in the loss of certain verbal capacities.

In the usual case, patients with left-hemisphere damage may be unable to read or spell out words or understand syntax (the rules of digital selection and combination in language); those with right hemisphere damage may be unable to recognize humor or appreciate poetry; unable to comprehend figures of speech, taking them literally; unable to maintain the connecting thread or theme of a narrative (as in a novel); unable to appreciate nuances and levels of meaning in communication, including non-verbal communication; and unable to interpret a tone of voice.

These are all failures of metacommunication (failures to distinguish between levels of communication and reality) (Chapter 1, Chapter 6). Each includes the many-dimensioned, qualitative, and relational communication typical of the non-verbal (analog and iconic) contextual markers that frame the content of verbal communication (Chapter 8). These are markers that communicate about the relationship between people in communication, social, political, economic, interpersonal, sexual, mutual, and of course also pathological.

The commonest distinctions between the complementary functions of the two hemispheres describe the left brain as rational, analytical, and step-by-step, and the right brain as intuitive, synthesizing, and holistic.

In most people, says Campbell in *Grammatical Man* (1982, pp. 239–40), the left hemisphere specializes in numbers, analytic thought, speech, and handling information in sequence. The right hemisphere is better at dealing with space, pictures, and multiple and simultaneous connections between items of information.

> The right side tends to use a 'top-down' strategy, processing information as a whole, perceiving its full meaning, rather than approaching it 'bottom-up', using the parts to construct the whole. ... In the case of language the right hemisphere thinks in terms of entire sentences, rather than single words, and is sensitive to the way sentences fit into paragraphs.

The coding system for recognizing faces, he adds, is right brain; that for recognizing objects is left brain. According to Elkhonon Goldberg and Louis Costa,

> the right hemisphere is the brain's jack-of-all-trades, a generalist that addresses new problems without preconceptions and tries many solutions until it hits on one that works. The left hemisphere, in contrast, is a specialist, solving familiar problems quickly and efficiently by using established methods (Finn, 1983, p. 103).

For example, whereas most people use the right brain to distinguish melodies (Kimura, 1973), professional musicians use the left. New faces are first recognized by the right brain, but once they have become familiar, they are recognized by the left. It appears that once any task becomes practiced and its solution stereotyped the left hemisphere takes over from the right (Finn, 1983).

The two hemispheres communicate with each other by means of a large bundle of nerve fibers called the corpus callosum, but these channels do not become effective until about the age of 2, and do not become fully formed until about the age of 10. This delay in maturity may allow the two hemispheres to develop more or less independently of each other in early life. It appears that genetic potential, biological development, and family and social experience all play a part in defining the eventual channels of communication between the two, and there is no reason to assume that all the information is shared by both sides. The extent, kind, and degree of information exchange via the corpus callosum still remains largely unknown (Campbell, 1982, p. 241), as do the same characteristics of the left hemisphere and right hemisphere memories.

Table 7.1 reproduces a classification of the functions of the two hemispheres drawn up in 1971 by the psychologist Paul Bakan, who described the left brain as predominantly digital and the right brain as predominantly analogic.

Table 7.1: Functions of the cerebral hemispheres (Bakan, 1971).

Left-brain functions	Right-brain functions
verbal	pre-verbal
analytic	synthetic
abstract	concrete
rational	emotional
temporal	spatial
digital	analogic
objective	subjective
active	passive
tense	relaxed
euphoric	depressed
sympathetic	parasympathetic
propositional	appositional

For a century before research on 'split-brain' patients whose corpus callosum had been cut to relieve epileptic seizures (they are still able to live normal lives), the digital and verbal bias of Western scientists led to the assumption that the left hemisphere was always dominant, or ought to be; and the great strides made in the study of language disorders led some to call the right hemisphere passive, non-responsive, inferior in cognitive capacities (which are predominantly digital functions), even when studying patients with right-hemisphere language capacities. With the advent of studies such as that by Doreen Kimura cited below, however, which showed right-hemisphere superiority in many of our most important non-verbal tasks, the relationship between the two hemispheres is now described as 'complementary dominance', with each side taking over when exercising its particular specialties.

Table 7.2: Distinctions in function between the cerebral hemispheres: hearing and vision (Kimura 1973). Like sensation and motor activities hearing is almost completely crossed. Vision, however, differs in that the left hemisphere receives information from the right half of the visual field of each eye, and the right hemisphere, information from the left half.

Left-brain specialization	*Right-brain specialization*
Hearing (right ear)	*Hearing* (left ear)
words	melodies
spoken numbers	
vowels	vowels
syllables	coughing, laughing, crying, sighing (human non-speech sounds)
backward speech	
nonsense syllables	
unknown language being spoken	
Vision (right half of both fields)	*Vision* (left half of both fields)
words	drawing
letters	building models from a plan or picture
perception of the slant of a line	finding one's way from place to place
	orientation in space (spatial information in the third dimension, position of objects in space)
	direct analysis of information about the external environment
monocular information	monocular and binocular information, stereoscopic depth perception

Robert Finn reports that Goldberg and Costa, who view the left brain as the specialist and the right brain as the generalist, have found some support for their view in recently discovered anatomical distinctions between the hemispheres:

> The right hemisphere contains many long fibers that connect widely separated regions of the brain, each specialized for different aspects of information processing. This hemisphere can thus mobilize a wide range of resources to attack a novel problem.

In contrast,

> the left hemisphere contains shorter fibers that provide rich interconnections within a region to facilitate detailed processing of more well-defined tasks. In addition, the right hemisphere contains larger volumes of 'associative cortex', the functions of which, although not well understood, apparently comprise the brain's most complex levels of information processing (p. 103)

Table 7.3: Joseph Bogen's psychological distinctions (1977) between left-brain and right-brain modes of knowing (and therefore modes of communication), as quoted by Campbell (1982, pp. 241–2).

left brain	right brain
intellect	intuition
convergent	divergent
intellectual	sensuous
deductive	imaginative
active	receptive
discrete	continuous
abstract	concrete
realistic	impulsive
propositional	imaginative
transformational	associative
lineal [straight-line]	nonlineal
historical [diachronic]	timeless [synchronic]
explicit	tacit
objective	subjective

Campbell adds to Table 7.3 an *explication de texte*:

> At the risk of generalizing about conclusions that are already general, one can say that the left-hand column [in Table 7.3] suggests the presence of constraints more than the right-hand

column does. Linguistically, it is more Chomskyan than the other, referring to what speakers of language cannot do rather than what they can do. There is less uncertainty, a sense of fewer possibilities, on the left side. The categories suggest that information [on the left side] is coded in ways which are more strictly organized, more formal, stable, and free from error. They refer to modes of thought in which structure is of great importance, but structure of the kind in which one component is fitted to another, by a single connection, leaving no room for ambiguity or for multiple relationships.

Continuing with Bogen's list, Campbell goes on to define in more detail some of the relations between the two hemispheres:

Convergent implies the idea of meaning shrinking into the confines of the well-formed, grammatical sentence, rather than carrying many interpretations. *Deductive* describes an analytical type of reasoning, sentences in which the predicate is already contained, logically, in the subject: 'All bachelors are unmarried men'. The *propositional* style of language is of the true-or-false variety, a declaration. *Lineal* events are more rigorously ordered than nonlineal events; their redundancy is greater. And the *explicit* is more firmly committed to present reality than is the tacit. Is it any surprise, then, that the left hemisphere is the primary seat of language?

Sequential forms of order, in which items or events succeed one another discretely are typical of the left hemisphere. They are constructed by excluding possibilities. At each moment in the process, one item is selected from an array of other possible items (and combined with others), resulting in a convergence on a goal much as we converge on our own front door in returning home, much as we converge on the point of a sentence.

By exclusion, one abstracts something from a context. By inclusion, that something is fitted into a context (p. 243).

The right hemisphere has no preference so marked as that of the left for spoken language. Campbell continues:

It may be that the ability to make radical changes in the structure of information, to convert it from one code to another by means of formal and highly constrained rules, marks the essential difference between the two hemispheres. And this is because the speech code is one of the most, if not the most powerful, complex, and intricate in the entire brain (p. 243).

The right brain is poor at comprehending consonants and syntax (whether this might result from inhibition communicated across the corpus callosum by the left brain is not yet clear, he notes).

Even in split-brain patients, with no communication between the hemispheres, whereas the right brain can understand the meaning of word pairs like 'ache' and 'lake', it does not realize that the two words rhyme (Chapter 8).

For all its linguistic limitations, the right brain may nevertheless be an active partner in sophisticated uses of language. Language may be regarded simply as structure or form, says Campbell, but the result is that 'speech becomes too innocent' (p. 244):

> Meaning converges into the sentence instead of diverging out into wider contexts. The right hemisphere corrects this tendency to constrain meaning. It makes the brain as a whole less literal-minded.

The right brain probably plays a dominant role in the understanding of the 'many shades and levels of meaning' in poetry. It is sensitive to rhythm and sound and tempo, and not merely to content (the passage from Alexander Pope's *Essay on Criticism* in Chapter 5 illustrates this to perfection).

As the psychologist Howard Gardner has said, left-hemisphere activity on its own 'is like reading the script of a play instead of going to see it' (p. 245).

It is the right hemisphere that knows what words connote (or mean), what associations they have, and not simply what they denote (or signify), as well as what they refer to:

> It can recognize the ridiculous and the innappropriate, and be aware that words and sentences are embedded in a wide matrix of relationships.

The right hemisphere, then, is 'more worldly' than the left. It is the source of our sense of humor, for the left hemisphere alone is too literal-minded for jokes.

We can say that the right brain is receptive to metaphor; the left is dominated by metonymy.

Campbell rewrites Joseph Bogen's 1977 list of distinctions between left and right coding styles (see Table 7.4), and brings out the contextual functions of the right hemisphere, including its capacity to provide concepts or patterns that create order and information out of apparent chaos, disorder, or noise (p. 249).

Table 7.4: Jeremy Campbell's modification of Bogen's classification of left- and right-brain coding styles (1982, pp. 247–8).

Left	*Right*
literal	metaphorical
innocent	sophisticated
denoting	connoting
contrasting	comparing
banal	rich
bottom-up	top-down
verbal	non-verbal
innappropriate	appropriate
exclusion	inclusion

Erain Zaidel, a psychologist at the University of California, thinks that the right-brain supplies concepts and contexts for the computational style of the left brain. The right brain may be the hemisphere that assimilates novel information and 'embeds it in the context of the familiar'. Novelty introduced by the right becomes a matter of practice suitable for control by the left. Zaidel suggests that the right brain is the seat of a special kind of intelligence, intelligence based on experience, even wisdom, an intelligence that continues to develop throughout life (p. 251).

The most recent research suggests that intelligence is not a single quality (measurable quantitatively by so-called IQ tests). Many forms or species of intelligence, including body intelligence, appear to be native to human beings (Gardner, 1983).

Finally, in comparing relative left- and right-brain dominance in linguistic communication itself, Campbell cites two passages from the work of the rhetorician W. Ross Winterowd (1980). Winterowd, using passages from compositions diagnosed as schizophrenic, gives two worst-case illustrations. The first is strongly left brain (digital) and propositional:

> The subterfuge and the mistaken planned substitutions for that demanded American action can produce nothing but the general results of negative contention and the impractical results of misplacement, of mistaken purpose and unrighteous position, the impractical serviceabilities of unnecessary contradictions. For answers to this dilemma, consult Webster.

(One notes that the example contains nine negative expressions; negation is presumably a mainly or wholly left brain operation.)

The next passage is predominantly right brain (iconic) and relational, displaying some of the features of Bogen's list in Table 7.3:

I hope to be home soon very soon. I fancy chocolate eclairs.
Doenuts [sic]. I want some Doenuts. I do want some golden syrup,
a tin of golden syrup or treacle, jam . . . See the Committee about
me coming home for Easter my twenty-fourth birthday. I hope
all is well at home, how is Father getting on. Never mind there is
hope, heaven will come, time heals all wounds.

The English essays of university students, Winterowd adds, are 'only
a shade less schizoid' than these two samples. In the first, says
Winterowd, 'we have the ghost of coherence without the substance of
tangible content; in the other, the cup of meaning runneth over' (p.
252).

The first is dominated by metonymy; the second, by metaphor.

In the integrated brain, 'these two polar styles' coexist and co-operate
to a greater or lesser extent. Campbell summarizes (pp. 252–3):

The left brain prefers a tightly organized sequential pattern of
relations, excluding possibilities, singling things out, fitting parts
together step by step, contrasting rather than comparing. The right
brain contributes pattern, too, but it appears to be a pattern of
meaning, a network of semantic connections that form a wordly
context into which the structures of the left brain can fit and find
their place.

(If the left brain is regarded as 'system', we can say that the right brain
is its environment.)

The right brain can show that information does not always mean
what it appears to mean. It can make 'semantic sense out of semantic
noise':

The right brain is more conceptual than computational, but it does
not specialize in chaos. It seeks out order and supplies order.
Memory . . . needs not only an abstract structure, a 'syntax', but
also a personal [and collective] context of meaning, where the
strange becomes familiar and the familiar strange (p. 253).

Researchers report that people with right-hemisphere damage were
uncertain as to what was significant and what was not in stories
presented to them, failing to make appropriate patterns of connections
in the plot, and not dealing well with context. People with right-
hemisphere defects, said Howard Gardner and Suzanne Hamby in a
paper written in 1979,

lack anchorage with respect to the external world: they were
uncertain of their own status in relation to diverse social

environments or literary creations, and thus, they cannot
appropriately distance themselves . . . It is as if the left hemisphere
is a highly efficient, but narrowly programmed linguistic computer;
the right hemisphere constitutes the ideal audience for a humorous
silent film, but only the two hemispheres together can appreciate
all four of the Marx brothers (p. 246).

CHAPTER 8

Montage analytic and dialectic: The right-brain revolution

A: What is a question that is also its own answer?
B: Why not, 'Why not?'
A: 'Why not?'? Why not!

THOMAS MUNNECKE: Letter to the *Scientific American* on the paradoxes of self-reference discussed by Douglas Hofstadter in 'Metamagical Themas' (1981)

FIGURE 8.1: (a) *La Condition humaine (The Human Condition)* by the Belgian surrealist René Magritte (1898–1967), completed in 1936. (b) *La Trahison des images* (The treachery of Images), Magritte 1928–29 (see pp. iv, 210). In *Vicious Circles and Infinity* (1975), Patrick Hughes and George Brecht comment on the picture in the window as follows:

> Magritte presents what might be called the *paradox of the realistic painter*. By making the representation of the easel exactly contiguous with [= 'exactly overlap'] the representation of the real world, Magritte plunges us into paradox. Magritte said of this picture: 'In front of a window, as seen from the interior of a room, I placed a picture that represented precisely the portion of landscape blotted out by the picture. For instance the tree represented in the picture displaced the tree situated behind it, outside the room. For the spectator it was simultaneously inside the room, in the picture, and outside, in the real landscape, in thought.'

In another terminology, Magritte creates a three-level 'tangle in the rules' of perception (Gregory Bateson) via a 'strange loop' (Douglas Hofstadter): a 'vicious circle', which in this case is a metaphoric paradox that alternatively creates and collapses the distinctions in logical typing, or levels of communication, between the symbolic, the imaginary, and the real. In Hofstadter's words (1979; p. 10), a strange or self-reflexive loop exists when 'by moving upwards (or downwards) through the levels of some hierarchical systems, we unexpectedly find ourselves right back where we started.' See also pp. iv, 210, 244, 256–7.

8.1 Negation

In the Preface to the *Phenomenology of Mind* (1807), Hegel wrote of the 'seriousness, the pain, the patience, and the labor of the negative'. There are few philosophers to whom negation was more significant: he believed its 'divine power' to be the source of progress.

The painting of the pipe labelled 'This is not a pipe' by René Magritte (1898–1967) – the 1930s apostle of comedy and horror, mysticism and ambiguity, and above all self-referential communication about communication in art (as in the two illustrations in Figure 8.1) – suggests to me what Hegel might have thought about negation – the most misjudged operation in semiotic – had he had a sense of humor.

If we ask ourselves just what is not a pipe in Magritte's metaphoric image, we find at least six respectable answers, each of them depending for their validity on the framing of the message:

This [pipe] is not a pipe –
This [image of a pipe] is not a pipe –
This [painting] is not a pipe –
This [sentence] is not a pipe –
[This] this is not a pipe –
[This] is not a pipe –

and presumably take our pick.

Of the strategic function of the negative the philosopher, poet, and culture critic Kenneth Burke (b. 1897) said more than once:

There are many notable aspects of language, such as classification, specification, abstraction, which have their analogues in purely nonverbal behavior. But the negative is a peculiarly linguistic resource. And because it is so peculiarly linguistic, the study of man as the specifically word-using animal requires special attention to this distinctive marvel, the negative.

There are three types of negation, the first syntactic, the second psychological, and the third an imaginary term for a notable kind of real event:

First: *Syntactic 'not'* (or any equivalent term). Ordinary 'not' is called 'syntactic' because it depends for its effects on its place in the sentence. As a communication about an affirmation, 'not' is not of the same logical type, or level of communication, as the other words in the sentence in which it appears.

Second: *Verneinung (verneinen)*: 'I know what you're thinking', says the patient to the analyst, 'but that man in my dream is *not* my father' (he is of course). This is an example of 'denial', the term chosen by

Freud to define a common defensive process by which we keep an unwanted fact repressed from conscious awareness. (*Verneinung* also means 'negation', 'the negative', and sometimes 'contradiction'.)

(The repressed information remains present in the 'deep memory' of the Freudian unconscious or primary system, as distinct from ordinary memory, which for Freud is the 'preconscious', which along with consciousness, forms the secondary system.)

By stating the information along with a 'not', we show that we are acquainted with the message, at one level of communication (German *Kenntnis*, French *connaissance*), but that at another level we fail to recognize its significance (*Verkenntnis, méconnaissance*).

The solution, at yet another level, is what Hegel insisted on as recognition (*Erkenntnis, reconnaissance*). By recognizing the fact we already knew, we know we know it, and its meaning changes in the process.

Other examples of psychological (and indeed ideological) denial:

- 'I don't want to hurt you, but . . .'
- 'We're not saying we're not at fault, but . . .'
- 'I wouldn't call you "nigger" (you're not like the others), but . . .'
- 'Just because I called you "girl" doesn't mean I'm putting you down . . .'
- 'I'm not denying anything I did not say, but . . .'

– and so on. In psychological denial, the negation is a pointed affirmation.

Third: *Aufhebung (aufheben)*: This is an amphibious word meaning in German both 'suppress' and 'conserve' (as well as 'abolish' or 'neutralize', and 'maintain' or 'keep'), with the basic sense of 'lift up'. Freud uses it in his 1925 article, 'Negation', when he says that a denial (*Verneinung*) suppresses and conserves the repression (*Verdrängung*) of what it denies. The term was used by Hegel and those he influenced to stand for the so-called 'negation of the negation' in the dialectic of ideas supposedly at the origin of reality.

For Hegel the real is rational and the rational is real. The 'negativity of the dialectic' is the supposedly self-generating and self-renewing source of motion, growth, and change in nature, society, and history.

An idea or concept is posited or put forward (forming a thesis, literally 'set down, placed'); it is said to be negated by its opposite (its antithesis); the fusion of thesis and antithesis is then said to be negated by the 'negation of the negation', producing the synthesis – which becomes the thesis to be negated at the next stage of the supposedly inevitable dialectical process.

(The originator of the terms thesis, antithesis, and synthesis was

Johann Fichte (1762–1814), who regarded knowing as an act of creation, rather than discovery, and who, like Hegel, considered the dialectic to be a teleological process leading to a predesigned and necessary end, such as 'God', the 'Absolute', the 'Divine Idea', and so on.)

The synthesis 'suppresses and conserves' both thesis and antithesis, but at a new level and in a new context, the context created by the dialectical process itself. The synthesis thus bears with it the insignia of its origins – its memory, in fact.

In 1847, in *The Poverty of Philosophy*, Marx pastiched Hegel in these words:

> . . . In what does the movement of pure reason consist? To pose, oppose and compose itself, to be formulated as thesis, antithesis and synthesis, or, better still, to affirm itself, to deny itself and to deny its negation . . .
>
> But once it has placed itself in thesis, this thesis, this thought, opposed to itself, doubles itself into two contradictory opposites, the positive and the negative, the yes and no. The struggle of these two antagonistic elements, comprised in the antithesis, constitutes the dialectic movement. The yes becoming no, the no becoming yes, the yes becoming at once yes and no, the no becoming at once no and yes, the contraries balance themselves, neutralize themselves, paralyze themselves. The fusion of these two contradictory thoughts constitutes a new thought which is the synthesis of the two. This new thought unfolds itself again in two contradictory thoughts which are confounded in their turn in a new synthesis.

It can be seen at once that this is largely nonsense. While the imagery is suggestive and the both-and capacities of dialectics are clearly stated, the thought model is one-dimensional, making no distinction between levels; 'pure' reason (so-called) is not, as we would expect, a principle of in-formation (which could give the Hegelian schéma some metaphorical credibility), but an (impossibly absolute) matter-energy force; the supposedly inherent binary opposition between positive and negative is simply a mechanical or electromagnetic metaphor, with no relevance to living nature or human history; and the categories of 'no', 'not', 'denial', 'opposition', 'antagonism', 'antithesis', and 'contradiction' are hopelessly confused. The Hegelian *Aufhebung* is imaginary.

There is no general 'dialectics of nature', as Engels fervently believed – for him even the strata of geology were examples of the so-called 'negation of the negation' – but wherever we find information at work in nature or society, we find processes of many kinds that may quite properly be called 'dialectical' in the modern sense. The symmetrical and either/or opposition between the nineteenth-century categories of 'materialism' and 'idealism' is replaced by the both-and, multilevel, and open system dialectics of the symbolic, the imaginary, and the real.

There is a real dialectic of production, reproduction, communication, and exchange, a real dialectic of learning, a real dialectic of invention and technological innovation, a real dialectic of paradigms in scientific inquiry, and a real dialectic of conflict in the illegitimate hierarchy between dominant and subordinate in the social and economic structure, whether defined by class, race, or sex.

In the dialectic of invention and science and history unexpected novelty emerges from the insoluble conflicts or tangled contradictions – the undecidable paradoxes – of the old system, often quite suddenly but also over centuries, and a new technique, a new machine, a new understanding, a new mode of production, a new social order becomes dominant over the old, which survives in a subordinate role marking the distinction in the continuity between the past and the future created by the system's radical change in structure.

(Structural change is distinct from mere functional change within the context of the existing structure, as in the case of the reform of certain of the working conditions in the factories and mines of nineteenth-century England, conditions originated by the structural revolution of capitalism itself. In natural history a functional change is an adaptation, often reversible, of individual organisms within a given population; a structural change, impossible for the individual, is expressed by the evolution of a new species.)

In this way the old system creates and passes through the boundary of an *Aufhebung* – not to be translated 'negation' – by means of which the old order forms the basis of and at the same time gives way to the new, and the whole, as a whole, survives. Here the previously subordinate or unnoted becomes dominant or critically important, noise becomes information, disorder forms the basis of new order.

The structural changes are continuous but in retrospect we detect a discontinuity: the process displays emergent qualities. In every instance of change – in analytic logic change is impossible to explain – the paradox of the discontinuous in the continuous comes in and out of being like the Cheshire Cat.

As with the evolution of a new species, however, we can usually tell what is on one side or the other side of the boundary between old and new (or between the original system and the metasystem emerging out of it), even if we cannot precisely locate the boundary itself. (It is like a 'Dedekind cut', an imaginary discontinuity inserted into the continuity of the real numbers so as to make an operational distinction between 'smaller than x' and 'greater than x'.) No one, for example, will deny the reality of the steam-powered industrial revolution, which followed on the water, wind, and muscle-powered machine revolution of the sixteenth and seventeenth centuries, but to date it between 1750 and 1850 is a matter of historical convenience and convention rather than crisp fact.

Changes in levels and structure through changes in context are among the commonest of events in organic nature. When in the process of development the continuously growing embryo displays emergent qualities, such as the beating of a heart, during the process by which the originally genetically identical cells, all carrying the same genetic information, differentiate and become distinct kinds of tissue, as the original information is reinterpreted at each more complex level of organization and in each new context, we call this process the 'programmed development' of new structures. When genetic variation governed by information and tested by the environment of natural selection, results – in a minute number of cases – in a new species, this 'non-programmed' or originally accidental emergence of new structures is the matter of evolution.

The dialectic of learning is marked by what the Gestalt psychologists of the early twentieth century called the 'Aha! experience'. Here order is reordered; disorder creates order; noise becomes information; knowledge becomes recognition; and as if by a discontinuous jump between levels there emerges a new whole, a new pattern, a newly coherent form (German *Gestalt*).

In Freud the dialectic of learning is called the 'theory of deferred action' or 'learning-after-the-event' (*Nachträglichkeit*). (Learning is a form of adaptation, and adaptation in complex systems is time and duration dependent.) The same information, enduring through memory, takes on new meanings in new contexts in time and space. The fact that Freud uses this notion largely to explain the sudden comprehension of the sexual content of childhood events as the child passes through puberty (thus ending the so-called 'latency period') should not deter us from recognizing its far more general importance. Learning-after-the-event is the agent of maturity and the origin of wisdom.

In Bateson the concept of levels of learning – at the first level the mere reception of information (zero learning), then the comprehension of the information by putting it into the context of other information (learning), then the comprehension of the diversity of contexts to put the information in (learning how to learn) – has the same dialectical form, including the apparent discontinuity between levels.

In Marx, Engels, Eisenstein, Mao, and others the key is learning through conflict.

In Latin learning is *docendo didici*: 'I learnt by teaching'.

The before and after of the dialectical event are of distinct logical types. Whether in the dialectic of ideas, the work of invention, the paradigms of science, the revolutions of history, or learning-after-the-event, the 'Aha! experience' and its equivalents in action mark a new level of organization or patterning that produces a reinterpretation of the past, a rereading, in a new context, of the logical typing and other relationships of past events, and thus a re-evaluation of the future.

Given that 'dialectic' means 'the art of conversation' in Greek, it is altogether appropriate that, viewed in the abstract, this 'rereading in a new context', this 'reframing of logical types', this 'shift in levels of communication', this emergence of novelty 'after-the-event' all follow exactly the same pattern as that of the well-made joke:

Mr Abraham, driven to desperation by the endless delays of a tailor who was making him a pair of trousers, finally cried, 'Tailor, in the name of heaven, it has already taken you six *weeks*!'
'So?'
'*So*, you ask? Six weeks for a pair of pants? *Riboyne Shel O'lem*! God in heaven! It took God only six days to create the *universe*!'
'*Nu*', shrugged the tailor, 'look at it . . .'

The story is from *The Joys of Yiddish* (1968, p. 309), by Leo Rosten, the creator of H*Y*M*A*N K*A*P*L*A*N.

The punchline collapses levels, changes the context, reframes what went before, and remakes the structure of the story. Life is life, history is history, and jokes are jokes because in going forward we come to understand them by reading backwards.

It is not true that the 'law of non-contradiction' is violated in the dialectical perspective. In the first place dialectical (or process) logic includes and uses analytic (or static) logic as its necessary complement. Without the 'either/or' of analytic logic decision is impossible. Where the two differ is that dialectical logic, the logic of levels used throughout this book, is not simply an 'either/or' and 'all-or-none' logic, nor is it based on choosing between one 'side' or the other of pairs of mutually exclusive alternatives in a single dimension, such as the binary oppositions in Aristotle's world view, or the similar oppositions in the structural anthropology of Claude Lévi-Strauss.

The dialectical leap that results in the discrete Event of Events, the change in levels, the framing of new contexts, the repatterning and restructuring of the old order, has nothing to do with 'not', 'negation', or (Hegel's) so-called 'third law of dialectics': the 'negation of the negation'. Negation is a linguistic operation not found in nature or history or communication between organisms.

Nor do dialectical change or dialectical logic have anything essential to do with the other two supposed 'laws' of dialectics: the 'transformation of quantity into quality (and vice versa)', and the 'interpenetration of (binary) opposites' ('Action and reaction are equal and opposite', says Newton's Third Law of Motion). These ideas are obsolete – the simplest reason for this being that they deal only with matter-energy in motion and take no account of information.

'Not'

To return now to the role of 'not' in language, thought, and reality. It seems best to do this in point form, for ease of reference, as several of these remarks are quite technical:

1   Ordinary syntactic 'not' and the other negative particles and prefixes are not the same as 'no'. Like 'yes', 'no' can be communicated without using language, as when we shake our head, which is a form of refusal, rather than negation. A digital syntax with a hierarchy of levels, as in language and digital computers, is essential to 'not', which cannot be communicated without it.

2   Benedict Spinoza (1632–77) said that 'every definition of a boundary is a negation' (*omnis determinatio est negatio*), meaning that every definition negates or excludes all other definitions. 'Not' *may* be used in this way to signify absence, zero, opposition, or exclusion. But the only time this usage is correct is when (in analytic logic) the framing of the negation allows only one other (binary) possibility, as is the case for the binary code (1,0) of the digital computer, where 'not-1' has no alternative but to mean '0' ('if not *a*, then *b*'; cf. pp. 313, 316).

(This is true so long as the computer does not fall into an electronic paradox called by engineers the 'synchronizer glitch' (*Scientific American*, April 1973, pp. 43–4). Here a flip-flop circuit, out of phase with the clock of the central processor, fails to choose between a flip and a flop, and thus remains in an undecided ('metastable') state between continuity and discontinuity, which one theorist compares to Zeno's paradoxes of motion.)

3   Like the prohibition of incest, 'not' never appears in the animal world. There are good grounds for doubt whether apes taught to communicate by American Sign Language, switchboards, feltboards, and the like can ever master the levels of syntax necessary to use 'not' (as distinct from 'no' or rejection or refusal). In Bateson's words (he uses the traditional terminology of opposition): 'An animal has to say the opposite of what it means to mean the opposite of what it says'.

4   'Not-1' is not the same as 'minus-1', for 'not-1' is a general category of being, while 'minus-1' is a particular number in arithmetic.

5   'Not' has no opposite. 'I' cannot be the opposite or the 'other

side' (of the coin) of 'not-I', for 'I' is a particular, whereas 'not-I' is a general relation englobing the rest of the universe. 'Not-I' is the environment of the system 'I', and open system and environment are not of the same level of logic, communication, or reality.

6 The German logician Gottlob Frege (1848–1925) argued in 'Negation', published in 1919, that although judgment depends on negation, it does not depend on an 'opposition', at a single level, between two kinds of assertions, one affirmative and the other negative. All that is logically necessary for judgment, says Frege, is 'an assertion and a negative word'. This is to define 'not' as a metastatement, at one level, about another statement, at another level. In speech, as Victoria Fromkin points out (1973), the negative word in a sentence is defined phonologically after the structure of the sentence is formed.

7 Zero, which is the boundary between the positive and negative numbers (thus neither positive nor negative) and subject to special rules, such as the prohibition against dividing by zero, is a 'metanumber', a rule about numbers (especially in the syntax of place notation) – neither real nor imaginary, but symbolic. 'Not' is not the same as zero, but as the boundary between 'A' and 'not-A', it is a 'metaword', a rule about words, a word with the symbolic function of changing the meaning of all the other words associated with it.

8 Zero mediates between the positive and negative numbers at a single level; 'not' mediates between positive and negative statements at a potentially infinite number of levels.

9 Denial (*Verneinung*), using 'not', is distinct from refusal, rejection (*Verwerfung* in Freud), and disavowal (*Verleugnung*), communicated without using 'not'. (In Freud's view, denial and repression are typical of neurosis; rejection and disavowal are typical of schizophrenia or psychosis; cf Lacan and Wilden, 1968; Wilden, 1980b).

10 Unlike digital computers, which use a discrete code, analog computers and other communicational devices using continuous codes, such as lengths, motions, electrical potentials, and so on (a slide rule or the dial of an analog-digital watch, for example, considered without their digital scales), cannot represent zero. They can approximate the truth function 'and' in analytic logic, but not the truth functions 'or', 'if-then', 'if and only if', or 'not' – all of which involve digital communication. Where the digital computer answers 'either/or', the analog computer answers 'more-or-less'.

11 According to Freud we never find a 'not' coming from the uncon-

scious, nor can 'not' be represented in the visual and sensory code of dreams.

12   As the boundary between 'A' and 'not-A', 'not' is neither 'A' nor 'not-A'.

This enables us to write the Three-Way Rule:

The Three-Way Rule: The minimum number of connections required to establish a relationship is three: system, environment, and the boundary mediating between them.

Negative numbers

As Martin Gardner pointed out in his 'Mathematical Games' in the *Scientific American* for June 1977, it was not until the seventeenth century that mathematicians began to feel comfortable with negative numbers and the 'law of signs': plus times plus equals plus, plus times minus equals minus, and – as W. H. Auden recalled from school:

> Minus times minus equals plus.
> The reason for this we need not discuss.

The Greeks, who loved geometry, thought of numbers as rather like pebbles (as did the Romans), and liked to diagram their mathematics, did not believe in negative numbers – Aristotle was even reluctant to call 1 a number, because, he said, numbers measure pluralities, and the numeral 1 is the measuring unit, not a plurality.

(As the unit of measure the number 1 (unity) is distinct in logical type from the other integers (pluralities). The integers thus display at least three levels of logical typing: zero, one, and more than one.)

In the seventeenth century Descartes spoke of negative roots as 'false roots' and Pascal thought it nonsense to call a quantity less than zero a number. Negative numbers, represented in calculation by black rods, with positive numbers represented by red rods, were however in use in China during the Han period (between about 200 BCE and 200 CE). In the seventh century Hindu mathematicians, who were already using a systematic algebra and a sign for zero in the modern sense (the concept appears in Sanskrit in the fifth century), began using negative values (marked with a special sign) for debtor-creditor relations. The ordinary plus and minus signs we use for what are called 'signed' or 'directed numbers' were first used in the fifteenth century in Germany as warehouse marks for 'over' and 'under' a standard weight.

The first known zero appears in the Babylonian place-value system in about 250 BCE (Ifrah, 1981).

Gardner explains that negative numbers are not the same as those used in subtraction. A shepherd or a child can take six sheep or cows from ten sheep or cows with no difficulty, but a 'negative sheep' is harder to imagine than a ghost sheep or the imaginary sheep we count to overcome insomnia. Says Gardner:

> A ghost cow has at least some kind of reality, but a negative cow is less real than no cow. A cow from a cow leaves nothing, but adding a negative cow to a positive cow, causing both to vanish like a particle meeting its antiparticle, seems as ridiculous as the old joke about the individual whose personality was so negative that when he walked into a party, the guests would look around and ask 'Who left?'.

> 'Well, now that we *have* seen each other', said the Unicorn, 'if you'll believe in me, I'll believe in you. Is that a bargain?'
> 'Yes, if you like', said Alice.
> LEWIS CARROLL: *Alice Through the Looking Glass* (1871)

8.2 Framing and punctuation

Juxtaposition:

> A man awakens suddenly in the middle of the night, bolts up in bed, stares ahead intensely, and twitches his nose. If you cut now to an image of clouds drifting before the full moon, the audience is primed for a wolf-man adventure.

However:

> If you cut to a room where two people are desperately fighting a billowing blaze, the viewers realize that through clairvoyance, a warning dream, or the smell of smoke, the man in bed has become aware of danger.

But:

> If you cut to a distraught wife defending her decision to commit her husband to a mental institution, they will understand that the man in bed is her husband and that the dramatic tension will surround the couple.

And:

> If you're editing an Alfred Hitchcock movie, the juxtaposition of

the man and the wife will immediately raise questions in the viewers' minds about foul play on the part of the woman (p. 2).

So say Ralph Rosenblum and Robert Karen in their 'film editor's story': *When the Shooting Stops . . . The Cutting Begins* (1979). Rosenblum is the editor.

Editing means selection and combination; selection and combination result in a convergence of constraints:

you can cut from the just-awakened protagonist clutching the blankets to his chest to a stranger standing in the shadows at the foot of the bed, pointing a gun and talking in a menacing fashion.

Or

you can cut from the startled sleeper sitting up in bed to a tight close-up of his face, which reveals the terror in his eyes as the menacing voice of the gunmen, unseen by the audience, is heard on the soundtrack (p. 7).

The choice will depend on

the degree of tension you want to generate, whether you want the tension to be muted or to reach climax proportions, your concern about repetitive images and moods, your desire to avoid clichés.

The final set of choices for this combination of just two shots will include picking out from the raw footage the strongest acting performance or best 'take', the best camera angle, and the precise moment to cut the shot and make the transition. Shaping, rhythm, or movement begun in shot A may be completed or carried through in shot B. Every selection and combination is critical, for although audiences are not aware of ordinary editing – Hollywood 'continuity editing' is the work of an invisible hand – they are as much affected by it as they are by a writer's style (p. 7), and often more so.

For the editor, the twenty to forty hours of film actually shot by the director are the axis of cinematic metaphor. The one to three hours of metaphors selected and combined in the final print are the axis of cinematic metonymy.

In editing, the raw shots are

selected, tightened, paced, embellished, arranged, and in some scenes given artificial respiration, until the author's and director's vision becomes completely translated from the language of the script to the idiom of the movies (p. 5).

What editing and montage show is that while shot A frames the following shot B, shot B also reframes shot A, resulting in a 'seeing-after-the-event' just like learning-after-the-event.

Report, command, and question

Montage also illustrates the fact that no communication can be analyzed or understood only at the manifest level on which it occurs. Just like signals in the nervous or hormone systems of the body, every message in a communication system is both a *report* (about a situation, about another message) and a *demand* or *command* (to respond in some way, including silence), as well as a *question* (about the response).

'I love you' reports a state of feeling ('I'm in love'); asks a question ('Do you love me?'); and makes a demand ('Love me too').

Shot A, the startled man, reports a state, say fear, surprise, shock, or sudden recognition. It also demands or invites an interpretation and a response: 'fear (and so on) in relation to what?'. Shot B, say the wife committing her husband to an institution, answers that question and at the same time invites a response to the message created, at another level, by the combination of A and B (which is neither A nor B, but nevertheless remembers them). If shot C shows the wife in the proverbial arms of another man, then A and B suggest deception and conspiracy; if shot C shows the husband beating his wife, then A and B communicate self-defense and justice.

The emergent quality in each case is an emergent meaning, and a meaning is a relationship.

Nowhere in the universe of matter-energy can a later event change an earlier event in this way, the dialectical way.

Content and relationship

The report/command aspects of a message are part of a more general distinction: *content* and *relationship*. In any given message any information that does not communicate report necessarily communicates relation. The content aspect of a message is the relationship between the message and what it is about; its relationship aspect is ultimately the relationship between the communicators – symbolic, imaginary, and real – and that between the communicators and their environment(s).

The relationship aspect of a message is thus a message about how to take the message as a whole.

Relationship almost invariably contextualizes content; content more rarely contextualizes relationship. The relationship aspect of the message is not necessarily consciously exchanged or understood. It may also be expressed simultaneously in another mode of communication

– as when a threat is accompanied by a wink, a 'no' by a nod, an enthusiastic greeting by a stiff-armed handshake.

Relationship concerns the perspective, orientation, framing, and punctuation of messages.

Punctuation

Consider the problem of translating a sequence of signs in one notation into another notation. Assume that a perspective tells us that we are dealing with signs. Assume that an orientation tells us that a certain sequence of signs are numbers. Assume that the framing of the message tells us that the sequence is in binary notation (base 2). What does 00000101001110010110111 signify in decimal (base 10)? (In the decimal system, each leftward place is 10 times the last; in the binary system it is twice the last.)

Without knowing how the binary sequence is punctuated, we cannot translate it. Although in mathematical information theory ('signal theory') the quantitative information content of the sequence remains the same no matter how we partition it, its qualitative content, its meaning, changes when its framing or punctuation changes.

If the sequence is punctuated so that every sign represents a single message (0,0,0,0,0,1, . . .), then the sequence means in decimal exactly what it means in binary. If it is punctuated as pairs of signs, however (00,00,01, . . .), the binary sequence means in decimal: 0, 0, 1, 1, 0, 3, 2, 1, 1, 3, 1, 3. If its punctuation is by triplets, then the binary sequence means in decimal: 0, 1, 2, 3, 4, 5, 6, 7. And if the whole sequence is punctuated as a single message, then it means in decimal 342,391.

Perspective

A perspective can be said to serve two main functions: It acts as a many-dimensioned and many-valued 'filter' that decides what will be considered as information and what will be rejected as noise (or not perceived at all); it also provides the structure(s) by which the information received is made intelligible.

Perspective, orientation, framing, and punctuation can be considered as a four-level hierarchy in which the lower levels are normally constrained by the higher levels and depend on them for their existence, or more precisely here, where all levels are concerned with the organization of information, for their structure.

Under ordinary circumstances, then, a perspective constrains and mediates all orientations within the perspective; an orientation constrains and mediates all frames within the orientation; a frame constrains and mediates all punctuations within the frame.

Thus if a perspective constraining an orientation is inadequate or incorrect, no amount of reorientation within the perspective's constraints can put the perspective right. The same is true for the other three levels: So long as the hierarchy of constraints remains unchanged, changes at the lower levels cannot correct errors or inadequacies at the higher levels. In these circumstances the hierarchy is a dependent hierarchy.

(In hierarchies of perception and communication what is a perspective in one order of complexity may correspond to a punctuation in a higher one. Similarly, what is merely a punctuation of perception and communication in another order may correspond to a perspective in a lower one.)

Under other conditions, however, and notably in every instance of the several kinds of dialectical change outlined in this chapter, the constraints at the higher levels may be broken, outflanked, or restructured by innovation at the lower levels. The higher levels then become temporarily dependent on the outcome of events at the lower levels, and the normal relationship of 'top-down' constraint and dependency will not be restored until the structural changes set off by the innovation have run their course.

This kind of hierarchy is therefore called a 'semi-dependent hierarchy'.

In being semi-dependent the hierarchy of perspectives and punctuations is similar to that existing between strategy and tactics. In the two-term model, framing corresponds to strategy, and punctuation, to tactics.

An innovation at the tactical level can have strategic effects. For example, Cromwell's selection of religiously dedicated men for the New Model Cavalry first used at Marston Moor in 1644 in the English Civil War, combined with his new kind of cavalry charge and above all with the Ironsides' training in strict battlefield discipline, not only made sure of Parliament's victory over King Charles I and the Royalists that day, but also changed the battle strategy of future wars.

Similarly with technological innovation. Before the nineteenth century, a multitude of tactical advances in metal-working, the control of mechanical motions, and machine design and construction – in clocks and watches, automata (mechanical, hydraulic, and pneumatic), water mills, the pumping engines used in mines and in ornamental water displays in aristocratic gardens, programmed water organs and music boxes, as well as programmed weaving machinery (the Jacquard loom), and the 'automatic systems of machinery' (including cybernetic control systems) in the eighteenth-century windmill, the most advanced machine of its day, and finally the reciprocating steam engine – all these interrelated developments over a period of two hundred years amidst the first capitalist revolution eventually made possible the

modern factory system, which, along with the reduction of labor potential (creativity) to a commodity, radically changed the strategy of work
and the nature of social life.

In another terminology this process of dialectical change corresponds
to a situation where novelty at the message level in a system comes to
break through the constraints of its code, restructuring the code so that
previously unheard-of messages become possible. In the early centuries
of the 400-year-long capitalist revolution, for example, the mercantile
'bourgeoisie' ('townspeople') represented no more than one particular
set of messages constrained by the dominant codes of feudal relations
and manorial production. By the mid-nineteenth century in England,
however, when the industrial bourgeoisie won political and economic
power over the agrarian capitalists, they are no longer merely messages
in the system, but the embodiment of the newly dominant codes of the
newly dominant mode of production, industrial capitalism.

A Mickey Mouse film breaks the rules of common sense more
violently than any book ever written, yet because it is seen it is
perfectly intelligible. Try to describe it in words and you will fail;
worse, nobody will listen to you.

GEORGE ORWELL: Review of Henry Miller's *Black Spring* in 1936.

8.3 Cliché clinches

Dwell for a moment on Ralph Rosenblum's warning against clichés in
editing film – a cliché is what is left of an image that has been worked
to death – and recall that the great French stylist, Gustave Flaubert
(1821–80), a man prepared to spend a day or more on a single sentence,
compiled a dictionary of 'received ideas' never to be used in writing
novels. He feared the cliché because in uttering it he was no longer
speaking his own ideas, the received idea was speaking him.

In 'Politics and the English Language', written in 1946, George
Orwell attacked the clichés in English meant to be political English:
dying metaphors, verbal false limbs, vague terms, pretentious diction,
meaningless words, mechanical composition, prefabricated phrases,
sheer incompetence, and outright lying:

In our time, political speech and writing are largely the defence of
the indefensible. Things like the continuance of British rule in
India, the Russian purges and deportations, the dropping of the
atom bombs on Japan, can indeed be defended, but only by
arguments which are too brutal for most people to face. . . . Thus
political language has to consist largely of euphemism, question-

begging and sheer cloudy vagueness. Defenseless villages are bombarded from the air, the inhabitants driven out into the countryside, the cattle machine-gunned, the huts set on fire with incendiary bullets: this is called *pacification*.

'Political language', he says, 'is designed to make lies sound truthful and murder respectable, and to give an appearance of solidity to pure wind' (pp. 153, 157).

In 'The Prevention of Literature', written in 1945–6, he had said:

Political writing in our time consists almost entirely of prefabricated phrases bolted together like the pieces of a child's Meccano set. ... To write in plain, vigorous language one has to think fearlessly, and if one thinks fearlessly one cannot be politically orthodox (p. 168).

He ends the essay 'Politics and the English Language' with six rules for writing to be read:

1   Never use a metaphor, simile, or other figure of speech which you are used to seeing in print.
2   Never use a long word where a short one will do.
3   If it is possible to cut out a word, always cut it out.
4   Never use the passive where you can use the active.
5   Never use a foreign phrase, a scientific word or a jargon word if you can think of an everyday English equivalent.
6   Break any of these rules sooner than say anything outright barbarous.

According to Ernest Bahrac, who drove a camera dolly shooting boy-loves-girl movies at the RKO studios for over twenty years, there were in 1955 just seven basic clinches:

1   First Love, or Sophomore Struggle. Wild-eyed, awkward, elbowish, with no finesse.
2   The Give-in. Love-about-to-be-rewarded fade-out.
3   The Wedding Clinch. Ernest calls this 'dang nigh spiritual'.
4   The Commuter. Door-scrambling husband beats a hasty exit.
5   The Wolf Clinch. A calculated assault, usually accompanied by sweet music, soft lights, champagne.
6   The Would-be-Romeo. Least subtle and most ambitious tactics, sometimes involving a wrestling match.
7   Home-Again. The welcome-home embrace for the truant. Usually the climax to a mouth-on collision (quoted by Denis Myers in *Secrets of the Stars*, 1955, p. 118).

Also in 1955 (p. 119) Andre Doran, President of the Southern California Cosmetologist Society, announced that Hollywood recognizes just six kinds of (feminine) lips: the Tempting (Constance Smith) . . . the Knowing (Ann Sheridan) . . . the Lingering (Linda Darnell) . . . the Sultry (Susan Hayward) . . . the Worldly (Joan Crawford) . . . and the Cheery (Betty Grable).

The best kisses, says Ernest, 'always let the girl's [sic] nose come in front of the man's cheek'.

Milton Berle: 'Wait a minute. Are you knocking this country? Are you saying something against America?'
Terry Thomas: 'Against it! I should be positively astounded to hear of anything that could be said for it. Why, the whole bloody place is the most unspeakable matriarchy in the whole history of civilisation. Look at yourself. And the way your wife and her *strumpet* of a mother [Ethel Merman] push you through the hoop. As far as I can see American men have been totally emasculated. They're like slaves. They die like flies from coronary thrombosis, while their women sit under hairdryers eating chocolates and arranging for every second Tuesday to be some kind of Mothers Day.'
    It's a Mad, Mad, Mad, Mad World (1963), directed by Stanley Kramer

8.4 Film stereotypes of American women

In an important article Joseph W. Baunoch and Betty E. Chmaj of Wayne State University have carefully identified sixteen strategic stereotypes of women in American film, providing us with a semiotic dictionary of the 'nature of woman' according to Hollywood from the 1930s to the mid-1970s.

These stereotypes are by no means confined to Hollywood, of course. As ideological and working images necessary to the colonization of women by men (most of whom are colonized by other men), they appear in one form or another, mainly negative, wherever women are oppressed.

In what follows I am summarizing Baunoch and Chmaj's article, omitting the numerous films they cite as examples.

Their categories are:

- THE PILLARS OF VIRTUE: the Sweet Young Thing, The Perfect Wife, the Gracious Lady, Mother/Mammy/Mom/Ma.

LIPS ARE THE DOORWAY
TO THE HEART . . . .

This is what Andre Doran, President of the Southern California Cosmetologist Society, declares. He lists six basic types of lips—the Tempting, with the lower lip full, lush, challenging, the upper defiant, "a provocative combination". . . the Knowing, arched like Cupid's Bow, yet firm and decisive . . . the Lingering, soft and understanding . . . the Sultry, a heavily dipped lower lip "pulsating with warmth," a calculating upper lip guarding it . . . . the Worldly, long, exquisite, usually parted . . . the Cheery, with upturned lips like a smile about to be born. . . .

Susan Hayward,
the Sultry.

Constance Smith,
the Tempting.

Ann Sheridan,
the Knowing.

Betty Grable,
the Cheery.

Joan Crawford,
the Worldly.

Linda Darnell,
the Lingering.

- THE GLAMOR GIRLS: the Femme Fatale, the Sex Goddess, the Showgirl, the Cool Beauty.
- THE EMOTIVE WOMAN: the Long-Suffering Lady, the Vixen, the Sexually-Frustrated Neurotic.
- THE INDEPENDENT WOMAN/THE NEW WOMAN: the Career Girl, the Regular Gal, the Durable Dame, the Brassy Modern, the Liberated Modern.

The details follow:

A The Pillars of Virtue

1 The Sweet Young Thing
As sacred as Mom – in America – she is 'a chaste charmer, whether child, waif, girl next door, or Pollyanna. Warm and wholesome, she looks at the world with wide-eyed innocence. The eternal girl-woman and apple-pie symbol of all that is good.'
Representative stars: Janet Gaynor (1929–38), Shirley Temple (1934–40), Doris Day (1948–69), June Allyson (1944–53), Julie Andrews (1964–69).

2 The Perfect Wife
'Often the elder sister to the Sweet Young Thing,' she is 'more chic and sophisticated in the thirties and forties than later', but 'remains throughout film history the supportive, enduring, good-humored, comely (though not often overtly sexy – less so, certainly, in later decades) complement to her mate and bastion of the American Home.'
Representative stars: Myrna Loy (1934–52), June Allyson (1954–59), Eve Marie Saint (1957–present).

3 The Gracious Lady
Although sharing many of the attributes of the Perfect Wife, 'she was something more: the focal point of her dramas rather than a supporting peg. Virtuous, compassionate, intelligent, witty, and in her own elegant, genteel way, always able to face whatever crisis confronted her'. She could be 'strong and independent, freely giving of her strength to sustain her man without loss of dignity'.
Representative stars: Irene Dunne (1930–52), Greer Garson (1939–55), Deborah Kerr (1947–present).

4 Mother/Mammy/Mom/Ma
'Aproned, over-forty, and beyond sex, another bastion of the American Home, usually bolstering from the background'. She is 'the quintessence of strength, constancy, approachability, and integrity who would

sacrifice all for the family. Not until the fifties and sixties does this tower of selflessness give way in film to the "Great American Bitch'" (e.g. Angela Lansbury) 'moms who blight instead of brace'.

Representative stars: Fay Bainter (1934–53), Hattie McDaniel (1932–48) (also Ethel Waters), Jane Darwell (1930–56) – who played the role in over three hundred films.

B   The Glamor Girls

1   The Femme Fatale

'Dietrich, as a *femme* at her most *fatale* in *The Devil is a Woman* [1935], tells the hero, "I came to see if you were dead. If you loved me enough, you would have killed yourself." Although most film *fatales*, including Dietrich herself, aren't really such lethal witches, even the most Americanized carries a hint of destructiveness. A woman of mystery and allure, she is the exotic conqueror of the submissive male in a world of romance, intrigue, and shadows.'

Representative stars: Marlene Dietrich (1930–57), Rita Hayworth (1941–57), Hedy Lamarr (1938–57), Ava Gardner (1946–64).

2   The Sex Goddess

'Another temptress, but open rather than mysterious, straightforward rather than devious, brassy rather than sinister. Her guise is whorish but her heart is often as generous as her proportions'. 'By the forties the brassiness gives way to cuddliness and by the sixties (as a reflection of an alienated, automated age?) it sometimes descends to a zombie-like, plastic, super-womanishness'.

Representative stars: Mae West (1932–40), Jean Harlow (1930–37), Lana Turner (1941–55), Marilyn Monroe (1950–62), Raquel Welch (1966–present).

3   The Showgirl

'The Sweet Young Thing with spangles. Although glamorized and greasepainted, she is essentially a "good kid": affable, wholesome, reliable, with "the-show-must-go-on" in her blood. Curiously, a less overtly theatrical personage than many of her performing sisters, she often experiences a metamorphosis from chorus kicker or cheap honky tonk singer or the prettier part of a song-and-dance team into Lady and Star at the film's end. When backstage musicals fade in the fifties, she fades with them'.

Representative stars: Ruby Keeler (1933–37), Alice Faye (1936–43), Betty Grable (1940–55), Judy Garland (1940–54).

4 The Cool Beauty

'The "white" lady, the goddess on a pedestal: aristocratic, imperturbably and impeccably groomed. Often an heiress or a princess', she draws respectful glances 'rather than leering appraisals from men. Copulation with such a creature, if at all imaginable, could cause frostbite. After the fifties, the Cool Beauty, too, disappears.'
Representative stars: Constance Bennett (1929–39), Gene Tierney (1940–55), Alexis Smith (1940–59), Grace Kelly (1951–56).

C The Emotive Woman

1 The Long-Suffering Lady

'The noble martyr who tearfully but courageously suffers the slings and arrows. Her agonizing is usually the result of the abusiveness and/or infidelities and/or weaknesses of a man (or men); on other occasions her antagonist might be a thankless child, malicious gossip, or disease (physical or mental). Popular with feminine audiences, she "complies with woman's image of herself as long-suffering" (Leslie A. Fiedler). Interestingly and paradoxically, many stars who made the type a specialty were equally adept at portraying her opposite, the Vixen.'
Representative stars: Greta Garbo (1930–37), Bette Davis (1937–64), Joan Crawford (1945–62), Barbara Stanwyck, Susan Hayward, Olivia de Havilland, and others (1940s and after), Katherine Hepburn (1951–present).

2 The Vixen

'Overpowering and destructive, a more lethal antagonist than the *femme fatale*, the neurotic, vindictive, castrating bitch-woman'.
Representative stars: Bette Davis (1934–1970s), Joan Crawford (1931–1967), Barbara Stanwyck (1930–56), Susan Hayward (1942–61), Elizabeth Taylor (1963–present).

3 The Sexually-Frustrated Neurotic

'The perennial outsider, the misfit, the unfulfilled woman, whose lonely, empty life is vitalized almost solely by her own hysterical outbursts'.
Representative stars: Miriam Hopkins (1936–43), Agnes Moorehead (1942–60), Mercedes McCambridge in *All the King's Men* (1949), Rosalind Russell in *Picnic* (1955), individual roles by Ingrid Bergman, Bette Davis, Shelley Winters, and others.

OVERLEAF FIGURE 8.3: An anonymous poster for Ernst Lubitsch's *Angel* (1937), with Marlene Dietrich, Herbert Marshall, and Melvyn Douglas. In the original poster Dietrich appears in color; her lover, in a twilight grey-green.

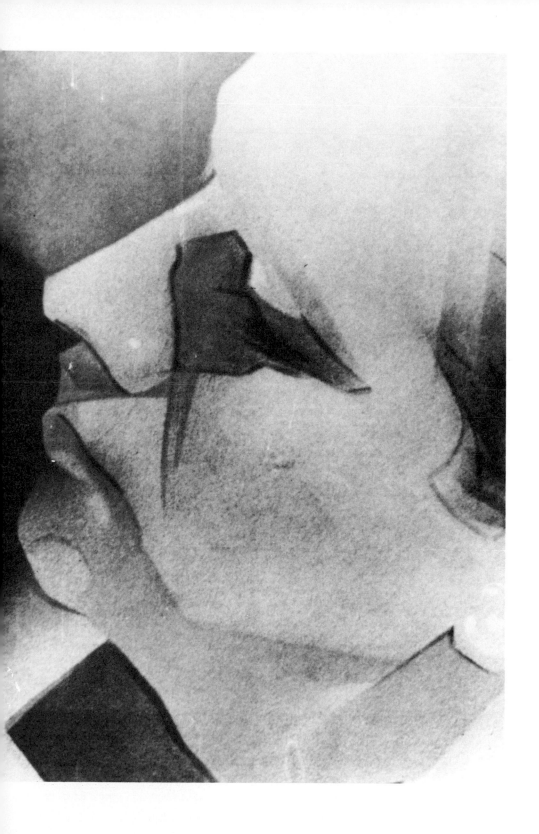

D   The Independent Woman (at times the 'New Woman' or the 'Modern Woman')

1   The Career Girl
'Ambitious and productive, tailored and crisp; triumphant in a dismayed man's world (until her final-reel conversion into a lovestruck, "fulfilled" female). The Career Girl as a star type, along with most of her Modern Woman sisters, all but disappears after the forties.'
Representative stars: Jean Arthur (1935–48), Katherine Hepburn (1933–52), Claudette Colbert (1939–46), Rosalind Russell (1940–52).

2   The Regular Gal
'Earthbound and salty, another female who holds her own in the male world but men like her better; the wise-cracking "good Joe", comfortable "pal" or "buddy".' The masculine terms used to describe her are assumed to be complimentary.
Representative stars: Joan Blondell (1930–56), Ginger Rogers (1930–50), also Anne Sheridan, Patricia Neal, and Eve Arden (in supporting roles).

3   The Durable Dame
'Behind her battleaxe exterior beats the proverbial heart of gold (or, in recent caricatures of the type, as with Bette Davis, a "one hundred percent camp" malignancy)'. 'A lovable, earthy old rock, too tough to be a relic and too honest for the prescribed niceties', she 'weathers the world, one way or another, and only death can demolish her.'
Representative stars: Marie Dressler (1930–33), Marjorie Main (1937–57), Bette Davis (1961–1970s).

4   The Brassy Modern
'As brash as the Regular Gal but bouncier and more volatile; a bombshell – likeable, rambunctious, and non-stop in her quest, whether for a man or anything else, comes on strong but makes them laugh.'
Representative stars: Ethel Merman (1934–53), Betty Hutton (1942–52), Barbra Streisand (1968–present).

5   The Liberated Modern
'The newest of the types, good-looking in her own way', she appeared in the mid-sixties. '"Liberated" in any of several ways, she may be prominent as a career woman of a newer kind (whether as teacher, model, tramp)', and '"free" in a new way (free of stereotypes, for instance). Unlike most American Dreaming sisters, she sets her life-goals beyond the husband-and-home-in-the-suburbs.' 'Usually self-reliant, razor-sharp, alienated, and tough but pretty.'
Representative stars: Jane Fonda (1965–present), Julie Christie

(1965–present), Faye Dunaway (1967–present), Glenda Jackson (1970–present).

(Male stereotyping of women is taken up again and its pathology analyzed in terms of its basic code – (Virgin) Mother, Wife, Whore, and Witch (Bitch) – in *Man and Woman, War and Peace: The Strategist's Companion*, 1987.)

Give Coleridge one vivid word from an old narrative; let him mix it with two in his thought; and then (translating terms of music into terms of words) 'out of three sounds he [will] frame, not a fourth sound, but a star'.

JOHN LIVINGSTONE LOWES: *The Road to Xanadu* (1930)

8.5 Montage

As Frank Thomas and Ollie Johnston explain in *Disney Animation* (1981, pp. 64–5), just two drawings of a head, the first with it leaning towards the right shoulder and the second with it turned to the left and the chin slightly raised, can be used to communicate a multitude of images – merely by varying the timing. The timing is changed by inserting between these two extremes of motion other drawings called, what else? 'inbetweens'. An 'inbetween' fills one or two frames of film at 24 frames a second (the best frequency is one drawing for every two frames of film).

With no inbetweens we see the character struck by a tremendous force. With one inbetween the character has merely been hit by a brick. With two inbetweens the character has a nervous tic, an uncontrollable twitch. With three inbetweens the character is dodging the brick. With four the character is turning to give a crisp command, 'Get going!', 'Move it!'. With five inbetweens the character is more friendly, the movement less agitated, 'Over here!', 'Come on – hurry up!'. With six inbetweens the character is watching someone attractive cross the street. With seven the character is trying to get a better look. With eight the character is scanning a shop window, looking for an item desired. With nine the character is appraising something, considering it thoughtfully. With ten inbetweens we see the character stretching aching muscles from head to toe.

In 1902, to save money on a ten-minute film called *The Life of an American Fireman*, Edwin S. Porter began with a fireman dreaming of a woman and child in danger (conveyed by double exposure), dissolved to a close-up of a fire alarm and a hand reaching into the frame to set it off, cut to stock footage of firemen bursting into action in the firehouse, then to an external shot of the fire engine racing to the scene, and ended with the fireman rescuing the mother and child about to be overcome by smoke. The audience was excited and delighted; nothing like this had ever been done before. Porter had invented editing, and with editing the modern film (Rosenblum and Karen, 1981, pp. 35–7).

Within two decades of mostly silent film, through D. W. Griffith, Vsevolod Pudovkin, Sergei Eisenstein, Fritz Lang, and others, and culminating in the visual revolution of Abel Gance's *Napoleon* (1927), the entire syntax basic to shooting, editing, and projecting the modern film had been invented, uncovered, or discovered – largely by D. W. Griffith, the man who invented Hollywood.

David Wark Griffith (1875–1948) was the first filmmaker to develop a coherent and conscious 'grammar' of film. His fluid and integrative rhythms, as in his depiction of the family, the home, filial duty, white supremacy, community, country, and tradition, set the style for the 'continuity editing' of future Hollywood films, while his use of rapid crosscutting generated excitement, tension, and climax (Mast, 1974).

Griffith's two basic discoveries were the effects of composition and cutting. Through experience, with little conscious theorizing but great singleness of purpose, Griffith

> developed the texture, the look, the feel, and the tone of the individual shot, as well as the rhythms, the meaning, the kinetic sensations, and the intellectual commentary of joining the shots (Mast, 1974).

He treated individual shots or takes as 'words' to be combined into scenes as if into 'sentences', combined scenes into sequences as if into 'paragraphs', and paragraphs into plots as if into arguments. (Note that film is not a language.) And his films were arguments, for Griffith was the first director to use the motion picture as a means of presenting through his eyes an interpretation of human values, historical events, and social change. Projecting into his films the values of his class, caste, race, and sex, as well as his uniquely personal views, Griffith invented the overtly ideological film.

Among his cinematic innovations (largely worked out in the more than 150 films he directed between 1908 and 1913): He divided continuous scenes into separate shots (saving money on actors); changed camera angles to change mood and message (he was also the first to use a truck-mounted camera to film a speeding train); integrated panning and tracking shots into his emotional and narrative grammar of film; moved in on the actors with medium shots and close-ups, improving acting at the same time by suppressing the exaggerated gestures typical of the stage; cut from actors to the subject of their thoughts and back again; employed the flashback; used the extreme long shot contrasted with the extreme close up; expanded time and space as needed for suspense; used a 'concrete symbolism' of objects – hats, wrenches, flowers, telephones, pistols, animals, and so on – to communicate meanings, emotions, and contexts; added musical scores cued to his films' effects; used color tinting (blue, orange, yellow, green, or red) to intensify the emotional tone of particular sequences; created the high-tension 'Griffith last-minute ending' by developing the parallel montage (cutting from one simultaneous action to another, typically between attacker, victim, and rescuer racing to the scene); and eventually cut his scenes shorter and shorter, eliminating the superfluous, each shot focusing attention on a 'single essential fact' as if it were a single essential word (Mast, 1974; Rosenblum and Karen, 1981, pp. 37–40).

Griffith's hoped-for masterpiece, *Intolerance* (1916), was a cinematic and commercial failure. But Sergei Eisenstein, the next great master of a new kind of editing, later said of it: 'All that is best in the Soviet film has its origins in *Intolerance*.'

Beginning his 1938 article 'Word and Image' with Lowes' remarks on Coleridge quoted at the head of this section, Eisenstein starts the analysis of his mode of montage with the fact that 'two film pieces of any kind, placed together, inevitably combine into a new concept, a new quality, arising out of that juxtaposition'. Such an emergence of novelty (whether in perception or understanding) always occurs, he says, when two or more distinct facts, phenomena, objects, qualities, or messages are juxtaposed. There is a 'universal tendency', he avers, for us to make out of the contiguity of two or more qualities a unity that surpasses its parts.

This he compares with Lewis Carroll's 'portmanteau words' – 'frumious', for example, composed of 'furious' and 'fuming' – and with Freud's examples of 'condensation' in his work on jokes – 'the Christmas alcoholidays', for instance (*The Film Sense*, 1947, pp. 6–7).

Splicing two shots together resembles 'not so much a simple sum of one shot plus another shot – as it does a *creation*' (p. 7). He quotes Kurt Koffka from *The Principles of Gestalt Psychology* (1935, p. 126):

It has been said: The whole is more than the sum of its parts. It is more correct to say that the whole is something else than the sum of its parts, because summing is a meaningless procedure, whereas the whole-part relationship is meaningful.

Eisenstein defines an image as a selection and combination of representations: at midnight the hands of a clock form a *representation* of 12 pm; the *image* of midnight consists of all the representations associated with that hour. A montage, he says, is a sequence of representations that when combined together create a dynamic image or images, not so much of a story or chain of events, as with narrative editing, as of a complex of meanings, values, attentions, and emotions.

In the montage a chain of originally separate icons merges into one. Although these are presented to consciousness (and, one adds, to the unconscious) one after the other, in sequence, the pattern of the whole is preserved in the sensations and memory (pp. 16–17).

There follows his definition of montage:

> *Representation A* and *representation B* must be so selected from all the possible features within the theme that is being developed, must be so sought for, that their *juxtaposition* – that is, the juxtaposition of *those very elements* and not of alternative ones – shall evoke in the perception and feelings of the spectator the most complete *image of the theme itself* (p. 11).

Eisenstein takes an example from the narrative poem *Poltava* (1829) by the popular and radical Aleksandr Pushkin (1799–1837), considered the greatest of Russian poets (p. 48). The image is that of flight by night, secrecy, escape:

> But no one knew just how or when
> She vanished. A lone fisherman
> In that night heard the clack of horses' hoofs,
> Cossack speech and a woman's whisper . . .

Having told the reader in the first two lines that Marya has vanished, says Eisenstein, Pushkin 'wanted to give him the experience as well. To achieve this, he turns to montage':

> Clack of horses' hoofs.
> Cossack speech.
> A woman's whisper.

'Three shots', says Eisenstein. And then a fourth, not in sound but sight:

> And eight horseshoes had left their traces
> Over the meadow morning dew.

The image is complete.

Every edited film is of course a montage; what Eisenstein brought to film was both a new kind of montage within the film and the theory to teach it with. As Gerald Mast says (1974, p. 525):

> Eisenstein was the greatest magician and musician of montage. He manipulated the kinetic rhythms of editing so successfully that an audience was never aware of manipulation, only of the film's

tension, energy, and excitement. Eisenstein's theory of montage was one of collision – a crash of images from cut to cut, the images contrasting in light, shading, length, texture, size, speed, or emphasis.

Others find Eisenstein's 'dialectic montage' or 'montage of contradictions' – notably in his first feature film *Strike* (1924) – too arty, too showy, and often too unrealistic for the modern eye.

In this Eisenstein's approach differed decisively from the 'linking', 'constructive', or 'structural' montage of his contemporary Vsevolod Pudovkin (1893–1953). Pudovkin stressed sequence and 'natural' succession rather than conflict, a more lyrical and graceful mode of composition, using montage to underscore particular dramatic effects rather than using it as a major vehicle of the filmic experience itself. (In practice both Eisenstein and Pudovkin used the mode of montage associated with the other as well as their own.)

Of Eisenstein's celebrated montage of the massacre on the Odessa Steps in *The Battleship Potemkin* (1926), Ralph Rosenblum says that it 'remains for editors everywhere the single most intimidating piece of film ever assembled' (p. 51).

But Eisenstein's definition of montage just quoted – as the precise juxtaposition of 'representation A' and 'representation B' (and no others), so as to evoke in the spectator 'the most complete image of the theme itself' – is more restrictive than it can be or needs to be. The definition implies that the director's conscious intention can be completely expressed by the two images selected, which, given the necessary participation of the spectator, is unlikely; it suggests moreover that no other perceptions, feelings, or meanings will or should arise, which is impossible, given the vast range of unconscious intentions and the diversity of the audience; and it suggests also that the image produced by the juxtaposition is novelty only for the viewer, and not also an image full of surprises for the director as well (a position Eisenstein abandons elsewhere in his text).

Novelty

Novelty is the faithful companion of natural evolution, history, and human creativity, both individual and collective. It is the unexpected emergence of novelty, its surprise value, its creation of order (or information) from disorder (or noise) that mainly distinguishes the dialectical process from the mere cycles of repetition with which it is often confused. Both Eisenstein and Mao, for example, equate dialectics with the oscillation between opposites described by the Chinese ideology of the two cosmic forces of yin and yang (which are also said to form an 'identity' or 'unity' of opposites, like positive and negative electricity).

There are four further points of distinction. Unlike oscillating or cyclic systems, the dialectical process is irreversible, just as evolution and history are irreversible.

Secondly, unlike the simple harmonic motion of cyclic physical systems such as pendulums, radio waves, resonating atoms, or the sine waves of AC current (which are matter-energy cycles subject to ordinary physical regularities or 'laws'), dialectical change is not a change of motion, but a transformation of organization. Dialectical changes are not matter-energy processes, but semiotic ones. They are changes in levels and types of complexity governed by information.

Thirdly, real physical systems, as well as their imaginary equivalent in the yin-yang system, are closed systems. Their real or imaginary sources of energy are internal to the system involved, and not external, as is the case for open systems, including dialectical systems, all of which depend on their relationships to their (often multiple) environments for sustenance and survival – and often for the origin of certain kinds of change.

Fourthly, the physical systems discussed are not only closed to new inputs of matter and energy (physical negative entropy), they are also closed to new information or order (semiotic negative entropy). The same is true for the imaginary yin-yang system. A system closed to new order (and thus also to disorder) is incapable of the creation of order from disorder that is the hallmark of dialectical change.

Working with the Soviet composer Sergei Prokofiev on *Alexander Nevsky* (1938), Eisenstein created what he called 'vertical montage'. Just as an orchestra score is written in several staffs or registers, one for each group of instruments, so that the horizontal development of each part being played is accompanied by a vertical structure that relates all the parts together, so is vertical montage a combination of simultaneous themes at several levels progressing successively through time along a horizontal axis.

(The continuity of the film shot as we perceive it is not to be confused with the effectively invisible level at which it consists of discrete frames.)

In order to create the vertical montage, says Eisenstein in 'Synchronization of Senses' (*The Film Sense*, 1947, pp. 74–5), he drew on his experience of the silent film, on the *polyphonic* montage

> where shot is linked to shot not merely through one indication – movement, or light values, or stage in the exposition of the plot, or the like – but through a *simultaneous advance* of a multiple series of lines, each maintaining an independent compositional course and each contributing to the total compositional course of the sequence.

For Eisenstein the three central media of montage are dialectical conflict, 'organic' (or 'embryonic') novelty (sometimes he calls it 'molecular'), and the communication of the deepest of emotions. As he had said in 1929 in an article on film form, and in another of the same year comparing the principles of cinema with the structure of the Chinese ideogram and the Japanese Kabuki play, and as he said again in 1944 in 'Dickens, Griffith, and the Film Today' (reprinted in *Film Form* in 1949):

> The shot is by no means the *element* of montage.
> The shot is the montage *cell*.
> Just as cells in their division cell-differentiation form a phenomenon
> of another order, the organism or embryo, so, on the other side
> of the dialectical leap from the shot, there is montage.

Montage may also be the expansion of a contradiction within a shot to a contradiction between shots, creating out of conflict a novel and in some sense always unexpected unity (p. 236).

In his concept of the close-up – understood not so much as a simple change of viewpoint but rather as a statement about the value of what is seen – Eisenstein uses a language model that has only to be translated into a semiotic one (film is not a language) to remain valid today:

> The principal function of the close-up in our cinema is – not only
> and not so much to *show* or to *present*, as to *signify*, to *give
> meaning*, to *designate* (p. 238).

One understands montage, he says, not merely as a means of producing effects,

> but above all as a means of *speaking*, a means of *communicating*
> ideas, of communicating them by way of a special film language,
> by way of a special form of film *speech* (p. 245).

Montage is allied with the originally imagistic value of words, he adds, with the figure of speech, with metaphor and metonymy (pp. 246–8). The secret of the structure of montage is in fact 'the secret of *the structure of emotional speech*' (p. 249).

He quotes an example of the distinction between 'logical' and 'affective' speech (both have of course their own logic) from *Language* (1925) by Joseph Vendryes. In the formal syntax of the written tongue, one says for example:

> The man that you see sitting down there on the beach is the one I
> saw being robbed at the station yesterday.

In speaking one would say:

> You see that man – the one over there – he's sitting on the beach – well! I saw him yesterday – he was at the station – he was being robbed!

In the affective sentence the formal syntax dissolves into the juxtaposition of metaphors. Of this spoken form Vendryes says:

> The verbal image is one though it forms a kind of kinematical development. But whereas in the written tongue it is presented as a whole, when spoken it is cut up into short sections whose number and intensity correspond to the speaker's impressions, or to the necessity he feels for vividly communicating them to others.

Responds Eisenstein (p. 250): 'Isn't this an exact copy of what takes place in montage?'

Montage, Eisenstein concludes, is neither written nor spoken speech, but rather a third variety in which the affective and emotional structure functions in 'an even more full and pure form': *inner speech* – speech enriched, he says, by *'sensual thinking'*.

Here the interplay of conflict and resolution, unity and diversity, light and shadow, motion and movement, metaphor and metonymy, similarity and contiguity, image and representation, continuity and discontinuity, and logic and feeling creates the 'organic unity of a higher order' that for Eisenstein the master artisan is the goal of montage.

Translated into semiotic terms Eisenstein's richly meaningful metaphors of the 'sensual thinking' of montage are images of the ecology of analog and iconic communication, images dominated primarily by the holistic and intuitive logic of the right brain rather than by the digital and rational logic of the left – for (analog and iconic) sensing, sensuality, and emotion are not simply the context of (digital) reason, they are the reason for reason itself.

'Contrariwise', continued Tweedledee, 'if it was so, it might be; and if it were so, it would be: but as it isn't, it ain't. That's logic'.
LEWIS CARROLL: *Alice Through the Looking-Glass* (1871)

8.6 Both-and and either/or

Dialectic is not simply a way of knowing; it is the way of life itself. The dialectical way includes the analytical way as its necessary complement, and neither of them violates the principle of non-contradiction.

When analytic logic says 'either A or not-A', it means this:

either A *or* not-A

– a choice. When analytic logic says 'both A and not-A' it means this:

both A *and* not-A

– a contradiction.

When dialectical logic says 'both A and not-A', it means this:

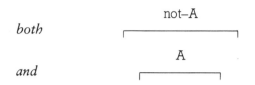

– a dependent hierarchy between open system and environment.

Analytic logic is a single-level and static logic, outside time and change. It is the symmetrical logic of classical physics.

Dialectical logic is a many-leveled and dynamic logic, within time – and dependent, like learning, on duration.

The both-and of analytic logic is a secondary relationship derived by addition from its basic operation of division, either/or. The perspective of analytic logic is thus '*either* either/or *or* both-and'.

The both-and of dialectical logic is a primary relationship derived by connection from relations between levels, such as the both-and relation between open system and environment. The perspective of dialectical logic is thus '*both* both-and *and* either/or'.

Amid the seeming confusion of our mysterious world, individuals are so nicely adjusted to a system, and systems to one another and to a whole, that, by stepping aside for a moment, a man exposes himself to a fearful risk of losing his place forever.

NATHANIEL HAWTHORNE: *Wakefield* (1835)

8.7 Montage analytic and dialectic

Table 8.1 lists some functional distinctions between the cerebral hemispheres suggested by the argument of this and the preceding chapter.

It seems likely that the left hemisphere is mainly concerned with tactics, while the right hemisphere is mainly concerned with strategy. Most of the qualities considered by Carl von Clausewitz to be essential to the character of the strategist are associated with right brain functions. The same is true of context theory, the new view (see below).

Let us recall from Chapter 7 that people with right-hemisphere damage were uncertain as to what was significant and what was not

Table 8.1: Some distinctions between the functions of the cerebral hemispheres suggested by the argument of this and the preceding chapter

left-hemisphere specialization	*right-hemisphere specialization*
analytic, deductive	dialectic, synthetic
computation	emulation
exclusive (either/or)	inclusive (both-and)
order from order	order from disorder
identity, familiarity, symmetry	novelty, change, asymmetry
convergent	divergent
system, text	environment, context
content	relationship
sequence	simultaneity
verbal, propositional	non-verbal, imaginative
words, numbers, letters	models, plans, pictures
digital and iconic	iconic and analog
signification	meaning
literal	figurative
rational, intellectual, lineal	poetic, humorous, intuitive
solipsistic	interpersonal
punctuation	orientation
competition	co-operation
win/lose	win/win
metonymy	metaphor
logistics	reconnaissance
bottom up	top down
tactics	strategy

in stories presented to them, failing to make appropriate patterns of connections in the plot, and not dealing well with context. According to Howard Gardner and Suzanne Hamby, writing in 1979, people with right-hemisphere damage,

> lack anchorage with respect to the external world: they were uncertain of their own status in relation to diverse social environments or literary creations, and thus they cannot appropriately distance themselves (Campbell, 1982, p. 246).

'It is as if the left hemisphere is a highly efficient, but narrowly programmed linguistic computer', while 'the right hemisphere constitutes the ideal audience for a humorous silent film, but only the two hemispheres together can appreciate all four of the Marx brothers.'

The 400-year-old capitalist revolution in economics and society has been a mainly left-brain, digital revolution. In modern society, emotion and feeling, which are typically analog or iconic states, are commonly divorced from (digital) reason. Images, icons, and ideas not expressed or expressible in words are regarded as not worth thinking. Digital information and digital coding – the form taken by signification in language, by commodities in production, by value in relations of exchange, and by creativity when measured in labor time – have come to dominate their context of analog and iconic communication (including graphics, film, and television), just as 'all/or/none' has come to dominate 'more-or-less', 'either/or' to dominate 'both-and', competition to dominate co-operation, exchange value to dominate use value, and short-range survival value to dominate long-range survival value.

The subject of digital communication is divorced from the subject of analog communication, the subject of 'mind' from the subject of 'body', and the subject of creativity from the subject of work.

A revolution is a strategic envelopment of the system in which it arises. It is a radical change in the basic structure and grand strategy of a dominant science, philosophy of life, society, or economic system. Revolutions are the processes by which solutions impossible in one system are uncovered by turning it into a new one. The system survives, not by staying the same but by a radical transformation, a radical change in values and structure.

If it is true that only a social, economic, and political revolution can solve the crises of state and private capitalism, East and West, and provide us with a real future, it is also true that if that revolution is not primarily a right-brain, contextual, many-dimensioned, diverse, and open-system revolution, then it will not be a revolution but a rearrangement.

These are the words of the right-brain strategists.

FRONTISPIECE: The Commander of the Guard in the *The Princess Radiant* playing at the Haymarket in London in 1851 helps to launch Mrs Bloomer's new invention.

Envoi

Women in Production: The Chorus Line 1932–1980

a videotape montage by Rhonda Hammer and Anthony Wilden, edited by Frank Campbell and Rhonda Hammer

> We should talk less and draw more. Personally, I would like to renounce speech altogether and, like organic nature, communicate everything I have to say in sketches.
>
> JOHANN WOLFGANG VON GOETHE (1749–1832)

Media literacy

Terry Ramsaye begins his elegant history of the motion picture, *A Million and One Nights*, published in 1926, with a remark as true today as it was in the golden age of the silent film:

> In the public mind and in the consciousness of many of its students the motion picture seems a magic thing, born yesterday and full of growth this morning. But magic and miracles always fade in the light of information. It is the vastness of what we do not know which creates the great astonishments (p. xxxvii).

It is not astonishing that most people are highly literate in the many kinds of non-verbal communication used by the video media, whether by that we mean the movies, magazines, picture books, or television. What is astonishing is the extent to which this literacy in the social media is unconscious, inarticulate, and unrecognized.

The Chorus Line, a 55-minute montage of fifteen musical numbers from eleven Hollywood films and one Broadway show, is designed to make this unconscious literacy conscious. Literacy is power – for whoever has command of it – and *The Chorus Line* invites the viewer to take command of the medium on display.

As an anthology of popular dance and a 50-year visual history of Hollywood, the montage puts at the viewers' disposal a concise and representative record of the way the most important social values – relations between people – have been communicated to the public over the past fifty years by the best people in the business.

The Chorus Line speaks to the eyes and ears in many ways: through its chronicle of popular stars, popular wisdom, and popular music;

WOMEN IN PRODUCTION
THE CHORUS LINE
1932-1980

The Program: This one-hour program is a selective video history of the chorus line. It is also a record of the way social relations have been depicted in one medium of popular entertainment. The production numbers we have selected for study depict relations of class, race, sex, and nationality. Each production number has been chosen both for what it portrays and for the high quality of the way it portrays it.

The Stars: Cab Calloway, Marlene Dietrich, Cary Grant, Ruby Keeler, James Cagney, Eddie Cantor, Ethel Merman, Lucille Ball (as a 'Goldwyn Girl', twice), Eddie Foy Jr., George Chakiris, Rita Moreno, Zero Mostel, Gene Wilder, Joel Gray, Liza Minnelli, John Hurt, the cast of the Broadway production of **A Chorus Line**, and several hundred working women.

The Montage

Blonde Venus, 1932	'Hot Voodoo'
Footlight Parade, 1933	'By a Waterfall'
	'Shanghai Lil'
Murder at the Vanities, 1934	'Where Do They Come From?'
	'Soothe Me'
Kid Millions, 1934	'Ice Cream'
Roman Scandals, 1934	The Roman Market
	'Keep Young and Beautiful'
Here Come the Waves, 1944	'Here Come The Waves'
The Pajama Game, 1957	'Hurry Up!'
West Side Story, 1961	'America'
The Producers, 1968	'Springtime for Hitler'
Cabaret, 1972	'Welcome'
The Naked Civil Servant, 1975	
A Chorus Line, 1980	'One'

The Directors: Josef von Sternberg, Lloyd Bacon (Busby Berkeley), Mitchell Leisen, Roy Del Ruth, Frank Tuttle (Busby Berkeley), Mark Sandrich, George Abbott and Stanley Donen (Bob Fosse), Robert Wise, (Jerome Robbins), Mel Brooks, Bob Fosse, Jack Gold, Michael Bennett.

Format: One hour, ¾" cassette, B&W and colour. The cassette should be played back with an amplifier and two speakers in place of the audio output of the television monitor. For audiences bigger than about 35 persons, two monitors should be used.

For further information and Program Guide, write: The Chorus Line, c/o Department of Communication, Simon Fraser University, Burnaby, B.C., Canada.

FIGURE E.1:   Program for *The Chorus Line* (1982).

through the history of the art of moving pictures; through the shift from the visual codes of black and white to those of color; through its diversity of musical and visual styles; through its historical context of depression, war, and peace; through the repetition of patterns depicting the same relations of domination and subordination (and sometimes relations of equality) in otherwise very different numbers; through the ways in which the dancers and their directors innovate at the same time as they salute the best work of their predecessors; and through the increasing artfulness of the means of representation.

As the montage unfolds the dance numbers lose their apparent innocence as 'mere entertainment' and reveal themselves as complex social messages. Here one can recognize in the information clutter of our society the stereotyped and often violent images of human relationships that the social media, and especially the media of entertainment, teach us to value and accept.

Spatial images (*Raumbilder*) are the dreams of society. Wherever the hieroglyphics of these images can be deciphered, one finds the basis of social reality.

SIEGFRIED KRACAUER: 'Labor Exchange'.
Frankfurter Zeitung, June 17, 1930

The montage

The Chorus Line is a sequence of fifteen production numbers from eleven films (and one Broadway show), all made between 1932 and 1980, selected from more than a hundred examples collected over three years (October 1978–October 1981). We made our selections on the grounds of pertinence, style, diversity, and, above all, quality in design and execution, then assembled them in chronological order. Each selection is preceded by a simple black and white silent screen intertitle (styled after D. W. Griffith's), giving the title and date of the film and the title of the musical number.

Our first draft was a reconnaissance and study tape that ran two-and-a-half hours with 37 selections. This we used to develop our own literacy in the genre, paying close attention to the original editing, the musical and visual rhythms, and the interplay of cinematic forms in each musical number. We soon rejected about half the material as failures of entertainment.

The second draft, shown at Simon Fraser University in October 1981, ran for eighty minutes (our goal was sixty minutes) with 19 individual numbers. The 55-minute version, for which we re-edited several of the selections from the 1930s and 1940s (cutting eight minutes from Busby Berkeley's 'By a Waterfall', for example), is now in its fifth and final edition (1982).

The final version includes opening and closing credits and a montage within the montage: a rapid edit trailer framing the opening credits with a selection of the images to come. This was edited to the rhythm of the rehearsal number from the Broadway musical *A Chorus Line*; the montage ends with the finale from that show.

Except for the last title before the final credits – 'It's the patterns that connect' (Gregory Bateson) – *The Chorus Line* employs no verbal commentary. The result is a simple and logical basic assembly in which every selection becomes a commentary on every other – both simultaneously and successively. At the same time the historical sequence of the pieces reveals the basic codes by means of which the messages of the musical are created and continue to evolve.

Some viewers, often teachers, have objected to the lack of narration. Others have welcomed its absence. In evaluating the third edition of the montage in March 1982, an upper levels undergraduate student at Simon Fraser had this to say:

> Originally I was perplexed and dismayed: 'Just what are these characters [the producers] saying?' . . . I listened intently to what others had to say, their questions and criticisms, keeping a low profile at the back of the room. I was still left with the feeling that something was amiss. And then I discovered what it was: I was so bloody used to being told what to see and think that I lacked the ability to form opinions and clarify meanings from information presented visually. From that point on, viewing *The Chorus Line* became a lesson in visual literacy . . . The idea that 'unaware learning' was going on first came as a dreadful shock . . . It wasn't until the epistemology of levels became a way of seeing *The Chorus Line*'s beauty that it could be appreciably understood.

Another viewer, a woman in her seventies, simply said: 'This is self-education. You let them make up their own minds.'

By taking the production numbers out of their original contexts and putting them into the context of each other, we found that we were greatly increasing the quality and quantity of the accessible information of the film-text. Without at first realizing it, we were transforming what would ordinarily be merely message information – the actual details of a given production number in a particular film – into coding information – the repetition in many modes and styles of the basic semiotic patterns of the Hollywood musical. What had previously been invisible, unnoted, or disregarded as noise emerged, as if from nowhere, as novel information. Pattern after pattern joined the patterns that connect.

> Those things which we see with our eyes and understand by means of our senses are more clearly to be demonstrated than if learned by means of reasoning.
>
> GEORGIUS AGRICOLA: *De ortu et causis subterraneorum* (1546)*

Learning

The Chorus Line is an exercise in the dialectic of learning. The viewer who finds the selections from the 1930s too distant in time or otherwise difficult to read – difficult to fit into a coherent pattern – has less of a problem with the later ones, even though the choreography, like the stereotyping, greatly increases in subtlety as we approach the present. The earlier selections provide the context necessary to make fuller sense of the later ones.

At the same time, the later selections become the context of the earlier ones and in the process they change the latter's meanings. Only within and between goalseeking, adaptive open systems with complex memories can the present change the past in this way, the dialectical way.

Thus at one level the viewer is learning (largely unconsciously) through the passage of time, by the process of duration or *durée* (Henri Bergson). At another level the viewer is repeatedly 'learning after the event' (Sigmund Freud) – re-reading old information in a new context, and seeing new meanings emerge as a result. At another level yet, the viewer is 'learning how to learn' (Gregory Bateson) – using the experience of the earlier selections as a model to appreciate the later ones, and using the context of the later numbers to reinterpret the meanings of the earlier pieces.

The videotape is not a linear collection of information. The viewer does not simply move from point to point gathering more and more information as the tape unwinds, but repeatedly breaks through the frames defining the limits and levels of what has previously been learnt or understood, both consciously and unconsciously, and comes to view the same information in a new frame, at a new level of learning. There is a characteristic discontinuity here, a sudden moment of recognition,

---

* Agricola (1494–1555), the German classicist, humanist, and physician known as the 'father of mineralogy', was among the first to base his science on observation and inquiry in the field. His major work *De re metallica* (1556), the first extensive study of mining and mine technology, is illustrated by several hundred detailed woodcuts.

a newly emergent gestalt, an 'Aha! experience', a distinct jump in levels of communication, a restructuring of patterns of information, and ultimately a transition from message to code.

In these and other ways *The Chorus Line* makes its content understood by communicating its own explanation.

No culture will give popular nourishment and support to images or patterns which are alien to its dominant impulses and aspirations.

MARSHALL McLUHAN: *The Mechanical Bride* (1951)

The mass ornament

The Chorus Line contains four extravaganzas by Busby Berkeley (1895–1976): 'By a Waterfall' and 'Shanghai Lil' from *Footlight Parade* (1933), and the slave market and 'Keep Young and Beautiful' from *Roman Scandals* (1934). Ex-Lieutenant Berkeley, thoroughly conversant with military spectacles, was the song and dance director who invaded Hollywood from Broadway in the early 1930s and developed the spectacular, kaleidoscopic 'girlie' number in which scores of female bodies and above all female legs are used like interchangeable parts to create optical, organic, and mechanical patterns in motion, dramatically portrayed by Busby's trademark, the top-down (and bottom-up) shot.

As Jack Zipes of the University of Wisconsin at Milwaukee pointed out at a showing of *The Chorus Line* at the Institute for Twentieth Century Studies in November 1983, Busby's dance teams had their origins in the music halls and night clubs of the 1920s. The 'girlie geometry' of these shows had been analyzed by the German critic Siegfried Kracauer.

Writing in May 1931 of the Tiller Girls (a celebrated American dance troupe who first performed in Berlin in the early 1920s, during the German inflation), in his essay 'Girls and Crisis', Kracauer had recalled:

In that postwar era, in which *prosperity* appeared limitless and which could scarcely conceive of unemployment, the [Tiller] Girls were artificially manufactured in the USA and exported to Europe by the dozens. Not only were they American products; at the same time they demonstrated the greatness of American production. I distinctly recall such troupes in the season of their glory. When they formed an undulating snake, they radiantly illustrated the virtues of the conveyor belt; when they tapped their feet in fast tempo, it sounded like *business, business*; when they kicked their

FIGURE E.2: One of the kaleidoscopic patterns from the famous title sequence of *Dames* (1934), directed by Busby Berkeley for Warner Bros. The object in the center is a cherry.
Reprinted from: Clive Hirschhorn: *The Hollywood Musical* (1981).

FIGURE E.3: A publicity shot from Busby Berkeley's 'By a Waterfall' in Lloyd Bacon's *Footlight Parade* (1933).
Reprinted from: Ted Sennett: *Hollywood Musicals* (1981).

legs with mathematical precision, they joyously affirmed the progress of rationalization; and when they kept repeating the same movements without ever interrupting their routine, one envisaged an uninterrupted chain of autos gliding from the factories into the world, and believed that the blessings of prosperity had no end.

In 'The Mass Ornament', published in the *Frankfurter Zeitung* in July 1927, six years before Hitler came to power, Kracauer had pointed to a 'change of taste' taking place in the field of physical culture. It began with the Tiller Girls, he says:

These products of American 'distraction factories' are no longer individual girls, but indissoluble female units whose movements are mathematical demonstrations. Even as they crystallize into patterns in the revues of Berlin, performances of the same geometrical exactitude are occurring in similarly packed stadiums in Australia and India, not to mention America. Through weekly newsreels in movie houses they have managed to reach even the tiniest village. One glance at the screen reveals that the ornaments consist of thousands of bodies, sexless bodies in bathing suits. The regularity of their patterns is acclaimed by the masses, who themselves are arranged in row upon ordered row (p. 67).

In *From Caligari to Hitler* (1947), Kracauer argued that German film of the twenties and early thirties displayed the authoritarian disposition that led to German fascism (Witte, 1975). One could trace a line of development leading from Fritz Lang's *Nibelungen* of 1924 to Leni Riefenstahl's *Triumph of the Will* ten years later, the official film of the Nazi Party Convention in Nuremberg in 1933 (Figure E.4).

According to Karsten Witte's introduction (1975) to 'The Mass Ornament', in Kracauer's view, Riefenstahl's technique in *Triumph of the Will* depends on an overwhelming subjugation or submission of the masses to the power of the director as dictator. In the film, the patterns formed by massed humanity in the stadiums of Nazi Germany, 'collaborate in deepening the impression of Fate's irresistible power'. This use of people as 'human ornaments' denotes 'the omnipotence of dictatorship'. In both film and reality, this is the *mass ornament* of Kracauer's 1927 article. As he put it in 1947:

The innumerable rows of the various Party formations composed *tableaux vivants* across the huge festival grounds. These living ornaments not only perpetuated the metamorphosis of the moment, but symbolically presented masses as instrumental superunits. . . . The film also includes pictures of the mass ornaments into which this transported life was pressed at the [Party] Convention. They

FIGURE E.4: Director Leni Riefenstahl (left) shooting up into the face of a Hitler Youth leader in the making of *Triumph of the Will* (1934). From a Nazi cigarette card of the time, published in Dresden.

FIGURE E.5: Police units performing at the Berlin Sports Palace in 1934. One of a set of 156 pocket-sized photographs, *Das Neue Reich*.

appeared as mass ornaments to Hitler and his staff, who must have appreciated them as configurations symbolizing the readiness of the masses to be shaped at will by their leaders.

As he had said twenty years earlier, 'The hands in the factory correspond to the legs of the Tiller Girls' (p. 70). The first produces commodities for those who control the means of production; the second produces images for those who control the means of representation.

Both come face to face with the products of their alienated creativity; both may believe their mass produced relationships to be 'part of the natural order of things', eternal and unchangeable, and thus beneath notice, not to be discussed.

Certainly the legs of the Tiller Girls, and not the natural units of their bodies, swing in unison with one another; and certainly the thousands in the stadium are also one single star. But this star does not shine, and the legs of the Tiller Girls are the abstract signs of their bodies.

In both the Busby Berkeley musical and the Nazi pageant of the 1930s, what we see created in the mass ornament is a structure without a subject in the discourse of the Other for which the medium is the masses.

An analysis of the simple surface manifestations of an epoch can contribute more to determining its place in the historical process than judgments of the epoch about itself.

SIEGFRIED KRACAUER: 'The Mass Ornament' (1927)

Responses

'I am male', said one Simon Fraser viewer in November 1983:

I am overwhelmed, shocked, disgusted, blown away.
I can now understand the sickness that manifests itself as pornography.
I don't want to think about it any more now.
After that one needs a rest.

Another man in the same upper levels film course found the montage 'extremely painful to watch'. A woman said:

FIGURE E.6: The mass ornament.

It nauseates me, paralyzes me. I don't know what the hell it is going to take to change woman's position.

A woman in another course said:

I didn't realize that this hatred of women already existed so long ago – I am plenty aware that it exists today and is getting worse.

Many people take a both-and attitude: an evident delight at the superb dancing in many of the cuts, and an outspoken disgust at the portrayal of non-whites and women. Some people remain quiet, others express amazement at something they did not suspect existed, a few struggle to reject or trivialize what they have seen, and some respond almost as if the program were a personal attack.

Three examples follow. The first is from a mature male student in an upper levels film course at Simon Fraser:

Scopophilia is alive and well and living on Canadian video. Merciless without narrator. Makes its point mercilessly.

The second is from a lower levels communications course at York University in Toronto:

1. Being a male, it really didn't bother me the way women were treated – anyway it was just a movie. 2. It should be a boost for women because in most of the films they were actually working and not stay [sic] at home making babies.

The third is from Simon Fraser:

How uninteresting, how boring, how repulsive.

Another man at York wrote that the montage really opened his eyes to the exploitation of women from past to present:

Hips, legs, and breasts are the focal points in all scenes, from workers to prostitutes to wives – the many roles of women.

A woman student at Simon Fraser in 1984 said that she wanted to enjoy the dancing but that the videotape 'produced a pervasive sense of fear and confusion ... The film quite simply brought out a lot of my own hang ups, and the entire process caused me disgust and anxiety'.

A woman student in Toronto remarked:

FIGURE E.7: *Ku Klux Kuties* (1980).

I found all takes very violent – especially the [female slave market in *Roman Scandals*]. Watching the musicals out of context of the movies highlighted all the aspects of what you are trying to show, especially the degradation of women. I am not a feminist but I was shocked at the end – masculine authority and male chauvinism.

Another Toronto student simply wrote:

I really felt sick during many of the cuts.

Another said:

Your presentation was a very powerful visual onslaught which left me feeling enraged at the degradation of the human spirit through violence, racism, and sexism as demonstrated in the movie.

An upper levels Simon Fraser student summed up the program by saying:

Instead of *Women in Production* your title should be *The Production of Women*.

A woman in the same class wrote:

I was totally 'blown away' by this piece when I first saw it. I was speechless but my mind would not stop working.

A year later another woman said:

It is an awful, gruelling video. It was good to be reassured, though, that I'm not paranoid. The world really is misogynist.

Two students singled out for comment the short (35-second) musical segment from *The Naked Civil Servant* (1975), with John Hurt playing Quentin Crisp. In this clip a man in a blue pinstripe at a bus stop takes one look at Crisp's manner and make-up, then brings his heel down hard on Crisp's sandaled instep. Next, as Crisp steps aside to let a woman in black pass him in a doorway, her lips curl and she slaps him in the face. The first comment is from an upper levels class at Simon Fraser:

I liked the [scene from] *The Naked Civil Servant* because I am impressed by the courage of this man who is bisexual and struggles for his own rights in society. It was a good representation when the woman hit this man in the face because a bisexual person is considered a deviant in society. People can only accept the things they often see. People usually resist change.

The second comment is from a lower levels student at York:

More scenes like *The Naked Civil Servant* should be thrown into the production. The shock value was incredible and that one small section crammed in far more than several sequences together. It is perhaps the shortest visual essay in history. The timing for it was perfect.

The last response we will quote comes from an upper levels male student at Simon Fraser:

Each segment makes an important statement about woman and her role in our society. This point is presented in such a way that one can neither refute it nor stop watching it.

We were just as startled and intrigued by our results as the viewers have been and continue to be. Since 1981 we have shown the montage to dancers, anthropologists, film makers, critics, futurologists, artists, semiologists, philosophers, therapists, friends and relations, and people off the street. Whether in Vancouver, Kitchener, Waterloo, or Toronto, or in Los Angeles, San Francisco, Salt Lake City, or Milwaukee, or in

Santa Cruz, Davis, Irvine, or New York, or at the 'McLuhan et 1984' Conference in Paris in December 1983, we have yet to hear of a neutral response to this production.

We could not have asked for better evidence that communication in society cannot be divorced from social and personal values, that communication cannot be 'objective' – and that in the production and reproduction of the dominant ideology visual images and visual structures are undoubtedly more important than mere verbal ideas.

Lastly, we did not expect that *The Chorus Line*, a cultural anthropology of Hollywood (and a study in the strategy of male supremacy), would take us so quickly and directly into an ethnography of the audience.

Bonaparte said that the secret of war lies in the secret of communication. He also said:

> To make oneself understood by the people one must first speak to the eyes.

This is the motto chosen by Francis Coppola for the modern reconstruction of Abel Gance's *Napoleon* (1927), whose passionately structured levels of vision in motion – besides their appeal to despotism – speak for themselves.

> We have been trained to think of patterns, with the exception of those of music, as fixed affairs . . . In truth, the right way to think about the pattern which connects is to think of it as primarily . . . a dance of interacting parts . . .
> GREGORY BATESON: *Mind and Nature: A Necessary Unity* (1979)

The message 'This is play'

In watching animals at play Gregory Bateson recognized that 'play' differs from 'combat' in much the same way that 'nip' differs from 'bite'. Play is symbolic combat; nips are symbolic bites. How is it, he asked himself, that the animals know that a nip is not a bite? By communicating about their communication. In order that a 'nip' not be confused with a 'bite', the animals must be exchanging a general message, at one level, about all their other messages, at another level. This Bateson called 'The message "This is play"'.

The evolution of play thus meant the emergence of a new level of communication (metacommunication) in the coding of messages between animals.

The Chorus Line is of course a communication about communication in the modern visual and musical codes, as well as a communication about communication, period.

Watching *The Chorus Line* is to experience the emergence of meta-communication in the montage and in one's own understanding. The montage cuts through any and all illusions one may have about 'entertainment' by using Hollywood to communicate about itself.

But why did we retain these illusions when we saw the dance numbers in the context of the original film? It is as if the original film were framing the dance numbers by the message 'This is play', whereas *The Chorus Line* tells us 'This is combat'.

An Actor is not a machine, no matter how much they want to say you are.

MARILYN MONROE (1926–1962)

Left and right

Media literacy may be numeral and verbal (mainly functions of the left cerebral hemisphere); it may also be non-verbal, and especially musical and visual (mainly functions of the right cerebral hemisphere). Media literacy is simply the capacity to transfer and translate between the left and right brain at will – without forgetting that most non-verbal information is too rich in meaning to be translated into words.

Media literacy is literacy in communication, whatever its shape or form. But visual imagery – a right brain specialty – is almost invariably ambiguous and open to multiple interpretations. Language imagery – a left brain specialty – may be ambiguous too, but not to the same extent; and language is capable of great precision when properly used.

But the more precise we are in language, the less diverse is the information our words can bear. Conversely, the less precise we are in the visual mode of communication, the more diverse is the information our visual images can bear. Media literacy is the capacity to combine the digital precision and low diversity of language (which is predominantly digital and iconic) with the analog and iconic ambiguity and high diversity of visual and other non-verbal modes of communication.

Context, reconnaissance, and novelty – specialties of the right brain – are essential here. The more contextualized (and thus the more structured) information is, the easier it is to read, mark, learn, recall, and use it on your own account. As a teaching tool, one basic goal of *The Chorus Line* is to link the words of left brain learning with the images of right-brain learning so closely that no one easily forgets what the montage has to show.

> Strategy is the study of communication.
> WILHELM VON WILLISEN. Quoted by T. E. Lawrence in *The Seven Pillars of Wisdom* (1935)

Strategy

We soon realized that *The Chorus Line* was as novel and meaningful as its design was traditional and classically simple. Quality and elegance were essential. Television is such an urgent competitor for attention that in video anything less than the best may leave you without an audience. That is why we got our quality from Hollywood. That is why we let the production numbers themselves create the orchestration for the tape. That is why there is no narration. That is why our only comment is 'It's the patterns that connect'.

We wanted to expose Hollywood to the critical eye; we took Hollywood as our guide. Hollywood provided the keys to ideological ciphers we didn't suspect existed.

The Chorus Line takes the material of entertainment and transforms it into an exposé. It takes the Hollywood original and by changing its context turns its emotional power back on itself.

Sun Tzu says: 'Attack the opponent's strategy'. *The Chorus Line* is not only an attack on Hollywood's strategy, but also a strategic envelopment of that strategy — accomplished by using the right brain's capacities in melody and vision as our instruments of strategic reconnaissance. The strength of *The Chorus Line* lies in its use of the arms of the Other. *The Chorus Line* is guerrilla theater. *The Chorus Line* is true.

I return to the strategic envelopment and the guerrilla strategy in the companion to this volume, *Man and Woman, War and Peace: The Strategist's Companion* (1987).

Postscript

Context theory/Théorie des contextes: The new science*

The Incomparable Mr. *Isaac Newton* gives but these Three Laws of Motion, which may be truly called *Laws of Nature*.

1. That every Body will continue in its State, either of Rest, or Motion uniformly forward in a [Straight] Line, unless it be made to change that State by some Force impressed upon it.

2. That the Change of Motion is proportional to the moving Force impressed; and is always according to the Direction of that [Straight] Line in which the Force is impressed.

3. That *Reaction* is always equal and contrary to Action; or, which is all one, the mutual Actions of two Bodies one upon another are equal, and directed towards contrary Parts: As when one Body presses and draws another, 'tis as much pressed or drawn by that Body.

JOHN HARRIS: *Lexicon Technicum Or An Universal English Dictionary of Arts and Sciences* (1704)

1 Revolt

The scientific revolution of the past fifty years had its origins in a revolt against simplicity.

This was not the quantum-relativistic revolution of the turn of the century (continuing in nuclear physics through the twenties), the revolution we associate with multiple dimensions in space and time, astrophysics, matter-energy, quantum theory, the splitting of the atom, the speed of light, and ballistic missiles.

It is the Shannon Revolution of the 1930s and 1940s: the definition of information (coded variety);

In the 1950s we had learned about the quantum-relativistic (matter-energy) revolution via the latest media marvel: the mass-market paperback. Among my favorites are George Gamow's *One Two Three ...*

*This is a more extensive version of a paper originally delivered at the first French conference on Gregory Bateson, held at Cérisy-la-Salle in Normandy in the summer of 1984, directed by the Belgian scholar Yves Winkin, editor of *La Nouvelle communication* (1982). For background see especially Ray Holland, *Self and Social Context* (1977); also Voloshinov, *Marxism and the Philosophy of Language* (1930, pp. 9–41, 45–106); and Bateson, *Steps to an Ecology of Mind* (1972, pp. 3–58, 177–93, 279–308, 399–410, 448–66).

Infinity, written in 1947 and sold as a Mentor Book for 50 cents in 1954 (illustrated by the author), and the Penguin book, *The Strange Story of the Quantum*, by Banesh Hoffman. Others are the Time-Life series on science for suburbia, published in 1964, and the four-volume paperback series *The World of Mathematics* – classic original texts from the history of mathematics (including John Von Neumann (1903–1957) on the 'general and logical theory of automata', a pathbreaking paper on general purpose digital computers) – edited, explained, and introduced by James R. Newman and published by Simon & Schuster between 1950 and 1960.

The theory of relativity in physics discovered by Einstein (1879–1955) vastly influenced the disciples of 'subjective relativism' ('all opinions are equal'), as well as their cousins in anthropology, the 'cultural relativists' ('all cultures are equal'). This is the easy way: If everything is relative to everything else, then nobody is ultimately responsible for anything at all. Values? Ethics? Who cares?

The uncertainty principle uncovered by Werner Heisenberg (1901–1976) in nuclear physics ('all observations are equally uncertain') had similar relativist effects. (The observation disturbs the observed.) Many anthropologists, sociologists, psychologists, and ideologues turned this physical matter to reductionist and other ends.

The 'principle of complementarity' articulated by Niels Bohr (1885–1962) – particles are waves and waves are particles, depending on what you want to say about them – had a lesser influence, going as it did 'against the grain' (if the metaphor be permitted) of the long dominant logic: analytic logic. This is the either/or, digital, diagnostic logic of science, mechanicking, and making certain kinds of yes/no decisions in everyday life. It has little place for dialectical and both-and logics of process, levels, and change.

Early quantum theory gave strategic reinforcement to the dominant either/or, digital, and matter-energy perspective of the so-called 'hard sciences' (basically physics and chemistry); gave currency to 'reductionism' or 'scientism' (sociology aping mechanics or biology, for instance, reducing distinct levels and kinds of communication and reality the one to the other, reducing the more complex to the less complex); and made its mark on every other academic discipline besides.

This went down well with those who maintained the modern version of the reductionist illusion of Laplace (1740–1827), that ultimately everything will be explained in the 'really real' domain of 'hard science' (as distinct from 'social fluff', by which is meant the social sciences).

It was very strange. Because you couldn't 'pin them down', as the saying goes, perfectly respectable people in science and philosophy actually wondered whether electrons (all of which are so equal that if two exchange places, nothing has happened) might have 'free will'.

Today we have millions of glossy science magazines aimed at the educated updraft of the Sixties Generation – *Science Digest* (Hearst), *Omni* (Bob Guccione), *Discover* (Time-Life), *Science 85* (the American Association for the Advancement of Science) – bringing the strange story of the quantum back to the ideological front again, under the label of 'quantum weirdness'.

This means not recognizing that matter-energy exists independently of its being perceived, but information does not.

Is this backward journey really necessary?

Political

For the classic liberal, the quantum-relativistic theory had three useful political translations and one conjuring trick:
- Everyone is an individual atom separated from every other.
- Everyone is equal.
- Everything is relative to everything else.
- Both-and is either/or (or vice versa).

The basic structure of the liberal ideology rests on the illiberal belief that there are 'two sides to every question' – and no real hierarchies of power, where the questioner has the power and authority to harm the person or family or other treasured relations of the one under interrogation.

By its very structure capitalist liberal theory (born in the English Revolution of 1642–88) ignores the fact that many questions have many 'sides' (religion is the best example); that certain questions and kinds of questions – such as racism and torture – have only one side; and that other problems can't be defined by the word 'sides' at all, since they don't have any to start with.

Let it not be forgotten, however, that classic capitalist liberalism also strengthened the legal doctrines of equality before the law and due process in and out of court (called 'natural justice' in English common law), as well as the complex rights of contract, besides the other 'rights of man' (the 'rights of woman' is another matter). They protected free speech as far as that was possible, and brought to the university the doctrine of academic freedom: protection from the clumsier forms of censorship – really a privilege.

The 1950s

In the 1950s, with McCarthy, the cold war, and the witch hunts, it had been 'back to the bombshelter', with flyboy films largely funded by the Strategic Air Command sending multi-engine jets roaring across 85 million American television screens in 1959 (up from 1.5 million in 1950), six times as many as the rest of the world combined (Britain was second with 10.5 million sets).

The Administrations of the 1950s had the faculty on their knees. But then came Sputnik, in 1957 – and in the United States, at least, education suddenly became the biggest game in town.

The explosion of education during the Super Sixties was paid for by the huge economic boom – and mortgage on the future – caused by the Vietnam War (1945–75).

In the 1950s you had retreated into your hopefully impregnable foxhole (Kafka's 1931 'Burrow' reincarnated), where the doctrine of 'all ideas are equal' held sway and one easily swallowed the solipsism invented mainly by Descartes (1596–1650). But here at least you couldn't be attacked (you hoped), because you had already agreed that everybody else's ideas were just as good as your own (most of which you had in fact got from somewhere else, but that's another matter).

This is not, however, a point of view that will get you safely across Times Square, or through the Place de la Concorde, or round the Marble Arch.

Ideas

In philosophy, film, literature, civics, civility, and polity the 1950s were centered on Europe. Those were the days of long books full of long words like the 'phenomenology' of Edmund Husserl (1859–1938) ('study the thing itself') – a 'phenomenon' means simply 'what comes to light, appears' – or German existentialism ('I am what I say'), or, in its French version, 'I am what I do' – not to mention the almost single-handed revival of Hegel by Alexandre Kojève at the Ecole Normale in Paris (5ᵉ Section) in the 1930s, whose most celebrated lecture, that on the 'master-slave dialectic', had the misfortune to be published in 1939.

Suddenly, in the 1950s and early 1960s, there dropped into the scientific complex the New Marx (the 'humanist of 1844'); the New Freud (Freud [1856–1939] the theoretician of communication and semiotic, viz. the work of Jacques Lacan [1901–1981]); the New Structuralism, i.e. the work of the French anthropologist Claude Lévi-Strauss (b. 1908), notably *The Elementary Structures of Kinship*, first published in 1949, and whose autobiographical *Tristes Tropiques* was a best-seller in 1955; and the myriads working in cybernetics, operations research, systems theory, engineering, systems ecology, code-breaking, and communication theory (much of the work derived from World War II). There was also the New Therapy: the 'anti-psychiatric' R. D. Laing (b. 1927) and Thomas Szasz (b. 1920); the double-bind, communicational, family-centered 'Palo Alto School' following the work of Gregory Bateson (1904–1980) (not to mention the short-lived pseudo-Gestaltism of Fritz Perls, in whom even Hitler would have found encouragement). Each was back to back with every other; and back to back with the logical positivists in literature as well, the New Critics ('all contexts are equally irrelevant').

The 1960s

The outpouring of radically new information in the 1960s (c. 1964–1974) and the rebirth of natural, political, and social ecology (including the Mother Earth movement) was influenced in both the United States and Europe by popular 'intellectual' or 'artistic' movements whose existence depended directly upon the level and degree of their authors' and disciples' insulation from the real life of working people – working people whose alienated creativity sustains the entire system – whether that insulation was primarily mediated by class, race, or sex (or one or more of the same).

Some of the more extravagant – and pessimistic, defeatist, or crudely cynical – post-war results were 'the theatre of the absurd' ('all meanings are equal'), minimal art ('all junk is equal'), random music ('all notes are equal'), and the political-literary-moral all-rounder: 'life is a game' ('all games are equal'), not to mention the 'structure without a subject' ('all subjects are equally irrelevant').

Here the act of scholarship and the scholar's obligation to the people who pay the bills – the taxpayers – became a farce: You simply used the texts to play the game. Reality and people disappeared.

I'm OK, you're OK. I think therefore I am. Do your own thing. I'm all right, Jack. Right.

All this, and much more, was the contradictory and eventually provocative set of processes, movements, information, and events which most explosively joined daily life (the US draft) with the student revolt (draft deferment) in 1968 – the year of the Tet Offensive (with the US Embassy under siege), the year of the assassination of Martin Luther King and Robert F. Kennedy, the year of still fiercer 'inner cities' rebellions against white oppression – extending even to Baltimore, Maryland, although hardly a match for the machine-gunning of ghetto tenements in Detroit – the year the Russians invaded Czechoslovakia to put an end to 'liberal communism', the year Richard Nixon was elected President of the United States, the year that James D. Watson published *The Double Helix* (the discovery of the structure of the genetic code), the year the Pope banned all artificial means of birth control, the year the British tested the 'second class' British passport on India, Pakistan, and the Caribbean, the year the middle and upper class Protestant oppression of the largely working-class Catholics of Northern Ireland brought fighting in the streets, with no protection for Catholics from Protestant police, the year that Vietnam-caused inflation first went out of control, the year of what became known as the 'police riot' against the protesters at the Democratic National Convention in Chicago, the year the barricades of Paris exploded, the year the Mexican Army stormed the campus of the University of Mexico and shot 200 students stone dead, the year that broke the century.

The point was, nevertheless, that we felt that we could make a difference, individually and collectively, and differences we made, whether in combating racism in universities and hospitals, or in white-only Baltimore bars. And because masses of people from the governing and middle classes joined in the opposition to the war, thousands upon thousands of lives were saved.

We can still make a difference today (with a little help from our friends) – and in any case who is there left to do it?

But protest was privilege, too – the 1960s Peace Movement, with the exception of such as Mohammed Ali and Stokely Carmichael ('Hell, no! We won't go!'), was a movement organized, dominated, and sexualized in the US and elsewhere by White Anglo Saxon Protestant Western men. Not counting the Vietnam Veterans Against the War, and the combat troops who used their own methods of resistance, most of us were people whose family, children, age, and social status gave us the privilege of not joining the rest of the boys in Vietnam.

There is of course much more to say about the unprecedented explosion of life and death in the 1960s. It was an explosion of feeling and emotion, good, bad, and just plain horror; a time of pride in living up to democratic principles; an unprecedented chance to fight for civil rights; a many-layered montage of moving exposures to distinctly different, contradictory, and often utterly pathological contexts; a time of wars of independence and police-state repressions, East and West; a time of people newly born and suddenly dead; and a time to extend responsibility, courtesy, and humanity to others (symbolized by the complementarity of the V-sign and the clenched fist) – and a time of villainy, treachery, and atrocity – as every veteran knows.

The 1960s were the explosion of the context of life itself.

Information

In the 1950s and 1960s biology had taken the crown from physics with the deciphering of DNA. Here molecular biology was dealing not just with matter-energy, but with molecules carrying biologically coded information that could tell other parts of the living open system what to do – and how and when to do it – besides being able to repair and reproduce the system as well.

It was then that scientists realized for the very first time that although you must of course have matter and energy available in living (open) systems, it is information and information alone that is the key to life on earth.

This was the 'second theorem' revolution (Shannon's understanding of the necessity of redundancy to create and protect structure), eloquently explained by Jeremy Campbell in *Grammatical Man: Information, Entropy, Language, and Life*, published by Simon & Schuster in 1982.

At the Bell Labs at AT&T in the 1940s Claude E. Shannon (b. 1916) was the first person to give a mathematical (probabilistic) definition of the physical signals of the most important word in life: 'information', which he colloquially called 'novelty' or 'surprise' (unexpected order, rather than the (physically) expected chaos).

Information is the basis of 'negative entropy' (open system order or organization, in systems which export the entropic disorder they create into their environments), as distinct from the 'positive entropy' of physics (closed system disorder or disorganization in systems which accumulate their entropic disorder until they arrive at a state of relative randomness or disorganization (maximum entropy) from which no further work can be obtained).

Complexity

The fifty-year-old revolt against simplicity made the neglected topic of complexity, or more accurately, *organized complexity* (constrained diversity), into a subject worthy of attention by scientists – biologists, ecologists, philosophers, humanists, culture critics, and others.

This many-leveled revolution in favor of diversity is coming about at a time when we know for a fact that we may all end up nuked or puked.

Our long-range future – if we have one – is now utterly dependent on those in power coming to understand the basic fact of the new science: that the open system that destroys its environment ultimately destroys itself.

Organized complexity is the fount of life, liberty, and novelty on the planet earth.

Simplicity, sameness, and symmetry

We didn't realize it at the time, but in recognizing the structures of complexity as positive and intriguing scientific, social, and personal values in the 1960s, we had also discovered that we were all uniquely diverse goalseeking adaptive open systems – or, as the texts would put it:

goalseeking, goalchanging, adaptive, self-regulating (homeostatic), self-reproducing, open systems, ruled by hierarchies of constraints, structurally conservative, governed by information and by positive and negative feedback – systems open to the environments in space and time that permit their production, reproduction, and repair, systems that import matter-energy and information (order) and export (what is for us) entropy (disorder, noise).

We knew in the early 1960s that the old order in the life and social sciences was being subverted, on both sides of the Atlantic, by a largely 'context-free', 'structural', and 'linguistic' view from France and by a largely 'context-sensitive', 'systemic', 'semiotic', and 'ecological' view from the various English-speaking spheres – all of which were centered on communication, for without communication there is no memory, and without memory there is no life.

The new outlook, which we may now call *context theory*, is a revolution in science and understanding, a jump to a new level of theory and practice, a new level of patterns which connect, a strategic envelopment of the old inlook.

The inlook view is dominated by matter-energy, one-to-one linear causality, forces, atoms, singularity, closure, one-dimensionality, determinism, symmetry, sameness, simplicity, competition, short-range survival, and the past.

Context theory, in contrast, is oriented to information, goalseeking, constraint, relationships, reciprocity, levels of reality, levels of responsibility, levels of communication and control, requisite diversity, innovation, openness, cooperation, the capacity to utilize unexpected novelty, and thus towards long-range survival and the future.

Symmetry, sameness, and simplicity. Simplicity, much admired by the ancient Greeks, became one of the great idols of modern science when Isaac Newton astounded the world of physics, religion, and philosophy by setting out the principles of mechanical motion in just three sentences in plain Latin, later translated into plain English.

Sameness has Newtonian roots also. Eighteenth-century philosophers sought to apply Newton's atomistic and mechanical principles directly to the analysis of society and the individual, inventing a reductionist and completely imaginary theory of 'social physics' in the process.

After James Clerk Maxwell produced the first unified field theory of electromagnetism in the mid-nineteenth century, theorists sought to reduce the information manifested in human communication to the matter-energy level of 'fields of mental force'. When the new machine, the steam engine, was the miracle of the day (beginning about 1800), the favored thought-models spoke of pressures, heads of steam, pivotal moments, pendulums swinging, reciprocation, power, and so on in an 'energy currency'.

Not to be outdone, the theologians, the vitalists, and many others clung to the organic model of human reality, but mechanical invention after invention weakened what argument they had left.

When popular cars first acquired hydraulic brakes (servomechanisms) in the 1920s and 1930s – a 1939 Plymouth Coupe, for one – the theory of the human being as a servomechanism very soon appeared. One after another, the emergence of an innovation, sometimes in science, but much more often in technology, has given rise to all or part of an attitude to life.

Inversely, a social attitude – this is especially obvious in the case of militarism, morality, and modern economics – may be projected as a model onto living nature.

As an example of projecting technology onto life, clockwork is still a favorite. As an example of projecting social relations onto nature, a popular model in molecular biology was the factory – but the word-processing or montage model is more recently a vigorous competitor.

Cybernetics

Information theory, cybernetics, and linguistic theory began to subvert the mechanical and bioenergetic view (the Newtonian-Cartesian view) in the 1930s. In the war of 1939–1945, besides the early information processors or 'bombes' used to crack the Enigma codes, the anti-aircraft 'computers' called 'predictors' were converted to radar gunsights, and a new type of machine – a machine with feedback between input and output (or between itself and its context or its target), a machine dependent on information, communication, and control: the cybernetic machine – was once again recognized. By the late 1950s cybernetic theory had displayed the requisite diversity to illuminate other fields, mainly physiology, linguistics, biology, anthropology, economics, psychology, and political science.

Symmetry displays a similar Newtonian and Cartesian lineage (for Descartes the mind or soul is an idea, the body is a robot, and 'I am what I think'). Symmetry and symmetrization are treated in detail in *Man and Woman, War and Peace: The Strategist's Companion* (1987) – for the moment we need only note the theory of irreversible (non-symmetrical, non-commutative) thermodynamic processes taking place in systems far from equilibrium ('dissipative structures'), as developed by the Belgian Nobel Laureate Ilya Prigogine (b. 1917), to recognize here a fundamental restructuring of the strategy of science – based on a late blooming 'existentialist' revolution (sixty years after the *Being and Time* (1927) of the later Nazi Martin Heidegger (1889–1976) and forty years after the *Being and Nothingness* (1943) of the later Marxist Jean-Paul Sartre (1905–1980) – as expressed by Prigogine in the 'existential' title of his 1980 book: *From Being to Becoming: Time and Complexity in the Physical Sciences.*

Reductionism

The rattling reductionism of the old science – the 'flattening out' of levels of relationship, the reduction of qualities to quantities, the crossing of boundaries between qualitatively distinct orders of complexity without realizing it, the reduction of diversity to variety and complexity to simplicity – is quite amazing when you reflect on it. For over a century there have been just two generally accepted scientific models of reality, even in the structural anthropology of Claude Lévi-Strauss:

- the *organized variety* or *organized simplicity* of Newtonian dynamics (e.g. the solar system), which concerns completely determined, symmetrical (reversible), closed systems of minimal variety (like the balls on a pool table) and is incapable of dealing adequately with more than two bodies at the same time;
- the *unorganized variety* of the kinetic theory of heat, as in the case of a gas, whose temperature is a statistical product of the varying velocity of individual molecules cannoning about in the 'bloomin', buzzing confusion' of the microworld. Here causality is a statistical probability. No Newtonian or deterministic prediction is possible, no linear causality (the effect is proportional to the cause) nor lineal (straight-line) causality is recognizable in the system, which is closed to matter-energy and to information.

The 'unorganized *variety*' of the model was wrongly labeled 'unorganized *complexity*' by the general systems theorists, who based their views on the thermodynamics of gases (the relation between speed of molecular motion and elevated temperature). But the only distinction between molecules in this kinetic theory (literally 'moving theory') is the 'random' variety of their motions, which are variations of a single logical type.

By defining diversity – the constituent of complexity – as a combination of two or more varieties of distinct kinds or levels of reality or logical type, we see that the system discussed displays no diversity. Rather than being a chaotic *complex* system (unorganized diversity), a gas in thermodynamics is a chaotic *simple* system (unorganized variety).

These two closed system models lack the requisite diversity (including the requisite levels of logical typing) to model living and social systems in any remotely scientific, much less humanist, way. The reason is that the dominant (normative) science and philosophy of the last generation got itself hamstrung by a set of imaginary oppositions between *le hasard et la nécessité* (chance and necessity, the title of a book by the French Nobelist, Jacques Monod [1910–1976]); between order and disorder; and between determinism and so-called chaos (not to mention determinism and so-called 'free will').

The result was that any set of relations that could not be fitted – or if necessary, jammed – into one or other of the two quantitative models was generally regarded as 'not science', notably by physicists and positivists, many of whom did not, however, refrain from pontificating about 'non-scientific' subjects – culture, 'human nature', society, history, ideology, war – in their spare time, whether they had any scholarly or empirical claim to expertise on the topic or not.

Logic

There are three kinds of analytic logic. In type A, the basis of the other two, there is a digital gap between either 'true' or 'false', and between 'all/or/none'. In Type B, called 'many-valued' logic – a recent version is called 'fuzzy logic' (*Discover*, February 1985) – the 'either' and the 'or' are the end points of a one-dimensional scale of more-or-less probabilities: a black-grey-white analog spectrum between probably 'absolutely true' (labeled 1) and probably 'absolutely false' (labeled 0). Type C is an all/or/none logic of mutually exclusive binary oppositions in which the negation or criticism of the one means the affirmation of the other, which is (by often unconscious and imaginary definition) the only possible or thinkable alternative ('if not *a*, then *b*') (cf. *Wall Street Journal*, 26 August 1986, p. 26).

There is an imaginary opposition in the old models between mechanical *order* (organized simplicity) and thermodynamic *disorder* (unorganized simplicity). But since apparent disorder is the source – and the environment – of order, they are not of the same logical type (they form a dependent hierarchy), and thus cannot legitimately be 'opposed' to each other.

(A popular model of analytic logic extends from the perfect and absolute order of a crystal (organized variety), at one extreme, to the apparently chaotic disorder of a gas (unorganized variety), at the other.)

But life is simply not like that.

Alfred North Whitehead (1861–1947), the organicist philosopher of process, had a word for the physicists and their models – rhythm:

A crystal lacks rhythm from excess of pattern, while a fog is unrhythmic in that it exhibits a patternless confusion of detail.

Kenneth Burke came at the same question in another way when he wrote in *The Philosophy of Literary Form* (1957):

You have explained the complex in terms of the simple – and the simple is precisely what the complex is not.

Consequently, rather than proceeding from the 'simple' to the 'complex' (as seventeenth century 'empiricists' and ideologists like John Locke (1632–1704) thought we could and we should), context theory proceeds from the complex to the *structures of complexity*, including their environments.

Context theory is a strategic reorientation of that network of theories we have variously called information theory, communications theory, cybernetics, kinesthetics, semiotics, and systems theory.

And just as Monsieur Jourdain in Molière's *Le Bourgeois Gentil-homme* (1670) discovered that he was speaking prose without realizing it, so also will many people in many disciplines recognize that they are doing context theory, now that it has a name.

Not all biology is psychology, but in my view *all* psychology *is* biology.

JERRE LEVY, pioneer in the study of 'split brain' patients, as quoted in *Omni*, January 1985.

2 Lexicon

I have set out in Table P.1 a vocabulary of the main distinctions between the ecosystemic, cybernetic, semiotic, and informational perspective of context theory and the 300-year old matter-energy perspective.

The new outlook, which itself has ancient roots, both includes the old inlook and goes beyond it. The two views are not and cannot legitimately be 'opposed' to each other (as they would be in the liberal view), because they are not of the same logical type.

Thus the traditional matter-energy perspective is neither rejected nor refuted by context theory, but part of it, and used wherever it works, as in the study of earthquakes. And with a little fudging here and there, Newton still takes you to the moon and back – as long as Shannon rides along.

All the sensations from our senses are telegraphed along our nerves to our brains, and are sorted out there . . . The result on the brain is to form a sort of electric pattern, perhaps rather like an illuminated advertisement sign.

DR W. EDWARDS in *The Wonders of Science*, a high-school text (1958)

Table P.1: Context theory: Lexicon

A The old view (excludes B)	B The new view: (includes A)
matter-energy (conserved)	information (created and destroyed)
medium	message
real	symbolic, imaginary, and real
the physical level of complexity	the biological, social, and cultural levels of complexity
closed systems (not dependent on their environments)	open systems (dependent on their environments), 'dissipative structures' (Ilya Prigogine)
solar system, clockwork, heat engine, force field	organism in milieu, system in environment, ecosystem, population, community, social system, information network
mass, inertia, force, momentum, charge, etc.	codes, messages, information, noise, redundancy
motion	evolution, development, history
mechanism	process
action and reaction	report, command, question, response (message)
organization of matter-energy by matter-energy relations (in principle reversible)	organization of matter-energy and information by information (irreversible)
atomistic	holistic
entities, objects	relationships
relations between entities	relations between relations
patterns	patterns of patterns
few or no levels	many levels of organization, communication, and reality
relative simplicity	great complexity
system outside observer	observer in system
synchronic (not dependent on time)	diachronic (dependent on time)
classical machines	cybernetic machines, robots, computers
isolate variables	recognize codes
'bottom up' analysis (simple to complex)	'top down' analysis (from complexity to the structures of complexity)
apparently single-level logic	explicitly hierarchical logic

A The old view (excludes B)	B The new view: (includes A)
digital yes/no, either/or logic (Type A)	many-valued and many-leveled logic,
an either/or one-dimensional spectrum (black-grey-white) between 'true' and 'false' (Type B)	
a logic of binary opposition (if not *a*, then *b*) (Type C)	
either either/or *or* both-and (both-and is subordinate to either/or)	*both* both-and *and* either/or (both-and is dominant over either/or)
analytic (taking apart)	dialectic (putting together)
force, (Newtonian) causality	goalseeking, constraint
outside the context of ordinary space and time	development, evolution, and history, within specific contexts in space and time
linear (proportional) and lineal (straight-line) causality	goalseeking within hierarchies of constraints, positive and negative feedback (mutual causal processes), self-differentiation, self-reproduction
determinism, probability	instructions for production and reproduction
closed to novelty	open to novelty
order from order	order from disorder
equilibrium, non-equilibrium, or random states internal to system	self-regulation in relation to environment(s), order through oscillation
energy source in system	energy source in environment
present effects are the result of past causes	present effects are the result of the interrelation of programmed instructions, future goals, and environmental constraints, including natural and social selection, and socialization
no memory	dependent on memory (genetic, neurological, social, individual, preconscious, unconscious, etc.)

A The old view (excludes B)	B The new view: (includes A)
the system is (a) the sum of its parts (Newtonian mechanics); (b) more than the sum of its parts (theology, early general systems theory)	the system is *other* than its parts (not a sum of anything) (Gestalt psychology)
context-free (actually or potentially)	context-constrained, context-sensitive
'laws of nature', 'natural law'	codes of messages, rules of behavior
closed systems tending towards increasing disorder (positive entropy)	open systems maintaining or increasing order (neutral or negative entropy)
entropy increases in system	entropy increases in environment
physics, chemistry, biology, and ultimately classical information theory (Shannon and Weaver)	biology, ecology, cybernetics, systems theory, communication theory (semiotics), the human and social sciences
physical and chemical change	natural evolution, production and reproduction, organic growth, social development, human history, and social, political, and economic revolution

3 Some axioms of communication

Here I have jotted down, in no particular order, as many of the axioms of communication in context theory that presently come to mind:

- All behavior is communication (Bateson). (Whatever else it also is, all behavior is communication.)
- Society is impossible without history; communication is impossible without memory.
- Every act communicates messages at many levels, conscious and unconscious.
- In living and social systems, silence is communication.
- In living systems, the organism cannot not communicate.
- In social systems, the person cannot not communicate.
- In a communications system, nothing never happens (Ray Birdwhistell).
- Every message, organic or social, is both a report and a command

(Warren McCulloch), as well as a question (Bateson). (Whatever its source or context, a message is a report about some situation or other, a command to respond in some way, and a question about the appropriate response.)

- Communication signifies the processing of information.
- Communication is not the same as understanding.
- Understanding takes place at a level distinct from that of the communication of information which makes understanding possible. A so-called 'failure to communicate' is in fact a failure to understand, which may bespeak relations of pathological communication.
- Communication is a function of organized complexity (constrained diversity)
- Communication is an attribute of open systems.
- Systems involving or simulating life or mind are open systems, dependent on their environment.
- The environment of an open system is of a higher logical type than the systems it sustains.
- An open system may be organic, ecological, social, economic, and/or abstract (i.e. epistemological, ideological).
- Intention may be conscious or non-conscious, but outside of legal concerns, what ultimately counts are effects.
- No communication can be adequately understood or analyzed solely at the level at which it occurs.
- Communication always involves levels of communication (levels of reality, levels of logical typing).
- Every message involves at least four levels of organization: perspective (which constrains) orientation (which constrains) framing (which constrains) punctuation.
- The more complex and diverse a system is, the more complex and diverse its modes and levels of communication will be.
- Information may be analog (continuously variable), or digital (discretely coded), or both at once, in which case the information is iconic.
- Information communicates both content and relationship.
- Inorganic nature is the ecological basis of organic nature.
- Inorganic and organic nature are the ecological basis of society.
- Society is part of nature, and nature is part of society, but they are not the same parts.
- The production and reproduction of whatever is known as the 'means of subsistence' is the ecological and economic basis of all other social relations.
- Social relations, including production, exchange, and reproduction, are dependent both on matter-energy and on information.

- The medium is not the message, it is the means of communication.
- Information is distinct from the matter-energy medium that carries it.
- Mind is an attribute of social relations, individual and collective, conscious, preconscious, and unconscious.
- Brain, nervous system, hormone system, gene system, and so on are the organic or biological basis of the social and individual category of mind.
- There are as many kinds of intelligence as there are modes of communication.
- Information may be symbolic, imaginary or real.
- Real information stands for real relations and events.
- Imaginary information appears to be independent of its context. In the positive sense, the imaginary is essential to invention, intuition, imagination, and vision. In the negative sense, the imaginary is essential to perversion and pathology, especially in colonization, where real hierarchies of power are first decontextualized and second symmetrized or inverted.
- Symbolic information is information standing for other information, which may itself be symbolic, imaginary, or real.
- Memory in communication may be genetic, neurological, immunological, unconscious, non-conscious, personal, and/or social.
- Communication is impossible without coding.
- A code is not of the same level of communication, reality, or logical type as the messages it makes possible for goalseekers to construct, send, or receive.
- A code is a set of constraints, a code of rules, that permits goal-seekers (i.e. communicants) mediated by the code to construct mutually understandable messages.
- A code always includes a syntactic or ordering function (similar to the role of logistics in strategy).
- A code may be primarily semantic, having to do with the organization of sensing, meaning, and/or signification.
- A code may be primarily pragmatic, having to do with the organization of various kinds of value, notably use value, exchange value, and survival value.
- Semiotic freedom is the relative freedom to produce, reproduce, and communicate within the constraints of a code or codes.
- Information is the ground or basis of sensing; sensing is the ground of meaning; and meaning is the ground of signification.
- Sensing is coded information; meaning is coded sensing; signification is coded meaning.
- Survival value is the basis of both (digital) exchange value and

(iconic) use value. Both kinds of value are created in production and expressed in exchange.

- The simplest kind of information is coded variety (W. Ross Ashby), a signal.
- Two or more kinds of variety constitute at least one kind of diversity.
- Relations of communication and organization may take the form of difference, distinction, opposition, contradiction, and paradox.
- Difference, the ground of distinction, is defined as analog (continuously coded). Distinction, the ground of opposition, contradiction, and paradox, is digital (discontinuously coded).
- Language is a communication system found only in human societies. No naturally evolved animal communication, including dolphins, insects, and apes, has been shown to possess all the characteristics of language.
- Language is distinguished from other modes of communication mainly by (a) our use of abstractions, syntactic negation, and tense, and (b) our use of language to talk about its own characteristics.
- Teaching language to apes is no exception to the distinction between language and other modes of communication. Apart from unconscious cuing by the investigators, the domesticated dependence on humans it requires is a social intervention into nature. It is a product of the social order of reality (history), not of the natural order (evolution).
- Objectivity in communication is imaginary.
- Subjectivity is both unique and real, but also collective.
- Metacommunication (communication about communication) signifies:
  - (a) communication about communication in general (e.g. this sentence);

    (b) communication about a particular communication (e.g. 'This message is in English');

    (c) communication in one mode of communication about the communication of another mode (e.g. a threat accompanied by a wink, or a wink accompanied by a threat).

Metacommunication of type (a) is restricted to human society. Meta-communications of types (b) and (c) are found throughout the human and animal worlds, notably in play. To distinguish 'play' from 'fight', and 'co-operative competition' from 'competitive competition', a meta-message is required, the equivalent of 'this is play' (Bateson).

Mutual agreements about meta-messages are agreements to change

– or 'reframe' – one or more of the dominant codes of constraints (the rules of the context) shared by the communicants.

> Awareness of self and social context is highly developed and becomes explicitly stated in captive animals that have been taught a laboratory sign language. Another fascinating finding reveals how strongly cultural an animal the chimpanzee is ... Miss Goodall's book [displays] an animal uncannily similar to ourselves ... Perhaps we now need to use more imagination in converse with these extraordinary 'people'.
>
> JOHN H. CROOK: Review of Jane Goodall's *Chimpanzees of Gombe* in the *New York Times* for 24 August 1986.

4 Reduction of the reduction

According to the popular thesis of sociobiology outlined in the review just quoted – the thesis by which success in the future is measured against individual 'reproductive fitness' (leaving a large number of biological progeny) – I ought to be out chasing the opposite sex instead of writing this book. That way instead of influencing you and the future, I could be out siring any number of unknown and thus completely uninfluenceable descendants. brought up by absolute strangers.

The result of artificially reducing people to animals, as sociobiology does, is that animals can be artificially raised to the status of people, as sociobiology also does. For the sociobiologists to make any seriously favorable comparison between the sign systems and other relations of primates, at one level, and human relations and language, at another, is to depend on a reductionism that must rank among the seven blunders of the world. I'll believe the social side of sociobiology the day the first chimp writes a book.

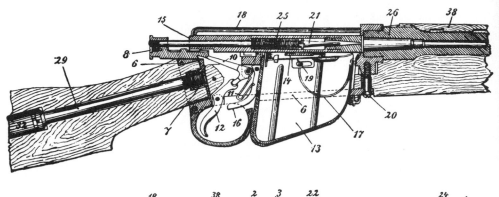

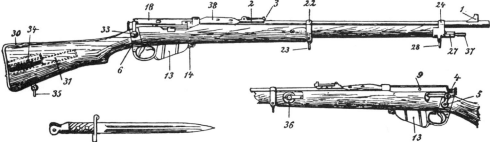

Fig. 1.   The Lee-Enfield-Rifle 1895

1. Foresight	14. Cut off	27. Bayonet catch
2. Bed of Backsight	15. Bolt	28. Piling swivel
3. Leaf of Backsight	16. Magazine Catch	29. Butt bolt
4. Aperture backsight	17. Magazine Spring	30. Butt plate
5. Screw for ditto	18. Body	31. Oil bottle
6. Cover	19. Magazine platform	32. Butt bolt head
7. Butt bolt screw	20. Connecting screw	33. Bolt knob
8. Cocking piece	21. Striker	34. Pull through
9. Screw Ejector	22. Lower Band	35. Butt swivel
10. Sear	23. Lower band swivel	36. Dial-Sight
11. Sear Spring	24. Upper Band	37. Cleaning rod
12. Trigger	25. Main Spring	38. Hand guard.
13. Magazine	26. Chamber	

Bibliography

I hate quotations.

RALPH WALDO EMERSON (1803–1882)

Bibliographical note

The bibliography is divided into four parts.

Part A, *The 20th Century War*, is a selective list of the references and background readings for the opening essay, 'The Naming of Parts and the 20th Century War'.

Part B, *Illustrated Media*, originally drawn up as a guide for students, is a selection of pictorial material on the social media, including war, technology, and toys, designed to complement and contextualize the mainly verbal information of Part A.

Part C, *The Strategy of Communication*, forms the main bibliography beginning with Chapter One.

Part D, *Reference Works*, lists works of reference and general utility.

The booklist should be treated as representative rather than as complete. It is in many respects quite personal and dominated by works read over the past four years. It includes books only recently brought to my attention; books I have come across by accident; books suggested by students (for which many thanks); and books bought years ago that for some reason I finally decided to sit down and read.

Part A: The 20th century war

Note: Part A lists all books directly referred to in the opening essay, along with details of other sources, background material, and suggestions for further reading.

For each major event or period referred to I have tried to find one or more reasonably reliable sources that deal with the matter in a strategical way. For the 20th century the reader may also consult the always informative but not always critical accounts in the 20 volumes of Purnell's illustrated *20th Century* (1979), edited by A. J. P. Taylor and others; or the 1976 *History of the 20th Century* by Octopus; or some similarly general source. In dealing with the more controversial events, such as the Spanish Civil War (1936–39) or the Algerian War of Independence (1954–62), I have listed several sources.

I have also drawn up a representative cluster of military texts (continued in Part B). Taken together, and especially when read in the light of Susan Brownmiller's *Against*

Our Will (1975), these are decisive evidence of the merciless New Model Strategy developed out of the defeat in the Indochina War.

Today the post-Vietnam strategy is readily made flesh in medieval brutality: in state terrorist tactics and the technology of torture, new and old, constantly refined by the ever-expanding stormtrooper elites around the world.

To these military readings I have added a selection of books of the kind read by middle and upper class boys of my grandfather's generation (b. 1885), my father's generation (b. 1908), and my own (b. 1935), as well as some other treasures unearthed in the secondhand trade.

On examination forty years after the event, these 'boy's books' are not at all the 'good clean fun' or the 'ideal worlds' we imagined them to be. They are suffused throughout with an ideology of retribution, if that's the word I want – an ideology of (white) might makes right. They present on the whole a view of 'justice' that unconsciously prepares the mind for the unjust act. They ignore the common basis of social organization: 'natural justice' in English common law and 'due process' in the more advanced capitalist democracy of the United States.

The result of this unconscious learning is disastrous to civil society. As if by the inherent godliness of priests, or the awful majesty of law, or the divine right of kings, the ideology of retribution – the self-righteous punishment of real and imaginary wrongs – turns into what every colonizer recognizes as the strategy of colonialism: The absolute right of 'absolute good' (the colonizers) to do absolutely anything to absolutely anyone they have defined as criminal, immoral, animal, or evil.

Vengeance is mine, saith the Lord, I will repay.

Most of the illustrated works relevant to 'The Naming of Parts and the 20th Century War' will be found in Part B. Illustrations are in black and white (b&w) unless otherwise stated, and remarked on only when particularly instructive.

Adams, Ian
  1981 S: Portrait of a Spy. Toronto: Virgo Press. [On the trail of a 'Canadian Philby' directing Royal Canadian Mounted Police counterespionage for the KGB: a fictional treatment of events.]
Adams, Jean, and Margaret Kimball, with Jeanette Eaton
  1942 *Heroines of the Sky*. With 30 photographs. Garden City, N.Y.: Junior Literary Guild and Doubleday, Doran & Co.
Alinsky, Saul
  1971 *Rules for Radicals*. New York: Vintage, 1972.
Allan, Ted, and Sydney Gordon
  1952 *The Scalpel, the Sword: The Story of Dr. Norman Bethune* [1890–1939]. Boston: Little, Brown & Co.
Allen, Charles, editor, with Helen Fry
  1979 *Tales from The Dark Continent: Images of British Colonial Africa in the Twentieth Century*. London: André Deutsch/British Broadcasting Corporation (BBC). Macdonald Futura edition, 1980.
Allen, Charles, editor, with Michael Mason
  1975 *Plain Tales from the Raj: Images of British India in the Twentieth Century*. London: André Deutsch/BBC. Macdonald Futura edition, 1976.
Allen, Peter
  1982 *The Yom Kippur War* [1973]. New York: Charles Scribner's Sons.
Alvarez, Manuel
  1980 *The Tall Soldier*. Toronto: Virgo Press. [Alvarez's search for the man from the Mackenzie-Papineau Battalion who saved his life as a boy during the Spanish Civil War, 1936–39.]

Anderson, Charles R.
1982 *The Grunts* (1976) and *Vietnam: The Other War*. Novato, Ca.: Presidio Press.
Anon
1937 *Chums Annual 1936–7*. To the Boys of the Empire upon which the Sun never sets. With over 200 cuts and decorations. London: Amalgamated Press
1952 *Film Fun Annual 1952*. London: Amalgamated Press.
1985 *Clandestine Operations Manual for Central America*. English translation of *Psychological Operations in Guerrilla Warfare*. Cornville, Arizona: Desert Publications.
Associated Press
1982 Mounting oil debts, trade deficits threaten to collapse world economy. *Vancouver Sun*, May 31, 1982.
Atkin, Ronald
1980 *Dieppe 1942: The Jubilee Disaster*. London: Macmillan.
The Australian Military Forces
1965 *Ambush and Counter Ambush*. With 11 drawings. Boulder, Colo.: Paladin. Facsimile reprint.
Baker, Mark
1981 *Nam: The Vietnam War in the Words of the Men and Women Who Fought There*. New York: Wm. Morrow.
Balchen, Colonel Bernt, Major Corey Ford, and Major Oliver Lafarge
1944 *War Below Zero: The Battle for Greenland*. Foreword by General H. H. Arnold, Commanding General, Army Air Forces. With map and 15 pages of photographs. Boston: Houghton Mifflin/The Army Air Forces Aid Society.
Barker, A. J.
1971 *The Rape Of Ethiopia 1936*. New York: Ballantine's Illustrated History of the Violent Century (hereafter Ballantine's Violent Century).
Baritz, Loren
1985 *Backfire: A History of How American Culture Led Us into Vietnam and Made Us Fight the Way We Did*. New York: Ballantine.
Beaumont, Roger A.
1974 *Military Elites: Special Fighting Units in the Modern World*. Indianapolis and New York: Bobbs-Merrill.
Boase, Wendy
1979 *The Sky's the Limit: Women Pioneers in Aviation*. New York: Macmillan.
Beckwith, Col. Charlie A., and Donald Knox
1983 *Delta Force: The U.S. Counter-Terrorist Unit and the Iran Hostage Rescue Mission*. New York and London: Harcourt Brace Jovanovich. [Beckwith introduced British Special Air Service methods, derived from imperial days, to the United States in the 1960s.]
Beesly, Patrick
1982 *Room 40. British Naval Intelligence 1914–1918*. New York: Harcourt Brace Jovanovich.
Bell, William
1936 The way of a white man: A thrilling tale of the Canadian lumberlands. Daily Mirror, publisher, *The Pip & Squeak Annual for 1936*, pp. 200–3.
Ben-Porat, Yeshayahu, Eitan Haber, and Zeev Schiff
1976 *Entebbe Rescue*. Introduction by Yitzhak Rabin. Tr. by Zmora, Bitan, Modan Publishers. New York: Delacorte, 1977.
Beresford, Major C. F. C.
1886 "The Field Telegraph", Its use in war and its employment in the late expeditions in the Soudan and South Africa. *Journal of the Royal United Service Institution*, pp. 673–600. Scheips, ed., 1980, vol. II.

Berkeley, Humphry
    1969 *The Power of the Prime Minister*. London: George Allen & Unwin; New York: Chilmark Press [see Young 1941].
Bermant, Chaim
    1975 *London's East End: Point of Arrival*. London and New York: Macmillan, 1976.
Bernstein, Carl, and Bob Woodward
    1974 *All the President's Men*. New York: Warner, 1976.
Bérubé, Allan
    1984 Coming out under fire: The untold story of the World War II soldiers who fought on the front lines of gay and lesbian liberation. *Mother Jones*, February–March.
Besançon, Julien, compiler
    1968 *"Les Murs ont la Parole": Journal Mural Mai 68: Sorbonne Odéon Nanterre Etc*. Paris: Tchou. [Graffiti from the events of May 1968.]
Beveridge, Senator Albert J.
    1900 Speech on the Philippines, January 4, 1900. Mendenhall, et al., eds., 1948, pp. 299–301.
Blainey, Geoffrey
    1966 *The Tyranny of Distance: How Distance Shaped Australia's History*. Melbourne: Macmillan, 1975.
Borrer, Dawson
    1848 *Narrative of a Campaign against the Kabaïles of Algeria: With the Mission of M. Suchet to the Emir Abd-el-Kader for an Exchange of Prisoners*. London: Longman, Brown, Green, and Longmans.
Bowle, John
    1974 *The Imperial Achievement: The Rise and Transformation of the British Empire*. With 26 illustrations. Harmondsworth, Middlesex: Penguin, 1977.
Bowman, Constance
    1944 *Slacks and Callouses*. Illustrated by Clara Marie Allen. New York and Toronto: Longmans, Green & Co. [An art teacher and an English teacher build bombers on their summer vacation.]
Boyle, Andrew
    1979 *The Climate of Treason: Five who Spied for Russia*. London: Hutchinson.
The Boy's Own Paper
    n.d. *The Boy's Own Annual*. With hundreds of illustrations, a number in color. London, 1884–1885 (7th volume); 1887–1888 (10th volume); 1888–1889 (11th volume); 1890–1891 (13th volume); 1913–1914 (36th volume); 1916–1917 (39th volume).
Bradley, La Verne
    1944 Women at Work. With 23 Illustrations. *National Geographic*, 86/2 (August), pp. 193–220.
Breckenridge, Major Robert P.
    1942 *Modern Camouflage. The New Science of Protective Concealment*. With a chart of the 9 official Army camouflage colors and 132 photographs and diagrams. New York and Toronto: Farrar & Rinehart.
Briggs, William, publisher
    1924 *Young Canada: An Illustrated Annual for Boys throughout the English-speaking World*. With over 250 illustrations, some in color. Toronto: Wm. Briggs. Forty-fifth volume.
Broadfoot, Barry
    1977 *Years of Sorrow, Years of Shame: The Story of the Japanese Canadians in World War II*. Garden City, N.Y.: Doubleday.

Brough, James
    1975 *The Prince and the Lily: The Story of Edward VII and Lillie Langtry*. London:
          Coronet, 1978.
Brown, Anthony Cave
    1982 *The Last Hero: Wild Bill Donovan*. The biography and political experience of
          Major General William J. Donovan, founder of the OSS and 'father' of the
          CIA. New York: Times Books.
Browne, Douglas G.
    1941 *Private Thomas Atkins: A History of the British Soldier from 1840 to 1940:
          A Panorama of Gallantry*. With 16 illustrations. London and Melbourne:
          Hutchinson.
Brownmiller, Susan
    1975 *Against Our Will: Men, Women and Rape*. New York: Simon & Schuster.
          Bantam edition 1976.
Buckley, Tom
    1984 *Violent Neighbors: El Salvador, Central America and the United States*. New
          York: Times Books.
Butler, Ewan
    1963 *Amateur Agent: A Story of Black Propaganda during World War II*. London,
          Toronto, Wellington, and Sydney: Harrap. [A Special Operations Executive
          (SOE) agent in the Middle East and Sweden.]
Butler, Samuel
    1872 The book of the machines. *Erewhon*. New York: Dutton, 1965, pp. 140–63.
Caesar, Julius
    1917 *The Gallic War* [58–52 BCE]. Facing translation by H. J. Edwards. Cambridge,
          Mass.: Harvard University Press; London: Heinemann, 1979. [Written in plain
          Latin, Caesar's *Commentaries* have been a standard component of the Classics
          curriculum for centuries (see Xenophon).]
Carter, Hodding, III
    1986 Reagan's different brand of statism. *Wall Street Journal*, July 3.
Cassell and Co., publishers
    1916 *The Canadian Girl's Annual*. Compiled by the editor of *Little Folks*. With
          numerous sketches and cuts, and 20 full-page illustrations in b&w and color.
          London, New York, Toronto, and Melbourne.
Capek, Karel
    1921 *R.U.R. (Rossum's Universal Robots). Of Men and Machines*. Ed. by Arthur
          O. Lewis, Jr. New York: Dutton, 1963, pp. 3–58.
Chadwick, John
    1958 *The Decipherment of Linear B*. Harmondsworth, Middlesex: Penguin, 1961.
Chandos, John
    1984 *Boys Together: English Public Schools 1800–1864*. Newhaven: Yale University
          Press. [Excellent example of the 'public school mind'.]
Charteris, Leslie
    1951 *The Second Saint Omnibus* [1933–51]. Garden City, N.Y.: Doubleday Crime
          Club.
Cherniavsky, Michael
    1980 *25 Short Pieces*. Waterloo, Ont.: University of Waterloo.
Childers, Colonel James Saxon
    1943 *War Eagles: The Story of the Eagle Squadron*. With 104 photographs. New
          York and London: Appleton-Century.
Chilton, Paul, and Crispin Aubrey, editors
    1983 *Nineteen Eighty-Four in 1984: Autonomy, Control and Communication*.
          London: Comedia [9 Poland Street, London, W1V 3DG].

Chomsky, Noam
  1967 *American Power and the New Mandarins*. London: Chatto & Windus, 1969.
Churchill, Randolph S.
  1966 *Winston S. Churchill: Youth 1874–1900*. Cambridge: Riverside Press; Boston: Houghton Mifflin.
Clausewitz, Carl von
  1832 *On War*. Tr. by O. J. Matthijs Jolles. New York: The Modern Library, 1943.
Clébert, Jean-Paul
  1961 *The Gypsies*. Tr. by Charles Duff. Harmondsworth, Middlesex: Penguin, 1969.
Courrière, Yves
  1968 *La Guerre d'Algérie I: Les Fils de la Toussaint*. Paris: Fayard.
  1969 *La Guerre d'Algérie II: Le Temps des léopards*. Paris: Fayard.
Creswicke, Louis
  n.d. *South Africa and the Transvaal War*. With over 200 photographs, color plates, portraits, and maps. Edinburgh: T. C. & E. C. Jack. Six volumes.
Crompton, Richmal
  1933 *William – The Rebel*. Illustrated by Thomas Henry. London: George Newnes Limited, 1942. [One of a series of 23 books.]
Culhane, Claire
  1972 *Why is Canada in Vietnam?* Toronto: NC Press.
Daily Express, publisher
  n.d. *Rupert: The Daily Express Annual*. London: Beaverbrook Newspapers. Various dates.
Daily Mirror, publisher
  1936 *The Pip & Squeak Annual for 1936*. London. Fourteenth number.
Danylchuk, Jack
  1985 Former adviser on Star Wars calls defence system a fraud. *The Globe and Mail*, July 10.
Davis, Forrest
  1941 *The Atlantic System: The Story of Anglo-American Control of the Seas*. New York: Reynal & Hitchcock.
Davis, R. G.
  1975 *The San Francisco Mime Troupe: The First Ten Years*. Introduction by Robert Scheer. With 57 prints, drawings, and photographs, and a 26-page flip book. Palo Alto, Ca.: Ramparts Press.
Davy, M. J. Bernard
  1941 *Air Power and Civilization*. London: George Allen & Unwin. [An early refutation of the supposed effects of strategic bombing.]
de Jonge, Alex
  1978 *The Weimar Chronicle: Prelude to Hitler* [1918–33]. With 100 photographs. New York and London: Paddington Press.
Department of the Army, Washington, D.C.
  1965 *Special Forces Operational Techniques* (FM 31–20). Boulder, Colo.: Paladin, 1982. [For the Paladin (U.S.) catalog see the reference section.]
  n.d. *U.S. Special Forces Recon Manual (Elite Unite Tactical Series)*. U.S. Institute for Military Assistance. Sims, Ark.: Lancer Militaria, 1982.
de St Jerome, John
  1972 *The Brothers' War: Biafra and Nigeria* [1967–70]. Boston: Houghton Mifflin.
de Tocqueville, Alexis
  1840 *Democracy in America*. The Henry Reeve text, revised by Francis Bowen. Ed. by Phillips Bradley. New York: Vintage, 1943. Vol. I, 1835; vol. II, 1840.
Dietrich, Noah, and Bob Thomas
  1972 *Howard: The Amazing Mr. Hughes*. Greenwich, Conn.: Fawcett.

Diskin, Martin, editor
   1984 *Trouble in Our Own Backyard: Central America and the United States in the Eighties*. New York: Pantheon.
Dixon, Alex
   1941 *Tinned Soldier: A Personal Record 1919–1926*. London: Jonathan Cape. [Dixon became a friend of T. E. Lawrence when the latter joined the Tank Corps.]
Doggett, F. C., editor
   n.d. *The Cigarette Card News and Trade Card Chronicle*. Somerton, Somerset: The London Cigarette Card Company. Monthly.
Douglas, David C.
   1969 *The Norman Achievement 1050–1100*. Berkeley: University of California Press.
Douglas, W. A. B., and Brereton, Greenhous
   1977 *Out of the Shadows: Canada in the Second World War*. Toronto, Oxford, and New York: Oxford University Press.
Dower, John W.
   1986 *War Without Mercy: Race and Power in the Pacific War*. New York: Pantheon.
Dowling, Colette
   1981 *The Cinderella Complex: Women's Hidden Fear of Independence*. New York: Pocket Books.
Doyle, Arthur Conan
   1900 *The Great Boer War*. London: Smith, Elder, & Co.
Drake, Francis Vivian
   1943 *Vertical Warfare*. With 59 photographs and 7 line cuts. The bombing program of the US and British air forces. Garden City, N.Y.: Doubleday, Doran and Co.
Dranoff, Linda Silver
   1977 *Women in Canadian Life: Law*. Toronto: Fitzhenry & Whiteside.
Dupuy, Colonel Trevor, U.S. Army, Ret.
   1980 *The Evolution of Weapons and Warfare*. Indianapolis and New York: Bobbs-Merrill.
Dyer, Gwynne
   1985 *War*. New York: Stoddart. From Dyer's National Film Board Television Series.
Dyson, Freeman
   1984 *Weapons and Hope*. New York: Harper & Row.
Edwards, G. B.
   1981 *The Book of Ebenezer Le Page*. A novel of Guernsey life. Harmondsworth, Middlesex: Penguin, 1982.
Eisenhauer, Captain A. L. 'Ike', and Robin Moore with Robert J. Flood
   1976 *The Flying Carpetbagger*. With 16 pages of photos. New York: Pinnacle Books. [The story of Robert Vesco's Boeing 707 pilot and aide.]
Ellison, Ralph
   1951 *Invisible Man*. New York: Vintage, 1963.
Elstob, Peter
   1973 *Condor Legion*. New York: Ballantine's Violent Century. [The Nazi state terrorists who bombed the defenseless city of Guernica, spiritual capital of the Basques, on market day, Monday, April 26, 1937.]
Emerson, Gloria
   1972 *Winners and Losers: Battles, Retreats, Gains, Losses and Ruins from a Long War*. New York: Random House, 1976.
Epstein, Jason
   1970 *The Great Conspiracy Trial: An Essay on Law, Liberty and the Constitution*. New York: Vintage, 1971. [Trial of the Chicago Eight, including Rennie Davis,

Dave Dellinger, Tom Hayden, Abbie Hoffman, Jerry Rubin, and Bobby Seale. See also Walker, 1968.]

Ezard, John
  1984 'Secret' of GIs' deaths saddens E-boat chief. *Manchester Guardian Weekly*, April 29, p. 7.

Farwell, Byron
  1967 *Prisoners of the Mahdi*. The story of the Mahdist Revolt [1884–1898]. New York: Harper & Row.
  1981 *Mr Kipling's Army: All the Queen's Men*. With 30 illustrations. New York and London: Norton.
  1984 *The Ghurkas*. New York: Norton.

Faughnan, Thomas
  1879 *Stirring Incidents in the Life of A British Soldier. An Autobiography*. Toronto: Hunter, Rose and Co, 1880. Second edition.

Fenwick, Bryan, editor
  1938 *The Speed Omnibus*. Illustrated in b&w and color. London and Glasgow: Collins, 1948.

Ferguson, Ted
  1980 *Desperate Siege: The Battle of Hong Kong* [December 1941]. Garden City, N.Y.: Doubleday.

Finnemore, John
  n.d. *The Empire's Children*. With numerous photographs. Toronto: Musson, c. 1920.

Fisher, David, and Anthony Read
  1984 *Colonel Z. The Secret Life of a Master of Spies*. New York: Viking 1985.

Fleming, Peter
  1940 *The Flying Visit*. Drawings by David Low. London: Jonathan Cape.
  1956 *Operation Sea Lion: The Projected Invasion of England in 1940*. New York: Simon & Schuster, 1957.

Flying Magazine
  1977 *Pilot Error: Anatomies of Aircraft Accidents*. New York, Cincinnati, Toronto, London, and Melbourne: Van Nostrand Reinhold.

Foot, M. R. D.
  1966 *S O E in France: An Account of the Work of the British Special Operations Executive in France 1940–1944*. With 15 pages of photographs. London: HMSO History of the Second World War. [Portraits include Virginia Hall, Noor Inayat Khan, Yvonne Baseden, and Jean Moulin.]

Ford, Brian
  1969 *German Secret Weapons: Blueprint for Mars*. Ballantine's Violent Century.

Fuller, Major-General J. F. C.
  1932 *Armored Warfare*. Military Classics IV. Harrisburg, Pa: Telegraph Press, 1943. First American edition.
  1961 *The Conduct of War 1789–1961*. London: Methuen University Paperbacks, 1979.

Fussell, Paul
  1975 *The Great War and Modern Memory*. New York and London: Oxford University Press.

Galbraith, John Kenneth
  1954 *The Great Crash 1929*. Boston: Houghton Mifflin, 1961.
  1967 *The New Industrial State*. Boston: Houghton Mifflin.

General Staff, War Office
  1912 *Field Service Regulations Part One: Operations 1909*. London: HMSO. Reprinted with Amendments, 1912.

Gilliam, Dorothy Butler
  1978 *Paul Robeson All-American* [1899–1976]. With 20 photographs and an index of plays and films. Washington, D.C.: The New Republic Book Company.
Goff, Stanley, Robert Sanders, and Clark Smith
  1982 *Brothers: Black Soldiers in the Nam.* Novato, Ca.: Presidio Press; London: Arms and Armour Press.
Gold, Wilmer
  1985 *Logging As It Was: A Pictorial History of Logging on Vancouver Island.* Victoria, B.C.: Morriss.
Gordon, Don E.
  1981 *Electronic Warfare: Element of Strategy and Multiplier of Combat Power.* New York, Oxford, Toronto, and Sydney: Pergamon Press.
Goulden, Joseph
  1983 *Korea: The Untold Story.* New York: McGraw-Hill.
Gowing, T.
  1892 *A Soldier's Experience, or, A Voice from the Ranks, Showing the Cost of War in Blood and Treasure: A Personal Narrative of the Crimean Campaign, from the Standpoint of the Ranks; the Indian Mutiny and Some of its Atrocities; the Afghan Campaigns of 1863. Together with Some Things not Generally Known. By One of the Royal Fusiliers.* Nottingham: Printed for the Author by Thos. Forman and Sons.
Graham, Hugh Davis, and Ted Robert Gurr, co-directors
  1969 *Violence in America: Historical and Comparative Perspectives.* Studies by 50 scholars from various disciplines. A report submitted to the National Commission on the Causes and Prevention of Violence. New York: Bantam.
Graham-White, Claude, and Harry Hopkins
  1913 *The Air King's Treasure: A Story of Adventure with Airship & Aeroplane.* London, New York, Toronto, and Melbourne: Cassell.
Groom, Winston, and Duncan Spencer
  1983 *Conversations with the Enemy: The Story of Pfc Robert Farwood.* New York: G. P. Putnam's Sons. [Captured by the Viet Cong in 1965, Garwood was held prisoner until 1979 (the war ended in 1975).]
Gung-Ho
  1984 Rainbow Warriors: The dedicated gung-ho eco-guerrillas of Greenpeace. A Gung-Ho elite unit staff report. *Gung-Ho* (February), pp. 42–51, 67–71.
Gurd, Eric
  1942 *Cigarette Cards: An Outline.* London: The Cartophilic Society of Great Britain.
H., Captain, late R.N.
  1885 Boy Life Afloat II: The Gratings. London: *The Boy's Own Paper*, vol. 7, no. 333, Saturday, May 30. [Eye-witness of British sailors being flogged to death in 1865.]
Haggard, H. Rider
  1885 *Three Adventure Novels: She, King Solomon's Mines, and Allan Quatermain.* New York: Dover, 1951.
Halberstam, David
  1969 *The Best and the Brightest.* Greenwich, Conn.: Fawcett Crest Books, 1973. [How America became involved in Vietnam.]
  1979 *The Powers That Be.* New York: Dell, 1980. [The media barons.]
Harrison, Gordon
  1978 *Mosquitoes, Malaria and Man.* New York: Dutton.
Hart, Liddell
  1934 *A History of the World War 1914–1918.* London: Faber & Faber. The 1930 edition revised and enlarged.

Haugland, Vern
    1979 *The Eagle Squadrons: Yanks in the RAF 1940–1942.* New York: Ziff-Davis.
Hayens, Herbert
    1902 *For the Colours: A Boys' Book of the Army* [1066–1900]. With 33 illustrations. London, Edinburgh, and New York: Thomas Nelson.
Hayes, Carlton J. H.
    1941 *A Generation of Materialism 1871–1900.* With 62 illustrations drawn from unusual sources. New York: Harper Torchbooks, 1963. Rise of Modern Europe Series.
Hemingway, Ernest, editor
    1942 *Men at War: The Best War Stories of All Time.* New York: Bramhall House, 1979.
Henty, G. A.
    n.d. *Orange and Green: A Tale of the Boyne and Limerick* [1690–91]. Illustrated by Gordon Browne R.I. London and Glasgow: Blackie & Son. [The Orangist (Protestant) victory under William III after England's 'glorious revolution' of 1688, when the Catholic James II was deposed.]
    n.d. *Bonnie Prince Charlie: A Tale of Fontenoy and Culloden* [1745–46]. Illustrated by Gordon Brown. London and Glasgow: Blackie & Son.
    1897 *The Young Buglers: A Tale of the Peninsular War* [1808–14]. With 8 illustrations by John Proctor and 11 battle plans. London: Griffith Farran Browne & Co.
    1901 *With Buller in Natal Or, A Born Leader.* With 10 illustrations by W. Rainey R.I. London, Glasgow, and Dublin: Blackie & Son. [The South African War, 1899–1900.]
    n.d. *With the Allies to Pekin: A Tale of the Relief of the Legations.* With 4 illustrations, a map, and color frontispiece. London and Gasgow: Blackie & Son, c. 1901. [The Boxer Rebellion of 1899–1901.]
Herm, Gerhard
    1975 *The Celts: The People who Came out of the Darkness.* London: Weidenfeld & Nicolson; New York: St. Martin's, 1977.
Hersh, Seymour M.
    1983 *The Price of Power: Kissinger in the Nixon White House.* New York: Summit Books. [The 'wimp factor' and the prolongation of the Vietnam War.]
Hibbert, Christopher
    1978 *The Great Mutiny: India 1857.* New York: Viking.
Higham, Charles
    1983 *Trading With the Enemy: An Exposé of the Nazi-American Money Plot 1933–1949.* New York: Dell, 1984.
Hoar, Victor, and Mac Reynolds
    1969 *The Mackenzie-Papineau Battalion.* Toronto: Copp Clark. [Proportionate to population more Canadians volunteered to serve in the International Brigades supporting the Republic in the Spanish Civil War than nationals of any other nation.]
Holmes, Richard, and Anthony Kemp
    1982 *The Bitter End: The Fall of Singapore 1941–42.* Chichester: Antony Bird Ltd.
Hopkins, J. Castell, and Murat Halstead
    1900 *South Africa and the Boer-British War, Comprising an Authentic History of the Dark Continent.* With over 70 pages of sketches and photographs. Toronto War Book Publishing Co. Two volumes.
Horne, Alistair
    1977 *A Savage War of Peace: Algeria 1954–1962.* Harmondsworth, Middlesex: Penguin, 1979. [Francophile.]

Horne, Charles F.
    1894   *Great Men and Famous Women: A Series of Pen and Pencil Sketches of the
            Lives of More than 200 of the Most Prominent Personages in History.* New
            York: Selmar Hess. Two volumes each: *Soldiers and Sailors, Statesmen and
            Sages, Workmen and Heroes,* and *Artists and Authors.*
Horsley, Reginald
    n.d.   *Romance of Empire: New Zealand.* With a map and 12 color reproductions
            from drawings by A. D. M'Cormick R.I. London and Edinburgh: T. C. & E.
            C. Jack, c. 1907. [A series on Australia, Canada, India, South Africa, the Land
            of the Golden Trade (West Africa), and the Outposts of Empire.]
Hoyt, Edwin P.
    1981   *Guerilla: Colonel von Lettow-Vorbeck and Germany's East African Empire*
            [in World War I]. New York and London: Macmillan/Collier Macmillan.
Hughes, Terry, and John Costello
    1977   *The Battle of the Atlantic.* With over 400 photographs. London: Collins; New
            York: The Dial Press/James Wade. ['The first complete account of the origins
            and outcome of the longest and most crucial campaign of World War II'.]
Hurd, Douglas
    1967   *The Arrow War: An Anglo-Chinese Confusion 1856–1860.* London: Collins;
            New York: Macmillan. [The first Opium War (1839–42) was an attack on
            China by Britain; in the second or 'Arrow' war Britain was allied with France.]
Infantry Magazine, editors
    1983   *A Distant Challenge: The U.S. Infantryman in Vietnam, 1967–1972.* Foreword
            by General William C. Westmoreland. Nashville: The Battery Press. [A series
            of appreciations and reflections by U.S. officers.]
Jackson, Gabriel
    1974   *A Concise History of the Spanish Civil War.* With 152 photographs, cartoons,
            and maps. London: Thames & Hudson, 1980.
Jackson, G. Gibbard
    n.d.   *Motoring by Land, Sea and Air.* Illustrated in b&w and color. London: Thomas
            Nelson, c. 1925.
Jackson, Peter
    1982   British came 'close to defeat' in Falklands. *Manchester Guardian Weekly,*
            September 19.
James, C. L. R.
    1938   *The Black Jacobins: Toussaint L'Ouverture and the San Domingo Revolution*
            [1791–1803]. London: Allison & Busby, 1980. New edition.
Johns, Captain W. E.
    1936   *Biggles & Co.* Oxford: Oxford University Press.
    1943   *Spitfire Parade.* Oxford: Oxford University Press.
    1945   *Worrals on the War Path.* Venture Books for Girls. Toronto: Musson.
    1959   *The Biggles Book of Heroes.* London: Max Parrish.
Jones, C. Sheridan, and Alfred Miles
    n.d.   *Heroic Deeds of Great Men.* With numerous cuts and 7 color plates. London,
            Paris, and New York: Raphael Tuck & Sons, Publishers to Their Majesties
            the King and Queen, c. 1925.
Jones, Gwyn
    1968   *A History of the Vikings.* London, New York, and Toronto: Oxford University
            Press.
Jones, R. V.
    1978   *Most Secret War: British Scientific Intelligence 1939–45.* London: Hamish
            Hamilton; New York: Coronet.

Kahn, Leon
 1978 *No Time To Mourn: The True Story of a Jewish Partisan Fighter*. Vancouver,
    B.C.: Laurelton Press [1194 Wolfe St, Vancouver, B.C.].
Karas, Thomas
 1983 *The New High Ground: Systems, Strategies, and Weapons of Space Age War*.
    New York: Simon & Schuster.
Kaucher, Dorothy
 1947 *Wings over Wake*. Across the Pacific by Pan American Clipper in 1937. With
    20 pages of photographs. San Francisco: John Howell.
Keegan, John
 1976 *The Face of Battle*. New York: Viking.
Kerner, Otto, chairman
 1968 *Report of the National Advisory Commission on Civil Disorders*. Introduction
    by Tom Wicker. With 32 pages of photographs. New York: Bantam.
Kevin, Kelley
 1982 *The Longest War: Northern Ireland and the IRA*. Dingle, Co. Kerry: Brandon;
    Westport, Conn.: Lawrence Hill; London: Zed Books.
Kiaulehn, Walter
 n.d. The Anaconda System: America's contribution to the conduct of war (c. 1942).
    Signal: Hitler's Wartime Picture Magazine. Ed. by S. L. Mayer. Englewood
    Cliffs, N.J.: Prentice-Hall, 1976. [A German account of Sherman's 'locust
    strategy' in the devastation of Georgia in 1864–5.]
Kilfeather, T. P.
 1969 *The Connaught Rangers*. Dublin: Anvil Books, 1980.
Klickmann, Flora, editor
 1929 *The Girl's Own Annual*. With hundreds of illustrations, some in color. London:
    Woman's Magazine and the Girl's Own Paper.
Knightley, Phillip
 1975 *The First Casualty: The War Correspondent as Hero, Propagandist, and Myth
    Maker*. New York and London: Harcourt Brace Jovanovich.
Kolko, Gabriel
 1985 *Anatomy of a War: Vietnam, the United States, and the Modern Historical
    Experience*. New York: Pantheon.
Korda, Michael
 1979 *Charmed Lives: A Family Romance*. New York: Avon, 1981. [The Korda
    brothers and the British film industry.]
Korngold, Ralph
 1944 *Citizen Toussaint* [c. 1743–1803]. London: Victor Gollancz/New Left Book
    Club, 1945.
Kruger, Rayne
 1959 *Good-bye Dolly Gray: The Story of the Boer War*. London: Cassell.
Laffin, John
 1973 *Americans in Battle*. London: J. M. Dent and Sons.
Lane, Peter
 1971 *Revolution*. With over 50 illustrations. London: Batsford. World Wide Series.
Langworthy, John Luther
 1912 *The Aeroplane Boys, Or The Young Sky Pilot's First Air Voyage*. Chicago and
    New York: M. A. Donohue & Co.
Lawrence, Christie
 1947 *Irregular Adventure*. Introduction by Evelyn Waugh. London: Faber & Faber.
    [Twelve months with partisans in Yugoslavia after escaping from the Germans
    in 1941.]
Leed, Eric J.
 1979 *No Man's Land: Combat and Identity in World War I*. Cambridge, London,

New York, New Rochelle, Melbourne, and Sydney: Cambridge University Press, 1981.

Letts, Charles, publisher
n.d.   *The Raid Spotter's Pocket Book and Log*. London, c. 1941.

Levy, 'Yank' Bert
1964   *Guerrilla Warfare* [1942]. Introduction by Franklin Mark Osanka. Ed. by Robert K. Brown, editor and publisher of *Soldier of Fortune*. Boulder, Colo.: Paladin, 1964. [On loan from Britain in 1942–43, Bert Levy, born in Hamilton, Ont., and veteran machine gunner of WWI and the International Brigades in Spain, taught the first official guerrilla warfare courses in the United States.]

Lewis, Anthony
1985   Morbid fear of Soviets is fuelling the arms race. *Toronto Globe & Mail*, November 19.

Ley, Willy
1944   *Rockets: The Future of Travel Beyond the Stratosphere*. New York: Viking.

Lindsey, Robert
1986   Long-term woes seen for California economy. *New York Times*, September 28.

Lipset, Seymour Martin, and Sheldon S. Wolin, editors
1965   *The Berkeley Student Revolt: Facts and Interpretations*. Garden City, N.Y.: Anchor. [The Free Speech Movement in the fall of 1964: the first big student action of the 1960s.]

Lucas, E. V.
1907   *Highways and Byways in Sussex*. Illustrated by F. L. Griggs. London, Bombay, Calcutta, Melbourne, New York, Boston, Chicago, Atlanta, San Francisco, and Toronto: Macmillan.

MacInnes, Colin
1961   *England, Half English*. London: MacGibbon & Kee.

McLaren, Peter
1980   *Cries from the Corridor: The New Suburban Ghettos*. Markham, Ont.: Paper-jacks, 1981.

MacLaren, Roy
1978   *Canadians on the Nile 1882–1898*. Vancouver, B.C.: University of B.C. Press.

Maclear, Michael
1981   *The Ten Thousand Day War: Vietnam 1945–1975*. New York: St Martin's.

McLuhan, Marshall
1964   *Understanding Media: The Extensions of Man*. London: Routledge & Kegan Paul.

McWhiney, Grady, and Perry D. Jamieson
1982   *Attack and Die: Civil War Military Tactics and the Southern Heritage*. University, Ala.: University of Alabama Press.

Magdoff, Harry
1969   *The Age of Imperialism: The Economics of U.S. Foreign Policy*. New York and London: Modern Reader Paperbacks.

Mahan, Captain A. T.
1900   *The War in South Africa: A Narrative of the Anglo-Boer War from the Beginning of Hostilities to the Fall of Pretoria*. Introduction by Sir John G. Bourinot, Clerk of the Canadian House of Commons. With over 200 illustrations in b&w, sepia, and color. New York: Peter Fenelon Collier & Son.

Malcolm X
1964   *The Autobiography of Malcolm X, as told to Alex Haley*. New York: Ballantine, 1976.

Mallin, Jay, and Robert K. Brown
    1979 *Merc: American Soldiers of Fortune.* New York and London: Macmillan/
          Collier Macmillan.
Malone, Colonel Dick
    1946 *Missing from the Record.* Toronto: Collins.
Malone, Lt-Col. Richard, editor
    1944 *The Maple Leaf Scrapbook: Souvenir Book Printed in Belgium at Cost Price
          to Forces Overseas.* Brussels: No. 3 Canadian Public Relations Group.
Manchester, William
    1978 *American Caesar: Douglas MacArthur 1880–1964.* New York: Dell.
Manvell, Roger
    1974 *Films and the Second World War.* With over 80 stills. London: J. M. Dent;
          New York: Delta, 1976.
Mao Tse-Tung
    1937 *Mao Tse-Tung on Guerrilla Warfare.* Tr. with an introduction by Brigadier
          General Samuel B. Griffith US Marine Corps (Ret.). New York and Wash-
          ington, 1961. [A reprint of the 1941 original, with an additional note.]
Markham, Beryl
    1942 *West with the Night.* San Francisco: North Point Press, 1983
Marquis, T. G.
    1900 *Canada's Sons on Kopje and Veldt.* With 91 illustrations. Toronto: Canada's
          Sons Publishing Co.
Mason, Robert
    1983 *Chickenhawk.* New York: Viking.
Mauldin, Bill
    1971 *The Brass Ring: A Sort of Memoir.* Illustrated by photographs and Mauldin
          cartoons 1941–51. New York: Norton.
Mellen, Joan
    1977 *Big Bad Wolves: Masculinity in the American Film.* With 41 stills. New York:
          Pantheon.
Mendenhall, Thomas C., Basil D. Henning, and Archibald S. Foord, editors
    1948 *The Quest for a Principle of Authority in Europe: 1715–Present.* New York:
          Holt, Rinehart & Winston, 1964.
Michael, Franz, with Chung-Li Chang
    1966 *The Taiping Rebellion: History and Documents.* Seattle and London: Univer-
          sity of Washington Press.
Mikes, George
    1946 *How to Be An Alien: A Handbook for Beginners and More Advanced Pupils.*
          Nicolas Bentley drew the pictures. London: Andre Deutsch, 1961.
Miller, Stuart Creighton
    1982 *"Benevolent Assimilation": The American Conquest of the Philippines
          1899–1903.* New Haven: Yale University Press.
Millis, Walter
    1931 *The Martial Spirit.* New York: The Literary Guild of America. [A critical
          account of the Spanish American War of 1898 and American operations in
          Cuba and the Philippines.]
Ministry of Information
    1942 *We Speak from the Air: Broadcasts by the R.A.F.* London: HMSO.
    1943 *Roof over Britain: The Official Story of the A.A. Defences 1939–1942.* With
          some 20 illustrations. London: HMSO.
Mitchison, Naomi, editor
    1932 *An Outline for Boys & Girls and Their Parents: Science, Civilisation, Values.*
          Illustrated by Wm Kermode & Ista Brouncker. London: Victor Gollancz Ltd.

[Part III includes Dancing and Drama, Or The First Pattern of Life; Visual Art, Or The Pattern Set Down; and Writing, Or The Pattern Between People.]

Moorehead, Alan

1956 *Gallipoli*. London: Hamish Hamilton.

Morella, Joe, Edward Z. Epstein, and John Griggs

1973 *The Films of World War II*. Introduction by Judith Crist. With over 300 stills. Secaucus, N.J.: Citadel.

Morin, Edgar

1969 *Rumour in Orléans*. Tr. by Peter Green. New York: Pantheon, 1971.

Mulvaney, Charles Pelham, A.M., M.D.

1885 *The History of the North-West Rebellion of 1885. Comprising a Full and Impartial Account of the Origin and Progress of the War, of the Various Engagements with the Indians and Half-Breeds, of the Heroic Deeds Performed by Officers and Men, and of Touching Scenes in the Field, the Camp, and the Cabin; Including a History of the Indian Tribes of North-Western Canada, their Numbers, Modes of Living, Habits, Customs, Religious Rites and Ceremonies, with Thrilling Narratives of Captures, Imprisonment, Massacres, and Hair-Breadth Escapes of White Settlers, Etc. By Charles Pelham Mulvaney, A.M., M.D., Formerly of No. 1 Company, Queens Own Rifles . . . assisted by a well-known journalist. Illustrated with Portraits of Distinguished Officers and Men, Maps, Diagrams and Engravings*. With 56 illustrations. Toronto: A. H. Hovey & Co. Facsimile: Toronto: Coles, 1971. [The Gatling Gun used in the expedition was under the command of an American advisor appointed by the manufacturer.]

Mydans, Carl, and Shelley Mydans

1968 *The Violent Peace*. New York: Atheneum. New edition.

Myers, Gustavus

1914 *A History of Canadian Wealth*. Introduction by Stanley B. Ryerson. Toronto: Lorimer, 1972

Navasky, Victor S.

1980 *Naming Names*. Harmondsworth, Middlesex, and New York: Penguin, 1981. [The House Un-American Activities Committee, the Hollywood blacklist era, and the ethics of informing.]

Neufeld, Charles

1900 *Under the Rebel's Reign: A Story of Egyptian Revolt*. With 54 illustrations by Charles Sheldon. London: Wells Gardner, Darton & Co.

O'Ballance, Edgar

1977 *The Secret War in the Sudan 1955–1972*. London: Faber & Faber. [Begins with an overview 1821–1936.]

Oberdorfer, Don

1971 *Tet!*. Garden City, N.Y.: Doubleday.

Obst, Lynda Rosen, editor

1977 *The Sixties*. With over 50 full page photographs. Designed by Robert Kingsbury. New York: Random House/Rolling Stone.

Octopus Books, publisher

1976 *History of the 20th Century*. Introduction by Allan Bullock. With over 500 illustrations mostly in color. London: Octopus/Phoebus/BPC.

O'Neill, Ralph, with Joseph F. Hood

1973 *A Dream of Eagles*. Boston and San Francisco: Houghton Mifflin. [Proving the route of the New York, Rio, and Buenos Aires Airline in the 1920s in Sikorsky flying boats.]

Orwell, George

1938 *Homage to Catalonia*. Harmondsworth, Middlesex: Penguin, 1980.

1939 Boys' weeklies. *Inside the Whale and Other Essays*. Harmondsworth, Middlesex: Penguin, 1979, pp. 175–203.

1949 *Nineteen Eighty-Four*. Harmondsworth, Middlesex: Penguin, 1979 [see Chilton and Aubrey, 1983].

Packard, Vance

1957 *The Hidden Persuaders*. New York: Pocket Books, 1968.

1972 *A Nation of Strangers*. New York: David McKay.

Page, Bruce, David Leitch, and Phillip Knightley

1981 *The Philby Conspiracy*. New York: Ballantine.

Pakenham, Thomas

1979 *The Boer War*. New York: Random House.

Parker, Ernest

1964 *Into Battle 1914–18: A Seventeen-Year-Old Boy Enlists in Kitchener's Army*. Foreword by Sir Arthur Bryant. London: Longmans.

Patterson, R. M.

1951 *Dear Mother: Letters from Rossall 1911–1917*. Private printing.

1952 *Dangerous River*. London: Panther; Sidney, B.C.; Gray's.

Peden, Murray

1978 *Fall of an Arrow*. With numerous photographs. Stittsville, Ont.: Canada's Wings [see Dow 1979].

Perrett, Bryan

1983 *Lightning War: A History of Blitzkrieg*. Foreword by General Sir John Hackett. London: Panther, 1985.

Pincher, Chapman

1978 *Inside Story: A Documentary of the Pursuit of Power*. London: Sidgwick & Jackson.

Post, Wiley, and Harold Gatty

1931 *Around the World in Eight Days: The Flight of the Winnie Mae*. Introduction by Will Rogers. Garden City, N.Y.: Garden City Publishing Co.

Power, James R.

1959 *Brave Women and their Wartime Decorations*. New York: Vantage Press.

Pratt, Fletcher

1942 *What Every Citizen Should Know About Modern War*. With 42 drawings. New York: Norton.

Price, Alfred

1977 *Blitz on Britain 1939–1945*. With over 100 photographs. London: Ian Allen.

Pugsley, William H.

1945 *Saints, Devils and Ordinary Seamen: Life on the Royal Canadian Navy's Lower Deck*. With 26 photographs. Toronto: Collins, 1946.

Purcell, Hugh

1973 *The Spanish Civil War*. With 50 photographs and maps. London: Wayland; New York: G. P. Putnam's Sons. The Documentary History Series.

Ramparts Magazine

1966 *A Vietnam Primer*. San Francisco.

Ranelagh, John

1981 *Ireland: An Illustrated History*. London: Collins.

Raskin, Marcus G., and Bernard B. Fall, editors

1965 *The Viet-Nam Reader*. New York: Vintage, 1967. Revised edition.

Rawlings, Leo

1972 *And the Dawn Came Up Like Thunder*. With 119 paintings by the author. Foreword by Admiral of the Fleet The Earl Mountbatten of Burma. Potters Bar, Herts.: Rawlings, Chapman Publications. [Building the Burma railway for the Japanese in World War II.]

Reeves, Thomas
    1982   *The Life and Times of Joe McCarthy: A Biography*. New York: Stein & Day.
Reuter
    1985   Star Wars ineffective, writer says. *Toronto Globe and Mail*, November 14.
           [The writer in question is Roland Pretty, editor of *Jane's Weapons Systems*.]
Rice, Desmond, and Arthur Gavshon
    1984   *The Sinking of the Belgrano*. London: Secker & Warburg.
Rohatyn, Felix G.
    1982   The state of the banks. *New York Review of Books*, November 4, pp. 3–8.
Rothschild, Emma
    1983   Delusions of Deterrence: Review of *Department of Defense Annual Report to
           the Congress, Fiscal Year 1984* by Caspar W. Weinberger. *New York Review
           of Books*, April 14, pp. 40–50.
Rose, Robert A.
    1976   *Lonely Eagles: The Story of America's Black Air Force in World War II*. Los
           Angeles: Tuskegee Airmen Inc. Western Region [1675 Virginia Road, Los
           Angeles, Ca. 90019].
Ryerson, Stanley Bréhaut
    1960   *The Founding of Canada: Beginnings to 1815*. Toronto: Progress Books.
    1975   *Unequal Union: Roots of Crisis in the Canadas 1815–1873*. Toronto: Progress
           Books. Second edition.
Santoli, Al
    1981   *Everything We Had: An Oral History of the Vietnam War by Thirty-three
           Americans Who Fought It*. New York: Random House.
    1985   *To Bear Any Burden: The Vietnam War and Its Aftermath In the Words of
           Americans and Southeast Asians*. New York: E. P. Dutton.
Santos-Dumont, Alberto
    1904   *My Airships: The Story of My Life*. With 46 illustrations. New York: Dover,
           1973.
Saul, S. B., editor
    1970   *Technological Change: The United States and Britain in the 19th Century*.
           London and New York: Methuen.
Saunders, John Monk
    1927   *Wings*. Based on the Paramount picture directed by William A. Wellman.
           Illustrated with scenes from the photoplay. New York: Grosset & Dunlap.
Schaller, Michael
    1979   *The U.S. Crusade in China, 1938–1945*. New York: Columbia University
           Press.
Scheips, Paul J., editor
    1980   *Military Signal Communications*. New York: Arno Press, 1980. Two volumes.
Schoenberner, Gerhard
    1969   *The Yellow Star: The Persecution of the Jews in Europe 1933–1945*. With
           over 200 photographs. Tr. by Susan Sweet. New York: Bantam, 1979.
Scholes, Robert and Eric S. Rabkin
    1977   *Science Fiction: History – Science – Vision*. London: Oxford University Press.
Setton, Kenneth M.
    1966   The Norman Conquest. With the Bayeux Tapestry in full color. *National
           Geographic*, 130/2, pp. 206–51.
Sheehan, Neil, Hedrick Smith, E. W. Kenworthy, and Fox Butterfield
    1971   *The Pentagon Papers: The Secret History of the Vietnam War*. As published
           by *The New York Times*. New York, London, and Toronto: Bantam.
Shih, Vincent Y. C.
    1967   *The Taiping Ideology: Its Sources, Interpretations, and Influences*. Seattle and
           London: University of Washington Press, 1972 [see Michael 1966].

Shriver, Sargent
    1964   Ambassadors of good will, the Peace Corps. With reports from Peace Corps
           volunteers from Bolivia, Tanganyika, Gabon, Turkey, Sarawak, and Ecuador.
           National Geographic, 126/3, pp. 297–345.
Shuler, Marjorie
    1938   *A Passenger to Adventure*. With 15 photographs. New York and London: D.
           Appleton-Century Co. [Round-the-world by clipper.]
Simpson III, Charles M.
    1983   *Inside the Green Berets: The First Thirty Years: A History of the U.S. Army
           Special Forces*. Novato, Ca.: Presidio Press.
Smith, Bradley
    1983   *The Shadow Warriors: O.S.S. and the Origins of the C.I.A.* New York: Basic
           Books.
Solinas, PierNico, editor
    1973   *Gillo Pontecorvo's The Battle of Algiers*. A film written by Franco Solinas.
           New York: Charles Scribner's Sons.
Stevenson, William
    1976   *A Man Called Intrepid: The Secret War*. New York: Ballantine, 1977.
    1983   *Intrepid's Last Case*. New York: Villard Books.
Storey, Donald R., and J. Anthony Boeckh
    1974   Kondratieff and the supercycle: Deflation or runaway inflation? *The Bank
           Credit Analyst* (October), pp. 12–38.
Stuebing, Doug
    n.d.   *Dieppe 1942*. Toronto: Clarke, Irwin & Co. Jackdaw C8.
Summers, Jr., Colonel Harry G.
    1982   *On Strategy: A Critical Analysis of the Vietnam War*. Novato, Ca.: Presidio
           Press, 1983.
Sun Tzu
    1963   *The Art of War* [c. 400–320 BCE]. Tr. and annotated with an introduction by
           Brigadier General (ret.) Samuel B. Griffith, U.S. Marine Corps. Foreword by
           Basil Liddell Hart. London and New York: Oxford Paperbacks, 1981. [This
           is Griffith's 1960 Ph.D. thesis and the most reliable modern translation.]
    1983   *The Art of War*. Edited and with a foreword by James Clavell. New York:
           Delacorte. [The Lionel Giles translation, modified at will by Clavell.]
Taber, Richard
    1965   *The War of the Flea: Guerrilla Warfare Theory and Practice*. London: Paladin,
           1977.
Taylor, A. J. P.
    1969   *War by Time-Table: How the First World War Began*. London: Macdonald &
           Co.; New York: American Heritage Press.
Taylor, A. J. P., J. M. Roberts, Alan Bullock, et al., editors
    1979   *20th Century*. With thousands of illustrations, mostly in color. Milwaukee,
           Toronto, Melbourne, and London: Purnell Reference Books. Twenty volumes.
Terry, Wallace
    1984   *Bloods: An Oral History of the Vietnam War by Black Veterans*. New York:
           Random House.
Thayer, George
    1969   *The War Business: The International Trade in Armaments*. New York: Discus/
           Avon, 1970.
Thomas, Hugh
    1977   *The Spanish Civil War*. Harmondsworth, Middlesex: Penguin. Third edition,
           revised and enlarged.

Thomas, Lowell
    1943 *These Men Shall Never Die*. Illustrated with official photographs; approved by the War Department. Philadelphia and Toronto: John C. Winston Co.
Thomas, Lowell, and Rex Barton
    1937 *Wings Over Asia: A Geographic Journey by Airplane*. Philadelphia: John C. Winston Co.
Thomas, Tony
    1976 *The Great Adventure Films*. With over 350 stills. Secaucus, N.J.: Citadel, 1980.
The Times, publisher
    1916a The Dardanelles Campaign and The spirit of Anzac. London: *The Times History of the War*, vol. 6, pp. 81–160.
    1916b The extermination of the Armenians. London: *The Times History of the War*, vol. 8, pp. 353–92.
Towner, J. R. B.
    1984 Rehearsal that came to secret grief. Letter to the *Manchester Guardian Weekly*, May 6 [see Ezard 1984].
Trotti, John
    1984 *Phantom over Vietnam: Fighter Pilot USMC*. Novato, Ca.: Presidio [31 Pamaron Way, Novato, CA 94947].
Union of Concerned Scientists
    1984 Reagan's Star Wars. *New York Review of Books*, April 26. pp. 47–52. Illustrated. [Excerpts from the UCS Report on 'Space-Based Missile Defense'.]
Vagts, Alfred
    1937 *A History of Militarism Civilian and Military*. New York: The Free Press; Toronto: Collier-Macmillan. Revised edition, 1959.
Vallières, Pierre
    1968 *White Niggers of America*. Tr. by Joan Pinkham. Toronto and Montreal: McClelland & Stewart.
Van Wagenen Keil, Sally
    1979 *Those Wonderful Women in their Flying Machines: The Unknown Heroines of World War II*. New York: Rawson, Wade.
Veitch, Colonel R. H., R.E.
    1894 General Charles George Gordon [1833–1885]. Horne, ed., 1894, vol. 6, pp. 384–91.
Verney, John
    1955 *Going to the Wars: A Journey in Various Directions* [1937–45]. London: Collins.
Vespa, Amleto
    1938 *Secret Agent of Japan*. London: Victor Gollancz/New Left Book Club.
Vicary, Peter T.
    1984 Rehearsal that came to secret grief. Letter to the *Manchester Guardian Weekly*, May 6 [see Towner 1984].
Wain, Barry
    1986 Why we were in Vietnam. Review of W. S. Turley, *The Second Indochina War* (1986). *Wall Street Journal*, August 11.
Walker, Daniel, director, Chicago Study Team
    1968 *Rights in Conflict: "The Chicago Police Riot"*. The violent confrontation of demonstrators and police during the week of the Democratic National Convention of 1968. A report submitted to the National Commission on the Causes and Prevention of Violence. With 176 pages of photographs. New York: Signet.
Warshaw, Tessa Albert
    1980 *Winning by Negotiation*. New York: Berkley Books, 1981.

Weaver, Carolyn
    1984 The killing of Laura: Crimes of passion: Boyfriends who kill. *Mother Jones*, 9/11 (February–March), pp. 32–9.

Welchman, Gordon
    1982 *The Hut Six Story: Breaking the Enigma Codes*. New York: McGraw-Hill.

Wells, H. G.
    1899 *Three Prophetic Science Fiction Novels: The Time Machine, A Story of Days to Come, and When the Sleeper Wakes*. New York: Dover, 1960.
    1933 *The Shape of Things To Come*. New York: Macmillan.

Westerman, Percy F.
    1926 *The War of the Wireless Waves*. London, Edinburgh, Glasgow, New York, Toronto, Melbourne, Cape Town, and Bombay: Oxford University Press.

Wheatcroft, Geoffrey
    1986 *The Randlords: The Exploits and Exploitations of South Africa's Mining Magnates*. New York: Atheneum.

White, Theodore H., and Annalee Jacoby
    1946 *Thunder Out of China*. New York: William Sloane.

Wicksteed, Bernard
    1947 *It's Fun Finding Out*. Drawings by Osbert Lancaster. London: The Daily Express.

Wills, Garry
    1969 *Nixon Agonistes: The Crisis of the Self-Made Man*. New York: Signet.

Wilson, H. W.
    1901 *With the Flag to Pretoria: A History of the Boer War of 1899–1900*. With maps, plans, and hundreds of sketches and photographs. London: Harmondsworth Bros. Two volumes.
    1902 *After Pretoria: The Guerilla War*. London: Amalgamated Press. Two volumes.

Wilson, Michael, screenwriter
    1978 *Salt of the Earth* [1953]. With stills from the film. Commentary by Deborah Silverton Rosenfelt. Old Westbury, N.Y.: The Feminist Press.

Wodehouse, P. G.
    1924 *The Inimitable Jeeves*. Harmondsworth: Penguin, 1982.
    1934 *Right-Ho, Jeeves*. Harmondsworth: Penguin, 1982.

Woodcock, George
    1975 *Gabriel Dumont: The Métis Chief and his Lost World*. Edmonton, Alta.: Hurtig. [Dumont was Louis Riel's guerrilla general in the Northwest Rebellion of 1885.]

Woodham-Smith, Cecil
    1953 *The Reason Why*. Harmondsworth, Middlesex: Penguin, 1960.

Woodward, Bob, and Carl Bernstein
    1976 *The Final Days*. With Scott Armstrong and Al Kamen. New York: Simon & Schuster.

Wyden, Peter
    1979 *The Bay of Pigs: The Untold Story* [1961]. New York: Touchstone, 1980.

Xenophon
    1922 *Anabasis* [c. 394 BCE]. Facing translation by Carleton L. Brownson. Cambridge, Mass.: Harvard University Press; London: Heinemann, 1968. The Loeb Classical Library. [The march of the Ten Thousand Greeks from Sardis in Asia Minor to the gates of Babylon in 401 BCE and thence back to the Greek coast of the Black Sea, where they built ships, the most famous fighting retreat in history. Xenophon (c. 43–c. 355 BCE) the Athenian commanded the rearguard, the most dangerous post of all; his strategic and tactical sense was unequalled in the ancient world before Alexander. Written in plain Greek, the

Anabasis has been a standard component of the Classics curriculum for centuries (see Caesar).]

Yass, Marion

1973 *The Great Depression*. London: Wayland; New York: G. P. Putnam's Sons. The Documentary History Series.

Yeats-Brown, Francis

1930 *The Lives of a Bengal Lancer*. New York: Viking.

Young, G. M.

1941 *The Government of Britain*. With 16 illustrations and 12 color plates. London: Wm. Collins. Britain in Pictures Series. [See Berkeley 1969.]

Ziman, H. D.

1944 Canadians fight like Dervishes writes Englishman. Malone, ed., 1944, p. 40.

Part B: **Illustrated media**

Note: Illustrated books on the South African War (1899–1902) will be found in Part A.

Abbot, Willis J.

1914 *The Nations at War: A Current History. By Willis J. Abbot, Assisted by a Staff of Photographers, Foreign Agents, and Writers of Authority on International Relations, Military and Naval Tactics, History, Armament, Geography, Topography, Languages, Ethnology, Food Supply, and All the Other Phases of the World's Greatest War*. Illustrated with many plates in color, photographs from private sources, maps, charts, and diagrams. New York: Syndicate Publishing Co.

Adler, Alan

1977 *Science Fiction and Horror Movie Posters in Full Color* [1933–1973]. With 44 full-page illustrations. New York: Dover.

The Aero

1911 *The Aero. Incorporating "Flying" (Established 1902) and "The Airship"*. With photographs, sketches, and technical drawings. London: Iliffe & Sons Limited. Four volumes from vol. I, no. 1.

Air Historian Magazine

1974 *Australia's Airmen at War*. With over 100 illustrations, including color. Sydney, Wellington, and London: A. H. & A. W. Reed.

Air Ministry

1928 *Air Publication 129. Royal Air Force. Flying Training Manual. Part I. Flying Instruction*. With photographs, sketches; plans, and technical drawings. London: HMSO.

1943 *Tee-Emm*. With cartoons by Fougasse and others. London: HMSO. Monthly RAF training memoranda.

Alderson, Frederick

n.d. *The Comic Postcard in English Life*. With over 100 illustrations in b&w and color. Newton Abbot: David & Charles.

Anderson, Allan, and Betty Tomlinson, editors

1978 *Greetings from Canada: Canadian Postcards from the Edwardian Era 1900–1916*. With over 300 reproductions, some in color. Toronto: Macmillan.

Anon

n.d. *Combat Craft Part 2*. Military manual with 30 numbered photographs and sketches, no text. Source unknown.

1895 *Soldiers of the World.* Bristol: W. D. & H. O. Wills (hereafter Wills). Set of 100 cards. [All cigarette cards listed are in color unless otherwise noted.]

1899 *The British Army. By a Lieutenant-Colonel in the British Army. With Twenty-Seven Full-Page Plates (Thirteen Being in Colours) and Thirty Illustrations and Diagrams in the Text.* Bound by the publishers in the actual material used for the uniforms of our Soldiers in South Africa, etc., known as "Khaki". London: Sampson Low, Marston & Co.

1900 *Our Colonial Troops.* London: W. & F. Faulkner, 90 cards.

n.d. *Beauties.* Jersey Lily Cigarettes. Liverpool: Wm. Bradford. Five cards known (not located), c. 1900.

1904 *British Empire Series.* Players' Navy Cut. Nottingham: John Player & Sons (hereafter Players), 50 cards.

1905 *Riders of the World.* Players, 50 cards.

1906 *[Campaign Medals]* [1778–1901]. Wills, 50 cards.

1910a *Arms and Armour.* Capstan Navy Cut. Wills, 50 cards.

1910b *Aviation.* Wills Overseas (Australia), 75 cards.

1910c *Types of the Commonwealth Military Forces* [Australia]. Wills Overseas (Australia), 50 cards.

1912 *British Warriors: From 55 B.C. to A.D. 1855.* Liverpool: Cope Bros., 50 cards.

1914a *Overseas Dominions (Australia).* Wills, 50 cards.

1914b *Overseas Dominions (Canada).* Wills, 50 cards.

1914c *Regimental Uniforms of Canada.* Imperial Tobacco Co. of Canada, 55 silks.

1915a *Recruiting Posters.* Wills, 12 cards.

1915b *Famous Inventions.* Wills, 50 cards.

n.d. *With the First Canadian Contingent.* With 101 mounted half-tones. London: Hodder & Stoughton; Toronto: Musson Book Co., c. 1916.

1916a *The Anzac Book Written and Illustrated in Gallipoli by the Men of Anzac.* With 13 color plates and numerous photographs, decorations, and cartoons. London, New York, Toronto, and Melbourne: Cassell.

1916b *Oh, Canada! A Medley of Stories, Verse, Pictures, and Music Contributed by Members of the Canadian Expeditionary Force.* With 27 plates, some in color. London: Simpkin, Marshall, Hamilton, Kent & Co.

1916c *Military Motors.* Wills, 50 cards.

1916d *Women on War Work.* London and Montreal: Carreras Black Cat Cigarettes, 50 cards.

1917 *Britain's Part in the War.* Wills, 24 cards.

1923 *Struggle for Existence.* Players, 25 cards.

1924 *Do You Know?* Second series. Wills, 50 cards.

1925a *Units of the British Army and R.A.F.* Wills, 50 b&w photograph cards.

1925b *Poster Pointers.* Mac Fisheries, 12 large cards. [Posters by Irene Fawkes, C. Lovat Fraser, and M. McLeish.]

1927 *Engineering Wonders.* Wills, 50 cards.

1930a *Regimental Standards and Cap Badges.* Players, 50 cards.

1930b *Speed.* Wills, 50 cards.

1930c *History of Naval Dress.* Players, 50 cards.

1932 *Dandies.* From paintings by Christopher Clark R.I. Players, 25 large cards.

1933a *Parteitag der N.S.D.A.P. Nürnberg 1933.* Dresden, 50 b&w photograph cards.

1933b *Das Neue Reich.* Dresden, 156 b&w photograph cards.

1934 *The Kensitas Album of National Flags.* London: J. Wix & Sons, 60 silks.

1935a *The Kings and Queens of England.* Players, 50 cards in their special album.

1935b *Henry.* London: Kensitas Cigarettes, 50 large cards in their special album.

1936a *International Airliners.* Players, 50 cards in their special album.

1936b *Empire Air Routes.* London: Lambert & Butler, 50 cards.

1936c *The World of Tomorrow.* Glasgow: Stephen Mitchell & Son, 50 b&w cards.

[Includes shots from the films *The Tunnel*, *High Treason*, and Alexander Korda's *Things to Come* (1936), screenplay by H. G. Wells.]

1937a *This Mechanized Age*. Second series. London: Godfrey Phillips, 50 cards.

1937b *The R.A.F. at Work*. Ipswich: W. A. & C. Churchman (hereafter Churchmans), 48 large cards.

1938a *British Railways*. Senior Service Cigarettes. Manchester: J. A. Pattreioux, 50 large b&w photograph cards.

1938b *Modern Wonders*. Ipswich: Churchmans, 48 large cards.

1938c *Military Uniforms of the British Empire Overseas*. Players, 50 cards in their special album.

1938e *Interesting Events in British History*. London: Typhoo Tea, 25 long cards.

n.d. *Modern Warfare* [c. 1938]. Source unknown, 50 b&w photograph cards.

1939a *Wings over the Empire*. Churchmans, 48 large cards.

1939b *Cycling 1839–1939*. Players, 50 cards in their special album.

1939c *Life in the Royal Navy*. Churchmans, 48 cards.

1939d *Air Raid Precautions*. Churchmans, 48 large cards.

n.d. *"It All Depends on Me"*. London: Ministry of Information, c. 1940, 25 large cards.

1942 *Soldiering On: The Australian Army at Home and Overseas Prepared by Some of the Boys*. With photographs, cartoons, and 16 color plates. Canberra: Australian War Memorial.

1944 *Jungle Warfare: With the Australian Army in the South-West Pacific*. Canberra: Australian War Memorial.

n.d. *Meet the Members: A Record of the Timber Corps of the Women's Land Army*. With 12 photographs. Bristol: Bennett Brothers, c. 1944.

1960 *Jersey Past and Present*. Channel Isles: Ching's Silk Cut Cigarettes, 24 large cards.

Applebaum, Stanley, editor

1977 *Scenes from the 19th Century Stage in Advertising Woodcuts* [c. 1860–74]. With 268 woodcuts and 25 other illustrations. New York: Dover; London: Constable.

Argüelles, José, and Miriam Argüelles

1972 *Mandala*. With over 100 illustrations, a number in color. Berkeley and London: Shambhala Publications.

Arnold, Eve, et al.

1985 *The Fifties. Photographs of America*. Introduction by John Chancellor. New York: Pantheon.

Arwas, Victor

1978 *Belle Epoque: Posters and Graphics* [1890–1914]. With over 100 illustrations, 18 in color. London: Academy Editions; New York: Rizzoli.

Ash, Brian, editor

1977 *The Visual Encyclopedia of Science Fiction*. A documented pictorial checklist of the SF world – concepts/themes/books/mags/comics/films/TV/radio/art/fandom/cults/personal commentaries by the greatest names in SF writing. With indexes, time charts, a glossary of terms, and over 350 illustrations in b&w and color. London: Trewin Copplestone; New York: Harmony.

Badeau, John S., et al.

1975 *The Genius of Arab Civilization: Source of Renaissance*. With 211 illustrations, mostly in color. London: Westerham Press; New York: New York University Press.

Bairnsfather, Bruce

1943 *Jeeps and Jests*. New York: G. P. Putnam's Sons.

Barnouw, Erik
  1981 *The Magician and the Cinema.* With 71 illustrations. Oxford and New York:
        Oxford University Press.
Bateson, Gregory, and Margaret Mead
  1942 *Balinese Character: A Photographic Analysis.* With 100 pages of photographs.
        New York: Special publications of the New York Academy of Sciences, 1962.
Baynes, Ken
  1970 *War: Art and Society One.* With over 100 illustrations, some in color. London:
        Arts Council of Great Britain; Boston: Boston Book and Art, publisher.
Baxter, John
  1971 *The Cinema of Josef von Sternberg.* With over 80 stills. London: A. Zwemmer;
        New York: A. S. Barnes & Co.
Beck, Henry Houghton
  1898 *Cuba's Fight for Freedom and the War with Spain. A Comprehensive, Accurate
        and Thrilling History of the Spanish Kingdom and its latest and fairest Colony;
        the long Struggle of Cuba for Freedom and Independence; the Intervention of
        the United States and the Fierce War with Spain that followed. A Record of
        Oppression and Patriotism, of Cruelty and Valor, and above all the triumph
        of the Stars and Stripes.* With 64 photographs and artists' sketches, including
        maps. Philadelphia: Globe Bible Publishing Co.
Bengough, J. W.
  1886 *A Caricature History of Canadian Politics.* Toronto: The Grip Printing and
        Publishing Co. One volume edition with 134 cartoons: Toronto: Peter Martin
        Associates, 1974.
  1895 *The Up-to-Date Primer: A Book of Lessons for Little Political Economists, in
        Words of One Syllable with Pictures.* London: Funk & Wagnalls. Toronto:
        Peter Martin Associates, 1975. Facsimile edition.
Benham, W. Gurney
  1931 *Playing Cards: History of the Pack and Explanations of its many Secrets.* With
        242 illustrations, 102 in color. London and Melbourne: Ward, Lock & Co.
Bennett, Peter, editor
  1979 *The Child Celebrated in Illustration.* Design by Dreadnaught. With over 125
        reproductions, mostly in color, of the work of famous illustrators. Toronto:
        Jonathan/James Books. Markam (Ontario), Harmondsworth (Middlesex), New
        York, Ringwood (Australia), and Auckland: Penguin.
Berton, Pierre
  1975 *Hollywood's Canada.* With 109 stills. Toronto: McClelland & Stewart.
Birdsall, Steve
  1973 *Log of the Liberators: An Illustrated History of the B-24.* With over 250
        photographs and color drawings. Garden City, N.Y.: Doubleday.
Black, Mary
  1976 *American Advertising Posters of the Nineteenth Century* [1842–1897]. With
        101 full page illustrations, 34 in color, from the Landauer Collection of The
        New York Historical Society. New York: Dover.
Blackwell's, publisher
  1979 *A Centenary Catalogue of Antiquarian and Rare Modern Books.* With 236
        illustrations. Oxford.
Blaine, Hon. James G., Secretary of State, et al.
  1892 *Columbus and Columbia: A Pictorial History of the Man and the Nation
        Embracing A Review of Our Country's Progress, A Complete History of
        America, A New Life of Columbus and an Illustrated Description of the Great
        Columbian Exposition. Embellished with over Five Hundred Engravings,
        Maps, Charts, Diagrams, and Illustrations in Oil Colors by the Great Masters.*
        Richmond, Va.: B. F. Johnson & Company. Four books in one volume.

Bliss, Sands & Co, publishers
    1898   *The Motograph Moving Picture Book*. New York: Dover; London: Constable, 1975. Facsimile edition: *The Magic Moving Picture Book*.
Boardman, R. W., et al.
    1963   *Printing and the Mind of Man: Catalogue of a Display of Printing Mechanisms and Printed Materials Arranged to Illustrate the History of Western Civilization and the Means of the Multiplication of Literary Texts since the XV Century*. With 33 plates, one in color. Assembled at the British Museum and at Earl's Court London. Published by Messrs F. W. Bridges & Sons Ltd and the Association of British Manufacturers of Printers' Machinery (Proprietary) Ltd.
Bogle, Donald
    1973   *Toms, Coons, Mulattoes, Mammies, & Bucks: An Interpretive History of Blacks in American Films*. With 55 illustrations. New York: Viking; Toronto: Macmillan.
Bonds, Ray, editor
    1979   *The Vietnam War: An Illustrated History*. Foreword by General William C. Westmoreland. With more than 550 photographs, over 40 maps and diagrams, and a full-color technical section. New York: Crown; London: Salamander.
Bonn, Franz
    1878   *The Children's Theatre*. Esslingen, Germany: J. E. Schreiber. London: Kestrel; New York: Viking, 1978. Facsimile pop-up book.
Bonn, Thomas L.
    1982   *UnderCover. An Illustrated History of American Mass Market Paperbacks*. Harmondsworth, Middlesex: Penguin.
Booth-Clibborn, Edward, and Daniele Baroni
    1979   *The Language of Graphics*. With more than 1000 illustrations, over 530 in color. Tokyo: Mondadori-Kodansha, 1979; New York: Harry N. Abrams, 1980. [Based on the seven-volume *Graphic Design of the World* published by Kodansha in Tokyo in 1974–76.]
Boraiko, Allen A.
    1984   The Laser: 'A splendid light' for man's use. *National Geographic*, 165/3, pp. 335–63. [Front cover carries the first laser hologram – an American Eagle – to be printed by a major magazine.]
Bridgeman, Harriet, and Elizabeth Drury, editors
    1977   *Society Scandals*. With 48 contemporary prints, paintings, cartoons, and photographs. Newton Abbot, London, North Pomfret (VT), and Vancouver: David & Charles.
Bruton, Eric
    1979   *The History of Clocks and Watches*. With over 600 illustrations from photographs, many in color. London: Orbis.
Buchheim, Lothar-Günther
    1976   *U-Boat War*. With 205 contemporary photographs by the author. Tr. by Gudie Lawaetz. New York: Alfred A. Knopf, 1978.
Buckley, V. C.
    1979   *The Good Life: Between the Two World Wars with a Candid Camera*. With 197 snaps by the author. New York: William Morrow.
Buhler, Michael
    1978   *Tin Toys 1945–1975*. With 108 photographs in color by Ian Hessenberg. London: Bergström & Boyle Books.
Burke, James
    1978   *Connections*. With over 200 illustrations. London: Macmillan; Boston and Toronto: Little, Brown and Co.

Cadwalladar and Nudnick [Patrick W. Nerney and Paul Clemens]
    1957 *The Little Black Book: A Manual for Bachelors.* Illustrated by R. Taylor. Garden City, N.Y.: Doubleday.
Canby, Courtlandt
    1963 *A History of Rockets and Space.* With 56 pages of illustrations, many in color. New York: Hawthorn Books.
Carlisle, Norman, Reginald Cleveland, and Jonathan Wood
    1945 *The Modern Wonder Book of the Air.* With some 200 photographs and sketches. Philadelphia and Toronto: John C. Winston Co.
Cassell and Co., publishers
    n.d. *Cassell's History of the Russo-Japanese War* [1904–5]. With hundreds of photographs, sketches, diagrams, and maps. London, Paris, New York, and Melbourne. Six volumes.
Cassier's Magazine
    1899 *The Electric Railway Number.* With over 600 photographs, diagrams, drawings, sketches, and decorations. London.
Ceram, C. W.
    n.d. *Archaeology of the Cinema.* With 293 illustrations. New York: Harcourt, Brace & World.
Chandler, David
    1974 *The Art of Warfare on Land.* With 40 illustrations in color, including 18 photographs of model soldier war games, and about 250 in b&w, including maps and diagrams. London, New York, Sydney, and Toronto: Hamlyn.
Chant, Christopher, Dr W. C. Beaver, Brigadier Shelford Bidwell, William Fowler, Richard Humble, Alon Kadish, and Brigadier W. F. K. Thompson
    1978 *Airborne Operations: An Illustrated Encyclopedia.* Ed. by Philip de Ste Croix. With hundreds of photographs, many in color, 15 full page color drawings, numerous color panels, and a 16-page technical section in color. London: Salamander; New York: Crescent, 1979.
Chapman & Hall, publisher
    1849 *A History of Wonderful Inventions.* Illustrated with numerous engravings on wood, several in color. London.
Chapuis, Alfred, and Droz, Edmond
    1949 *Les Automates: Figures artificielles d'hommes et d'animaux.* With 488 photographs and 18 color plates. Neuchâtel: Editions du Griffon.
Choay, Françoise
    1969 *The Modern City: Planning in the 19th Century.* With over 50 illustrations. New York: Braziller.
Cirker, Hayward, and Blanche Cirker, editors
    1971 *The Golden Age of the Poster* [1891–1899]. With 70 European and American posters in color. New York: Dover; London: Constable.
Clarke, Arthur C.
    1974 *Voice Across the Sea.* With 32 illustrations. London: William Luscombe/ Mitchell Beazley. [Transatlantic telegraph cable, 1866; telephone cable, 1956; commercial communications satellite, 1965.]
Clarke, Donald, editor
    1978 *The How It Works Encyclopedia of Great Inventors & Discoveries.* With 100 photographs, many in color, and over 100 other illustrations. London: Marshall Cavendish, 1982.
Clarke, Donald, editor, and Chris Lower, designer
    1974 *The Encyclopedia of Transport.* With 139 photographs and 87 illustrations in color, and 64 b&w photographs. London: Marshall Cavendish, 1981.
Collins, publisher
    1958 *The Wonders of Science: The Story of Man's Achievements in Invention,*

Science and Industry. With 5 plates in color and over 300 photographs, sketches, and technical drawings. London and Glasgow.

Cormac
　1982　*Cormac Strikes Back: Resistance Cartoons from the North of Ireland*. London: Information on Ireland.

Cornwell, E. L., editor
　1972　*The Pictorial Story of Railways*. With hundreds of photographs and other illustrations, mostly in color. London, New York, Sydney, and Toronto, 1974.

Coughlin, Tom
　1968　*The Dangerous Sky: Canadian Airmen in World War II*. With some 100 photographs. Foreword by Douglas Bader. Toronto: Ryerson.

Csida, Joseph, and June Bundy Csida, editors
　1978　*American Entertainment: A Unique History of Popular Show Business*. From the pages of *Billboard* magazine. New York: Billboard Publications.

Daily Telegraph
　1955　*100 Years in Pictures, As Described in Contemporary Reports from* The Daily Telegraph. London: The Daily Telegraph. Centenary Supplement.

Darracott, Joseph, editor
　1974　*The First World War in Posters*. With 75 works, 48 in color, from the Imperial War Museum, London. New York: Dover; London: Constable.

Day, John
　1980　*Engines: The Search for Power*. With contemporary photographs of modern and preserved machines [many in color], detailed cut-away drawings of engines of all types, schematic artwork to explain principles and practice, and diagrams to show the relationship of types and their evolution. London: Hamlyn; New York: St Martin's.

de Bono, Edward, editor
　1974　*Eureka! An Illustrated History of Inventions from the Wheel to the Computer*. With over 500 illustrations, mostly in color. London: Thames and Hudson; New York: Holt, Rinehart and Winston, 1979.

de Givry, Grillot
　1929　*The Illustrated Anthology of Sorcery, Magic and Alchemy*. With 10 plates and 366 other illustrations. Tr. by J. Courtenay Locke. New York: Causeway Books, 1973.

de la Calle, C., et al.
　1962　*Les Origines de la civilisation technique*. With 113 figures and 48 plates. Paris: Presses Universitaires de France. Histoire générale des techniques: General editor Maurice Dumas. Volume I.

Department of the Army
　1965　*Special Forces Handbook ST31–180*. With cartoons, line drawings, technical sketches, graphs, and maps. Washington, D.C. Issued by Army Ft McPherson, Georgia, 425/67. Boulder, Colo.: Paladin, n.d. [For the Paladin catalog, see the reference section.]

Devens, R. M.
　1880　*Our First Century: Being a Popular Descriptive Portraiture of the One Hundred Great and Memorable Events of Perpetual Interest in the History of Our Country, Political, Military, Mechanical, Social, Scientific and Commercial: Embracing also Delineations of all the Great Historic Characters Celebrated in the Annals of the Republic; Men of Heroism, Statesmanship, Genius, Oratory, Adventure and Philanthropy. With Additions to the Present Time. Splendidly Illustrated with Several Hundred Plates, Portraits, and Other Embellishments*. Springfield, Mass.: C. A. Nichols & Co.; Chicago: Hugh Heron.

The Diagram Group, London
1980 *Weapons: An International Encyclopedia from 5000 BC to 2000 AD.* With over 2500 illustrations. New York: St. Martin's.
Dickens, Charles
1838 *The Adventures of Oliver Twist.* Illustrated by stills from the film by David Lean. London: Paul Elek and World Film Publications, 1948.
Dickens, Homer
1968 *The Films of Marlene Dietrich.* With over 400 photographs. New York: Citadel, 1970.
Diderot, Denis, editor
1763 *A Diderot Pictorial Encyclopedia of Trades and Industry.* Ed. by Charles Coulston Gillispie: 485 plates from the *Encyclopédie.* New York: Dover. Two volumes.
Dille, Robert C.
1964 *The Collected Works of Buck Rogers in the 25th Century* [1929–64]. Introduction by Ray Badbury. New York: Bonanza Books, 1969.
Doggett, Frank
1981 *Cigarette Cards and Novelties.* London: Michael Joseph.
Doré, Gustave
1862 *The Doré Illustrations for Dante's Divine Comedy.* With 136 plates. New York: Dover; London: Constable, 1976.
Doré, Gustave, and Blanchard Jerrold
1872 *London: A Pilgrimage.* With 180 illustrations by Gustave Doré. New York: Dover, 1970.
Dubuisson, M. et al.
1965 *Les premières étapes du machinisme.* With 317 figures and 48 plates. Paris: Presses Universitaires de France. Histoire générale des techniques: General editor Maurice Dumas. Twelve contributors, volume II.
1968 *L'Expansion du machinisme.* With 447 figures and 48 plates. Paris: Presses Universitaires de France. Histoire générale des techniques: General editor: Maurice Dumas. Seventeen contributors, volume III.
Düttman, Martina, Friedrich Schmuck, and Johannes Uhl
1980 *Color in Townscape.* With thousands of illustrations. Tr. by J. W. Gabriel. San Francisco: W. H. Freeman.
Eams, John Douglas
1979 *The MGM Story: The Complete History of Fifty-Four Roaring Years* [1924–1978]. All 1723 films of MGM described and illustrated in b&w and color. New York: Crown. Revision of 1975 edition.
Ehmcke, Fritz H.
1907 *Graphic Trade Symbols by German Designers.* From the 1907 Klingspor Catalog. With 293 symbols and 54 other illustrations. New York: Dover, 1974.
Emde, Heiner
1968 *Conquerors of the Air: The Evolution of Aircraft 1903–1945.* With 92 three-views in color by Carlo Demand, and b&w scale drawings of pictured machines. Lausanne: Edita S.A.; New York: Bonanza Books.
Erdman, David V., annotator
1974 *The Illuminated Blake: All of William Blake's Illuminated Works with a Plate-by-Plate Commentary.* Garden, City, N.Y.: Anchor.
Escher, Maurits C.
1960 *The Graphic Work of M. C. Escher.* With 76 prints. Tr. from the Dutch by John E. Brigham. New York: Hawthorne Books, n.d. New and revised edition.
Essoe, Gabe
1968 *Tarzan of the Movies: A Pictorial History of More than Fifty Years of Edgar*

Rice Burrough's Legendary Hero [1913–1965]. With over 400 photographs. Secaucus, N.J.: The Citadel Press.

Estren, Mark James
1974 *A History of Underground Comics*. San Francisco: Straight Arrow Books [625 Third Street], distributed by Quick Fox, Inc., New York.

Everett, Marshall
1904 *Exciting Experiences in the Japanese-Russian War: A Complete History of Japan, Russia, China and Korea. Relation of the United States to the Other Nations. Causes of the Conflict. Startling Stories of the War as Told by the Heroes Themselves. Wonderful Descriptions of Battles. Thrilling Personal Experiences. Exciting Stories of Bravery. Superb Heroism. Daring Exploits. Vivid Stories of Japanese Cunning. History of Each Battle Told by Both the Japanese and Russian Commanders. Illustrated with a Vast Gallery of Photographs of Battle Scenes, War Incidents and the Leaders on Both Sides* [and over 50 newspaper cartoons]. [New York:] Henry Neil.

Feldman, Edmund Burke
n.d. *Varieties of Visual Experience: Art as Image and Idea*. With over 1100 pictures and 100 colorplates in visual essays that illuminate the text. Englewood Cliffs, N.J.: Prentice-Hall; New York: Harry N. Abrams. Second edition (c. 1971).

Fellowes, Air-Commodore P. F. M., L. V. Stewart Blacker, Colonel P. T. Etherton, and Squadron Leader The Marquess of Douglas and Clydesdale
1933 *First Over Everest: The Houston-Mount Everest Expedition 1933*. Foreword by John Buchan. With 57 photographs. London: John Lane The Bodley Head.

Ferris, Richard
1910 *How to Fly, or The Conquest of the Air: The Story of Man's Endeavours to Fly and of the Inventions by which he has Succeeded. Illustrated by over 150 Half-tones and Line Drawings, Showing the Stages of Development from the Earliest Balloon to the Latest Monoplane and Biplane*. London, Edinburgh, Dublin, and New York: Thomas Nelson and Sons.

Fitzsimons, Bernard, editor
1969 *The Illustrated Encyclopedia of 20th Century Weapons and Warfare*. London: Purnell & Sons; Phoebus/BPC Publishing, 1977. Distributed by Columbia House. Twenty-four volumes.

Flexner, Stuart Berg
1982 *Listening to America: An Illustrated History of Words and Phrases from our Lively and Splendid Past*. New York: Simon & Schuster.

Floherty, John J.
1934 *'Board the Airliner': A Camera Trip with the Transport Planes*. With over 50 striking photographs. Garden City, N.Y.: Doubleday, Doran, 1937.

The Ford Motor Company
1929 *Book of Instruction: Ford Trimotor All-Metal Monoplane*. Fully illustrated by photographs, technical drawings, exploded views, diagrams, and charts. Dearborn, Michigan; Arcadia, Ca.: Post-Era Books, 1977. Facsimile edition.

Freedman, Jill
1981 *Street Cops*. New York: Harper & Row.

Freeman, Roger A.
1977 *B-17 Fortress at War*. With over 250 photographs, several in color. New York: Charles Scribner's Sons.

Furhammer, Leif, and Folke Isaksson
1968 *Politics and Film*. With 150 photographs. Tr. by Kersti French. New York and Washington, D.C.: Praeger. Swedish text revised and updated for the English edition, 1971.

Gallo, Max
1974 *The Poster in History*. With over 350 illustrations, mostly in color. Tr. by A.

and B. Mayor. London: Hamlyn; New York: New American Library. Abridged edition, 1975.

Garrett, Richard
1976 *Clash of Arms: The World's Great Land Battles* [1066–1944]. With numerous contemporary paintings, prints, and photographs, many in color. London: Weidenfeld & Nicolson.

Gartmann, Heinz
n.d. *Science as History: The Story of Man's Technological Progress from Steam Engine to Satellite.* With 51 photographs and many other illustrations. Tr. by Alan G. Readett. London: Hodder & Stoughton.

Geddes, Norman Bel
1932 *Horizons.* With 221 illustrations. New York: Dover, 1977. Facsimile reprint. [The Streamline Age.]

Geraghty, Tony
1982 *This is the SAS: A Pictorial History of the Special Air Service Regiment.* With over 300 photographs. London: Arms and Armour Press.

Ghyka, Matila
1946 *The Geometry of Art and Life.* With drawings and diagrams. New York: Dover, 1977.

Giedion, Siegfried
1948 *Mechanization Takes Command: A Contribution to an Anonymous History.* With 501 illustrations. London: Oxford University Press; New York: Norton, 1969.

Gilbert, James
1975 *The World's Worst Aircraft.* With numerous illustrations. New York: St Martin's.

Gillon, Jr., Edmund Vincent, editor
1969 *The Gibson Girl and Her America: The Best Drawings of Charles Dana Gibson* [1894–1905]. Introduction by Henry C. Pitz. With 163 illustrations. New York: Dover.

Gimpel, Jean
1976 *The Medieval Machine: The Industrial Revolution of the Middle Ages.* With numerous illustrations. New York: Holt, Rinehart & Winston.

Golding, Harry, editor
n.d. *The Wonder Book of Railways for Boys and Girls.* With nearly 100 illustrations in tinted b&w and color. London and Melbourne: Ward, Lock and Co., c. 1911 (first edition). Others in the series: *The Wonder Book of the Navy,* c. 1924 (entirely new edition); *The Wonder Book of Ships,* c. 1925 (eleventh edition); *The Wonder Book of Wonders,* c. 1925 (third edition); *The Wonder Book of Aircraft,* c. 1929 (sixth edition); *The Wonder Book of Engineering Wonders,* c. 1930 (second edition, revised); *The Wonder Book of How It's Done,* c. 1936; *The Wonder Book of Would You Believe It?,* c. 1939; *The Wonder Book of Aircraft,* c. 1940 (ninth edition); *The Wonder of the R.A.F.,* c. 1941; *The Wonder Book of the R.A.F.,* c. 1950 (entirely new edition); *The Wonder Book of Aircraft,* c. 1954 (new edition).

Good, Richard
1978 *Watches in Colour.* With 86 photographs in color and 28 b&w photographs and technical drawings. Poole, Dorset: Blandford Press. With a glossary of terms.

Goodenough, Simon
1979 *Tactical Genius in Battle.* Ed. and introduced by Len Deighton. With over 100 photographs and prints, and over 100 battle plans. London: Phaidon.

Graves, Charles L.
1921 *Mr. Punch's History of Modern England* [1840–1874]. With numerous

cartoons. London, New York, Toronto, and Melbourne: Cassell & Co. Two volumes.

Greener, W. W.
1910 *The Gun and its Development*. With over 700 illustrations. New York: Bonanza Books/Crown Publishers, c. 1967. Facsimile of the ninth edition (first edition 1881).

Griffith, Richard, and Arthur Mayer
1957 *The Movies: The Sixty-Year Story of the World of Hollywood and its Effect on America from Pre-Nickelodeon Days to the Present*. With more than 1000 photographs. New York: Bonanza Books.

Griffith, Richard, Arthur Mayer, and Eileen Bowser
1981 *The Movies*. With almost 1500 photographs. New York: Simon & Schuster.

Grooch, William Stephen
1936 *Skyway to Asia*. With 31 photographs. New York and Toronto: Longmans, Green and Co.

Gruenhagen, Robert W.
1976 *Mustang: The Story of the P-51 Fighter*. Illustrated with photographs, diagrams, graphs, and technical drawings. New York: Arco Publishing Co. Revised edition.

Gunston, Bill
1976 *Night Fighters: A Development and Combat History*. Illustrated with photographs, diagrams, and maps. Cambridge: Patrick Stephens.

Gunston, Bill, editor
1979 *The Illustrated Encyclopedia of the World's Rockets & Missiles*. With over 550 photographs, many in color, and an 8 page color fold-out. London: Salamander; New York: Crescent.

Gunther, John, and Bernard Quint
1956 *Days to Remember: America 1945–1955*. With over 600 photographs. New York: Harper.

Hackett, General Sir John
1983 *The Profession of Arms*. With over 180 illustrations, a number in color. London: Sidgwick & Jackson; New York: Macmillan.

Hackleman, Charles W.
1924 *Commercial Engraving and Printing: A Manual of Practical Instruction and Reference Covering Commercial Illustrating and Printing by all Processes for Advertising Managers, Printers, Engravers, Lithographers, Paper Men, Photographers, Commercial Artists, Salesmen, Instructors, Students and all Others Interested in these and Allied Trades*. With 2054 illustrations of all types including steel plate engravings, plates and photogravures, a number in color, printed on 17 different kinds of paper. Indianapolis, Indiana: Commercial Engraving Publishing Co. Second printing, revised.

Haeckel, Ernst
1904 *Art Forms in Nature*. With 100 plates, comprising over 1000 drawings. New York: Dover; London: Constable.

Hammerton, J. A., editor
n.d. *Peoples of All Nations: Their Life Today and the Story of their Past. By Our Foremost Writers of Travel Anthropology & History. Illustrated with upwards of 5000 Photographs, numerous Colour Plates, and 150 Maps*. The work of more than one hundred writers of distinction and some three hundred expert photographers. London: The Amalgamated Press Ltd., c. 1920. Seven volumes.

n.d. *The New Punch Library*. London: The Educational Book Company, c. 1932. Twenty volumes. Notably: *Mr Punch's Cavalcade: A Review of Thirty Years*; *Mr Punch and the Services*; *Mr Punch in War Time*; and *Mr Punch on His Travels*.

Hansen, Zenon
  1977 *The Goodyear Airships*. With hundreds of illustrations, including technical drawings. Bloomington, Ill.: Airship International Press.
Harper, Harry
  1928 *A Day on the Airway*. London: Sarony Silk Cut Virginia Cigarettes. Set of 25 cards in their special album.
  n.d. *The Romance of a Modern Airway*. Introduction by Air Vice-Marshal Sir Sefton Brancker. Illustrated by 100 special photographs selected by the author. London: Sampson Low, Marston & Co., c. 1930.
Hatfield, D. D.
  1972 *Howard Hughes H-4 'Hercules'*. With over 100 illustrations. Hatfield History of Aeronautics, Northrop Institute of Technology, Inglewood, Ca. Los Angeles: Historical Airplanes.
Hawk, Ellison
  n.d. *The Marvels and Mysteries of Science*. With over 500 illustrations. London: Odhams Press.
Heck, J. G., editor
  1851 *The Complete Encyclopedia of Illustration*. With 500 plates comprising thousands of illustrations. Tr. by Spencer F. Baird. New York: Crown, 1979.
Heyn, Ernest V., et al., editors
  1972 *A Century of Wonders: 100 Years of Popular Science*. With about 1000 drawings and photographs, some in color. Garden City, N.Y.: Doubleday.
Hiley, Michael
  1979 *Victorian Working Women: Portraits from Life*. With some 200 photographs, stereocards, sketches, cartoons, and cuts. London: Gordon Fraser Gallery; Boston: David R. Godine, 1980.
Hillier, Mary
  1976 *Automata and Mechanical Toys: An Illustrated History*. With 193 photographs and 32 color plates. London: Jupiter.
Hirschhorn, Clive
  1979 *The Warner Bros. Story* [1918–78]. Every Warner Bros. feature film described and illustrated. London: Octopus; New York: Crown.
  1981 *The Hollywood Musical*. Every Hollywood musical to the present day: 1344 films described and illustrated. London: Octopus; New York: Crown.
Hohlwein, Ludwig
  1976 *Hohlwein Posters in Full Color* [c. 1905–1935]. With 45 full page reproductions. New York: Dover; London: Constable. [His National Socialist posters are not included.]
Hollander, Nicole
  1981 *"That Woman Must Be On Drugs": A Collection of Sylvia*. New York: St Martin's Press.
  1982 *"Mercy, it's the revolution and I'm in my bathrobe": More Sylvia*. New York: St Martin's Press.
Holme, Bryan
  1982 *Advertising: Reflections of a Century* [1880–1980]. With over 350 illustrations, mostly in color. New York: Viking.
Holmes, Rand H.
  1972 *The Collected Adventures of Harold Hedd*. Comic strip in b&w. Vancouver, B.C.: The Georgia Straight.
Hopkins, Anthony
  1979 *Songs from the Front and the Rear: Canadian Servicemen's Songs of the Second World War*. Edmonton, Alta.: Hurtig.
Horn, Maurice
  1977 *Women in Comics*. New York and London: Chelsea House.

Hornung, Clarence P., editor

1932 *Handbook of Designs and Devices.* 1836 basic designs and their variations. New York: Dover. Revised and enlarged edition, 1946.

1956 *Handbook of Early Advertising Art Mainly from American Sources* [c. 1750–1880]. With hundreds of illustrations. New York: Dover Books. Third edition.

Humbert, Claude

1972 *Label Design from the Earliest Times to the Present Day.* With 1000 illustrations. Tr. by Nicholas Fry (English) and R. M. Ostheimer (German). London: Thames & Hudson. Text in English, French and German.

Humphreys, Henry Noel

1867 *A History of the Art of Printing from its Invention to its Widespread Development in the Middle of the 16th Century. Preceded by a Short Account of the Origin of the Alphabet and the Successive Methods of Recording Events and Multiplying Ms. Books before the Invention of Printing. With One Hundred Illustrations Produced in Photo-Lithography by Day & Son, Limited, Under the Direction of the Author.* London: Bernard Quaritch.

Hunter, Prof. H. H.

n.d. *Super Ju-Jitsu: "The Hunter" superior system of Self-defence under all circumstances for Police Officers and Prison Guards: Personally instructed members of the Royal Canadian Mounted Police, Toronto, Ont.; Stratford City and Hamilton City Police, Ontario; leading Police Forces, England; Secret Service Officials; students of Upper Canada College, Toronto; Asnbury College, Ottawa, Etc.* With over 100 photographs. Hamilton, Ont.: The Times Job Print. Two parts.

Ingells, Douglas J.

1966 *The Plane that Changed the World: A Biography of the DC-3.* With over 200 illustrations. Fallbrook, Ca.: Aero Publishers, Inc.

Ingells, Douglas J., and Ralph Dietrick

1968 *Tin Goose: The Fabulous Ford Trimotor.* With over 100 illustrations. Fallbrook, Ca.: Aero Publishers, Inc.

Jane, Fred T., founder

1938 *Jane's All the World's Aircraft 1938.* Compiled and edited by C. G. Grey and Leonard Bridgman. London: Sampson Low Marston & Co, 1938. Newton Abbot, Devon: David & Charles Reprints, 1972.

Jenkins, Alan

1976 *The Thirties.* With over 200 illustrations, a number in color. London and Toronto: William Heinemann.

Joyce, T. Athol, and N. W. Thomas, editors

1908 *Women of All Nations: A Record of Their Characteristics, Habits, Manners, Customs and Influence.* With 25 plates in color and 647 illustrations in b&w. London, Paris, New York, Toronto and Melbourne: Cassell and Company, Limited. Two volumes.

Keay, Carolyn

1975 *American Posters of the Turn of the Century.* With over 150 illustrations, including 80 full page posters, 12 in color. London: Academy Editions; New York: St Martin's.

Keegan, John, and Joseph Darracott

1981 *The Nature of War.* With 255 illustrations, many in color. Don Mills, Ont.: Jonathan-James Books; New York: Holt, Rinehart & Winston.

Kemp, Lieut.-Commander P. K., R.N. (Retd.)

n.d. *The Boys Book of the Navy.* With over 150 photographs, sketches, and technical drawings. London: Burke, 1960. Revision of 1953 edition.

Kenton, Warren
  1974 *Astrology: The Celestial Mirror.* With 146 illustrations, 30 in color. New York: Avon.
Kerrod, Robin
  1980 *The Way It Works: Man and His Machines.* With over 400 illustrations in color. London: Octopus.
Kery, Patricia Frantz
  1982 *Great Magazine Covers of the World.* New York: Abbeville.
Klossowski de Rola, Stanislas
  1973 *Alchemy: The Secret Art.* With 65 plates in b&w and color and 30 pages of prints. London: Thames & Hudson; New York: Avon.
Koch, H. W.
  1981 *The Rise of Modern Warfare 1618–1815.* With over 400 paintings, prints, maps, and charts, many in color. London: Bison Books; Englewood Cliffs, N.J.: Prentice-Hall.
Koenig, W. J.
  1980 *Americans at War: From the Colonial Wars to Vietnam.* Illustrated with over 500 photographs and rare prints, including 150 in color. London: Bison; New York: G. P. Putnam's Sons.
Kreuger, Miles, editor
  1975 *The Movie Musical from Vitaphone to 42nd Street* [1926–1933] As reported in *Photoplay.* With over 400 illustrations. New York: Dover; London: Constable.
Kyle, David
  1977 *The Illustrated Book of Science Fiction Ideas and Dreams.* With over 300 illustrations, many in color. London, New York, Sidney, and Toronto: Hamlyn.
Landery, Charles
  1940 *Mr Smith Goes to Washington.* London: J. M. Dent & Sons. A novel adapted from Frank Capra's Columbia picture [1939].
Leacock, Stephen, et al.
  1944 *Canada's War At Sea.* With 12 color plates, many photographs, and 100 pages of advertisements. Montreal: Alvah M. Beatty, 1948.
Le Bris, Michel
  1981 *Romantics and Romanticism.* With 124 b&w illustrations and 90 reproductions in color. Tr. Barbara Bray and Bernard C. Swift. Geneva: Editions d'Art Albert Skira; New York: Rizzoli International Publishers.
Lehner, Ernst
  1950 *Symbols, Signs & Signets.* With 1355 cuts from many cultures, from early times to 1900. New York: Dover Books; London: Constable, 1969.
Levey, Michael F., editor
  1976 *London Transport Posters* [1908–1976]. With 80 plates, mostly in color. London: Phaidon.
Levy, Allen
  1974 *A Century of Model Trains* [1870–1970]. With over 500 illustrations, 187 in color. London: New Cavendish Books, 1978
Ley, Willy, Dr Wernher Von Braun, Or Heinz Haber, Hugo Gernsback, et al.
  1953 *The Complete Book of Outer Space.* With over 150 photographs, prints, sketches, and technical drawings. New York: Maco Magazine Corp.
Logan, Ian, and Henry Nield
  1977 *Classy Chassy: American Aircraft "Girl Art" 1942–1953: A Book of Paintings the Art Historians Have Missed.* With over 80 photographs and artists' sketches, mostly in color. London: Mathews, Miller and Dunbar; New York: A & W Visual Library.

Loke, Margarett, editor and commentator
1980 *The World As It Was 1865–1921: A Photographic Potrait from the Keystone-Mast Collection.* With over 220 reproductions of stereographs. Preface by Paul Theroux. New York: Summit Books.
Love, Brian, compiler
1978 *Play the Game: The Book that You Can Play! Over 40 Games from the Golden Age of Board Games* [c. 1775–1930]. With accompanying illustrations, a number in color. London: Michael Joseph.
Low, David
1940 *Europe Since Versailles.* A cartoon history. Harmondsworth, Middlesex, and New York: Penguin.
1941 *Low on the War: A Cartoon Commentary of the Years 1939–41.* With 142 cartoons. New York: Simon & Schuster.
McLoughlin Bros., publisher
n.d. *The Magic Mirror: An Antique Optical Toy.* With 24 anamorphic prints in color and the magic mirror. New York: Dover; London: Constable, 1979.
McLuhan, Marshall
1951 *The Mechanical Bride: Folklore of Industrial Man.* With 32 reproductions of newspaper pages, advertisements, film posters, book jackets, and comic strips. Boston: Beacon Paperbacks, 1968.
Maltin, Leonard
1980 *Of Mice and Magic: A History of American Animated Cartoons.* New York, London, and Scarborough, Ont.: New American Library.
Marsh, Jean
1978 *The Illuminated Language of Flowers.* With over 30 drawings in color by Kate Greenaway. New York: Holt, Rinehart & Winston.
Marzio, Peter C.
1979 *The Democratic Art: Chromolithography 1840–1900: Pictures for a 19th-Century America.* With 126 plates, mostly in color, and some 40 figures. London: Scolar Press; Boston: David R. Godine.
Mauldin, Bill
1945 *Up Front.* New York: Henry Holt.
Mayer, S. L., editor
1976 Signal: *Hitler's Wartime Picture Magazine.* London: Bison; Englewood Cliffs, N.J.: Prentice-Hall.
Meggendorfer, Lothar
1887 *International Circus.* London: Kestrel Books; New York: Viking, 1979. [Color reproduction of the pop-up book, considered to be Meggendorfer's masterpiece.]
Mercer, F. A., and W. Gaunt, editors
1937 *Modern Publicity: The Annual of Art and Industry 1936–7.* With 8 four-color illustrations and hundreds of reproductions in b&w. London and New York: The Studio.
Mercer, F. A., and Grace Lovat Fraser, editors
1941 *Modern Publicity in War.* With 8 color illustrations and hundreds of repro-ductions in b&w, and 31 pages of advertisements. London and New York: The Studio.
Miller, Ernestine, editor
1980 *The Art of Advertising: Great Commercial Illustrations from the Early Years of Magazines* [c. 1900–1920]. With 29 full page advertisements in color. New York: St Martin's.
Miller, Joni K., and Lowry Thompson
1978 *The Rubber Stamp Album.* With over 250 illustrations and how and where to buy over 5000 rubber stamps. New York: Workman Publishing.

Miller, Kelly

1919 *Kelly Miller's History of The World War for Human Rights: An Intensely Human and Brilliant Account of the World War and For What Purpose America and the Allies Are Fighting and the Important Part Taken by the Negro. Including The Horrors and Wonders of Modern Warfare, The New and Strange Devices, etc. "Fighting for the Rights of Mankind and for the Future Peace and Security of the World".* With 128 photographs, and sketches and maps. Washington, D.C.: Austin Jenkins Co.

Ministry of Information

1941 *Bomber Command: The Air Ministry Account of Bomber Command's Offensive Against the Axis: September 1939–July 1941.* With over 100 photographs, diagrams, and maps. London: HMSO.

1946 *Merchant Airmen: The Air Ministry Account of British Civil Aviation 1939–1944.* With over 100 photographs, diagrams, and maps. London: HMSO.

Moore, Patrick

1984 *Travellers in Space and Time.* With over 80 illustrations in color. Garden City, N.Y.: Doubleday.

Morella, Joe, Edward Z. Epstein, and John Griggs

1973 *The Films of World War II.* Introduction by Judith Crist. With over 300 photographs. Secaucus, N.J.: Citadel.

Morgan, Hal, and Dan Symmes

1982 *Amazing 3-D: Gum Cards – Photos – Movies – Comics. Overflowing with more than 150 illustrations in incredible 3-D, 17 full-color plates of movie posters and comic book covers, and your own 3-D glasses!* Boston and Toronto: Little, Brown and Co., 1983.

Morris, Charles

1901 *The History and Triumphs of the Nineteenth Century Embracing Descriptions of the Decisive Battles of the Century and the Great Soldiers Who Fought Them; the Rise and Fall of Nations; the Changes in the Map of the World, and the Causes which Contributed to Political and Social Revolution; Discoverers and Discoveries; Explorers of the Tropics and Arctics; Inventors and Their Inventions; the Growth of Literature, Science and Art; the Progress of Religion, Morals and Benevolence in All Civilized Nations. Embellished with Nearly 100 Full-Page Half-Tone Engravings, Illustrating the Greatest Events of the Century, and 100 Portraits of the Most Famous Men in the World.* Washington, D.C.: W. E. Scull.

Morris, Eric, Christopher Chant, Curt Johnson, and H. P. Willmott

1975 *Weapons & Warfare of the 20th Century: A Comprehensive and Historical Survey of Modern Military Methods and Machines.* With over 700 technical drawings and photographs in b&w and color. London: Octopus, 1976.

Mullen, Chris

1979 *Cigarette Pack Art.* With hundreds of illustrations in b&w and color, many enlarged. London: Ventura; Toronto: Totem.

Nevill, Ralph

1909 *British Military Prints.* With 146 illustrations, mostly in color. London: The Connoisseur Publishing Co.

Newell, Gordon, and Joe Williamson

1959 *Pacific Coastal Liners.* With over 200 photographs. New York: Bonanza Books.

The New Yorker

1951 *Twenty-fifth Anniversary Album 1925–1950.* New York: Harper & Brothers.

Nister, Louis
   1892 *Revolving Pictures.* With six revolving scenes in color. New York: Philomel
       Books/Intervisual Communications, 1979. Facsimile.
O'Ballance, Edgar
   1961 *The Story of the French Foreign Legion.* With 16 photographs, 4 prints, and
       10 maps. London: Faber & Faber.
Odhams Press, publishers
   n.d. *Pageant of the Century* [1900–33]. Foreword by H. W. Morton. With over
       2000 sepiatone photographs. London, c. 1934.
Ollman, Bertell
   1978 *Class Struggle: To prepare for life in capitalist America – an educational game
       for kids from 8 to 80.* New York: Class Struggle, Inc. [487 Broadway, New
       York 10013].
Ott, Frederick W.
   1979 *The Films of Fritz Lang* [1919–1961]. With more than 500 photographs.
       Secaucus, N.J.: Citadel.
Parker, Derek, and Julia Parker
   1975 *The Natural History of the Chorus Girl.* With over 100 illustrations, some in
       color. London: David & Charles; New York: Bobbs-Merrill.
Peck, C. B., editor
   1952 *Locomotive Cyclopedia of American Practice: Definitions, Drawings and Illus-
       trations of Diesel, Steam, Electric and Turbine Locomotives for Railroad,
       Industrial and Foreign Service; Their Parts and Equipment; Descriptions and
       Illustrations of Locomotive Shops and Servicing Facilities: Fourteenth Edition
       1950–52. Compiled and Edited for the Association of American Railroads –
       Mechanical Division.* With several thousand illustrations and advertisements
       of all types, some in color. New York: Simmons-Boardman.
Philippe, Robert
   1980 *Political Graphics: Art as a Weapon.* With over 350 illustrations of all kinds
       from the 16th century to the present day, many in color. Milan: Arnoldo
       Mondadori; New York: Abbeville Press.
Philips, Baxter
   1975 *Cut/The Unseen Cinema.* New York: Bounty.
Pienkowski, Jan
   1979 *Haunted House.* With six pop-out scenes in color. London: Wm. Heinemann;
       Los Angeles: Intervisual Communications, Inc.
Pressland, David
   1976 *The Art of the Tin Toy* [1825–1975]. With 645 illustrations in b&w and color.
       London: New Cavendish Books, 1979.
Protheroe, Ernest
   n.d. *The Book of Ships.* With 8 color plates and 48 half-tone illustrations. London
       and Glasgow: Collins' Clear-Type Press, c. 1930.
Pulos, Arthur J.
   1983 *American Design Ethic: A History of Industrial Design to 1940.* With some
       350 unusual photos, engravings, ads, and drawings. Cambridge, Mass., and
       London: MIT Press.
Punch
   1941 *Punch and the War. "Punch" Carries On during War Time, and the Work of
       her Artists Presents, as Nothing Else Can, a Revealing Picture of Life on the
       Beleaguered Island and Affords an Insight into the Amazing Spirit of the
       British People.* With 120 pages of cartoons. Garden City, N.Y.: Blue Ribbon
       Books.

Purcell, Hugh
    1973   *The Spanish Civil War.* With many illustrations. London: Wayland; New York: G. P. Putnam's Sons. The Documentary History Series.

Raemakers, Louis
    1916   *Raemakers War Cartoons.* London and Montreal: Carreras Cigarettes. Set of 140 cards.

Rawson, Philip, and Laszlo Legeza
    1973   *Tao: The Chinese Philosophy of Time and Change.* With 196 illustrations, 33 in color. London: Thames & Hudson.

Ray, William, and Marylis Ray
    1974   *The Art of Invention: Patent Models and their Makers.* With over 125 illustrations, many in color. Princeton: The Pyne Press.

Reichardt, Jasia
    1978   *Robots: Fact, Fiction and Prediction.* With 280 illustrations, 12 in color. London: Thames & Hudson.

Riley, Frank, editor
    n.d.   *Meccano Magazine.* Liverpool: Meccano Ltd. Issues from 1946 to 1964. [Later editor: Geoffrey Byrom.]

Rip Off Press
    1973   *The Best of the Rip Off Press.* Volume 1. San Francisco: Rip Off Press Inc. [Box 14158, San Francisco, CA. 94114.] Gilbert Shelton, Jaxon, Robert Crumb, Fred Schrier, Dave Sheridan, Spain Rodriguez, Greg Irons, Robert Williams, Jim Franklin, S. Clay Wilson, and Foolbert Sturgeon.

Ross, Andy
    1977   *Stirling Cycle Engines.* With some 50 prints and photographs. Phoenix, Arizona: Solar Engines.

Runes, Dagobert D.
    1963   *Despotism: A Pictorial History of Tyranny.* With over 120 illustrations. New York: Philosophical Library.

Russell, Thomas H.
    1915   *The World's Greatest War: Sinking of the Lusitania and Other Atrocities. A Thrilling Story of the Most Sanguinary Struggle of All the Ages, Its Battles and Strategy; with a Concise Account of the Causes that Led the Nations of Europe into the Awful Conflict. By Thomas H. Russell, A.M., LL.D. Noted Historical and Military Writer, Member American Historical Association, Formerly of the British War Office; 2nd Devon (Prince of Wales' Own) Volunteers, and 12th Middlesex (Civil Service) Rifles. With Introductory Chapter by William King Pattison, President of the British Empire Association, Etc. Exciting Personal Experiences from the Bloodstained Battlefields of Europe. Over 100 Actual Photographs, Maps, and Authentic Drawings. Special Article on "The Canadian Contingent" by John A. Cooper, Editor, "The Canadian Courier".* Brantford, Ont.: The Bradley-Garretson Co.

Russo, Vito
    1981   *The Celluloid Closet: Homosexuality in the Movies.* With over 120 stills and other photos. New York and London: Harper Colophon Books.

Sadoul, Jacques
    1973   *2000 A.D.: Illustrations from the Golden Age of Science Fiction Pulps (Hier L'An 2000)* [1926–1953]. With 175 pages of illustrations, a number in color. Chicago: Henry Regnery, 1975.

Schoenberner, Gerhard
    1969   *The Yellow Star: The Persecution of the Jews in Europe 1933–1945.* With over 150 photographs. Tr. by Susan Sweet. New York: Bantam, 1979.

Schorsch, Anita
1979 *Images of Childhood: An Illustrated Social History*. With over 120 illustrations, 20 in color. New York: Mayflower Books.
Schreuders, Piet
1981 *The Book of Paperbacks. A Visual History of the Paperback*. With hundreds of illustrations in b&w and color. Tr. by Josh Pachter. London: Virgin.
Sennett, Ted
1981 *Hollywood Musicals*. With 420 illustrations, 110 in color. New York: Harry N. Abrams Inc.
Sharpe, Roger C.
1977 *Pinball!* With over 120 photographs, mostly in color, by James Hamilton. New York: Dutton.
Sheckley, Robert
1978 *Futuropolis: Impossible Cities of Science Fiction and Fantasy*. With 154 illustrations, many in color. London: Bergström & Boyle; New York: A & W Visual Library.
Shepard, E. H.
1979 *The Work of E H Shepard* [1879–1976]. With over 300 drawings and paintings, many in colour. Ed. by Rawle Knox. London: Methuen Children's Books; New York: Schocken, 1980.
Shepp, Daniel B.
1900 *Story of One Hundred Years: A Matchless Record of the Greatest Century of Historic Time: A Comprehensive View of the Political and Military Events, the Social, Intellectual and Material Progress, and the General State of Mankind in All Lands Embodying Detailed and Accurate Accounts of all Things of Importance and Interest, from 1801 to 1900, Inclusive. Profusely Illustrated from Historic Paintings and Engravings and from Special Drawings made expressly for this work*. Philadelphia: Globe Bible Publishing Co.
Shulman, Arthur, and Roger Youman
1966 *How Sweet it Was: Television: A Pictorial Commentary*. With 426 pages of photographs. New York: Bonanza Books.
Sietsema, Robert, compiler
1978 *Weapons and Armor*. With over 1400 illustrations. New York: Hart Picture Archives.
Singer, Charles, E. J. Holmyard, and A. R. Hall
1958 *A History of Technology*. With numerous illustrations. Oxford: Oxford University Press. Five volumes.
Skinner, Michael
n.d. *U*S*A*F*E: A Primer of Modern Air Combat in Europe*. Photography by George Hall. Novato, Ca.: Presidio Press.
Sklar, Martin A.
1964 *Disneyland: The Behind-the-Scenes Story of How It Was Done . . . of the Man Who Made It Possible . . . and of the Millions of Visitors Who Have Helped Make It the Happiest Place on Earth*. With 70 pages of pictures in color. Los Angeles: Walt Disney Productions, c. 1977.
Smith, Whitney
1975 *Flags through the Ages and Across the World*. With more than 2250 illustrations, mostly in color. New York, St Louis, San Francisco, Auckland, Johannesburg, Kuala Lumpur, London, Montreal, New Delhi, Sao Paulo, Singapore, Sydney, Toronto: McGraw-Hill.
Spilhaus, Athelstan
1983 Those wonderful old mechanical toys. Illustrated in color. *Encyclopaedia Britannica Yearbook for 1984*, pp. 24–45.

Spoto, Donald
  1978 *Camerado: Hollywood and the American Man.* With over 75 stills. New York: Plume. ['My hope is to be provocative rather than probative – not to prove any predetermined hypothesis (that men have been mistreated, for example, or that they have been treated childishly, patronizingly, cruelly, or accurately) . . .']

Springer, John
  1980 *Forgotten Films to Remember – And a Brief History of Fifty Years of the American Talking Picture.* With some 250 stills. Secaucus, N.J.: Citadel.

Stanley, Sir Henry M.
  1878 *Through the Dark Continent Or, The Sources of the Nile around the Great Lakes of Equatorial Africa and down the Livingstone River to the Atlantic Ocean.* With maps and 139 illustrations. London: Sampson Low, Marston & Co., 1879. Eighteenth edition.

Stettinius, Jr., Edward R.
  1944 *Lend-Lease: Weapon for Victory.* With over 60 photographs, maps, and drawings. New York: Macmillan.

Stockbridge, Frank Parker
  1920 *Yankee Ingenuity in the War.* With 170 photographs and drawings. New York: Harper.

Strandh, Sigvard
  1979 *A History of the Machine.* With over 300 illustrations, many in color. Tr. by Ann Henning. New York: A&W Publishers.

Strang, Herbert, editor
  n.d. *The Blue Book of British Naval Battles.* With 8 color plates, 11 illustrations in b&w, and numerous decorations. London: Henry Frowde/Hodder & Stoughton.

Strauss, Walter L., editor
  1972 *The Complete Engravings, Etchings and Drypoints of Albrecht Dürer.* With 120 illustrations. New York: Dover.

Strong, Roy
  1978 *Recreating the Past: British History and the Victorian Painter.* With 186 illustrations, 13 in color. London: Thames & Hudson; New York: The Pierpoint Morgan Library.

Suarès, J.-C., and David Owen
  1978 *Flight: A Poster Book.* With 32 full page posters in color and other illustrations in b&w. New York: Harmony Books.

Swift, Jonathan
  1727 *Gulliver's Travels.* With the illustrations from the French edition of 1838 by J. J. Grandville. Arlington, Va.: Great Ocean Publishers, 1980. Text of the Dublin edition of 1735.

Talbot, Fred A.
  n.d. *Cassell's Railways of the World.* With 18 plates and about 1000 photographs, plans, technical drawings, and maps. New York: Simmons-Boardman, c. 1925. Two volumes.

Taylor, The Rev. Isaac
  1830 *Scenes of Commerce, By Land and Sea; Or, "Where Does It Come From?" Answered. For the Amusement and Instruction of Tarry-at-Home Travellers.* With 54 illustrations. London: John Harris.

Taylor, John W. R.
  1974 *A History of Aerial Warfare.* With 41 illustrations in color, including 12 special paintings, and about 250 in b&w. London, New York, Sydney, and Toronto: Hamlyn.

Thomas, Frank, and Ollie Johnston
  1981 *Disney Animation: The Illusion of Life*. With 489 color plates and thousands of illustrations in b&w, including a 500-page flip book. New York: Abbeville Press.
Thomas, Tony
  1976 *The Great Adventure Films*. With over 350 stills. Secaucus, N.J.: Citadel Press, 1980.
Thompson, Sir Robert, consultant editor
  1981 *War in Peace: An Analysis of Warfare since 1945.* With 80 diagrams and 120 maps in color, and over 500 photographs. Introduction by John Keegan. London: Orbis Publishing.
Time-Life Books
  1950 *Life's Picture History of World War II*. New York: Time Inc.
  1964 *Life Science Library: Machines*. By Robert O'Brian and the Editors of *Life*. With hundreds of illustrations, many in color. New York: Time Inc. In the same series: *Mathematics* (1964).
  1967 *Time Capsule/1923: A History of the Year Condensed from the Pages of Time*. New York: Time Inc.
  1968 *Age of Progress* [1830–1914]. Ed. by S. C. Burchell. Illustrated in b&w and color. New York: Time-Life Books.
  1970 *This Fabulous Century*. New York: Time-Life Books. Six volumes, 1870–1950.
  1973 *The Best of Life*. New York: Avon/Flare Books, 1975.
  1974 *The Old West: The Gunfighters*. Alexandria, Va.: Time-Life Books. In the same series: *The Women* (1974).
  1977a *Life Goes to War: A Picture History of World War II*. Boston and Toronto: Little, Brown and Co. A Time-Life Television Book.
  1977b *World War II: The Battle of Britain*. Alexandria, Va.: Time-Life Books. In the same series: *The Home Front: U.S.A.* (1978); *The Secret War* (1981); and *The Aftermath: Europe* (1983).
Time Magazine
  1983 *The Most Amazing 60 Years in History*. Special anniversary issue, October 5, 1983.
Tod, Ian, and Michael Wheeler
  1978 *Utopia: The Perfect Society Visualized by the World's Greatest Utopian Writers, Painters, Poets and Architects*. With over 125 illustrations, many in color. London: Orbis; New York: Harmony Books.
Todd, Pamela, and David Fordham, editors
  1980 *Private Tucker's Boer War Diary*. With over 110 photographs, prints, and maps. London: Elmtree Books.
Trent, Paul
  1975 *Those Fabulous Movie Years: The 30s*. With 188 pages of photographs, some in color. Barre, Mass. and New York: Barre Publishing/Crown Publishers.
Tripp, William R.
  1976 *Presidential Campaign Posters* [1828–1976]. With over 60 illustrations. New York: Drake Publishers.
Turner, Patricia, illustrator
  n.d. *Little Red Riding Hood: A Peepshow Book*. London: Folding Books Ltd.
Underwood, John W.
  1972 *Acrobats In The Sky*. With about 300 illustrations. Glendale, Ca.: Heritage Press.
Unger, Frederic William, and Charles Morris
  1904 *Russia and Japan and a Complete History of the War in the Far East. Profusely Illustrated by Half-Tone Engravings and Special Artists' Drawings*. [New York:] W. E. Scull.

Upton, Florence K.
  1909 *Golliwogg in the African Jungle*. Verses by Bartha Upton. With 31 full page
         color illustrations. London, New York, and Bombay: Longmans, Green & Co.
The U.S. Playing Card Company
  n.d.   *Spotter Cards: International Aircraft Silhouettes*. Cincinatti, Ohio, c. 1943.
Van Amerongen, C., editor and translator
  1963 *How Things Work: The Universal Encyclopedia of Machines*. With over 300
         illustrations. Tr. and adapted from the revised German edition of *Wie Funk-
         tionert Das?*. London: George Allen & Unwin; St Albans, Herts.: Paladin,
         1974. Volume I.
Van Riemsdijk, J. T., and Kenneth Brown
  1980 *The Pictorial History of Steam Power*. With hundreds of illustrations, mostly
         in color. London: Octopus.
Verne, Jules
  1865 *The Annotated Jules Verne: From the Earth to the Moon: Direct in Ninety-
         seven Hours and Twenty Minutes. The Only Completely Rendered and Anno-
         tated Edition*. By Walter James Miller. With engravings from the first illustrated
         edition (1872). New York: Thomas Y. Crowell; Toronto: Fitzhenry and White-
         side, 1978.
War Resisters League
  1972 *In Woman's Soul*. The 1972 Peace Calendar and Appointment Book. With
         numerous illustrations and quotations. [WRL 339 Lafayette St, New York
         10012.]
  1976 *To Secure Peace and Liberty: Creative Nonviolence in the American Past*. The
         1976 Peace Calendar.
  1977 *What Did You Learn in School Today? A Statement on the Liberation of
         Education*. The 1977 Peace Calendar.
  1979 *While There is a Soul in Prison: Statements on the Prison Experience*. The
         1979 Peace Calendar.
Watkins, Julian Lewis
  1949 *The 100 Greatest Advertisements: Who Wrote Them and What They Did
         [1852–1958]*. Foreword by Raymond Rubicam. New York: Dover Books;
         London: Constable. Revised and enlarged edition, with 13 new advertisements,
         1959.
Webster, H. T.
  1953 *The Best of H.T. Webster: A Memorial Collection [1914–1953]*. New York:
         Simon and Schuster.
Wentz, Budd
  1977 *Ready-to-Make Photo & Scene Machines: Antique Optical Inventions Recre-
         ated*. San Francisco: Troubador.
Wheeler, Harold F. B.
  1916 *The Story of Lord Kitchener*. With illustrations by famous artists. London:
         Harrap.
White, Jr., John H.
  1972 *Early American Locomotives*. With 147 Engravings. New York: Dover.
Whitehouse, P. B., J. B. Snell, and J. B. Hollingsworth
  1978 *Steam for Pleasure*. With over 200 photographs and maps, some in color.
         London and Boston: Routledge & Kegan Paul.
Wickler, Wolfgan
  1968 *Mimicry in Plants and Animals*. With numerous illustrations, many in color.
         Tr. by R. D. Martin. New York and Toronto: McGraw-Hill. World University
         Library.

Wilden, Anthony, compiler

1982 *I Want Out: A Pictorial Supplement to The 20th Century War 1880–1982.* Unpublished xerox.

Wilk, Max

1973 *Memory Lane: The Golden Age of American Popular Music 1890–1925.* With 128 music covers in color and 36 pages of sheet music. New York: Ballantine, 1976.

Williams, Archibald

n.d. *Let Me Explain.* With over 150 sketches, diagrams, and photographs. London: Wells Gardner, Darton & Co, c. 1914.

n.d. *How It is Made: Describing in simple language how various Machines and many Articles in common use are manufactured from the Raw Materials.* With 198 photographs, sketches, drawings, circuits, and other diagrams. London, Edinburgh, Dublin, and New York: Thomas Nelson & Sons, c. 1915.

Williams, C. J.

n.d. *Greenacre, Or the Edgeware-Road Murder. Presenting an Authentic and Circumstantial Account of this Most Sanguinary Outrage of the Laws of Humanity; and Showing, upon the Confession of the Culprit, the Means he Resorted to, in order to Effect his Bloody Purpose; Also his Artful and Fiendlike Method of Mutilating his Murdered Victim, The Inhuman Manner in which he afterwards Disposed of the Mangled Body and Limbs, and his Cold-blooded Disposal of the Head of the Unfortunate Female, on the Eve of their Intended Marriage; with a Full Account of the Facts which led to the Discovery of the Atrocious Deed, His Apprehension, Trial, Behaviour at the Condemned Sermon, and Execution.* With a hand colored fold out. Derby: Thomas Richardson, c. 1840.

Willmot, Ned, and John Pimlott

1979 *Strategy and Tactics of War: Land – Sea – Air.* With over 150 photographs, prints, maps, sketches, and technical drawings, many in color. London: Marshall Cavendish; Secaucus, N.J.: Chartwell Books.

Wilson, Simon

1976 *Beardsley.* With 50 plates. London: Phaidon; New York: Dutton.

Winchester, Clarence, A.R.Ae.S.I, editor

1938 *Wonders of World Aviation. To be Completed in about 45 Weekly Parts.* With a color plate in each part and hundreds of photographs and diagrams. London: Amalgamated Press.

Winton, John

1976 *Air Power at Sea 1939–45.* With over 120 photographs and maps. Toronto: Griffin Press.

Wise, Terence

1977 *Military Flags of the World.* Illustrated by Guido Rosignoli. London: Blandford; New York: Arco Publishing.

Wood, J. E. R., editor

1946 *Detour: The Story of Oflag IVC.* Prose, poetry, and pictures from a Canadian officers' prison camp. London: The Falcon Press.

Woodward, David

1978 *Armies of the World 1854–1914.* With 150 photographs. New York: G. P. Putnam's Sons.

Woodward, John, and George Burnett

1892 *A Treatise on Heraldry.* With over 150 illustrations, mostly plates in color, including gold and silver. Edinburgh and London: W. & A. K. Johnston. Two volumes.

Wykes, Alan
    1970 *The Nuremburg Rallies*. With over 100 photographs: New York: Ballantine's Violent Century.
Yank
    1945 *The Best from Yank the Army Weekly*. With over 100 cartoons and 44 pages of photographs. New York: Dutton.
Yanker, Gary
    1972 *Prop Art*. Over 1000 contemporary political posters. New York: Darien House; Greenwich, Conn.: New York Graphic Society.
Young, G. M.
    1941 *The Government of Britain*. With 12 plates in colour and 16 illustrations in b&w. London: William Collins. Britain in Pictures series. Second edition.
Zucker, Irving, compiler
    1964 *A Source Book of Advertising Art*. With over 5000 cuts from turn of the century France. New York: Bonanza Books.

Part C: The strategy of communication

This is the bibliography for Chapters 1 to 8, the Envoi, and the Postscript.

Abbott, Edwin A.
    1884 *Flatland: A Romance of Many Dimensions*. Oxford: Blackwell, 1978.
Acker, Lewis F.
    1939 Communication systems of the American Indians. *Signal Corps Bulletin* (January–March). Scheips, ed., 1980, vol. 1, pp. 63–70.
Adorno, T. W., et al.
    1950 *The Authoritarian Personality*. With numerous tables and figures. New York: Wiley, 1967. Studies in Prejudice, ed. by Max Horkheimer and Samuel H. Flowerman. Two volumes.
Agricola, Georgius
    1556 *De re metallica [On Metals]*. Tr. by Herbert Hoover and Lou Henry Hoover (1912). New York: Dover, 1950.
Antrim, Don
    1983 Your memory stands accused. *Science Digest*, November, pp. 76–7.
ARTnews
    1921 [Abbott Handerson] Thayer [1850–1921], father of camouflage, dead: Distinguished American painter was discoverer of the theory of protective coloration among animals. Diamonstein, ed., 1977, p. 56.
Ashby, W. Ross
    1952 *Design for a Brain*. London: Science Paperbacks, 1966. Revised edition, 1960.
    1956 *An Introduction to Cybernetics*. London: Chapman and Hall; New York: Wiley, 1966.
Atlan, Henri
    1979 *Entre le crystal et la fumée: Essai sur l'organisation vivante*. Paris: Seuil.
Aubrey, Crispin, and Paul Chilton, editors
    1983 *Nineteen Eighty-Four in 1984: Autonomy, Control and Communication*. London: Comedia.
Bain, David, and Bruce Harris, editors
    1973 *Mickey Mouse: Fifty Happy Years*. With 253 pages of illustrations, many in color. New York: Harmony, 1977.

Bakan, Paul
1971 The eyes have it. *Psychology Today*, April.
Baldwin, Gordon C.
1970 *Talking Drums to Written Word.* New York: Norton.
Balzac, Honoré de
1843 *Lost Illusions.* Tr. by Kathleen Raine. New York: The Modern Library.
1844 *Les Paysans.* Paris. [See Lukács, 1938, pp. 21–46.]
Baran, Paul A., and Paul M. Sweezy
1966 *Monopoly Capital: An Essay on the American Economic and Social Order.* New York: Modern Reader Paperbacks.
Bardin, Desdémone
1974 *Diphtongues et lutte de classes.* Preface by Léandre Bergeron. Montréal: Editions Québécoises.
Bar-Hillel, Yenoshua
1967 Theory of types. *The Encyclopedia of Philosophy.* Ed. by Paul Edwards. New York and London: Macmillan/Collier Macmillan, vol. 8, pp. 168–72.
Bateson, Gregory
1926 On certain aberrations of the red-legged partridges *Alectoris rufa* and *saxatilis. Journal of Genetics*, 16, pp. 101–23 (with William Bateson).
1943a Cultural and thematic analysis of fictional films. *Transactions of the New York Academy of Sciences*, series 2, 5/4, pp. 72–8. Reprinted in *Personal Character and Cultural Milieu.* Ed. by Douglas G. Haring. Syracuse, N.Y., 1948, pp. 117–23.
1943b An analysis of the Nazi film *Hitlerjunge Quex* [1933]. New York: Museum of Modern Art Film Library. Mimeographed. [A copy of the first three reels of this film, with analytic titles by Bateson, is in the Museum of Modern Art Film Library in New York (see also Bateson 1953a).]
1946a The pattern of an armaments race, Part I: An anthropological approach. *Bulletin of the Atomic Scientists*, 2/5–6, pp. 10–11.
1946b The pattern of an armaments race, Part II: An analysis of nationalism. *Bulletin of the Atomic Scientists*, 2/7–8, pp. 26–8. [Both articles reprinted in *Personal Character and Cultural Milieu.* Ed. by Douglas G. Haring. Syracuse, N.Y., 1948, pp. 85–88, 89–93.]
1947 Atoms, nations, and cultures. *International House Quarterly*, 11/2, pp. 47–50.
1953a An analysis of the Nazi film *Hitlerjunge Quex* [1933]. *The Study of Culture at a Distance.* Ed. by Margaret Mead and Rhoda Métraux. Chicago: University of Chicago Press. [Abstract by Margaret Mead of Bateson's original text (see Bateson 1943b).]
1953b The position of humor in human communication. *Cybernetics: Circular Causal and Feedback Mechanisms in the Biological and Social Sciences: Transactions of the Ninth Conference* (Princeton, N.J.: March 20–21, 1952). Ed. by Heinz von Foerster. New York: Josiah Macy, Jr. Foundation, pp. 1–47. [The Macey Conferences were the first on the new perspective that developed from the massive increase in knowledge and experience in all the sciences associated with information during World War II: communications, cryptanalysis, information theory, coding theory, computers, systems theory, systems analysis, operational research, and the cybernetics of self-regulating or self-steering systems, notably the first cruise missile (the German V-1) and the first true ballistic missile (the V-2).]
1953c Metalogue: About games and being serious. *ETC.: A Review of General Semantics*, 10, pp. 213–17.
1956 The message 'This is play'. *Group Processes: Transactions of the Second Conference* (October 1955, at Princeton, New Jersey). Ed. by Bertram Schaffner. New York: Josiah Macy, Jr. Foundation, pp. 145–242.

1958 *Naven: A Survey of the Problems Suggested by a Composite Picture of the Culture of a New Guinea Tribe from Three Points of View*. Cambridge: Cambridge University Press; New York: Macmillan, 1937. Second edition: Stanford: Stanford University Press. [The 1958 epilog makes explicit the (non-mechanistic) cybernetic and systems perspective implicit in the original. Omitted from the French translation.]

1972 *Steps to an Ecology of Mind: Collected Essays in Anthropology, Psychiatry, Evolution, and Epistemology*. San Francisco, Scranton, London, and Toronto: Chandler/Intext; New York: Ballantine. [The Chandler edition includes an index; the Paladin edition omits the metalogues. Except for the metalogue of 1953, none of the items listed above appear in the 1972 collection.]

1979 *Mind and Nature: A Necessary Unity*. New York: Bantam.

Bateson, Gregory, Don D. Jackson, Jay Haley, and John Weakland
1956 Toward a theory of schizophrenia. *Behavioral Science*, 1, pp. 251–64. Reprinted in Bateson 1972, pp. 201–27. [The announcement of the double bind theory.]

Bateson, Gregory, and Margaret Mead
1942 *Balinese Character: A Photographic Analysis*. New York: Special publications of the New York Academy of Sciences, 1962.

Bateson, Mary Catherine
1972 *Our Own Metaphor: A Personal Account of a Conference on The Effects of Conscious Purpose on Human Adaptation*. New York: Alfred A. Knopf.

Becker, Carl L.
1932 *The Heavenly City of the Eighteenth-Century Philosophers*. New Haven: Yale University Press, 1959.

Belsham, W.
1805 *History of Great Britain*. London: Verner and Hood. Second edition. Five volumes.

Berger, John
1972 *Ways of Seeing*. With Sven Blomberg, Chris Fox, Michael Dibb, and Richard Hollis. Harmondsworth, Middlesex: Penguin.

Bergeron, Léandre
1978 *The History of Quebec: A Patriote's Handbook*. Tr. by Baila Markus. Toronto: NP Press. Updated edition.

Berlin, Isaiah
1939 *Karl Marx: His Life and Environment*. New York: Galaxy, 1961.

Bernard, Claude
1865 *An Introduction to the Study of Experimental Medicine*. Tr. by Henry Copley Greene. New York: Collier, 1961.

Bernstein, Basil
1971 *Class, Codes and Control*. London: Routledge & Kegan Paul [notably pp. 143–230].

Bertalanffy, Ludwig von
1968 *General Systems Theory*. New York: Braziller.

Birdwhistell, Ray L.
1970 *Kinesics and Context*. New York: Ballantine, 1972.

Blackburn, Robin, editor
1972 *Ideology in Social Science*. London: Fontana.

Blake, William
1965 *The Poetry and Prose of William Blake*. Ed. by David V. Erdman. Commentary by Harold Bloom. Garden City, N.Y.: Anchor, 1970.

Bloom, Floyd E.
1981 Neuropeptides. *Scientific American*, 245/4, pp. 148–68.

Boas, George
  1929 *The Major Traditions of European Philosophy*. New York and London: Harper.
  1959 *Some Assumptions of Aristotle*. Philadelphia: Transactions of the American Philosophical Society for Promoting Useful Knowledge, 1970. New series: vol. 49, part 6.
Boas, Marie
  1962 *The Scientific Renaissance 1450–1630*. With 17 illustrations. New York: Harper Torchbooks. The Rise of Modern Science series, ed. by A. Rupert Hall.
Bochner, Salomon
  1968 Continuity and discontinuity. *Dictionary of the History of Ideas*. Ed. by Philip P. Wiener. New York: Scribner's, vol. 1, pp. 492–504.
Boman, Thorlief
  1960 *Hebrew Thought Compared with Greek*. Tr. by Jules L. Moreau. New York: Norton, 1970. Second edition.
Borko, Harold, editor
  1962 *Computer Applications in the Behavioral Sciences: The role of the computer as a research tool*. With numerous photographs, figures, tables, diagrams, pictograms, and flow charts. Englewood Cliffs, N.J.: Prentice-Hall. ['Written in connection with a research project sponsored in the public interest by the System Development Corporation, Santa Monica, California'.]
Boston Women's Health Book Collective
  1971 *Our Bodies, Ourselves: A Book By and For Women*. New York: Simon and Schuster, 1973.
Brand, Stewart
  1974 *II Cybernetic Frontiers*. Conversations with Gregory Bateson. New York: Random House.
Braudel, Fernand
  1979a *The Structures of Everyday Life: The Limits of the Possible*. Tr. revised by Siân Reynolds. London: Collins; New York: Harper & Row, 1981. Civilization and capitalism 15th–18th centuries, volume I.
  1979b *The Wheels of Commerce*. Tr. revised by Siân Reynolds. London: Collins; New York: Harper & Row, 1982. Civilization and capitalism 15th–18th centuries, volume II.
Braverman, Harry
  1974 *Labor and Monopoly Capital: The Degradation of Work in the Twentieth Century*. New York and London: Monthly Review Press.
Brockman, John, editor
  1977 *About Bateson*. New York: Dutton.
Bronowski, J., and Bruce Mazlish
  1960 *The Western Intellectual Tradition*. Harmondsworth, Middlesex: Penguin. Reprinted with revisions, 1970.
Browne, Sir Thomas
  1967 *The Prose of Sir Thomas Browne*. Ed. by Norman J. Endicott. New York: Norton, 1972.
Brown, J. A. C.
  1963 *Techniques of Persuasion: From Propaganda to Brainwashing*. Harmondsworth, Middlesex: Penguin.
Brownmiller, Susan
  1975 *Against Our Will: Men, Women and Rape*. New York: Simon and Schuster. Bantam edition 1976.
Buckley, Walter
  1968 *Sociology and Modern Systems Theory*. Englewood Cliffs, N.J.: Prentice-Hall.

Buckley, Walter, editor
  1968 *Modern Systems Research for the Behavioral Scientist*. Chicago: Aldine.
Bunker, Stephen G.
  1985 *Underdeveloping the Amazon. Extraction, Unequal Exchange, and the Failure of the Modern State*. Chicago: University of Illinois Press.
Burnet, John
  1892 *Early Greek Philosophy*. Cleveland, Ohio: Meridian Books, 1964. Fourth edition, 1930.
Burns, Tom, and S. B. Saul, editors
  1967 *Social Theory and Economic Change*. London: Social Science Paperbacks, 1972.
Butterfield, Herbert
  1931 *The Whig Interpretation of History*. Harmondsworth, Middlesex: Penguin, 1973.
Cade, Toni, editor
  1974 *The Black Woman*. New York: Signet.
Campbell, Jeremy
  1982 *Grammatical Man: Information, Entropy, Language and Life*. New York: Simon and Schuster.
Carson, Rachel
  1962 *Silent Spring*. Introduction by Paul R. Ehrlich. Greenwich, Conn.: Fawcett, 1970.
Chambers, W., editor
  1876 *The Book of Days: A Miscellany of Popular Antiquities in Connection with the Calendar, Including Anecdote, Biography, & History; Curiosities of Literature; and Oddities of Human Life and Character*. Numerous engravings. London and Edinburgh: W. & R. Chambers. Two volumes.
Chambon, Pierre
  1981 Split genes. *Scientific American*, 244/5, pp. 60–71.
Changeux, Jean Pierre
  1983 *L'Homme neuronale*. Paris: Fayard.
Chase, Allen
  1980 *The Legacy of Malthus*. Urbana and London: University of Illinois Press.
Cherniavsky, Michael, and Arthur J. Slavin, editors
  1972 *Social Textures of Western Civilization: The Lower Depths*. Volume I: From classical antiquity to the 15th century. Lexington, Mass. and Toronto: Xerox.
Cherniavsky, Michael, Arthur J. Slavin, and Stuart Ewen, editors
  1972 *Social Textures of Western Civilization: The Lower Depths*. Volume II: From the 16th century peasant wars to the mid-1960s. Lexington, Mass. and Toronto: Xerox.
Chesler, Phyllis
  1974 *Women and Madness*. New York: Avon.
Chomsky, Noam
  1957 *Syntactic Structures*. The Hague: Mouton.
Cipolla, Carlo M., editor
  1970 *The Economic Decline of Empires*. London: University Paperbacks.
Clausewitz, Carl von
  1832a *Vom Kriege: Auswahl*. Ed. by Ulrich Marwedel. Stuttgart: Philip Reclam Jun., 1981.
  1832b *On War*. Trans. by O. J. Matthijs Jolles. New York: The Modern Library, 1943.
Coe, Richard M., and Anthony Wilden
  1978 Errore. *Enciclopedia Einaudi*. Torino: Einaudi Editore, vol. 5, pp. 682–711.

Collingwood, R. G.
1945 *The Idea of Nature.* New York: Galaxy, 1960.
Commoner, Barry
1971 *The Closing Circle: Nature, Man, and Technology.* New York: Bantam, 1973.
1972 Man's debt to nature. *International Herald-Tribune*, June 5, 1972.
Cooper, David, editor
1968 *The Dialectics of Liberation.* Harmondsworth, Middlesex: Penguin. [Papers from a conference between R. D. Laing, Gregory Bateson, Jules Henry, John Gerassi, Paul Sweezy, Paul Goodman, Lucien Goldmann, Stokely Carmichael, Herbert Marcuse, and David Cooper.]
Cornford, F. M.
1932 *Before and After Socrates.* Cambridge: Cambridge University Press, 1965.
Corrigan, Philip, and Derek Sayer
1985 *The Great Arch: English State Formation as Cultural Revolution.* Oxford: Blackwell's Paperbacks.
Crosson, Frederick J., and Kenneth M. Sayre, editors
1967 *Philosophy and Cybernetics.* Essays delivered to the Philosophic Institute for Artificial Intelligence at Notre Dame University. New York: Simon and Schuster, 1968.
Daly, Herman E., editor
1973 *Toward a Steady-State Economy.* San Francisco: W. H Freeman.
Daly, Mary
1978 *Gyn/Ecology: The Metaethics of Radical Feminism.* Boston: Beacon. [Essential for the history of female castration.]
Danchin, Antoine
1983 *L'Oeuf et la poule: Histoires du code génétique.* Paris: Fayard.
Darnell, Jr., James E.
1983 The processing of RNA. *Scientific American*, 249/4, pp. 90–100.
Debord, Guy
1977 *Society of the Spectacle.* Detroit: Black and Red. [P.O. Box 9546, Detroit, Michigan, 48202.]
de la Haye, Yves, editor
1979 *Marx & Engels on the Means of Communication: The movement of commodities, people, information & capital.* New York: International General.
Deregowski, J. B.
1972 Pictorial perception and culture. *Scientific American*, 227/5, pp. 82–8.
1984 *Distortion in Art: The Eye and the Mind.* London and Boston: Routledge & Kegan Paul.
Detwyler, Thomas R.
1971 *Man's Impact on Environment.* New York: McGraw-Hill.
Deutsch, Karl W.
1966 *The Nerves of Government: Models of Political Communication and Control.* With a new introduction 1962–1966. New York: The Free Press; London: Collier-Macmillan.
Dowling, Colette
1981 *The Cinderella Complex: Women's Hidden Fear of Independence.* New York: Pocket Books.
Dumouchel, Paul, and Jean-Pierre Dupuy, editors
1983 *L'Auto-organisation: De la physique au politique.* Paris: Editions du Seuil. [Proceedings of a conference at Cérisy-la-Salle, June 10–17, 1981. Papers by Isabelle Stengers, Henri Atlan, Maurice Milgram, Cornelius Castoriadis, René Girard, Edgar Morin, Yves Barel, and others.]
Dunn-Rankin, Peter
1978 The visual characteristics of words. *Scientific American*, 238/1, pp. 122–30.

Eckhart, Meister
   1941 *Meister Eckhart: A Modern Translation.* Tr. by Raymond Bernard Blakney.
         New York: Harper Torchbooks, n.d.
Edwards, Betty
   1979 *Drawing on the Right Side of the Brain: A Course in Enhancing Creativity
         and Artistic Confidence.* Los Angeles: J. P. Tarcher; Boston: Houghton Mifflin.
Edwards, Richard C., Michael Reich, and Thomas E. Weisskopf, editors
   1978 *The Capitalist System: A Radical Analysis of American Society.* Englewood
         Cliffs, N.J.: Prentice-Hall. Second edition.
Ehrenreich, Barbara, and Deirdre English
   1973a *Witches, Midwives, and Nurses: A History of Women Healers.* Old Wester-
         bury, N.Y.: The Feminist Press.
   1973b *Complaints and Disorders: The Sexual Politics of Sickness.* Old Westerbury,
         N.Y.: The Feminist Press.
   1978 *For Her Own Good: 150 Years of the Experts' Advice to Women.* New York:
         Anchor.
Eigen, Manfred, William Gardiner, Peter Schuster, and Ruthild Winkler-Oswatitsch
   1981 The origin of genetic information. *Scientific American,* 244/4, pp. 88–118.
Eis, Egon
   1959 *The Forts of Folly: The History of an Illusion.* Tr. by A. J. Pomerans. London:
         Oswald Wolff.
Eisenstein, Sergei
   1947 *The Film Sense.* Ed. and tr. by Jay Leyda. New York: Harvest Books.
   1949 *Film Form.* Ed. and tr. by Jay Leyda. New York: Harvest Books.
Eliade, Mircea
   1973 *Australian Religions.* Ithaca and London: Cornell University Press.
Ellul, Jacques
   1954 *The Technological Society [La Technique ou l'enjeu du siècle].* Introduction
         by Robert K. Merton. Tr. by John Wilkinson. New York: Vintage, 1964.
   1962 *Propaganda: The Formation of Men's Attitudes.* Tr. by Konrad Kellen and
         Jean Lerner. New York: Vintage, 1973.
Emery, F. E., editor
   1969 *Systems Thinking: Selected Readings.* Harmondsworth, Middlesex: Penguin,
         1971.
Engels, Frederick
   1967 *Selected Writings.* Ed. by W. O. Henderson. Baltimore: Penguin.
Epstein, Irving R., Kenneth Kustin, Patrick De Kepper, and Miklos Orban
   1983 Oscillating chemical reactions. *Scientific American,* 248/3, pp. 112–23 [see
         Prigogine].
Erlich, Victor
   1955 *Russian Formalism: History – Doctrine.* New Haven: Yale University Press,
         1981. Revised 1965.
Fanon, Frantz
   1952 *Black Skin, White Masks: The Experiences of a Black Man in a White World.*
         Tr. by C. L. Markmann. New York: Grove Press, 1967.
   1963 *The Wretched of the Earth.* Tr. by Constance Farrington. New York: Grove
         Press, 1968.
Farrington, Benjamin
   1964 *The Philosophy of Francis Bacon.* Chicago: Phoenix.
Fekete, John
   1977 *The Critical Twilight: Explorations in the ideology of Anglo-American literary
         theory from Eliot to McLuhan.* London and Boston: Routledge & Kegan Paul.

Finn, Robert
  1983a New split brain research divides scientists. *Science Digest*, September, pp. 54–5, 103.
  1983b Memory. *Science Digest*, November, pp. 72–5.
Firestone, Shulamith
  1970 *The Dialectic of Sex: The Case for Feminist Revolution.* The *human* alternative to 1984 – a slashing attack on male supremacy that charts the end of the sexual class system. Chapter 6 might change your life. New York: Bantam, 1971. Revised edition.
Flecker, H. L. O., et. al.
  1931 *A Shortened Psalter for use in Christ's Hospital Chapel.* Horsham, West Sussex.
Flinn, M. W.
  1967 Social theory and the industrial revolution. Burns and Saul, eds., 1967, pp. 9–34.
Fraser, Douglas
  1968 *Village Planning in the Primitive World.* New York: Braziller.
Freire, Paulo
  1969 *Pedagogy of the Oppressed.* Tr. by M. B. Ramos. Sommers, Ct.: Seabury Press, 1971.
Frege, Gottlob
  1919 Negation (*Die Verneinung*). *Logical Investigations.* Ed. by P. T. Geach. Tr. by P. T. Geach and R. H. Stoothoff. Oxford: Blackwell, 1977, pp. 30–53. [First published in *Beiträge zur Philosophie des deutschen Idealismus*, vol. 1, pp. 143–57.]
Freud, Sigmund
  1925 Negation (*Die Verneinung*). *Standard Edition*, 19, pp. 235–9.
  1974 *The Complete Psychological Works of Sigmund Freud (Standard Edition).* Ed. by James Strachey. London: Hogarth Press. Twenty-four volumes, 1953–74.
  1954 *The Origins of Psycho-analysis: Letters to Wilhelm Fliess 1887–1902.* Ed. by Marie Bonaparte, Anna Freud, and Ernst Chris. Tr. by Eric Mosbacher and James Strachey. London: Imago.
Fried, Albert, and Ronald Sanders, editors
  1964 *Socialist Thought: A Documentary History.* Garden City, N.Y.: Anchor.
Fromkin, Victoria A.
  1973 Slips of the tongue. *Scientific American*, 224/3, pp. 106–9.
Fromm, Erich
  1961 *Marx's Concept of Man.* With a translation from Marx's *Economic and Philosophical Manuscripts [of 1844]* by T. B. Bottomore. New York: Ungar.
Galbraith, John Kenneth
  n.d. *Money: Whence It Came, Where It Went.* Boston: Houghton Mifflin.
Gamow, George
  1947 *One Two Three . . . Infinity: Facts and Speculations of Science.* Illustrated by the author. New York: Mentor, 1954.
Gardner, Howard
  1983 *Frames of Mind: The Theory of Multiple Intelligences.* New York: Basic Books.
Gardner, Martin
  1960 *The Annotated Alice.* New York: Bramhall House.
  1980 Monkey business. *New York Review of Books*, March 20.
Gelb, I. J.
  1952 *A Study of Writing.* Chicago: Phoenix, 1974. Second edition.
George, Susan
  1977 *How the Other Half Dies: The Real Reasons for World Hunger.* New York: Universe Books.

Gillmore, Parker (Ubique)

  1888 *Days and Nights by the Desert, with Numerous Illustrations.* London: Kegan Paul, Trench & Co.

Girard, René

  1961 *Deceit, Desire, and the Novel [Mensonge romantique et vérité romanesque]: Self and Other in Literary Strucure.* Tr. by Yvonne Freccero. Baltimore: Johns Hopkins, 1965.

Godelier, Maurice

  1966 Structure and contradiction in *Capital.* Blackburn, ed., 1967, pp. 334–68.

Goldmann, Lucien

  1955 *Le Dieu caché: Etude sur la vision tragique dans les Pensées de Pascal et dans le théâtre de Racine.* Paris: Gallimard. Tr. as *The Hidden God* by Philip Thody: New York: Humanities, 1963. International Library of Philosophy and Scientific Method.

Gould, Stephen Jay

  1981 *The Mismeasure of Man.* New York and London: Norton.

Griffith, D. W.

  1972 *The Man Who Invented Hollywood: The Autobiography of D. W. Griffith.* A memoir and some notes edited and annotated by James Hart, including the unfinished autobiography of the film master. Louisville, Kentucky: Touchstone.

Hall, Edward T.

  1959 *The Silent Language.* New York: Fawcett World Library.

  1966 *The Hidden Dimension.* Garden City, N.Y.: Doubleday Anchor Books, 1969.

Hammer, Rhonda

  1981 *The Pattern Which Connects: The Communicational Approach.* Simon Fraser University. Unpublished MA thesis.

Hammer, Rhonda, and Anthony Wilden

  1981 *METROPOLIS in 30 Minutes.* Burnaby, B.C.: Simon Fraser University/Instructional Media Center. Videotape montage, 30 minutes. Broadcast December 10.

  1982 *Women in Production: The Chorus Line 1932–1980.* Videotape montage, 55 minutes (5th edition).

  1984 *Busby Berkeley and The Mechanical Bride: From Flying Down To Rio to The Lullaby of Broadway 1932–1935.* Videotape montage, 35 minutes.

Hargrave, John

  1940 *Words Win Wars: Propaganda the Mightiest Weapon of All.* London: Wells Gardner, Darton & Co.

Harris, Marvin

  1968 *The Rise of Anthropological Theory: A History of Theories of Culture.* New York: Thomas Y. Crowell.

  1971 *Culture, Man, and Nature.* New York: Crowell.

  1974 *Cows, Pigs, Wars and Witches.* New York: Vintage, 1975.

  1977 *Cannibals and Kings.* New York: Vintage, 1978.

Haskell, Molly

  1973 *From Reverence to Rape: The Treatment of Women in the Movies.* New York: Holt, Rinehart and Winston.

Hassenstein, B.

  1970 *Information and Control in the Living Organism.* London: Chapman and Hall; New York: Barnes & Noble, 1971.

Hawkins, Gerald S.

  1966 *Stonehenge Decoded.* Garden City, N.Y.: Doubleday.

Hegel, G. W. F.

  1832 *The Philosophy of History.* Trans. by J. Sibree (1899). New York: Dover, 1956.

Heilbroner, Robert, and Lester Thurow
1982 *Economics Explained.* Englewood Cliffs, N.J.: Prentice-Hall.
Herndon, James
1968 *The Way it Spozed To Be: A report on the classroom war behind the crisis in our schools.* New York: Bantam, 1969.
Heninger, Jr., S. K.
1977 *The Cosmographical Glass: Renaissance Diagrams of the Universe.* With 117 illustrations. San Marino, Ca.: The Huntington Library.
Hesse, Eckhard H.
1975 The role of pupil size in communication. *Scientific American,* 233/5, pp. 110–19.
Hewlett, Sylvia Ann
1986 *A Lesser Life: The Myth of Women's Liberation in America.* New York: Morrow.
Heyer, Paul
1982 *Nature, Human Nature, and Society: Marx, Darwin, Biology, and the Human Sciences.* Westport, Conn., and London: Greenwood Press.
Hill, Christopher
1967 *Reformation to Industrial Revolution.* Harmondsworth, Middlesex: The Pelican Economic History of Britain.
Hobsbawm, E. J.
1968 *Industry and Empire: From 1750 to the Present Day.* Harmondsworth, Middlesex: The Pelican Economic History of Britain.
Hodges, Andrew
1983 *Alan Turing: the Enigma.* New York: Touchstone.
Hoffman, Banesh
1947 *The Strange Story of the Quantum.* Harmondsworth, Middlesex: Penguin, 1965. Revised 1959.
Holt, John
1964 *How Children Fail.* New York: Delta.
Holland, Ray
1977 *Self and Social Context.* London: Macmillan.
Horowitz, David, editor
1968 *Marx and Modern Economics.* New York and London: Modern Reader Paperbacks.
Hudson, Derek
1945 *British Journalists and Newspapers.* London: Collins. Britain in Pictures.
Hughes, Patrick
1983 *More on Oxymoron: Foolish Wisdom in Words and Pictures.* Harmondsworth, Middlesex: Penguin.
Hughes, Patrick, and George Brecht
1975 *Vicious Circles and Infinity.* New York: Doubleday; Harmondsworth, Middlesex: Penguin, 1978.
Humez, Alexander, and Nicholas Humez
1981 *Alpha to Omega: The Life & Times of the Greek Alphabet.* Boston and London: David R. Godine/Kudos & Godine, 1983.
Hyman, Stanley Edgar
1951 *The Tangled Bank: Darwin, Marx, Frazer and Freud as Imaginative Writers.* New York: Grosset & Dunlap: The Universal Library, 1962.
Idris-Soven, Ahmed, Elizabeth Idris-Soven, and Mary K. Vaughan, editors
1978 *The World as a Company Town: Multinational Corporations and Social Change.* The Hague: Mouton; Chicago: Aldine.
Ifrah, Georges
1981 *From One to Zero.* Tr. by Lowell Blair. New York: Viking Penguin, 1985.

The Institute of Race Relations
   1982   *Patterns of Racism: Book Two*. London.
Jantsch, Erich
   1980   *The Self-Organizing Universe*. Oxford, New York, Toronto, Sidney, Paris, Frankfurt: Pergamon Press. The Systems Science and World Order Library, General Editor: Ervin Laszlo.
Jackson, T. A.
   1947   *Ireland Her Own: An Outline History of the Irish Struggle*. Ed. by C. Desmond Greaves. London: Lawrence & Wishart, 1976.
Jakobson, Roman
   1966   Two aspects of language and two types of aphasic disturbances. Jakobson and Halle, 1966, pp. 67–96.
   1972   Verbal communication. *Communication*. San Francisco: W. H. Freeman, pp. 39–44.
Jakobson, Roman, and Halle, Morris
   1966   *Fundamentals of Language*. The Hague: Mouton, 1971. Revision of 1956 edition.
Jonas, Gerald
   1983   Engineers come down to earth. *Science Digest*, October, pp. 90–1, 102.
Jordan, Z. A.
   1967   *The Evolution of Dialectical Materialism: A Philosophical and Sociological Analysis*. London, Bombay, Calcutta, Madras, Melbourne, and Toronto: Macmillan; New York: St Martin's Press.
Kahl, Joachim
   1968   *The Misery of Christianity*. Tr. by N. D. Smith. Harmondsworth, Middlesex: Penguin, 1971.
Kahn, Charles H.
   1968   Empedocles. *The Encyclopedia of Philosophy*. Ed. by Paul Edwards. New York and London: Macmillan/Collier Macmillan, vol. 1, pp. 496–9.
Kaplan, E. Ann, editor
   1978   *Women in Film Noir*. London: British Film Institute, 1980.
Kasanin, J. S., editor
   1944   *Language and Thought in Schizophrenia*. New York: Norton, 1964.
Kasner, Edward, and James Newman
   1940   *Mathematics and the Imagination*. With drawings and diagrams by Rufus Isaacs. New York: Simon & Schuster, 1949.
Keller, Evelyn Fox
   1983   *A Feeling for the Organism: The Life and Work of Barbara McClintock*. New York and San Francisco: W. H. Freeman.
Kepes, Gyorgy, editor
   1965   *Education of Vision*. Vision + Value Series. New York: Braziller.
   1966   *Sign Image Symbol*. Vision + Value Series. New York: Braziller.
Keynes, John Maynard
   1936   *The General Theory of Employment Interest and Money*. London, Melbourne, and Toronto: Macmillan, 1967.
Kimura, Doreen
   1973   The asymmetry of the human brain. *Scientific American*, 228/3, pp. 70–8.
Kline, Morris, editor
   1968   *Mathematics in the Modern World: Readings from Scientific American*. San Francisco: W. H. Freeman.
Kohl, Herbert
   1967   *36 Children*. With illustrations by R. G. Jackson, III. Harmondsworth, Middlesex: Penguin, 1972.

Kojève, Alexandre
  1947 *Introduction to the Reading of Hegel*. New York: Basic Books, 1968. [Selections from the French collection, edited by Raymond Queneau. Notes of lectures delivered in Paris in the 1930s.]
Koshland, Jr., D. E.
  1973 Protein shape and biological control. *Scientific American*, 229/4, pp. 52–64.
Koyré, Alexandre
  1957 *From the Closed World to the Infinite Universe*. New York: Harper Torchbooks, 1958.
Kracauer, Siegfried
  1927 The mass ornament. Tr. by Barbara Correll and Jack Zipes. *New German Critique*, no. 5, Spring 1975, pp. 67–76.
  1947 *From Caligari to Hitler: A Psychological History of the German Film*. With 56 stills. Princeton: Princeton Paperbacks
Kramer, Heinrich, and James Sprenger
  1486 *Malleus Maleficarum: The Hammer of the Witches*. Tr. with introduction, bibliography, and notes by the Rev. Montague Summers (1928). New York: Dover Books, 1971. With a new introduction (1948).
Kuhn, Thomas S.
  1962 *The Structure of Scientific Revolutions*. Chicago: University of Chicago Paperbacks, 1970. Second edition, enlarged. The International Encyclopedia of Unified Science, 2/2.
Lacan, Jacques, and Anthony Wilden
  1968 *Speech and Language in Psychoanalysis*. Baltimore: Johns Hopkins Paperbacks, 1981. Original title: *The Language of the Self*.
Laing, R. D.
  1960 *The Divided Self*. Harmondsworth, Middlesex: Penguin.
Lakoff, George, and Mark Johnson
  1980 *Metaphors We Live By*. Chicago and London: University of Chicago Paperbacks.
Lane, Michael, editor
  1970 *Introduction to Structuralism*. New York: Basic.
Langer, Susanne K.
  1942 *Philosophy in a New Key: A Study in the Symbolism of Reason, Rite, and Art*. Cambridge, Mass.: Harvard University Press; New York and Toronto: Mentor Books. Second edition, 1951.
  1962 *Philosophical Sketches*. A study of the human mind in relation to feeling, explored through art, language, and symbol. Baltimore: Johns Hopkins; New York: Mentor Books, 1964.
Lawrence, Vera Brodsky
  1975 *Music for Patriots, Politicians, and Presidents: Harmonies and Discords of the First Hundred Years*. New York and London: Macmillan/Collier Macmillan.
Leder, Philip
  1982 The genetics of antibody diversity. *Scientific American*, 245/5, pp. 102–15.
Lee, Richard, and Irven Devore, editors
  1968 *Man the Hunter*. Chicago: Aldine.
Leenhardt, Maurice
  1947 *Do Kamo: La personne et le mythe dans le monde mélanésien*. Paris: Gallimard.
Lenhard, Lane
  1983 The dynamic brain. *Science Digest* (December), pp. 65–7, 118–19.
Levinson, Stephen E., and Mark Y. Liberman
  1981 Speech recognition by computer. *Scientific American*, 244/4, pp. 64–76.

Lévi-Strauss, Claude
    1949 *The Elementary Structures of Kinship.* With a new introduction. Tr. by J. H.
          Bell, J. R. von Sturmer, and R. Needham. Boston: Beacon Press; London:
          Social Science Paperbacks, 1969. Second edition.
    1958 *Structural Anthropology.* Tr. by C. Jacobson and B. G. Schoepf. Garden City,
          N.Y.: Anchor, 1963.
    1962 *La Pensée sauvage.* Paris: Plon.
    1964 *Le Cru et le cuit.* Paris: Plon.
Lewin, Roger, editor
    1978 *Darwin's Forgotten World* [the Galapagos Islands]. Special photography by
          Sally Anne Thompson. With 189 color plates and an extract from Darwin's
          Voyage of the Beagle (1831–36). London: Bison; Los Angeles: Reed.
Lewis, Arthur O., Jr., editor
    1963 *Of Men and Machines.* New York: Dutton. [Readings from Karel Capek,
          Lewis Mumford, Ralph Waldo Emerson, Robert Frost, Walt Whitman, Sir
          Francis Bacon, Carl Sandburg, Adam Smith, Isaac Asimov, Samuel Butler,
          Stephen Crane, Emily Dickinson, Kurt Vonnegut Jr., Byron, Stephen Spender,
          Mark Twain, W. H. Auden, George Orwell, E. M. Forster, E. E. Cummings,
          Aldous Huxley, C. P. Snow, Ray Bradbury, and others.]
Lewontin, R. C., Steven Rose, and Leon J. Kamin
    1984 *Not In Our Genes: Biology, Ideology, and Human Nature.* New York:
          Pentheon.
Lipset, David
    1980 *Gregory Bateson: The Legacy of a Scientist.* Englewood Cliffs, N.J.: Prentice-
          Hall; Boston: Beacon Paperbacks, 1982.
Lovejoy, Arthur O.
    1936 *The Great Chain of Being.* Cambridge, Mass.: Harvard University Press, 1974.
    1948 *Essays in the History of Ideas.* New York: Capricorn, 1960.
Lovejoy, Arthur O., Gilbert Chinard, George Boas, and Ronald S. Crane, general editors
    1935 *Primitivism and Related Ideas in Antiquity.* Baltimore: Johns Hopkins. A
          Documentary History of Primitivism and Related Ideas, vol. I.
Lowen, Alexander, M.D.
    1967 *The Betrayal of the Body.* London: Collier.
Lukács, Georg
    1916 *The Theory of the Novel: A historico-philosophical essay on the forms of
          great epic literature.* Tr. from the German by Anna Bostock. London: Merlin;
          Cambridge, Mass.: MIT Press, 1971.
    1938 *Studies in European Realism.* Introduction by Alfred Kazin and a new preface
          (1948) by the author. New York: Grosset & Dunlap, The Universal Library,
          1964.
MacCannell, Dean, and Juliet MacCannell
    1983 *The Time of the Sign.* Bloomington, Indiana: Indiana University Press.
MacLean, Paul
    1973 *A Triune Concept of the Brain and Behaviour.* Toronto: University of Toronto
          Press.
McLuhan, Marshall
    1962 *The Gutenberg Galaxy: The Making of Typographic Man.* Toronto: University
          of Toronto Press. 1966.
McNeill, William H.
    1976 *Plagues and Peoples.* Garden City, N.Y.: Anchor.
    1982 *The Pursuit of Power: Technology, Armed Force, and Society since A.D. 1000.*
          Chicago: University of Chicago Press.

Maldonado, Tomas
   1970 *Environnement et idéologie (Vers une écologie critique)*. Tr. by Giovanni
        Joppolo from the Italian original by Einaudi. Paris: 10/18.
Mantoux, Paul
   1961 *The Industrial Revolution in the Eighteenth Century*. Tr. by Marjorie Vernon.
        London: Methuen, 1970. Revision of 1928 edition.
March, Lionel, and Philip Steadman
   1971 *The Geometry of Environment*. London: University Paperbacks, 1974.
Margalef, Ramon
   1968 *Perspectives in Ecological Theory*. Chicago: University of Chicago Press.
Margulis, Lynn
   1971 Symbiosis and evolution. *Scientific American*, 225/2, pp. 48–57.
   1981 Symbiosis and the evolution of the cell. *Encyclopaedia Britannica 1982 Year-
        book of Science and the Future*, 1981, pp. 104–21.
Marney, Milton C., and Nicholas M. Smith
   1964 The domain of adaptive systems: A rudimentary taxonomy. *General Systems
        Yearbook*, vol. 9, pp. 107–33.
Marshall, Herbert
   1983 *Masters of the Soviet Cinema: Crippled Creative Biographies*. London and
        Boston: Routledge & Kegan Paul.
Marshall, Herbert, editor
   1978 *Sergei Eisenstein's The Battleship Potemkin*. With a number of stills. New
        York: Avon.
Marx, Karl
   1844 *Economic and Philosophic Manuscripts of 1844*. Ed. by Dirk J. Struik, with
        an introduction and glossary. Tr. by Martin Milligan. New York: International
        Publishers, 1964.
   1847a *Misère de la philosophie: Réponse à la* Philosophie de la misère *de M.
        Proudhon*. Paris: 10/18, 1964. [Extracts from Proudhon followed by the orig-
        inal text of Marx.]
   1847b *The Poverty of Philosophy*. Introduction by Frederick Engels. New York:
        International Publishers, 1971. Corrected text of 1892. See also: Marx-Engels:
        Collected Works. New York: International Publishers, Volume 6 [1845–1848],
        1976, pp. 105–212.
   1956 *Selected Writings*. Tr. by Tom Bottomore. New York: McGraw-Hill.
Marx, Karl, and Frederick Engels
   1845 *The Holy Family, or Critique of Critical Criticism: Against Bruno Bauer and
        Company*. Marx-Engels *Collected Works*, vol. 4, pp. 3–211.
   1846 *The German Ideology*. London: Lawrence & Wishart, 1965.
   1959 *Basic Writings on Politics and Philosophy*. Ed. by Lewis S. Feuer. Garden City,
        N.Y.: Anchor.
Mason, Philip
   1971 *Patterns of Dominance*. London, Oxford, and New York: Oxford University
        Press.
Mast, Gerald
   1974 History of motion pictures. *Encyclopaedia Britannica* (15th edition), vol. 12,
        pp. 511–39.
Mast, Gerald, and Marshall Cohen
   1979 *Film Theory and Criticism: Introductory Readings*. New York and Oxford:
        Oxford University Paperbacks. Revision of 1974 edition.
Matthews, Robert W., and Janice R. Matthews
   1978 *Insect Behavior*. New York, Chichester, Brisbane, and Toronto: Wiley-
        Interscience.

Mauss, Marcel
    1925 *The Gift.* Tr. by Ian Cunnison. New York: Norton, 1967.
Mayr, Otto
    1969 *The Origins of Feedback Control.* Cambridge, Mass.: MIT Press, 1970.
Mazia, Daniel
    1974 The cell cycle. *Scientific American,* 230/1, pp. 55–64.
Meadows, Donella H., Dennis L. Meadows, Jorgen Randers, and William W. Behrens III
    1972 *The Limits to Growth: A Report for the Club of Rome's Project on the Predicament of Mankind.* New York, Washington, and London: Universe Books/Potomac Associates/Earth Island/The Club of Rome.
Memmi, Albert
    1957 *The Colonized and the Colonizer.* Tr. by Howard Greenfeld. Boston: Beacon Paperbacks, 1969.
Merchant, Carolyn
    1980 *The Death of Nature: Women, Ecology and the Scientific Revolution.* San Francisco: Harper & Row.
Moore, Jr., Barrington
    1966 *Social Origins of Dictatorship and Democracy.* Boston: Beacon Paperbacks; Harmondsworth, Middlesex: Penguin.
Morgan, Robin, editor
    1970 *Sisterhood is Powerful.* New York: Vintage.
Moscovici, Serge
    1972 *La Sociéte contre nature.* Paris: 10/18.
Mother Jones
    1979 *The Corporate Crime of the Century.* San Francisco. November issue.
Muller, John P., and William J. Richardson
    1982 *Lacan and Language: A Reader's Guide to Ecrits.* New York: International Universities Press.
Munitz, Milton K., editor
    1957 *Theories of the Universe: From Babylonian Myth to Modern Science.* New York: The Free Press, 1965. Library of Scientific Thought.
Murchie, Guy
    1954 *Song of the Sky: An Exploration of the Ocean of Air.* Illustrations by the author. Boston: Houghton Mifflin.
Myers, Denis
    n.d. *Secrets of the Stars.* London: Odhams.
Nathanson, James A., and Paul Greengard
    1977 'Second messengers' in the brain. *Scientific American,* 237/2, pp. 108–19.
Needham, Joseph
    1956 *Science and Civilisation in China.* Cambridge: Cambridge University Press. Volume two: *History of Scientific Thought.* With the assistance of Wang Ling.
Nelson, Benjamin
    1949 *The Idea of Usury: From Tribal Brotherhood to Universal Otherhood.* Chicago: University of Chicago Press, 1969. Second edition, enlarged.
Nelson, Joyce
    1983 As the brain tunes out, the TV admen tune in. *Common Ground,* Winter 1983–84, issue 5, pp. 38–9. Originally in the *Toronto Globe & Mail,* April 16, 1983.
The New Internationalist
    1984 *Economics in seven days: A short-cut through the book.* By Peter Stalker. Oxford: New Internationalist Publications, no. 134 (April). [Women do 66 per cent of the work in the world, but receive a mere 10 per cent of the income.]

Newton, Sir Isaac
1953 *Newton's Philosophy of Nature: Selections from his Writings.* Ed. and annotated by H. S. Thayer. Introduction by John Herman Randall, Jr. New York
and London: Macmillan/Collier Macmillan. The Hafner Library of Classics
Number Sixteen.
Nicholas of Cusa
1453 *The Vision of God, or The Icon.* Tr. by Emma Gurney Salter. New York:
Ungar, 1969.
Nichols, Bill, editor
1976 *Movies and Methods: An Anthology.* Berkeley and London: University of
California Press.
Nicolaus, Martin
1972 The unknown Marx. Blackburn, ed., 1972, pp. 306–33.
Norman, Donald A.
1982 *Learning and Memory.* San Francisco: W. H. Freeman.
Norris, John
1692 *A Collection of Miscellanies.* London. Second edition.
Northrop, F. S. C., and Helen H. Livingston, editors
1964 *Cross-Cultural Understanding: Epistemology in Anthropology.* New York,
Evanston, and London: Harper & Row.
W. W. Norton, publishers
1979 *The Norton Anthology of English Literature: Volume 2: The Romantic Period,
the Victorian Age, and the Twentieth Century.* Ed. by M. H. Abrams, George
H. Ford, and David Daiches. New York and London. Fourth edition.
Novick, Richard P.
1980 Plasmids. *Scientific American,* 243/6, pp. 103–27.
Ogden, C. K.
1932 *Opposition: A Linguistic and Psychological Analysis.* Introduction by I. A.
Richards. Bloomington and London: Indiana University Press; New York:
Midland Books, 1967.
Oldendorf, William H., and William Zabielski
1982 Liquid lightning in your nerves. *Science Digest,* May, pp. 82–3, 116.
Orwell, George
1946 The prevention of literature. *Inside the Whale and Other Essays.* Harmond-
sworth, Middlesex: Penguin, 1979, pp. 159–75.
1946 Politics and the English language. *Inside the Whale and Other Essays.*
Harmondsworth, Middlesex: Penguin, 1979, pp. 143–58.
Padover, Saul K.
1978 *Karl Marx: An Intimate Biography.* New York: Mentor. Abridged edition,
1980.
Paine, Thomas
1791 *The Rights of Man.* With a biographical introduction by Philip S. Foner.
Secaucus, N.J.: Citadel Press, 1948, 1974.
Pascal, Gabriel
1670 *Pensées.* In *Oeuvres complètes.* Ed. by Jacques Chevalier. Paris: Pléïade, 1954,
pp. 1079–1345.
Pattee, H. H., editor
1973 *Hierarchy Theory: The Challenge of Complex Systems.* New York: Braziller.
[Includes important articles by Clifford Grobstein and Herbert A. Simon.]
Peirce, Charles Sanders
1940 *Philosophical Writings of Peirce.* Ed. by Justus Buchler. London: Routledge
and Kegan Paul; New York: Dover, 1955.

Piaget, Jean
    1968 *Structuralism*. Tr. and ed. by Chaninah Maschler. New York: Basic Books, 1970.
Piattelli-Palmarini, Massimo, editor
    1980 *Language and Learning: The [1975] Debate between Jean Piaget and Noam Chomsky*. Cambridge, Mass.: Harvard University Press.
Pickhardt, Irene
    1983 Sexist piglets: Studies show that sex-stereotyping is part of childhood. *Parents* (December), pp. 32–8.
Pietsch, Paul
    1983 The mind of a microbe: Can thought occur where no brain is found? *Science Digest* (October), pp. 68–72, 104.
Pimentel, David, et al.
    1973 Food production and the energy crisis. *Science*, vol. 182, pp. 443–9.
Platt, John
    1970a Hierarchical restructuring. *General Systems Yearbook*, vol. 15, pp. 46–54.
    1970b *Perception and Change*. Ann Arbor: University of Michigan Press.
Pollard, Sidney
    1968 *The Idea of Progress*. Harmondsworth, Middlesex: Penguin.
Polunin, N., editor
    1972 *The Environmental Future*. London: Macmillan.
Polyani, Karl
    1944 *The Great Transformation*. Foreword by Robert M. MacIver. New York and Toronto: Farrar & Rinehart.
Polyani, Karl, Conrad M. Arensberg, and Harry W. Pearson, editors
    1957 *Trade and Market in the Early Empires: Economies in History and Theory*. Chicago: Henry Regnery, 1971.
Porta, Giambattista della
    1589 *Natural Magick* [1558–89]. New York: Basic Books, 1965. Facsimile of the English translation of 1658.
Postman, Neil
    1979 *Teaching as a Conserving Activity*. New York: Delacorte.
Postman, Neil, and Charles Weingartner
    1971 *Teaching as a Subversive Activity*. New York: Delta; Harmondsworth, Middlesex: Penguin.
Priestley, Joseph
    1762 *The Theory of Language and Universal Grammar*. Farnborough, Hants.: Gregg International Publishers, 1971. Facsimile edition.
Prigogine, Ilya
    1980 *From Being to Becoming: Time and Complexity in the Physical Sciences*. San Francisco: W. H. Freeman.
Prigogine, Ilya, and Isabelle Stengers
    1979 *La Nouvelle alliance: Métamorphose de la science*. Paris: Gallimard.
Rambusch, E. J. C.
    1881 Visual signalling. *Journal of the Royal United Service Institution*, vol. 25, no. 112, pp. 614–37. Scheips, ed., 1980.
Ramsaye, Terry
    1926 *A Million and One Nights: The History of the Motion Picture*. New York: Simon & Schuster.
Ranelagh, John
    1981 *Ireland: An Illustrated History*. London: Collins.
Rappaport, Roy A.
    1968 *Pigs for the Ancestors*. New Haven, Conn.: Yale Paperbacks.

1971a The flow of energy in an agricultural society. *Scientific American*, 225/3, pp. 116–32. Also in *Energy and Power*. San Francisco: W. H. Freeman, 1971.

1971b Nature, culture, and ecological anthropology. *Man, Culture and Society*. Ed. by Harry L. Shapiro. Oxford: Oxford University Press. Only in the second edition.

Read, Herbert

1964 *The Philosophy of Modern Art*. London: Faber & Faber.

Richards, Paul W.

1973 The tropical rainforest. *Scientific American*, 229/6, pp. 58–67.

Rifkin, Jeremy, with Ted Howard

1980 *Entropy: A New World View*. Afterword by Nicholas Georgescu-Roegen. New York: Bantam, 1981.

Rius

1976 *Marx for Beginners*. London: Writers and Readers Publishing Co-operative; New York: Two Continents.

Rosen, Marjorie

1974 *Popcorn Venus: Women, Movies, and the American Dream*. New York: Avon.

Rosenblum, Ralph, and Robert Karen

1979 *When the Shooting Stops . . . the Cutting Begins: A Film Editor's Story*. New York: Viking, 1979; Harmondsworth, Middlesex: Penguin, 1980.

Rosenfield, Israel, Edward Ziff, and Borin Van Loon

1984 *DNA for Beginners*. London and New York: A Writers and Readers Documentary Comic Book.

Rosten, Leo

1968 *The Joys of Yiddish*. New York: Pocket Books.

1982 *Hooray for Yiddish! A Book About English*. New York: Touchstone.

Ruchames, Louis, editor

1969 *Racial Thought in America: Volume 1: From the Puritans to Abraham Lincoln: A Documentary History*. New York: Grosset & Dunlap's Universal Library.

Ruesch, Jurgen, and Gregory Bateson

1951 *Communication: The Social Matrix of Psychiatry*. With a new preface. New York: Norton, 1968.

Russell, Bertrand

1959 *Wisdom of the West*. With 313 pages of illustrations in b&w and color. New York: Crescent Books, 1977.

Sahlins, Marshall

1972 *Stone Age Economics*. Chicago: Aldine.

Salthouse, Timothy A.

1984 The skill of typing. *Scientific American*, 250/2, pp. 128–35.

Sambursky, S.

1954 *The Physical World of the Greeks*. Tr. from the Hebrew by Merton Dagut. London: Routledge & Kegan Paul, 1963.

Sambursky, S., editor

1974 *Physical Thought from the Presocratics to the Quantum Physicists: An Anthology*. New York: Pica.

Sartre, Jean-Paul

1937 *The Transcendence of the Ego*. Tr. by F. Williams and R. Kirkpatrick. New York: Noonday, 1957.

1939 Une idée fondamentale de Husserl. *Situations I*. Paris: Gallimard, 1947, pp. 31–5.

1946 *Anti-Semite and Jew (Réflexions sur la question juive)*. Tr. by George J. Becker. New York: Schocken Books, 1948, 1968.

1964 *The Words*. Tr. by Bernard Frechtman. New York: Braziller, 1964; Greenwich, Conn.: Fawcett Premier Books, 1968.

Saussure, Ferdinand de
  1916 *Course in General Linguistics.* Ed. by Charles Bally, Albert Sechehaye, and Albert Riedlinger. Tr. by Wade Baskin. New York: McGraw-Hill, 1966.
Sayre, Kenneth M., and Frederick J. Crosson, editors
  1963 *The Modeling of Mind: Computers and Intelligence.* New York: Clarion, 1968.
Schapiro, Mark
  1982 Seeds of disaster. *Mother Jones* (December), pp. 11–15, 36–7. [The reduction of the genetic diversity of world seed stocks by commercial exploitation.]
Schatzman, Morton
  1974 *Soul Murder: Persecution in the Family.* New York: Signet. [The definitive refutation of Freud's theory of paranoia (1911), which was based on his reading of Dr Daniel Paul Schreber's *Memoirs of my Nervous Illness* (1903).]
Scheips, Paul J., editor
  1980 *Military Signal Communications.* New York: Arno Press. Two volumes. Historical Studies in Telecommunications.
Schmandt-Besserat, Denise
  1978 The earliest precursor of writing. *Scientific American,* 238/6, pp. 50–9.
Schon, Donald A.
  1963 *Invention and the Evolution of Ideas.* London and New York: Tavistock/Methuen; Social Science Paperbacks.
Schreber, Daniel Paul
  1903 *Memoirs of my Nervous Illness.* Translated and edited, with introduction, notes, and discussion, by Ida Macalpine and Richard A. Hunter. London: Wm. Dawson, 1955.
Schwartz, Bernard
  1974 *The American Heritage History of the Law in America.* New York: American Heritage Publishing Co.
Scientific American Books
  1970 *The Biosphere.* San Francisco: W. H. Freeman.
  1971 *Energy and Power.* San Francisco: W. H. Freeman.
  1972 *Communication.* San Francisco: W. H. Freeman.
  1978 *Evolution. Scientific American,* 239/3 (September). Special issue.
  1982a *The Mechanization of Work. Scientific American,* 247/3 (September). Special issue.
  1982b *Human Communication: Language and its Psychobiological Bases.* San Francisco: W. H. Freeman.
Sebeok, Thomas A., editor
  1960 *Style in Language.* Cambridge, Mass.: MIT Press. [Articles by Dell Hymes, Roman Jakobson, George A. Miller, Charles E. Osgood, I. A. Richards, René Wellek, and others.]
Selsam, Howard, and Harry Martel
  1963 *Reader in Marxist Philosophy.* New York: International Publishers, 1968.
Service, Elman R.
  1971 *Profiles in Ethnology.* New York: Harper & Row, 1971. Revised version of 1958 and 1963 editions.
Shannon, Claude E., and Warren Weaver
  1949 *The Mathematical Theory of Communication.* Urbana: University of Illinois Press, 1964.
Shapiro, Evelyn, and Barry Shapiro, editors
  1979 *The Women Say/The Men Say: Women's Liberation and Men's Consciousness: Issues in Politics, Work, Family, Sexuality, and Power.* New York: Delta.
Shepard, Paul, and Daniel McKinley, editors
  1969 *The Subversive Science: Essays toward an Ecology of Man.* Boston: Houghton Mifflin.

Shepherd, Gordon M.
  1978 Microcircuits in the nervous system. *Scientific American*, 238/2, pp. 98–103.
Shurkin, Joel
  1984 *Engines of the Mind: A History of the Computer*. New York, W. W. Norton.
Simonis, Yvan
  1983 L'Anthropologie dans la stratégie. Simonis, ed., 1983, pp. 97–114.
Simonis, Yvan, editor
  1983 *Guerres et Stratégies*. Special issue of *Anthropologie et Sociétés*, vol. 7, no. 1.
Sloane-Evans, William Sloane
  1854 *A Grammar of British Heraldry, Or The Art of Blazon*. London: J. R. Smith. Second edition.
Sluzki, Carlos E., and Donald C. Ransom, editors
  1976 *Double Bind: The Foundation of the Communicational Approach to the Family*. New York: Grune & Stratton.
Smith, Alfred G., editor
  1966 *Communication and Culture: Readings in the Codes of Human Interaction*. New York, Toronto, and London: Holt, Rinehart & Winston.
Smith, John Maynard, editor
  1982 *Evolution Now: A Century after Darwin*. In association with *Nature*. San Francisco: W. H. Freeman, 1983.
Smith, Whitney
  1975 *Flags through the Ages and Across the World*. With more than 2250 illustrations, mostly in color. New York, St Louis, San Francisco, Auckland, Johannesburg, Kuala Lumpur, London, Montreal, New Delhi, Sao Paulo, Singapore, Sydney, Toronto: McGraw-Hill.
Spender, Dale
  1982 *Women of Ideas (and What Men Have Done to Them)*. London and Boston: Routledge & Kegan Paul; Ark Paperbacks, 1983.
Springer, Sally P., and Georg Deutsch
  1985 *Left Brain, Right Brain*. San Francisco: W. H. Freeman. Second edition.
Stanton, Elizabeth Cady
  1895 *The Woman's Bible*. Published in New York by the Arno Press in 1974 as *The Original Feminist Attack on the Bible*.
Stearns, Forrest W., and Tom Montag
  1974 *The Urban Ecosystem: A Holistic Approach*. The Institute of Ecology/National Science Foundation (Research Applied to National Needs). Stroudsburg, Pa.: Dowden, Hutchinson & Ross; New York: Halsted Press/John Wiley.
Sterne, Lawrence
  1767 *The Life and Opinions of Tristram Shandy, Gentleman*. Ed. and annotated by James Aiken Work. New York: Odyssey, 1940.
Stone, Lawrence
  1977 *The Family, Sex and Marriage in England 1500–1800*. New York, Hagerstown, San Francisco, and London: Harper & Row.
Stover, Leon E.
  1974 *The Cultural Ecology of Chinese Civilization: Peasants and Elites in the Last of the Agrarian States*. New York: Mentor.
Storey, Donald R., and J. Anthony Boeckh
  1974 Kondratieff and the supercycle: Deflation or runaway inflation? *The Bank Credit Analyst* (October), pp. 12–38.
Sullivan, J. W. N.
  1933 *The Limitations of Science*. New York: Mentor, 1952.
Summers, Anne
  1975 *Damned Whores and God's Police: The Colonization of Women in Australia*. Harmondsworth, Middlesex: Penguin, 1980.

Sweezy, Paul M.
    1942 *The Theory of Capitalist Development.* New York and London: Modern Reader Paperbacks, 1968.
Taber, Robert
    1965 *The War of the Flea: Guerrilla Warfare Theory and Practice.* London: Paladin, 1970. Updated 1969.
Tannahill, Reay
    1980 *Sex in History.* New York: Stein and Day.
Thomas, Lewis
    1974 *Lives of a Cell.* New York: Bantam, 1980.
Thompson, E. P.
    1963 *The Making of the English Working Class.* New York: Pantheon/Vintage Books, 1966.
Thornhill, Randy
    1980 Sexual selection of the black-tipped hangingfly. *Scientific American* (June), pp. 162–72.
Tributsch, Helmut
    1982 *How Life Learned to Live: Adaptation in Nature.* Cambridge, Mass.: MIT Press.
Tuchman, Barbara W.
    1958 *The Zimmerman Telegram.* New York: Ballantine, 1979. New edition 1966.
    1978 *A Distant Mirror: The Calamitous 14th Century.* With maps and illustrations. New York: Alfred A. Knopf, 1979.
Turim, Maureen
    1981 Symmetry/asymmetry and visual fascination. With a number of film stills. *Wide Angle,* 4/3, pp. 38–47. [Includes an analysis of the 'spectacular symmetries' of thirties dance films.]
Turner, Victor
    1974 *Dramas, Fields, and Metaphors.* Ithaca and London: Cornell University Press.
Tustin, Arnold
    1952 Feedback. *Scientific American,* 187, pp. 48–55.
Uexküll, Jakob von
    1934 *Mondes animaux et monde humain, suivi de Théorie de la signification* [1940]. Illustrated by George Kriszat. Tr. by Philippe Muller. Paris: Gonthier, 1965.
Université Libre de Bruxelles
    1963 *Problèmes d'une sociologie du roman. Revue de l'Institut de Sociologie.* [Articles by Lucien Goldmann, George Lukacs, René Girard, Nathalie Sarraute, Alain Robbe-Grillet, and others.]
Unwin, Nigel
    1984 The structure of proteins in biological membranes. *Scientific American,* 250/2, pp. 78–94.
Ure, Andrew
    1861 *The Philosophy of Manufactures.* London. Expanded version of the 1830 edition, by P. L. Simmonds.
Van Heijenoort, John
    1967 Logical paradoxes. Edwards, Paul, ed., 1967, vol. 5, pp. 45–51.
Vayda, Andrew, editor
    1969 *Environment and Cultural Behavior: Ecological Studies in Cultural Anthropology.* American Museum Sourcebooks in Anthropology. Garden City, N.Y.: The Natural History Press.
Vidal, Gonzalo
    1984 The oldest eukaryotic cells [cells with nuclei]. *Scientific American,* 250/2, pp. 48–57.

Voloshinov, V. N.
   1929   *Marxism and the Philosophy of Language*. Tr. by Ladislav Matejka and I. R.
         Titunik. New York and London: Seminar Press, 1973.
von Foerster, Heinz
   1980   Epistemology of communication. In Woodward, ed., 1980, pp. 18–27.
von Neumann, John
   1958   *The Computer and the Brain*. New Haven: Yale University Press, 1967.
Vuong, Thanh H.
   1984   *Un modèle cogitif et décisionnel de fabrication des stratégies de changement*.
         Québec: Université Laval. Unpublished Ph.D thesis.
Vygotsky, L. S.
   1938   *Thought and Language*. Ed. and trans. by E. Haufman and G. Vakar.
         Cambridge, Mass.: MIT Press, 1962.
Wallerstein, Immanuel
   1976   *The Modern World System: Capitalist Agriculture and the Origins of the
         European World Economy in the Sixteenth Century*. New York and London:
         Academic Press. Text edition.
Warshaw, Tessa Albert
   1980   *Winning by Negotiation*. New York: Berkley Books, 1981.
Warusfel, André
   1969   *Les Mathématiques modernes*. Paris: Le Seuil.
Watson, James D.
   1968   *The Double Helix: A Personal Account of the Discovery of the Structure of
         DNA*. Harmondsworth, Middlesex: Penguin, 1971.
Watzlawick, Paul
   1976   *How Real is Real? Confusion, Disinformation, Communication*. New York:
         Vintage, 1977.
Watzlawick, Paul, Janet Beavin, and Don D. Jackson
   1966   *The Pragmatics of Human Communication: A Study of Interactional Patterns,
         Pathologies, and Paradoxes*. New York: Norton; Toronto: George J. McLeod.
Weibel, Kathryn
   1977   *Mirror, Mirror: Images of Women Reflected in Popular Culture*. Garden City,
         N.Y.: Anchor.
Weiss, Paul A., et al.
   1971   *Hierarchically Organized Systems in Theory and Practice*. New York: Hafner.
White, George Abbott, and Charles Newman, editors
   1972   *Literature in Revolution*. New York, Chicago, and San Francisco: Holt, Rine-
         hart and Winston.
White, Morton
   1955   The decline and fall of the absolute. *The Age Of Analysis: 20th Century
         Philosophers*. Boston: Houghton Mifflin; New York: Mentor Books, 1963,
         pp. 13–21.
White, Jr., Lynn
   1962   *Medieval Technology and Social Change*. London, Oxford, and New York:
         Oxford University Paperbacks, 1976.
Whorf, Benjamin Lee
   1956   *Language, Thought and Reality: Selected Writings*. Ed. by John B. Carroll.
         Cambridge, Mass.: MIT Press, 1966.
Whyte, Lancelot Law
   1960   *The Unconscious Before Freud*. Garden City, N.Y.: Anchor, 1962.
   1965   Atomism, structure and form. *Structure in Art and in Science*. Ed. by Gyorgy
         Kepes. New York: Braziller, pp. 20–8.
Wickler, Wolfgang
   1968   *Mimicry in Plants and Animals*. With numerous illustrations, many in color.

Tr. by R. D. Martin. New York and Toronto: McGraw-Hill. World University Library.

Widgery, David
  1983 Reclaiming Orwell. Aubrey and Chilton, eds., pp. 15–23. [An exposé of Orwell's elitism and defeatism in *Nineteen Eighty-Four*.]

Wiener, Norbert
  1948 *Cybernetics: Or Control and Communication in the Animal and the Machine*. Cambridge, Mass.: MIT Press, 1969.
  1950 *The Human Use of Human Beings: Cybernetics and Society*. Garden City, N.Y.: Anchor, 1954. Second edition.

Wilden, Anthony
  1953 Flea market. *The Outlook*, no. 14, p. 25.
  1965 An editorial. *The Stag* (Summer).
  1966a Jacques Lacan: A partial bibliography. *Yale French Studies*, vol. 36–7, pp. 263–8. Also in: *Structuralism*. Ed. by Jacques Ehrmann. New York: Anchor, 1970, pp. 253–60.
  1966b Freud, Signorelli, and Lacan: The repression of the signifier. *American Imago*, vol. 23, pp. 332–66.
  1968 *Par divers moyens on arrive à pareille fin*: A reading of Montaigne. *Modern Language Notes*, vol. 83, pp. 577–97.
  1969a Death, desire, and repetition in Svevo's *Coscienza di Zeno*. *Modern Language Notes*, vol. 84, pp. 98–119.
  1969b Marcuse and the Freudian model: Energy, information, and *Phantasie*. *Salmagundi*, vol. 10–11, pp. 196–245. Also in: *The Legacy of the German Refugee Intellectuals*. Ed. by Robert Boyers. New York: Schocken, 1972.
  1970 Montaigne's *Essays* in the context of communication. *Modern Language Notes*, vol. 85, pp. 454–78.
  1971a Review of O. Mannoni: *Freud*. *Psychology Today* (August), pp. 8, 12.
  1971b Epistemology and the biosocial crisis: The difference that makes a difference. *Coping with Increasing Complexity*. Ed. by D. E. Washburn and D. R. Smith. New York: Gordon & Breach, 1974, pp. 249–70.
  1971c Review of Piaget: *Structuralism*. *Psychology Today* (October), pp. 10, 13.
  1972a L'Ecriture et le bruit dans la morphogénèse du système ouvert. *Communications*, vol. 18, pp. 48–71. Special Issue: *L'Evénement*, ed. by Edgar Morin.
  1972b Libido as language: The structuralism of Jacques Lacan. *Psychology Today*, vol. 5, no. 12 (May), pp. 40–2, 85–9.
  1972c Analog and digital communication: On negation, signification, and the emergence of the discrete element. *Semiotica*, vol. 6, no. 1, pp. 50–82.
  1972d Structuralism, communication, and evolution. *Semiotica*, vol. 6, no. 3, pp. 244–56.
  1972e On Lacan: Psychoanalysis, language, and communication. *Contemporary Psychoanalysis*, vol. 9, no. 4, pp. 445–70.
  1972f Review of Leiss: *The Domination of Nature*. *Psychology Today* (October), pp. 28, 30, 32.
  1972g *System and Structure: Essays in Communication and Exchange*. London: Tavistock. London & New York: Social Science Paperbacks, 1977.
  1973a Ecology and ideology. Idris-Soven and Vaughan, eds., 1978, pp. 73–98.
  1973b Review of Bateson: *Steps to an Ecology of Mind*. *Psychology Today* (November), pp. 138, 140.
  1974 Ecosystems and economic systems. *Cultures of the Future*. Ed. by M. Maruyama and Arthur Harkins (Ninth Congress of Anthropological and Ethnological Sciences) (*World Anthropology Series*) The Hague: Mouton; Chicago: Aldine, 1978, pp. 101–24.

1975a Piaget and the structure as law and order. *Structure and Transformation: Developmental Aspects.* Ed. by Klaus F. Riegel and George L. Rosenwald. (*Origins of Behavior Series*) New York: Wiley, pp. 83–117.

1975b The scientific discourse: Knowledge as a commodity. Illustrated in b&w. *MAYDAY,* vol. 1, no. 1, pp. 69–77.

1975c Ecology, ideology, and political economy. Burnaby, B.C.: Simon Fraser University. Unpublished ms., xeroxed.

1976a Changing frames of order: Cybernetics and the *machina mundi.* Woodward, ed., 1979, pp. 219–41.

1976b *Communication in Context: A Systems Perspective.* Burnaby, B.C.: Simon Fraser University. Unpublished ms., xeroxed.

1978 Communicazione. *Enciclopedia Einaudi,* vol. 3, pp. 601–95.

1979a Informazione. *Enciclopedia Einaudi,* vol. 7, pp. 562–628.

1979b Culture and identity: The Canadian question, *Why? Ciné-Tracts,* vol. 2, no. 2, pp. 1–27.

1979c *Le Canada imaginaire.* Tr. by Yvan Simonis. Québec: Presses Coméitex.

1980a *The Imaginary Canadian.* Vancouver: Pulp Press.

1980b *System and Structure: Second Edition.* London: Tavistock; New York: Methuen. Social Science Paperbacks. With a new introduction and critical notes.

1980c *Greetings from Canada.* Six broadsheets. Printed for the author by Pulp Press, Vancouver.

1981a Semiotics as praxis: Strategy and tactics. *Recherches sémiotiques/Semiotic Inquiry,* vol. 1, no. 1, pp. 1–34. [This article was the plan for what became *The Rules Are No Game* and *Man and Woman, War and Peace.*]

1981b Ideology and the icon: Oscillation, contradiction, and paradox. An essay in context theory. *Iconicity: The Nature of Culture. Essays in Honor of Thomas Sebeok.* Ed. by Paul Bouissac, Michael Herzfeld, and Roland Posner. Tübingen: Stauffenberg Verlag, 1986, pp. 251–302.

1982a Postscript to 'Semiotics as Praxis: Strategy and Tactics'. *RSSI,* vol. 2, no. 2, pp. 166–70.

1982b *I Want Out: A Pictorial Supplement to The 20th Century War: 1880–1982.* Burnaby, B.C.: Simon Fraser University. Xeroxed.

1983a *Système et structure: Essais sur la communication et l'échange.* Tr. by Georges Khal. Montréal: Boréal Express [5450 ch. de la Côte-des-Neiges, Montréal, Qué., H3T 1Y6]; Paris: Distique [9, rue Edouard-Jacques, 75014, Paris]. Revised edition of Wilden 1980, with two new chapters.

1983b Teaching Media Literacy. *Symposium on Interdisciplinary Aspects of Academic Disciplines.* Bellingham. Wash.: Western Washington University, pp. 335–48.

1983c La Guerre du 20e siècle et Penser la stratégie. Tr. by Yvan Simonis. *Anthropologie et Sociétés:* 'Guerres et Stratégies', vol 7, no 1, pp. 3–38.

1984a Montage analytic and dialectic. *American Journal of Semiotics,* 3/1, pp. 25–47.

1984b In the penal colony: The body as the discourse of the Other. *Semiotica,* 54-1/2 (1985), pp. 33–85. Special issue on violence edited by Nancy Armstrong.

1985 Context theory: The new science. *RSSI,* 5/2 (1986), pp. 97–116.

1987 *Man and Women, War and Peace: The Strategist's Companion.* London and New York: Routledge & Kegan Paul.

Wilden, Anthony, and Tim Wilson

1976 The double bind: Logic, magic, and economics. *Double Bind: The Foundation of the Communicational Approach to the Family.* Ed. by C. E. Sluzki and D. C. Ransom. New York: Grune & Stratton, pp. 263–86.

Wilson, Edward O.
  1972 Animal communication. *Communication*. San Francisco: W. H. Freeman, pp. 29–36.
Winkin, Yves, editor
  1981 *La Nouvelle Communication*. Paris: Seuil. [G. Bateson, R. Birdwhistell, E. Goffman, E. T. Hall, D. Jackson, A. Scheflen, S. Sigman, and P. Watzlawick.]
Witherspoon, Alexander M., and Frank J. Warnke, editors
  1963 *Seventeenth-Century Prose and Poetry*. New York: Harcourt, Brace & World. Second edition.
Witte, Karsten
  1975 Introduction to Siegfried Kracauer's 'The mass ornament'. Trans. by Barbara Correll and Jack Zipes. *New German Critique*, no. 5, pp. 59–66.
Wolfe, Martin, editor
  1972 *The Economic Causes of Imperialism*. New York: Wiley.
Woodward, John, and George Burnett
  1892 *A Treatise on Heraldry*. Edinburgh and London: W. & A. K. Johnston. Two volumes.
Woodward, Kathleen, editor
  1979 *The Myths of Information: Technology and Postindustrial Culture*. Madison, Wisc.: Coda Press; London: Routledge & Kegan Paul.
Zaretsky, Eli
  1976 *Capitalism, the Family and Personal Life*. New York: Harper & Row.

Part D: Reference works

Allègre, Christian, Michel Bélair, Michel Chevrier, Georges Khal, and Michel St-Germain
  1977 *Le Répertoire québécois des outils planétaires*. Montréal: Editions Alternatives/ Editions Mainmise; Paris: Flammarion.
Anon
  1860 *A New Dictionary of Quotations from the Greek, Latin, and Modern Languages. Translated into English, and Occasionally Accompanied with Illustrations, Historical, Poetical, and Anecdotal*. Philadelphia: J. B. Lippincott. From the last London edition.
Auden, W. H., and Louis Kronenberger
  1962 *The Faber Book of Aphorisms*. London: Faber and Faber.
Baden-Powell, Robert
  1932 *Scouting for Boys. A Handbook for Instruction in Good Citizenship*. Norwich: Fletcher & Son, 1980. New edition.
Bartlett, John, compiler
  1882 *Familiar Quotations*. New York: Blue Ribbon Books, 1919 (10th edition); New York and Toronto: Little, Brown and Co., 1955 (13th edition); New York and Toronto: Little, Brown and Co., 1968 (14th edition).
Barraclough, Geoffrey, editor
  1979 *The Times Atlas of World History*. London: Times Books
  1982 *The Times Concise Atlas of World History*. London: Times Books. Completely revised.
Bartholomew, John
  1944 *The Comparative Atlas of Physical and Political Geography*. London: Meiklejohn & Son. 32nd edition.

Brand, Stewart, editor
 1974 *Whole Earth Epilog: Access to Tools*. New York and Harmondsworth, Middlesex: Penguin.
 1981 *The Next Whole Earth Catalog: Access to Tools*. New York and Toronto: Random House.
Brennan, Joseph G.
 1961 *A Handbook of Logic*. New York and London: Harper & Row. Second edition.
Brewer, The Rev. E. Cobham
 1870 *The Dictionary of Phrase and Fable, Giving the Derivation, Source, or Origin of Common Phrases, Allusions, and Words that have a Tale to Tell*. New York: Avenel Books, 1978.
Brooks, Tim, and Earle Marsh
 1981 *The Complete Directory to Prime-Time Network TV Shows 1946–present*. New York: Ballantine. Revised edition.
Buck, Carl Darling
 1949 *A Dictionary of Selected Synonyms in the Principal Indo-European Languages: A Contribution to the History of Ideas*. With the co-operation of colleagues and assistants. Chicago and London: University of Chicago Press, 1971.
Bullock, Alan, and Oliver Stallybrass, editors
 1977 *The Fontana Dictionary of Modern Thought*. London: Fontana/Collins. US title: *A Dictionary of 20th Century Culture*.
Burnam, Tom
 1975 *The Dictionary of Misinformation*. New York: Ballantine.
Burton, Philip Ward
 1974 *Advertising Copywriting*. Columbus, Ohio: Grid. Inc. Third edition.
Byrne and Spon, editors
 1874 *Spons' Dictionary of Engineering, Civil, Mechanical, Military, and Naval*. With hundreds of technical drawings and technical terms in French, German, Italian, and Spanish. London and New York: E. & F. N. Spon. Three volumes plus Supplement.
The Canadian Union of Public Employees
 1982 The hazards of video display terminals. *The Facts*, April. [Condensed version of the full report.]
Carnegie Steel Co., publisher
 1930 *Carnegie Pocket Companion, Abridged Edition: Information and Tables for Engineers and Designers and other Data Pertaining to Structural Steel Manufactured by Carnegie Steel Company, Subsidiary of United States Steel Corporation*. Pittsburgh.
Carter, E. F.
 1966 *Dictionary of Inventions and Discoveries*. London: Frederick Muller. Second revised edition 1974: Stevenage, Herts.: Robin Clark: 1978.
Casagrande, Bob
 1982 *Better Black-and-White Darkroom Techniques*. Master Class Photography Series. Englewood Cliffs, N.J.: Prentice-Hall.
Cassell, Peter, Galpin & Co., publishers
 1885 *Cassell's Illustrated History of England: New and Revised Edition*. From the earliest period to the passing of the Franchise Bill (1884). London, Paris, and New York. Ten volumes.
Cavendish, Marshall, publisher
 1978 *The How It Works Encyclopedia of Great Inventors & Discoveries*. With hundreds of illustrations, many in color. London, 1982.
Chevalier, Jean, and Alain Gheerbrant, editors
 1969 *Dictionnaire des symboles*. Mythes, rêves, coutûmes, gestes, formes, figures,

couleurs, nombres. With numerous illustrations. Paris: Seghers, 1973. Four volumes.

Cirlot, J. E.
1962 *A Dictionary of Symbols.* With 32 plates and numerous illustrations in the text. Foreword by Herbert Read. Tr. by Jack Sage. London: Routledge & Kegan Paul; New York: Philosophical Library.

Coe, Richard M.
1981 *Form and Substance: An Advanced Rhetoric.* New York: Wiley.

Cohen, J. M., and M. J. Cohen, editors
1960 *The Penguin Dictionary of Quotations.* Harmondsworth, Middlesex: Penguin, 1967.

Cole, Stephen, editor
n.d. *For Your Eyes Only: An Open Intelligence Summary of Current Military Affairs.* Amarillo, Tex.: Tiger Publications [P.O. Box 8759]. Bimonthly.

Colombo, John Robert, editor
1974 *Colombo's Canadian Quotations.* Edmonton, Alta.: Hurtig Publishers.

Correspondence Education Branch
n.d. *English for Adults II.* Victoria, B.C.: B.C. Ministry of Education.

Darby, H. C., and Harold Fullard, editors
1970 *The New Cambridge Modern History Atlas.* Cambridge and New York: Cambridge University Press, 1978. Corrected reprint.

Davidoff, Henry
1942 *The Pocket Book of Quotations.* New York: Cardinal Books, 1953.

Dick, William Brisbane
1873 *Dick's One Hundred Amusements for Evening Parties, Picnics, and Social Gatherings, containing New and Attractive Parlor Games, clearly Illustrated by means of Witty Examples showing how each may be most successfully played. Surprising Tricks, easy of performance. Musical and other Innocent Sells. Comical Illusions fully described, very startling in their effects, and presenting little or no difficulty in their preparation. A variety of new and ingenious Puzzles.* With over 50 illustrations. New York: Something Else Press/ Joyous Harper Books, 1967. Facsimile edition.

Dickson, Paul
1982 *Words: A Connoisseur's Collection of Old and New, Weird and Wonderful, Useful and Outlandish Words.* Illustrated with photographs and drawings. New York: Delacorte.

Dunnigan, James F.
1982 *How To Make War. A Comprehensive Guide to Modern Warfare.* New York: William Morrow.

The Economics Press, Inc.
n.d. *How to Communicate Ideas.* From the book by Richard Borden *Public Speaking as Listeners Like It* (1935). Fairfield, N.J. Supplied by *Front Line Management* in 1982.
1977 *How to Dream Up Dollar-Saving Bright Ideas!* Fairfield, N.J.

Edwards, Paul, editor
1967 *The Encyclopedia of Philosophy.* New York and London: Macmillan/Collier Macmillan. Eight volumes.

Encyclopaedia Britannica
1974 *The New Encyclopaedia Britannica.* Chicago: H. H. Benton. Fifteenth edition. Thirty volumes.

Featherstone, Donald F.
1972 *War Games through the Ages.* With photographs, maps and battle plans. London: Stanley Paul, 1973. Vol. I: 3000 B.C. to 1500 A.D.; vol. II: 1420 to 1783.

Fougasse and McCulloch
1935 *You Have Been Warned: A Complete Guide to the Road.* London: Methuen, 1936. Seventh edition.
Gallenkamp & Co., suppliers
n.d. *Illustrated Catalogue of Scientific Apparatus and Instruments for Educational Purposes.* Contractors to The War Office, Colonial and Indian Governments, Crown Agents for the Colonies, London County Council, Government of Spain, Sudan, etc., and Imperial Chemical Industries. On Admiralty List. Technico House, London (c. 1935). Tenth edition.
Gibson, Walter B., editor
1974 *Hoyle's Modern Encyclopedia of Card Games, Rules of All the Basic Games & Popular Variations.* Illustrated. New York: Doubleday.
Gilpin, Alan
1966 *Dictionary of Economic Terms.* London: Butterworth's. Second edition, revised, 1970.
Glover, Samuel
1948 *Pros and Cons: A Newspaper Reader's and Debater's Guide to the Leading Controversies of the Day.* (First edition by J. B. Askew, 1896). London: Routledge & Kegan Paul. Eleventh edition.
Grahame-White, Claude, and Harry Harper
1916 *Learning to Fly: A Practical Manual for Beginners.* With 10 photographs. London: T. Werner Laurie, Ltd.
Grant, James
n.d. *British Battles on Land and Sea.* With hundreds of illustrations. London, Paris, and New York: Cassell, Petter, Galpin & Co., c. 1885. Four volumes.
Green, Jonathon
1984 *Newspeak: A Dictionary of Jargon.* London and Boston: Routledge & Kegan Paul.
Grun, Bernard
1979 *The Timetables of History: A Horizontal Linkage of People and Events.* Based on Werner Stein's *Kulturfahrplan* of 1946. New updated edition. New York: Touchstone, 1982.
Halliwell, Leslie
1977 *The Filmgoer's Companion.* New York: Avon, 1978. Sixth edition.
Hansen, Soren, and Jesper Jensen, with Wallace Roberts
1971 *The Little Red Schoolbook.* Tr. by Berit Thornberry. London: Stage 1; New York: Pocket Books.
Harris, Jay S., and the Editors of *TV Guide* Magazine, compilers and editors
1978 *TV Guide: The First 25 Years.* New York: Simon and Schuster.
Harris, John
1704 *Lexicon Technicum Or An Universal Dictionary of Arts and Sciences.* London. Volume I. New York and London: Johnson Reprint Corporation, 1966. Facsimile edition. Volume II, 1710.
Harris, John
1824a *The Infant's Grammar, Or A Picnic Party of the Parts of Speech.* Illustrated in color. London: Scolar Press, 1977. Harris's Cabinet of Amusement and Instruction.
1824b *Punctuation Personified.* Illustrated in color. London: Scolar Press, 1978.
Harvey, Sir Paul, editor
1937 *The Oxford Companion to Classical Literature.* Oxford: Oxford University Press, 1959.
Harvey, Sir Paul, and J. E. Heseltine, editors
1959 *The Oxford Companion to French Literature.* Oxford: Oxford University Press, 1961.

Herman, Lewis
    1952 *A Practical Manual of Screen Playwriting for Theater and Television Films.*
        New York and Scarborough. Ontario: Meridian Books, 1974.
Holley, Frederick S., compiler
    1979 *Los Angeles Times Stylebook.* New York, London, and Scarborough:
        Meridian, 1981.
Hornstein, Lillian Herlands, et al., editors
    1956 *The Reader's Companion to World Literature.* New York: Mentor, 1962.
Hurst, Walter E., and William Storm Hale
    1973 *Film Superlist: 20,000 Motion Pictures in the U.S. Public Domain.* Hollywood,
        Ca.: 7 Arts Press. Volume 8 of the Entertainment Industry Series. [6253
        Hollywood Boulevard, Suite 1100, Hollywood & Vine, Hollywood, CA
        90028.]
Izard, Ralph S., Hugh M. Culbertson, and Donald A. Lambert
    1977 *Fundamentals of News Reporting.* Dubuque, Iowa: Kendall/Hunt. Third
        edition.
Jones, Barry, and M. V. Dixon
    1981 *The Rutledge Dictionary of People.* New York: Rutledge.
Kael, Pauline
    1982 *5001 Nights at the Movies: A Guide from A to Z.* New York: Holt, Rinehart &
        Winston.
Kidron, Michael, and Ronald Segal
    1981 *The State of the World Atlas.* London and Sydney: Pan Books.
Kinder, Hermann, and Werner Hilgemann
    1964 *The Anchor Atlas of World History.* Tr. by Ernest A. Menze. Maps designed
        by Harald and Ruth Bukor. Garden City, New York: Anchor Books, 1974.
        Two volumes. Published in Britain by Penguin.
Kirschner, Stephen, Barry J. Pavelec, and Jeffrey Feinman, compilers
    1979 *The Rule Book.* Garden City, N.Y.: Dolphin.
Langer, William L., editor and compiler
    1948 *An Encyclopedia of World History, Ancient, Medieval, and Modern, Chrono-
        logically Arranged.* Cambridge: The Riverside Press; Boston: Houghton
        Mifflin. Revised edition.
Laplanche, J., and J.-B. Pontalis
    1967 *Vocabulaire de la psychanalyse.* Paris: Presses Universitaires de France.
Levi, Peter
    1980 *Atlas of the Greek World.* With 60 maps and 500 illustrations, 350 in color.
        Oxford: Elsevier; New York: Facts on File.
Link Belt Limited
    1924 *Link-Belt General Catalog No. 400 (1924 Reprint).* With thousands of illus-
        trations. Philadelphia, Chicago, Indianapolis, Toronto, and Montreal: The
        Link-Belt Company.
The London Cigarette Card Co., publishers
    1985 *The Catalogue of British and Foreign Cigarette Cards 1888–1985* [Sutton
        Road, Somerton, Somerset TA11 6QP].
Luke, Carmen
    1982 Television and children: A bibliography 1975–1981. Burnaby, B.C.: Depart-
        ment of Education, Simon Fraser University. Mimeographed.
McCulloch, J. R.
    1852 *A Dictionary, Practical, Theoretical, and Historical, of Commerce and
        Commercial Navigation. Illustrated with Maps and Plans. A New Edition,
        Corrected, Enlarged, and Improved; with a Supplement.* London: Longman,
        Brown, Green, and Longmans.

MacDonald, Sandy A. F.
   1963 *From the Ground Up*. Ottawa: Aviation Publishers. 20th revised edition.
Macksey, Joan and Kenneth, editors
   1975 *The Guinness Guide to Feminine Achievements*. Enfield, Middlesex: Guinness Superlatives.
Mair, Roslin
   1979 *Key Dates in Art History from 600 BC to the Present*. Oxford: Phaidon.
Maltin, Leonard, editor
   1982 *1983–84 TV Movies: Everything You Want to Know and More about 15,000 Movies now Being Shown on Regular and Cable TV*. New York: New American Library. Revised edition.
   1983 *The Whole Film Sourcebook*. New York and Scarborough, Ont.: Plume Books.
Manguel, Alberto, and Gianni Guadalupi
   1980 *The Dictionary of Imaginary Places*. Illustrated by Graham Greenfield. Maps and charts by James Cook. Toronto: Lester & Orpen Dennys; New York: Macmillan.
Manvell, Roger, general editor
   1972 *The International Encyclopedia of Film*. London: Rainbird Reference Books; New York: Bonanza Books, 1975.
Margulis, Lynn, and Karlene V. Schwartz
   1982 *Five Kingdoms: An Illustrated Guide to the Phyla of Life on Earth*. San Francisco: W. H. Freeman.
Märklin, Gebr., & Cie, GmbH, publishers
   1976 *The Märklin Train and Toy Catalog*. Württ. Illustrations in color.
Matthew, Donald
   1983 *Atlas of Medieval Europe*. With 64 maps and 293 illustrations, 175 in color. Oxford: Equinox; New York: Facts on File.
Maunder, Samuel
   1876 *The Biographical Treasury: A Dictionary of Universal Biography*. Revised and enlarged by William L. R. Cates. London: Longmans, Green, & Co. Thirteenth edition.
Mencher, Melvin
   1981 *News Reporting and Writing*. Dubuque, Iowa: Wm. C. Brown Co. Second edition.
Merriam-Webster
   1965 *Webster's Biographical Dictionary*. G. & C. Merriam Co.
Meyers, Warren b.
   1967 *Who Is That? The Late Viewer's Guide to the Old Movie Players*. New York: Bell.
Miller, Casey, and Kate Swift
   1980 *The Handbook of Nonsexist Writing*. New York, London, and Sydney: Barnes & Noble.
Moulds, George Henry
   1966 *Thinking Straighter*. Dubuque, Iowa: Kendall Hunt.
Murdock, George P.
   1967 *Ethnographic Atlas*. Pittsburgh: University of Pittsburgh Press.
Murray Cards (International) Ltd., publisher
   1985 *Catalogue of Cigarette and Other Trade Cards*. [51 Watford Way, Hendon Central, London NW4 3JH].
Murray, Jocelyn, editor
   1981 *Cultural Atlas of Africa*. With 96 maps and 333 illustrations, 248 in color. Amsterdam: Elsevier; New York: Facts on File.
Needham, Joseph
   1954 *Science and Civilisation in China*. With the assistance of Wang Ling, K. G.

Robinson, Lu Gwei-Djen, Ho Ping-Yu, and others. Cambridge: Cambridge University Press. Volume 2: 'History of Scientific Thought' (1956); Volume 4, Part 1: 'Physics and Physical Technology', Section 26: 'Physics' (1962); Part 3, Section 27: 'Engineering, Mainly Mechanical' (1956); Sections 28 and 29: 'Civil Engineering and Nautics' (1971).

Newman, James R., editor
1956 *The World of Mathematics*. Four volumes: *Men and Numbers; The World of Law and the World of Chance; The Mathematical Way of Thinking;* and *Machines, Music and Puzzles.* New York: Simon & Schuster.

Oxford University Press, publishers
1928 *The Compact Edition of the Oxford English Dictionary* [1878–1928]. Oxford, 1971.
1953 *The Oxford Dictionary of Quotations.* Oxford, 1977. Second edition.

Paddington Press
n.d. *Time Lines: Science and Inventions: 1900 Years of Discoveries.* New York and London: Paddington Press/The Diagram Group. Foldout time chart.
n.d. *World History: 5000 Years of the Rise and Fall of Civilizations.*
n.d. *The Twentieth Century.*

Paladin Press
1984 *The Action Library Catalog.* Boulder, Colorado: Paladin Press, vol. 14, no. 2. [P.O. Box 1307, Boulder, Colo., 80302].

Palmer, R. R., editor
1957 *The Rand McNally Atlas of World History.* New York, Chicago, and San Francisco: Rand McNally.

Partridge, Eric
1961 *A Dictionary of Slang and Unconventional English.* London: Routledge & Kegan Paul, 1974. Fifth edition. *Supplement* to the Dictionary, 1970. Eighth edition.
1977 *A Dictionary of Catch Phrases.* London: Routledge & Kegan Paul.

A. & F. Pears, Ltd, publisher
1940 *Pears' Cyclopaedia: Twenty-two Complete Works of Reference in one Handy Volume of nearly 1,000 pages.* Ed. by Leslie W. E. Sherwood and ten specialists. Isleworth, near London.

Pei, Mario
1966 *Glossary of Linguistic Terminology.* Garden City, N.Y.: Anchor.

Pickard, Lieutenant Colonel Edward E., U.S. Army Corps of Engineers
1951 *The Military Instructor.* With 102 illustrations. Harrisburg, Pa.: Military Service Publishing Co.

Pitman, Sir Isaac
190 *Pitman's Book-Keeping Simplified.* London, Bath, and New York: Sir Isaac Pitman & Sons.

Reader's Digest
1973 *Reader's Digest Complete Do-it-yourself Manual.* Montreal: Reader's Digest Association (Canada) Ltd.

Red River Cereal
1941 *Flags of Empire.* Toronto and Montreal: Maple Leaf Milling Co.

Reese, W. L.
1980 *Dictionary of Philosophy and Religion: Eastern and Western Thought.* New Jersey: Humanities Press; Sussex: Harvester Press.

Richardson, Alan, editor
1950 *A Theological Word Book of the Bible.* New York: Macmillan, 1971.

Robert, General Henry M., Corps of Engineers, U.S.A.
1876 *Pocket Manual of Rules of Order for Deliberative Ceremonies: Part I. Rules of Order. A Compendium of Parliamentary Law, Based upon the Rules and*

Practice of Congress. Part II. Organization and Conduct of Business. A Simple Explanation of the Methods of Organizing and conducting the Business of Societies, Conventions, and Other Deliberative Assemblies. Chicago: Scott, Foresman and Co., 1906. Three hundred and forty second thousand. Revised 1893 and 1904.

Roud, Richard, editor
1980 Cinema: A Critical Dictionary. London: Secker & Warburg; New York: Viking. Two volumes.

Runes, Dagobert D., editor
1964 Dictionary of Philosophy. Paterson, N.J.: Littlefield, Adams & Co. Fifteenth edition.

Shapiro, Evelyn, editor
1973 Psycho-Sources: A Psychology Resource Catalog. New York and Toronto: Bantam.

Shepherd, William R.
1964 Historical Atlas. New York: Barnes & Noble, 1967. Ninth edition, corrected.

Sills, David L., editor
1968 International Encyclopedia of the Social Sciences. New York: Macmillan/The Free Press; London: Collier-Macmillan, 1972. Seventeen volumes.

Simon, Oliver
1963 Introduction to Typography. Ed. by David Bland. London: Faber and Faber. Revision of 1954 edition.

Singer, Charles S., E. J. Holmyard, A. R. Hall, Trevor I. Williams, editors
1958 A History of Technology. With numerous illustrations. Oxford: Oxford University Press. Five volumes.

Steinberg, S. H.
1949 Historical Tables 58 B.C. – A.D. 1945. London: Macmillan.

Strandh, Sigvard
1979 A History of the Machine. With over 300 illustrations, many in color. Tr. by Ann Henning. New York: A&W Publishers.

Strong, James
1890 The Exhaustive Concordance of the Bible Showing Every Word of the Text of the Common English Version of the Canonical Books, and every Occurrence of each Word in Regular Order; together with a Comparative Concordance of the Authorized and Revised Versions including the American Variations; also Brief Dictionaries of the Hebrew and Greek Words of the Original, with References to the English Words. New York and Nashville: Abingdon Press, 1967 (27th printing).

Thorndike, Lynn
1958 A History of Magic and Experimental Science. New York and London: Columbia University Press, 1964. Eight volumes, 1923–58.

Thoules, Robert H.
1930 Straight and Crooked Thinking. London: Pan Books, 1963. Revised and enlarged edition.

University of Chicago Press, publishers
1982 The Chicago Manual of Style. Chicago and London. Thirteenth edition, revised and expanded.

Urdang, Laurence, editor
1981 The Timetables of American History. Introduction by Henry Steele Commager. New York: Touchstone, 1983.

Ure, Andrew
1839 A Dictionary of Arts, Manufactures, and Mines: Containing a Clear Exposition of their Principles and Practice. Illustrated with 1240 engravings on wood. London: Longman, Orme, Brown, Green, & Longmans.

Vincent, Benjamin, editor and compiler
    1889   *Haydn' Dictionary of Dates and Universal Information Relating to All Ages and Nations Containing the History of the World to the Autumn of 1889.* London, New York, and Melbourne: Ward, Lock and Co. Nineteenth edition.
Wallace, Amy, David Wallechinsky, and Irving Wallace, compilers
    1983   *The Book of Lists no. 3.* New York, London, Toronto, and Sydney: Bantam Books.
Wallace, Carlton
    1951   *The Schoolboy's Pocket Book.* London: Evans Bros., 1959.
Wallace, Irving, David Wallechinsky, Amy Wallace, and Sylvia Wallace, compilers
    1979   *The Book of Lists no. 2.* New York, London, Toronto, and Sydney: Bantam Books.
White, Wilbur W.
    1947   *White's Political Dictionary.* Cleveland and New York: World Publishing Co.
Wiener, Philip, editor
    1968   *The Dictionary of the History of Ideas.* New York: Charles Scribner's Sons, 1973. Four volumes and index.
Wilhelm, Richard, and Cary F. Baynes, translators
    1950   *The I Ching or Book of Changes.* Foreword by C. G. Jung. Preface by Hellmut Wilhelm. New York: Bollingen Foundation; Princeton: Princeton University Press, 1980. Third edition, 1967.
Williams, Raymond
    1983   *Keywords: A Vocabulary of Culture and Society.* Completely revised and expanded to include over twenty new words. London: Fontana. Original edition 1976.
Wintle, Justin
    1983   *The Dragon's Almanac: Chinese, Japanese and other Far Eastern Proverbs.* London and Boston: Routledge & Kegan Paul.
Woods, Ralph L., editor
    1951   *The Businessman's Book of Quotations.* New York, London, and Toronto: McGraw-Hill.

Name index

Note: This index is followed by a chronological index of battles, campaigns, and wars, then by the subject index.

Acheson, Dean, 39
Acker, Lt-Col. Lewis F., 98
Adams, Eddie, 52
Adams, Elizabeth (Lizzie), 18
Adams, John, 144
Agricola, Georgius, 287
Aldworth, Lt-Col. W., 9
Alexander, 5, 79, 214–15
Ali, Mohammed, 308
Allen, Woody, 69–70
Allyson, June, 263
Andrews, Julie, 263
Arden, Eve, 268
Aristotle, 79–81, 90, 153, 154, 155, 176, 198, 250
Arnett, Peter, 28
Artemidorus, 214–15
Arthur, Jean, 268
Ashby, W. Ross, 77, 172, 183, 189, 190, 192, 320
Atkin, Ronald, 11, 12
Azemilcus, 214

Bacon, Lloyd, 290
Bacon, Sir Francis, 58, 87, 208
Baden-Powell, Ernest, 260
Bainter, Fay, 264
Bakan, Paul, 235
Baldwin, Gordon, 165
Ballard, Ada Margaret, 4, 18, 19, 61
Ballard, Ada Margaret (Peggy), 18
Ballard, George Edward, 16, 61
Ballard, George Harold, 4, 16, 21, 23, 61, 324
Ballard, Lilian Elizabeth, 3, 18, 19, 61, 63
Barnouw, Erik, 69
Bateson, Gregory, 76, 88, 105, 167, 189, 194, 195, 201, 203, 230, 244, 249,

251, 286, 287, 298, 303n, 306, 317, 318, 321
Baunoch, Joseph W., 261ff.
Bean, 'Judge' Roy, 17
Becker, Carl, 83
Belsham, W., 141
Bennett, Constance, 265
Bergman, Ingrid, 265
Bergson, Henri, 287
Berkeley, Busby, 286, 288, 289, 290, 293
Berkeley, George, 83
Berle, Milton, 261
Bertalanffy, Ludwig von, 131, 178
Beveridge, Albert J., 30, 54
Birdwhistell, Ray, 124, 318
Bjerg, Kresten, 226
Blake, William, 82, 207–8
Blondell, Joan, 268
Bloom, Floyd, 227, 228
Bloomer, Amelia, 282
Boas, George, 79, 80, 81
Boehme, Jakob, 135
Bogen, Joseph, 237, 239, 240
Bohr, Niels, 304
Boltzmann, Ludwig, 185
Boudicca, 44–5
Boulles, Charles de, 154, 155
Boulton, Matthew, 189
Boyle, Robert, 155
Bradley, Gen. Omar, 39
Brecht, George, 244
Brentano, Franz, 178
Browne, Douglas G., 24, 25
Browne, Sir Thomas, 128, 181
Brownmiller, Susan, 27, 28, 323
Buckley, Walter, 190
Bunker, Ellsworth, 52
Burke, Edmund, 144

Burke, Kenneth, 245, 313
Burnett, George, 211
Burns, Robert, 3
Butcher, Harry, 13
Butler, Samuel, 70

Cade, Jack, 44
Caesar, Julius, xiii
Calame-Griaule, G., 135
Calley, Lt. William L., Jr, 7
Cameron, Norman, 203
Campbell, Frank, 283
Campbell, Jeremy, 188, 234–42, 278, 309
Cannon, Walter, 233
Cardigan, Lord, 10
Carmichael, Stokely, 308
Carroll, Lewis, 79, 169–70, 254, 271, 276
Chambers, R., 231
Changeux, Jean Pierre, 229
Chaplin, Charles, 207
Charles I, 45, 118, 258
Charles V, 220
Chase, Allen, 151
Chaucer, Geoffrey, xiii, 173
Chayevsky, Paddy, 193
Cherniavsky, Michael, xiii
Chiang Kai-shek, 27, 39
Chmaj, Betty E., 261ff.
Chomsky, Noam, 150, 177, 238
Christie, Julie, 268
Chu Hsi, 89–80
Chu Teh, Gen., 27–8
Churchill, Winston S., 5, 6, 9, 12, 26
Clausewitz, Carl von, 8, 37, 102, 167, 277
Colbert, Claudette, 268
Coleridge, Sammuel Taylor, 269, 271
Collingwood, R. G., xiv, 82
Conan Doyle, Arthur, 8
Condillac, Etienne Bonnot de, 198
Constable, John, 73
Cooper, A. A., 129
Cooper, Gary, 28
Coppola, Francis Ford, 298
Corneille, Pierre, xiii
Costa, Louis, 234, 237
Crawford, Broderick, 29
Crawford, Joan, 261, 262, 265
Crerar, Gen. Harry, 6, 10
Crick, Francis, 186
Crisp, Quentin, 297
Cromwell, Oliver, 258
Cronje, Gen. Piet, 7–8

Crook, John H., 321
Ctesibius of Alexandria, 189
Cudworth, Ralph, 129

Darnell, Linda, 261, 262
Darwell, Jane, 264
Darwin, Charles, 144
Darwin, Erasmus, 144
Davis, Bette, 265, 268
Day, Doris, 263
De Bono, Edward, 190
Dedekind, J. W. R., 248
de Havilland, Olivia, 265
Deregowski, J. B., 210
Descartes, René, 88, 178, 224, 253, 306, 311
De Wet, Gen. Christiaan, 7
Dickens, Charles, 207, 275
Dietrich, Marlene, 264, 266
Disney, Walt, 151–3
Dobrizhoffer, Martin, 135
Doran, Andre, 261
Douglas, Melvyn, 266
Dowling, Colette, 46–7
Dressler, Marie, 268
Dryden, John, 173
Dunaway, Faye, 269
Dunn, Lt. A. R., 10
Dunne, Irene, 263
Dunn-Rankin, Peter, 187
Dürer, Albrecht, 156, 158

Eddington, Sir Arthur S., 184
Edward VII, 17
Edwards, Private, 25
Edwards, W., 314
Einstein, Albert, 304
Eisenhower, Gen. Dwight D., 13, 39
Eisenstein, Sergei, 91, 207, 219, 249, 270, 271–3, 274–6
Eliade, Mircea, 93, 112, 113–16, 117, 161, 163
Eliot, George, 71
Elizabeth I, 44, 118, 220
Emerson, Ralph Waldo, 219, 323
Empedocles of Agrigentum, 153
Ennals, Richard, 42
Escher, Maurits C., 203
Ezard, John, 12, 13

Faraday, Michael, 190
Faye, Alice, 264
Fichte, Johann, 247
Finn, Robert, 232, 234, 235, 237

Fitzgibbon, 1st Earl of Clare, 141
Flaubert, Gustave, 259
Fleischer, Max, 152
Fludd, Robert, 162, 164–5
Fonda, Jane, 268
Fourier, Charles, 117
Franco, Gen. Francisco, 36
Franklin, Benjamin, 144
Fraser, Douglas, 100, 136
Freeman, Eugene, 160
Frege, Gottlob, 252
French, English, 43
Freud, Sigmund, 23, 123, 136–7, 150,
    198, 210, 202, 205, 214–29, 232,
    246, 249, 252, 271, 287, 306
Fromkin, Victoria A., 181, 252
Fulton, Robert, 58

Galbraith, John Kenneth, 42
Galileo, 88, 126, 143
Galton, Francis, 144
Gamow, George, 303
Gance, Abel, 139, 270, 298
Garbo, Greta, 265
Gardner, Ava, 264
Gardner, Howard, 239, 240, 241, 278
Gardner, Martin, 140, 169, 170, 253–4
Garland, Judy, 264
Garson, Greer, 263
Gatty, Harold, 110, 213
Gaynor, Janet, 263
Gillmore, Parker, 131
Girouard, Lt. Edouard Percy Cranwell, 8
Goebbels, Joseph P., 21
Goethe, Johann Wolfgang von, 75,
    175–6, 283
Goldberg, Elkhonon, 234, 237
Goldmann, Lucien, 113
Goldstein, Kurt, 200, 201–3
Goodall, Jane, 321
Gordon, Gen. Charles George, 26
Goulden, Joseph, 39
Grable, Betty, 261, 262, 264
Grattan, Henry, 142
Greengard, Paul, 227
Griaule, Marcel, 135
Griffith, D. W., 206, 207, 270–1, 275

Haase, Gen. Conrad, 11
Halle, Morris, 179, 180
Hamby, Suzanne, 241, 278
Hamilton, Gen. Ian, 14
Hammer, Rhonda, 86, 283ff.
Hammurabi, 146

Handcock, Lt., 33
Hannay, Col. O. C., 9
Harlow, Jean, 264
Harriman, W. Averell, 39
Harris, John, 129–30, 303
Harris, Marvin, 102, 105, 107, 118–19,
    121, 135, 138
Harris, Walter L., 156
Hassenstein, B., 188
Hawkins, Gerald S., 146–9, 165–6
Hawkins, John, 220
Hawthorne, Nathaniel, 277
Hayward, Susan, 261, 262, 265
Hayworth, Rita, 264
Hegel, G. W. F., 79, 82–7, 88, 89, 156,
    160, 245, 246–7, 250, 306
Heidegger, Martin, 311
Heine, Heinrich, 215
Heisenberg, Walter, 171, 304
Heninger, S. K., Jr., 128, 155, 156–60
Henry VI, 44
Henry VIII, 44, 118
Henty, G. A., 32
Hepburn, Katherine, 265, 268
Heraclitus, 84, 153
Heston, Charlton, 31
Hicks Pasha, 26
Hilton, Robert, 189
Hindle, Brook, 229–30
Hippel, Frank von, 40
Hirschhorn, Clive, 289
Hitler, Adolf, 22, 36, 50, 291, 293, 307
Hoffman, Banesh, 304
Hofstadter, Douglas, 243, 244
Holland, Peter, xii
Holland, Ray, 303n
Holmes, Oliver Wendell, Jr., 123
Hooper, Stephen, 189
Hopkins, Miriam, 265
Hughes, Patrick, 244
Hugo, Victor, xiii
Hume, David, 198
Hurt, John, 297
Husserl, Edmund, 178, 306
Hutton, Betty, 268
Huxley, Aldous, 120
Huyghens, Christian, 69

Isidore of Seville, 154, 157

Jackson, Glenda, 269
Jackson, Harold, 40
Jackson, John Hughlings, 204

Jakobson, Roman, 177, 178, 179, 180,
181, 197–8, 199–201, 202, 204–7
James II, 118
Jefferson, Thomas, 144
Johnson, Lyndon B., 7, 40, 50, 52
Johnson, Samuel, 112
Johnston, Ollie, 152, 269
Jomini, Antoine, 48
Jonas, Gerald, 229
Jowett, Marion, 16

Kafka, Franz, 306
Kahn, Charles H., 153
Karen, Robert, 254–5, 270, 271
Kasanin, J. S., 201
Keeler, Ruby, 264
Kelly, Grace, 165
Kennedy, John F., 39, 40
Kennedy, Robert F., 307
Kerr, Deborah, 263
Kimura, Doreen, 235, 236
King, Martin Luther, Jr., 307
Kipling, Rudyard, 23, 30–1, 43, 54
Kircher, Athanasius, 69
Kissinger, Henry, 37–8
Kitchener, Gen. Lord, 6–9, 25–6, 32
Koffka, Kurt, 271
Kojève, Alexandre, 306
Kondratiev, N. D., 34, 35
Koyré, Alexandre, 79
Kracauer, Siegfried, 285, 288, 291, 293
Kramer, Stanley, 261

Lacan, Jacques, 201, 205, 215, 306
Laing, R. D., 199, 306
Lamarr, Hedy, 264
Lang, Fritz, 270, 291
Langley, Samuel P., 146
Langtry, Mrs Lillie, 17
Lansbury, Angela, 264
Laplace, Pierre Simon de, 304
Lashley, 228
Lawrence, T. E., 300
Le Breton, Jane, 17
Lee, Edmund, 190
Leenhardt, Maurice, 133–4
Leibniz, G. W. von, 129
Lenin, V. I., 82
Lévi-Strauss, Claude, 82, 92, 94, 101–2,
104, 106, 115–16, 150, 165, 177,
178, 250, 306, 312
Levy, Jerre, 314
Lévy-Bruhl, Lucien, 137
Li, Ch'üan, 140

Locke, John, 142, 198, 208, 314
L'Ouverture, General Toussaint, iv
Lovejoy, A. O., 79, 130, 222
Lowes, John Livingstone, 269, 271
Loy, Myrna, 263
Lucan, Lord, 10

MacArthur, Gen. Arthur, 29–30
MacArthur, Gen. Douglas, 29
McCambridge, Mercedes, 265
McCarthy, Joe, 305
McCulloch, Warren, 318
McDaniel, Hattie, 264
Machaut, Guillaume de, 173
Machiavelli, Niccolo, 118
McKinley, William 29
Maclear, Michael, 41
McLuhan, Marshall, 288
McNamara, Robert, 40
Magritte, René, iv, 210, 244–5
Main, Marjorie, 268
Mao Tse-tung, 28, 82, 249, 273
March, Lionel, 90, 107
Markham, Francis, 220
Marquis, T. G., 9, 10
Marschak, Alexander, 148
Marshall, Herbert, 266
Maruyama, Magoroh, 190
Marx, Karl, xv, 150, 247, 249, 306
Mary II, 118
Mast, Gerald, 270, 271, 272–3
Mauss, Marcel, 134
Maxwell, James Clerk, 185, 190, 310
Mayr, Ernst, 190
Mazia, Daniel, 75
Mead, Thomas, 189
Mee, Arthur, 86–7
Merman, Ethel, 261, 268
Miller, Henry, 259
Mohammed Ahmed, the Mahdi, 23, 24,
25
Moira, 2nd Earl of, 141
Moliere, xiii, 314
Monod, Jacques, 312
Monroe, Marilyn, 264, 299
Montgomery, Gen. Bernard Law, 6
Moorehead, Agnes, 265
Moorehead, Alan, 14
Morant, Lt. Breaker, 33
More, Henry, 129
Mountbatten, Lord Louis, 6
Munnecke, Thomas, 243
Munois, Guy de, 211
Murchie, Guy, 110–11

Murdock, George P., 119–20
Mussolini, Benito, 36
Myers, Denis, 260
Mylands, Carl, 41
Mylands, Shelley, 41
Myrdal, Gunnar, 126

Napier, Gen. Sir Charles, 141
Napoleon, 1, 8, 37, 45, 298
Nathanson, James A., 227
Neal, Patricia, 268
Needham, Joseph, 89–90
Newman, James R., 304
Newton, Isaac, 88, 190, 208, 251, 303,
    310, 314
Nicholas II, 32
Nicholas of Cusa, 82
Nietzsche, Friedrich, 196, 204
Niven, David, 29, 31
Nixon, Richard M., 37–8, 39, 307
Nolan, Capt. Lewis E., 6
Norris, John, 129, 130

Oberdorfer, Don, 51
Ogden, C. K., 74, 80
Oldendorf, William H., 227, 228
Orwell, George, 21, 22–3, 62–3, 120,
    259–60
Otter, Lt-Col. W. D., 9

Paine, Thomas, 143, 144
Pakenham, Thomas, 33
Parmenides, 84, 153
Partridge, Eric, 46
Pascal, Gabriel, 80, 113, 224, 253
Pattee, H. H., 176
Peirce, Charles S., 160–1, 177
Pepys, Samuel, 69
Perls, Fritz, 307
Philip of Macedon, 5, 79
Philo Judaeus, 115
Plato, 79, 80, 81, 83, 90, 176, 198, 231
Plotinus, 127, 231
Polunin, N., 193
Pope, Alexander, 173, 239
Porta, Giambattista della, 88–9
Porter, Edwin S., 269–70
Post, Wiley, 110, 213
Priestley, Joseph, xiii, 143–5
Prigogine, Ilya, 171, 311, 315
Primaudaye, Pierre de la, 128
Prokofiev, Sergei, 274
Proust, Marcel, 131
Pudovkin, Vsevolod, 270, 273

Pushkin, Aleksandr, 272
Pythagoras, 126, 154, 155, 231

Racine, Jean Baptiste, xiii
Raffray, Herbert, 17
Raffray, Jack, 17
Raffray, Jessie Le Breton, 16, 17
Raglan, Lord, 6
Ramos, Gen. Fidel, 40
Ramsaye, Terry, 283
Reagan, Ronald, 42, 49–50, 54–5
Reeves, Richard, 69
Rennie, John, 189
Rhodes, Cecil, 37
Rider, Major, xiii
Riefenstahl, Leni, 21, 291, 292
Riel, Louis, 26
Ritterbush, Philip, 158
Roberts, David S., xi-xv
Roberts, Field Marshal Lord, 6
Roberts, Maj-Gen. John, 6, 10, 11, 12
Robertson, Etienne, 68
Rogers, Ginger, 268
Rollo, 45
Rosenblum, Ralph, 69–70, 254–5, 259,
    270, 271, 273
Rosten, Leo, 217–18, 250
Rothschild, Baron, 215
Rousseau, Jean-Jacques, 67, 208, 211
Rusk, Dean, 52
Russell, Bertrand, 84, 167
Russell, Rosalind, 265, 268

Sahlins, Marshall, 94, 113, 121
Saint, Eve Marie, 263
Sapir, Edward, 137
Sartre, Jean-Paul, 178, 311
Saussure, Ferdinand de, 177, 179–80
Savery, Thomas, 88
Schiller, J. C. Friedrich von, xiv, 95
Schirren, Oberleutnant Hans, 12
Schmandt-Besserat, Denise, 149
Schnösenberg, Capt. Richard, 11
Schrödinger, Erwin, 185
Scott, Sir Walter, 231, 232
Sennett, Ted, 290
Service, Elman R., 96, 98, 116
Shah of Iran, 37–8
Shakespeare, William, xiii, 44
Shannon, Claude E., 173–4, 180, 185–8,
    192, 303, 309, 314
Shepherd, Gordon M., 227
Sheridan, Ann, 261, 262, 268
Sherman, Gen. William T., 8

Shults, Jim, 51–4
Simon, William E., 38
Singlaub, Gen. John, 51
Sloane-Evans, W. Sloane, 207, 213, 219, 221
Smith, Alexis, 265
Smith, Constance, 261
Smith, Whitney, 141
Smith-Dorrien, Maj-Gen. H. A., 9
Southern, John, 190
Spilhaus, Athelstan, 59, 229
Spinoza, Benedict, 251
Stalin, Joseph, 35, 36
Stanner, W. E. H., 93, 114
Stanwyck, Barbara, 265
Statius, Caecilius, 89
Steadman, Philip, 90, 107
Stowe, Harriet Beecher, 18
Strauss, Walter L., 156, 158
Stravinsky, Igor, 176
Streisand, Barbra, 268
Strethlow, T. G. H., 93, 115, 116
Stubbs, William, xv
Sullivan, Harry Stack, 126, 201
Sun Tzu, xii, 47–8, 49, 140, 150, 300
Sun Yat-Sen, 32
Szasz, Thomas, 306
Szilard, Leo, 185

Tacitus, 44
Taylor, A. J. P., 323
Taylor, Elizabeth, 265
Temple, Shirley, 263
Tenniel, Sir John, 81
Thomas, Frank, 152, 269
Thomas, Leslie, 13
Thomas, Terry, 261
Thornhill, Randy, 122–3
Tierney, Gene, 265
Tone, Franchot, 28
Tone, Theobald Wolfe, 141
Towner, J. R. B., 13
Toynbee, Arnold, xv
Troubetzkoy, Nikolai, 177, 178
Truman, Harry, 39
Turner, Lana, 264
Turner, Victor, 134–5
Tzu Hsi, 31

Uspenskij, Gleb Ivanovič, 196–7

Van Praagh, Dr. G., xiii
Vendryes, Joseph, 275–6
Vico, Giambattista, 211

Vinci, Leonardo da, 90
Voloshinov, V. N., 142, 303n
Von Foerster, Heinz, 175, 186
Von Neumann, John, 304
Vo Nguyen Giap, Gen., 34
Von Uexküll, Jakob, 109
Von Willisen, Wilhelm, 300

Warshaw, Tessa Albert, 48–9
Warusfel, André, 106
Waters, Ethel, 264
Watson, James, 186, 307
Watt, James, 144, 189, 190
Weaver, Warren, 173–4, 180, 186
Wedgwood, Josiah, 144
Weil, André, 106
Welch, Ràquel, 264
Wellington, 1st Duke of, 24
Wells, H. G., 15, 36, 37
West, Mae, 264
Westmoreland, Gen. William, 7, 52
White, Morton, 86
Whitehead, Alfred North, 313
Whyte, Lancelot Law, 129, 184
Wiener, Norbert, 133, 186, 190, 195, 198
Wigan, L. W., 231–2
Wilden, Alan, 16, 43, 44, 57
Wilden, Dennis, 16
Wilden, Dorothy Reeve, 19, 61
Wilden, Frank Clover, 16, 17, 19–20, 57, 61, 63, 324
Wilkins, Maurice, 186
William I, 44, 45
William III, 118
Wilson, E. O., 122
Winkler, Captain, 110
Winterowd, W. Ross, 240–1
Winters, Shelley, 265
Wise, Terence, 141
Witte, Karsten, 291
Wittgenstein, Ludwig, 87
Wolseley, Lord, 26
Woodward, John, 211
Wordsworth, William, 127, 170, 231

Xenophon, xiii

Yanker, Gary, 2

Zabielski, William, 227, 228
Zaidel, Erain, 240
Zeno of Elea, 251
Zimman, H. D., 23
Zipes, Jack, 288

Index of battles, campaigns, and wars

Note: This index is in chronological order. The subject index follows.

Retreat of the Ten Thousand (401 BCE), xiii

Conquests of Alexander (331–323 BCE), 79

Alexander's Siege of Tyre (322 BCE), 214–5; casualties, 215

Caesar's Gallic War (58–52 BCE), xiii

Boudicca's Revolt (61 CE), 44–5; casualties, 44–5

Hastings (1066), 44, 46

Kentish Rebellion (1450), 44

Fall of Constantinople (1453), 5

Wars of the Roses (1455–85), 44, 118

English Revolution (1642–88), 45, 118

Second Anglo-Dutch War (1665–67), 34

War of the Spanish Succession (1702–13), 34

Seven Years War (1756–63), 34

American War of Independence (1775–83), 34

French Revolution (1789–), 144

Revolutionary and Napoleonic Wars (1789–1815), 34, 35, 45

United Irish Rebellion (1798–99), 141

War of 1812 (1812–14), 34, 46

Waterloo (1815), 24

First Opium War (1839–42), 26, 32

US-Mexican War (1846–48), 34, 35

Taiping Rebellion (1851–64), 26

Crimean War (1854–56), 6, 14

Balaklava (1854), 6

Second Opium War (the Arrow War) (1856–60), 26, 32

'Indian Mutiny' (the Great Rebellion) (1857–9), 28

American Civil War (1861–65), 8, 34, 35

Sherman's March to the Sea (1864–65), 8

Red River Rebellion, (1869–70), 26

Zulu War (1879), 24

Sudanese War of Independence (1881–98), 23–6

Tamai (1884), 24–25

Abu Klea (1885), 24

Fall of Khartoum (1885), 26

Ashanti Campaign (1896), 33

Matabele Rising (1896), 33

Omdurman (1898), 8, 25–6, 28; casualties, 26

Spanish-American War (1898), 28, 35

Philippine-American War ('Philippine Insurrection') (1898–1906), 28–31; casualties, 31

Boxer Rebellion (1899–1901), 31–2

Second South African War (Anglo-Boer War) (1899–1902), 6–10, 12, 14, 32–3; casualties, 14; civilian, black, 32–3

Siege of Mafeking (1899–1900), 33

Spion Kop (1900), 9; casualties, 9

Paardeberg (1900), 6, 7–8, 9–10, 14; casualties, 6, 9–10

Russo-Japanese War (1905), 32

Balkan Wars of Independence (1912–13), 5

World War I (1914–18), 4, 8, 11, 15, 21, 34, 35, 36, 50, 56; casualties, 15–16, 56

Retreat from Mons (1914), 4; casualties, 4

Extermination of the Armenians (1915), 5; deaths, 5

Dardanelles Campaign (Gallipoli) (1915–16), 4, 5–6, 14–15; casualties, 5–6, 14

Japanese Invasion of Manchuria (1931), 36
The Holocaust (1933–45), 5, 15; deaths, 5, 15
Sino-Japanese War (1933–45), 39; casualties, 15
Italo-Abyssinian War (1935–41), 35
Spanish Civil War (1936–39), 26, 36
World War II (1939–45), 3–4, 15, 16, 21, 29, 33–4, 36–7, 56; casualties, 15–16, 56
Battle of Britain (1940), 10
Dieppe (1942), 6, 10–12; casualties, 6, 10–11
Slapton Sands (1944), 12–14; casualties, 12–14
Liberation of the Netherlands (1944–45), 23
Chinese Civil War (1945–49), 39
Wars between 1945 and 1983, 41, 56; casualties, 41, 56
First Indochina War (1946–54), 26, 39; casualties, 41

Korean War (1950–53), 34, 39, 52; casualties, 39
Dien Bien Phu (1954), 34
Algerian War of Independence (1954–62), 26; casualties, 26
Vietnam War (Second Indochina War) (1955–75) (escalated 1965; US withdrew 1973), 34, 35, 37, 38, 40–1, 50–1; casualties, 41
Bay of Pigs (1961), 39
Civil War in Northern Ireland (1966–   ), 29
Tet Offensive (1968), 29, 51–2, 307; casualties, 52
My Lai Massacre (1968), 7; deaths, 7
Russian Invasion of Czechoslovakia (1968), 307
Zimbabwean War of Independence (1972–80), 26
Russian Invasion of Afghanistan (1979–   ), 26
Falklands War (1982), 49
US Invasion of Grenada (1984), 54–5

Subject index

Notes (1) Pages 315–19 of the Postscript are not included in this index.
(2) For battles, campaigns, wars, and casualties see the chronological index following the name index.
(3) Pairs of terms separated by a slash refer to left and right brain functions respectively.

A and not-A, 252, 253, 277; *see also* 'if not *a*, then *b*'
absolute, 85, 86
abstract: and concrete, 137; confused with concrete, 202–3
abstract/concrete, 230, 235, 237
abstraction: impaired, 202–3; mapping and, 107
A Chorus Line (1980), 284, 286
act, inability to: in dreams, 218; *see also* negation
action and reaction, equal and opposite, 250, 303
Action Stories, 22
active, 159–60, 235, 237; opposed to passive, 80
active/passive, 235
active/receptive, 237
actor, as machine, 299
adaptation, 107, 249
adaptive *see* goalseeking
Adventure, 21
Aeneas, 92
affect, displaced, 215
affinities: and opposition between qualities, elements, 159–60
affirmation: and negation, 245–6, 251–2; and negative word, 252
Aha! experience, xiii, 249, 250, 288
Akaruio Bokodori, 92, 94
Alexander Nevsky (1938), 274
all/or/none, 16, 199, 222, 225, 227, 250, 279, 313
alphabet, divine, 128

ambiguity: of analog, iconic, right-brain information, 224, 238, 299
analog *see* information
analogia, 164–5
analogy, 198; visual, 164–5
analytic/dialectic, 278; *see also* analytic/synthesizing; dialectic; logic, analytic; logic, dialectical;
analytic/synthesizing, 234, 235; *see also* analytic/dialectic
ancestors, 92–4, 96, 113–16; feminine, 116
Angel (1937), 266–7
animals, communication with, 140, 320–1
animation, 151–3, 197, 269
antagonism, 247
anthropology, structural, 79, 94, 101–2, 104–9, 177–9, 310
anti-defeatism, 43, 46
antithesis: and thesis, synthesis, 84–5, 246–7
aphasia, 197–207
appearance *see* reality
appositional *see* propositional
appropriate/inappropriate, 240
approximation, 218
aristocracy, 94, 96, 119–20
armes parlantes (canting arms), 211
arms race, 36–42; and exponential growth, positive feedback, 38, 42, 190
arms, talking, 211
arrangement, 184

artforms: metonymic, metaphoric, 210, 244–5
articulation, 145; double, 139
Arunta, 93, 112, 113–14, 116–17
assertion: and negative word, 252
associative *see* transformational
astronomy, 120, 146–50, 165–6
asymmetry *see* symmetry
attitudes: as communication, 151–3
attraction, 153, 160
attribute, 198
aufheben (lift and conserve), 84, 246
Aufhebung (lifting and conserving), 246; as boundary, 248; imaginary, 247
authoritarianism, xii, 51
axis mundi (center of the world), 149, 161, 163; imparts structure, 113–14; *see also* mediation; orientation
Azande, 103

back to front: not symmetrical, 80–1
banal/rich, 240
battle: communication in, 140–1
battle standard: as telegraph to the wings, 141
battles, index of, 405–6
Battleship Potemkin (192), 273
Beau Geste (1939), 29
before: in imaginary opposition with after, 80
beginning: head as, 207
behavior: and determinism, free will, 79; living, is communication, 69
being: as becoming, 83; great chain of, as inverted dependent hierarchy, 129–30; in imaginary opposition with non-being, 80
Being and Nothingness (Jean-Paul Sartre, 1943), 311
Being and Time (Martin Heigegger, 1927), 311
beliefs, 91, 132; *see also* ideology; value
Besetzung (investment of interest, cathexis), 178
biases: systematic, 126
'big man' system, 119, 121
Bild (image, form), 214
Bilderschrift (pictograph, hieroglyphic), 214
bilingualism: and aphasia, 200
bind double, iv, 203, 210, 244; *see also* oscillation; paradox; wave
Birth of a Nation (1915), 207
bisexuality, 297

bit, 173, 175, 180–1, 186, 188, 192
Blonde Venus (1932), 284
blood lust, 9, 22
blunders, xv; strategic, 5–12, 39; tactical, 5–6, 8–14, 26; *see also* defeat; victory
body: as environment of mind, 82; as robot, 311; intelligence, 24; role in perception, conception, language, meaning, 226; subject of, 279; *see also* communication; nature
boom and bust cycle, 34–9; and war, 34–6, 37; *see also* arms race; depression; oscillation; semiotic; systems, cyclic; wave
Bororo, 92, 93, 98, 100, 101–2
both A and not-A, 277
both-and, 48, 62, 70, 74, 88, 126, 195, 225, 247, 248, 277, 278, 279, 304, 305
both both-and *and* either/or, 277
bottom-up/top-down, 48, 234, 240, 278; *see also* left-brain functions; right-brain functions boundary: and *Aufhebung*, 248; and 'not', negation, 251, 253; and zero, 252; between A and not A, 253; between levels, orders of complexity, 75–7, 167–70, 192, 312; between nature and culture, mediated by totemism, 115–16; between non-state and state societies, 94; cell membrane, 75; crossing *see* reductionism; digital, 222–4; iconic, 222–4; in schizophrenia, 203; mediating between system and environment, 115–16, 161, 253; neither system nor environment, 253; of language, labor, and kinship, 104, 168–9; organic, inorganic, 74–7, 168; *see also* environment; figure-ground relation; system; system, closed; system, open
boundless: and limit, 84
Le Bourgeois gentilhomme (Molière, 1670), 314
'boy's books', 324
The Boy's Own Paper, 22
'boy's weeklies', 22–3
brain development, 151; and environment, 232, 233, 236, 241–2; and selective stabilization, 229; *see also* left-brain functions; right-brain functions
brotherhood of men, xii, 46, 112
bullying, xi, 15, 22, 51

'The Burrow' (Franz Kafka, 1931), 306
business: and Tiller Girls, 288
bust *see* boom and bust

Cabaret (1972), 284
capacity; carrying, 107, 113, 165;
    creative, 165; productive, 167;
    productive, underuse of, 113, 121
capital: in imaginary opposition with
    labor, 82
capitalism: and booms, busts, 34–6, 37;
    and militarism, 37; and war, 34–8,
    41–2, 49; and survival, 105;
    destruction of other systems, 194;
    industrial, 194, 208; mercantile, 194;
    state and private, 35, 36, 49, 279;
    totalitarian, 50; *see also* revolution,
    capitalist
Captain Marvel, 21
Cartesianism, 86, 88, 306, 311
cash cropping; and hybrids, monoculture,
    wage labor, 194
caste, 119
castration, female, 118, 371
catch phrases, 43, 46
cathexis and intentionality, 178
    deficits, 41–2
causality: and metonymy, 198; and past,
    future, 78; as contiguity, in dreams,
    218; cybernetic, 78; efficient,
    newtonian, 78, 89, 303; final, 129–30;
    lineal (straight line), 303, 312; linear
    (proportional), 72, 303, 312; matter-
    energy, 76, 78; statistical, 312; *see also*
    constraint; goalseeking
cell: differentiation, 170; division, 275;
    membrane, 75; montage, 275
center: imparts structure, 114;
    organizing, 142; *see also axis mundi*;
    orientation
chance: in imaginary opposition with
    necessity, 312; *see also* chaos; disorder
chang (ordinary), 150
change, 81, 83, 85, 153, 246; adaptation
    to, 117; and analytic logic, 61, 277;
    and perspective, orientation, framing,
    punctuation, 258; and the four
    elements, 159–60; as an illusion, 153;
    as restructuring from below, 258–9;
    cyclic, 163, 274; environmental, 105,
    107, 274; dialectical, 248–51, 258–9,
    273–4, 275; dialectical, governed by
    information, 274; functional, 248;
    irreversible, 274; linear, lineal, 72, 163,

303, 312; of levels, 249, 258, 274;
    structural, 248–50, 279; survival
    through, 279; tactical, strategic, 258;
    technological, 258–9; uncommitted
    potential for future, 105, 194; *see also*
    causality; development, dialectic;
    disorder; evolution; history; mutation;
    noise; order
changeless, 83, 85
channel(s); and redundancy, 188;
    capacity of, 190, 192; coding,
    message, 161; correction, 192
chaos, 309; and order, 84; and right-brain
    functions, 239, 241; disorder as
    relative, 72, 135, 183; in imaginary
    opposition with determinism, 312–13;
    order from, 84, 239, 241; *see also*
    disorder; order
characteristics, acquired, 76
Cheyenne, 98, 99
chhi (matter-energy), 89–90
ch'i (extraordinary), 150
chiefs, types and origins of, 120, 121
chimpanzees, 320–1
The Chorus Line (1982): characteristics
    of, 283–5, 300; communicates its own
    explanation, 288; finale, 286; making
    of, 285–6, 300; opening montage,
    286; responses to, 286, 293, 295–8
churinga, 113, 116
cigarette cards, 20–1
Cinderella complex, 46–7
circle, vicious, 244
circumcision, 112
civilization, 95, 112, 117, 120
class; absence of, 119; ruling, 119–21;
    women as the original working, 108,
    120, 121; working, 3, 22; *see also*
    colonization; state
class distinction: hereditary, between men
    and women, 108
clichés, 249–61
clinches, 260–1
clitorectomy, 112
clockwork, 20, 56–7, 311
close-up, 207; and meaning, 275
code, 181, 188; acoustic, phonemic, 177,
    179, 181; and context, 72, 184; axis
    of the, 197, 202; binary, 239, 251, 257;
    continuous, discrete repertoire, 151–3,
    197; continuous, squash and stretch,
    152–3; from message to, 286–8;
    mediates communicants, messages,
    161; of English, 201; of higher logical

type than message, 152–3, 161; of
rules, and deep structure, 149–50,
161; speech, 223, 239; switching,
bilingual, 200; *see also* code-message
system; code-to-code; coding;
diversity; mediation; metaphor;
selection; variety
code-message system, 202; and context,
72, 183–4; and the four elements,
154–5, 157, 159–60; in aphasia,
197–205; minimum requirements for
communication, 72, 161, 184, 253;
restructured by innovation from
below, 259; *see also* code; code-to-
code; coding; mediation
code-to-code translation, 107, 109, 147,
200, 238
coding, 72, 175; analog, digital, iconic,
222–5; analog, iconic, 222–5, 279;
and context, order, goalseeking, 72,
184; and receiver, 72, 225; and
representation, 192; and sensing,
meaning, signification, 185, 225; and
substitution, 200, 206; digital, 222–5,
230, 240, 278, 279; disorder, in
aphasia, 199–204; flexibility of, 192;
iconic, 222–5, 240, 279; requisite
diversity of, 192; *see also* code;
communication; diversity;
information; mediation; selection;
variety
co-evolution, 105, 116, 163, 194
cogito (I think), 178
collective: and subjective, objective, 125
collision, contrast, contradiction,
montage of, 273
colonization, 12, 23, 26–9, 31, 45–7, 49,
83, 324; and Cinderella complex,
46–7; of men by men, 261; of women
by men, 46–6, 261; *see also* class; war
colors: primary, 150, 153; symbolic
meanings of, 220–1
combat: and play, 298–9
combination: and contexture, 198–200,
204–5, 215, 217–18; and selection,
94–5, 151, 153, 155, 156, 159–60,
197–200, 202, 204, 209, 211, 215,
255, 271; principle of, 153, 160;
without complexity, 174–5; *see also*
message; metonymy
command, 118, 190; and report,
question, 256, 318
commodities, 225, 279, 293
common sense, rules of, 259

communication, 10, 61, 69–70, 75, 93,
94, 98, 100, 101, 113, 118, 124, 129,
136, 137–8, 140, 141, 152–3, 171–2,
175, 184, 188, 197, 201, 202, 276,
279, 298; about communication, 104,
139, 205, 245, 298–9; and command,
control, 118, 190; and content,
relationship, 256–7; and emanation,
129–31, 163; and report, command,
question, 255–6; animal, human,
320–21; behavior is, 69; body, 76,
128, 137–8, 145, 153, 225; in
nervous, hormone system, 224, 226–9;
is oriented, transitive, 124, 161; levels
of, 61, 103, 104, 139, 205, 224, 234,
245, 252, 256, 288, 298–9; means of,
62, 91, 285, 293; minimum
requirements for, 161, 253; non-
verbal, 59, 61, 67, 70, 87, 132, 136–9,
151–3, 245, 283, 299; origins of, 93;
strategy as, 300; the secret of war, 298;
verbal, linguistic, *see* language; visual,
59–61, 67–9, 82, 87, 136, 138–9,
140–1, 209–16, 218–19, 221, 225,
229–30, 232–4, 236–7, 240–2,
254–6, 259, 269–76, 278–9, 283–93,
299–300; *see also* code; code-message;
code-to-code; coding; information;
film; language; left-brain functions;
literacy; media; montage; right-brain
functions
communism, xv, 51, 54
comparing *see* contrasting
comparison: and metaphor, 198
competition: and co-operation, 225;
dominating co-operation, 279; in
nature, leads to diversity, 42, 194;
under capitalism, leads to monopoly,
42, 194; with human, natural
environments, 165
competition/co-operation, 278
complementarity, 304
complex: not simple, 313, 314
complexity: and combination, 174–5;
and constraint, diversity, 172–6; and
redundancy, rules, 188; attention to,
184; biological, 73, 185, 189; change
in levels of, 274; creation of, 94;
increasing, 71, 168, 170, 189, 194;
levels, orders of 71, 73–7, 167–8, 192;
logical typing of, 167–8; loss of, 193;
organized, 309–10; reduction of levels
of, 192, 304, 312; structure(s) of, 175,
309, 314; unorganized, 312; *see also*

constraint; diversity; levels; logical typing

composite: persons, ideas, structures, words, 215, 218

composition and cutting: D. W. Griffith's grammar of, 270–1

comprehensive: the more, the less, 198

computation, 223, 224, 240, 241; and emulation, 229–30, 278

computation/emulation, 278

computer: analog, 222–3, 227, 252; digital, 222–3, 229–30, 251, 252; linguistic, 242, 278

concepts: discrete, class, 222

conceptuality: and sensuality, 163, 165

concrete see abstract

condensation: and displacement, 198, 202, 205, 214–18; and montage, 271; in dreams jokes, 214–18; see also code; dream; metaphor; similarity

condition(s): for communication, 72, 161, 202; for relationship, 253

La Condition humaine (René Magritte, 1936), 243, 244

configuration: and attention to complexity, 184

conflict: dialectical, 275, 276; hegelian, 83–4; of race, class, sex, 248

connections: and metonymy, 198; logical, in dreams, 218; minimum required to establish relationship, 161, 253

connotation, 185, 224, 239, 240

connoting see denoting

conquest, 118–21; at any cost, 8, 9, 55–6

conscious see unconscious

conscience, double, 232

consciousness, 246; intentionality of, 178; political, 46–7; see also unconscious

conspiracy theory, 92

constitution as grammar of liberty, 143

constraint(s), 70, 73–4, 77–9, 103, 168, 172–6, 188, 189; and innovation from below, 257–9; code of, 150, 161; complexity and, 167–70, 172–5; convergence of, 255; creativity and, 71, 77, 175; goalseeking within, 76, 77–9; hierarchy of, 74, 77–9, 133, 168, 182; left-brain functions and, 237–8; mediation and, 161, 165, 257–8; not causes, forces, 175; semi-dependent hierarchy of, 258; take advantage of, 77; see also code; complexity; diversity; mediation

content: and context, 256; and relationship, 225–6, 256–7, 278, 318; and system, structure, relation to environment, 102, 105

content/relationship, 256–7, 278

context 179, 308, 310; and closed systems, 60, 86; and coding, 72, 184; and content, relationship, 256–7; and learning how to learn, 249; and metaphor, metonymy, 198–9; and relationship, 225; and relativism, 306; and right-brain functions, 230, 233, 234, 239, 240, 241, 278; and text, 278; as message system, memory, map, 98; bound, 200; change of, 249, 286–8, 296, 299, 300; deficient, 204; exclusion from, 238; free, 310; human, 70–1; inclusion in, 238, 279; in displacement jokes, 217; loss of, 204–5; minimum of, 187; no information without, 184; of open systems, 60, 61, 62; of message, 199, 202; of reason, 86, 276, 279; of word order, sentence, 199, 200; relative to, 183; rereading in a new, 249, 250, 286–8; sensitive, 310; see also combination; environment; text

contexere (to weave), 134

contexture, 198–200, 202, 204–5, 215, 217–18; see also combination

contiguity, 198, 202, 205, 206, 210, 215, 217, 222; as dream sign for cause and effect, 218; see also combination; contiguity disorder; displacement; metonymy

contiguity disorder, 197–9, 204–6; dreams and, 218; literature and, 206; see also contiguity

continuity, 98, 197, 222, 224, 248, 274, 275; represents thirdness, 160

continuous see discrete

contradiction, 59, 101, 218, 247, 277; and identity, 224; and opposition, 101; between men and women, 101; montage of, 173; tangled, 248

contrast, 206

contrasting/comparing, 240, 241

control; cybernetic, 189–92, 195; requisite diversity of, 190, 192

convergent, 255

convergent/divergent, 237, 238, 239, 278

conversation; and dialectic, 84, 87; pictures and, 79

co-operation: and competition, 225, 278,

279; and correspondences, 135; in
organicist perspective, 80, 83, 87–9;
with nature, 116; *see also* competition
corpus callosum, development of, 235
correspondences, 154, 156; and co-
operation, 135
cortex, cerebral, 233
cosmos: and form, matter, 162–5; and
teleology, 78; as animate being, 86,
126, 154–5; as text, idea, poem, book,
128; finite, closed, 83; informed by
ideas, 88; mapping of, 115
coughing, 236
counter-insurgency, 26–7, 28–9, 31–3,
51–2; and concentration camps, 32;
and rape, 27–8, 32
creation, 87, 91, 113, 115
creativity, 69; alienated, 293; and
constraint, 71, 77, 175; and power,
59; as commodity, 259, 279; subject
of, 279
crying, 236
cubism: and metonymy, 206
cuing, unconscious, 140
culture, 73, 74, 76–7, 85; and genetic
potential, 229, 233, 235; and nature,
101, 116–17; and totemic code as
mediator, 116–17; as means of
representation, 168; in imaginary
opposition to nature, 82; is symbolic,
imaginary, real, 77; popular, 138, 288;
power of, 105
cut, Dedekind, 248
cybernetes (pilot), 115
cybernetics, 78, 90, 178, 179, 186,
189–92, 222–3
cycle: closed system, 274; logical,
paradoxical, 203; of repetition,
273–4; ritual, business, 203; yin-yang,
273–4; *see also* oscillation; wave

Daily Express, 33
Daily Telegraph, 22, 23, 28
Dames (1934), 289
de-development, of other societies, 194
de-diversification, 194
deductive/imaginative, 237, 238
deductive/synthetic, 278
defeat: strategic, tactical, 34, 50, 51–2
defeatism 43, 46–7, 53–4, 55, 63
deferred action, theory of, 249
definition, digital, 224; *see also*
denotation; signification
déjà vu, 231–2

demon, Maxwell, 185
dendrites, 226, 227, 229
denial, negation, 218, 245–6, 247, 252
denotation, 185, 224, 239; *see also*
signification
denoting/connoting, 240
dependency: and colonization, Cinderella
complex, 46–7; technological, 194
dependent *see* hierarchy; system
depersonalization, 232
depressed *see* euphoric
depression; of 1873–96, 35–6, 37; of
1929–41, 36; and recession, 35; *see
also* boom
derealization, 232
descent: marriage and, 105–7;
matrilineal, 101; patrilineal, 106
designation, 275
desire, 198; in dreams 214–15; *see also*
displacement; metonymy
despotism, 45, 94, 118, 291, 293, 298
determinatio (definition, limit), 251
determinism, 47, 76, 95, 105; and free
will, 79; in imaginary opposition with
chance, chaos, free will, 312–13
deus absconditus (hidden God), 113
development, embryonic, 170–1, 249,
275
deviation amplification, 190; *see also*
feedback, positive
deviation reduction, 190; *see also*
feedback, negative
diachrony, 198, 202, 237
diachrony/synchrony, 237
diagnosis, 59–62
dialectic, xiii, 62, 153, 246–51, 273–4,
276–9; and negativity, 245, 246; and
transformation of organization, 274;
confused with language, 247–8;
confused with matter-energy, motion,
248; confused with oscillation, 273–4;
hegelian, 84–6, 245, 246–7, 250;
imaginary, 86, 246–7; irreversible,
273–4; governed by information, 274;
not cyclic, 273–4; not matter-energy,
261, 274; of concepts, ideas, 84–6,
246, 249; of jokes, 250; of learning,
248–50, 287–8; of open systems,
248–51; real, 248–51; semiotic, 261,
274; so-called laws of, 247, 250–1; *see
also* Aha! experience; change; gestalt;
event; logic, dialectical
dictatorship, 45, 94, 118, 291, 293;
Stuart, 45, 118; Tudor, 118

difference, 92–3, 130, 180, 222, 223; *see also* continuity; continuous; distinction; information
differentiation; cell, 170, 249, 275; principle of, 153, 160
digital/analog, 235
digital and iconic/iconic and analog, 278
digital *see* coding; code; discrete; information; repertoire
dignity, xi, 46–7
disavowal, 218, 252
discipline: and skill, training organization, morale, 55; tactical, 25, 56
discontinuity, 93–4, 98, 153, 222, 237, 276, 287; dialectical, 84–5, 248–9
discontinuous/continuous, 248–9, 275, 276; *see also* great chain of being; code; information; repertoire
discourse: and language, 182; dominant, 88, 132–3; has a subject, 132–3; male, female, 132; of the Other, 293
discrete/continuous, 222–3, 237; *see also* code; information; repertoire
disorder: as environment of order, 313; as relative chaos, 72, 135, 183; from order, 117, 183–5, 239, 241, 248, 273, 274, 278; logical typing of, 313; in imaginary opposition with order, 313; relative to context, 183; entropic, 309, 310, 313; *see also* information from noise; innovation; novelty; order
disorganization, 135, 183, 185, 309; *see also* disorder; entropy; order; organization
displacement: and condensation, 198, 202, 205, 211, 215–18; and jokes, 215, 217–18; in dreams, 215; linguistic, 215, 217–18; of meaning, 217–18; *see also* metonymy
distinction, 92–3, 130, 170, 181, 222; and opposition, 156; between levels, 223; class, 108; *see also* difference; discrete; information
distinctive features, 176–7, 179, 180–2, 223
distraction factories, 291
divergent *see* convergent
diversion *see* displacement
diversity: and ambiguity, precision, 299; and boundary, 76; and competition, 42, 194; and complexity, 76, 172–5, 176, 309, 312; and constraint, 172–5, 309; and differentiation, 153, 160; and

future, 279; coded, 135, 188, 225; as combination of varieties, 172–3, 312; destruction of, 193–4; genetic, individual, social, 76, 105; homogenization of, 194; increasing, 71, 194, 279; loss of, 42, 194; organized, 172, 309; reduction, neutralization of, 192–5, 312; requisite, 189–92, 279, 312; structural, 193–4; unity and, 176; *see also* complexity; constraint; variety
divide-and-rule, 44, 47, 49, 120
DNA, 75, 109, 175, 183, 186, 189, 197, 223, 229
Dogon, 135–6
dominant: and both-and, either/or, 277; and subordinate, 80, 248; *see also* domination
domination, 279; and imaginary oppositions, 82; and symmetrization, 82; and subordination, 80, 248, 285; and the mass ornament, 291, 293;
double bind, iv, 203, 210, 243, 244
The Double Helix (James Watson, 1968), 307
doubling time, 38
down, up and: not symmetrical, 79, 80–1
drawing: and communication, 283; and melody, 208; and right-brain functions, 236; and speech, 283
dream(s): absence of negation in, 252–3; and metaphor, metonymy, 215; and tense, negation, contradiction, 224; content, text, thoughts, 214–15, 218–19; interpretation of, 136–7, 198, 202, 205, 211, 214–19, 22; not a language, 214, 215, 219; of society, 285; work, 214–15, 218–19; *see also* condensation; displacement; jokes; metaphor; montage
dream time: and history, 114–17; and life on earth, 115; and memory, 114–15; and orientation, *axis mundi*, 113–17, 135, 149, 161–3, 165; and origins of reality, 93; and symbolic geography, 114–16, 117–18; as locus of reference, mediation, 135; *see also* ideology; memory
dualisms, 84
due process, 305, 324
duration, 249, 277; learning through, 287
dureé (duration), 287

ecology, 42, 56, 179, 193–5

economy, subsistence, 113
ecosystem: and diversity, stability, 193–5; fittest, 76, 195; natural, social, 75
editing, 254–6, 271–3; continuity, 255, 270; invention of, 269–70; narrative, 271; *see also* montage
effect *see* cause
efficiency, energy conversion, 194
either A or not-A, 277
either either/or *or* both-and, 277
either/or, 48, 59, 60, 61, 74, 83, 126, 177, 222, 225, 233, 248, 250, 252, 277, 278, 279, 304, 305; and analytic logic, types A, B, C, 313; *see also* logic, analytic; more or less
electricity: and unity, identity of opposites, 273; as model for opposites, 247
The Elementary Structures of Kinship (Claude Lévi-Strauss, 1949), 306
elements, discrete: code, repertoire of, 92, 94, 153, 222; *see also* information, digital
elements, the four: and five Chinese, 153; and love and strife, 153, 160; and mediation, 159–61; as code-message system, 153–60, 161, 162–3; oppositions, affinities between 80, 159; rules for, 159–60; structure of, 154–5, 157, 159; the fifth, 153
emanation, 128; as communication, 129, 130, 163; as information, 163; from God, 87, 129, 130, 163
emblems, 219–21
emergence: and condensation, 271; and creation, 271; and dialectic, 246–51; and framing, 256; and learning, 249; and montage, 256, 271, 274–6, 286–8; and recognition, 246–7; and restructuring, 250, 258–9; and transcendence, 84; in development, evolution, 249; in jokes, 250; of juxtaposed metaphors, 276; of kinship, language, labor, 75; from message to code, 259, 286–8; of novelty, 273–6; of whole, gestalt, 249, 271, 288; structural, 250, 249, 258–9; *see also* Aha! experience; dialectic; evolution; history; innovation; qualities, emergent; learning; novelty
emotion, 70, 76, 152, 225; and montage, 275–6; as environment of reason, 82; in imaginary opposition with reason, 82;
emotional *see* rational
emulation, 278; learning by, 59, 229–30; *see also* computation
end, 129–30
energy, 74; and information, 71–3; conservation of, 184; conversion efficiencies, 194; free and bound, 184; internal, external source of, 274; psychic, 215; *see also* matter-energy; thermodynamics
engine, steam, 190–1
engineering, 17, 57–9, 229–30
entertainment, 62, 71, 91, 113, 285, 299, 300
entities and relations, 178–9
entropy: as missing information, 185; negative, 185, 187; of the planet, 194; of pollution, 74; physical, semiotic, 274; positive, 74, 194, 309, 310
envelopment: strategic, 279, 300
environment: and boundary, 74–7, 104, 115–16, 161, 167–70, 192, 223–4, 251–3, 312; and reduction of diversity, 193–5; and right-brain functions, 230, 233, 234, 239, 240, 241, 278; and system, structure, rules, content, 102, 105; and Three-Way Rule, 253; as message system, map, memory, 96, 98–101, 114–15, 117–18; both system and, 194, 195; brain development and, 229, 232, 233, 236, 242; carrying capacity of, 107, 113, 121, 165; code-message system and relation to, 161, 202; entropy, increases in, 185; exploitation, destruction, of, 82, 86; in dependent hierarchy, 73–5, 82, 86, 133, 168; internal, external, 170; 'not', as boundary between system and environment, 253; of closed systems, 60; of complexity, 314; of higher logical type than open system, 252, 253, 277; of order, 313; open system, dependent on, 60, 73, 74, 76, 86, 102, 105, 165, 168, 179, 183–4, 185, 278, 279, 309; *see also* context; ecosystem; system
epistemology, bioenergetic, 88, 314–17
equality, 106, 121
Erkenntnis (recognition), 246
eroticism, 22
error, 187

esse est percipi ('To be is to be perceived') (Berkely), 83
essential and non-essential, 203
eternal return, 163, 231
ethics, 49, 62
euphoric/depressed, 235
event: dialectical, 249, 250; functional, 229; great, 114–15; lineal, 238; mythical, 114–15; unique, closed, separate, 61
evolution, 273; and embryonic development, 249; and extinction, revolution, 194; Darwinian, Lamarckian, 76; divergent, 194; natural, 71, 75, 76, 117, 183–5, 248, 249, 273; not teleological, 78–9; *see also* emergence; history; novelty
evolutionism, 112
ewekë, 134
exceptions to rules, 103–4
exchange, 67, 72, 75; kinship, 104–8; of women, 94; *see also* communication; value
exclusion, competitive, 194
exclusion/inclusion, 238, 240, 241, 279
exogamy, 104–5; and adaptivity, flexibility, 107; function of, 107
expansion, territorial, 120–1
expect the unexpected, 17
experience, 198, 229, 230, 233; organizing center of, 142
explicit/tacit, 237, 238
extinction, 74; and evolution, revolution, 194; *see also* Rule
eye, 219, 221; speaking to the, 298

faces, recognition of, 234–5
factory: model, 311; system, 259
familiar/unfamiliar, 234–5, 240, 241
familiarity/novelty, 278
family, 46–7
fascism, 22–3, 27, 50
fate and dictatorship, 291
fear: and Cinderella complex, 46–7
features *see* distinctive features
feedback: and doubling time, 38; and output, input, 191; exponential, 38, 42, 189–91; negative, positive, 189–91
feeling, 87, 91, 276; *see also* emotion; meaning; sensing
Field Service Regulations, 1912 (War Office), 55
field theory, 310
55 Days at Peking (1963), 31

Fight Stories, 22
figurative, 167; and literal, in similarity disorder, 200–3; not the literal, 146; confused with literal, 234; *see also* literal
figure of speech (trope), 200, 219, 224, 239, 275; inability to comprehend, 234
figure-ground relation, 205, 209–11; and schizophrenic, paradoxical, oscillation, iv, 203–4, 210, 244
film, 62–3, 69, 77, 206–7, 242, 259–61, 269–76; and fascism, 291, 293; and stereotypes of American women, 261–9; compared with speech, language, 138–40, 269–76; not a language, 138–40, 269–76; *see also* montage
Financial Times, 22
fitness, reproductive, 320–1
flags, functions of, 140–1
flanking movements, 119
flexibility: and kinship, exogamy, 107; and structural diversity, 194; and uncommitted potential for future change, 105, 194
floursack, half-filled, 153
fluctuation *see* oscillation
Footlight Parade (1933), 284, 288, 290
force, 77, 78, 90, 303
forgetting, 198
form, 114, 175–6, 187; and conceptuality, sensuality, 163, 165; and function, 149; and information, 87; and matter, 88–9, 130, 162–5; Aristotelian, 80, 88, 90; Bacon on, 87; and sensation, 165; communication by changes in, 152–3; hierarchy of, 130; human, as pattern for structure, 154–5, 164; in equilibrium with matter, 163, 165; modules of, 187; new, 249; pyramid of, 162, 164–5; *see also* gestalt; whole
Fortune, 51, 54
The Four Feathers (1939), 49
framing, 125, 222, 234; and perspective, orientation, punctuation, 257–8; and punctuation, 254–6; and strategy, 258; logical, 251; new, 287
free will: and goalseeking within constraints, 79; and determinism, 79; in imaginary opposition with determinism, chaos, disorder, 313
freedom: and constraint, 79; and

necessity, 79, 84, 313; semiotic, 77–8, 181–2
frequency modulation, 226, 227
From Being to Becoming: Time and Complexity in the Physical Sciences (Ilya Prigogine, 1980), 311
front to back: not symmetrical, 79
full, opposed to empty, 80
functions *see* left-brain functions; right-brain functions; truth
future, 279; re-evaluation of, 250
'Fuzzy Wuzzy' (Rudyard Kipling, 1892), 23

gap: digital, 93, 223, 313; synaptic, 226–9
Gem, 22
general and particular, 60, 252
generalist *see* specialist
generosity: in the other societies, 108, 119, 121; and the origins of chiefs, ruling classes, 121
genes, 76, 105, 107; levels of, 189
geography, symbolic, scientific, 114–16, 117–18; *see also* environment; topology
geometry, 120
gestalt, emergent, 288; *see also* emergence; qualities
Gestalt (form), 249
gesture, 143, 145
giftgiving, 92, 121, 134
goalchanging, 79
goalseeking, 77–9, 86, 103, 150, 153, 167, 178, 184, 309–10; and coding, 72, 161; and mediation, 72, 161; teleonomy, 79, 129; within constraints, 78–9; *see also* adaptive; communication; systems, open
God, 30, 47, 79, 83, 87, 154, 162, 163, 164, 165, 231, 247; as perfectly communicative, 129; hidden, 113; objective, 125, 126; voice, word of, 126–8; *see also* logos
govern, 172–3
government, 195
governor, centrifugal, 189–91
grammar, 150, 151, 153–60, 219; and constitution, liberty, 143; and naming, 201; of composition and cutting, 270–1; universal, 143–5
The Green Hornet, 21
ground *see* figure-ground
growth, 72, 190, 246; and arms races, 38,

42, 190; and doubling time, 38; exponential, 38, 42, 190; *see also* feedback, positive
Gunga Din (1939), 49
Gung-Ho, 50–4

hands *see* legs
handwriting, 187
harmony, 202; and melody, 198
Hawaiians, 94, 103
head, 207, 210, 219
hemispheres, complementary dominance of cerebral, 232–4, 236; *see also* left-brain functions; right-brain functions
Henry VI, Part 2, 44
heraldry, 208–13, 216, 219–21
Here Come the Waves (1944), 284
heterogeneity, 176; *see also* complexity; diversity; perfection
hierarchy: and series, 80; hierarchy, dependent, 73–4, 86, 126, 133, 167–70, 171, 185; dependent, between A and not-A, 277; dependent, between I and not-I, 251–2; dependent, between order and disorder, 313; dependent, inverted, 130; dependent, between quality and quantity, 126; dependent, symmetrized, 82, 205; illegitimate, of power, 80, 305; linguistic, 205; logical, 60, 102; mechanical, 57, 60; of constraints, 77–9, 167–9, 172–3, 175, 176, 310; of form, matter, being, 130; of logical typing, 168; of rules, 103; of strategy and tactics, 258; of variety, 60; orientation of, 86; semi-dependent, of perspective, orientation, framing, punctuation, 257–8; symmetrization, inversion of, 82, 205; *see also* levels; logical typing
hieroglyphics, 207, 211, 214, 285
historical/timeless, 237
history, xiii-xv, 71, 76, 78–9, 82–3, 85–6, 184, 185, 246, 250, 274; and memory, xiv, 62–3; and surface manifestations, 293; innovations translated into traditional patterns, 117; sacred, 114, 115; strategic and tactical, xiv; television and, 62–3; visual, 283; *see also* geography
holistic, 234, 276; *see also* step-by-step; whole; whole-part relation
Hollywood, 283, 286, 288, 300
homeostasis (steady state), 178, 189, 192
homogeneity, 176, 194

homophobia, 297
hormone system, 224, 226–9
Hotspur, 21
humor, 239, 242; inability to appreciate, 234; *see also* jokes
humours, the four, 154–6, 158
hunting, cybernetic, 193
hybrids: and cash cropping, monoculture, wage labor, 194

I and not-I, 251–2
iconic *see* boundary; coding; digital; information
icons, 279; and senses, meaning, 225; visual, flags as, 140–1; *see also The Chorus Line*; communication; non-verbal, ideas; images
idealism: in imaginary opposition with materialism, 83, 248; metaphysical, 83, 130
ideas, 91, 129; and reality, 82–3; and relativism, 306; association of, 198; clear and distinct, 224; communication of, in montage, 275; hegelian dialectic of, 846, 246–7; history of, 79; in imaginary opposition with reality, 83; mind as, 306; play on, 217; role in society, history, 83, 117–18
identification, 205, 218
identity (a=a), 200; and Cinderella complex, 46–7; and contradiction, 224; for others, 117; in kinship, geneaology, 92, 96–7, 117; logical, 200, 224; national, personal, 46
identity/novelty, 278; *see also* innovation; negation; novelty
ideograph, 182
ideology, 83, 113–17, 192, 193, 208; and change, 92, 117; and origins, 91–4, 113; and Cinderella complex, 46–7; as ground of truth, 91; and television, 63; dominant, 91–2, 288, 298, 300; imaginary and real, 91, 116; imaginary, symbolic of real, 116, 163, 165; of 'boy's books', 324; of 'boy's weeklies', 21–3; of retribution, 324; non-verbal, 298; production, reproduction of, 293, 298, 300; role of visual images, structures in, 298; verbal and non-verbal, 219, 261; *see also The Chorus Line*; colonization; defeatism; dream time; image; imaginary
ideostructure, 98

if not *a*, then *b*: and 1, 0, of digital computer, 251; logic of binary opposition (Type C), 313, 316
if . . . then, 224
illiteracy, strategic, 48
image, 91, 197, 200, 286; body, 96–7; alien, 288; ambiguity of, 299; and representation, 271, 276; as dreams of society, 285; for image, 198; non-verbal, 225, 279; spatial, and social reality, 285; popular, 288–94; verbal, 207–8, 276; visual, 136, 209–16, 219–21, 225; *see also The Chorus Line*; communication, non-verbal; figurative; icons; ideas; metaphor; metonymy
imaginary, 67, 113, 214–15, 244, 248, 252; and culture, 77; and real, 67, 86, 146; and symbolic, real, 67–9; and symmetrization, inversion, 82, 205; not the real, 146; symbolic of real, 116, 165; *see also* opposites
imagination, 59, 67, 69; *see also* image
imaginative *see* deductive; propositional
imperialism: and conquest states, 120–1; and 'manhood', male supremacy, 31, 54–5; education in, 21
impulsive *see* realistic
inappropriate *see* appropriate
inbetweens, 269
incest: prohibition of, 102–5, 251; enigma of, exceptions to, 103
inclusion *see* exclusion
independence, 46
indeterminacy, 178
individual: abstract, 84; biological, 70, 74, 76, 77; human, social, 70, 74; *see also* self
individuality, 230
inequality, 119–21; *see also* class
infanticide, 112
infinite: God as, 83; Hegel on, 85; progress, 83, 175–6
infinity, infinities: analog, digital, 223
inflation, 34, 35–6, 41, 42, 190; doubling time, 38; out of control by 1968, 307–8
information: analog, 61, 93, 222–5, 235, 279, 299; and coding, context, 184; and emanation, 163; and entropy, 184–5, 187, 309; and redundancy, 185, 187–8, 189; and sensing, meaning, signification, 185, 225; and surprise value, 175, 186, 187, 188, 273,

209; binary-digital, 177; binocular, monocular, 236; coded, 135, 185, 225, 286; contextualized, 299; dependent on perception, 72, 305; digital, 61, 93–4, 151, 153, 222–5, 235, 240–1, 252, 279, 299; distinct from matter-energy, 70, 71–3, 88–9, 153, 163, 171–2, 183, 185, 251; from noise, 117, 183–4, 239, 241, 248, 249, 257, 273, 274, 278; iconic, 139, 153, 222–5, 240-1, 279, 299; *li* as, 90; loss of, 192; mathematical definition of, 185, 188, 309; numerical, 299; organizes other information, 72, 103; potential, 185, 188; rereading, in next context, 249, 250; rules as stored, 188; spatial, 236; symbolic, imaginary, real, 67–9; uncoded, 135, 185, 224, 286; *see also* diversity; noise; novelty; order; variety
infrastructure, 178
initiation, 112, 115–16
innocent/sophisticated, 240
innovation, 120, 248; absorbed into myth, 117; and emulation, 230; and right-brain functions, 229, 230, 233, 240; and rulebreaking, 103; from below, 258–9; strategic, 119; strategic and tactical, 258–9; technological, 258–9; *see also* invention; novelty; order from disorder
instability, ecosystemic, 193
intellect/intuition, 234, 237
intellectual/intuitive, 278
intellectual/sensuous, 237
intelligence, 240
intentionality, 178
interest: compound, 190; investment of, 178; *see also Besetzung*; growth, exponential
'interpenetration of opposites', 250
interpersonal *see* solipsistic
Intolerance (1916), 271
intonation, 145, 217–18
Introduction à la lecture de Hegel (Àlexandre Kojève, 1933–9; ed. Raymond Queneau, 1947), 306
intuition *see* intellect
intuitive, 276, 278; *see also* intellectual; rational
invention, 67, 90, 190, 248, 249, 258–9; *see also* innovation; novelty
inversion: of dependent hierarchy, 82, 130; of figure and ground, 203; *see also* symmetrization

It's a Mad, Mad, Mad, Mad World (1963), 261

jargon, 209, 211
Jerusalem (William Blake, 1804), 207–8
jokes, 123, 198, 202, 205, 211, 215–19, 250, 251; condensation, 215–17; displacement, 215–18
jump, in levels of communication, 249, 250, 275, 288; *see also* dialectic; event; emergence; figure-ground; learning; whole-part relation
justice, natural, 305, 324
juxtaposition, 254–5; and emergent novelty, meaning, 271, 272, 273; in montage, 254–6, 269–76; of metaphors, 276

Kariera, 106–7
Kenntnis (knowledge), 246
kinship, 67, 92–5, 101–2, 105–8, 116, 209; and class, race, 105; and etiquette, 95, 116; and language, labor, 75, 94; language model of, 94; origins of, 92–3; role in state, non-state societies, 94–5; system, structure, 105–8; *see also* memory
knowledge, 129; and information, sensing, meaning, signification, 185, 225; and literacy, 58; and recognition, 246, 249; constituents of, 185, 225; of principles, codes, structures, strategy, 58; fingertip, 60, 225, 230; levels of, 185, 225; *see also* unconscious
kosmos, 126
Ku Klux Kuties (1980), 296

labor: and big man systems, 121; and kinship, language, division of, 75, 94, 120; division of, 94, 120; environment of capital, 82; in imaginary opposition with capital, 82; types of, 94, 120; wage, and cash cropping, hybrids, monoculture, 194
labor potential: as commodity, 259; *see also* creativity
lakshana (sign), 134
langage, 132–3
language, 59, 67, 70, 87, 124–5, 126–9, 130–1, 133–40, 144–5, 196–208, 223, 225, 226, 230, 232–42, 246–7, 251–3, 259–60, 275–9, 299; american sign, 140; and ambiguity,

diversity, precision, 299; and
classification, specification, abstraction,
245; and communication, 59, 67, 70,
87, 124–5, 126–9, 130–40, 144–5;
and communication, speech, as models
of reality, 134–6; and discourse,
132–3; and dreams, 214, 215, 219;
and film 138–9; and kinship, labor, 75,
94, 95; and negation, 245–6, 251–3;
and theology, objectivity, 126–30; and
thought, reason, 138; as goalseeking
system, 178; capacities of, 95;
ecological validity of, 130; film is not,
275; learning, 199–201; levels of, 133,
139, 140, 200–1, 205; no primitive,
112, 137; not a statement, 132; part of
human reality, 132; perfect, 126, 130;
Priestley on, 144–5; role of body in,
226; schizophrenic, 202–3, 224,
240–1; structure of, 151, 176–82; see
also left-brain functions; right-brain
functions
langue, 133, 202
Laos, 40
lap dissolve, 207
law, codes of, 120
leap, dialectical, 275
learning, 230; after-the-event, 23,
249–50, 287; and brain development,
selective stabilization, 229, 232–3,
236, 241–2; and context, 249, 286,
287; bottom-up, tactical, 48; by
emulation, 59, 61, 229–30; by
example, 62; by experience, 62; by
reasoning, 287; by seeing, sensing,
287; conscious, unconscious, 286, 287;
dialectic of, 249–51, 287–8; how to
learn, 249, 287; levels of, 249, 287;
through conflict, 249; through
duration, 249, 287; time and duration
dependent, 249, 287; top-down,
strategic, 48; unconscious, 61, 286;
zero, 249
left-brain functions, 48, 59, 61, 87, 197,
230, 231–42, 277–8
legs, 219; and mass ornament, 288, 291,
293; and means of communication,
representation, 293; hips, breasts, 295
letters: and words, numbers, 236, 278;
and left-brain function, 236, 278;
feature recognition of, 187
levels: and reductionism, 192, 304, 312;
discontinuity between 223, 249, 250,
287; epistemology of, 286; figure and

ground, iv, 201, 203–4, 210, 244; loss
of, 201, 203–4; of communication and
reality, 61, 72–3, 79–80, 86, 126,
139, 149–50, 151, 154, 155, 161,
167–70, 176–82, 189, 201, 249, 250,
275, 288; of complexity, organization,
73–5, 167–9, 172, 176, 182, 250,
274; of language, 133, 139, 140,
176–82, 189; of learning, 249–50,
287–8; of logic, 201; of logical typing,
126, 169–72; of structure, 176–82; of
syntax, 151; symmetrization of, 80, 82,
205; see also logical typing;
metacommunication
li (organization, information), 89–90
liberalism, 305
Life, 51
life: and non-life, 74–6; as quest, 85;
systems involving or simulating, 72, 78
The Life of an American Fireman (1902),
269
lineal/intuitive, 278
lineal/non-lineal, 237
linguistics, 177–82; structural, 79,
176–81; synchronic, diachronic, 177
literacy: conscious, unconscious, 283; in
silent film, 207; is power, 58, 283;
machine, and men and women, 58;
non-verbal, 283, 299; strategic, 47–9,
58; visual, 68, 286, 299; see also
learning; media literacy
literal/figurative, 239, 240, 278
literal/metaphorical, 240
The Lives of a Bengal Lancer (1935), 28
living as a sacred act, 112
logic, analytic, 59–62, 224, 232; analog-
digital (Type B), 313, 316; and change,
248, 250, 277; complement to
dialectic, 250; diagnostic, 59–60, 304;
digital (Type A), 313, 316; excludes
change, dialectic, 61, 250; ignores
levels of communication and reality,
61; included in dialectical logic, 250;
many-valued, 313, 316; non-
contextual, one-dimensional, static,
closed system, 6, 60–2; of binary
opposition (if not a, then b) (Type C),
251, 313, 316; outside time and
change, 277; single-level, static, 60–2,
250, 277; symmetrical, 277, 278; treats
events as unique, closed, not part of
any pattern, 61; see also information,
digital
logic: and feeling, 276; diagnostic,

59–62; digital, rational, 276; holistic, 276; in dreams, 218–19; intuitive, 276; left brain *see* left-brain functions; many-valued, 313; right brain *see* right-brain functions; *see also* logic, analytic; logic, dialectical; logical typing

logic, dialectical, 62, 304; and open system, 60, 62; asymmetrical, 278; contextual, many-leveled, relational, 62; and non-contradiction, 250, 276; includes analytic logic, 250; many-leveled, 277, 316; time and duration dependent, 277; *see also* dialectic

logical/ecological, 232

logical typing, 86, 126, 169–72, 224, 314; and complexity, 267–70; and dialectical event, joke, 249–50; and emergent qualities, iv, 167–70, 210, 244; collapsed, iv, 210, 243, 244; confusion of, 201; hierarchies of, 167–70; of code, message, 161; of environment, system, 252; of integers, zero, 253; of 'not', 245; of order, disorder, 313; of past, 250; of symbolic, imaginary, and real, 243–4; requisite levels of, 191–2, 312; *see also* communication; hierarchy; levels; logic

logistics/reconnaissance, 278

logos, 87, 135

logos (principle), 93

loop, strange, iv, 210, 243, 244

love (attraction), principle of unity and combination, 153, 160

lying, and truth, 260

machines: literacy in, 56–60, 61; the five simple, 58; the three basic, 58

macrocosm and microcosm, correspondences between, 135, 136, 154–6, 157, 162–4

Magnet, 22

man, misuse of term, 71

mana, 96

'manhood', 27, 31, 54–5

many *see* one

many-dimensioned, 234, 279

many-valued, 313

map, mapping, 98, 107–11, 117; and territory, 108–9, 147; of environment, 114–16; of kinship structure, 101; not the territory, 146; structuring information, 107; village plans, 99–102; *see also* code-to-code translation

The Maple Leaf, 23

marae, 96, 98

marked, unmarked, 179, 181

marker, as bearer of information, 72–3, 140, 234

marriage and descent, 105–7

The Marvel Family, 21

the mass ornament, 288–94

masses as medium, 291–3

materialism, 83; in imaginary opposition with idealism, 248

materiality (sensuality) and conceptuality, 163, 165; *see also* form

matriarchy, 101; US as, 261

matrilineality, 101

matter: mind and, 84, 87; pyramid of form and, 162, 164–5; *see also* form

matter-energy: distinct from information, 71–3, 153, 163, 171–2, 183, 185, 251; exists independent of perception, 72, 305; *see also* information

Mbuti, 100, 101

meaning, 95, 103, 138–9, 151, 152, 186, 204, 222, 224, 234, 270; and information theory, 186, 188; and orientation, mediation, reference point, 114–15; and redundancy, 188; and right-brain functions, 239–42; and sensing, signification, 185, 225; and signification, 185, 223, 225, 239, 278; and structure, 188, 197; and thirdness, 160; anticipation of, 188; as coded sensing, 185, 225; displacement of, 217–18; figurative, 200; intentionality of, 178; new, 249; *see also* connotation; denotation; signification

means: and ends, 62; of communication, 62, 71, 285, 293; of production, reproduction, 167–9, 239; of representation, 168, 169, 284, 293

Meccano, 57–9, 260

mechanism, 86, 87, 88, 131; *see also* organicism

méconnaissance (failure to recognize), 246

media, 70–1; and socialization, 125; social, 62, 70–2, 91, 96, 125, 283, 285; video, 283; *see also* media literacy

media literacy, 68; and left-, right-brain functions, 299; conscious, 283; unconscious, inarticulate, unrecognized, 283; verbal, non-verbal,

299; *see also* communication, visual; literacy

mediation, 72, 85, 114, 135, 160–1, 165, 202, 252; and code, message, 161; and constraint, 161, 257–8; and creative capacity, 165; and mediated, 161; and system-environment relation, 165, 253; and the four elements, 159–61; and thirdness, 160, 253; by the other, 124; locus of, 135; locus of, not individual, 165; of boundary between system and environment, 253; of personal identity, 117; of third term, 160, 253; of totemism, between nature and culture, 115–16; orientation of, 161, 163; triangle of, 161, 202; *see also* *axis mundi*; code-message; orientation

medium, 71, 72, 88, 109, 145, 160; and message, memory, 62–3; masses as, 293

melancolia, 156, 158

melody, 208, 236; and harmony, 198, 202; recognition, of 234

memory, 95, 225, 231–2, 247, 249; deep, 224; preconscious, ordinary memory, 224, 232, 246; social, topological, symbolic, 96, 98–101, 114–15, 117–18; television and, 62–3; the lasting word, 133–5; unconscious, 224, 232, 246; unwritten, 96, 98; *see also* dream time; trace; unconscious

men: and women, hereditary class distinction, 108; brutalized by other men, 27, 50–1

message: and content, relationship, 256–7, 278; and innovation, 257–9; as report, command, question, 256; axis of the, 198, 202; deep, surface structure of, 150; organism as, 132; not intransitive, 124; 'this is play', 298–9; transition to code, iv, 210, 244, 286–8; *see also* code; code-message system; contiguity; displacement; metonymy

message disorder: in aphasia, 199, 204–6

metabolism, 72

metacommunication, 104, 139, 205, 245, 320; and play, 298; emergence of, 298–9; failures of, 234; *see also* communication; levels; logical typing; metalanguage

metalanguage, 139, 169–70, 206; loss of, in contiguity disorder, 205; loss of, in similarity disorder, 200–3; *see also* metacommunication

metanumber, zero as, 252

metaphor: and affective speech, 241; and condensation, favored in dreams, 202, 215–16; and condensation jokes, 214–15; and contiguity disorder, 204–5, 206; and metonymy, 197–8, 239, 241, 278; and metonymy, in verbal image, 207–8; and montage, 275, 276; and paradox, 210, 243–4; and rebus, 211, 216; and right-brain functions, 197, 239, 278; cinematic, 225, 275, 276; dominant in affective speech, 241, 276; dominant over metonymy, in contiguity disorder, 199, 204–5; in art, 210, 243, 244; is meant, 146, 167, 201; juxtaposition of, 276; meaning figure of speech, 200, 201, 224, 240; studies of, 206; way of, 206–7; *see also* code; condensation; similarity

metaphorical *see* literal

metaphysics, 80

metarules, 103, 104

metasystem, 248

metaword, 'not' as, 252

meter, poetic, 206

metonymy: and rebus, 211, 216; dominant in abstract language, 240; dominant over metaphor, in similarity disorder, 199, 201; and displacement, in dreams, jokes, 198, 215–19; and left-brain functions, 197, 239, 278; and metaphor, 197–8, 239, 241, 278; and metaphor, in verbal image, 207–8; and montage, 275; and rebus, 211, 216; and similarity disorder, 199–203; cinematic, 255, 275, 276; in art, cubism, 206, 210; lack of studies of, 206; way of, 206–7; *see also* message; displacement; contiguity

metonymy/metaphor, 197–8, 239, 241; 278

milieu, social, as organizing center, 142

militarism: and manliness, monarchism, 21; and social control, 37; as a power on its own, 42

mimicry, 123

mind: and body, brain, 76; and matter, 84, 87; as master of the universe, 85, 87; as pure form, 165; in imaginary opposition with body, 82; subject of, 279; systems involving or simulating life or, 72, 78; *see also* form; information; soul; subject

minus-1, not-1, 251
mirror image, 85
misogyny, xii, 69, 295, 297
Mitteilung (communication), dreams as, 136
mobility, superior, answers superior numbers, 7
mode of production, reproduction, 167–9
model, modelmaking: and plans, pictures, 236, 278; and right-brain functions, 57–9, 230, 236, 278; synchronic, 106–8; *see also* language; mechanism; communication; montage; organicism; semiotics
monoculture, and hybrids, cash cropping, wage labor, 194
monopoly, 194; economic competition leading to, 42
montage, 254–6, 269–76; and verbal image, 276; and designation, signification, meaning, 275; and emergent novelty, qualities, 271, 272, 273; and figures of speech, 275; and imagistic value of words, 275; and juxtaposition, 271, 272, 273, 276; of metaphors, 276; and sensual thinking, 276; as affective speech, 276; as inner speech enriched by sensual thinking, 276; and speech, logical, affective, 275–6; as a complex of meanings, values, emotions, 271–2; as a means of communicating ideas, 275; as a means of speaking, 275; as a special film language, a special form of film speech, 275; condensation and, 271; defined, by Eisenstein, 271–3; developed by Griffith, 270–1; dialectic of, 273; Eisenstein on, 271–6; in semiotic terms, 275, 276; invented by Porter, 269–70; language model of, 275–6; linking, connective, 273; metaphoric, 207; not a language, 275; of collision, contrast, contradiction, 273, 275; organic model of, 275; parallel, 207, 271; poetic, 272; shot as montage cell, 275; structure of, affective and emotional, 276; structure of, is the structure of emotional speech, 275; vertical, polyphonic, 274; *see also* film; metaphor; metonymy
morale: and skill, organization, training, discipline, 55; essential to success, xi, 7, 43, 55; failure of, 7

more-or-less, 177, 179, 22, 225, 252, 279, 313; *see also* both-and; either/or
morphemes, 176–82
morphology, 175–6
motion: circular, simple, eternal, 80–1; lineal (straight line), 303; lineal (effect is proportional to cause), 303; Newton's laws of, 303; Newton's third law, 250–1; simple harmonic, 203, 274; to be composed by inventor, 59
murder, 260
Murder at the Vanities (1934), 284
Murinbata, 114
music, 198, 208, 283, 285, 300; patterns of, 298
mutation, 117, 183–4
myth of origins, 92–4, 113–15
mythology, judeo-christian, lineal, not cyclic, 163

Nachträglichkeit (learning after the event), 249
The Naked Civil Servant (1975), 284, 297
name, not the thing, 146
naming, 169, 205, 224; and metaphor, 200–3; and metonymy, 198, 205; in contiguity disorder, 204–5; in similarity disorder, 200–3
naming of parts, 27, 58, 63, 302, 322
Napoleon (1927), 270, 298
narrative, inability to follow, 234, 241
natural: in imaginary opposition with unnatural, 80
nature: and culture, 94, 101, 104; and history, 82; and nurture, 76; and totemic code, as mediator, 115–16; book of, 128; communicates in sketches, 283; competition in, leads to diversity, 42; in imaginary opposition with culture, 82; no general dialectics of, 247; organicism, 88; stewardship of, 115; *see also* complexity; culture; inorganic; levels; organic; real; society
navel, 210
navigation, South Sea, 109–11
necessity, 74, 79; in imaginary opposition with chance, 312
negation, 224, 240, 245–7, 248, 251–3; absent from analog, 224; absent from dreams, the unconscious, 218, 252–3; and denial, 218, 245–6, 247, 252; by opposition, exclusion (if not *a*, then *b*), 251, 313, 316; framing of, 251; Frege

on, 252; in dreams, 218; peculiar to language, 245, 250; role in Hegel, 245, 246–7; Spinoza on, 251; syntactic, 95, 139, 245, 251–3; *see also* denial; logical typing; 'not'; zero

'negation of the negation', 246–7, 250–1; Marx on, 247

neither-nor, 253

neurons, 224, 226–9

neurosis, 252

newsreels, 291

newtonianism, 86, 88, 303, 310, 311

Nibelungen (1924), 291

Nineteen Eighty-Four (George Orwell, 1949), 62–3

'no', 139, 200; distinct from 'not', as refusal, 251, 252; yes and, 247; *see also* negation

no, 133–4

noise, 135, 185; and redundancy, 188, 189; apparent, 239; information from, 183–4, 239, 241, 248, 249, 273–4, 286–7; reduction of, 190, 192; semantic, 241; source of new patterns, 189; *see also* disorder; information; variety

non-contradiction, principle of, 250, 276

non-lineal, 299–30; *see also* lineal; linear

non-state societies, 94–5, 118–20, 121

non-verbal *see* verbal

non-white, as environment of white, 82

'not', syntactic, 95, 224, 243; absent from analog, 224; absent from dreams, the unconscious, 252–3; and identity operation, 224; and zero, 224, 251–3; as a boundary between system and environment, 251, 252–3; as a metaword, 252; as a metastatement, 252; as a rule about words, 252; distinct from 'no', rejection, refusal, 251; neither A nor not-A, 253; *see also* denial; negation; 'no'

not-1: and minus-1, 251; as environment of 1, 251–2

noumenon, 178

nous (mind), 88, 128

novelty, 71, 185, 229, 230, 233, 240; accepted into traditional patterns, 117; and montage, juxtaposition, 271, 273, 275; embryonic, organic, 275; emergence of, 248, 250, 273–4, 275, 286–7, 299; *see also* dialectic; emergence; history; innovation; invention; montage; qualities, emergent

numbers, 234; and logical typing of integers, 253; and words, letters, 278; and zero, one more than one, 252, 253; negative, 252, 253–4; real, 223, 248; spoken, 236; whole, 223, 253

objective/subjective, 235, 237

objectivity *see* God

objects, recognition of, 234

opinions: and relativism, 304

opposites, oppositions; and affinities between elements, qualities, 154, 155, 156, 159–60; and distinction, 156; Aristotelian, 79–81; binary, 178, 179, 181, 247, 250, 251, 313, 316; binary logic of, 313, 316; binary, single level, 79, 82; change into, 81, 159; confused with contradiction, 101; diametrical, 80; either/or, 74, 83, 247–8, 313; equal and, 250, 303; imaginary, 82, 83; imaginary, between chance and necessity, order and disorder, determinism and chaos, free will, 312–13; imaginary, between idealism and materialism, 248; imaginary, between subjectivity and objectivity, quality and quantity, 125, 126; 'interpenetration' of, 250; meaning of, 79–82; mutually exclusive, 250; negation by, 246–7, 313; 'not' has no, 251; oscillation between, 273; polar, 80; representation by, 218; subjectivity has no, 125; symmetrical, 247–8; symmetrized, 80, 82; transcendence of, by mediation, 160; unity, identity of, 82, 273; 'unmediated', 159; *see also* double bind; contradiction; difference; distinction; either/or; imaginary; paradox

oppression, collaborating in one's own, 47

order: and attention to compexity, 184; and chaos, dualism of, 84; and disorder, spirit of, 135; and dream time, 93–4, 113–17; and right-brain functions, 241; and thirdness, 160; from disorder, 117, 183–5, 239, 241, 248, 273, 274, 278; from order, 117, 185, 278; in imaginary opposition with disorder, 312–13; logical typing of, 313; natural, of things, 283;

organic, embryonic, and montage, 275; relative to environment, 72, 135, 183; through oscillation, 117; sequential, 238; syntax, 93–5; *see also* complexity, levels of; disorder; information; noise

order from order/order from disorder, 278

ordering, and attention to complexity, 184

organicism, 86, 88–9, 126–7, 130–1, 154

organism, 76, 82, 175–6; as message, 133; as open system, 71; cosmic, 86, 126, 135, 154–5

organization, 91, 103; and attention to complexity, 184; and complexity, 175–6; and constraint, 77–8; and information, 72–3; and skill, training, discipline, morale, 55; and reorganization, spirit of, 135; as information, 183, 184; biological, social, 71, 168, 171; coding of, requires context, 184; levels of, 90; *Li* as, 90; origins of, 71; unperceived, 135; *see also* complexity; order

organizing center: of utterance, experience, 142

orientation, 223; and *axis mundi*, 113–14, 161–3, 165; and perspective, framing, punctuation, 257–8; and right-brain functions, 236, 278; and symbolic geography, dream time, 112–17; imparts structure, 114; of Stonehenge, 148; point of reference, 163; *see also* mediation

origins: and ideology, 91–4, 113–17; and meaning, 115; myths of, 92–4, 113–15

ornament, the mass, 288–94

oscillation: and simple harmonic motion, 203–4, 273–4; between figure and ground, 203; between metaphor and metonymy, 206; between opposites, 273; between yin and yang, confused with dialectic, 273–4; cybernetic, 193; cyclic, 273–4; matter-energy, 203, 273–4; neurological, 233; of cosmos, between unity and diversity, 153, 160; semiotic, governed by information, 203, 274; paradoxical, 203–4; pathological, 203; yin and yang, as closed system, 274; *see also* double bind; motion; paradox

Other, the, 124; discourse of, 293

otherness, 180

others, 124

overproduction, 36, 41; paradox of, 37

ownership, stewardship, 114–15

'pacification', 26, 27–8, 51–2, 260; *see also* counter-insurgency

painting, and drawing, melody, 208

The Pajama Game (1957), 284

paradigmatic, 202

paradox: figure-ground, 203; metaphorical, 244; of overproduction, 37; of the realistic painter, 244; pipe, iv, 210, 244; undecidable, 248; *see also* oscillation

parallelism, metrical, 206

parasympathetic *see* sympathetic

parole, 202

part for whole *see* metonymy; whole

particular and general, 60, 200, 252

parts: interchangeable, 57–9, 288; pattern as a dance of interacting, 298; *see also* gestalt; metonymy; whole

past: logical typing of, 250; rereading of, 250

patriarchy, 94, 104

patrilineality, 106

pattern, 72, 88, 90, 93, 107, 110–11, 114, 132, 133, 183, 189, 206, 224, 239, 240, 249, 288, 289, 291, 313; as a dance, 298; excess of, lack of, 313; that connects, xiii, 18, 23, 188, 230, 298, 300

perceptions, 271, 273; and body, 226; and entropy, 185; information dependent on, 72, 305; matter-energy; independent of, 72, 305; *see also* perspective

perfection, 130, 153; and communication, 129, 144; and complexity, change, simplicity, 80, 176; and morphology, 175–6; and progress, 83, 176; structural, 126

personality: split, 197; *double conscience*, 232

perspective: and orientation, framing, punctuation, 257–8; traditional, semiotic, organicist, 86, 88–9, 126–31; *see also* dream time; ideology

phenomenology, 84, 178

The Philosophy of Literary Form: Studies in Symbolic Action (Kenneth Burke, 1941, 1957), 313

phonemes, 176–82; loss of, in contiguity disorder, 205
photosynthesis, 75
phrén (mind), 153
physiognomy, 128
pictures, 234; and conversation, 79; and plans, models, 236, 278; and right-brain functions, 236, 278; *see also* right-brain functions
place notation, and zero, 252
plans: and models, pictures, 236, 278; and right-brain functions, 236, 278; village, 99–100, 136; *see also* right-brain functions
play, 21, 57–9, 71; and combat, 298–9; and metacommunication, 298–9; on words, ideas, 217; *see also* message
plenitude, principle of, 30
plurality, and one, unity, zero, 253
pneuma (breath), 88, 89
poetry, 206, 211, 219, 224, 239, 278; inability to appreciate, 234
poles, magnetic, terrestrial, 80
pollution, 56; and reduction of diversity, 193–4; entropic disorder of, 74
polygyny, 96, 100, 101, 106, 108, 121
popular sayings, 43
population increase, 119; doubling time, 38
pornography, 22–3, 293
position, strategic: of Dardanelles, Malacca Straits, 5; of Philippines, 29–30; *see also* strategy
posterity, writing and, 145, 320–1
potential: genetic, 105, 107, 229, 233, 235; genetic, social, 76; graded, 227; uncommitted, for future change, 105, 194; *see also* redundancy
power: and divine right, 45; and rape, 27; education in exercising, 59; emotional, 300; division of, 45; hierarchies of, 80; literacy is, 58; male, xi, 21–3, 54, 116, 120, 136, 298; not principles, 144; of fate, dictatorship, 291, 293; of God, 27; of reason, 85–7; of television, 63; social, 98, 118–21; transfer of, 230; *see also* class; literacy; state; strategy; stratification
precision *see* ambiguity
preconscious memory, 224, 232, 246; *see also* unconscious
pretending to pretend, 123
pre-verbal *see* verbal
priesthood, 95, 120, 149

'primitive', 112–13, 136, 137
principle: creative, 135; *li* as, 90; of unity, diversity, 153, 160; of yin and yang, 153, 160, 273–4
probability: and analytic, many-valued logic, 313; and information, entropy, 175, 184, 186–7, 188
The Producers (1968), 284
production, 72, 95; intensification of, 119–21; means of, 293; modes of, 167–9; surplus, 113
progress: evolutionist, 112; infinite, 83, 176
propositional/appositional, 235
propositional/imaginative, 237, 238, 240, 278
providence, 79
psychology, 321; gestalt, 249, 271; reduced to biology, 314
psychosis *see* schizophrenia
Punch, 22, 36
punctuare (to prick, point), 209
punctuation, 125, 183, 209–10, 222, 257, 278; and framing, 254–8; and left-brain functions, 278; and perspective, orientation, framing, 257–8; and tactics, 258
puns, 211–13
puzzle *see* rebus

qualities: dominant, 159; emergent, 168, 170–2, 248, 249, 256, 271; oppositions, affinities between, 159–60; rules for, 159–60; the four, 154–7; *see also* Aha! experience; complexity; dialectic; montage; novelty; quality
quality, 192, 233; and pattern which connects, 230; and quality, 126, 184; reduced to quantity, 193–4, 312; transformation of quantity into (and vice-versa), 250–1; *see also* complexity; diversity; qualities
quantum theory, 303–5
quest, 85, 231
question: and report, command, 256, 318; that answers itself, 243; two sides to every, 305; *see also* qualities
quipu, 120

racism, xii, 22, 32–3, 295, 296, 305
railroad switching, 87
randomness, 183, 184, 185; *see also* chaos; disorder, relative

rank, 96–7, 115, 119–20
rape, 27–8, 32, 33, 45, 47
ratio, signal to noise, 223
rational, 278; and real, 82–7, 246
rational/emotional, 235
rational/intuitive, 234
rationalism, linguistic, 87, 240, 279; *see also* left-brain function; logic, analytic
Raumbilder (spatial images), 285
read, inability to, 234
The Real Glory (1939), 28
real, reality, xiii, xiv, 82–4, 131, 139, 222, 244, 248, 252; and animation, 153, 269; and language, 82–7, 130, 132, 240–1, 279; and myth, origins, 91, 93, 114–15, 117; and symbolic, imaginary, 67–9, 244; confused with symbolic, 200–1; deep structure of, 126, 154, 155; levels of, 61, 72–4, 80, 82, 86, 234; loss of, 231–2; matter-energy is, 72, 305; rational and, 82–7, 246; social basis of, 285; *see also* complexity; levels; logical typing; ideology; ideas; images; imaginary; symbolic
realism, and metonymy, 206
realistic/impulsive, 237
reason, 87, 89, 246–7; and emotion, 82, 225, 235, 276; cunning of, 85, 87; digital, 225, 235, 279; in imaginary opposition with emotion, 82; reasons for, 276; *see also* left-brain functions; logic, analytic; rational
reasoning, dramatical, 123
rebus, 211, 213, 214–15, 216
receptive *see* active
receptivity, neural, 228
reciprocity, 116, 121
recognition, 51, 70, 79, 107, 187, 246, 249, 285, 287
recognize, failure to, 246
reconnaissance, 285, 299, 300
reconnaissance *see* logistics
reconnaissance (recognition), 246
redistribution, by chief, 'big man', 121
reductionism, 86, 192, 193–4, 304, 312, 320, 321; *see also* coding; complexity; diversity, requisite; information; levels; quality
redundancy, 185, 238; and anticipation, 188; and noise, 188, 189; as structure, 188, 309; is relative, 187–8; of lineal events, 238; transitional, 229
referent, 87, 124, 206

refusal, 139, 251, 252; *see also* negation; rejection; disavowal; 'no'; 'not'
regulation, cybernetic, 190–2; *see also* self-regulation
rejection, 218, 252
relations, relationships, 72, 76, 79, 198, 225, 238, 240–1, 256, 293; between relations, 178–80; content and, 256–7, 278; logical, in dreams, 218; minimum, 161, 253; not objects, entities, 126, 178–9; sequential, 241; social, economic, 167–9, 194, 283–4, 321; to environment, context, 60–2, 102, 105, 161, 165, 179, 183–4, 195, 202, 253, 256; *see also* boundary; context; environment; levels; mediation; system
relativism, and ideas, contexts, 306; and meanings, art, music, life, subjects, 307; and observations, 304; and opinions, 304; and uncertainty principle, 304; subjective, cultural, 125, 304
relativity, 183, 304
relaxed *see* tense
religion: state, 118, 120; women excluded from, 101, 112, 116; *see also* ideology; myth; theology
reorganization, 135; *see also* restructuring
repertoire, 175, 197, 219; discrete, non-discrete, 151–3, 185–6; *see also* code; coding; information
report, and command, question, 256, 318
representation: and image, simulation, 107, 200, 201, 223, 244, 271; by the opposite, 218; in dreams, jokes, 214–19; means of, 62, 168, 285, 293; of word, thing, 201; requisite diversity of, 192, 195; *see also* icons; ideas; images; left-brain functions; right-brain functions
repression, 218, 246
repression (*Verdrängung*), 218
'reproductive fitness', 320–1
repulsion, 153, 160
resources, control of, 119–21
responsibility, 46; and power, 62
res publica, 118
restraint, 189; *see also* constraint
restructuring, 248, 249, 250, 288; neural, 229, 233; from below, 258–9; *see also* Aha! experience; dialectic; innovation;

logical typing; novelty; order from disorder
return, eternal, 163
reversal, 218; *see also* inversion
reversibility, irreversibility, 171, 311
revolution, 83, 88, 117, 184, 185, 194, 314; and simplicity, complexity, 303–4, 309–11; as strategic envelopment, 279; capitalist, 156, 248–9, 278–9; English, 118; industrial, 248–9, 258–9; left brain, digital, 278; many-dimensioned, 279; quantum-relativistic, 303–5; right brain, contextual, 279; 'second theorem', 309; scientific, 303–11; socioeconomic, 248–50, 279; structural, 248, 279; *see also* change; disorder; innovation; novelty; order; restructuring
rhyme, 206, 239
rhythm, 225, 239; and montage, 270, 272; and pattern, 313; musical, visual, 285, 286
rhythmic, unrhythmic, and pattern, 313
rich *see* banal
right-brain functions, 59, 61, 87, 197, 231–42, 277–8; and models, emulation, 59, 61, 229–30
right, divine, 45
rigidity, 194
ritual, 203
ritualization, 122
Roman Scandals (1934), 284, 288, 296
romanticism, 206
Rover, 21
rule breaking, 62, 103, 260; *see also* innovation; novelty
rules, 62, 91, 93–5, 102–5, 115, 149, 150, 161, 175, 189, 219, 238, 259; about rules, 13–14, 17, 62, 102–3, 161; and system, structure, content, context, 102, 105, 161; and zero, 'not', 103, 104, 252; as stored information, 103, 188; exceptions to, 103, 104; for elements, qualities, 159–60; for writers, 260; kinship, 92–5, 100–9, 112, 116–17, 119, 121; legitimate, illegitimate, 18; levels of, 95, 103, 139, 161; of thumb, 43, 62; strategic and tactical, 102, 105; tangle in the, 244; *see also* code; innovation; law; novelty; Rules; rule breaking; strange loop
Rules; Bateson's Rule, 194; Chu Teh's

Rule, 27–8; the Colonial Rule, 49; the Democratic Rule, 49; the Environment Rule, 86; the Extinction Rule, 74; the Inevitable Rule, 86; the Media Rule, 63; Murphy's Rule, 13–14, 17; Orwell's Rule, 62; the Political Rule, 195; the Present Rule, 47; the Rule of Rules, 17, 49, 62; the Survival Rule, 195; the Three-Way Rule, 253; *see also* rule

sacrament, 143
sacred, and profane, men, women, 112, 114
sameness, and simplicity, symmetry, 310, 311
sanctity, 96
schizophrenia, 137, 198, 218, 252; and identity, 197; and *dejà-vu*, 232; and left, right-brain functions, 240–1; and similarity disorder, figure-ground, 200, 201–3; and speech, language, 198, 200–3; and oscillation, 201–3; as a security operation, 126
seeing: after the event, 256; and believing, telling, 122, 132; and learning, reason, 287; way of, 87; *see also* dreams; icon; image; right-brain functions
selection: and brain development, 229; and combination, 94, 95, 151, 153, 155, 156, 159–60, 197–200, 202, 204–5, 210, 215, 255, 271; natural, governed by information, 249; *see also* code; metaphor; similarity; substitution
self: and other, Other, 76, 125; consciousness of, 84; imaginary, 124; loss of, 46–7; *see also* individual; subject
self-defense, 55, 62
self-education, 286
self-hatred, 47
self-reference, paradoxes of, iv, 210, 243–5
self-regulation, 178, 189–92; *see also* cybernetics; homeostasis
self-respect, xi, 19, 43, 46, 47
sēma, sēmeion (sign), 142
semantic universality, 138
semantics, 139, 179–81, 206, 224, 226, 241; *see also* meaning; signification
semiotics, 124, 126–31, 138–41, 142–3
sender-receiver, 72, 161, 188
sense, 137, 138, 270; and sound, syntax,

173, 199, 214; semantic, 241;
suggested, 198; *see also* meaning;
sensing; signification
sensing, 87; and information, meaning,
signification, 185, 225; and learning,
187; as coded information, 185, 225;
see also emotion; information, analog,
iconic; meaning; sense; signification
sensitivity, neural, 228
sensuous *see* intellectual
sentence, 200, 204–5
sequence, 198, 202, 238, 341; *see also*
lineal; linear; step-by-step
sequence/simultaneity, 224, 234, 238,
241, 278; *see also* lineal; linear
set-up, and close-up, 207
shape, 114, 153; and squash and stretch,
152; *see also* form; gestalt; whole
The Shape of Things to Come (H. G.
Wells, 1933), 15, 37, 42
shot, and montage, 270, 274, 275
sighing, 236
signal, 140, 142, 175, 186; not the sign,
146
signatures, doctrine of, 128, 135
signification: and denotation, 185, 224,
239, 240; and information, sensing,
meaning, 185, 223, 225, 239, 275, 278,
279; anticipation of, 188; as coded
meaning, 185, 225
signification/meaning, 278
signifier, 140
signs, 127, 128, 131, 134, 202, 206; and
book of nature, 126–9; and
signatures, 128, 135; in dreams, 214;
meanings, 143; not the signified, 146;
see also semiotics; signal
signum (sign), 142
silence, 69–70, 71, 124
similarity, 198, 200, 202, 205, 206, 210,
224, 276; in dreams, jokes, 215–17,
221; *see also* similarity disorder
similarity disorder, 197–204; *see also*
condensation; metaphor; similarity
simile, 198; filmic, 207
simplicity, 84, 189; and analytic logic, 60;
and perfection, 80, 175–6; and
sameness, symmetry, 310, 311;
organized, 172, 312, 313; revolt
against, 303, 309; *see also* complexity;
diversity; variety
simulation, digital, 223
simultaneity, 218; and synchrony, code,

198, 202; *see also* sequence; step-by-
step
slips of the tongue, 181, 198, 218
society, 76, 77, 103, 115; and spatial
images, 285; and nature, 67, 70, 71,
75, 79, 85, 88, 91, 94, 104, 105,
167–9; without writing, 96–102,
114–17; *see also* history; self; state
sociobiology, 320–1
Soldier of Fortune, 41, 50–1, 54–5
solipsism (*solus ipse*: oneself alone), 306;
see also solipsistic
solipsistic/interpersonal, 278
sophisticated *see* innocent
soul, 86, 89–90, 127–8, 154, 207, 231
sound, 211, 239; and sense, syntax, 173,
199, 214
space, 222, 225, 234, 235, 236; between
words, 223
spatial images; and society, dreams, 285
spatial *see* temporal
specialist/generalist, 234, 237
species: and genus, 198; confused with
society, 71
speech, 127; and drawing, 283; and
language, discourse, 133–5, 234; and
sound, sense, 214; as model of reality,
communication, montage, 134–5,
270, 271, 275–6; backward, 236;
emotional, 275–6; inner, 87, 276; loss
of, 197–8, 204–5; parts of, 135; *see
also* communication, discourse;
language; memory; *parole*;
schizophrenia; word
spell, inability to, 234
squash and stretch, 151–3, 197
stability, ecosystemic, 193–4
stabilization, selective, 229
state: and Hegelian absolute, 85;
conquest, client, original, 56, 118–21;
steady (homeostasis), 178, 189, 192;
see also state societies
state societies, 94–5, 118–19, 120–1
status, social, 119–20
step-by-step/holistic, 230, 234, 238, 241;
see also lineal; linear; sequence
stereotypes, film, of American women,
261–9
stereotyping, 261–9, 285, 287
stewardship, possession, 115
strange loop, tangled rules, iv, 210, 244
strategists, 277, 279
strategy: and ethics, 49; and framing,
punctuation, 258; and male

supremacy, 58, 298; and right-brain, top-down learning, 48, 278, 279; and strategic envelopment, 300; as the study of communication, 300; attack the opponent's 48, 300; colonial, 12, 23, 26–9, 31–3, 45–7, 49, 54, 83, 261, 324; conscious, unconscious, 48; democratic, 49; grand, 279; guerrilla, xi, xii, 27–8, 51–2, 300; hierarchy of, 258–9; individual, collective, 48; in everyday life, 48, 58, 61; kamikaze, 56; literacy in, 58; 'locust', 8; male, and machine literacy, 58; of position, manoeuvre, 19; of terror, 27; post-Vietnam, 324; Sun Tzu on, 47–8; win-lose, zero sum, either/or, 48; win-win, 47–9; without tactics, is imaginary, 48; *see also* counter-insurgency; divide and rule; tactics

stratification, social, 96, 100, 119–21

stretch squash and, 151–3

strife (repulsion), principle of diversity and differentiation, 153, 160

Strike (1924), 273

structuralism, 79, 177–9; context-free, linguistic, 94, 310; *see also* anthropology; linguistics

structures, 91, 95, 175, 184, 187, 197, 198, 218, 257, 279, 298, 314; acoustic, 176–81; and orientation, center, 114, 161, 163, 165; and redundancy, pattern, 188, 238, 309; and rules, constraints, 95, 103; and system, rules, contents, environment(s), 102, 105; body as pattern for, 154–5; class, 119–21; deep, surface, 126, 149–50, 153–61, 165–6, 293; dissipative, 171, 311; kinship, 93–4, 101–2, 105–8; levels of, 176–83; mechanical, 57–60, 288; of brain, 226–9, 231–42; of form and matter, 162–5; of language, 150, 176–83; of qualities, elements, 153–60; of Stonehenge, 146–50, 165–6; social, 117, 18–21; steady (morphostasis), 178; symbolic of real, 165; without a subject, 293, 309; *see also* code; complexity; constraints; hierarchy; kinship; levels; mediation; restructuring; village plans

subject, 178, 200; and relativism, 304, 307; of discourse, 132; of creativity, work, mind, body, 279; structure

without, 293, 307; *see also* subjective; subjectivity

subjective *see* objective

subjectivity, in imaginary opposition with objectivity, 124–6

subordinate, subordination *see* dominant, domination

subordination; grammatical, 199–200; modes of production, 168; of parts, 176

substance, 85, 87, 90

substitute, 200, 215; *see also* code; dreams; metaphor; selection; similarity; substitution

substitution, 197–200, 202, 204, 215, 218, 221; *see also* code; dreams; metaphor; similarity; selection; substitute

succession, 224, 238, 241; and diachrony, 198, 202; *see also* sequence; step-by-step

summing, and whole, parts, 271

Superboy, 21

Supergirl, 21

Superman, 21

Superwoman, 21

supremacy, male, xii, 21–3, 54, 58, 116, 120, 134, 136, 298

surface manifestations, 293

surrealism, and metaphor, 206, 210, 244

survival, 73–4, 168, 274; long and short range, 82; long range, 42, 82, 132, 265, 194–5, 233, 279

switching: code, 200; railroad, 59

syllables, 236

symbiosis, 105

symbol, 142, 143; as word of the world, 135; not the symbolized, 146

symbolic, 206, 219, 244, 248, 252; and culture, 77; and imaginary, real, 67–9; confused with real, 201; of real, 116, 163, 165

symbolization, 139; in nature, 122

symmetrization: and inversion, 82, 130; of figure and ground, 203; of hierarchy, 80, 82, 205

symmetry, 164, 278; and sameness, simplicity, 310, 311; facial, 81; in depth, height, 81; two-sided, bilateral, horizontal, left-right, 80–2; *see also* opposite; opposition; symmetrization

symmetry/asymmetry, 278

sympathetic/parasympathetic, 235

symptom, 215

synchrony, simultaneity and, 198, 202
synecdoche, 198, 205, 207; *see also*
  metonymy
syntagmatic, 202
syntax: and 'not', 251; digital, 93–4, 151,
  223, 224, 234, 251; formal, informal,
  275–6; hierarchical, 219, 251;
  linguistic, 95, 137, 138, 139, 140, 173,
  199, 204, 206, 214; loss of, 204; of
  dreams, jokes, 214–19, 221; *see also*
  film; montage; semantics
synthesis, and thesis, antithesis, 84,
  246–7
synthesizing *see* analytic, deductive
system/environment, 278
systems: and structure, rules, content,
  environment, 102, 105–6; 'big man',
  119–21; coding of, and requisite
  diversity, 192; economic diversity of,
  193–5; factory, 259; nervous,
  hormone, 226–9; primary, secondary,
  232, 246; self-destructing, 82; *see also*
  boundary; communication;
  environment; goalseeking; kinship;
  closed; system; open
systems, closed, 60, 73, 83, 86, 309; and
  entropy, 184, 309, 312; chaotic,
  simple, 312; cybernetic, 189; cyclic,
  oscillating, 273–4; *see also* boundary;
  system, closed; system, open
systems, open, 60, 71–2, 73–4, 77–9, 82,
  86, 171, 192, 248, 278, 279; and
  entropy, 185; logical typing of, 252,
  253, 277; minimum requirements for,
  161, 253; of value, 72, 75; parts
  dependent on, 171; semiotic,
  oscillating, 273–4; self-referring, 85–6;
  see also boundary; communication;
  environment; goalseeking; structure;
  system; system, closed; teleonomy
systems theory, 172–9; context-sensitive,
  semiotic, ecological, 310

tactic *see* explicit
tactics, 7–12, 14, 23–6, 48, 49, 58, 61;
  and left-brain, bottom-up learning, 48,
  277, 278, 279; impossible without
  strategy, 48; kamikaze, 49; *see also*
  blunders; defeat; strategy; victory
tactics/strategy, 278
Tahitians, 96
taikns (token), 142
tangle in rules, strange loop, iv, 210, 244

teleology, 78, 128–30, 247; *see also*
  cause, final
teleonomy, 79, 129; *see also* goalseeking
telling, and seeing, 122
telos (goal, end), 78, 129
tempo, 239
temporal/spatial, 229, 234, 235
tense, linguistic, 224
tense/relaxed, 235
territory *see* map
text/context, 278
texture, of cinematic shots, 270, 273
textus (structure), 134
Thailand, 40
theater, guerrilla, 300
theology, and objectivity, 125, 126–30
theory: and practice, 143; information,
  173, 175, 185–8; signal, 175, 186;
  systems, 172–9, 310; thermodynamics,
  71, 171, 184–5, 311, 312; *see also*
  entropy
thesis: and antithesis, synthesis, 84,
  246–7
third term *see* mediation
thirdness, 160; *see also* mediation
thought, xiv, 69, 82, 85, 87, 95, 137,
  202–3, 214, 225, 229–30, 234, 246;
  see also left-brain functions; logic;
  memory; right-brain functions;
  unconscious
time, 184, 218, 222, 225; labor, 279;
  synchronic, diachronic, 177
Time, 51
timeless *see* historical
Times, Los Angeles, 51
timing, 269
token, 134, 142, 143
tone of voice, 145, 234
top-down *see* bottom-up
topology, 96, 98–101, 114
torture, 22–3, 26–8, 32, 33, 45, 47, 141,
  305, 324
totemism, mediates between nature and
  culture, 115–16
trace, memory, 96, 114, 229
La Trahison des images (René Magritte,
  1928–29), iv, 210, 244
transformational/associative, 237
transitivity, 124, 178
translation, code-to-code, 107, 109, 147,
  214
triangle: communicative, 165; of
  mediation, 161, 202; *see also* thirdness
the trinity, 160, 162

Tristes Tropiques (Claude Lévi-Strauss, 1955), 306
Triumph of the Will (1934), 21, 291, 292
truth, and lying, 260
truth functions: absent from analog, 224; absent from dreams, the unconscious, 252–4

Übertrangung (transfer, translation, transference), 136, 214
Umwelt (milieu), 109
uncertainty, 186, 194; and relativism, 304
unconscious, 95, 124, 129, 137, 140, 178, 201, 224, 231–2, 246, 273; absence of negation in, 252–3; and conscious, 82, 198, 214; and conscious, preconscious, 224, 232, 246; in imaginary opposition with conscious, 82
understanding, 70, 124, 201, 271; and redundancy, 188; and seeing, sensing, 287
unemployment, 36, 37, 42, 53
unity: and diversity, 153, 160, 276; and plurality, 253; in imaginary opposition with variety, 80; in montage, 271, 275, 276
universality, semantic, 138
up and down, not symmetrical, 79, 80–1
utterance, organizing center of, 142

value: communication of, 67, 91, 95, 279, 283, 285, 298; exchange, 194, 223, 225, 279; surprise, 175, 186, 187, 188; survival, 194–5, 273, 279; use, 223, 279; *see also* belief; ideology
variety, 150, 157, 181, 185, 192, 194, 225; and complexity, 172–3; and information, noise, redundancy, 72, 135, 182–4, 188; coded, uncoded, 72, 135, 172–3, 182–4, 185; hierarchy of, 60; organized, unorganized, 172, 312; requisite, 189; structural, 185; *see also* diversity; information; order
verbal/non-verbal, 219, 225, 230, 240, 261, 276, 278, 279
verbal/pre-verbal, 235
Verdichtung (condensation), 202
Verdrängung (repression), 246
Verkenntnis (failure to recognize), 246
Verleugnung (disavowal), 252
Verneinung (denial, negation), 245–6
Verschiebung (displacement), 202
Verwerfung (rejection), 252
victim: blaming self, 47; blaming the, 47,

53, 91, 116; *see also* Cinderella complex; colonization
victimization, xii, 46–7, 53, 91, 116
victory, tactical, strategic, 50, 51–2
violence, 22, 285, 296
volume, conservation of, 152–3
Vorstellung (presentation, representation), 201
vowels, 236

war, warfare: and booms, busts, 34–6, 37; and ethics, 27–8, 49, 55; and inflation, 34, 35–6, 38, 41, 42; and Kondratieff wave, 35; as business, politics, 34, 37; colonial, 27–9, 31–3, 39, 40–1, 55–6; guerrilla, people's xi-xii, 7, 26–9, 31, 32, 33, 51–2, 55; of conquest, 118–19, 120–1; on nature, 49, 56; peak, trough, 35; total, 16, 26–7; *see also* strategy
wave: Kondratieff, 35; navigation, 109–12; sine, 203
West Side Story (1961), 284
white: in imaginary opposition with non-white, 82
'The White Man's Burden' (Rudyard Kipling, 1899), 30–1
whole: emergent qualities of, 171; gestalt, 187; in imaginary opposition with part, 80; other than sum of parts, 271; *see also* whole-part relation
whole-part relation, 57, 80, 171, 176, 187, 188, 197, 198, 201, 204, 207–8, 217, 234, 271; *see also* metonymy; synecdoche
win-lose, win-win, 48–9, 278
wisdom, 87, 115, 119, 240, 249
wish fulfilment *see* desire
withdrawal: strategic, tactical, 19
women: and machine literacy, 22, 58; as hereditary class, 108; as original working class, 120; exchange of, 94, 104, 106–8; hatred of, xii, 69, 295, 297; stereotyping of, 261–9, 285, 287–91, 293; subordination of, 22, 58, 80, 94, 100, 101, 104, 106, 108, 112, 116, 120, 121, 132, 134
Wonder Woman, 21
word, 146, 234, 236; and image, 136, 197, 207–8; and *no, eweke, parole*, 133–4; as reference point, 135; composite, 215; in aphasia, 199–201, 204–5; of God *see* logos; of the world, 135; play on, 217; portmanteau, 271;

the lasting, 133–4; *see also* language;
left-brain functions; model; *parole*;
speech
word presentation, 224
work, 57–63; energy and, 184; physical,
logical, structural, 71; subject of, 279
world, external, 242
Wortvorstellung (word presentation),
224
writing, 95, 120, 205–6, 214; origins of,
148–9; political, 259–60; societies
without, 96–102, 114–17; *see also*
memory; trace

yes: and no, 247, 251, 252; and 'not',
251, 252; *see also* no, 'not'
yin and yang, 153, 160; confused with
dialectic, 273–4

Zeichen (sign), 214
zero: absent from analog computer,
unconscious, 224, 252; and 'not',
251–3; as a rule about numbers, 252;
as boundary, 104; invention of, 104,
253
zero sum game, 48
Zulu empire, 118–19